Rehabilitating Lawyers

Rehabilitating Lawyers

Principles of Therapeutic Jurisprudence for Criminal Law Practice

Edited by
David B. Wexler

Carolina Academic Press
Durham, North Carolina

Copyright © 2008
David B. Wexler
All Rights Reserved

Library of Congress Cataloging-in-Publication Data

Wexler, David B.
  Rehabilitating lawyers : principles of therapeutic jurisprudence for criminal law practice / by David B. Wexler.
      p. cm.
  Includes bibliographical references and index.
  ISBN 10: 1-59460-435-5 / ISBN 13: 978-1-59460-435-5 (alk. paper)
  1. Criminal lawyers--United States. 2. Practice of law--United States--Psychological aspects. 3. Therapeutic jurisprudence--United States. I. Title.

  KF299.C7W45 2008
  345.73001'9--dc22

2008015273

Carolina Academic Press
700 Kent Street
Durham, North Carolina 27701
Telephone (919) 489-7486
Fax (919) 493-5668
www.cap-press.com

Printed in the United States of America

To my wife, Ghislaine Laraque, with much love

Contents

Foreword by James P. Cooney III	xi
Acknowledgments	xv
Introduction	xvii
Part I · TJ and Criminal Law Practice	3
A. An Introduction to Therapeutic Jurisprudence	3
David B. Wexler, Therapeutic Jurisprudence: An Overview	3
B. Application to Criminal Law	11
i. A Tripartite Framework	11
David B. Wexler, A Tripartite Framework for Incorporating Therapeutic Jurisprudence in Criminal Law Education, Research, and Practice	11
ii. A Rehabilitative Consciousness	20
David B. Wexler, Therapeutic Jurisprudence and the Rehabilitative Role of the Criminal Defense Lawyer	20
Part II · Concerns and Critiques	45
A. Concerns Relating to Lawyering in Problem-Solving Courts	46
Tamar M. Meekins, "Specialized Justice": The Over-Emergence of Specialty Courts and the Threat of a New Criminal Defense Paradigm	46
B. Critique of TJ Lawyering Itself: A Conversation with a Critic	91
i. Mae C. Quinn, An RSVP to Professor Wexler's Warm Therapeutic Jurisprudence Invitation to the Criminal Defense Bar: Unable to Join You, Already (Somewhat Similarly) Engaged	91
ii. David B. Wexler, Not Such a Party Pooper: An Attempt to Accommodate (Many of) Professor Quinn's Concerns about Therapeutic Jurisprudence Criminal Defense Lawyering	129
iii. Mae C. Quinn, Postscript to an RSVP	137
iv. David B. Wexler, Author's Closing Comments	140

Part III • Practices and Techniques 143

    i. Tamar M. Meekins, You Can Teach Old Defenders New Tricks: Sentencing Lessons From Specialty Courts 144

    ii. Martin Reisig, The Difficult Role of the Defense Lawyer in a Post-Adjudication Drug Treatment Court: Accommodating Therapeutic Jurisprudence and Due Process 156

    iii. Orna Alyagon Darr, TJ and Zealous Advocacy: Tension and Opportunity 162

    iv. David B. Wexler, Therapeutic Jurisprudence and Readiness for Rehabilitation 169

    v. Joel Parris, Reinforcing Reform Efforts through Probation Progress Reports 181

    vi. Michael Crystal, The Therapeutic Sentence: Chicken Soup for an Ailing Criminal Court 183

    vii. Karine Langley, Affidavit 185

    viii. David Boulding, Fetal Alcohol and the Law 186

    ix. John V. McShane, Jailhouse Interventions, Treatment Bonds, and the So-Called "Recovery Defense" 193

    x. Robert Ward, Criminal Defense Practice and Therapeutic Jurisprudence: Zealous Advocacy through Zealous Counseling: Perspectives, Plans and Policy 206

    xi. Beth Bromberg, A Defense Lawyer's Perspective on the Use of Apology 225

    xii. Michael S. King, Therapeutic Jurisprudence, Criminal Law Practice and the Plea of Guilty 230

    xiii. JaneAnne Murray, Easing Your Client's Experience of Federal Prison 239

    xiv. Astrid Birgden, Dealing with the Resistant Criminal Client: A Psychologically-Minded Strategy for More Effective Legal Counseling 243

Part IV • Practice Settings and Clinical Opportunities 257

    i. Cait Clarke & James Neuhard, Making the Case: Therapeutic Jurisprudence and Problem Solving Practices Positively Impact Clients, Justice Systems and Communities They Serve 257

    ii. Gregory Baker & Jennifer Zawid, The Birth of a Therapeutic Courts Externship Program: Hard Labor but Worth the Effort 279

    iii. Bruce J. Winick & David B. Wexler, The Use of Therapeutic Jurisprudence in Law School Clinical Education: Transforming the Criminal Law Clinic 303

    iv. David B. Wexler, Crime Victims, Law Students, and Therapeutic Jurisprudence Training 323

    v. Kristin Henning, Defining the Lawyer-Self: Using Therapeutic Jurisprudence to Define the Lawyer's Role and Build Alliances that Aid the Child Client 327

Part V • Therapeutic Jurisprudence in a Comparative Law Context			351
	A. Barristers		352
	i.	The Honorable George Hampel QC, Therapeutic Jurisprudence — An Australian Perspective	352
	ii.	Patrick Mugliston, Should the Role of a Barrister Change to Enable the Adoption of a More Therapeutic Approach to the Practice of Law?	355
	B. Continental Approach		370
		Christian Diesen, Neither Freedom Fighter Nor Saboteur — Some Notes on the Role of the Defence Counsel in Sweden	370

About the Editor   387

Index   389

Foreword

James P. Cooney III*

I keep a different office than most lawyers. In one corner I have a full-sized skeleton who hangs by his head (I fancy him a male) and who wears a T-shirt for the 12th Human Remains Recovery Institute that I was given by a forensic pathologist from the "Body Farm." There is a camouflaged GI Joe on one of my shelves, given to me by a client who liked the way I "parachuted" into tough cases. I have an assortment of medical equipment—surgical stapling guns, needles, scalpels, syringes—constituting the general detritus of 25 years of defending malpractice cases. On the walls there are an assortment of courtroom sketches—I can watch as my hair slowly vanishes from drawing to drawing. There are framed newspaper headlines, photographs from articles and other courtroom sketches. There is even a large picture of my middle daughter with Eeorye. All of these surround my files and books and casebooks and pleadings.

One thing that is quite traditional in my office, though, is something that appears in nearly every lawyer's office that I have ever seen. It is as if we are all genetically programmed to know that if nothing else is in our offices, this one thing must be: a law license. My license, issued in 1984, is telling for what it says, and I glance at it from time to time to remind myself:

> Attorney and Counselor at Law

There it is: "Counselor at Law." For many people, that phrase simply means that a lawyer gives advice about the law—he or she offers "counsel." And, I am sure, for many lawyers that may be enough, or at least it is all that is asked of them.

---

* James P. Cooney III is a Partner in the law firm of Womble Carlyle Sandridge & Rice, PLLC, one of the "AmLaw 100" firms. Based in Charlotte, North Carolina, he is recognized as one of the best trial lawyers in the South. In 2000 he was the youngest attorney in North Carolina ever inducted into the American College of Trial Lawyers. In 2004, he was presented the William Thorp Pro Bono award for his representation of Alan Gell an innocent man wrongly convicted of murder and sentenced to death. The Gell case led to the establishment of one of the most comprehensive reforms in criminal law in the history of North Carolina. In 2006, he was recognized as one of the premier civil litigators in North Carolina, and in 2007 was selected as the top criminal trial lawyer in the State. In his career he has freed 5 men from Death Row and, in 2006 and 2007, was one of the defense attorneys who successfully defended the young men wrongfully charged with rape in what came to be known as the "Duke Lacrosse Rape case." He is a summa cum laude, Phi Beta Kappa, graduate of Duke University and received his law degree from the University of Virginia, where he was an editor of the *Virginia Law Review* and a member of the Order of the Coif.

For any attorney who practices trial law, and particularly trial law at its rawest—criminal defense, personal injury, domestic litigation—offering "counsel" does not begin to describe our task. We are, in the full-blooded meaning of the word, truly "counselors." If you have ever had the task of telling someone that they may go to jail, or lose their practice or their fortune, or that he or she has lost a marriage or a spouse, you use much more than your knowledge of the law to see your client through this crisis. Handling, coaching, coaxing, and above all else counseling another human being is the essence of the practice of law in these arenas. In many ways, trial law is as much about psychology and therapy as it is briefs and motions; for in the end, no matter the case, it is always about human beings and their emotions—and the cases will always be decided by other human beings and their emotions.

This book, and the concepts embodied in it, take the role of lawyer as "counselor" to the next level. It does so by positing that rather than simply counseling clients through a legal crisis—doing what it takes to preserve their humanity while representing them fully—a lawyer may need to act to ensure that his or her clients are treated through the process. The goal of such an approach—of "therapeutic jurisprudence"—becomes more than the survival of the client and the achievement of the best possible outcome. Rather, the goal now embraces a healing component, one in which the client may achieve the best possible outcome by becoming "better."

This is a radical concept. For many of us this approach has been in front of us, unknown, for years. In capital murder cases in which life itself is in the balance, defense attorneys have for years had clients evaluated, tested and oftentimes medicated. It is the unusual capital murder case in which a defendant is not diagnosed, finally, with a mental illness—sometimes treatable, often controllable—which, when exposed to therapy, recedes and suddenly the client is clearer, more rational, more human, than he has ever been.

The capital case, however, has always been therapeutic jurisprudence in the setting of a MASH unit—taking horribly damaged people and providing them with enough "therapy" so that they may try to survive the ordeal of the capital murder trial and its aftermath. This book and its chapters posit something altogether different, a proactive approach to "therapy" in a broad spectrum of cases, an approach that has at its core the concept that if the client can be made "better"—or even healed—that act will help both the client and the client's case.

This is in many ways both a simple and breath-taking proposition. It asks the attorney as zealous advocate to seek to heal—or at least begin to heal—the client as an explicit strategy in advocating the client's cause. It is in many ways the antithesis of how the lawyer—and particularly the trial lawyer—is often viewed and frequently portrayed: the hired gunslinger performing a task for money with little regard for anything other than winning. Yet, in its goal, therapeutic jurisprudence embodies the essence of the adversary process, but does so by turning it on its head. It contemplates a client who still makes the ultimate decisions, but is presented with choices beyond the strategic ones that present themselves in contested cases; rather, rehabilitative as well as litigative choices are now actively presented, and both merge to form a new paradigm for zealous advocacy.

Thus, therapeutic jurisprudence is the ultimate fulfillment of a lawyer's charge as "counselor" at law. It gives a potent and achingly human weapon to the advocate, and permits a lawyer to do well while actually doing some good. In this premise this concept is transformative—taken to the endpoint of its natural evolution, it promises to change the very way that law in this country is seen, practiced and taught. This is a change that I, and those clients who have sat in my office confronted with the reality of their situations, welcome and will benefit from.

James P. Cooney III
March 10, 2008
Charlotte, North Carolina

Acknowledgments

As always, many, many thanks to Carolina Academic Press and its President Keith Sipe for their interest in therapeutic jurisprudence and for the pleasure of working with them. Tim Colton (along with his superb production team of Karen Clayton and Kasia Krzysztoforska) has again worked tirelessly to usher the book through the production process. And much of the on-the-ground work has been done by my research assistant, Cristina Hernandez, at the University of Puerto Rico Law School, and by Lucy Hoffman, of the support staff at the University of Arizona, James E. Rogers College of Law. My deep thanks to all of them.

This book is dedicated to my wife, Ghislaine ("Gigi") Laraque, and she did the artwork for the book cover. Cuca del Rincon took my book jacket photo, and she and Jesus Maria ("Bibi") del Rincon created the jacket's graphic design. Although "Gigi, Cuca, and Bibi" may sound like a pre-school playgroup, they formed a superb artistic committee — and one that indeed "works and plays well together." I am very much indebted to them.

Introduction

Rehabilitating Lawyers. Surely, I don't really believe lawyers need to be "rehabilitated." Nor do I believe they should become therapists, in the business of actually and actively rehabilitating their clients.

Why then the "cutesy" *double entendre* title? Well, clearly as a hoped-for attention-grabber, an antidote for the more accurate but indisputably arid subtitle, "Principles of Therapeutic Jurisprudence for Criminal Law Practice."

Moreover, using "rehabilitating" in its "softer" sense, I do think—as many essays in this book demonstrate—that the therapeutic jurisprudence (TJ) perspective enables lawyers easily to inject an ethic of care into their practices and to serve as "positive change agents" for their clients.[1] And my hope and expectation is that a practice infused with therapeutic jurisprudence type approaches can help immeasurably to improve the image of lawyers—with their clients[2] and with the public at large[3]—and can, as well, enhance in a major way the professional and personal satisfaction derived from a life of lawyering.[4]

To be sure, many lawyers already practice along the lines suggested in this volume, whether or not they use the term "therapeutic jurisprudence." Those working in specific problem-solving courts (e.g., drug treatment court, mental health court) come quickly to mind, and the general criminal lawyer can learn much from these attorneys. Indeed, as we will see, many criminal defense attorneys practicing in general criminal courts also adopt such an approach.

The TJ community of scholars and practitioners can learn an enormous amount from these creative lawyers, and we should be continually encouraging them to write and to share their experiences. At the same time, my claim is that by familiarizing themselves with therapeutic jurisprudence and its interdisciplinary literature, and by invoking a TJ perspective explicitly and systematically, lawyers will see even more opportunities to practice in an enriched, beneficial and meaningful way.

Another aim of this book is to bridge the wide academic/practitioner divide that exists in the world of law. Commenting by e-mail on a recent essay of mine, a law professor wrote, "I don't think I have ever seen anything quite like this, in terms of connecting

---

1. Judging in a Therapeutic Key: Therapeutic Jurisprudence and the Courts 137 (Bruce J. Winick and David B. Wexler, eds.) (2003) (excerpting work of Michael D. Clark, MSW).
2. Marcus T. Boccaccini, et al., Development and Effects of Client Trust in Criminal Defense Attorneys, 22 Behavioral Science and Law 197 (2004).
3. Judging in a Therapeutic Key, supra note 1, at 132 (excerpting work of Judge Roger K. Warren).
4. Deborah J. Chase and Peggy F. Hora, The Implications of Therapeutic Jurisprudence for Judicial Satisfaction, 37 Coast Review 12 (2000).

the theoretical work on procedural justice and therapeutic jurisprudence with some very specific examples of what a thoughtful judge and a thoughtful defense lawyer are actually doing."

Unfortunately, and to me shockingly, this observation is largely true. More than fifteen years ago, Judge Harry Edwards, a former academic, wrote an article, famous at least in the world of law school teaching, entitled, "The Growing Disjunction Between Legal Education and the Legal Profession."[5] Judge Edwards was especially critical of interdisciplinary or "law and" scholarship, which he too often found to be of no value to the practicing profession. And in a *Harvard Law Review* essay published in 2006, another author claimed the disjunction comments to be "truer today than when Judge Edwards penned these words in 1992."[6]

But I am pleased to note that, even in the era of Judge Edwards' original indictment, he dropped an approving footnote characterizing therapeutic jurisprudence academic writing as "practical interdisciplinary scholarship."[7] And in this book I have sought further to create and nourish practical interdisciplinary scholarship. In fact, as it turns out, the lion's share of this book is composed of contributions from practitioners and their academic counterparts—faculty members attached to law school clinical programs. I very much hope the book will stimulate further scholarship from those sectors of the profession—and from their behavioral science counterparts.

The book itself is divided into five parts. Part I lays out a framework for therapeutic jurisprudence criminal law practice. Part II is devoted to a discussion of concerns and criticisms of the TJ approach. Part III, the most practical part of all, is dedicated to specific practices and techniques. Part IV explores settings where therapeutic jurisprudence skills can be practiced or honed. And Part V looks at TJ in a comparative law context, exploring issues in a continental context and in a profession distinguishing between barristers and solicitors.

In many ways, this entire project is a work in progress, and the enterprise will develop only through the input, reactions, and continued commentary of this broad interdisciplinary and international community. Interested persons can keep abreast and participate by visiting the website of the International Network on Therapeutic Jurisprudence at www.therapeuticjurisprudence.org and by joining its listserve or mailing list.

---

5. 91 Michigan Law Review 34 (1992).
6. Neil Kumar Katyal, "*Hamdan v. Rumsfeld*: The Legal Academy Goes to Practice", 120 Harvard Law Review 65, 66 (2006).
7. Harry T. Edwards, The Growing Disjunction Between Legal Education and the Legal Profession: A Postscript, 91 Michigan Law Review 2191, 2196 n. 20 (1993).

Rehabilitating Lawyers

Part I

TJ and Criminal Law Practice

This part seeks to introduce the reader to the therapeutic jurisprudence (TJ) perspective and to explore a framework for thinking about TJ in criminal law practice.

The Part opens with a very short, informal, and chatty introduction to TJ itself. It is a slightly revised version of a transcribed public lecture given at the Thomas Cooley Law School in Michigan and sponsored by its law review. Then, the material jumps to a specific criminal law focus. First, I propose a tripartite framework (relevant legal landscape, treatments and services, and practices and techniques) for viewing TJ in a criminal law context and for thinking about the competencies that need to be developed by the TJ criminal lawyer. Following that, I address various stages of the criminal process and explore how a lawyer's role might be enhanced and enriched by adding a TJ approach to the mix.

A. An Introduction to Therapeutic Jurisprudence

David B. Wexler,[1]
Therapeutic Jurisprudence: An Overview
(Revised and reprinted with permission from
17 Thomas M. Cooley Law Review 125, 2000)

Therapeutic jurisprudence is the "study of the role of the law as a therapeutic agent."[2] It focuses on the law's impact on emotional life and on psychological well-being.[3] These are areas that have not received very much attention in the law until now. Therapeutic jurisprudence focuses our attention on this previously underappreciated aspect, humanizing the law and concerning itself with the human, emotional, psychological side of law and the legal process.

Basically, therapeutic jurisprudence is a perspective that regards the law as a social force that produces behaviors and consequences.[4] Sometimes these consequences fall within the realm of what we call therapeutic; other times antitherapeutic consequences are produced.[5] Therapeutic jurisprudence wants us to be aware of this and wants us to

---

1. This is a slightly revised version of a public lecture given on October 29, 1999 at the Thomas M. Cooley Law Review Disabilities Law Symposium.
2. David B. Wexler & Bruce J. Winick, Law in Therapeutic Key: Developments in Therapeutic Jurisprudence xvii (1996) [hereinafter Key].
3. *See id.*
4. *See id.*
5. *See id.*

see whether the law can be made or applied in a more therapeutic way so long as other values, such as justice and due process, can be fully respected.[6]

It is important to recognize that therapeutic jurisprudence does not itself suggest that therapeutic goals should trump other ones.[7] It does not support paternalism, coercion, and so on.[8] It is simply a way of looking at the law in a richer way, and then bringing to the table some of these areas and issues that previously have gone unnoticed.[9] Therapeutic jurisprudence simply suggests that we think about these issues and see if they can be factored into our law-making, lawyering, or judging.[10]

Therefore, therapeutic jurisprudence is the study of therapeutic and antitherapeutic consequences of the law.[11] When we say the law, we mean the law in action, not simply the law on the books. The law can be divided into the following categories: (1) legal rules, such as "Don't Ask, Don't Tell"[12] or the Americans with Disabilities;[13] (2) legal procedures, such as hearings and trials;[14] and (3) the roles of legal actors and the behavior of judges, lawyers, and of therapists acting in a legal context.[15] Much of what legal actors do has an impact on the psychological well-being or emotional life of persons affected by the law.[16] I refer here, for example, to matters such as the dialogue that judges have with defendants or that lawyers have with clients.[17]

An example of a *legal rule* that could be examined from a therapeutic jurisprudence perspective is the "Don't Ask, Don't Tell" provision that bars military service for one who acknowledges being gay or bisexual.[18] The government is not permitted to ask about it, and so long as a recruit does not talk about it, there is supposedly no problem.[19]

One of the things that therapeutic jurisprudence does, however, is to tease out some of the more subtle, more unintended consequences of legal rules that may be antitherapeutic.[20] An interesting study of the "Don't Ask, Don't Tell" rule suggested that if someone is gay in the military and cannot talk about that, then that person may *also* be afraid to talk about many *other* things as well because those other things are likely to raise the question of the legally prohibited topic.[21] So where you went on vacation and with whom may be things you're not comfortable talking about because this topic could

---

6. *See id.*
7. *See id.*
8. *See id.*
9. *See id.*
10. *See id.*
11. *See id.*
12. Kay Kavanagh, *Don't Ask, Don't Tell: Deception Required Disclosure Denied*, in Key, *supra* note 2, at 343.
13. Michael Perlin, Address at the *Thomas M. Cooley Law Review Disabilities Law Symposium* (Oct. 29, 1999).
14. *See generally* Janet Weinstein, *And Never the Twain Shall Meet: The Best Interest of Children and the Adversary System*, 52 U. Miami L. Rev. 79 (1999) (providing a detailed analysis of legal procedures, hearings, and trials involving the custody of children).
15. *See generally* David B. Wexler, *Therapeutic Jurisprudence and the Criminal Courts*, in Key, *supra* note 2 (discussing therapeutic jurisprudence in a criminal court setting).
16. *See* Marjorie A. Silver, *Love, Hate, and Other Emotional Interference in the Lawyer/Client Relationship*, 6 Clinical L. Rev. 259, 293–94 (1999).
17. *See id.*
18. *See* Kavanagh, *supra* note 12, at 343.
19. *See id.* at 346.
20. *See id.* at 344–45.
21. *See id.*

raise the question of whether you're gay, and that is the prohibited conversational topic.[22]

Therefore, the author of the "Don't Ask, Don't Tell" article, Kay Kavanagh, suggested that the law, in practice, may cause great isolation, marginality, and superficiality in social relations for a gay person in the military, perhaps above and beyond what was anticipated when this provision was drafted.[23] Perhaps it was drafted with the thought that one's sexual life is personal, and that it makes sense, therefore, for us not to ask about it and for people not to talk about it.[24] It was perhaps based on the assumption that one's sexual life was a very isolated topic that doesn't spill over into other aspects of social life.[25] Kay Kavanagh's piece suggests, and I think with very good reason, that it *does* spill over into other areas; therefore, this is a richer look at that law and its implications.[26]

Therapeutic jurisprudence is a framework for asking questions and for raising certain questions that might otherwise go unaddressed. The answers to those questions are often empirical. Is Kay Kavanaugh right in suggesting that the rule has this chilling effect on other conversational topics?

Secondly, even if true empirically, there remains the normative question: what, if anything, should we *do* about that rule? Therapeutic jurisprudence sharpens the debate, focuses the debate; it does not really provide answers here, but it does bring these questions out into the open.

"Don't Ask, Don't Tell" is an example then of a *legal rule* and how it might be looked at from a therapeutic jurisprudence perspective.[27] Next, let's look at a *legal procedure*.[28]

An example of a legal procedure looked at through the lens of therapeutic jurisprudence is an article by Professor Janet Weinstein regarding child custody disputes.[29] Weinstein wrote about how the adversary process in a child custody context can be both traumatic for the child and damaging to the relationship of the parents who may, despite their divorce, need to have some kind of relationship in the future merely for the sake of the child.[30]

Weinstein's analysis is very interesting because it exposes how the adversary process encourages us to find the worst thing about the other party, to bring it out, and to talk about just how terrible that other parent is.[31] This is traumatic to children and, of course, damaging to the relationship of the parents.[32] Can there be other, less damaging ways of resolving these issues, such as through mediation or new mechanisms such as collaborative divorce. Therapeutic jurisprudence focuses on these creative explorations.[33]

Finally, an example of the third category is *legal roles*. This category examines the behavior of lawyers, judges, and other actors in the legal system.[34] For instance, the way

---

22. *See id.*
23. *See id.* at 344.
24. *See id.* at 353–54.
25. *See id.*
26. *See id.* at 353–64.
27. *See id.* at 343–63.
28. *See* Weinstein, *supra* note 14.
29. *See id.*
30. *See id.* at 123–24.
31. *See id.* at 86–88.
32. *See id.*
33. *See generally* David B. Wexler, *Therapeutic Jurisprudence and the Culture of Critique*, 10 J. Contemp. Legal Issues 263 (1999).
34. *See* Wexler, *supra* note 15, at 167–68.

the judge behaves at a sentencing hearing can actually, in and of itself, affect how someone who has been given probation complies with the conditions of that probation.[35]

In the simplest example, if a judge is not entirely clear in formulating a condition of probation, someone may not comply with the probationary terms because he or she never quite understood what it is that he or she was told to do or not to do.[36] How a judge behaves at a hearing can affect whether someone complies.[37] Later, I will come back to that issue and put it in a more complex context.

Therapeutic jurisprudence grew out of mental health law, the area that has been the main subject of the Thomas M. Cooley Law Review's Disabilities Law Symposium, from which these remarks are drawn.[38] Therapeutic jurisprudence cut its teeth on civil commitment, the insanity defense, and incompetency to stand trial.[39] It looked at the way in which a system that is designed to help people recover or achieve mental health often backfires and causes just the opposite.[40]

Therefore, a perspective developed recognizing that the law itself, know it or not, like it or not, sometimes functions as a therapeutic or an antitherapeutic agent.[41] This is, of course, highly relevant to mental health law. The therapeutic jurisprudence perspective, however, now applies to other legal areas, probably all legal areas. For example, the perspective applies to mental health law, criminal law, juvenile law, family law, and other areas. Personal injury law has also received attention.[42] We think of compensation in personal injury law as a way of trying with money to make someone whole; to put injured persons in a position that they would have been in if they hadn't been subjected to this accident.[43] It is clumsy, but it is designed to try to make them whole.[44]

What therapeutic jurisprudence adds to this mix is that compensation may *itself* affect the course of recovery.[45] Sometimes, time simply does not heal. Sometimes we see that people do not recover until a case is settled, for example, and sometimes they con-

---

35. *See id.* at 168.
36. *See id.* at 167–68.
37. *See* Donald Meichenbaum & Dennis C. Turk, Facilitating Treatment Adherence: A Practitioner's Guidebook (1987).
38. Address at the Thomas M. Cooley Law Review Disabilities Law Symposium (Oct. 29, 1999).
39. *See generally* David B. Wexler, Therapeutic Jurisprudence: The Law as a Therapeutic Agent (1990) (focusing on mental health issues).
40. *See id.* at 9. An early example that started me thinking along lines that culminated in the development of the therapeutic jurisprudence perspective was coming across a situation involving an Arizona statute that paid the transportation costs to the state hospital only for court-committed patients, not for voluntary ones, thus legislatively creating an incentive for involuntary hospitalization. See David B. Wexler, Stanley E. Scoville, et al, The Administration of Psychiatric Justice: Theory and Practice in Arizona, 13 Ariz. L. Rev. 1, 58 n.186 (1971).
41. *See* Wexler & Winick, *supra* note 2, at xvii. I wrote the first paper on therapeutic jurisprudence, explicating and naming the perspective, for a 1987 National Institute of Mental Health law-mental health workshop. I was asked to write within the general area of law and therapy, and decided to sharpen my focus by concentrating not on law and therapy but rather on law as therapy, as therapy through law, thereby offering a conceptual framework for therapeutic jurisprudence as a discrete field of inquiry. For an historical account, see generally David B. Wexler, The Development of Therapeutic Jurisprudence: From Theory to Practice, 68 Revista Jurídica Universidad de Puerto Rico 691(1999).
42. *See* Daniel W. Shuman, *The Psychology of Compensation in Tort Law, in* Key, *supra* note 2, at 438.
43. *See id.*
44. *See id.* at 441.
45. *See id.* at 433.

sciously or unconsciously exaggerate or accentuate the injury.[46] Thus, compensation can independently affect a person's healing process,[47] above and beyond its theoretical purpose.[48] Therapeutic jurisprudence encourages people to think about that and study it to see if there are certain ways that we can lessen that impact.[49] In summary, then, therapeutic jurisprudence started as a new twist on mental health law and has now become a mental health twist on law *in general,* and in all legal areas.

One of the things therapeutic jurisprudence tries to do is to look carefully at promising literature from psychology, psychiatry, clinical behavioral sciences, criminology and social work to see whether those insights can be incorporated or brought into the legal system.[50] In this respect therapeutic jurisprudence is very different from the early days of mental health law, where the effort was really just to see what was *wrong* with this sort of literature or testimony.[51] Again, there were good reasons for that early emphasis; however, an exclusive focus on what is wrong, rather than also looking at what might be *right* and how we might *use* some of this material, is seriously shortsighted.

Current therapeutic jurisprudence thinking encourages us to look very hard for promising developments, even if the behavioral science literature itself has nothing to do with the law. It also encourages people to think creatively about how these promising developments might be brought into the legal system.[52] An example links back to the earlier discussion of the judge's role in setting probation conditions or conditions on someone being conditionally released from a mental hospital after a judgment of not guilty by reason of insanity.[53]

Facilitating Treatment Adherence is a book written by psychologists on psychological principles that could help doctors and other health care providers have their patients adhere better to medical advice.[54] It is not specifically about psychiatry, although it could include that medical specialty, and it had nothing at all to do with law.[55] But the words "facilitating treatment adherence," approached from a therapeutic jurisprudence angle, were exciting to me.[56] I wondered whether the law could use any of this to facilitate a probationer's compliance with conditions of probation, and to facilitate an insanity acquittee's compliance with conditions of release from an institution.[57]

Those principles dealt first with some very common sense things, such as speaking in simple terms.[58] Patients sometimes may not comply with medical advice because they just never really quite got the message.[59] They were not told in simple terms what the doctor was suggesting they do, or they were not asked before they left, "Now, let's make sure you've got this straight. Tell me what you intend to do, how often you're going to

---

46. *See id.*
47. *See id.*
48. *See id.*
49. *See id.* at 443–44; *see also* Katherine Lippel, *Therapeutic and Anti-Therapeutic Consequences of Workers' Compensation,* 22 Int'l J. L. & Psychiatry 521 (1999).
50. *See* Wexler, *supra* note 2, at xvii.
51. *See* Wexler, *supra* note 15, at 167–77.
52. *See id.* at 167.
53. *See* Meichenbaum & Turk, *supra* note 37, at 159–60.
54. *See* Meichenbaum & Turk, *supra* note 37.
55. *See id.*
56. *See id.*
57. *See* Wexler, *supra* note 15, at 165.
58. *See* Meichenbaum & Turk, *supra* note 37, at 81, 116.
59. *See id.* at 76.

take these pills? Do you take them with meals or without meals? How often do you take them?"[60] Thus, noncompliance sometimes results from insufficient clarity in giving instructions.[61]

Another principle that Meichenbaum and Turk dealt with was signing a behavioral contract.[62] When people sign behavioral contracts, they are more likely to comply with medical advice than if they do not.[63] Also, if they made a public commitment to comply, to persons above and beyond the health care provider, they were more likely to comply.[64] Relatedly, if family members were informed of what patients were to do, those patients were more likely to comply.[65]

It is interesting to think about how these principles might operate in a legal setting.[66] For example, if a judge is looking at a proposal for an acquitted insanity patient to be conditionally released from a hospital or when a judge is deciding whether to grant probation in a sentencing hearing, the court could conceptualize the conditional release as a type of behavioral contract: I will agree to give you probation if you will agree to abide by these conditions.

One can also envision a hearing as a forum in which an insanity acquittee or criminal defendant makes a public commitment to comply.[67] You might also see whether agreed-upon family members might be present at that hearing.[68]

These are ways of trying to bring these psychological health care compliance principles into a legal setting. Now, will they work the same way in that setting? That is the kind of empirical question that therapeutic jurisprudence suggests or raises but does not answer.

Should we do it? Is it going to be too time consuming? Do judges have the time to do this? That's the normative question that gets raised by all of this. But I suggest that we're now asking questions that otherwise we might not be asking at all.

Another way in which therapeutic jurisprudence has tried to use information from behavioral science relates to cognitive distortions of offenders, especially sex offenders.[69] Many therapists suggest that in order to take a first step in the treatment of offenders, one needs to tackle offender denial or minimization.[70] The offenders also need to take responsibility and to be accountable.[71] They need to overcome the cognitive distortions of denial and minimization, such as "I didn't do it," or "I did it but it wasn't my idea," and "I did it and it was my idea but it wasn't for sexual gratification."[72]

A question therapeutic jurisprudence would ask is whether the law in practice operates to foster cognitive restructuring or whether it actually perpetuates cognitive distor-

---

60. *See id.* at 122.
61. *See id.* at 113.
62. *See id.* at 164–73.
63. *See id.* at 164.
64. *See id.* at 124–25.
65. *See id.*
66. *See id.* at 164.
67. *See* Wexler, *supra* note 15, at 167–68.
68. *See id.* at 168.
69. *See id.* at 159.
70. *See id.*
71. *See id.* at 159, 161–62.
72. *See id.* at 159.

tions.[73] One area we might examine is the plea process. When judges take guilty pleas, and most people do plead guilty, there is a requirement that the court find that the plea is voluntary and that there is a factual basis for the plea.[74] There are different ways that judges behave in accepting pleas from offenders, and some legal anthropologists who have actually gone into the courtrooms have categorized and classified these judicial behaviors.[75]

Some judges are very "record oriented."[76] They try to avoid dealing with the defendant because he could "muck up" the record.[77] Instead, they look to statements of the prosecutor, the defense counsel, or something in the file that will establish the factual basis for the plea.[78] Those courts involve the defendants minimally.[79]

Other judges have an open colloquy with the defendant, such as: "Okay, you realize this is the offense that you're pleading to. Please tell me in your own words what happened, when, and so on."[80] The second type of judicial behavior might be a bit better than the first because it takes that first step of confronting denial, minimization, and encouraging an offender to take responsibility.[81]

The next example concerns rights and responsibilities and their relationship to rehabilitation.[82] I have been interested in some recent literature that relates to relapse prevention planning principles and how they may be brought into the law.

For years there was a real pessimism in rehabilitation and rehabilitative efforts.[83] Starting in the 1970s, when Martinson suggested that nothing really worked, there was a long period of time when people were giving up on rehabilitation.[84]

More recently, it looks like there are certain kinds of rehabilitative programs and packages, particularly the cognitive/behavioral variety, that look rather promising.[85] One type of these cognitive behavioral treatments encourages offenders to think through the chain of events that lead to criminality and then tries to get the offenders to stop and think in advance.[86] This will enable an offender to figure out two things: (1) what are the high risk situations, in my case, for criminality or juvenile delinquency; and (2) how can the high risk situations be avoided, or how can the situations be coped with if they arise?[87]

---

73. *See id.*
74. *See id.* at 159–60.
75. *See id.* at 159–64.
76. *See id.* at 163.
77. *See id.*
78. *See id.* at 162–63.
79. *See id.* at 163.
80. *See id.* at 161–62.
81. *See id.*; *see also* Katherine Corry Eastman, *Sexual Abuse Treatment in Kansas's Prisons: Compelling Inmate to Admit Guilt*, 38 Washburn L. J. 949 (1999); Jonathon Kadan, *Therapy for Convicted Sex Offenders: Pursuing Rehabilitation Without Incrimination*, 89 J. Crim. L. & Criminology 347 (1998).
82. *See* Dr. Robert Miller, Address at the *Thomas M. Cooley Law Review Disabilities Law Symposium* (Oct. 29, 1999).
83. *See generally* Robert Martinson, *What Works? Questions and Answers About Prison Reform*, 35 Public Interest 22 (1974) (stating that the evidence did not suggest that rehabilitation worked).
84. *See id.*
85. *See* James McGuire, What Works: Reducing Reoffending (McGuire ed., 1995).
86. *See* Jack Bush, *Teaching Self-Risk Management to Violent Offenders, in* McGuire, *supra* note 85, at 139, 141.
87. *See id.*

These situations may be things such as realizing you are very much at risk on Friday nights after having partied with such and such person. The offender may decide that he or she shouldn't go out Friday nights. This determination is a way of avoiding high risk behaviors.[88] Instead of going out on Friday night with Joe and getting into trouble, the offender may choose to stay home. But what happens the next night when Joe calls or what happens when Joe knocks on the offender's door?

Therapists have developed approaches of working with these issues, and of having offenders prepare relapse prevention plans.[89] There are also certain programs, like "reasoning and rehabilitation" type programs, that teach offenders cognitive self change, to stop and think and figure out consequences, to anticipate high risk situations, and to learn to avoid and cope with them.[90]

These programs seem to be reasonably successful.[91] One of the issues that I am interested in now, from a therapeutic jurisprudence standpoint, is how this might be brought into the law. In one obvious sense, these problem-solving, reasoning and rehabilitation type of programs can be made widely available in correctional and community settings.[92] A way of linking them even more to the law, of course, would be to say that as a condition of probation or parole, one might have to attend or complete one of these courses.[93]

A more subtle way of thinking about this in therapeutic jurisprudence terms, however, is to ask how reasoning and rehabilitation can be made part of the legal process *itself*.[94] The suggestion here is that if a judge or parole board becomes familiar with these techniques and is about to consider someone for probation, the judge might say, "I'm going to consider you but I want you to come up with a type of preliminary plan that we will use as a basis of discussion. I want you to figure out why I should grant you probation and why I should be comfortable that you're going to succeed. In order for me to feel comfortable, I need to know what you regard to be high risk situations and how you're going to avoid them or cope with them."[95]

If that approach is followed, courts will be promoting cognitive self-charge as part and parcel of the sentencing process itself.[96] The process may operate this way: "I realize I mess up on Friday nights; therefore, I propose that I will stay home Friday nights." Suddenly, it is not a judge imposing something on you. It's something you are coming up with so you should think it is fair. You have a voice in it, and presumably your compliance with this condition will also be better.[97]

I hope I have given you an idea of what therapeutic jurisprudence is through these examples, and how it tries to achieve therapeutic goals through the very operation of the legal system itself. The remainder or this volume will further introduce principles of Therapeutic Jurisprudence and will suggest how Therapeutic Jurisprudence may inform criminal law practice.

---

88. *See id.*
89. *See* Christine Knott, *The STOP Programme: Reasoning and Rehabilitation in a British Setting*, in McGuire, *supra* note 84, at 115.
90. *See* Knott, *supra* note 89.
91. *See id.*
92. *See id.*
93. *See id.*
94. *See* David B. Wexler, *How The Law Can Use What Works: A Therapeutic Jurisprudence Look at Recent Research in Rehabilitation*, 15 Behav. Sci. & L. 365, 367 (1997).
95. *See id.* at 367–68.
96. *See* Knott, *supra* note 85, at 117.
97. *See id.*

B. Application to Criminal Law

i. A Tripartite Framework
David B. Wexler, A Tripartite Framework for Incorporating Therapeutic Jurisprudence in Criminal Law Education, Research, and Practice

(Reprinted with permission from
Florida Coastal Law Review 95, 2005)

Slowly but surely the practice of law—or at least the practice of some lawyers—is beginning to change. The change is in the direction of practicing in a more holistic way, of lawyering with an ethic of care, and, as a recent popular book put it, of "law reform as if people mattered."[1]

Much of the change relates to the therapeutic jurisprudence ("TJ") perspective and to its movement from theory to practice. Practical therapeutic jurisprudence scholarship relates to judging, legal counseling, numerous aspects of clinical legal education, and most recently, criminal law practice.[2]

This essay seeks to facilitate the development of criminal lawyering by offering a simple yet useful model of the components or ingredients of a therapeutic jurisprudence criminal law practice. These components—which I hope will promote inquiry and facilitate teaching—can perhaps best be illustrated by a concrete case. Interestingly, and perhaps significantly, the case I have selected is, in its facts and legal import, an "ordinary" one, not unlike the steady diet of cases handled by criminal defense lawyers.

I. A Representative Case

The case is *United States v. Riggs*,[3] involving a federal firearm violation by one formerly convicted of a felony. According to the opinion, the chronological facts are as follows:

1. Riggs suffers from paranoid schizophrenia and, without medication, experiences auditory hallucinations and paranoia.[4]

2. These symptoms began to assert themselves approximately two years before his first arrest on Maryland state charges of drug distribution and possession of a

---

1. Mark Satin, Radical Middle: The Politics We Need Now 54–55 (2004).
2. *See* International Network on Therapeutic Jurisprudence, http://www.therapeutic jurisprudence.org (last visited Aug. 28, 2005) (providing a bibliography). On criminal law practice, see David B. Wexler, *Therapeutic Jurisprudence and the Rehabilitative Role of the Criminal Defense Lawyer*, 17 St. Thomas L. Rev. 743 (2005); Cait Clarke & James Neuhard, *Making the Case: Therapeutic Jurisprudence and Problem Solving Practices Positively Impact Clients, the Justice Systems and Communities They Serve*, 17 St. Thomas L. Rev. 781 (2005); David B. Wexler, *Some Reflections on Therapeutic Jurisprudence and the Practice of Criminal Law*, 38 Crim. L. Bull. 205 (2002) [hereinafter *Some Reflections*]; Martin Reisig, *The Difficult Role of the Defense Lawyer in a Post-Adjudication Drug Treatment Court: Accommodating Therapeutic Jurisprudence and Due Process*, 38 Crim. L. Bull 216 (2002); Astrid Birgden, *Dealing with the Resistant Criminal Client: A Psychologically-Minded Strategy for More Effective Legal Counseling*, 38 Crim. L. Bull. 225 (2002).
3. United States v. Riggs, 370 F.3d 382 (4th Cir. 2004), *vacated by* 125 S. Ct. 1015 (2005).
4. *Id.* at 383.

shotgun found during a subsequent search of his home.[5] However, Riggs did not receive any psychiatric treatment until *after* his arrest.[6]

3. Riggs began taking oral medication to control the schizophrenia, and was sentenced on the state charges to three years probation, which he successfully completed.[7]

4. At some point Riggs failed to take his medication for two or three days,[8] began hallucinating, and believed people were trying to hurt him.[9] The parties agreed Riggs's failure to take his medication was the cause of Riggs's later legal trouble.[10]

5. A few days after discontinuing his medication Riggs was stopped for driving a vehicle with expired plates.[11] Riggs was clutching his jacket and refused to show his hands.[12] A pat-down frisk revealed a .22 revolver in Riggs's jacket, leading to the federal firearm violation.[13]

6. Riggs pled guilty to the federal offense and resumed taking his oral medication.[14] Moreover, after the federal arrest, Riggs's mother began reminding Riggs daily to take his oral medication, and his treating physician started Riggs on long-acting intramuscular injections of antipsychotic drugs—drugs that remain in the bloodstream for a month, assuring adequate medication even if he failed to take the oral medication.[15]

7. Riggs was on pre-sentence release for almost two years.[16] That period was marked by its uneventful nature, during which Riggs took his medication without incident.

8. At the federal sentencing hearing, evidence was presented regarding the intramuscular injections, Riggs's oral medication compliance, and his mother's role in providing reminders.[17] Moreover, "Riggs emphasized to the court that he wanted to continue taking his medication, an intent that his consulting clinical psychologist believed."[18]

9. Under the then-existing sentencing guidelines, the district court granted a diminished capacity downward departure and sentenced Riggs to three years probation, of which twelve months was to be served under home confinement with an electric home monitoring system. The court did not believe the nonincarcerative downward departure to be barred by a need to protect the public:

> I really do think that to the extent one can tell, based upon the facts as they now exist, things are under control, that you have been taking your medication, your mother is making sure, and ... [your] treating

---

5. *Id.* at 391 (Duncan, J., dissenting).
6. *Id.*
7. *Id.* at 383.
8. *Id.* at 391 (Duncan, J., dissenting).
9. *Id.* at 383.
10. *Id.* at 391 (Duncan, J., dissenting).
11. *Id.* at 383.
12. *Id.*
13. *Id.*
14. *Id.* at 384.
15. *Id.*
16. *Id.*
17. *Id.* at 390 (Duncan, J., dissenting).
18. *Id.*

> physician is making sure you take your medication, and as long as you do that I think you are going to be law abiding.[19]

For our heuristic purposes, the preceding facts are more or less sufficient. In terms of the human drama and legal niceties, however, there is more to the story. The government appealed—on public protection grounds—the district court's grant of the downward departure. A divided panel of the Fourth Circuit agreed with the government, vacated the sentence, and remanded for resentencing. The majority noted that "although Riggs has been complying with his treatment program, we see no adequate assurance in the record that he will continue to do so."[20] The dissent strongly disagreed with the position that, despite the apparent success of Riggs's treatment plan, "the possibility that the defendant *might*, at some future time, decide not to take his medications requires the defendant's incarceration to protect the public."[21] But significantly, *Riggs* was decided before—and was ultimately vacated and remanded in light of—the United States Supreme Court's landmark decision in *United States v. Booker*,[22] which in essence converts the federal sentencing guidelines from mandatory to advisory only and subjects imposed sentences to a "reasonableness" review.

Before proceeding to piece together the components of TJ lawyering, two observations are in order. First, the thrust of *Booker* is likely to lead federal courts to pay greater attention to general factors in sentencing, including treatment and rehabilitative goals.[23] In any case, after *Booker*, the sort of probationary sentence imposed by the district court in *Riggs* should be less likely to be reversed on appeal. *Booker*, if it is not undone by Congress, surely ushers in the distinct possibility of a true therapeutic jurisprudence perspective in federal criminal court.

Next, recall that Riggs's symptoms surfaced two years before his initial arrest, but that Riggs did not receive mental health treatment until after he was arrested. It was not until his second arrest that his medication regimen was augmented by a monthly intramuscular injection.

This noteworthy, but not at all uncommon, sequence of events underscores the difficulty of the position of those who "prefer that the judicial system was out of the business of organizing and providing social services to individuals and families,"[24] or who oppose "making the judiciary more like the public health arena."[25] Of course, the more

---

19. *Id.* at 384.
20. *Id.* at 386.
21. *Id.* at 387 (Duncan, J., dissenting) (emphasis in original).
22. United States v. Booker, 125 S. Ct. 738 (2005).
23. *See, e.g.*, the treatment-oriented provision in 18 U.S.C. §3553(a)(2)(D), which is receiving much post-*Booker* attention. United States v. Ranum, 353 F. Supp. 2d (E.D. Wis. 2005); United States v. Jones, 355 F. Supp. 2d (D. Me. 2005). In fact, on remand, when the Fourth Circuit considered its *Riggs* opinion in light of *Booker*, it reinstated its earlier opinion reversing and remanding for re-sentencing. But the now unanimous panel recognized the greater flexibility wrought by *Booker*, as well as the appropriateness of a "reasonableness" review. United States v. Riggs, 410 F.3d 136, 137 (4th Cir. 2005).

Even before *Booker*, a federal judge wrote an op-ed piece in the New York Times urging a more flexible and therapeutic approach for the federal justice system. *See* Donald P. Lay, *Rehab Justice*, N.Y. Times, Nov. 18, 2004, at A31.

24. Jennie J. Long, *Book Review of Winick and Wexler (eds.) Judging in a Therapeutic Key*, 40 Crim. L. Bull. 541, 542 (2004) (book review).
25. Jessica Pearson, *Special Issue: Models of Collaboration in Family Law: The Bookshelf: Bruce J. Winick and David B. Wexler (Eds.), Judging in a Therapeutic Key: Therapeutic Jurisprudence and the Courts*, 42 Fam. Ct. Rev. 384, 385 (2004) (book review).

"macro" issues of prevention, treatment, and services need to be seriously and vigorously addressed.[26] The legal profession needs to be an important participant and advocate in this venture.[27] But as the facts of *Riggs* suggest, no matter what the available resources, the criminal justice system will often function as a legal emergency room.[28] There is thus a crucial role for lawyers and courts to concern themselves with treatment issues at the "micro" level[29] of the individual case and client. Let us then turn to the nature of TJ criminal lawyering.

II. The Components of TJ Criminal Lawyering

Several factors facilitated the district court's decision to grant Riggs a probationary sentence. Riggs's mental condition seemed very much "under control," according to the court, thanks to the medication. Riggs was receptive to taking the medication, was reminded daily by his mother, and was, in any case, administered a monthly long-acting intramuscular injection. Moreover, the adequacy of the treatment plan was evidenced by an almost two year period of successful pre-sentence release.

For pedagogical purposes, the above factors can be helpfully grouped into three categories: (1) treatment and social service resources (here, the availability and suitability of both the oral and intramuscular medication); (2) the legal landscape (the ability under the law to defer sentence and permit a period of pre-sentence release); and (3) the less obvious and more nuanced category that we might call theory-inspired practices (reflected here by the involvement of defendant's mother and, arguably, by the positive and reinforcing judicial remark that matters were "under control"). The remainder of this essay will explore further this tripartite classification or, in keeping with the standard vocabulary of the therapeutic jurisprudence "lens,"[30] will look at the criminal lawyer's potential role through a TJ trifocal.

A. Treatment and Social Service Resources

The availability of treatment is of course an essential ingredient in TJ criminal lawyering—and, ideally, in preventing many of the incidents that trigger the involvement of the criminal justice system. Services are necessary for mental health problems, such as was encountered in *Riggs*, as well as for substance abuse, domestic violence, child abuse, and the like.

Lawyers need to have a basic understanding of these problem areas and of the programs designed to deal with them. Through judicial colleges and associations, judges are beginning to receive basic instruction in these areas,[31] and lawyers and law students likewise need an exposure to this material. An introductory course in social work and social welfare, especially if brought to life by a series of guest speakers from local programs and agencies, would be a wonderful addition to the law school curriculum.[32]

---

26. *See* Long, *supra* note 24; Pearson, *supra* note 25.
27. Wexler, *Some Reflections*, *supra* note 2.
28. Of course, as a matter of policy, we would surely want to avoid a situation where treatment and services are provided and are available *primarily* through the courts, thereby in essence rewarding criminal behavior. Pearson, *supra* note 25, at 386 ("Will we reward criminal behavior with jobs, housing, and education?").
29. Long, *supra* note 24, at 542.
30. *E.g.*, Law in a Therapeutic Key: Therapeutic Jurisprudence and the Courts xix (David B. Wexler & Bruce J. Winick eds., 1996).
31. *See* National Judicial College, http://www.judges.org (last visited Aug., 26, 2005).
32. *See, e.g.*, Rosalie Ambrosino et al., Social Work and Social Welfare: An Introduction (5th ed. 2005). The University of Arizona is planning to offer just such a course as part of its law school curriculum.

Mostly, of course, this overall category is the proper province of the mental health, social work, and criminal justice fields, but lawyers need to grasp the essentials and need to know how to relate to, ask questions of, and coordinate with those allied professions: Is this a condition that can be improved by medication? Is there any kind of appropriate long-acting medication available for patients who are forgetful about daily medication-taking?

The need for basic knowledge and inter-professional cooperation, moreover, extends as well to "jobs, housing, food, education, and health care."[33] For we cannot "address the causes of recidivism without creating jobs for offenders or places where they can live"[34] and cannot adequately tackle problems of domestic violence and child abuse and neglect when breadwinners cannot find jobs.[35]

Lawyers are not equipped to be social science researchers delving into the efficacy of treatment programs. But lawyers should be competent consumers and conveyors of that research. They can synthesize and draw bottom-line conclusions about the research.[36] They can, moreover, serve as compilers of (and, when appropriate, complainers about) their clients' experiences in given programs.[37] Working in partnership with social workers, the legal profession—especially in law school clinics and public defender offices—can embody this material in useful up-to-date manuals of services and resources.[38] Lawyers acutely aware of service shortcomings can, especially if they are institutional defenders,[39] advocate freely for needed programs and resources.

B. *The Legal Landscape*

Much like the first category—treatment and social services resources—is primarily in the province of social work, but nonetheless sometimes influenced by the needs of clients of the legal profession, the present category, focusing on the legal landscape, is quite clearly in the lawyer's domain, yet ideally shaped by therapeutic considerations. At issue here are the various legal provisions, usually statutory, that facilitate or impede the practice of therapeutic jurisprudence in a given jurisdiction.

As was suggested during the earlier discussion of the *Riggs* case, a rigid, inflexible sentencing scheme, especially one characterized by mandatory incarcerative penalties, is surely a major impediment. By contrast, the ability to defer the imposition of sentencing, also involved in *Riggs*, is surely a major facilitator. The deferral can allow rehabilitative efforts to get meaningfully underway, and can, as in *Riggs*, allow for gauging their likely success.[40]

---

33. *See* Pearson, *supra* note 25, at 386.
34. *Id.*
35. *Id. See also* Long, *supra* note 24. This task shows the blurring of law and social work as well as the blurring of functions between criminal defense lawyers and civil legal aid lawyers.
36. *E.g.*, David R. Katner, *A Defense Perspective of Treatment Programs for Juvenile Sex Offenders*, 37 CRIM. L. BULL. 371 (2001).
37. A book by a physician could serve as a model for attorneys: LONNY SHAVELSON, HOOKED: FIVE ADDICTS CHALLENGE OUR MISGUIDED DRUG REHAB SYSTEM (2001).
38. *See* SUSAN GOLDBERG, CANADA'S NATIONAL JUDICIAL INSTITUTE, JUDGING FOR THE 21ST CENTURY: A PROBLEM-SOLVING APPROACH (2005), *available at* http://www.nji.ca/Public/documents/Judgingfor21scenturyDe.pdf (last visited Aug. 28. 2005) [hereinafter JUDGING FOR THE 21ST CENTURY] (an excellent judicial manual).
39. Wexler, *Some Reflections*, *supra* note 2.
40. BRUCE J. WINICK, REDEFINING THE ROLE OF THE CRIMINAL DEFENSE LAWYER AT PLEA BARGAINING AND SENTENCING: A THERAPEUTIC JURISPRUDENCE/PREVENTIVE LAW MODEL, IN PRACTICING THERAPEUTIC JURISPRUDENCE: LAW AS A HELPING PROFESSION 245 (Dennis P. Stolle et al. eds., 2000) [hereinafter PRACTICING TJ]; United States v. Flowers, 983 F. Supp. 159 (E.D.N.Y. 1997). In

Jurisdictions may differ markedly in the "TJ-friendly features" of their legal landscapes, or at least in the extent to which certain facilitative features are present, absent, or ambiguous. A comparative law analysis—within the United States and internationally—can yield promising proposals as well as creative implementation efforts.

For instance, in some jurisdictions, sentencing may be deferred, either indefinitely or for a limited period, in the sole discretion of the court.[41] However, in other jurisdictions—such as Canada—the situation is less clear, although in practice sentencing is often deferred if both the defense and the Crown consent.[42] At the other end of the criminal process, some jurisdictions allow for motivating and rewarding an offender by the possibility of early termination of probation,[43] or parole,[44] whereas others do not permit or are silent on the possibility.[45]

With regard to probationary sentences in general, the therapeutic jurisprudence literature recommends, in addition to the possibility of early termination, a process of ongoing judicial supervision by means of periodic review hearings.[46] The review process is meant to monitor compliance—of both the offender and the social service agencies—and, in cases of successful offender compliance, to provide an opportunity for the court to reinforce and praise the offender's efforts.[47]

American jurisdictions seem rather "TJ-friendly" regarding the possibility of follow-up hearings for probationers. Apparently, so is Canadian law.[48] New Zealand law, however, is not.

In New Zealand, once a sentence of supervision has been imposed, the case may come back to court only upon application by the probation officer or the offender; routine review hearings on the court's own initiative are apparently not contemplated.[49] When there is more than a single charge, New Zealand judges have at times creatively, if necessarily clumsily, implemented the law to allow for periodic review hearings.

---

traditional TJ terminology, deferral of sentence could be regarded as an "opportunity spot." See PRACTICING TJ, *supra*, at 61.

41. PRACTICING TJ, *supra* note 40. In Western Australia, the court may defer sentencing, but for only a period of six months. Sentencing Act, 1995, c. 16(1)-(2) (W. Austl.).

42. JUDGING FOR THE 21ST CENTURY, *supra* note 38, at 33. Section 720 of the Canadian Criminal Code states that "a court shall, as soon as practicable after an offender has been found guilty, conduct proceedings to determine the appropriate sentence to be imposed." Provincial Court Judge Sharon Van de Veen notes that the section seems not to permit deferred sentencing unless the words "as soon as practicable" are interpreted and include an offender undergoing a treatment program to assist the court in determining an appropriate sentence. Clarifying—and facilitating—legislation is expected soon. S. L. Van de Veen, A Canadian Response to Professor David Wexler's Presentation Entitled A Dozen Therapeutic Jurisprudence Principles For Use in Sentencing (Mar. 2005) (unpublished manuscript, on file with author, presented in Vancouver, B.C., Apr. 1, 2005).

43. ARIZ. REV. STAT. § 13-901(E) (2004).

44. JOAN PETERSILIA, WHEN PRISONERS COME HOME 211 (2003) ("goal parole").

45. *Id. See also* David B. Wexler, *Spain's JVP (Juez de Vigilancia Penitenciaria) Legal Structure as a Potential Model for a Re-Entry Court*, 7(1) CONTEMP. ISSUES IN L. 1, 7 (2004) [hereinafter *Spain's JVP Law*].

46. David B. Wexler, *Robes and Rehabilitation: How Judges Can Help Offenders Make Good*, 38 CT. REV. 18 (2001) [hereinafter *Robes and Rehabilitation*]. For a general resource on the use of therapeutic jurisprudence in judicial settings, most of which is pertinent in the criminal context, see JUDGING IN A THERAPEUTIC KEY: THERAPEUTIC JURISPRUDENCE AND THE COURTS (Bruce J. Winick & David B. Wexler eds., 2003) [hereinafter TJ JUDGING].

47. Wexler, *Robes and Rehabilitation*, *supra* note 46.

48. Hon. Judge Sherry L. Van de Veen, *Some Canadian Problem Solving Court Processes*, 83(1) CANADIAN B. REV. 91, 136–38 (2004).

49. Sentencing Act, 2002, § 54 (N.Z.).

Through implementation, the law has been converted into what we might call a "fairweather friend" by the device of holding one charge back and making it a condition of bail that the sentence of supervision imposed on the *other* charge be complied with. The court can then hold review hearings on the held-back charge.[50]

Although New Zealand law and American law differ considerably regarding judicial authority after the imposition of a probationary sentence, even American law does not ordinarily contemplate judicial involvement after the imposition of an *incarcerative* sentence. The absence of judicial branch authority over incarcerated offenders has hampered efforts to create "re-entry" courts to ease offenders, perhaps through a judicially supervised conditional release process, back into society.[51] In the United States, if discretionary release of a prisoner does exist, the authority resides in the executive branch, typically with a parole board.[52] However, with a 'just desert' model of criminal sentencing, even that discretionary power has been largely eroded.[53]

Spain, however, recognizes judicial authority over prisoners. There, judges monitor an offender's progress through three correctional levels, and can grant, monitor, and revoke conditional release. In a recent essay, I examined certain "TJ-friendly features" of the Spanish law and proposed the Spanish legal structure as worthy of consideration in the construction of United States re-entry courts.[54] From a therapeutic jurisprudence perspective there are several attractive features of the Spanish law:

1. Conditional release authority resides in a single judge rather than a multi-member board, allowing for the possibility of developing a one-to-one relationship between the judge and the offender, thereby increasing the judge's motivational influence.[55]

2. The judge's role begins at the time of incarceration (much earlier than when the offender becomes eligible for conditional release), allowing the judge, from the beginning, to monitor—and motivate—the offender's progress in the correctional environment.[56]

3. Under the statute, if a prisoner has served a certain portion of the imposed sentence, is in the third (the highest) classification level, and has a good behavioral record and prognosis, conditional release should follow. Conditional release is not automatic once an offender serves a certain portion of the sentence (which would sap the system of motivational strength), nor does release lie in the unfettered discretion of the judge (which could lead to arbitrariness, help-

---

50. Interview with Judge John Walker, Provincial Court Judge (Jan. 31, 2005). The procedure can also be employed, under section 25 of the Sentencing Act of 2002, with a deferred sentence accompanied by review hearings on the deferred charge. *Id.*
51. *Spain's JVP Law, supra* note 45.
52. An exception is in the codes of several tribal nations, where tribal courts often have the authority to grant parole. *E.g.*, Tohono O'Odham Nation Law and Order Code §1.11(5): "A person convicted of an offense and sentenced to jail may be paroled after he or she has served at least half of the particular sentence with good behavior." With such a "TJ-friendly feature," the Tohono O'Odham are well-positioned to create a re-entry court. Logistics are favorable as well, since offenders are incarcerated in a jail on the reservation itself, which is by no means always the case with tribal governments.
53. *Spain's JVP Law, supra* note 45, at 3.
54. *Id. passim.*
55. *Id.* at 4.
56. *Id.* at 4–5.

lessness, frustration, and rage). Rather, a standard of "constrained discretion" seems to meet both therapeutic and justice objectives.[57]

4. The judge can set appropriate conditions, including conditions for follow-up hearings, as part of the release process.[58]

The illustrations provided in this section are rather random. They are drawn from the existing therapeutic jurisprudence literature and from the author's brief exposure, during professional visits, to the legal provisions of some other nations. Obviously, a careful, systematic examination of the criminal code in a given jurisdiction will reveal a great many instances of provisions friendly or hostile to a therapeutic jurisprudence approach. It would likely also call attention to provisions which, if used creatively, could pave the way for an increased therapeutic jurisprudence practice. For instance, the therapeutic jurisprudence literature suggests the value of "behavioral contracting" to set appropriate conditions of probation.[59] It has been suggested by a Canadian judge that the simple "allocution" provision requiring judges to ask offenders whether they have anything to say before sentence is imposed could, combined with the pre-sentence guidance and preparation provided clients by defense counsel, constitute a convenient context for discussing and setting the terms of a behavioral contract.[60]

The careful examination of criminal codes for their therapeutic jurisprudence potential is a crucial enterprise and a very fertile field for TJ criminal law education, research, and practice. Relevant provisions and practices should be embodied in local practice manuals.[61] Indeed, at some time in the future, we may just have enough accumulated knowledge and thinking to propose a "model" TJ component of a criminal code.

C. Theory-Inspired Practice

It is not at all uncommon, of course, for a lawyer to try to postpone a pending case and attempt to connect a client with an appropriate treatment or service. In fact, increasingly, some lawyers are envisioning such activities as the core of their professional role.[62] They intend, in essence, to specialize in knowing appropriate treatments and programs, in accessing those services for their clients, and in navigating the legal landscape so as to achieve a rehabilitative result. These lawyers, then, will seek to develop expertise in the first two categories — the treatments and the relevant law — already discussed in this essay.

But in order to most effectively engage criminal clients in rehabilitative enterprises, there is an important third dimension to the role, the somewhat fancy-sounding category of Theory-Inspired Practices, a name I have chosen principally for its appropriate acronym, TIPs.[63] If the first examined category — treatment and services — is primarily in the mental health/social work realm, and if the second category — the legal landscape — is primarily in the legal realm, the final category — theory-inspired practices — is overwhelmingly and vigorously interdisciplinary.

---

57. *Id.* at 5–6.
58. *Id.* at 6.
59. *E.g.*, TJ JUDGING, *supra* note 46, at 213, 227.
60. *See* Van de Veen, *supra* note 42 (discussing allocution under Section 726 of the Canadian Criminal Code).
61. *E.g.*, JUDGING FOR THE 21ST CENTURY, *supra* note 38.
62. *E.g.*, Cait Clarke & James Neuhard, *From Day One: Who's in Control as Problem Solving and Client-Centered Sentencing Take Center Stage*, 29 N.Y.U. REV. L. & SOC. CHANGE 11 (2004).
63. The term, however, is also accurate insofar as the suggestions are actually more "inspired" by theory than they are "based" on such theory.

Being robustly interdisciplinary, the theory-inspired practices category's thrust is to search for promising developments and insights in the relevant mental health/social work/criminal justice disciplines and to explore creatively how those insights might best be brought into the realm of lawyering. Behavioral science titles that have inspired my own efforts in therapeutic jurisprudence/criminal law scholarship include Donald Meichenbaum and Dennis C. Turk, *Facilitating Treatment Adherence: A Practitioner's Guidebook*,[64] James McGuire's edited collection entitled *What Works: Reducing Reoffending*,[65] and Shadd Maruna's *Making Good: How Ex-Convicts Reform and Rebuild Their Lives*.[66]

The third category is somewhat more nuanced and subtle than the other two categories. Nonetheless, intuitive and psychologically-sensitive lawyers and judges are likely to already employ a number of devices that are completely consistent with the TIPs literature.

For example, in the *Riggs* case, Riggs's mother was enlisted to provide reminders regarding Riggs taking his daily medication. The notion of involving a family member for such purposes is noted as a worthwhile ingredient of facilitating treatment adherence.[67] Likewise, the district court's statement that Riggs seemed to have matters "under control" serves not only as a statement of factual/legal relevance, but, according to the literature, likely serves as well to reinforce and maintain the offender's successful reform efforts.[68]

While it is likely that sensitive lawyers and judges will intuit and use several techniques that happen to be supported by the therapeutic jurisprudence literature, it is also extremely likely that without periodic exposure to the pertinent TJ literature, the actual use of recommended TIPs will be hit-and-miss and few and far between. For instance, the therapeutic jurisprudence literature, in addition to promoting the involvement of family (like Riggs's mother) in the treatment process, suggests a great many additional techniques, such as behavioral contracting,[69] to enhance client adherence to treatment plans. The practice TIPs are meaningful because they suggest not merely the importance of lawyers contemplating rehabilitative efforts from day one, but also *how* lawyers might guide clients along a promising rehabilitative path.

The TIPs category, therefore, gives lawyers practice tips on the "how" of effective TJ criminal lawyering. These practice tips are sometimes called TJ's "principles"[70] or "instrumental prescriptions."[71] The information provided in the TIPs or principles in-

---

64. Donald Meichenbaum & Dennis C. Turk, Facilitating Treatment Adherence: A Practitioner's Guidebook (1st ed. 1987). This work prompted David B. Wexler, *Health Care Compliance Principles and the Insanity Acquittee Conditional Release Process*, 27 Crim. L. Bull. 18 (1991).
65. What Works: Reducing Reoffending (James McGuire ed., 1995). This work inspired, for example, David B. Wexler, *Relapse Prevention Planning Principles for Criminal Law Practice*, in Practicing Therapeutic Jurisprudence: Law as a Helping Profession 237 (Dennis P. Stolle et al. eds., 2000).
66. Shadd Maruna, Making Good: How Ex-Convicts Reform and Rebuild Their Lives (1st ed. 2001). Maruna's work led me to write *Robes and Rehabilitation*, supra note 46, and *Some Reflections*, supra note 2.
67. *See* sources cited *supra* note 64.
68. *See* sources cited *supra* note 66.
69. *See supra* note 64.
70. TJ Judging, *supra* note 46, at 105.
71. Robert F. Schopp, *Therapeutic Jurisprudence: Integrated Inquiry and Instrumental Prescriptions*, 17 Behav. Sci. & L. 589 (1999).

cludes: *how* lawyers can put clients at ease by according them "voice" and "validation;" *how* lawyers can develop a respectful—and influential—relationship with their clients; *how* lawyers can reduce perceptions of coercion and give clients a meaningful choice to opt in or out of particular programs; *how* lawyers can work with clients to increase empathy to victims and increase also the genuineness of any acceptance of responsibility or tendered apology; *how* lawyers can help clients develop relapse prevention strategies, engage in efforts of behavioral contracting, and propose a plan for conditional release on probation or parole; *how* lawyers can work with clients to increase offender compliance with release conditions; and *how* lawyers can recognize client strengths and reinforce client efforts at desistance from crime.[72]

III. Conclusion

At least for some attorneys the nature of criminal law practice is changing, and the indications are that the change will continue to gain strength and numbers. With this growing transformation, criminal law education and research will also change. I hope this essay will contribute to the overall effort by suggesting an organizational framework, or at least a springboard for future discussion, of the important and interesting issues involved.

ii. A Rehabilitative Consciousness
David B. Wexler, Therapeutic Jurisprudence and the Rehabilitative Role of the Criminal Defense Lawyer

(Reprinted with permission from
17 St. Thomas Law Review 743, 2005)

Introduction

Therapeutic Jurisprudence ("TJ") is maturing, moving rather rapidly from the world of theory to the world of practice.[1] It is only natural, therefore, for Therapeutic Jurisprudence to work its way into the law school curriculum and, as this special law review issue attests, into legal clinics and clinical legal education.

In the area of criminal law, the practical side of Therapeutic Jurisprudence has, to date, been reflected more in judicial activity than among the practicing bar. Judicial interest is mounting internationally, especially in the areas of drug abuse, mental illness, domestic violence, and related concerns of the criminal justice system. Indeed, judges are the principal intended audience for the recently published book entitled *Judging in a Therapeutic Key: Therapeutic Jurisprudence and the Courts*.[2]

---

72. All of these, and more, are discussed from a judicial perspective in TJ JUDGING, *supra* note 46. In my Therapeutic Jurisprudence courses at the University of Arizona and the University of Puerto Rico, I ask the law students to explore how those principles can best be employed by practicing lawyers. A specific therapeutic jurisprudence scholarship on criminal lawyering is, however, now emerging. *See supra* note 2.

1. For information about Therapeutic Jurisprudence and how it has evolved over time through the present, *see generally* The International Network on Therapeutic Jurisprudence, *at* http://www.therapeuticjurisprudence.org (last visited Mar. 13, 2005); *see also* PRACTICING THERAPEUTIC JURISPRUDENCE: LAW AS A HELPING PROFESSION (Dennis P. Stolle et al. eds., 2000) [hereinafter PRACTICING].

2. JUDGING IN A THERAPEUTIC KEY: THERAPEUTIC JURISPRUDENCE AND THE COURTS (Bruce J. Winick & David B. Wexler eds., 2003) [hereinafter JTK].

Since judges are in an enviable position to influence local legal culture and climate,[3] it is likely that courts will encourage the development of a criminal law bar attuned to these concerns.[4] Indeed, even without a push from the judiciary, some lawyers have begun to practice criminal law in a specifically therapeutic key.[5] Mostly, interested lawyers will likely augment a traditional criminal law practice with the more holistic approach suggested by Therapeutic Jurisprudence, and the present article seeks to point interested practitioners in that direction.

Some lawyers may even decide to go "all the way," and to limit their criminal law practice to a concentration in Therapeutic Jurisprudence. For instance, in *The How and Why of Therapeutic Jurisprudence in Criminal Defense Work*,[6] Dallas, Texas attorney John McShane provides a brief overview of his perspective and his practice:

> Application of therapeutic jurisprudence in criminal defense work involves a threshold recognition that most criminal defense attorneys and the criminal justice system generally address the symptoms of the client's legal problem rather than the cause. For example, in the classic case of the habitual driving under the influence (DUI) offender, the symptom is the repeated arrests and the cause is usually alcoholism. It is the long-standing policy of the firm of McShane, Davis and Nance to decline representation of this type of defendant unless he or she contractually agrees to the therapeutic jurisprudence approach. If this approach is declined by the potential client, referral is made to a competent colleague who will then represent the client in the traditional model.[7]

Referral to outside counsel is also made if the defendant has a viable defense. In the criminal arena, therefore, the firm "focuses solely on rehabilitation and mitigation of punishment."[8] Representation is agreed to if the client is in turn willing "to accept responsibility for his actions, submit to an evaluation, treatment, and relapse prevention program, and to use this approach in mitigation of the offense in plea bargaining or the sentencing hearing."[9] McShane seeks to defer disposition of the case so as "to allow the client the maximum opportunity to recover."[10] A packet of mitigating information is assembled and eventually submitted to the prosecutor in an effort at plea bargaining, or, failing that, to the court at sentencing. The packet consists of items such as "AA Meeting Attendance Logs, urinalysis lab reports, reports of evaluating and treating mental health

---

3. *E.g.*, Dave Moore, *Lessons Learned in Washington's King County*, COLUMBIA DAILY TRIB., Feb. 8, 2004 at 3 (detailing how "King County Superior Court Judge Patricia Clark led the charge to call 120 people to the table" to reform the juvenile justice system); *see also* Judge Leonard P. Edwards, *The Juvenile Dependency Drug Treatment Court of Santa Clara County, California*, in JTK, *supra* note 2, at 39–40. Studying how judges and others change the legal culture would be a significant strand of ethnographic/legal scholarship, and clinical law faculty would likely be in an excellent position to undertake such work.

4. *See* Judge Michael Marcus, *Archaic Sentencing Liturgy Sacrifices Public Safety: What's Wrong and How We Can Fix It*, 16 FED. SENT. REP. 76 (2002) (setting out Judge Marcus's views on sentencing and instructing attorneys on how to argue sentencing matters before him).

5. David B. Wexler, *Some Reflections on Therapeutic Jurisprudence and the Practice of Criminal Law*, 38 CRIM. L. BULL. 205, 205 (2002) (unpublished paper, on file with author).

6. JOHN V. MCSHANE, THE HOW AND WHY OF THERAPEUTIC JURISPRUDENCE IN CRIMINAL DEFENSE WORK (2000).

7. Wexler, *supra* note 5, at 206–07.

8. *Id.* at 207.

9. *Id.*

10. *Id.*

professionals, and letters of support from various people in the community such as AA sponsor, employer, co-workers, clergyman, family, and friends."[11]

There is much more to this, of course, and there are indeed a variety of models that criminal defense attorneys might use in practicing Therapeutic Jurisprudence. Although McShane and his firm have chosen to refer a client to outside counsel unless the client chooses, from the beginning, to accept responsibility, that course of action is in no sense required. As noted earlier, a lawyer might well choose to practice "traditional" criminal law, but infuse the practice with Therapeutic Jurisprudence concerns throughout the process. Indeed, as we will see, a TJ criminal lawyer can play an essential role even after conviction in the appeal process, in release planning, in prisoner reentry, and beyond.

In the present article, I will identify the potential rehabilitative role of the attorney from the beginning stages—possible diversion, for example—through sentencing and even beyond—through conditional or unconditional release, and possible efforts to expunge the criminal record. This article has two principal purposes; first, to call for the explicit recognition of a TJ criminal lawyer, and to provide, in a very sketchy manner, an overview of that role; second, to propose an agenda of research and teaching to foster the development of the rehabilitative role of the criminal lawyer.[12] While much of the proposed research would discuss the rehabilitative potential of applying the current law therapeutically, practitioners and scholars working in this area will also naturally have occasion to consider alternative approaches, resulting in proposals for law reform.[13]

The agenda is intended as a warm invitation to several communities, each of which, if so inclined, could contribute mightily to this effort, which ultimately should result in journal articles, practice manuals, anthologies, and texts. The most obvious community consists of involved practitioners[14] and, especially, their academic counterparts, the community of clinical law professors. Law school clinical teaching and scholarship are

---

11. *Id.*
12. Of course, the legal profession alone cannot "solve" the problem of criminality or rehabilitate persons involved in the criminal justice system. *See* Jessica Pearson, 42 Fam. Ct. Rev. 384 (2004) (reviewing Judging in a Therapeutic Key: Therapeutic Jurisprudence and the Courts (Bruce J. Winick & David B. Wexler, eds. 2003) (critiquing the ability of courts to achieve rehabilitation). But criminal lawyers can make a dent, salvage some lives, work with other professionals and advocate for services and changes in policy. Crucially important, too, but almost entirely ignored to date, are the potential therapeutic roles of prosecutors and police officers. For groundbreaking efforts in these areas see Carolyn Coops Hartley, *A Therapeutic Jurisprudence Approach to the Trial Process in Domestic Violence Felony Trials*, 9 Violence Against Women 410 (2003); *see also* Ulf Holmberg, Police Interviews with Victims and Suspects of Violent and Sexual Crimes; Interviewees' Experiences and Interview Outcomes (2004) (unpublished doctoral dissertation, Stockholm University) (on file with the Stockholm University Department of Psychology).
13. *E.g.*, David B. Wexler, *Spain's JVP ('Juez de Vigilancia Penitenciaria') Legal Structure as a Potential Model for a Re-entry Court*, 7 Contemp. Issues in L. 1 (2003/2004) [hereinafter Wexler, S*pain's JVP*].
14. John V. McShane, *The Need for Healing*, 89 A.B.A. J. 59, 59 (2003); Robert Ward, *From Courtroom Advocacy to Systems Advocacy: Lessons Learned by a Drug Court Public Defender* (March/April 2000), *available at* http://www.nlada.org/Defender/Defender_IndigentDef/NLADA/Defender/Defender_IndigentDef/Publications/Indigent_Defense/Defender_Indigent_Archive/MarchApril2000/March April2000/MarchApril_DrugCourts (last visted Mar. 14, 2005); Martin Reisig, *The Difficult Role of the Defense Lawyer in a Post-Adjudication Drug Treatment Court: Accommodating Therapeutic Jurisprudence and Due Process*, 38 Crim. L. Bull. 216 (2002); Mae C. Quinn, *Whose Team am I on Anyway? Musings of a Public Defender About Drug Treatment Court Practice*, 26 N.Y.U. Rev. L. & Soc. Change 37, 37 (2000–2001).

uniquely suited to address many of the issues raised later in this article.[15] Another relevant community is that of social workers, criminologists, psychologists, and the like, some of whom are connected with law school clinics[16] or are working as practitioner-scholars in the Therapeutic Jurisprudence area.[17] Finally, academics working in Therapeutic Jurisprudence and in criminal law, especially in sentencing and corrections,[18] would be highly valuable partners in this enterprise. So would their students, and a number of the topics raised below might indeed serve as interesting and useful exercises for course papers.

It is time, then, to begin to sketch more clearly the role and practice setting of the TJ criminal lawyer, taking into account certain important skills, legally-relevant doctrines, and the kind, content, and timing of certain important conversations with clients. In the effort of constructing an agenda, my approach will be to cite much of the relevant literature, but not generally to synthesize or summarize it in any detail. My main objective is to provide interested others with a jumping-off point, and to pose questions and suggest avenues of future inquiry.

The reader will note immediately that the proposed attorney-client relationship bears virtually no resemblance to many shameful systems of indigent defense, where crushing caseloads allow for little client contact and where the only real objective is to secure a decent deal on a plea. But legal clinics need to teach excellence, to push for expanded legal horizons, and to model and point the way to the provision of first-rate legal services. They cannot succumb to mimicking the structural ineffective assistance of counsel exhibited in many public sector defense programs. Indeed, this article ends with a discussion of the structure of legal services, and proposes that very area as one deserving the creative efforts of clinical legal scholarship.

1. The Criminal Lawyer as Change Agent

Before proceeding to particular stages in the criminal process, and looking at the criminal defense lawyer's potential rehabilitative role in each, we need to address a more general and basic set of issues. A typical initial response to a proposed broadening of the traditional role of defense counsel is, "Hey, I'm not a therapist." True, a lawyer is

---

15. Legal clinics could readily produce valuable faculty-supervised, student-researched local TJ manuals, detailing relevant local statutory provisions, cases, and forms.

16. The manuals described above could also include descriptive information on local treatment programs, perhaps prepared by cooperating clinic students from social work, criminology, and psychology, again working under faculty supervision.

17. Michael D. Clark, *Change Focused Drug Court: Examining the Critical Ingredients of Positive Behavior Change*, 3:2 Nat'l Drug Ct. Inst. Rev. 35, 56–57 (2001); Eric Y. Drogin, *From Therapeutic Jurisprudence ... to Jurisprudent Therapy*, 18 Behav. Sci. & L. 489, 490 (2000); Hartley, *supra* note 12, at 412; John Q. La Fond & Sharon G. Portwood, *Foreword: Preventing Intimate Violence: Have Law and Public Policy Failed?*, 69 UMKC L. Rev. 3, 13 (2000); Robert G. Madden & Raymie H. Wayne, *Social Work and the Law: A Therapeutic Jurisprudence Perspective*, 48:3 Soc. Work 338, 339–40 (2003); Robert G. Madden & Raymie H. Wayne, *Constructing a Normative Framework for Therapeutic Jurisprudence Using Social Work Principles as a Model*, 18 Touro L. Rev. 487, 501 (2002); James McGuire, *Maintaining Change: Converging Legal and Psychological Initiatives in a Therapeutic Jurisprudence Framework*, 4 W. Criminology Rev. 108, 118 (2003); James McGuire, *Can the Criminal Law Ever be Therapeutic?*, 18 Behav. Sci. & L. 413 (2000); Carrie J. Petrucci, *Apology in the Criminal Justice Setting: Evidence for Including Apology as an Additional Component in the Legal System*, 20 Behav. Sci. & L. 337, 340, 359 (2002); Leonore Simon, *A Therapeutic Jurisprudence Approach to the Legal Processing of Domestic Violence Cases*, 1 Psychol. Pub. Pol'y & L. 43, 50 (1995).

18. *See* Nora V. Demleitner et al., Sentencing Law and Policy (2004).

not a therapist or social worker, and is not expected to be. But, as social worker and drug court consultant Michael Clark makes clear,[19] lawyers (and others in the legal/judicial system) can nonetheless be quite effective as "change agents."

Clark notes that, if change is forthcoming, the lion's share of change will come from the client, together with whatever internal or social strengths and supports can be mustered. Client "hope and expectancy" accounts for another chunk of the change. And a whopping amount of positive change is attributable to "relationship" factors—the connection between client and change agent (e.g., relations characterized by empathy, acceptance, encouragement). Much rehabilitative work lies in encouraging active and meaningful client participation, in developing a strong relationship between client and change agent, and in fostering client hope and expectancy. Writing in the context of drug courts, Clark underscores that "all professionals working with drug court participants, especially judges, lawyers, and probation officers, may adopt and utilize techniques that most effectively induce positive behavior change."[20]

Clark and others have written about how a professional can strive to develop a relationship of respect[21] and trust,[22] and about the importance of giving a client "voice"—of clients being able to "tell their story,"[23] unconstrained by rigid notions of legal relevance.[24] Important, too, are matters of emotional intelligence and cultural competence.[25]

These skills—on building a strong interpersonal relationship, on attentive listening, and on becoming an "effective helper"[26]—can be acquired and improved by lawyers, and are increasingly important components of law school courses on interviewing and counseling and in legal clinics. Proposals are now emerging, too, to introduce lawyers and law students to techniques of "motivational interviewing."[27] Keeping the impor-

---

19. Michael D. Clark, *A Change-Focused Approach for Judges*, in JTK, *supra* note 2, at 137, 137.
20. *Id*. at 147.
21. *Id*. at 148 (*e.g.*, respectful communication, eye-contact, attentive listening).
22. Marcus T. Boccaccini et al., *Development and Effects of Client Trust in Criminal Defense Attorneys: Preliminary Examination of the Congruence Model of Trust Development*, 22 BEHAV. SCI. & L. 197 (2004) (stating that lawyers should invite client participation, take client phone calls, ask for suggestions, and listen to suggestions).
23. Clark, *supra* note 19, at 142.
24. *Cf*. Jack Susman, *Resolving Hospital Conflicts: A Study on Therapeutic Jurisprudence*, in LAW IN A THERAPEUTIC KEY (David B. Wexler & Bruce J. Winick eds., 1996) 907, 909–10 (stating that patients prefer informal dispute resolution proceedings, for such proceedings allow for greater dialogue); Thomas D. Barton, *Therapeutic Jurisprudence, Preventive Law, and Creative Problem Solving: An Essay on Harnessing Emotion and Human Connection*, 5 PSYCHOL. PUB. POL'Y & L. 921, 921 (1999).
25. Marjorie A. Silver, *Emotional Competence, Multicultural Lawyering and Race*, 3 FLA. COASTAL L.J. 219, 220–21 (2002); Carolyn Copps Hartley & Carrie J. Petrucci, *Practicing Culturally Competent Therapeutic Jurisprudence: A Collaboration Between Social Work and Law*, 14 WASH. U. J.L. & POL'Y 133 (2004); Marjorie A. Silver, *Emotional Intelligence and Legal Education*, 5 PSYCHOL. PUB. POL'Y & L. 1173, 1173 (1999).
26. Richard Sheehy, *Do You Have the Skills to be an Effective Helper*, FLA. B. NEWS, May 15, 2002, available at http://www.flabar.org/DIVCOM/JN/JNNews01.nsf/cb53c80c8fabd 49d85256b5900678 f6c/b82d3f3cd077d99c85256bb200527098?OpenDocument (last visited Mar. 16, 2005).
27. Astrid Birgden, *Dealing with the Resistant Criminal Client: A Psychologically-Minded Strategy for More Effective Legal Counseling*, 38 CRIM. L. BULL. 225 (2002) (stating that motivational interviewing, or MI, finds a line between a "heavy handed" approach and "hands off" approach). For a bibliography on motivational interviewing, including discussion of the impact a helping professional can have on a client's stages of change, go to http://www.motivationalinterview.org/library/index.html (last visited Mar. 13, 2005).

tance of these skills always in mind, we may now turn our attention to the lawyer's role in various stages of the criminal process.

2. Diversion and Problem solving Courts[28]

Lawyers need to be versed in the various treatment programs available in their jurisdictions,[29] and in informal and formal schemes for diversion. Diversion is sometimes spelled out by statute, and may operate either pretrial or post-adjudication (deferral of judgment). In diversion, issues often arise regarding the appropriateness of conditions, such as those relating to drug testing or to search and seizure.[30] A worthwhile interdisciplinary research project would be to detail the law and practice of diversion in a particular jurisdiction. The written product could be preserved as part of a practice manual, and could be periodically updated.

Problem solving courts, such as drug treatment courts ("DTCs"), may also operate pre- or post-adjudication; increasingly, they operate post-guilty plea. Lawyers need to know about these courts, their programs, their eligibility requirements,[31] and about the actual functioning of the courts and programs,[32] including rates of successful graduation versus the 'flunk out' rate, and the amount of time an average client might expect to spend in jail (for being sanctioned) under a DTC program as compared to expected jail time in the conventional system.[33]

There is emerging literature on the role of counsel in this area,[34] given the non-traditional aspects and atmosphere of DTCs and other problem solving courts ("PSC"). One

---

28. *See generally* JTK, *supra* note 2; DEMLEITNER ET AL., *supra* note 18, at 546–56.

29. This is true, of course, whether we are talking diversion, sentencing, or parole. For a good example of scholarship in this area, see David R. Katner, *A Defense Perspective of Treatment Programs for Juvenile Sex Offenders*, 37 CRIM. L. BULL. 371 (2001).

30. Terry v. Superior Court, 86 Cal. Rptr. 2d 653, 666 (Cal. Ct. App. 1999). Conditions may also be imposed when one is released pretrial on bail or on one's own recognizance. In *In re* York, 9 Cal. 4th 1133, 1151 (Cal. 1995), the California Supreme Court upheld conditions, such as random drug testing and unannounced searches, beyond those relating to assuring the defendant's presence in court. For a discussion of conditions of release, *see infra* Part 5. In Alabama v. Shelton, 535 U.S. 654, 656 (2002), the Supreme Court discussed the availability of 'pretrial probation' (adjournment in contemplation of dismissal), and noted that the conditions imposed under that arrangement are basically the same as those available under 'regular' probation.

31. In New South Wales, Australia, where the drug court is statutorily based, the drug court, in written opinions, decides eligibility requirements and other interpretative matters. *See* Lawlink New South Whales, *Caselaw New South Wales*, at http://www.lawlink.nsw.gov.au/lawlink/caselaw/ll-caselaw.nsf/pages/cl_index (last visisted June 4, 2005) [hereinafter New South Wales]. A body of case law is developing. For some TJ implications of this development for the lawyer's role, *see infra* Part 6.

32. For example, one of my students at the University of Puerto Rico reported that clients in one area of the island were expected to enroll in a treatment program that involved little more than hour upon hour of daily prayer.

33. *See* Mark A.R. Kleiman, *Drug Court Can Work: Would Something Else Work Better?*, 2 CRIMINOLOGY & PUB. POL'Y 167 (2003) (stating that recent research suggests a client, although successful in the program, may spend about as much time in jail under DTC as under the traditional criminal justice option). In terms of their actual functioning, the operation of DTCs has been affected in several jurisdictions by the passage of drug treatment initiatives. These initiatives generally mandate treatment and probation, and forbid incarceration, for qualifying defendants. The initiatives have been worrisome to some DTC judges, for the laws may remove the motivational "stick" of possible incarceration. *See* Michael M. O'Hear, *Statutory Interpretation and Direct Democracy: Lessons from the Drug Treatment Initiatives*, 40 HARV. J. ON LEGIS. 281, 289–90 (2003).

34. For the most recent contributions, see generally Cait Clarke & James Neuhard, *From Day One: Who's in Control as Problem Solving and Client-Centered Sentencing Take Center Stage*, 29

of the most important issues relates to the client's consent to opt out of the 'ordinary' criminal justice system and into a PSC program. In an important article, former drug court defense attorney Martin Reisig underscores the necessity of obtaining true client consent to enter the program.[35] According to Reisig, obtaining adequate client consent is always important, but it is clearly crucial in post-adjudication jurisdictions, given the fact that fully one-third of those who enter a DTC program may flunk out of it and be returned to the criminal court not to stand trial, but as a convicted defendant. Real consent is crucial, says Reisig, for purposes of due process. Moreover, consent is important therapeutically as well: imagine how 'sold out' a client may feel being rushed into a DTC program from which he/she later flunks out, only then to face the court as an already convicted defendant.

Reisig notes that, even in a therapeutically-oriented law practice, the criminal defense lawyer needs to convince the client that the strengths and weaknesses of the case can, and will, be evaluated more or less along traditional lines.[36] A study of clients in mental health court revealed that those who believe they have a real choice regarding participation also feel less perceived coercion than do others.[37] Yet, a number of clients reported that they were unaware they had a choice.[38]

Apparently, some clients do not understand a general statement, made by the judge to the courtroom audience as a whole, regarding voluntary participation. This suggests the need for a change in the judicial role and, in any case, suggests a highly significant role for counsel. Although observations of mental health court reveal "there is little that reflects traditional 'lawyering' as the attorneys are relegated to relatively minor roles in the hearings,"[39] pre-selection legal advice and counseling are essential.

An important exercise in law clinics might be to consider the kind of dialogue a lawyer might have with a client about the pros and cons of opting into DTC or mental health court. What information should be provided the client regarding the program,

---

N.Y.U. Rev. L. & Soc. Change 11 (2004); William H. Simon, *Criminal Defenders and Community Justice: The Drug Court Example*, 40 Am. Crim. L. Rev. 1595 (2003); Jane M. Spinak, *Why Defenders Feel Defensive: The Defender's Role in Problem Solving Courts*, 40 Am. Crim. L. Rev. 1617 (2003). For a recent defense of the traditional model, see Abbe Smith, *The Difference in Criminal Defense and the Difference it Makes*, 11 Wash. U. J.L. & Pol'y 83 (2003). Melding therapeutic elements and traditional ones will lead to interesting discussions about accommodating conciliatory and adversarial postures. This is a crucial—perhaps *the* crucial—future issue, but, at this early stage, is beyond the scope of the present article. As evidenced by Clarke & Neuhard, *supra* note 34, at 36–47, this is a case where the general will flow from the specific; where concrete examples will be necessary to confront ethical issues. In the present article, I try to present important but relatively non-controversial aspects of the lawyer's role—aspects easy to accommodate in a traditional practice.

35. *See* Reisig, *supra* note 14 and accompanying text.

36. The conventional wisdom has it that the quicker the entry into a treatment program, the better. Judge Peggy F. Hora, Judge William G. Schma & John Rosenthal, *The Importance of Timing*, in JTK, *supra* note 2, at 178, 178. Be that as it may, the supposed advantage of early enrollment can be dwarfed by the due process considerations and by the anti-therapeutic aspects of having been rushed into a treatment track.

37. Norman J. Poythress et al., *Perceived Coercion and Procedural Justice in the Broward Mental Health Court*, 25 Int'l J.L. & Psychiatry 517, 526 (2002).

38. *Id.* at 530.

39. Roger A. Boothroyd et al., *The Broward Mental Health Court: Process, Outcomes, and Service Utilization*, 26 Int'l J.L. & Psychiatry 55, 67 (2003).

the nature of the treatment, the consequences of success or failure, the alternatives, the amount of incarceration one might expect under either option?[40]

What outcomes other than incarceration time might be important? Might success be measured not only by "graduation" rates, but also by small successful steps in peoples' lives? What if drug court participation gives many clients a new outlook on life, or a glimpse of a way to live life without drugs, or a family who now backs his or her efforts to get clean?[41]

Should the client, if free on bail (as many are), visit any of the treatment programs before making a decision? Should the client be invited or encouraged by counsel to sit in on a drug court session (typically open to the public) before making up his or her mind? Note that in many drug treatment courts, case calendaring is used to promote vicarious learning by clients—cases are ordered so as to give new clients a glimpse of the hard work, but also of the opportunity and hope for real recovery that lies ahead.[42] A lawyer, or paralegal, might play an important role in maximizing the vicarious learning by sitting through the session and explaining to the prospective DTC client exactly what is happening and why different clients are receiving different dispositions.

Legal clinics exploring the consent question should also consider how a client's active addiction impedes attentive listening and interacts with nuanced notions of consent. They should also ask how much effort is and should be expended in "regular" court to advise clients about the collateral consequences of a proposed plea—and should con-

---

40. Thus, the question asked critically by attorney Mae Quinn, "is it not a defense attorney's 'therapeutic jurisprudential' obligation to inquire whether certain drug court practices are perceived by client as confusing or too invasive ... ?" *See* Quinn, *supra* note 14, at 53 n.100. This question should be answered, assuming a correct understanding of Therapeutic Jurisprudence, with a resounding "yes."

41. These are all examples given by New South Wales Magistrate Neil Milson, as reported by Michael Pelly, *When Treatment is Scarier than Jail*, SYDNEY MORNING HERALD, February 26, 2004. Magistrate Milson's insights tie in nicely with the program development and evaluation research literature, where "outcomes" are defined as "measurable changes in the client's life situation or circumstances." PETER M. KETTNER ET AL., DESIGNING AND MANAGING PROGRAMS: AN EFFECTIVENESS BASED APPROACH 113 (2d. ed. 1999).

42. *See* Judge Peggy F. Hora et al., *Promoting Vicarious Learning Through Case Calendaring*, in JTK, *supra* note 2, at 300, 300–01:

> DTCs (Drug Treatment Courts) design the courtroom process itself to reinforce the defendant's treatment. The court may set up its daily calendar so that "first-time participants appearing in Drug Court ... are the last items on the session calendar. This gives them an opportunity to see the entire program in action, and know exactly what awaits them if they become a participant." The DTC may handle program graduates first in order to impart a sense of hope to the new and continuing program participants who may experience hopelessness at the beginning of the process. The court may then devote the next portion of the calendar to defendants who enter the court in custody. This procedure is designed to convey to all DTC participants the serious nature of the court and the gravity of the defendant's situation. This demonstrates that a violation of DTC rules may not get a defendant ejected from the program, but the court may use jail time as a form of "smart punishment" to get the defendant to conform to treatment protocol. Those DTCs that do not have treatment facilities in their jails recognize that incarceration represents a break in treatment for the individual. However, the shock of incarceration may serve to break down the person's denial of her addiction. Finally, the court handles the cases involving new defendants who wish to enter the DTC program. All of these procedures are founded on the therapeutic ideal that every aspect of a DTC can and does have a powerful impact on the success of the defendant in treatment.

Id.

sider whether enrollment in a treatment option should call for the same or a higher standard.

The drug court community sometimes speaks of the four "Ls" that drive people to treatment: lovers, livers, law, and labor. Clients typically opt for drug court and like programs when faced with loss of family, or health, or liberty, or employment.

Some practitioners and judges in the field thus feel that an overly complex consent procedure is not workable with many clients. Those experts believe a preferable approach would be to keep things simple and allow for an easy exit if the client wants out of the program. Such an easy exit should, of course, be especially consistent with a "pre-plea" kind of program.

3. Pleas and Sentencing Considerations[43]

It is always important to remember that the overwhelming majority of cases are resolved by plea,[44] and typically through a process of plea negotiation.[45] Accordingly, as noted earlier,[46] a TJ criminal lawyer will in appropriate cases try to assemble a rehabilitation-oriented packet to present to the prosecutor in hopes of securing a favorable plea arrangement. Failing that, the packet may be presented to a court at sentencing.

The area of plea negotiation is immense, and beyond the scope of this essay. What is within the essay's scope are some factors that may enter into a client's decision regarding a plea. For the most part, these factors have been the subject of case law, most notably under the federal sentencing guidelines. Here, the cases will be noted more for the relevant factors than for an interpretation of the federal guidelines.

Although the practice of TJ criminal law in federal court is an unexplored and very worthy research topic (and an excellent practice manual project), most TJ criminal lawyers will find themselves in state and local courts,[47] where there is typically greater flexibility than under the federal guidelines.[48]

---

43. *See generally* DEMLEITNER ET AL., *supra* note 18, at 405–32; JTK, *supra* note 2, at 165–76.

44. DEMLEITNER ET AL., *supra* note 18, at 405.

45. Plea negotiations may involve bargaining over the sentence or over the charge itself (an indirect way, of course, of affecting sentence). DEMLEITNER ET AL., *supra* note 18, at 413–25. The TJ literature has raised the question whether charge bargaining might feed into offender cognitive distortion and denial more so than sentence bargaining. *See* David B. Wexler, *Therapeutic Jurisprudence and the Criminal Courts*, in LAW IN A THERAPEUTIC KEY, *supra* note 24, at 157, 162 n.37. Therapeutic Jurisprudence thinking has also questioned whether "no contest" pleas feed into offender denial and minimization. *Id.* at 165–76.

46. *See supra* note 12 and accompanying text.

47. Another potential forum is tribal court, especially given the congruence of Therapeutic Jurisprudence with many indigenous dispute resolution practices. James W. Zion, Jr., *Navajo Therapeutic Jurisprudence*, 18 TOURO L. REV. 563 (2002).

48. Even in states with guidelines, the guidelines are not of the complex and mechanistic variety of the largely discredited federal guidelines. Kevin R. Reitz, *Model Penal Code: Sentencing Report* (2003), *available at* http://www.ali.org/ali/ALIPROJ_MPC03.pdf (last visited Mar. 15, 2005). A new ABA special commission report urges major changes in the criminal justice system, with "proposals that range from abandoning mandatory minimum sentences to better preparing prisoners for return to society." Terry Carter, *End Mandatory Minimums, ABA Commission Urges*, 3 No. 25 A.B.A. J. E-REPORT 1, June 25, 2004, WL 3 No. 25 ABAJEREP 1. In lieu of mandatory minimums, the report proposes the use of "guided discretion." *Id.* The Supreme Court's recent decision in United States v. Booker, 125 S. Ct. 738 (2005), discarding the mandatory force of the U.S. Sentencing Guidelines, will add flexibility to the federal sentencing scheme.

One factor that should enter into the determination of whether a client will go to trial or enter a plea is the likely loss, for one insisting on going to trial, of what in practice typically amounts to a 'plea discount'[49] for a defendant's saving the government the trouble of going to trial, and saving the victim and the government witnesses the trouble and often the trauma of a trial. Closely related to this is sentence leniency, often given for a defendant's 'acceptance of responsibility,' which will kick in more clearly if it occurs early in the process, and is perceived as genuine rather than as purely strategic.[50]

A genuine acceptance of responsibility—especially if coupled with an apology[51]—is generally regarded as therapeutically welcome by the victim[52] and as a good first rehabilitative step for the defendant. Other cooperative efforts, such as rendering substantial assistance[53] and pre-sentencing proactive repayment of victims[54] (which often, but not always, accompany a guilty plea), are also typically considered by the sentencing judge.[55]

The rub in all this, of course, especially as it relates to the role of the criminal lawyer, is that if courts regard these behaviors and gestures as being engaged in merely in the hopes of receiving a lesser punishment, the courts may find the acts to be without merit.[56] But there is also the other side to this coin: if a defendant does not plead guilty and goes to trial, he or she can, if convicted, expect to lose the typical "plea discount."[57] Moreover, if the defendant goes to trial, testifies, loses, and is regarded by the judge as having committed perjury at the trial, the court may well enhance the sentence further for this supposed obstruction of justice.[58]

In light of all the above, how should a defense lawyer go about advising a client, discussing these issues and potential consequences with a client, and trying to work with the client to create a genuineness even within a strategic legal context? Are there psychological approaches that may be useful? For example, one psychological approach to "empathy training" is a "perspective-taking" approach, where a psychologist working with an offender might ask the offender to re-enact the crime, playing the role of the victim:

> The offenders read heart-wrenching accounts of crimes like their own, told from the victim's perspective. They also watch videotapes of victims tearfully telling what it was like to be molested. The offenders then write about their own offense from the victim's point of view, imagining what the victim felt. They read this account to a therapy group and try to answer questions about

---

49. DEMLEITNER ET AL., *supra* note 18, at 305.
50. United States v. Jeter, 236 F.3d 1032 (9th Cir. 2001).
51. Petrucci, *supra* note 17.
52. *Cf.* Judge William G. Schma, *Judging for the New Millennium, in* JTK, *supra* note 2, at 87, 89 (victims prefer defendants to enter guilty pleas, rather than no contest pleas); *see also* Edna Erez, *Victim Voice, Impact Statements and Sentencing: Integrating Restorative Justice and Therapeutic Jurisprudence Principles in Adversary Proceedings*, 40 CRIM. L. BULL. 483 (2004); Stephanos Bibas & Richard A. Bierschbach, *Integrating Remorse and Apology into Criminal Procedure*, 114 YALE L.J. 85 (2004).
53. DEMLEITNER ET AL., *supra* note 18, at 318.
54. *Id.* at 341; United States v. Kim, 364 F.3d 1235 (11th Cir. 2004).
55. Michael O'Hear, *Remorse, Cooperation, and "Acceptance of Responsibility": The Structure, Implementation and Reform of Section 3E1.1 of the Federal Sentencing Guidelines*, 91 Nw. U. L. REV. 1507, 1510 (1997).
56. United States v. Martin, 363 F.3d 25 (1st Cir. 2004).
57. DEMLEITNER ET AL., *supra* note 18, at 314.
58. United States v. Dunnigan, 507 U.S. 87, 90–94 (1993); United States v. Grayson, 438 U.S. 41, 44–54 (1978).

the assault from the victim's perspective. Finally, the offender goes through a simulated reenactment of the crime, this time playing the role of the victim.[59]

It is interesting to consider how the "perspective-taking" approach could be imported into the law office. Might lawyers, preferably in combination with social workers or like professionals, create a "bank" of videotapes of victim statements, and ultimately suggest that a client, in preparing a written apology letter (or videotape), include a section where he or she imagines the many ways in which the crime likely affected the victim's life?[60]

4. Deferred Sentence and Post-Offense Rehabilitation

Recall that, in his practice, John McShane tries to delay the imposition of sentence for as long as possible,[61] and urges the client to begin to pick up the pieces and to engage in available rehabilitative efforts, whether they be attendance at Alcoholics Anonymous or a more elaborate treatment program. McShane emphasizes to the client that, up to this point, the existing evidence already, by definition, "exists"; it perhaps can be given a "spin," but it cannot be changed. On the other hand, suggests McShane, from here on out the client can build his or her own case, can help create evidence that is favorable and that can work to the client's advantage.

In order to accomplish some meaningful rehabilitation — rather than a mere gesture, however genuine — it is of course important to have some time on your side. For this reason, deferring the imposition of sentence can be highly important. Winick's writing on this topic[62] applauds Federal District Judge Jack B. Weinstein's on-point scholarly opinion in *United States v. Flowers*.[63] This is a topic that clearly deserves attention on the state law level, where defense attorneys will urge courts to defer sentence to allow rehabilitation to begin and to facilitate its progress.

Winick's article also summarizes the law under the federal sentencing guidelines allowing for post-offense rehabilitation efforts to be taken into account when sentence is eventually imposed.[64] This is a highly important area that also needs to be researched on a state-by-state basis. Some state courts may be explicit on the matter.[65] In others, post-

---

59. Allison R. Shiff & David B. Wexler, *Teen Court: A Therapeutic Jurisprudence Perspective*, in Law in a Therapeutic Key, *supra* note 24, at 287, 297.

60. Note that such a procedure would work even if we are dealing with an early stage in the proceedings, where a victim impact statement, Ariz. Rev. Stat. §13-4424 (2004), would not yet have been prepared. To establish the genuineness of an offender's apology, an expert witness—a professional who is not part of the offender's treatment team—might be called to counter any claim of malingering. See Bruce J. Winick, *Redefining the Role of the Criminal Defense Lawyer at Plea Bargaining and Sentencing: A Therapeutic Jurisprudence/Preventive Law Model*, in Practicing, *supra* note 1, at 245, 265–66.

61. See *supra* text accompanying note 10.

62. Winick, *supra* note 60, at 245, 267–71.

63. United States v. Flowers, 983 F. Supp. 159, 163–65 (E.D.N.Y. 1997).

64. Winick, *supra* note 60, at 258–63; Demleitner et al., *supra* note 18, at 342. United States v. Atlas, 94 F.3d 447 (8th Cir. 1996). For a recent case, see United States v. Smith, 311 F. Supp. 2d 801, 804–06 (E.D. Wis. 2004). Note that, in a formalistic bow to notions of equality, the federal arena does not permit the consideration of post-sentence rehabilitation efforts, for such efforts would only inure to the benefit of those whose convictions or sentences have been disturbed on appeal. See U.S. Sentencing Guidelines Manual §5K2.19 (Post-Sentencing Rehabilitative Efforts, 2003), *available at* http://www.ussc.gov/2003guid/5k2_19.htm (last visited Mar. 15, 2005). Post-sentence rehabilitative efforts *can*, however, be taken into account in connection with early termination of supervised release. *Id.*

65. Demleitner et al., *supra* note 18, at 343.

offense rehabilitation may not be the subject of case law, but may be the sort of factor that can be brought to bear where courts have considerable discretion in sentencing, perhaps under a statutory "catch-all" provision that allows for mitigation for "any other factor that the court deems appropriate to the ends of justice."[66]

5. Probation[67]

A client who successfully establishes a course of post-offense rehabilitation will typically hope for a probationary sentence in order to remain (relatively speaking) at liberty and to pursue a satisfying life path. The sanction of probation, when legally available for a given offense, is chock-full of Therapeutic Jurisprudence considerations,[68] which can inform and enrich the role of defense counsel. Some of the relevant psychological and criminological work relates to bringing into the probation area notions of psychological compliance principles,[69] relapse prevention principles,[70] and reinforcement of desistance from crime.[71] Let us consider some of these propositions and, following that, consider how they might be employed in the lawyer/client interaction. The assumption being made in these examples is that probation is legally available and that it is also a plausible disposition.

Regarding compliance, the suggestion is that adherence to probation conditions might be enhanced if probation is conceptualized more as a behavioral contract than as a judicial fiat. If certain family members are aware of the client's agreement to abide by certain conditions, that too is thought to increase the likelihood of compliance. Also, if a person is presented with some "mild counterarguments" regarding his or her likely compliance, the person may be encouraged to explain why "this time is different," and may thereby anchor himself/herself to the view that compliance is desirable and is now attainable.[72] Regarding relapse prevention, some promising rehabilitative techniques urge offenders to think through the chain of events that lead them to criminality so that they may be aware of patterns and of high risk situations (e.g., going to a disco on weekend nights). The offenders are then encouraged to think of ways of avoiding or coping with the high risk situation (e.g., not going to that disco on weekends, and going to a movie instead), and of ultimately embodying their thinking in a "relapse prevention plan" that they may employ in the future to reduce the risk of reoffending.[73] Regarding the reinforcement of desistance from crime, the literature suggests that desis-

---

66. Ariz. Rev. Stat. § 13-702(D)(5) (2003).
67. See generally Demleitner et al., supra note 18, at 519–34.
68. Faye S. Taxman & Meredith H. Thanner, *Probation from a Therapeutic Perspective: Results from the Field*, 7 Contemp. Issues in L. 39 (2004).
69. David B. Wexler, *Health Care Compliance Principles and the Judiciary*, in JTK, supra note 2, at 213, 213–26 [hereinafter *Health Care*].
70. David B. Wexler, *Problem Solving and Relapse Prevention in Juvenile Court*, in JTK, supra note 2, at 189, 189–99 [hereinafter *Problem Solving*].
71. David B. Wexler, *Robes and Rehabilitation*, in JTK, supra note 2, at 249, 249–54 [hereinafter *Robes*].
72. JTK, supra note 2, at 213–26.
73. *Problem Solving*, supra note 70, at 189–99. This is, of course, a highly skimpy and oversimplified summary of a meaty process. Moreover, the relapse prevention approach needs to be fused with an approach that looks at how offenders can lead "good lives," not simply at how they can avoid reoffending. Tony Ward & Claire Stewart, *Criminogenic Needs and Human Needs: A Theoretical Model*, 9 Psychol. Crime & L. 234 (2003). For a discussion of merging risk management and good lives considerations in the area of sex offenders, see Astrid Birgden, *Therapeutic Jurisprudence and Sex Offenders: A Psycholegal Approach to Protection*, 16 Sexual Abuse: J. Res. & Treatment 351 (2004).

tance is more a process than a specific event. Moreover, desistance can best be maintained if, especially in the early stages, it is reinforced through the recognition of respected members of the community.[74]

How might these 'principles'[75] be translated into law practice? Here are some ideas, presented as food for thought and discussion:

The defense lawyer could serve as a respected member of the community, proud of the client's efforts and positive about the client's prospects. The lawyer and client might talk about others who know the client and his/her genuine steps toward reform: an AA sponsor, the receptionist at the drug treatment clinic, a mental health professional, an employer, teacher, co-worker, member of the clergy, family member, and/or friend. The lawyer and client might decide which of them might approach which community figure regarding the willingness to provide a letter of support and the like.[76]

The lawyer might be guided by the relapse prevention principles to work with the client to come up with and to present to the court a proposed probationary plan.[77] The lawyer, perhaps working with a social worker or like professional, might engage the

---

74. *Robes, supra* note 71, at 249–54.

75. "At this exciting—but early—stage of development, these 'principles' must, of course, be taken more as suggestions for ongoing discussion, dialogue, and investigation than as hard and fast rules to be set in stone." JTK, *supra* note 2, at 105–06. A case that brings together many Therapeutic Jurisprudence principles, and is thus excellent for teaching purposes, is United States v. Riggs, 370 F.3d 382 (4th Cir. 2004). Riggs involves a case where, 1) the defendant's mental condition began to assert itself two years before his first arrest, but where he did not receive psychiatric treatment until after his arrest, thus indicating how the legal system often serves as a back-door social service agency; 2) sentence was deferred for nearly two years after his arrest for the offense in question (a second offense), thus allowing the defendant to indicate how this post-offense treatment plan was working; 3) where, because the offense in question was precipitated by Riggs forgetting to take his oral medication for a few days, the revised treatment plan was augmented by long-acting intramuscular injections of antipsychotic drugs and by Riggs' mother agreeing to remind him to take his daily oral medication; and where 4) the district judge reinforced Riggs' medically compliant and law-abiding behavior over the two year period during which sentence was deferred by stating on the record how things now seemed to be under control. *Id.* The district court accordingly ordered a downward departure because of Riggs' diminished mental capacity, and did not find the departure unavailable because of a likely danger to the public. The workable—and working—treatment plan, in the view of the district court, sufficiently alleviated public protection concerns. Riggs was accordingly sentenced to three years probation instead of being given a two or two and a half year incarcerative sentence. *Id.* at 384. A divided Fourth Circuit vacated the sentence and remanded the case for resentencing. *Id.* at 387. After deciding *U.S. v. Booker*, relating to the U.S. Sentencing Guidelines, the Supreme Court vacated and remanded *Riggs* to the Fourth Circuit. The *Riggs* case is an excellent vehicle for introducing a number of crucial Therapeutic Jurisprudence principles and techniques. The case also shows the potential of practicing Therapeutic Jurisprudence in the federal system, a topic that has received virtually no attention to-date.

76. *See* Wexler, *supra* note 5, at 214. The potential for introducing notions of Therapeutic Jurisprudence in federal court, recently advocated by Eight Circuit Judge Donald P. Lay, has been given a major boost by the Supreme Court decision in *Booker*, in essence converting the rigid U.S. Sentencing Guidelines into a set of advisory guideposts. *See* Donald P. Lay, *Rehab Justice*, N.Y. Times, Nov. 18, 2004, §A.

77. The proposed probationary plan would be derived from some of the relapse prevention principles, and may serve in a very rough way to start a client on the road to relapse prevention, but it is of course no substitute for a full-fledged relapse prevention program led by mental health professionals and trained probation officers. The lawyer's effort might more properly be viewed as resulting in a "safety" plan rather than in a true "relapse prevention" plan. Indeed, one of the proposed conditions of the probationary plan might be a client's full participation in a relapse prevention program, ultimately resulting in the preparation of a true relapse prevention plan. *Problem Solving*, *supra* note 70, at 198 n.2.

client in a discussion of the chain of events that has led to criminality or drug abuse and might encourage the client to recognize situations which, for the client, seem to be high risk. The lawyer can also prompt the client to consider ways in which the high risk situations can be best avoided.

In terms of the division of labor between lawyer and client, it is important to recognize that it is the *client* who should develop an appreciation of the high risk situations and their alternatives. The goal is for the client to recognize this and to buy into a change of behavior that should reduce the risk of criminality. It is thus important for the client to be fully involved in the thinking process, and lawyers should resist the temptation of thinking for the client and of proposing a plan for the client's acquiescence.

Perhaps the best role for the lawyer here is to prompt and prod the client by asking a series of questions. For instance, UK psychologist James McGuire has developed a course to teach problem solving skills to offenders, and some of the questions he employs are: "Does most of your offending behavior occur in the same place? At similar times of the day or week? In the presence of the same person or persons?"[78]

This is an area where psychologists and other professionals accustomed to the problem solving and relapse prevention approach might be very useful to lawyers. They might be able to suggest some interviewing techniques—or specific questions—to elicit from the client the high risk situations and ways of avoiding them. They may also be able to alert lawyers to the types of patterns and offense pathways often associated with particular offenses or offenders.

For example, youths usually get into car accidents not when driving alone but rather when other kids are in the car.[79] Criminologists and insurance companies—and now lawyers—may know this, but it is important for a youthful offender to personally realize it, and this may be accomplished by the lawyer engaging the client in what may appear to be a type of Socratic dialogue: "Well, when do you seem to get picked up for driving violations? Day or night? When you are alone or when you are with others? Which others? Your parents? Your friends?" And then, if the client recognizes that he or she gets into trouble when driving with certain peers, the lawyer might ask the client to propose a plan to reduce the likelihood of future violations or accidents, hopefully producing a response such as; "Well, I will make sure to drive alone, or with other kids only if an adult is present, or with Jane, who always wants me to drive carefully."

This questioning process could result in a preliminary probationary plan to be presented to the court. Note that the proposed conditions are now in essence coming from the client, not from the lawyer or the court, and thus should be understandable to the client and perceived as reasonable, enhancing the chance for compliance if probation is granted.[80] Probation under this scheme will look more like a behavioral contract than like judicial fiat.

---

78. *Problem Solving*, supra note 70, at 196.

79. Staff writer, *Passengers Hazardous to Teen Drivers*, Ariz. Daily Star, March 22, 2000, at A6. See generally L. H. Chen et al., *Carrying Passengers as a Risk Factor for Crashes Fatal to 16- and 17-Year-Old Drivers*, 283 JAMA 1578 (2000); R. Foss, *Reducing Fatal Crash Risk Among Teenaged Drivers: Structuring an Effective Graduated Licensing System*, 283 JAMA 1617 (2000). For a recent discussion of offense pathways, or offense process approaches, see Devon L. L. Polaschek, *Relapse Prevention, Offense Process Models, and the Treatment of Sexual Offenders*, 34 Prof. Psych.: Res. & Prac. 361 (2003).

80. A related dialogue springs from some of the research on risk management and the difference between "static" (unchanging) and "dynamic" (changeable) risk factors. Gender and race would be static risk factors, whereas drug use and employment status would be dynamic ones. One approach

Ideally, the client should play some role in presenting the proposal to the court, and a give and take might follow, leading to acceptance, modification, or, in disappointing cases, to rejection of the plan.[81] If the client is likely to speak to some of this in court, either proactively or at least in responding to the court's questions and concerns, the lawyer will need to prepare the client for the sentencing hearing.

As part of the preparation, the lawyer could present the type of 'mild counterarguments' that research suggests can be useful in grounding a client in the propriety of the present plan. For instance: "OK, now I want to ask you some questions that the judge or prosecutor might ask at the hearing, like: Why should I feel comfortable granting probation? Judge X granted you probation last time around, and probation was revoked very soon thereafter."

One would hope the client would personally come up with a suitable answer: "This time is different. I have been going to AA meetings for almost a year, and I have good attendance records. I have a job now, and I want to keep it. I don't go to that bar where I used to get into trouble. And I'm going to enroll in an anger management class that my lawyer and I visited a couple of weeks ago."

Knowing something about the compliance principles, including the fact that compliance is increased if some family or friends are aware of a client's proposed course of action, also suggests a role for the lawyer. The lawyer might discuss this with the client and suggest to the client the usefulness of having some agreed-upon family members or friends familiarize themselves with the proposed conditions and attend the hearing. But the lawyer should be clear that the client truly agrees with the idea of involvement of family and friends.

Ordinarily, if probation is granted, the court will have no further contact with the defendant unless revocation is sought for an alleged violation of the terms of probation. Some Therapeutic Jurisprudence writing, however, taking a page from the appar-

---

to risk management is the changing or elimination of dynamic risk factors, factors theoretically within the control of the individual under assessment. Emerging Therapeutic Jurisprudence literature suggests a motivational role for lawyers in prompting clients to change some dynamic risk factors so as to maximize liberty and, at the same time, to take a substantial step in the rehabilitative direction. *See* Bruce J. Winick, *Domestic Violence Court Judges as Risk Managers*, *in* JTK, *supra* note 2, at 201, 201–11. An interesting exercise in the risk management area is to ask what the lawyer-client conversation might look like. Keeping with the legal education analogy, might the lawyer in this context sometimes need to do a bit of "lecturing" rather than relying principally on the "Socratic method?" "It is known that factor X makes people more at risk for engaging in violent behavior. If you can change factor X, we can present that to the judge, and hopefully the judge will be impressed. Would you like to give that a shot? How?" Note that the proposed sharing of decision-making between lawyer and client taps into standard social work notions of client empowerment and self-determination. *See* Hartley & Petrucci, *supra* note 25, at 177.

81. Even if the plan is rejected, the effort was not necessarily wasted: the process may have started the client on a course of cognitive restructuring and relapse prevention, and these cognitive/behavioral changes can benefit the client even during incarceration and can surely be beneficial when planning for prison release and reentry. At some point, the lawyer should discuss with the client the usefulness of even the rejected plan, but of course should wait until the timing is right — until the dust settles and the client is able to think beyond having to face an incarcerative penalty. When a disappointing disposition occurs, this "long range" view of rehabilitation is also important in terms of defense counsel "believing in" the client and some of the client's strengths and achievements: "the defendant's forceful efforts and the intervention of a respected legal professional who 'believed in' the defendant may still, despite the setback, sow the seeds for eventual desistance on the part of the defendant." *See* Wexler, *supra* note 5 (referring to criminological work on offender desistance and the role of narrative development).

ently successful ongoing judicial supervision practices of drug treatment court, has urged ordinary criminal courts to schedule periodic review hearings in probation cases.[82]

Review hearings can monitor not only the defendant's compliance, but can also assess whether various agencies have been providing the offender with appropriate services.[83] If such hearings are held, defense counsel should recognize that there is a meaningful role to play even if all is going well.

Defense attorneys rapidly understand their role when violations are alleged and when revocation or other adverse sanctions will possibly result. But, attorneys can play an important role in routine review hearings by marshalling, with the client, impressive evidence of success, and presenting it to the court, thereby helping to reinforce desistance from criminal activity.[84]

Drug treatment courts also hold "graduation ceremonies" for clients who successfully complete the program. Graduates and their families attend, and applause is common. Again, receiving praise in this sort of official setting seems to be very meaningful. Accordingly, these ceremonies are not merely "ceremonial," but appear to have real rehabilitative value, and suggest an important, albeit unconventional, role for counsel.[85]

Given the drug court graduation experience, courts and counsel should consider some sort of in-court acknowledgement when probation is terminated. Indeed, when the probationary period has been going well, counsel should, when available under local law, move for the early termination of probation, hopefully accompanied by an in-court acknowledgement of the probationer's successful conduct.[86]

This overall approach to probation urges lawyers and clients to craft innovative, individually-tailored probation conditions. Yet, for other reasons, the notion of innovative probation conditions has recently come under attack, most notably in a fascinating and thorough article by Professor Andrew Horwitz.[87]

---

82. *Robes*, *supra* note 71, at 251.
83. This ties in with the "good lives" perspective mentioned earlier. *See* Ward & Stewart, *supra* note 73 and accompanying text.
84. *Robes*, *supra* note 71, at 251–52; *see also* Quinn, *supra* note 14, at 39 (counsel important at drug treatment court post-adjudication status hearings even when all is going well and when sanctions are not at issue). Caroline S. Cooper & Shanie R. Bartlett, *SJI National Symposium on the Implementation and Operation of Drug Courts*, available at http://spa.american.edu/justice/publications/juvrptt.htm. (last visited Jan. 27, 2005) (surveying drug court participants themselves report value in regular judicial contact). One DTC judge told me that, with retained counsel, to cut down on expenses, the judge only asks counsel to come to a review hearing if the judge expects "to be mean." This raises an interesting question regarding costs, therapeutic aims, and retained versus publicly-provided legal services.
85. *Robes*, *supra* note 71, at 251.
86. Ariz. Rev. Stat. § 13-901(E) (2002).
  The court, on its own initiative or upon application of the probationer, after notice and an opportunity to be heard for the prosecuting attorney, and on request, the victim, may terminate the period of probation or intensive probation and discharge the defendant at a time earlier than that originally imposed if in the court's opinion the ends of justice will be served and if the conduct of the defendant on probation warrants it.

Id.
  Under certain drug treatment initiatives, a similar court hearing can be held to underscore the "successful completion of treatment." Cal. Penal Code § 1210(c) (2004).
87. Andrew Horwitz, *Coercion, Pop-Psychology, and Judicial Moralizing: Some Proposals for Curbing Judicial Abuse of Probation Conditions*, 57 Wash. & Lee L. Rev. 75 (2000).

The Horwitz article should be required reading for lawyers and students contemplating a TJ-oriented criminal law practice. Horwitz details the many horrendous probation conditions sometimes employed by courts.[88] He notes, too, that such conditions are rarely reviewed by appellate courts, either because they were arrived at through plea negotiations, and are thus part of the deal accepted by the defendant, or, relatedly, because defendants are understandably reluctant to challenge conditions on appeal. This is because, in the event of success, the prevailing law would permit resentencing—and would therefore leave open the possibility of a sentence of incarceration.

His proposed solution is two-fold. First, he would leave the notion of innovative probation conditions to the legislature, and would basically restrict allowable conditions to those already common in the jurisdiction. Second, he would encourage defendants to appeal controversial conditions, and would disallow a sentencing court from imposing incarceration after a condition has been successfully challenged on appeal. It is hard to argue with anything Horwitz says about the abuses; they are really frightening. I wonder, though, if his proposed solutions might themselves pose some serious problems.

As noted above, Therapeutic Jurisprudence work urges defense lawyers to work with clients and helping professionals to craft and propose appropriate, responsive, innovative plans. Tying judges' hands to what is already common in the jurisdiction could therefore be a real impediment to lawyers trying to do more in the rehabilitative realm.

I also question whether it is wise to actually encourage defendants to challenge probation conditions on appeal. In many cases, they will challenge and lose. Will that only serve to increase their feeling that they have been treated unfairly? Would that be likely to adversely affect their compliance?

It would be helpful to learn, too, whether a study such as Horwitz' revealed any interesting/innovative cases where courts imposed unique but really appropriate conditions. My guess is that such conditions, if they exist, are even less likely to come to light in the appellate courts, but it would be useful to know what 'good' lawyering has led to in the area.[89]

Finally, Horwitz speaks of "netwidening." Apparently, many who have been subjected to unusual conditions were persons who, with or without such conditions, would have been sentenced to probation; thus, these troublesome conditions were simply "add ons," widening the net of governmental power over the probationers. I am nonetheless concerned that, under Horwitz' proposal, defendants themselves will not be able to suggest certain conditions, and courts will thus often be inclined to incarcerate offenders rather than to order probation.

---

88. Picture yourself having just been convicted of a relatively minor criminal offense. Imagine that you are living in a country in which the judge could prohibit you from participating in political speech or protest, prohibit you from associating with 'known homosexuals,' prohibit you from association with your spouse or fiancé, prohibit you from belonging to the religious organization of your choice, require you to submit to a search of your person or your home at any time of day or night, require you to wear a fluorescent pink bracelet proclaiming your offense, or banish you from the country altogether. This country must be an authoritarian dictatorship of some kind, a country that is not governed by a constitution or the rule of law, right? Wrong. This nation is the United States of America as the legal system exists today. A trial judge has imposed each of the sentences just listed, and an appellate court has allowed each to stand. *Id.* at 76.

89. A worthwhile project for clinic students might be to interview local lawyers and judges in an effort to determine creative, individually-tailored probation conditions that were never subject to appellate review.

None of this is intended to suggest that what Horwitz has unearthed is not really troubling, or that what has gone on is not truly outrageous. He surely makes the case. It is only that this is an extremely difficult—and fascinating—area of the law. Indeed, it provides considerable food for thought for TJ lawyering whether or not Horwitz' law reform approach is accepted. Consider, for example, the lawyering implications of the condition of probation upheld in the Wisconsin Supreme Court case of *State v. Oakley*.[90]

David Oakley, father of nine, was convicted of the Wisconsin felony of intentionally refusing to pay child support. In lieu of prison, the trial court sentenced him to probation, imposing as a condition that, during the probationary period, Oakley have no more children unless he could demonstrate his ability to support them and his other children.

Oakley challenged the condition, and the Wisconsin Supreme Court upheld it, putting in sharp relief the concerns expressed by Horwitz. But the case also raises another level of lawyering questions, worthy of attention in practice and clinical teaching:

Since the court upheld this controversial condition, is it the sort of condition that might ever be urged to a court by the *defendant*? One can imagine the following dialogue between lawyer and client:

> Lawyer: Ok, the court may want to let you stay in the community to continue your job and to start paying child support, for if it sentences you to prison, the payment of support would be out of the question. But still, is there any way we can try to convince the court of your genuine change of heart: that you don't want to continue to have children and to shirk your obligations to them?
>
> Client: Well, I could promise not to have any more kids; at least not until I get my act together and can support them.
>
> Lawyer: Would you be comfortable with such a promise?
>
> Client: Yeah; I really shouldn't have any more kids; I don't really want any more kids.

The point is that the types of behaviors (or non-behaviors) contemplated by many of these controversial conditions may be the subject of lawyer/client discussion. This is especially true if the conditions, though controversial, are deemed to be constitutional. If so, is there anything wrong with them being discussed by lawyer and client, by their being proposed by the client, especially if they may be the key to a non-incarcerative penalty?

Indeed, even if the courts were to hold a condition like the above to be unconstitutional, the underlying issue will not necessarily be swept from the judicial mind, and it may still be the subject of lawyer/client dialogue. Consider the following:

> Lawyer: The judge might want to give you a break and put you on probation so you can keep your job and start paying child support. But you already have nine kids, and this is freaking out the judge.
>
> Client: What if I promise not to have any more kids? I really don't want any more kids anyway.
>
> Lawyer: Well, the courts have said that such a promise would violate your constitutional rights, so they can't allow you to make such a promise, even if you want to.

---

90. See Wisconsin v. Oakley, 629 N.W.2d 200 (Wis. 2001); *see also* DEMLEITNER ET AL., *supra* note 18, at 520; Kelly R. Skaff, *Pay Up or Zip Up: Giving up the Right to Procreate as a Condition of Probation*, 23 ST. LOUIS U. PUB. L. REV. 399 (2004).

Client: Damn. So I go to jail because the judge thinks I might have more kids, even though I don't want more kids?

Lawyer: How else might we be able to convince the court that you won't have any more kids?

Client: What if I got a vasectomy? I thought about doing it a year ago, even spoke to a doctor, who said it's not a difficult procedure. I think he said it might even be reversible if I changed my mind in the future, but fat chance I would change my mind.

Lawyer: Are you really game for that? It may not be a difficult procedure, but it is a really significant thing to do.

Client: I think so. I'm surely willing to look into it. Like I said, I don't want any more kids anyway. Period.

Lawyer: Well, think about it. It might help. But there are no guarantees. If you do this, you still have to realize the judge might send you to jail. How would you feel in that case?

What all this suggests is that, with controversial and even potentially unconstitutional measures, lawyering may be involved. Although a 'behavioral contract' would not be possible in the case of unconstitutional conditions, the unilateral behavior of the client might eliminate the risk that will be of concern to the court. So, if presented with a fait accompli, the court might opt for probation rather than incarceration, although there is of course no guarantee.

These issues are set out as an area worthy of serious discussion. Should lawyers raise these topics? Should they not raise them but discuss them if clients bring them up? If they have a dialogue, can they do so in a way—again, an analogy to the Socratic method—that lessens the lawyer's role in suggesting these controversial procedures ("Listen, have you thought of getting a vasectomy? That might influence the court") but instead inches the client personally to think of and raise the point? Are there ethical or therapeutic distinctions between the two approaches?

6. Appeal

Following conviction, and especially after the imposition of an incarcerative sentence, the issue of an appeal will arise. With retained counsel, counsel and client will engage in a cost/benefit analysis of sorts. In most cases, however, the client will be indigent, and, given the right to appointed counsel in the first appeal,[91] there are no real disincentives to filing an appeal. Not surprisingly, therefore, the great bulk of appeals result in affirmances.

Therapeutic Jurisprudence considerations abound in the kind of conversations lawyers should have with clients both before an appellate brief is filed and in the aftermath of an appellate determination.[92] The relevant Therapeutic Jurisprudence literature

---

91. Douglas v. California, 372 U.S. 252 (1963).

92. In the event of an appellate reversal, counsel will need to explain what has happened and what comes next, especially in terms of possible new trials and the like. It is crucial, in such cases, that a client not think incorrectly that complete freedom has been won. Of course, all of this should ideally have been first explained to the client earlier, at the time counsel explained the arguments to be made and the relief sought. A valuable educational exercise would be for lawyers and law students to contemplate the kind of conversation to have with a client before a brief is filed and after an appellate ruling. Also to be considered is whether the conversation should be face-to-face or through correspondence. Of course, the post-ruling conversation will differ markedly if the appellate court reverses or affirms the court below. Mainly, the lawyer will be dealing with appellate affir-

on this topic actually relates to the therapeutic role of appellate courts, rather than to lawyers, but the concerns are closely connected.

Ronner and Winick have written about the antitherapeutic aspects of *per curiam* summary affirmances.[93] They note how an appellate ruling that says no more than "affirmed" may leave an appellant feeling that the court did not attend to his or her case. Ronner and Winick suggest that courts accord appellants a sense of "voice" by preparing very brief opinions that will at least indicate that the briefs have been read and understood. In essence, instead of a summary affirmance opinion, courts could write a type of "therapeutic" affirmance, though they would of course not be designated as such.[94]

The "real" way an appellant can be shown to have had "voice" is through a conversation with counsel, and, for that to happen, an appellate court opinion, however brief, is essential. Since criminal appeals are typically taken because there is nothing to lose, success on appeal is generally quite an uphill battle.

The appellate lawyer's task is a highly sensitive one. On the one hand, it is important for counsel to convey the message of voice and validation. On the other hand, it is crucial that counsel not simply serve as an apologist for an appellate affirmance; that appellant know that counsel is truly on the appellant's side, giving the case the best possible shot. The following remarks are intended to open a discussion about how to strike an appropriate balance.

If the appellate affirmance is much in line with what counsel anticipated (or feared), it is probably helpful for counsel to express that view to the client. "Yeah, as I feared, the

---

mances.

The present article discusses possible lawyer-client dialogue and conversations not only in the context of appeals, but also in the context of diversion decisions and in the context of formulating proposed conditions of probation and parole. Important as they are, these are only illustrative of the TJ-tinged conversations that can be had throughout the criminal process. For example, the nature—or at least the tone—of a conversation regarding a motion to suppress evidence may be a bit different from the conventional one when it is inspired by a TJ perspective. Legal clinics can discuss what these conversations might look like.

93. Amy D. Ronner & Bruce J. Winick, *The Antitherapeutic Per Curiam Affirmance*, in JTK, *supra* note 2, at 316, 316; *see also* Amy D. Ronner & Bruce J. Winick, *Silencing the Appellant's Voice: The Antiherapeudic Per Curiam Affirmance*, 24 SEATTLE U. L. REV 499, 500–07 (2000).

94. Interestingly, a debate currently raging in the federal arena might have an impact on the willingness of federal appellate courts to accept the therapeutic affirmance proposal (of course, the issue would be all the more important if it were transplanted to state appellate systems, where the great bulk of criminal appeals occur). The current debate is whether "unpublished" opinions— available to the parties and available online but not published in the reports—can properly be "cited" by lawyers. These opinions, prepared for the benefit of the parties only, are often not prepared with great care. The judges opposed to "citability" worry that, if these "junk law" opinions are allowed to be cited and quoted, courts will spend considerably more time in preparing them, thus adding significantly to the already immense workload of the appellate courts. *See generally*, Tony Mauro, *Judicial Conference Group Backs Citing of Unpublished Opinions*, LEGAL TIMES, April 15, 2004, *available at* http://www.law.com/jsp/article.jsp?id =1081792928522 (last visited April 23, 2005). Moreover, in connection with our particular concern, consider the following potential consequence: Courts willing to consider the proposal to write brief therapeutic affirmances in lieu of summary *per curiam* opinions might be willing to do so only if such affirmances could be short, skimpy, and not subject to citation. Indeed, under the prospect of citability, many of the short, unpublished opinions now being written might dry up and become the very *per curiam* summary affirmances under attack by Ronner and Winick. This is a fascinating issue. Without the Therapeutic Jurisprudence lens, the arguments appear to put concerns of justice (what some call "secret law") against concerns of workload and judicial efficiency. But from a Therapeutic Jurisprudence perspective, the justice issues are even richer, for now the "secret law" justice issue needs to be weighed against the procedural justice and Therapeutic Jurisprudence interests of some of the parties.

court reaffirmed what it had said five years ago in State v. Wilkins. We tried to get the court to overrule *Wilkins* or at least to limit it, and the court seemed to understand what we were arguing, but they didn't buy it." Unless counsel truly believes the appellate court was muddled, inattentive, or outright stupid, it would seem to be without much purpose so to characterize the ruling. Such a characterization suggests that the client was not accorded "voice" and "validation," even with a professional advocate speaking for the client, which would be likely to affect adversely the client's acceptance of the ruling and adjustment to the situation. In the great majority of cases, one would hope the appellate opinion would reflect the fact that the appellant—and thus the attorney as well—was accorded voice and validation.[95]

The conversation a lawyer might have with a client following an appellate ruling relates also to the conversation the lawyer should have had with the client earlier—when the appeal was filed or during the preparation of the appellate brief. Except when the attorney regards a case to be wholly without merit, a brief on the merits is likely to be filed. At that stage, it is important for the lawyer to explain the points and arguments to be made, but also to indicate the state of the prevailing law and the lawyer's general assessment of what the appellate court will do and why. This is to give the client a realistic view of what to expect, and it also sets the stage for the later conversation—the one following the appellate court's ruling.

And what if the lawyer finds the case completely without merit? *Anders v. California* allows the lawyer to move to withdraw, accompanied by a "minor brief" referring to anything in the record that may arguably support an appeal.[96] The more recent case of *Smith v. Robbins*, although it does not contemplate attorney withdrawal, and does not require the lawyer to characterize the case as frivolous, in some ways permits a lawyer to do even less than in *Anders*: to merely summarize the case, with references to the record, and to offer to brief any points suggested by the appellate court.[97]

A useful legal clinic exercise would be to discuss, keeping in mind the Therapeutic Jurisprudence considerations, what a lawyer faced with such a case should do, and what the lawyer/client conversation might look like. Might it be preferable for the lawyer to explain why the case, given the state of the law, seems without merit, but, in lieu of withdrawing, to offer to "dress up" the *Anders* brief as a short brief on the merits? Are there any ethical restrictions on such a strategy, such as an ethical obligation not to file a frivolous appeal?[98] If so, how might ethical considerations form part of the lawyer's conversation with the client on why another course of action seems in order?

7. Corrections, Re-entry, and Beyond

If a client is confronting an incarcerative sentence, the TJ criminal lawyer should, at some point, engage the client in a dialogue regarding the sentence and the future. Some of this discussion can occur in the legal context of an expected or hoped-for release or conditional release date.

---

95. These issues, and conversations, can be applied as well to the trial level when trial courts prepare written opinions, as does the drug treatment court of New South Wales. *See* New South Wales, *supra* note 31 and accompanying text.
96. Anders v. California, 387 U.S. 738 (1967).
97. Smith v. Robbins, 528 U.S. 259 (2000).
98. *Id*. at 278.

Relevant legal considerations will be earning and forfeiting good time credits,[99] including sentence reductions for engaging in certain treatment programs.[100] Crucially important, too, is whether the jurisdiction authorizes discretionary parole release and, if so, when the client will be eligible for parole consideration.[101]

Over the last couple of decades, as part of the development to reduce sentencing disparity, many jurisdictions have abolished discretionary parole eligibility, perhaps throwing the baby out with the bathwater by sapping the system of a tool to motivate prisoners and to orient them toward release. Recently, however, the crucial question of prisoner reentry has surfaced as a major concern of public policy.[102]

Proposals have emerged to reform and reinvigorate the parole process,[103] as well as to borrow from the drug court model and to create reentry courts.[104] A reentry court could have conditional release authority[105] or could operate post-unconditional release to work with ex-offenders who volunteer to participate in a program geared toward smoother reentry.[106]

This new urgency should carry with it a major role for lawyers—and a very major need for the creation of new structures for providing legal services in this arena. Constitutionally, the Sixth Amendment right to counsel is inapplicable because a "criminal proceeding" terminates with sentencing.[107] The Supreme Court has held that due process applies to a parole revocation proceeding,[108] and the due process right to assigned counsel at such hearings is determined on a case-by-case basis rather than as a hard and fast rule.

In terms of hearings regarding the potential *granting* of parole, as opposed to its potential revocation, matters are even worse. In the 1994 case of *Neel v. Holden*,[109] for example, the Utah Supreme Court ruled that a prisoner was not denied any rights when the parole board refused to allow Neel's *own* attorney to address the board. The court viewed "somewhat skeptically the suggestion that attorneys should be permitted to address the Board on their client's behalf in parole hearings."[110]

---

99. James B. Jacobs, *Sentencing by Prison Personnel: Good Time*, 30 UCLA L. Rev. 217 (1982).

100. Lopez v. Davis, 531 U.S. 230 (2001) (discussing operation and limitation of Federal Bureau of Prisons regulation according early release for completion of a substance abuse program). The U.S. Sentencing Commission's Ad Hoc Advisory Group on Native American Sentencing Issues recently proposed the adoption of a similar program for sex offender treatment. Report of the Native American Advisory Group, 26–30, Nov. 4, 2003, *available at* http://www.ussc.gov/NAAG/NativeAmer.pdf (last visited April 23, 2005).

101. Joan Petersilia, *What to Do? Reforming Parole and Reentry Practices, in* When Prisoners Come Home 171, 171 (2003).

102. *See id.*; *see also* Fox Butterfield, *Repaving the Long Road Out of Prison*, N.Y. Times, May 4, 2004, at 25A (discussing strong interest in reentry, and innovative programs to provide released inmates immediately with clothing, housing, mental health and drug treatment, and employment opportunities); Carter, *supra* note 48.

103. Petersilia, *supra* note 101.

104. Wexler, *Spain's JVP*, *supra* note 13.

105. *Id.*

106. Shadd Maruna & Thomas P. LeBel, *Welcome Home?: Examining the "Reentry Court" Concept from a Strengths-Based Perspective, in* JTK, *supra* note 2, at 255, 257.

107. Gagnon v. Scarpelli, 411 U.S. 778 (1973).

108. Morrissey v. Brewer, 408 U.S. 471 (1972).

109. Neel v. Holden, 886 P.2d 1097 (Utah 1994).

110. *Id.* at 1103 n.7; *see generally* Amanda N. Montague, *Recognizing All Critical Stages in Criminal Proceedings: The Violation of the Sixth Amendment by Utah in Not Allowing Defendants the Right to Counsel at Parole Hearings*, 18 BYU J. Pub. L. 249 (2003).

In Therapeutic Jurisprudence terms, there is much meaningful work for an attorney at the parole grant hearing stage. The prior detailed discussion of relapse prevention planning and probation is fully applicable.[111] That discussion proposes a very substantial role for the lawyer in working with the client and others to establish a plan—and proposed conditions—for conditional release.

Once the client has been released from confinement, conditionally or unconditionally, counsel can also help in the tremendously difficult task of reentry and readjustment.[112] On the strictly legal side, the client should be clearly informed of any imposed parole conditions. The possibility of parole revocation as well as the possible applicability of recidivist statutes[113] will underscore the high stakes involved in a return to criminality.

Unfortunately, the collateral consequences of a criminal conviction[114] are a further impediment to successful reentry, but they are crucial components of an important lawyer/client conversation.[115] On a slightly positive note, the restoration of some rights is possible,[116] and the lawyer can play an important role in restoration and expungement efforts.[117]

8. Structure of Legal Services

What is proposed in this essay is a rehabilitative role of the lawyer that extends beyond sentencing, into corrections, conditional or unconditional release, and to life in the community. Of course, such a role can be undertaken by attorneys in private practice, and, as we have seen,[118] some, like John McShane, are already moving in that direction.

There is also the possibility of innovative privately funded organizations, such as the Georgia Justice Project,[119] which is selective in the cases it takes, but which takes them with the objective of working with a defendant, win or lose, in a very broad, encompassing, and extensive way. Indeed, law school legal clinics could play a very major role in designing structures of legal services and in developing the role of the TJ criminal

---

111. *See supra* text accompanying notes 67–91.
112. Alan Feuer, *Out of Jail, Into Temptation: A Day in a Life*, in JTK, *supra* note 2, at 13–19. *See also* Butterfield, *supra* note 102; Anthony C. Thompson, *Navigating the Hidden Obstacles to Ex-Offender Reentry*, 45 B.C. L. Rev. 255 (2004) (a just-published excellent piece on the role of the lawyer in re-entry, and on the workings of the Offender Reentry Clinic at NYU law school).
113. Julian V. Roberts, *The Role of Criminal Record in the Sentencing Process*, 22 Crime and Just. 303 (1997).
114. Sabra Micah Barnett, *Collateral Sanctions and Civil Disabilities: The Secret Barrier to True Sentencing Reform for Legislatures and Sentencing Commissions*, 55 Ala. L. Rev. 375 (2004).
115. These collateral consequences accompany the conviction, and thus attach to probationers as well. Joshua R. DeGonia, *Defining a Successful Completion of Probation Under California's Expungement Statute*, 24 Whittier L. Rev. 1077 (2003).
116. *E.g.*, Ariz. Rev. Stat. §§ 13-904–912 (2004).
117. Margaret Colgate Love, *Starting Over With a Clean Slate: In Praise of a Forgotten Section of the Model Penal Code*, 30 Fordham Urb. L.J. 1705 (2003). These too could serve as reintegration ceremonies, or redemption rituals, praising and reinforcing the offender's desistance. *Robes, supra* note 71, at 250–51. Of course, some "collateral" consequences are purely informal rather than imposed by law: apartment complexes that may refuse to rent to those with a record, or employers who refuse to hire. Here is an area where the new reentry court concept may help, for landlords and employers may be more willing to consider one with a criminal record if the person is part of—or a graduate of—an official program. TJ criminal lawyers will need to play a role in the creation of these programs, and in informing clients of their existence, eligibility requirements, benefits, and potential costs.
118. *See supra* text accompanying notes 6–11.
119. Georgia Justice Project, *available at* http://www.gjp.org (last visited January 27, 2005).

lawyer. Finally, there is the question of whether and how Public Defender (PD) offices might also be structured to accomplish this sort of role.[120]

If publicly funded legal services are available only through sentencing and appeal (an issue that will be ultimately worthy of reconsideration given the growing importance of prisoner reentry, and of the potentially invaluable role of the lawyer in that enterprise), perhaps a privately funded or foundation funded agency could be set up, along modified Georgia Justice Project lines, to take over where the PD leaves off. And within the PD office, proper thought needs to be given to allowing at least some lawyers the opportunity to play an explicit TJ role.

Perhaps these TJ lawyers should conduct initial intake interviews, to assess a defendant's likely interest in pursuing a path that would most likely look to diversion (or participation in a problem solving court such as drug treatment court, mental health court, domestic violence court), plea negotiation, and sentencing. And those lawyers might then follow through representing clients for whom that path seems appealing.

PD offices will need to confront questions of relative caseload and will need to find ways of avoiding the development of intra-office resentment toward lawyers having a less frenzied daily diet. In part, the issue is not unlike the judicial view that sometimes regards problem solving courts as 'boutique' courts tapping a disproportionate share of the resources.[121]

In the PD office as well as the other settings of potential TJ criminal law practice, thought needs to be given, as well, to integrating other professionals—such as social workers—into the law office context. Some models already exist, but much more work will need to be done here. A worthwhile project would be to survey the structure of various PD offices along this dimension, to see how they are working, to compare and contrast them, and to propose a model for blending traditional and TJ approaches.

Conclusion

This essay has merely scratched the surface of the ways in which lawyers interested in Therapeutic Jurisprudence might invigorate and enlarge their traditional roles, but I hope it will motivate the development of a true TJ criminal defense bar[122] among pri-

---

120. With respect to legal clinics, Professor (and former DTC Judge) Greg Baker has established a legal clinic at the law school of William and Mary where supervised students play a role in DTC. Professor Baker's clinic is described under "Courses" in the website of the International Network on Therapeutic Jurisprudence. *Courses in Therapeutic Jurisprudence*, at http://www.law.arizona.edu/depts/upr-intj/intj-c.html (last visited Jan. 27, 2005). Gregory Baker & Jennifer Zawid, *The Birth of a Therapeutic Courts Externship Program: Hard labor but Worth the Effort*, 17 St. Thomas L. Rev. 709 (2005). The recent report of the ABA Justice Kennedy Commission speaks explicitly of law school clinics, and urges such clinics to represent prisoners in the reentry process, reestablishing themselves in the community, regaining legal rights, obtaining relief from collateral disabilities, and the like. ABA Justice Kennedy Commission, *Report to the House of Delegates*, available at http://www.abanews.org/nosearch/kencomm/rep121d.pdf (last visited Jan. 27, 2005). *See also*, Clarke & Neuhard, *supra* note 34, at 47 (suggesting an "intake unit," a "trial unit," a "negotiation team," and a "treatment unit"); Cait Clarke & James Neuhard, *Making the Case: Therapeutic Jurisprudence and Problem Solving Practices Positively Impact Clients, Justice Systems and the Communities they Serve*, 17 St. Thomas L. Rev. 779 (2005); *See also* Nancy Gist, *Foreword to The Executive Session on Public Defense*, 29 NYU Rev. L. & Soc. Change 1, 1–2 (2004).
121. Judge (rtr.) William F. Dressel, *Foreword to JTK*, *supra* note 2, at xiii–xiv.
122. The present article focuses on the role of the criminal defense attorney. A virtually untouched but crucial area of inquiry relates to the use of the Therapeutic Jurisprudence perspective in the role of the prosecutor in their dealings with defendants as well as with victims.

vate lawyers, public defenders, law school clinics, and privately-supported defense organizations. Additionally, I hope the essay will be useful in legal education, both in general courses in criminal law and procedure, to explicate and legitimate a non-traditional role, and in sentencing and correction courses. I especially hope it will find its way into clinical legal education. There, the topics explored here can be further developed in teaching, in practice, and in student research projects. After all, the legal clinics are where the initial training of many of tomorrow's criminal lawyers is likely to begin.

Professor Hartley recently addressed the question of the prosecutor's obligation to domestic violence victims. Note the following interesting conclusion:
> Some of the strategies I propose may not be legally necessary for successful prosecution. In cases involving overwhelming physical evidence or airtight eyewitness testimony introducing contextual evidence about the defendant's prior acts or rehabilitating the victim's credibility may seem superfluous. But allowing victims to describe the context of the violence and rehabilitating their character after a defense attack are essential to giving voice to and empowering women through due process.

Hartley, *supra* note 12. Note that Hartley is in essence arguing that the state has, through the operation of the law, caused some additional trauma to the victim (say, in opening her up to an attack on her credibility), and that the prosecutor might thus have a reason, even if not necessary to win the case, to use the law therapeutically—to "rehabilitate" the victim's credibility—and the victim herself. Therapeutic Jurisprudence thinking—but not published writing—has also turned to the prosecutor's obligation to child victim/witnesses. If a prosecutor develops a relationship with a child victim so as to prepare the child to be able to function effectively at an eventual trial, what happens to the relationship after the end of the trial? Will the child feel abandoned by an adult he or she has reluctantly come to trust? If so, what might a prosecutor do to avoid this? Might the prosecutor pair with a volunteer from a community agency so that the volunteer will play the major role and the prosecutor a secondary one? After the trial, the prosecutor might gradually, rather than abruptly, fade out, but the volunteer could maintain an ongoing relationship with the child. Besides the prosecution, there is an important role Therapeutic Jurisprudence can play in police behavior, as Swedish psychologist/police officer Ulf Holmberg has begun to document. Holmberg shows how some police interviewing techniques lead to better responses from both victims and persons accused of crime. *See* Holmberg, *supra* note 12.

Part II

Concerns and Critiques

Especially in a relatively new venture like therapeutic jurisprudence, concerns and critiques need to be taken and evaluated very seriously. That is the focus of this Part.

First, it is important to understand the relationship between therapeutic jurisprudence and problem-solving courts (drug treatment courts, mental health courts, domestic violence courts, community courts), two vectors of what is sometimes called the overall "comprehensive law movement". It is important to remember that these two vectors are close cousins rather than identical twins. They have different "ancestry," TJ as an academic venture studying legal arrangements and therapeutic outcomes, and problem-solving courts, especially drug treatment courts, as a practical and largely atheoretical on-the-ground creative response to revolving-door justice. TJ and problem-solving courts have learned much from one another—the relationship might even be seen as symbiotic—but they nonetheless remain in many ways distinct. For instance, TJ is in no sense "dependent" on problem-solving courts, and TJ principles and applications can and do flourish outside the problem-solving court context and, indeed, apart from a judicial context altogether. Similarly, since TJ asks *what* legal arrangements work and *why*, TJ principles can be seen as intimately tied to the functioning of problem-solving courts, but such courts are also fueled by many problem-solving factors other than therapeutic jurisprudence.

This book is especially geared to the use of TJ principles by general criminal lawyers. But given the close relationship of TJ and problem-solving courts, it is important for us to have a grasp of the concerns expressed regarding lawyering in the latter, and to be vigilant about so-called therapeutic goals not "trumping" legal and due process considerations. Accordingly, in the first selection of this Part, Professor Tamar Meekins calls attention to the serious constraints on lawyering that are often at play in the problem-solving court context. These are largely concerns I share, and I endorse as well Meekins' recent call for the development of a code of ethics for practice in such courts. Tamar Meekins, Risky Business: Criminal Specialty Courts and the Ethical Obligations of the Zealous Criminal Defender. 12 Berkeley Journal of Criminal Law 75 (2007).

Meekins also cautions against a constrained advocacy role leaping out of a problem-solving court setting into general criminal law practice, and I too am in full accord with that caution. But despite these concerns, Meekins acknowledges how much we can learn from problem-solving courts and from the dedicated and experienced practitioners who labor in them. In fact, in a subsequent section of the book detailing thoughtful and creative TJ-type lawyering practices and techniques, Meekins work is again featured, explaining, as her title in that Part says, that "You Can Teach Old Defenders New Tricks".

Unlike Meekins, Professor Mae Quinn does not focus her critique on systemically constrained advocacy in problem-solving courts. Instead, she takes aim at TJ itself, and at practicing criminal law with a TJ lens in general judicial settings, particularly as exemplified by my own writings. In the section of this Part entitled "A Conversation with a Critic," I present Quinn's critique in full and then respond, hoping to clarify, convince, and narrow the issues. Of course, it is the reader who must here serve as the ultimate judge.

A. Concerns Relating to Lawyering in Problem-Solving Courts

Tamar M. Meekins,[*] "Specialized Justice": The Over-Emergence of Specialty Courts and the Threat of a New Criminal Defense Paradigm
(Reprinted with permission from
40 Suffolk University Law Review 1, 2006)

"Power concedes nothing without a demand. It never did and it never will."[1]

"One can only imagine what criminal representation would look like if there were no ethical requirement of zealous criminal defense."[2]

"How arrogant and lazy and convinced of their own infallibility would the prosecution and court become if the defendant had no advocate?"[3]

Introduction

The sentiments embodied in the above statements, unfortunately, represent the everyday reality in some criminal specialty and treatment courts across the country. Over the past ten to fifteen years, many judges, court officials, legislators, academics, and other policy-makers confronted with rising recidivism and failed attempts to rid society of "the criminal element,"[4] embarked upon a campaign to address social

---

[*] Associate Professor and Clinical Director, Howard University School of Law.

1. Frederick A. Douglass, Aug. 4, 1857, available at http://www.buildingequality.us/Quotes/Frederick Douglass.htm. Douglass was not speaking of the criminal justice system when he made this statement, but rather the emancipation of North American slaves. The quote appears in several of Douglass's writings and speeches. See id. Though many individuals, groups, and causes use this quote in various forms, it aptly demonstrates the role of the defense lawyer—to demand and protect the rights of the criminal defendant in a criminal proceeding.

2. Abbe Smith, The Difference in Criminal Defense and the Difference It Makes, 11 Wash. U. J.L. & Pol'y 83, 128 (2003) (discussing role and significance of criminal defense lawyers in our adversary system).

3. Stanley A. Goldman, First Thing We Do, Let's Kill All the [Defense] Lawyers, 30 Loy. L.A. L. Rev. 1, 2 (1996) (noting criminal defense lawyers' importance).

4. Statistics show a significant increase in crime during the 1980s and early 1990s. In 1991, the homicide rate rose to 9.8 per 100,000 people. Since 1950, the rate exceeded this level only once. Federal Bureau of Investigation, Uniform Crime Reports, 1950–2002, available at http://www.fbi.gov/ucr/ucr.htm. Between 1985 and 1995, the reported rate of violent crime increased steadily from 557 per 100,000 people to 685, and peaked at 758 in 1991. U.S. Bureau of Justice Statistics, Reported Crime in the United States-Total (1985–1995), available at http://bjsdata.ojp.usdoj.gov/dataonline/Search/Crime/State/RunC rimeStatebyState.cfm. During the period from 1985–1995, the estimated number of persons arrested for drug abuse increased by more than nineteen percent. Federal Bureau of Investigation, Uniform Crime Reports, 1985–1995.

problems thought to lead to criminal activity. The so-called specialty courts or "problem-solving courts" are the embodiment of the therapeutic and restorative justice movements at work.[5] Hundreds of criminal court systems around the country have implemented various forms of courts which offer the promise of "specialized justice,"[6] to address a myriad of social issues, including drug addiction, domestic violence, sexual dysfunction, nuisance crimes, and homelessness.[7] An unintended and,

---

Several laws and initiatives emerged in an attempt to curb this increase in crime. The Comprehensive Crime Control Act of 1984 drastically changed the federal sentencing system and modified bail and forfeiture procedures. The Crime Control Act of 1990 authorized $ 900 million to help states improve their criminal justice systems by funding crime prevention programs and increasing the enforcement of drug laws. Lastly, the Violent Crime Control and Law Enforcement Act of 1994 allotted funds for crime prevention programs, increased the number of federal crimes punishable by death, contained a "three strikes" provision for felons, and permitted the prosecution of juveniles as adults when they commit certain federal offenses. See JoAnne O'Bryant, Congressional Research Service, Crime Control: The Federal Response 7–9 (Mar. 5, 2003), available at http://usinfo.state.gov/usa/infousa/society/crime/crimegun1.pdf. In the 1980s and 1990s, this federal legislation prompted some states' transition from indeterminate sentencing, which allowed judges and correctional officials broad discretion in sentencing and release decisions, to determinate sentencing. See Ben Trachtenberg, State Sentencing Policy and New Prison Admissions, *38 U. Mich. J.L. Reform 479, 479–530 (2005)* (reviewing state sentencing policies effect on prison populations). The most basic form of determinate sentencing is mandatory minimums, which require a person to serve a set percentage of their sentence regardless of their behavior in prison. By 1996, each state established some form of mandatory minimum covering a wide range of offenses. About half the states use sentencing guidelines that determine sentences based on the offense, the convict's criminal history, and other factors. States without sentencing guidelines developed other determinant sentencing laws, including "three strikes and you're out" for felons, broader definitions of criminal behavior, and the abolition of parole. See United States Sentencing Commission, Guidelines Manual §4B1.5 (Nov. 2004), available at http://www.ussc.gov/2004guid/gl2004.pdf; see also Bureau of Justice Assistance, U.S. Dep't of Justice, 1996 National Survey of State Sentencing Structures 29–30 (Sept. 1998), available at http://www.ncjrs.org/pdffiles/169270.pdf. In fact, the State of Virginia and the District of Columbia abolished parole for violent offenders in 1994 and 1998, respectively. See Truth in Sentencing Amendment Act of 1998, 1998 D.C. Stat. 12–165 (codified as amended at *D.C. Code §24-403.01 et seq.*); see also Virginia Criminal Sentencing Commission, A Decade of Truth-In-Sentencing in Virginia 2 (2005), available at http://www.vcsc.state.va.us/ReptCdPDFfinal.pdf. Additionally, to combat the proliferation of illegal drugs, Congress passed legislation that equated the possession of five grams of crack cocaine with the possession of five hundred grams of cocaine powder. See Comprehensive Crime Control Act of 1984 [CCCA], Pub. L. No. 98-473, tit II, 98 Stat. 1837, 1976 (1984) (codified at *18 U.S.C. §§5031*–5042). Minnesota was one of several states to introduce crack cocaine statutes similar to the federal statute, but it was struck down due to its discriminatory impact. *State v. Russell, 477 N.W.2d 886, 887 (Minn. 1991)* (stating "a far greater percentage of blacks than whites are sentenced for possession of three or more grams of crack cocaine under *Minn. Stat. §152.023* with more severe consequences than their white counterparts who possess three or more grams of cocaine powder").

5. Wendy Davis, Special Problems for Specialty Courts, 89 A.B.A. J., Feb. 2003, at 34–37; William H. Simon, Criminal Defenders and Community Justice: The Drug Court Example, *40 Am. Crim. L. Rev. 1595, 1602 (2003)*; see also Candace McCoy, The Politics of Problem Solving: An Overview of an Origins & Development of Therapeutic Courts, *40 Am. Crim. L. Rev. 1513, 1513 (2003)*. These courts have also been called "specialization of the judiciary," "treatment courts," "specialized courts," boutique courts, and therapeutic courts. See infra Part II.

6. "Specialized justice" refers to the notion of individualized, treatment-oriented, and problem-solving processing of cases and defendants through the criminal justice system.

7. Judge Morris Hoffman of Colorado believes that there are thousands of these courts in operation today. See Morris B. Hoffman, A Neo-Retributionist Concurs with Professor Nolan, *40 Am. Crim. L. Rev. 1567, 1568 (2003)* [hereinafter A Neo-Retributionist Concurs]; see also Timothy Casey, When Good Intentions are Not Enough: Problem Solving Courts and the Impending Crisis of Legitimacy, *57 SMU L. Rev. 1459, 1459 (2004);* Rodger M. McDaniel, Problem Solving Courts: A Role for the Judiciary in Meeting the Needs of Wyoming Children and Families, 27 Wyo. Law., Dec. 2004

as yet, largely ignored consequence of this burgeoning movement, however, may spell a threat to our adversary system. The standard premise behind these courts is the emasculation[8] of the traditional role of the criminal defender as a zealous advocate fighting against the system. Despite the importance of defenders insuring courts adhere to principles of substantive and procedural due process, the defender in specialty courts becomes, in most instances, a collaborator. He collaborates with the judge and prosecutors, thereby taking on a role that works to diminish the effectiveness of the defender overall, decreases the confidence defendants have in the outcome, and supports a culture of ineffectiveness and under-representation. More importantly, citizens most in need of justice and traditionally overrepresented in the

---

at 28;. Specialization in criminal courts has some counterparts in the civil court systems. For example, New York City established a commercial litigation court in the mid 1990s to hear breach of contract cases, and Los Angeles has explored establishing a business court to handle complex litigation. Civil specialty courts have won some praise and have also raised some concern. Davis, supra note 5, at 37–38. Additionally, Oregon has a state tax court and several administrative boards, such as the Land Use Board of Appeals and the Workers' Compensation Board that both have some court-like features and functions. Janine Robben, Who Decides?: Specialized Courts vs. the Jury of Peers, Or. St. Bar Bull., Apr. 2005, at 9. Irrespective of the implementation of specialty courts in the civil context, criminal specialty courts present more issues because they deal with fundamental constitutional rights and the liberty interests of clients. See Morris B. Hoffman, Therapeutic Jurisprudence, Neo-Rehabilitationism, and Judicial Collectivism: The Least Dangerous Branch Becomes Most Dangerous, *29 Fordham Urb. L.J. 2063, 2071 (2002)* [hereinafter Therapeutic Jurisprudence]. Beginning in the late 1800s, Juvenile courts were the first in the genre of specialty courts. This article makes no attempt to evaluate or address juvenile courts, but rather looks at the modern wave of specialty courts thought to have emerged with the first drug court in Miami in 1989. Drug courts, as a model of specialty courts, have become widespread, garnering the most attention, praise, funding, and analysis. Given their favored status by government funders, judges, attorneys, and some politicians, the level of criticism of drug courts has been low, and the model of treatment-based adjudication of cases serves as a model to deal with other issues in the criminal justice system.

8. I have intentionally used this strong word to describe what may be happening in some specialty courts because there is a danger that the traditional criminal defender will disappear in these courts and be replaced by a "team player." See supra Parts II & III.

9. Randall Kennedy, Race, Crime, and the Law 148 (1997). Randall Kennedy has pointed to a number of factors that contribute to the overrepresentation of minorities in the criminal justice system. Id. First, race has unduly become a proxy for an increased likelihood of criminal behavior. Id. Second, minorities have been adversely affected by discrimination in the jury selection process. Id. Third, analysis of relevant case law indicates a trend of prosecutors making racial appeals to the detriment of minority defendants in court. Id. Fourth, it has been demonstrated that prosecutors often charge minority defendants more harshly than they would others. Id. Fifth, individual judges have contributed to the overrepresentation of minorities in the criminal justice system with racially motivated sentencing decisions. Id. Lastly, federal and state anti-drug laws have had a discriminatory impact. Id.; *Russell, 477 N.W.2d at 887* (stating "a far greater percentage of blacks than whites are sentenced for possession of three or more grams of crack cocaine under *Minn. Stat. §152.023* with more severe consequences than their white counterparts who possess three or more grams of cocaine powder"). The results of these factors are that minorities, especially Blacks and Mexican Americans, are several times more likely to be arrested and incarcerated than Whites. See generally Randall Kennedy, Race, Crime, and the Law (1997) (detailing ways in which racism permeates U.S. criminal justice system). This problem is evident in the fact that while Blacks comprise twelve percent of the U.S. population, forty-four percent of all prisoners in the United States are Black. Matthew R. Durose, David J. Levin, & Patrick Langan, Felony Sentences in State Courts, Bureau of Just. Stat. Bull. (Oct. 2001), available at http://www.ojp.usdoj.gov/bjs/pub/ascii/fssc98.txt. Also, in twenty states the percentage of incarcerated Blacks is at least five times greater than their share of the resident population. Daniel Gray, New Studies Point to Crisis Among African American Men, Tenn. Trib., May 5, 2005, at 13A.

criminal justice system[9] may be adversely affected the most by this turn of events.[10] Statistics and research from specialty courts indicate that indigent criminal defendants and those from racial and ethnic minority groups are often over-represented in specialty courts, thus bearing more than their fair share of the danger of indifferent representation.[11]

In the majority of criminal specialty courts that have been developed and implemented in recent years, the defense lawyer is relegated to the role of team player whose only purpose serves to fulfill a constitutional mandate.[12] A client may face a significant period of incarceration due to a defender who does not zealously advocate for the dismissal of the case in appropriate circumstances, does not expose and challenge police abuse and illegality, does not voice the client's position, and does not challenge the automatic imprisonment of the defendant as a sanction for failed compliance.

Many other adverse consequences may also exist. Consider the following scenario that might occur in the courthouse hallway just prior to a defendant's first appearance in court on a misdemeanor drug possession case carrying a maximum penalty of 180 days in jail:

Attorney: Hello Mr. Defendant. My name is Attorney Advocate and the court has appointed me to represent you. To get done with this charge quickly, I think the best thing for you to do right away is to enter the community court program of community service and drug treatment. I've already talked to the prosecutor and he is willing to let you enter the program as long as you plead guilty to the charge and abide by the conditions of the program. You've been through this before, so let's just go in and plead ...

Defendant: You want me to plead guilty right now? I don't even know what evidence they have against me. How can I make that decision right now? Don't you have to get discovery or something? What am I charged with?

Attorney: Well, you know you were picked up for drugs. We don't really need to do any discovery right now because you've been offered this really good new program. You can go into a treatment program, and get off the drugs. You'll have to do some community service too, but that's not much. Not many people get this opportunity and we have to jump on it fast, because you might not get this offered to you later on. All we have to do is go in there and let the judge know that you want the program. Then she'll take your plea, you get released and start your treatment and community service.

Defendant: You're sure I'll get released if I enter the plea? You know I have a record.

---

10. See National Association of Drug Court Professionals, Resolution adopted by the Board of Directors, June 2001. The dangers of lackadaisical representation have seemingly been recognized by several groups who are champions of the specialty court movement. Id. For example, the National Association of Drug Court Professionals has enacted a resolution regarding indigent defense in drug courts. Id. Moreover, the National Legal Aid and Defender Association, a group that has been cautiously optimistic regarding these courts, has addressed this issue in several publications. Jim Neuhard & Scott Wallace, National Legal Aid & Defender Association, Ten Tenets of Fair and Effective Problem Solving Courts (Jan. 1, 2002), available at http://www.nlada.org/DMS/Documents/1019501190.93/document info (providing guidelines to increase fairness and effectiveness of problem solving courts).

11. McCoy, supra note 5, at 1513. See generally Hoffman, Therapeutic Jurisprudence, supra note 7.

12. U.S. Const. amend. VI; *Gideon v. Wainwright, 372 U.S. 335, 344–45 (1963)* (mandating right to counsel for indigent defendants).

Attorney: Well, all I know is that the prosecutor told me you have a prior felony drug conviction. The program works just like I told you. You have to be released to get the treatment.

Defendant: You keep saying treatment, treatment, treatment. What kind of treatment is it? How long is it? Do I go everyday? I have two small kids to take care of. I can't do community service every day.

Attorney: Its drug treatment. They do an assessment and decide what kind you need—what's appropriate for you.

Defendant: Who is "they"? Will it be group meetings, outpatient or what? I don't really need treatment; I'm not addicted. I was just caught holding some marijuana.

Attorney: Well, they always order treatment in these cases, so you're gonna have to do it anyway. The case will be called soon, so you have to sign this guilty plea form and waiver of jury trial. Take it and sign it. I have to go talk to some other clients that I have. I'll be back.

Defendant: But wait! Aren't we going to talk about the evidence they have against me? I think the police violated my rights when they stormed into my house.

Attorney: We can't get into that right now. We don't have time. If you don't want the program, then we can see if they violated your rights, but my experience in these cases is you do better if you just take the program. My advice is this is the best way to insure that you get out and don't get a bond today.

Defendant: I don't know. This is a big decision to make in just a few minutes. So, I won't get stepped back anytime in the program?

Attorney: Well, if you test positive or don't do the community service, there are sanctions, but not much. At most it's just a few days in jail.

Defendant: A few days in jail is a lot to me! I told you I have kids and I can't afford a babysitter.

Attorney: Well, we have about ten minutes before the case is called. I'll go talk to my other clients and you can talk to that program counselor over there (pointing). She can probably answer your questions and go over the forms with you.

Defendant: Okay. I can still challenge what the police did, right?

Attorney: No, because you have to plead guilty for the program. Just talk to the counselor, first. I'll be right back.

While the above scenario is fictional, it is representative of numerous accounts from clients that I have interviewed, lawyer-client interactions that I have witnessed in the hallways of the courthouse, and from some lawyers who believe that this is the correct approach to criminal defense practice in some specialty courts.[13] This scenario presents many ethical, attorney competence, and zealousness issues.[14] Similar interactions be-

---

13. I previously practiced for many years as a public defender in the District of Columbia Superior Court, and I currently practice as a clinical law professor. I had clients charged with all types of crimes and subject to all types of penalties, including some who have been processed in various specialty court models. The fictional scenario above reflects a conglomeration of what I saw and heard from clients, other lawyers, client family members, and student attorneys.

14. Many defender quality and ethical issues are apparent in this scenario, such as advising a client on a course of action without proper investigation and research, poor client interviewing skills, and non-protection of client confidentiality. See Richard C. Boldt, *Rehabilitative Punishment and the Drug Treatment Court Movement*, 76 Wash. U. L.Q. 1205, 1247–48 (1998). Some may even rise to the level of ineffective assistance of counsel as set forth in *Strickland v. Washington, 466 U.S. 668, 686 (1984)*.

tween clients and defense attorneys in these new specialty courts are unfortunately the norm and not the exception.

With the advent of the first drug court in Miami, Florida, in 1989, court systems in many states and localities created specialty courts, which seek to address the need for services and problems in defendants' lives that bear upon their ability to follow court orders and remain free of the criminal justice system. Some of these courts seek to integrate the community's voice in determining appropriate penalties and behavior modification systems that will appease community members as well.[15] Amidst these laudable goals, few have ventured to comment on the abandonment of the notion of adversarial justice in favor of a more treatment-oriented approach that emphasizes the team concept. Such an approach finds its roots in, and has been accepted by, other social science disciplines such as psychiatry, and is tied to several academic approaches to criminal law theory, namely rehabilitation, therapeutic jurisprudence, and restorative justice.[16] But the approach carries potential danger for the indigent or racial minority defendant who is counting on a committed zealous defender to be their voice, their sword, and their shield in the criminal justice system. The wide acceptance and silence regarding this model of criminal defense representation signals a change in the way our criminal justice system works.

Defenders, who litigate in these courts, encounter a dilemma between their instinctual desire to be an advocate for their clients and the desire to do whatever they can to seek treatment for their clients and keep them out of prison. As difficult as this dilemma is for a good number of committed defenders, an even more interesting issue concerns whether the nature of the treatment court and defenders' role in it negatively affect clients' interests by instigating a culture of indifference and incompetent advocacy.

Much debate can be found throughout legal literature concerning the efficacy of our adversary system and the role of the defender in the system.[17] Various legal scholars question the effectiveness of our system, pointing to its divisiveness on race and gender issues,[18] its disregard of the "search for truth,"[19] its resource-intensiveness and problematic functioning. However, very little has been written about the role of the defense

---

15. The Red Hook Community Justice Center in Brooklyn, New York, is often cited as an example of how a community can become vested in a problem-solving court. Red Hook has had many success stories and is often regarded as a shining example of the community court movement. See Red Hook Justice (Public Broad. Sys. 2003); see also Red Hook Justice, www.pbs.org/independentlens/redhookjustice/community.html (last visited Nov. 5, 2006) (focusing on experimental court in Red Hook, New York). There are many other questionable examples of specialty courts that are operating with the support of segments of the community. Privately funded specialty courts operate in several central business districts around the country and are supported financially by businesses and corporations. These businesses and corporations also receive direct benefits from the specialty courts, because defendants are often given sanctions which include community service jobs, such as removing graffiti and landscaping public areas. See Sundip Kundu, Privately Funded Courts and the Homeless: A Critical Look at Community Courts, 14 J. Affordable Hous. & Cmty. Dev. L. 170, 173–74 (2005).

16. See Hoffman, Therapeutic Jurisprudence, supra note 7, at 2067–68; Anthony C. Thompson, Courting Disorder: Some Thoughts on Community Courts, 10 Wash. U. J.L. & Pol'y 63, 98 (2002).

17. See Russell G. Pearce, Redressing Inequality in the Market for Justice: Why Access to Lawyers Will Never Solve the Problem and Why Rethinking the Role of Judges Will Help, 73 Fordham L. Rev. 969, 974 (2004).

18. See Carrie Menkel-Meadow, The Trouble with the Adversary System in a Post-Modern Multicultural World, 38 Wm. & Mary L. Rev. 5, 9 (1996).

19. See generally Gordon Van Kessell, Adversary Excesses in the American Criminal Trial, 67 Notre Dame L. Rev. 403, 406 (1992).

lawyer in the new non-adversarial problem-solving courts.[20] In fact, a review of the literature suggests that few legal scholars, court administrators, judges, and policy officials are willing to critique the effect of these courts on the litigants, the administration of justice, and the criminal justice system as a whole.[21] While some bold legal scholars and attorneys question the role of the criminal defense lawyer in these courts and call for more discussion and analysis of this crucial issue,[22] there still remains little academic discourse on the issue. This article will focus on the concept of the adversarial defender and the question of the proper role for that defender in specialty courts. Part I of this article examines the foundations of our adversary system and some varying philosophies regarding the role of the defense attorney. Part II discusses the practical reality of specialty courts and the changed role of the defense attorney who works in those courts. Finally, Part III sets out the major reasons why it is imperative that we critically examine this changed role of the defense attorney in specialty courts. This trend toward "specialized justice" is examined to determine if it can meet the need for competent and zealous criminal defense. Because academic discourse needs to explore real-world solutions, the article follows with a discussion of the dangers of this changed defender role. It finally concludes with an argument that specialty courts should not be completely abandoned,[23] but must move away from the team-player mandate toward defenders who are adversarial and zealous when litigating in specialty courts.

Part I: The Role of the Criminal Defense Lawyer in the Adversary System

Our adversary system of justice in the United States cannot function without the criminal defense lawyer.[24] In the criminal justice system, the defense lawyer is essential

---

20. See generally Cait Clarke & James Neuhard, From Day One: Who's in Control As Problem Solving and Client-Centered Sentencing Take Center Stage?, 29 N.Y.U. Rev. L. & Soc. Change 11 (2004); Thompson, supra note 16.

21. Several articles have been written, roundtable discussions transcribed, and reports developed about the efficacy of drug courts and their appropriateness as a model for this new type of court. The work has been primarily conducted by groups and individuals who are supportive of the model, either because of their status as a government agency funding these courts, as a judge who sits on these courts, or as a non-profit agency or association who promotes these courts. See generally The Nat'l Assoc. of Drug Court Professionals, Dept. of Justice (1997), Defining Drug Courts: The Key Components (1997) [hereinafter Defining Drug Courts], available at http://www.nadcp. org/docs/dkeypdf.pdf; Judith S. Kaye, Making the Case for Hands-On Courts, Newsweek, Oct. 13, 1999, at 13; Office of Justice Program, Mental Health Courts Program, http://www.ojp.usdoj.gov/ bja/grant/mentalhealth.html (last visited Nov. 5, 2006); Center for the Community Interest, Working With Courts and Prosecutors, http://www.communityinterest.org/neighborhoodsafety/resources/lawenforcement/working with courts and prosecut.htm (Dec. 2004). There seem to be a smaller number of articles or studies written by academics or independent organizations. See McCoy, supra note 5, at 1519 (noting some agencies have an "agenda" to promote development of drug courts). See generally Violent Crime Control and Law Enforcement Act of 1994, 42 U.S.C. §13701 (2000) (providing funds for state courts to implement drug courts).

22. Mae Quinn, Whose Team Am I on Anyway: Musings of a Public Defender about Drug Treatment Court Practice, 26 N.Y.U. Rev. L. & Soc. Change 37, 37 (2001); Kundu, supra note 15, at 180.

23. See infra Part VI. While some of the basic concepts of these problem-solving courts—specifically, their concentration on treatment and addressing social issues should, and can, be adapted to all courts in the criminal justice system—some urgent reforms are needed. Id.

24. Gerald W. Hardcastle, Adversarialism and the Family Court: A Family Court Judge's Perspective, 9 U.C. Davis L. Rev. 57, 60–68 (2005). The American adversary system includes several key features: disputes are resolved by an impartial decision maker after a presentation of the merits by partisans who present their respective positions, and litigants are seen as more "in charge" of the process. Id.

to keep the system honest and protect the interests and rights of the accused. Case law, scholarly commentary, and popular writings extol the criminal defense lawyer and her mission.[25] Depictions of the criminal defense lawyer can be found everywhere in our society; she is the subject of folklore, the central figure in media headlines, the protagonist in fictional television stories, the sometimes tragic and misunderstood character in blockbuster movies.[26] Judges, prosecutors, politicians, the media, and community members both respect and malign the criminal defense attorney. At any given time, the actions and calling of criminal defense attorneys, and particularly those that represent the indigent, are the subject of debate concerning standards of practice, ethical boundaries, and the breadth of their professional role.

Scholars debate the traditional view of the criminal defense attorney, her role and ethics in our legal system. The prevalent view has been clearly espoused by Professor Monroe Freedman in several seminal articles and books on the subject.[27] Professor Freedman's concept of the criminal defense attorney holds true every time I am appointed to represent a person accused of a crime; I am a partisan committed to the client and the client's expressed interests, whose zealousness and commitment to defend the client's rights is untempered and unmitigated. Freedman's criminal defense lawyer is unabashedly adversarial because there is no other avenue that will achieve her necessary ends. Those necessary ends are not just for the client, but because the criminal defense lawyer zealously and competently safeguards the client's position in the case, society's most precious rights and principles are upheld.[28] This traditional notion of the criminal defense lawyer and defense of the adversarial system is well supported in history and by legal scholars and practitioners.[29] Although it has been recast in different language, the underlying principles set forth by Freedman remain. Some cast the role of the criminal defense lawyer as a champion against the might and power of the state. These writers find support for a completely adversarial defense lawyer "whose loyalties must lay with the accused" as a necessary "bulwark against the possible overreaching of a sometimes too eager and powerful government."[30] Some see the job as essential to maintain the in-

---

25. See *Gideon v. Wainwright*, 372 U.S. 335, 344–45 (1963) (explaining defense counsel's fundamental role); see also supra notes 2, 3 and accompanying text (demonstrating necessity of criminal defense attorney). See generally Cristina C. Arguedas, Duties of the Criminal Defense Lawyer, 30 Loy. L.A. Rev. 7 (1996) (providing examples of criminal defense counsels' responsibilities); Abbe Smith, The Calling of Criminal Defense, *50 Mercer L. Rev. 443 (1999)* (describing nobility of criminal defense work throughout article).

26. Contemporary high profile criminal cases involving celebrities provide some of the most well-known examples: for example, Johnnie Cochran, the lead attorney in the O.J. Simpson trial; Pamela Mackey, who represented Kobe Bryant in recent rape allegations; and Mark Geragos, who initially represented Michael Jackson and later tried the Scott Peterson murder trial.

27. See Monroe H. Freedman, The Professional Obligation to Raise Frivolous Issues in Death Penalty Cases, *31 Hofstra L. Rev. 1167, 1168 (2003);* Monroe H. Freedman, How Lawyers Act in the Interests of Justice, *70 Fordham L. Rev. 1717, 1718–19 (2002);* Monroe H. Freedman, Ethics, Truth, and Justice in Criminal Litigation, *68 Fordham L. Rev. 1371, 1378 (2000);* Monroe H. Freedman, Our Constitutionalized Adversary System, *1 Chap. L. Rev. 57, 58 (1998);* Monroe H. Freedman, The Lawyer's Moral Obligation of Justification, *74 Tex. L. Rev. 111, 112 (1995).*

28. See Smith, supra note 2, at 87. Freedman seems to suggest that the right to counsel is the starting point for many other rights in the criminal justice system, including the right to trial by jury, right to confront witnesses, right to be free from compelled self incrimination, and the presumption of innocence. Id.

29. Johnnie L. Cochran, How Can You Defend Those People?, *30 Loy. L.A. L. Rev. 39, 42 (1996);* Charles Ogletree, Beyond Justifications: Seeking Motivations to Sustain Public Defenders, *106 Harv. L. Rev. 1239, 1242 (1993).*

30. Goldman, supra note 3, at 2.

tegrity of our criminal justice system. The defender's job is to "police the police, to audit the government, to speak for the accused, to fight for fairness and to rail against injustice."[31] In this conception, the criminal defense lawyer becomes David—the weaker, smaller opponent whose only weapon is the courage and strength to stand up for ideals and principles—against the prosecution's Goliath.[32] The defense attorney is then empowered to fight for the client's wishes; even though the defense can win by getting a not guilty verdict, that is not always the ultimate goal. Rather, ensuring procedural fairness and attention to the defendant's constitutional rights is of the utmost importance.[33]

Some writers embrace the notions of client-centered lawyering, where the defender's mission is to carry out the client's goals to the extent that they do not run afoul of ethical and legal requirements. This picture of an "aggressive defender" as some critics have labeled her, is duty-bound "to defend her client vigorously, aggressively and completely, within the bounds of the law."[34]

There are many who criticize and disavow Freedman's view of the criminal defense lawyer. Some are critical of the traditional view of the defender as too aggressive.[35] These scholars note the aggressiveness of all attorneys in our current adversary system. Professor Harry Subin calls it "ritualized aggression," and points to excesses in the system becoming the norm, rather than the exception.[36]

Some scholars reject the traditional view because they see the loyalty of the defender as equally divided among a duty to the client, duty to the court, and duty to the ethical boundaries that regulate the practice. For example, Professor Peter Fleming finds that the lawyer's responsibilities do not, and should not, end with the client, but rather continue to the court and the jury, which is the final arbiter.[37] He finds an overriding responsibility to "be fair and square with the evidence."[38] Professor Carrie Menkel-Meadow also explores the notion of the neutral lawyer who has neither client nor partisan cause, but who is able to build consensus and achieve or facilitate resolutions to disputes that further the goals of justice.[39]

Among the critics of the traditional view, Professor William Simon finds that Freedman's traditional or "Dominant View," as Simon calls it, may be the prevailing approach to describing a lawyer's role and ethical responsibilities, but that it is flawed.[40] Simon be-

---

31. Cochran, supra note 29, at 42.
32. Goldman, supra note 3, at 9.
33. The defense bar's mandate to ensure adherence to procedural justice principles is seen by a great number of defense attorneys as more important than winning trials. This makes sense given the small number of cases that actually result in a trial and result in a not guilty verdict.
34. Arguedas, supra note 25, at 7; see also William H. Simon, The Practice of Justice: A Theory of Lawyers Ethics 77 (1998); Michael P. Judge, Critical issues for Defenders in the Design and Operation of a Drug Court, Ind. Def., Nov.–Dec. 1997 (stating "defense function in the traditional adversarial system is to resist the government's charges and to avoid or minimize loss of liberty or other sanctions").
35. Smith, supra note 2, at 91 (noting Freedman's view of zealous defense attorneys).
36. Van Kessel, supra note 19, at 435. Van Kessel is an advocate of a non-adversary approach similar to some European systems. See id. at 435–58.
37. Peter Fleming, Jr., What Makes Us Different?, *30 Loy. L.A. L. Rev. 45, 45 (1996)*.
38. Id.
39. Carrie Menkel-Meadow, The Lawyer's Role in Deliberative Democracy, *5 Nev. L. J. 347, 349–50 (2004)*.
40. Simon, supra note 34, at 7–8.

lieves that the approach is too rigid and restrictive and does not allow lawyers to account for the range of considerations that confront a lawyer as a decision maker.[41] Simon argues that ethical decisions by lawyers should turn on "the underlying merits." His "Contextual View" compels the lawyer to take actions, such as considering the relevant circumstances of the particular case that seem likely to promote justice.[42]

Many lawyers who practice criminal law want to promote justice in a general sense; however, some contend that such a goal is more nuanced and difficult in the area of criminal law.[43] Simon, however, argues that the "Contextual View" is applicable to all lawyers, and he explicitly finds no merit in the notion that criminal defense is different or that defenders should be treated differently.[44] A criminal defense attorney in Simon's "Contextual View" frames his client's wishes by reference to how they promote justice in a particular context.[45]

Professor Simon addresses the role of defenders in specialty courts and finds that such an innovative change in the criminal justice system may be positive, but may require lawyers, especially defenders, to reinvent the way they see themselves.[46] Simon argues that team models embodied in drug courts raise problems, if they require "lawyers to violate ethical commitments fundamental to their role," or if the new skills lawyers have to embrace are similar to skills employed by lawyers outside of the criminal realm.[47] He concludes that the new courts do not require defenders to compromise their ethical responsibilities and the new skills they acquire are appropriate for lawyers in the criminal justice system.[48]

Reviewing the specialty court's model of defense lawyering by inquiring into new skill sets required of practitioners may not be an extensive enough measure. The need for defenders to acquire new skills is not a new or novel idea, but rather one that has been around for a very long time.[49] Many defenders recognize that in order to fully represent a client throughout all phases of the criminal justice system, they must take on various roles, including counsel, advisor, social worker, educator, and contract negotiator. When a defender takes a case to trial, particularly a serious felony case, the defender must learn the subject matter of many disciplines, including medical and physical sci-

---

41. Simon, supra note 34, at 9.
42. Simon, supra note 34, at 9. Simon also notes an alternative approach, the "Public Interest View," which holds that "law should be applied in accordance with its purposes, and litigation should be conducted so as to promote informed resolution on the substantive merits." Id. at 8. Simon describes the Public Interest View as rejecting the manipulation of form to defeat relevant legal purposes. Id. at 8.
43. See Smith, supra note 2, at 86.
44. Simon, supra note 34.
45. See Simon, supra note 34.
46. See Simon, supra note 5, at 1595.
47. See Simon, supra note 5, at 1595–96.
48. See Simon, supra note 5, at 1597.
49. Michael Pinard, An Integrated Perspective on the Collateral Consequences of Criminal Convictions and Reentry Issues Faced by Formerly Incarcerated Individuals, 86 B.U. L. Rev. 623, 677 (2005) (citing Edward D. Shapiro, Fresh Perspectives: The Practice of Holistic Lawyering, CBA Rec., Feb.–Mar. 2002, at 38). The notion of "holistic lawyering" in the criminal defense context recognizes that lawyers may have to focus on the "whole client," including non-criminal law problems. See id.; see also Cait Clarke, Problem-Solving Defenders in the Community: Expanding the Conceptual and institutional Boundaries of Providing Counsel to the Poor, 14 Geo. J. Legal Ethics 401, 409 (2001).

ence. In order to fully investigate a case or to seek an appropriate disposition or favorable sentencing outcome, the defender must think like a community organizer. It is nothing new that a defender must develop and nurture a plethora of skill sets. This is essential for the defender who fully and zealously represents clients in any court, including those of general jurisdiction or specialty courts.

Many defenders, however, question the team model through the ethical lens and find that defense representation in specialty courts may present a number of ethical challenges.[50] In a great number of specialty courts, defenders who participate according to the recognized and sanctioned model of those courts may well be violating "fundamental ethical commitments," and may be forced into a practice that ignores the client-centered model of representation that is predominant in the field.[51] Such a practice may violate the duty to competently and zealously represent a client, represent the client with diligence and promptness, maintain client confidences and secrets, or eschew practice that continues a conflict of interest.[52]

Professor Simon's "Contextual View" bears a resemblance to the lawyer model that is embraced by specialty court advocates. Specialty court advocates find that "adversarial advocacy is too adversarial," and promote a model of the criminal defender that focuses on collaboration and partnership; one in which traditional adherence to rights and challenges to government action are foregone in the name of treatment or problem-solving.[53] Specialty court proponents replace common notions of procedural justice and fairness with a resolution to succeed in treatment or problem-solving goals mandated by judges or treatment professionals. Justice in specialty courts focuses more on results than process, and the results may include treatment success for an individual client or wide ranging results such as a decrease in recidivism.[54] Such a retreat from traditional notions of procedural fairness may be dangerous in any court context, even one which focuses on beneficial treatment for defendants. In the criminal justice system, the defendant risks his life and liberty, faces stigma in the community, and is at a disadvantage in terms of resources and bargaining power.[55] An attempt to insure procedural fairness and institute a model that recognizes and supports procedural safeguards should be an essential component of specialty courts. Likewise, a careful review of the ethical challenges noted by defenders may result in the need for structural change in the prevailing specialty court model.

---

50. Quinn, supra note 22, at 50–54.
51. See Simon, supra note 5, at 1597; Jane Spinak, Why Defenders Feel Defensive: The Defender's Role in Problem Solving, 40 Am. Cr. L. Rev. 1617, 1618 (2003).
52. See Model Rules of Prof'l Conduct R. 1.1, 1.3, 1.4, 1.6, 1.7. Other ethical rules and proscriptions may also be jeopardized.
53. See Smith, supra note 2, at 93.
54. Hardcastle, supra note 24, at 57. Justice in a specialty courts, like in other courts, is seen by many as subjective. Id. at 69–71. Chief Judge Judith Kaye, an advocate for specialty courts, agrees that the public's perception of justice depends upon their perception of how a court is run and whether citizens are treated fairly. Such a perception places great weight on the notion of procedural fairness. Therefore, the protection of rights and general interests of a defendant should be at the forefront when determining how the court system operates. Id.; see also, Judith S. Kaye, Changing Courts in Changing Times: The Need for a Fresh Look at How Courts are Run, *48 Hastings L.J. 851, 853 (1997)*. Unfortunately, whatever conception of justice or lawyering is accepted as preferred in the criminal justice system, problems still persist with the quality of the lawyering especially for indigent criminal.
55. David Luban, Are Criminal Defenders Different?, 91 Mich. L. Rev. 1729, 1733 (1993); Smith, supra note 2, at 107–10.

Part II: The Nature and Foundations of Treatment Courts

Many officials and scholars theorize that frustration with the adversary system has in large measure led to the proliferation of specialty courts.[56] Upon closer review, however, it seems there are other reasons for the significant development in the administrative access to justice. Court officials, judges, and lawyers often report frustration with the "revolving door" of the courthouse, where charged persons are processed through the court on one charge and then a short time later on another.[57] Other reasons include the desire for increased court efficiency, better management of court dockets, and a desire to minimize the costs of the administration of justice, such as costs associated with building more and more prisons to warehouse offenders.[58] Some point to the overcrowded jails and prisons, where incarcerated persons learn to commit more dangerous crimes upon release, and whose release is dictated by unfair and unjust mandatory minimum sentences and sentencing guidelines.[59] The desire to reduce recidivism and better communities by decreasing quality of life crimes and increasing the defendant's accountability to the grassroots community is important.[60] This sometimes includes the desire to transform a community into a more economically productive one. Still, other theories exist that focus on politics and political ambition as the driving force behind the proliferation of some specialty courts. Some even point to the dissatisfaction of judges and lawyers on both sides of the table, who are unhappy with their jobs and feel that they are not making a difference.[61] Whatever the reasons for the proliferation, it seems clear that the movement toward "specialized justice" is here to stay, and may well expand into areas never thought of before.[62]

While many stakeholders in the criminal justice system have been instrumental in the formation of these courts, few activist defender agencies or defense lawyers have called for the implementation of these courts or played a prominent role in their initial design and development. Generally, the activist defense bar has been wary of the heavy reliance on sanctions, the increased role of the judge, and the non-adversarial nature of these courts.[63] In order to examine these and other concerns for the defense in specialty

---

56. See Morris B. Hoffman, The Drug Court Scandal, 78 N.C. L. Rev. 1437, 1439 (2000). Some also cite its ineffectiveness at addressing substance abuse issues which are prevalent among those who are subject to the coercive power of the criminal justice system. See Defining Drug.

57. I can remember, as many others who have been or are public defenders can no doubt relate, instances where a case is disposed of in court one morning with the defendant receiving a probationary sentence, and then receiving a call that same afternoon from family members, probation staff, or the court indicating that the same client has been rearrested on a new charge. See Defining Drug Courts, supra note 21; see also James L. Nolan, Redefining Criminal Courts: Problem-solving and the Meaning of Justice, 40 Am. Crim. L. Rev. 1541, 1541 (2003); Laurie O. Robinson, Community Court and Community Justice Commentary, 40 Am. Crim. L. Rev. 1535, 1535 (2003).

58. Nolan, supra note 57, at 1541; McCoy, supra note 5, at 1517–20; Defining Drug Courts, supra note 21. Professor McCoy calls it the "case overload crisis ... caused by the War on Drugs," and argues that it has led to a "management rationale" for the proliferation of specialty courts. McCoy, supra note 5, at 1518.

59. McCoy, supra note 5, at 1518.
60. McCoy, supra note 5, at 1518.
61. Nolan, supra note 57, at 1541.

62. Drug courts are entrenched in the court landscape. Some writers have estimated that there are over 1,700 across the country. See Casey, supra note 7, at 1459. Not surprisingly, some localities abolished or modified their drug courts when early results did not show the great reductions in recidivism that had been expected. Hoffman, A Neo-Retributionist Concurs, supra note 7, at 1567 (commenting on the example of Denver's drug court which was disbanded). Moreover, states will have to institutionalize funds into local budgets to keep courts going when federal funds are discontinued. See infra Part III.

63. See Clarke & Neuhard, supra note 20, at 19; Thompson, supra note 16, at 81 n.92.

courts, it is necessary to examine the foundations of the specialty courts, the goals they were initially designed to accomplish, the manner in which these courts actually work, and how these issues relate to the role of the defender in specialty courts.

A. Foundations of the Specialized Justice Movement

The trend to establish problem-solving courts began with the decline of the rehabilitative model of jurisprudence and the development of "therapeutic jurisprudence" and its sister theory, restorative justice.[64] These new theories are well-rooted in concepts of rehabilitation, although the traditional concept of rehabilitation has largely fallen out of favor.[65] Therapeutic jurisprudence and restorative justice theories emphasize that treatment is a desired goal of justice. Those theories maintain that the appropriate treatment will be provided by the court system, primarily because other governmental and social systems have failed to provide adequate social services, treatment, or incentives to insure that individuals do not resort to criminality. In essence, therapeutic and restorative justice regimes combine social work with law and attempt to correct the failures of social services systems.[66] Therapeutic jurisprudence theorizes that a closely controlled program of treatment results in less recidivism among offenders. The "treatment" addresses the problems or issues that led to the defendant's involvement in the criminal justice system and undertakes the appropriate treatment to cure or lessen the effects of the issues. Restorative justice principles focus on whether the regimen can restore all actors or stakeholders in the system, including defendants and victims, to their position prior to or irrespective of the criminality.[67] The "treatment" used in these courts is broadly described as an alternative to traditional forms of punishment, as it seeks to di-

---

64. McCoy, supra note 5, at 1513. According to several commentators, the rehabilitative model was abandoned in the 1970s when many scholars questioned whether the prison environment was suitable for rehabilitation, reform, and treatment of offenders. Greg Berman & Anne Gulick, Just the (Unwieldy, Hard to Gather, but Nonetheless Essential) Facts, Ma'am: What We Know and Don't Know about Problem-Solving Courts, 30 Fordham Urb. L. J. 1027, 1027–28 (2003) (citing Robert Martinson seminal, What Works? Questions and Answers about Prison Reform, 35 Pub. Int. 22 (1974)). See generally Hoffman, A Neo-Retributionist Concurs, supra note 7. Given the demise of the rehabilitative ideal, many different approaches were attempted to combat crime and recidivism. Rehabilitation was traditionally coupled with indeterminate sentencing, a sentencing structure that gave prison officials too much authority to determine the release of an incarcerated inmate. Legislators, judges, and court officials addressed indeterminate sentencing by enacting harsh sentencing schemes including the federal sentencing guidelines, the abolishment of parole, development of mandatory minimums, as well as the proliferation of the war on drugs. The rise of specialty courts and the therapeutic ideal are a response to the recent sentencing schemes in the United States, which resulted in inequity and injustice. See McCoy, supra note 5, at 1513 (discussing historical perspective on development and rise of "problem-solving" courts); see also supra note 4. Many believe the concepts of "therapeutic jurisprudence" and restorative justice were first introduced by Professors Bruce Winick and David Wexler in the 1980s. See Hoffman, A Neo-Retributionist Concurs, supra note 7, at 1568–70.

65. National Drug Court Institute, Critical Issues for Defense Attorneys in Drug Court 1 (Apr. 2003), available at http://www.ndci.org/CriticalIssues.pdf; Jim Neuhard & Scott Wallace, National Legal Aid & Defender Association, Ten Tenets of Fair and Effective Problem Solving Courts intro. (Jan. 1, 2002), available at http://www.nlada.org/DMS/Documents/1019501190.93/document info.

66. Jenny B. Davis, What I Like About My Lawyer: Happy Clients Speak Out on What Sets Their Lawyer Apart, 89 A.B.A. J., Jan. 2003, at 33. Professor Winick notes that when therapeutic jurisprudence was being developed, he attempted to see "if the law could be reshaped to make it into more of a healing force, a therapeutic force." Panel discussion, The Changing Face of Justice: The Evolution of Problem-Solving, 29 Fordham Urb. L.J. 1790, 1809 (2002).

67. McCoy, supra note 5, at 1524. Judge Hoffman argues against the notion of restoration of position. See Hoffman, Therapeutic Jurisprudence, supra note 7, at 2068.

vert low level offenders from incarceration. In the new specialty courts, the treatment approach uses coercive sanctions, including incarceration.[68] The use of coercion, especially the threat of imprisonment, militates in favor of a strong defense attorney presence both in the design and operation of specialty courts.[69]

B. The Practical Realities: How Treatment Courts Work

Exactly how do the new specialty courts work and what are they designed to do? These courts bring together new theories of justice, along with modifications in the structure and process of cases.[70] In most of these courts, the normal adjudicative process is modified to allow an alternative which combines treatment with sanctions or other conditions designed to modify behavior or punish the alleged offender.[71] When a defendant is deemed eligible for a particular specialty court program or treatment alternative, the defendant's case is placed on the specialty calendar, which theoretically allows the defendant to interact with one particular judge trained in the issues related to certain social problems.[72] These programs are then designed to have social workers, case managers, and other relevant professionals interact with the defendant in order to assess any treatment issues that may be present. The defendant is then court-ordered into an "appropriate" treatment modality or behavior modification program which may last from several months to more than a year.[73] In a growing number of jurisdictions, the treatment is available to the defendant only after a guilty plea is entered or many pretrial due process rights are waived.[74] This "post-adjudication" model is very attractive to prosecutors because the case is disposed of even though the defendant is receiving treat-

---

68. See Thompson, supra note 16, at 341–42. Other forms of "treatment" include restitution, mediation, community service, etc. Id.

69. Coercive pressure in the specialty court context often includes coercion in decision making. For example, the defendant often faces a choice between the prospect of jail time or immediate release from jail if he or she decides to immediately go into treatment. The defendant also faces a dilemma in deciding whether to accept sanctions by the court or to challenge alleged violations, whether to accept the advice of attorney, and other similar decisions.

70. Nolan, supra note 57, at 1543.

71. Nolan, supra note 57, at 1542–43 (introducing concept of "problem-solving" courts).

72. See Peggy Fulton Hora & William G. Schma, Therapeutic Jurisprudence and the Drug Treatment Court Movement: Revolutionizing the Criminal Justice System's Response to Drug Abuse and Crime in America, 74 Notre Dame L. Rev. 439, 476–78 (1999); Quinn, supra note 22, at 43–46. Substance abuse is the most notable social issue in which judges receive training.

73. Many arguments can be made as to whether the treatment ordered by these courts is appropriate for a particular defendant. Advocates of specialty courts, especially drug courts, insist that an assessment by case managers, drug treatment counselors, and/or social workers is made before a court orders a defendant into a particular course of treatment. Thus, they argue that the treatment is specially designed to address the particular defendant's treatment or other life issues, and therefore, the defendant can succeed in the treatment modality. See McCoy, supra note 5, at 1515. This "individual treatment plan" draws from medical and scientific principles that are found to combat drug addiction with constant monitoring and encouragement. See id.; see also Boldt, supra note 14, at 1224–25. However, the pro-specialty courts' lobby ignores the practical realities of what treatment is available to defendants in these courts. Court systems or court agencies often contract with a limited number of treatment providers who provide a limited number of treatment options. This limited array of treatment options fails to address the individual needs of the many defendants who come through the door of the drug court. See id. at 1227–28. For example, specialty courts may not have contracted with treatment providers who offer "dual-diagnosis" treatment which is appropriate for those defendants who may have mental health issues in addition to substance abuse problems.

74. See Nolan, supra note 57, at 1559 (discussing waived rights include right to speedy trial, jury trial, and preliminary hearing). Also, to enter the treatment court, a defendant will have to forego certain defenses that may establish reasonable doubt. Id.

ment.[75] Post-adjudication specialty courts have been criticized as contradicting the notion of treatment because they coerce the defendant to accept treatment and recognize addiction in order to avoid jail time.[76]

In a small number of jurisdictions, treatment programs or entrance into a specialized court is available as a condition of pre-trial release without any need for waiving important rights. Advocates contend that this is a better model for the specialty courts because the defendant's participation is voluntary.[77] There may, however, be consequences for those defendants who refuse the treatment alternative, or who accept it and later subsequently fail to meet any or all of its conditions.[78]

Although there are many types of specialized courts designed to focus on several different issues, there are several fundamental principles that characterize most of these courts.[79] In each of the fundamental principles incorporated in the specialty court, the potential for coercion, loss of liberty, or loss of protected rights is possible, and therefore this demonstrates the need for a zealous defender.

The treatment that is mandated for a particular offender is imposed early in the life of a case. Many advocates of specialty courts, particularly drug courts, including government and court officials, theorize that the time period shortly after an arrest of a defendant is the opportune time to intervene with treatment.[80] They argue that immediate treatment capitalizes on the crisis that has just occurred in the defendant's life.[81] They ignore the coercive effect of treatment at such a time in the defendant's life. This coercion is great because, in addition to the trauma of arrest and specter of jail time,

---

75. In the "post-adjudication" model, a defendant must initially enter a plea of guilty to the charged offenses or to a bargained for plea agreement in order to be eligible for the treatment program. Sentencing is postponed until the defendant completes treatment. If the defendant succeeds in treatment then she is guaranteed probation. If she is not successful in treatment, the defendant is sentenced in the normal manner. The post-adjudication model is somewhat favored by the prosecution as it permits them to close cases without regard to success or failure of treatment. In a pre-adjudication model, the defendant is allowed to enter treatment prior to any substantive disposition of the case. If the defendant is unsuccessful in treatment, the case returns to a pretrial stance, and the defendant can elect to go forward with a trial or challenge the constitutionality of police action. Prosecutors argue that it is a burden to their office to delay a case for an entire treatment period and then return to a trial posture.

76. Jim Neuhard & Scott Wallace, National Legal Aid & Defender Association, Ten Tenets of Fair and Effective Problem Solving Courts (Jan. 1, 2002), available at http://www.nlada.org/DMS/Documents/1019501190.93/documentinfo (pointing to Tenet 5 that expressly disfavors the post adjudication model). The tenet states that "the accused individual shall not be required to plead guilty in order to enter a problem solving court." Id. The primary reason is a guilty plea has no therapeutic value, but an argument can be made that a guilty plea requirement is a condition imposed by prosecutors acting in adversarial manner. For example, prosecutors may be protecting their position in the case rather than as a collaborator that has disavowed adversarialism. See infra Part III, at Section B.1.

77. Hora & Schma, supra note 72, at 521 (highlighting defendant's participation in drug treatment court as voluntary in every jurisdiction).

78. See Nolan, supra note 57, at 1560 (recounting statements of judges who push defendants into treatment court by veiled threat of jail time).

79. See supra Section C. (discussing different variations of specialty courts). Specialty courts address a variety of issues, such as domestic violence, weapons offenses, and mentally ill defendants.

80. Defining Drug Courts, supra note 21 (outlining third Key Component of drug courts).

81. Defining Drug Courts, supra note 21. Characteristics of the crisis include the stigma of being arrested, the requirement of attending court hearings on a regular and ongoing basis, the realization that jail time may be mandated, or the realization that the substance abuse or other problem is real and a change needs to be made.

the defendant must make an immediate decision at a time when he or she is in the throes of an addiction or facing other trauma. The reality, as in our fictional scenario, is that the defendant is placed in the untenable position of choosing between treatment, protection of the right to challenge the charges faced, and the expectation of zealous legal representation.[82]

In order to coerce compliance with the ordered course of treatment, the specialty court judge assesses and enforces a set of increasingly severe punitive sanctions, including jail time and community service, restitution and/or the abdication of rights or privileges.[83] These punitive sanctions are usually not negotiated by the defense prior to entrance or placement into the specialty court treatment program.[84] Indeed, an important principle of specialty courts is that, prior to any violation of a court mandate or sometimes prior to treatment, the defendant must agree that he or she will submit to the particular set of punitive sanctions. Often, the sanction is imposed automatically, without any opportunity for challenge by the defender.[85] Some defenders believe it futile to try to challenge the sanction. These defenders may not challenge the basis for the sanction, the imposition of the sanction, or the severity of it. Some may not even offer any mitigating evidence or argument to the judge on their client's behalf.[86]

Apart from the sanctions acknowledged by specialty court advocates, judges occasionally use public shaming techniques[87] to motivate defendants to comply with requirements of the specialty court program. There is frequent interaction between the judge and the defendant in specialty courts, since hearings are scheduled so the judge may determine the effectiveness of the defendant's treatment or the extent of compliance with the imposed conditions. The judge often inquires of the defendant in open court about particular aspects of the defendant's life and compliance with treatment,

---

82. See supra notes 12, 13 and accompanying text.

83. Boldt, supra note 14, at 1216; Nolan, supra note 57, at 1555. Some judges seek to lessen the impact of this coercion by using different terminology. Sanctions are seen as "providing help," "restructuring the defendant's lifestyle," "smart punishment," "motivational jail," or a "response." Id. at 1556–57. But a mere change in terminology does not take away from the nature of the measure as punitive and coercive. Professor Nolan notes that this "re-labeling" does not make the effect any less punitive. Id. at 1556.

84. The sanctions are often established during the design and planning phase of the specialty court. They may be predetermined by the judge and treatment officials, who may seek the input of the prosecutor and institutional defender. The treatment court judge, however, may incorporate sanctions that have not been predetermined or approved by the design and implementation committees.

85. Washington, D.C.'s drug court does allow for limited challenge by a stand-in defense counsel. When an alleged violation occurs, the court orders the defendant to appear before the judge at the next available court date. A stand-in attorney meets the client for the first time and determines if the client wishes to challenge the basis for the sanction. Few challenges are noted to the court. While this system of stand-in counsel is not ideal, it arose as a result of the drug court judges proceeding with sanctioning defendants for alleged violations without any counsel present. See supra Part II.D (discussing Washington's drug court).

86. Such inaction by defense counsel arguably violates ethical rules. Almost every state's ethics rules require zealous representation by the attorney. When the defender stands idly by and allows the judge to sanction the defendant, this inaction does not constitute zealous representation. See Model Rules of Professional Conduct R. 1.1.

87. Reintegrative and stigmatized shaming are major precepts of the restorative justice movement. Carren S. Oler, Unacknowledged Shame, Unresolved Family Cases, 38 Md. B.J. 12, 14–16 (2005); see also Anne-Marie McAlinden, The Use of "Shame" With Sexual Offenders, 45 Brit. J. Criminology 373, 376 (2005). The former is said to condemn the act and not the actor; whereas the latter uses different kinds of stigma and punishment to coerce and motivate actor to prevent recidivism. See generally John Braithwaite, Crime Shame and Reintegration (1989).

including asking questions that, if truthfully answered, may inculpate the defendant in criminal activity. In other circumstances, the judge may make statements to the defendant which tend to shame, coerce, chastise, or belittle the defendant for a certain behavior. At times the judge will publicly chastise the defendant, in very harsh tones, for his or her failure to move through the treatment process or to follow through with other aspects of the program. The defense attorney is expected to stand idly by while this interaction takes place.[88] Thus, public shaming presents another point in the specialty court process where the defense lawyer should be allowed to intervene on the defendant's behalf.

Specialty court advocates argue that the imposition of automatic sanctions is counterbalanced by a set of rewards that are essential to behavior modification and acceptance of treatment.[89] However, while sanctions in these specialty courts are swift and certain, actual or potential rewards for a defendant are less tangible, more long term, and of dubious effectiveness or worth to the client-defendant. Although, the social science experts seem to support the use of rewards in many court systems, financial restraints have prevented their use. Discussion regarding the benefits of rewards is abundant, and may in fact be convincing; however, actual conferring of tangible rewards is rare.[90] In fact, in some courts, the only reward seems to be that the judge will not get angry with the defendant for any failures in treatment. Sanctions, however, are abundant, and are served up with regularity. There is, therefore, no counterbalance to the sanctions and coercive measures utilized in specialty courts. A strong argument can be made that a reward, if any is given, must be one that is meaningful, empowering and of such a motivating level that it will help change the behavior of the defendant or complement the defendant's treatment in the specialty court.[91]

Specialty courts make use of a team approach. The team consists of the judge, the prosecutor, and the defense lawyer, who are all supposed to cast aside their traditional roles and work together to seek completion of the treatment modality for the defendant. Additionally, many of these courts involve non-legal actors, specifically drug treatment professionals, case managers, and social workers, as additional members of

---

88. Indeed, interruption by defense counsel often draws the ire of the judge, and often the judge will change the focus of the interaction with the defendant to an accusatory diatribe that endangers the continued liberty of the defendant.

89. Hoffman, Therapeutic Jurisprudence, supra note 7, at 2063. According to the disease model of treatment used in specialty courts and therapeutic justice movements, these rewards create a sense of achievement and help the defendant to accept their addiction. The disease model finds that the addiction is an uncontrollable, compulsive drug craving that is a "treatable brain disease." Timothy P. Ward, Note, Needing a Fix: Congress Should Amend the Americans with Disabilities Act of 1990 to Remove a Record of Addiction as a Protected Disability, 36 Rutgers L.J. 683, 691–94 (2005); see supra note 42. In an article critical of drug courts, the author notes that one judge allows participants to "draw from a fish bowl for prizes which may range from nothing ... up to a TV." Eric J. Miller, Embracing Addiction: Drug Courts and the False Promise of Judicial Interventionism, 65 Ohio St. L.J. 1479, 1498 (2004). I do not believe that conferring rewards is at all times meaningless. However, individual courts and judges need to be careful that the rewards are effective for a particular client-defendant with a particular problem.

90. Intangible rewards, such as praise by a judge or a graduation ceremony, have benefit and can have a powerful effect on a defendant's life, either through the fostering of self-esteem, motivation, and dignity, or through reinforcement of treatment goals and programming. Claire McCaskill, Combat Drug Court: An Innovative Approach to Dealing with Drug Abusing First Time Offenders, 66 UMKC L. Rev. 493, 498 (1998).

91. There is a wealth of social science literature on the therapeutic benefits of rewards in the treatment context. See generally Miller, supra note 89; supra note 86.

the team. In many instances, the non-legal team members have more interaction with the criminal defendant on a weekly or daily basis than the defendant's own lawyer. The defendant meets with these treatment professionals outside of the courtroom according to a proscribed regimen of court-ordered treatment or contact. Often the non-legal team members are able to take certain affirmative actions without the input of the judge, and they can mandate that the defendant engage in certain behavior and meet certain requirements. These mandates are often not subject to challenge by the defendant, and often are not even brought to the defense attorney's attention until some future court date, if ever.[92]

While the team approach is considered a central tenet of specialty courts, the enhanced and increased role of the judge is also very important to the operation of the program.[93] The usual model of a specialty court is to have a dedicated judge who presides over all of the cases assigned to the specialty court calendar. The theory is that the judge will develop special expertise on social issues and treatment approaches by repeatedly presiding over these types of cases.[94] In some treatment courts around the country, the specialty court judge has been in the same assignment for several years. In others, the judges may rotate through the specialty court, just like any other court assignment, staying for as long as one year or as short as a few months.[95] The role of the judge in specialty courts is distinctly different than in traditional courts, where the lawyers take on a more central role, thereby dictating the course of the litigation.[96] Of course, in a traditional setting, the defense attorney's role is as a representative of the defendant, and the attorney's actions must conform to the defendant's wishes and best interests.

The centrality of the judge's role in the specialty court is further evidenced by the scheduling of frequent hearings to ascertain the defendant's compliance with the court-ordered treatment. These hearings are often unnecessary from a criminal justice perspective, as they are scheduled when no issues exist requiring judicial intervention. Rather, they are often scheduled solely to give the defendant face time with the judge, who is perceived to be the leader of the treatment team. The theory is that regular interactions between the judge and the defendant increase the likelihood that a defendant will continue treatment, succeed in treatment, and not recidivate.[97] Treatment court ad-

---

92. Some examples of requirements imposed by non-legal team members, most often case managers, include imposing a curfew, forcing the defendant to keep certain job interviews, requiring the defendant to enroll in school programs, scheduling meetings with case manager or others, disclosing certain personal information to other service providers or the police, making unexpected and unannounced home visits, and imposing restrictions on freedom of association and travel.

93. McCoy, supra note 5, at 1529. Indeed, some of the most vocal supporters of drug courts today include jurists who preside over these courts. Defining Drug Courts, supra note 21 (pointing to Key Component 6 of drug courts). See generally Hora & Schma, supra note 72; Kaye, supra note 54; Nat'l Ass'n of Drug Court Professionals, A Level of Teamwork Not Often Seen: An Interview with Jeffrey S Tauber (Nov. 1997), available at http://www.nlada.org/DMS/Documents/998934264.745/Defenders% 20in%20Drug%20Courts.doc.

94. Davis, supra note 5, at 32; Defining Drug Courts, supra note 21 (highlighting Key Component 7 of drug courts).

95. In the Washington, D.C. trial court, judges are assigned to particular divisions of the court for three year periods. Within the three year rotations, they are assigned to different calendars each year, including the specialty court calendars. See infra Part II.D.

96. See supra note 25 and accompanying text (describing prominence of traditional defense attorney).

97. Defining Drug Courts, supra note 21 (outlining Key Component 7 of drug courts).

vocates further argue that the regular intervention of an authority figure in the defendant's life will "signal that someone cares and is closely watching."[98]

Finally and perhaps most significantly, the new treatment courts explicitly disavow adversarialism. In the specialty court, the team approach dictates that each side's goal is the defendant's success in the proscribed treatment program. Even in instances where the treatment is something more than substance abuse treatment, such as group counseling, punitive community service, or monetary restitution, the defense is required to support the completion of the "treatment." Judges frown upon any challenge or argument against the "treatment" or a modification to specifically support the defendant's particular circumstances. In some instances, a challenge to any aspect of the treatment can be seen as a material breach of the specialty court contract, thereby subjecting the defendant to sanctions or removal from the program.

C. Specialized Court Variations and Models

In the wake of the reported success and widespread acceptance of the drug court model, many other specialized courts have emerged. While the drug court model emerged earliest and fully embodies aspects of therapeutic justice, other models have emerged which utilize some of the same principles, particularly the team-oriented, multi-disciplinary, and non-adversarial approach.[99] These other models often encompass issues which cannot, and should not, fully embrace the use of treatment as a central tenet. Professor Candace McCoy reviewed the burgeoning literature on drug courts and therapeutic justice and found that the drug court model was applied to other therapeutic justice models, which primarily encompassed restorative justice principles and covered other social problems such as domestic violence or mental illness.[100] McCoy cautioned against equating these types of courts with drug courts, because the issues and methodologies are different.[101] She found that each different specialty court must be analyzed on its own terms.[102] Professor McCoy also notes that the emergence of greater numbers of these other specialized courts may mean that judges will increasingly delve into defendants' lives in ways that are inappropriate under the therapeutic approach.[103] She also notes that judges may not be properly trained to provide the appropriate therapeutic response.[104] While Professor McCoy did not evaluate any of these issues from the perspective of the appropriate role for the defense lawyer in the specialty court, her analysis supports the contention that the growth and expansion of the specialized court model has an inverse relationship to the effectiveness, competence, and zeal of criminal defenders in these courts. In other words, as the numbers and breadth of subject matter of these courts continues to grow, there may be a decline in the role of the traditional adversarial defense attorney.

---

98. See Defining Drug Courts, supra note 21. This justification, however, tends toward an overtly paternalistic model, which may serve to demoralize client-defendants and rob them of the ability to develop appropriate self-coping and self-reliance mechanisms that will allow them to resist the negative behaviors, such as substance abuse.
99. See Nolan, supra note 57, at 1543.
100. See McCoy, supra note 5, at 1524–25.
101. See McCoy, supra note 5, at 1513 n.11.
102. See McCoy, supra 5, at 1513 n.11. While I agree with Professor McCoy that these courts present many different issues and should be analyzed individually, several characteristics which are the subject of this article, including the role of the defense lawyer, have many of the same implications.
103. See McCoy, supra note 5, at 1533.
104. See McCoy, supra note 5, at 1533–34.

1. Domestic Violence Courts

Domestic violence is an issue that has plagued the criminal courts for many years, but only in recent years has a coordinated effort emerged to address the issue from a different perspective. New domestic violence courts have emerged in many jurisdictions after the reported success of the first domestic violence court in Brooklyn, New York.[105] These specialized courts are sometimes marked by a coordination of matters affecting an intra-family allegation of abuse.[106] For example, when an allegation of abuse is made, the court provides special services to the alleged victim, including assistance in filing and prosecuting a civil protection order, counseling services, and referrals to social services organizations. Additionally, the case is assigned to the domestic violence judge who gains access to and authority over any other legal matters involving the alleged victim and abuser, which can include any pending divorce, custody, or support matters. In theory, the court is "characterized by close monitoring and supervision by a specially trained judge," much like other specialized courts.[107] The judge often engages the defendant directly during court hearings and "assumes "multiple roles including acting as authority, motivator, problem solver, and monitor.'"[108] Some of these courts make use of anti-violence therapy, offering these services either before or after adjudication.[109] It is difficult to think of domestic violence courts as therapeutic, because therapy is such a small part of the process.[110] With community service requirements and liberal use of jail time as a sanction, many domestic violence courts emphasize punishment and retribution rather than treatment for the alleged abuser or protection and empowerment of the victim.[111] Additionally, some domestic violence courts place little emphasis on procedural due process for the defendant, who is often required to go forward in a contested civil protection order proceeding without counsel, while the alleged victim is represented by local prosecutors.[112]

2. Community Courts

Much literature has been produced regarding the community court model of specialty courts with particular focus on Red Hook Community Justice Center and the Midtown Community Court, both located in New York City.[113] Community courts are

---

105. Nolan, supra note 57, at 1544.
106. The term "intrafamily" is used to denote a broad range of matters in which the parties may have a domestic, familial-type relationship. For example, the D.C. Code defines an "intrafamily offense ... [as one] committed by an offender upon a person: (A) to whom the offender is related by blood, legal custody, marriage, having a child in common, or with whom the offender shares or has shared a mutual residence; or (B) with whom the offender maintains or maintained a romantic relationship, not necessarily including a sexual relationship." D.C. Code §16-1001 (2001).
107. See Nolan, supra note 57, at 1544.
108. Nolan, supra note 57, at 1544 (quoting Carrie J. Petrucci, Respect as a Component in the Judge-Defendant Interaction in a Specialized Domestic Violence Court that Utilizes Therapeutic Jurisprudence, 38 Crim. L. Bull. 268 (2002)).
109. Few of these courts offer or require anti-violence therapy, thereby missing an important opportunity to modify or ameliorate other issues in the intra-family unit, or to empower the complainant to seek additional resources when confronted with future domestic situations.
110. See McCoy, supra note 5, at 1531. While batterer's counseling is often a part of these courts, it is proscribed as a condition of probation, not as a treatment modality for the defendant. Id.
111. See Davis, supra note 5, at 37. Davis reports that the "emphasis on protecting victims makes courts too quick to lock up defendants" and the "strong momentum toward incarceration." Id.
112. This is the situation in Washington, D.C.'s Domestic Violence Unit. See infra Part II.D.
113. See Greg Berman & John Feinblatt, Problem Solving Courts: A Brief Primer (2001), available at http://www.courtinnovation.org/pdf/prob solv courts.pdf.

designed to exert social control on a target population to benefit the entire community.[114] The benefit from the community may take many forms: it decreases a specific type of crime in a particular area, it gets judges involved in local meetings with concerned citizens, it has residents and merchants advise the court of the community's needs and concerns, or it results in defendants performing community service jobs where the crime occurred.[115] Community courts most often concentrate on quality of life crimes, because of the "broken windows" theory which argues that unattended and unaddressed disorderly conduct can lead to an increase in the amount and seriousness of criminal behavior.[116]

As with other specialty courts, many due process concerns have been raised regarding community courts. Homeless people seem to be unfairly targeted and funding for some of these courts is provided by private business interests, who garner influence with the community court officials and judges.[117] Moreover, these courts may not address the root causes of the social problems faced by defendants. For example, where homelessness is a major issue in a community plagued by "quality of life" crimes, addressing the lack of affordable housing, or employment becomes paramount in trying to decrease the problems. Unfortunately, a majority of community courts lack any means to fundamentally address social issues.[118]

3. Mental Health Courts

Judge Ginger Lerner-Wren established the first mental health court in Broward County, Florida, in 1997 to focus mental health services and resources on defendants whose mental illness was the primary reason for their recidivism.[119] With the judge regularly monitoring their progress, defendants who are charged with "quality of life crimes," which are usually petty misdemeanors, are given access to community mental health treatment as a condition of release or as an attempt to divert them from the criminal justice system.[120] Sometimes the treatment is conditioned upon a guilty plea to the charged offense or a lesser included offense. As in drug court, the judge remains an integral part of the treatment team, which involves social workers and other professionals, and when a defendant fails to follow through with the treatment, the judge has the power to sanction and incarcerate the defendant where mental health treatment is involuntary.[121] When a defendant undergoes mental health treatment in jail, the treatment is

---

114. See McCoy, supra note 5, at 1517 n.10; see also Thompson, supra note 16, at 66; Jeffrey Fagan & Victoria Malkin, Theorizing Community Justice Through Community Courts, 30 Fordham Urb. L.J. 897, 900–01 (2003).

115. Kundu, supra note 15, at 170.

116. Kundu, supra note 15, at 172–73.

117. Kundu, supra note 15, 176–77.

118. Kundu, supra note 15, 179–80.

119. See Introduction, www.browarddefender.com/mhealth/volume i mental health.htm#Introduction (last visited Nov. 8, 2006). Other mental health courts are being implemented every year. See Amy Abern, Lutz is First Health Court Success Story, Sarasota Herald Trib., Jan. 25, 2006, at §B; John Koopman, An Alternative to Incarceration Behavioral Health Court Offers Counseling Criminal Defendants with Psychological Problems, San Francisco Chron., Jan. 23, 2006, at NEWS.

120. See Davis, supra note 5, at 33–34 (describing crimes such as trespassing and spitting in the street). This term is misleading, since all crime, particularly the serious violent crime, has a major impact on the perception of quality of life in a community. Unfortunately, very few specialized court programs exist to provide treatment and services to defendants charged with such violent offenses. Moreover, problems exist when the mental health court is used to criminalize homeless persons and people with mental health issues whose offenses are the result primarily of their living conditions.

121. Nolan, supra note 57, at 1544.

often inappropriate or insufficient. Additionally, the time spent in jail as a sanction for non-compliance often has a negative effect on the mental health of the defendant.[122]

The practice of requiring mental health treatment as a condition of probation or release from jail is susceptible to several criticisms. Chief among them is the notion that a defendant can be summarily jailed for curtailing mental health treatment or medication. This potential sanction exists irrespective of the possibility that the medication or other treatment may not work and that some medications can cause severe side effects. Defendants and their lawyers are left with a choice among a specific mental health treatment with the court's provider, no treatment at all, or no meaningful way to challenge the treatment that the court deems appropriate.[123]

4. Homeless Courts

The nation's first homeless court appears to have originated in July 1989 in San Diego, California. It was touted as a way of resolving outstanding bench and arrest warrants held by many homeless people in the city's shelters. The defendants were already enrolled in treatment programs in homeless shelters. Their advocates worked out deals between prosecutors and defenders in which the defendants would immediately plead guilty and be sentenced to continue in their programs. Thus, the court was able to clear up many outstanding warrants and cases. Since the first day of homeless court, San Diego have held similar proceedings once a month in a homeless shelter.[124] Other California jurisdictions have followed this example.[125]

Unfortunately, some of these proceedings are held in an informal atmosphere where there is little, if any, opportunity for a defendant and her lawyer to develop a relationship that facilitates the vindication of the defendant's wishes and/or position in the

---

122. Many advocates and critics alike criticize the notion of using sanctions to coerce mental health treatment for defendants with diagnosed problems. The Board of Directors of the National Mental Health Association has issued a policy statement calling for caution, the influence of state and local mental health associations, and the development of standards to shape the implementation and accountability of Mental Health Courts. See National Mental Health Assoc., Position Statement: Mental Health Courts (Nov. 17, 2001), available at www.nmha.org/position/mentalhealthcourts.cfm; see also Bureau of Justice Asst., Emerging Judicial Strategies for the Mentally Ill in the Criminal Caseloads: Mental Health Courts in Ft. Lauderdale, Seattle, San Bernardino and Anchorage (Apr. 2000), available at http://www.ncjis.gov/bja/mentalhealth/contents.html.

123. See generally Office of Justice Program, Mental Health Courts Program, http://www.ojp.usdoj.gov/bja/grant/mentalhealth.html (last visited Nov. 5, 2006). For more information on mental health courts, the Department of Justice's Bureau of Justice Assistance has many publications and resources for technical assistance and substantive advice. See id.

124. See Davis, supra note 5, at 33–34.

125. Alameda County, California, has developed a "homeless/caring court" that holds proceedings in a homeless shelter. See Superior Court of California, County of Alameda, Alameda County Creates Special Court Sessions for Homeless (June 17, 2005), available at http://www.court.info.ca. gov/programs/collab/documents/home less court press Release.pdf. The San Diego Homeless Court Program serves individuals who "demonstrate that they are willing to leave homelessness," and any outstanding warrants are dismissed in lieu of volunteering or attending mental health treatment or substance abuse counseling. See San Diego Association of Governments, San Diego Homeless Court Program: A Process and Impact Evaluation (June 2001), available at http://www.courtinfo.ca.gov/programs/collab/documents/2001S ANDAG HomelessCourtEvaluation.pdf. Los Angeles has also developed a similar program, however, individuals are eligible only if they have pending minor infractions or tickets for such offenses as jaywalking, fare evasion, or sleeping in public. See Public Counsel Law Center, Homeless Court Law Clerk at the Los Angeles City Attorney's Office, available at http://www.publiccounsel.org/internships/hclc.pdf.

court. Specifically, the speed and efficiency of the court become paramount, and little time is taken to make sure that defendants understand and agree with the proceedings.

5. Other Kinds of Specialty Courts

The landscape of specialized courts seems to continually expand with new subject matters or target populations being reviewed every year.

a. Prisoner Reentry Courts

The more than one-half million individuals returning to the community every year after a period of incarceration often face a plethora of issues affecting their ability to productively live in society. Many of these people remain under supervision by parole or probation authorities and are subject to conditions that restrict their liberty in different ways, ranging from drug testing to curfews to restrictions on association and residence. They often return to the community unprepared to secure meaningful employment, take care of responsibilities such as parenting and child support, combat lingering addiction, or resist the lure of criminal activity. Prisoner reentry courts represent an attempt to take the drug court model to a different level. Judges, who previously lost all control over a defendant once sentencing was completed, move into a role of "sentence manager, overseeing the convicted person's eventual return to the community."[126]

The Office of Justice Programs (OJP), which as an arm of the Justice Department has funded several reentry court experiments, defines this new court model as a court that manages the return of prisoners to the community using the authority of the court to apply graduated sanctions and positive reinforcement.[127] The Court is able to bring together resources to assist the individual and encourage positive behavior, specifically, refraining from recidivating. OJP has identified several core elements for these courts which are similar to the foundational principles for drug courts: assessment and treatment planning; regular status hearings to monitor progress; coordination of needed social services, including job training, housing, substance abuse; a system of graduated sanctions and rewards; and collaboration with community groups.[128]

A substantial number of reentry courts have emerged in the past five years as a result of Clinton Administration experimental pilot programs and other initiatives that focus on the broader problem of reentry into the community.[129] The provision of defender services in these courts is still questionable, especially since court systems rarely have any jurisdiction over the offenders, and therefore the reentry courts may not be under any mandate to provide legal representation for the clients.

b. Other Specialty Courts

Other specialty courts that have emerged in recent years include DUI Treatment Courts, Gambling Courts, Gun Courts and Prostitution or John Courts. These variations exhibit few, if any, characteristics of therapeutic jurisprudence, and are often marked by dedicated resources and focused court attention to address a particular problem.[130] They are marked by several restorative justice characteristics, as much at-

---

126. Shadd Maruna & Thomas P. LeBel, Welcome Home? Examining the "Reentry Court" Concept from a Strengths-based Perspective, 4 W. Criminology Rev. 91, 92 (2003).
127. Id.; see also McCoy, supra note 5, at 1518 (stating courts lack innovation or therapy, and only improve operations and resources of particular court units).
128. See Maruna & LeBel, supra note 126, at 92.
129. Developing sites include locations in California, Colorado, Delaware, Florida, Iowa, Kentucky, New York, Ohio, and West Virginia.
130. See McCoy, supra note 5, at 1517 n.10.

tention is placed on the notion that the offender must "pay back" the community in proscribed ways, such as community service projects and restitution.

D. Case in Point: Washington, D.C.'s Specialty Criminal Courts

Many jurisdictions have experimented with some form of specialty court. It is helpful to take a closer look at one such jurisdiction, even though it does not represent a model program or one that embodies a structure that has been adopted by a majority of jurisdictions. Washington is instructive because it has adopted and experimented with multiple kinds of specialized courts. Moreover, its specialized courts embody different models and features of defender participation. A review of this local court system may reveal typical or recurring issues that need to be addressed when considering the advancement of specialty courts, or when incorporating some of the precepts of therapeutic and restorative justice into other courts.[131]

Washington, D.C. is a city of about 600,000 people covering approximately sixty-nine square miles. Its system for the administration of justice is unique even among other cities with similar population demographics.[132] Because it is the nation's capital city with a limited system of home rule, its justice system has unique qualities that produce unique issues that have to be addressed.[133] The criminal division of the local trial court, Superior Court, is staffed by both federal and local prosecutors and cases are adjudicated by about sixty judges who are appointed by the President of the United States and confirmed by the U.S. Congress.[134] The Criminal Division handles over 15,000 misdemeanor cases each year and close to 10,000 felony cases.[135] Some statistics have shown that Washington has the "highest incarceration rate in the nation and longer prison sentences than any state."[136]

The District has a bipartite system for the delivery of indigent defense services. The Public Defender Service for the District of Columbia, created in 1971, is the institu-

---

131. Little empirical data has been captured with regard to the efficacy or outcomes of the participants in these specialty courts. Such a study is necessary. The information noted in this article is based upon my experience practicing in these courts, interviews with other lawyers and judges who often practice there, information garnered from annual court reports, and newspaper and other articles regarding these courts.

132. The District of Columbia's population in 2000 was 572,059, but it is estimated that it has declined by about three to four percent since that time. Sixty percent of the city's residents are African-American, and approximately thirty-one percent White. As of 1999, the city boasts about 248,338 households with a median income of $ 40,127. However, more than twenty percent of D.C. residents live below U.S. poverty guidelines. See U.S. Census Bureau, State & Country Quick Facts, District of Columbia (2005), available at http://quickfacts.census.gov/qfd/states/11000.html.

133. The District of Columbia has unique status with respect to its local governance. It is dependent upon congressional approval of many local laws and initiatives and depends upon a federal financial subsidy to operate. This has given Congress the authority to take over several essential city services, such as the prison system, and to impose guidelines and requirements on the local court systems. Yet D.C. residents are denied voting representation in the Congress. D.C. voters elect a delegate to the U.S. House of Representatives who does not have full voting rights. See D.C. Code §§1-201–1-207.71 (1973); National Capital Revitalization Act of 1998, D.C. Act 12-355 (Sept. 11, 1998).

134. The local prosecutor's office is the District of Columbia Office of the Attorney General. With regard to criminal cases, it prosecutes petty misdemeanor offenses and juvenile offenders. The United States Attorney for the District of Columbia prosecutes all other criminal offenses, including misdemeanor offenses such as drug crimes, domestic violence, and violent crimes such as robbery, rape, and murder.

135. 2003 D.C. Super. Ct. Ann. Rep. 50, available at http://www.dccourts.gov/dccourts/docs/AR04forDCC2.pdf.

136. Vincent Schiraldi, Editorial, Dealing with the District's Drug Users, Wash. Post, Nov. 2, 2002, at A24.

tional defender agency and by statute can take no more than sixty percent of the indigent cases that are processed in Superior Court.[137] The remaining cases are handled by hundreds of private attorneys who are paid by the court through a voucher system under the Criminal Justice Act.[138] Recently, the private defense bar reduced the number of private attorneys handling indigent criminal cases in an attempt to increase the standard of practice. Currently, only 250 attorneys have been certified by the Superior Court as possessing the requisite experience to receive appointments in indigent criminal cases.[139] These lawyers are also required to participate in continuing legal education training provided by the Public Defender Service or bar associations.[140]

For many years, Washington has been aggressive in its attempts to process the multitude of cases that flow through its courthouse doors. Like other urban jurisdictions, Washington faced an explosion of drug related crime in the early to mid 1980s, culminating in its dubious designation as the "murder capital."[141] Stakeholders in the criminal justice system began searching for ways to decrease crime rates and improve court efficiency. Community policing and prosecution developed, as well as the federal takeover of several local criminal justice functions, including corrections.[142] In 1995, Washington's City Council passed the Misdemeanor Streamlining Act, which reduced the maximum sentence for most misdemeanor offenses from one year to 180 days.[143] The major effect of the Act was to significantly reduce the number of charges eligible for a jury trial, thereby increasing the efficiency of the trial court to process cases.[144] At about the

---

137. See D.C. Code §11-2601 (creating Public Defender Service for the District of Columbia).
138. See Criminal Justice Act, D.C. Code §§11-2601–11-2609 (furnishing representation to indigents under the DC Criminal Justice Act (CJA Plan)).
139. See Superior Court of the District of Columbia Administrative Order Nos. 02-33 (eff. Jan. 1 2003) & 02-33 (July 17, 2000).
140. In December 2001, the Superior Court Chief Judge convened an Ad Hoc Committee to determine whether a continuing legal education (CLE) requirement should be instituted for private attorneys receiving appointments to indigent criminal cases. Upon the committee's recommendation, the Chief Judge signed an Administrative Order requiring eight hours of CLE training per year in approved subject areas in order to an attorney to continue to receive appointments by the court. See Superior Court of the District of Columbia Administrative Order No. 02-33 (eff. Jan. 1, 2003).
141. With the burgeoning northeast crack cocaine market, Washington endured a surge in violent crime in the late 1980s and early 1990s. See U.S. Bureau of Justice Statistics, Reported Crime in the United States-District of Columbia (1985–1995), available at http://bjsdata.ojp.usdoj.gov/data online/Search/Crime/State/RunCrimeStatebyState.cfm. The rise in the rate of murders per capita gained great media attention. See, e.g., Richard L. Berke, Capital's Government Denounced By Bennett, Opening Drug Drive, N.Y. Times, Apr. 11, 1989, at §A (stating District of Columbia has highest drug-related murders per capita); Richard Keil, Surge in Drug Killings Made 1988 Bloodiest Year in D.C. History, AP Online, Dec. 31, 1989, at Washington News (noting D.C. shared highest per capita murder rate in country); Last Year was the Bloodiest in D.C. History, AP Online, Jan. 2, 1989, at Washington News (discussing D.C.'s 371 murders and distinction of highest per capita murder rate).
142. National Capital Revitalization Act of 1998, D.C. Code §2-1219.29 (2001). Prisoners now are incarcerated in federal and state facilities, in part under a contractual payment system. The city also contracts with private prison corporations, including the Corrections Corporation of America, to house D.C. prisoners. These contractual relationships leave prisoners incarcerated many miles away from the city and their family resources. The city therefore has little, if any, control over treatment, educational or social services that may be provided for the prisoners. Several nonprofit agencies have initiated lawsuits to improve conditions and treatment of these prisoners.
143. Misdemeanor Streamlining Act, D.C. Code §16-705(b) (2006).
144. Id.

same time, the District's indeterminate sentencing scheme was abolished in favor of a determinate sentencing scheme without parole.[145]

1. Superior Court Drug Intervention Program

The movement for a drug court in the District began in 1994 when the city was awarded a five year, $ 5 million grant from the Department of Justice to operate an experimental drug court. Initially, the drug court operated with three separate dockets; when an appropriate case was brought into the system it was randomly assigned to either the control, sanctions, or treatment calendars.[146] The control docket continued with the normal adjudication procedures in criminal court, whereas the sanctions docket made liberal use of sanctions to coerce abstinence from drugs, which was determined through twice-weekly drug tests. The treatment court offered defendants a variety of options, including long-term inpatient treatment, group therapy, and acupuncture. After about two years, the treatment docket discontinued use of inpatient treatment programs in favor of day treatment programs.[147] As an essential component of the program, officials maintained statistical data to determine both the rate of success of this treatment modality and how this differed from normal adjudication. Eventually, after the initial experimental grant-funded period, the program settled to one calendar with a different judge assigned each year. The program, called the Superior Court Drug Intervention Program (SCDIP), is formally operated by the District's Pretrial Services Agency, which provides case management, treatment services, and compliance reporting for the program. The SCDIP is a pre-adjudication model that only accepts defendants with a demonstrated history of drug abuse who are charged with misdemeanor offenses. Potential eligibility is noted at the first court appearance and a subsequent assessment is conducted if the defendant is amenable to treatment. A defendant is accepted after the prosecution agrees to allow the case to be held in abeyance until the defendant completes a four-phase outpatient treatment process that can take up to one year to complete.

---

145. Legislation passed in 1997 by Congress changed sentencing practices in the District of Columbia. The National Capital Revitalization and Self Government Improvement Act of 1997 mandated the closure of the District's prison complex in Lorton, Virginia, transferred authority for parole to the federal government, allowed for federal funding of the local court system, established a sentencing commission charged with amending the D.C. Codes Sentencing provisions to ensure "just punishment" with good time calculated in accordance with federal law, and enacted a system of supervised release, instead of parole, following incarceration. See supra note 142 and accompanying text; see also D.C. Sentencing Commission Sentencing Reforms, http://www.sentencing.dc. gov/acs/cwp/view,a,3,q,589375,acsNavGID,1664,acsNav,-33149-,.asp (last visited Nov. 8, 2006).

146. Initially, the court admitted only those defendants charged with non-violent drug related felonies. Violent offenses were excluded and continue to be excluded from many drug courts nationwide because of federal regulations that must be complied with in order to be eligible for federal funding. See The Omnibus Crime Control and Safe Streets Act, 42 U.S.C. §3796ii (2000) (prohibiting admission of violent offenders to drug courts receiving funds from the U.S. Department of Justice, Drug Courts Program Office).

147. I suspect that the driving force behind the discontinuation of residential treatment programs was and continues to be cost. For example, residential drug treatment can cost five to seven times more than outpatient treatment. See Lisa R. Nakdai, Are New York's Rockefeller Drug Laws Killing the Messenger for the Sake of the Message?, 30 Hofstra L. Rev. 557, 562 (2001) (detailing costs faced by New York State for severe penalties for drug offenders); Michael L. Prendergast, M. Douglas Anglin & Jean Wellisch, Treatment for Drug-Abusing Offenders Under Community Supervision, 59 Fed. Probation 66, 72 (1995).

Sanctions are an integral part of the SCDIP drug court, and sanction hearings occur every afternoon. After an outcry by the defense bar denouncing the practice of holding sanction hearings without the defense attorney present, the SCDIP arranged to have one attorney assigned each day from the Public Defender Service (PDS) to appear in court in the afternoon to represent all defendants who are called in for a sanction that day. Usually, the defendant has violated a condition of treatment court, and it often results from a positive drug test. The PDS attorneys have no information about the client prior to the sanctions hearing and often do not have time to meet with the client prior to the hearing. At the sanctions hearing the judge asks the defense if they will contest the alleged violations. This rarely happens; if the defendant says that she wishes to contest the imposition of a sanction, some drug court judges will explain the process and reliability of urinalysis testing to the defendant. After a lengthy explanation by the judge, few, if any, defendants pursue a challenge to the imposition of a sanction. Sanctions are imposed for violation of conditions according to the guidelines of the treatment court. Individual judges sometimes depart from the guidelines for sanctions.

At regular status hearings which are scheduled for those enrolled in SCDIP, judges directly address the defendant. It is not infrequent for a judge to hold these hearings without the presence of a defense attorney. The hearing, however, is never held without a social worker, case manager, or other treatment professional present.

2. The Domestic Violence Unit

Washington's Superior Court began its Domestic Violence Court initiative in 1996 and incorporated a coordinated approach to the handling of domestic violence cases. Unlike drug court, which is merely a special calendar in the Court's Criminal Division, the Domestic Violence Unit(DV Unit) is a separate section of the court which combines criminal and family division matters in a central office. The DV Unit has a presiding judge and other judges and magistrates assigned to adjudicate domestic violence matters. One judge normally presides over both the criminal and civil matters relating to an abuse allegation in a family matter.[148] A prominent feature of the Domestic Violence Unit is the assistance it provides to victims seeking services or civil protection orders against alleged abusers. Victims are brought to the DV Unit and meet specially trained victims' advocates, who help them file requests for civil protection orders, and are given referrals for child care, shelter, job referrals, medical treatment, or other emergency services. Legal services are often offered to victims through collaboration with local clinical programs.

When a prosecution involving misdemeanor allegations of domestic violence begins, the case is assigned to one of three calendars. Usually, criminal court officials serve a civil protection order summons at the arraignment and immediately implement a temporary order. A hearing on the matter is scheduled on the same date as the status hearing in the criminal case. The attorney assigned in the criminal case is typically not assigned to represent the defendant in the accompanying civil matters.[149] On the day of the hearing, defendants and victims often meet with a DV Unit worker prior to appearing before the judge in the civil protection matter. The worker determines if a voluntary

---

148. Bill Miller, Domestic Violence Gets New Priority in District; Team of Judges, Courthouse Changes Announced, Wash. Post Nov. 5, 1996, at B3. A domestic violence case can therefore include divorce, paternity and support, criminal issues, and civil protection orders.

149. Some PDS attorneys appear with their clients during these civil hearings; however, private attorneys, appointed under the Criminal Justice Act, frequently do not, as they are not entitled to remuneration for their time or service.

civil protection order can be issued. The victim is often accompanied by a legal clinic volunteer or a prosecutor, while defendants have no legal representative. Defendants lacking legal counsel many times agree to protection orders including provisions which impact their liberty interests. The judge is informed of the consent agreement and makes inquiries of the parties during a hearing where no legal representative for the defendant appears. Additionally, this same judge or a different judge in the same unit will hear the criminal matter and can impose additional conditions of release based upon the conditions of the civil protection order, or involving other family-related matters.

With respect to the processing of the criminal case, the Domestic Violence Court has instituted a deferred sentencing program for those defendants found eligible by the prosecutors. This program is operated very similarly to a normal plea bargaining process. Cases where the defendant has no substantial criminal history, and where the victim does not allege significant injury, are deemed eligible by the prosecution for deferred sentencing. To take advantage of this program, the defendant must enter a plea of guilty and agree to a nine-month deferment of sentencing during which the defendant must attend domestic violence counseling, complete community service, and comply with any other conditions imposed by the judge. At the end of the deferment period, the guilty plea is withdrawn if the defendant has completed all the conditions imposed. In cases in which the defendant declines deferred sentencing, he can enter a plea bargain or proceed to trial. Prosecutors often proceed with trial in domestic abuse cases even when the alleged victim declines to testify.[150]

3. Prostitution Court

The Superior Court has experimented with an initiative designed to decrease the number of prostitution cases adjudicated in its misdemeanor branch. In 2003, the court set up a prostitution docket to "provide a more coordinated approach to dealing" with these cases, including the prostitutes and customers. This court attempted to refer those arrested for these crimes to drug or mental health treatment.[151] However, no special procedures or programs were included in this specialized court, so cases were handled in the ordinary fashion. The only program that routinely accepts defendants, only after the prosecution agrees to allow the defendant to enter the program, is a one-day program that focuses primarily on the public health risks of prostitution. The benefit to the community of the prostitution docket is unclear. Some police officers and prosecutors have noted that the court is now equipped to try the cases more quickly and efficiently.[152]

E. A Paradigm Shift?

How far will the expansion of specialized courts go? While states evaluate and implement new ideas for specialized courts, it remains to be seen whether this expansion will cause a radical and system-wide change in the way that justice is administered and conceived in the nation's courtrooms.

---

150. See supra note 122. Prosecutors often seek to introduce the hearsay spontaneous statements of the victims in lieu of live court testimony by the alleged victim. The recent Crawford decision, however, may have serious implications for this practice. See generally Crawford v. Washington, 541 U.S. 36 (2004).

151. Henri Cauvin, City's Prostitution Court Targets Defendants for Aid, Wash. Post, May 15, 2003, at B2.

152. The District does not have a formal Mental Health Court. After studying the issue for some time, the court implemented instead a diversion type program called "Options" that is available in all misdemeanor dockets. A client-defendant may enter this voluntary, pre-trial program to receive coordinated services. The judge adjudicating the case may view compliance with the program as an indicator that the court's sentence should reflect the defendant's changed circumstances.

Recently, some scholars have questioned whether the vast expansion of the specialty courts' methodology, which relies on therapeutic and restorative justice principles, signals a "paradigm shift" in the administration of justice landscape.[153] The shift would signal a vast change in the way courts are structured and the way in which actors within the court system, such as judges and lawyers, view and fulfill their duties. Additionally, it would signal a widespread concept of justice by the public that embraces new ideas, theories, and methodologies. Moreover, the change that might occur would become apparent in all aspects of the court system. The new principles and concepts would slowly, but methodically, infect the criminal court system including law enforcement, prosecutors, and criminal defenders. In this regard, the question becomes: has the specialty court movement and its way of doing business changed the criminal justice system's landscape in a broader sense?

One way to answer this question is to assess the extent to which major judicial groups have embraced the ideals of the specialty court movement. In recent years, several court officials, affinity agencies, and judicial organizations endorsed the specialty courts' therapeutic and restorative justice language. In a supportive joint resolution, the Conference of Chief Justices and the Conference of State Court Administrators described specialty courts as employing "principles and methods grounded in Therapeutic Jurisprudence, including integration of treatment services with judicial case processing, ongoing judicial intervention, close monitoring of and immediate response to behavior, multi-disciplinary involvement, and collaboration with community based, and government organizations."[154] Through this resolution, the judges and administrators seemed to endorse the notion of extending therapeutic jurisprudence to courtrooms nationwide. Additionally, many individual judges, most often those who played an integral role in setting up specialty courts or who preside over these courts, support the jurisprudence emanating from specialty courts.[155]

Like judicial groups, academics suggest that the emergence of specialty courts represents a paradigm shift in our criminal justice system.[156] Others have merely characterized the new specialty courts as an experiment that moves away from the traditional legal paradigm.[157]

On the other hand, some commentators believe it is too early to call the emergence of specialty courts a "paradigm shift." Professor Candace McCoy notes that many questions still linger as to whether the specialty courts will have the desired effect on problems in the criminal justice system.[158] She notes that it is unclear whether this new sys-

---

153. National Drug Court Institute, Critical Issues for Defense Attorneys in Drug Court 1 (Apr. 2003), available at http://www.ndci.org/CriticalIssues.pdf; see Nolan, supra note 57, at 1564–65 (calling it "overall transformation of the adjudicative setting according to the therapeutic paradigm").

154. See Nolan, supra note 57, at 1542.

155. See Hora & Schma, supra note 77, at 446–48. See generally Kaye, supra note 54; Nat'l Ass'n of Drug Court Professionals, A Level of Teamwork Not Often Seen: An Interview with Jeffrey S Tauber (Nov. 1997), available at www.nlada.org/DMS/Documents/998934264.745/Defenders%20in%20 Drug%20Courts.doc.

156. Professor James Nolan believes that the new courts do represent a paradigm shift in the criminal justice system. See generally JAMES L. NOLAN, REINVENTING JUSTICE: THE AMERICAN DRUG COURT MOVEMENT (2001).

157. Michael C. Dorf & Charles F. Sabel, Drug Treatment courts and Emergent Experimentalist Government, 53 Vand. L. Rev. 831, 837 (2000).

158. See McCoy, supra note 5, at 1532. Therapeutic jurisprudence, restorative justice and the specialty courts that they have engendered are not without their critics. Judge Hoffman argues that this new strain of rehabilitationism is "ineffective and dangerous," largely because of the "unchecked

tem will reduce recidivism, especially since there is currently no statistical data on recidivism that supports the contention. She also questions whether these courts will stand the test of time and reduced federal funding.[159] Many of the drug courts would not have been started but for the presence of substantial federal funding. To receive funding, the court had to be set up a certain way, which included instituting the collaborative team approach and the diminution of the adversary model.[160] A very real danger exists, however, that federal funding will not continue for these courts. The specialty courts will only be able to continue if states and localities step in and provide the funding for them.[161]

1. An Experiment Gone Too Far?

With the emergence of so many specialty courts, many are left to wonder if this is just a one time explosion with growth into new subject areas. Will the end result be that the overall administration of justice remains the same? For example, a "speedy homicide" court was recently enacted in Milwaukee, Wisconsin. This new court purported to use drug court methodology in the homicide context.[162] The sole purpose of the methodology, though, was to move cases along and prevent delay in the adjudication of these most series cases. While this is an attempt to solve a "problem" in the criminal justice system, it stretches logic to find any adherence to therapeutic or restorative justice principles, where there are no treatments and no services provided to the defendants.

The expansion of the new problem-solving courts may also cause an erosion of due process in contexts other than those involving a committed, zealous defender. Recently, in California, drug court judges lobbied for an extension of their authority so that they could order random searches of the residences of drug court defendants and the defendants themselves. They proposed an amendment to the penal statute that would allow these searches "at any time during the day or night, with or without probable cause...."[163] The judges rationalized that their proposal served therapeutic purposes; that is, with random checks, drug court judges could better monitor the efficacy of the treatment. This includes, among other things, the need for additional treatment, such as getting other family members involved in treatment and parenting classes.[164] Irrespective of the potential danger to our due process ideals, judges believed that through this additional information better therapeutic outcomes might be achieved for the drug court defendants.

One can only hope that the California proposal is an extreme example of the options being considered in the context of extending and expanding the specialty court model.

---

judicial power" in these courts. See Hoffman, supra note 11, at 2078. Judge Bamberger acknowledges the benefits of these courts but recognizes that courts of general jurisdiction will still need to incorporate different sentencing strategies in order to combat some of the same problems that are highlighted in specialty courts. See Phylis Bamberger, Specialized Courts: Not a Cure at All, 30 Fordham Urb. L.J. 1091, 1099–1101 (2003).

159. See McCoy, supra note 5, at 1516–17.

160. Many other guidelines were instituted, such as excluding violent offenses or offenders with a particular criminal history.

161. See McCoy, supra note 5, at 1531; see also Nat'l Ass'n of Drug Court Professionals, A Level of Teamwork Not Often Seen: An Interview with Jeffrey S Tauber (Nov. 1997), available at www.nlada.org/DMS/Documents/998934264.745/Defenders%20in%20Drug%20Courts.doc. However, localities will have to face the high cost of specialty courts.

162. Thomas P. Schneider & Robert C. Davis, Speedy Trial Homicide Courts, 9 Crim. Just. 24, 26–27 (1994).

163. See Nolan, supra note 57, at 1562.

164. See Nolan, supra note 57, at 1562.

This example illustrates the potential danger of unchecked judicial power, as well as the expansion of other ideals of the drug court methodology.

Only time will tell if the emergence of specialty courts mark a radical, system-wide change in the way criminal courts are administered. These new courts signal a significant movement away from some of the adversary system's key principles.

2. A New Criminal Defense Paradigm?

If the emergence of specialty courts indicates a paradigm shift in the administration of justice, then there is a real potential that the over-emergence of specialty courts signals the beginning of a paradigm shift in the role of the defense attorney in criminal court. That is, the Freedmanian, traditionalist view of the zealous, committed defender who rails against the system may be in decline as a model for defense representation. And, if the model is in decline, the reality often follows.

Certainly, a great number of defense attorneys have no objection to the therapeutic or restorative ideals of these new courts.[165] One of the realities of the treatment court movement is that it sometimes provides alternatives to incarceration even though the alternative may have multiple possibilities that are not readily apparent to the defendant. Some defense attorneys have even championed its principles.

A new criminal defense paradigm which puts a premium on a defender who does not vehemently assert the client's wishes would be an unfortunate byproduct of the positive benefits that specialty courts can bring. And ultimately, a new criminal defense paradigm is an indefensible change in our criminal justice system which may further lead to a decline in the levels of protection afforded to defendants.

Part III: The Good, the Bad and the Ineffective: Defender Roles in Theory and Practice

Defenders need to look at this as a new approach that requires a level of team work and partnership that is not often seen. It requires defenders to take a step back, to not intervene actively between the judge and the participant, and allow that relationship to develop and do its work, and basically to understand the importance of working within a team concept. It really does demand that they partner and work very closely with both the court, treatment, and their former adversary, the prosecutor.[166]

This comment about the role of defense lawyers in drug courts by Judge Jeffrey Tauber of the National Association of Drug Court Professionals succinctly summarizes the view of specialty court advocates who are strongly in favor of the main precepts of the specialty court movement. It asserts that defense counsel in specialty courts cannot function in their traditional role. In other words, those judges and officials who have designed the specialty courts require that the traditional adversarial role of the criminal defense attorney be subordinated to the notion of teamwork. Unfortunately, this means that the zealousness that is essential to the functioning of the defense attorney, as well as the intervention that is necessary to protect important rights, may be lost in specialty

---

165. See Quinn, supra note 22, at 73–74; Nat'l Ass'n of Drug Court Professionals, A Level of Teamwork Not Often Seen: An Interview with Jeffrey S. Tauber, (Nov.–Dec. 1997), available at http://www.nlada.org/DMS/Documents/998934264.745/Defenders%20in%20Drug%20Courts.doc#pitfalls.

166. Nat'l Ass'n of Drug Court Professionals, A Level of Teamwork Not Often Seen: An Interview with Jeffrey S. Tauber (Nov.–Dec. 1997), available at http://www.nlada.org/DMS/Documents/998934264.745/Defenders%20in%20Drug%20Courts.doc#pitfalls.

courts. In essence, the very premises of drug courts, and by extension other specialty courts, are at odds with standard notions of zealous advocacy.[167] The notion that the defense attorney in a specialty court must work as a team player engaged in the social rehabilitation of the defendant is antithetical to the traditional role of the criminal defense lawyer and invokes musings of the kindler, gentler defense practice advocated by Professor Simon.[168] In fact, some advocates argue that these new specialty courts "empower a new type of prosecutor and defense counsel," one that will press all of his or her energies toward serving the best interests of the defendant.[169] This is at least in so far as those best interests include treatment according to the modalities offered by the particular specialty court. According to the rhetoric, this new type of defender places a premium on the stated goals of the treatment court rather than on the defendant, and focuses all of his or her energy on that narrow goal.

Thus, the "role" of the defense attorney in specialty courts embodies no vestiges of the adversarial defender, and therefore takes on a "best interests" mantra. When a defendant is found to be in need of treatment by the court, prosecutor, social workers, or case managers, the defense attorney is expected to behave in a way that falls in line with the treatment recommendation and to act in a way that supports and furthers the treatment goals. The expected behaviors and actions of the defense attorney—what can be termed the "role markers"—are thus guided by the dictates of the court, and not the wishes of the defendant. Consequently, the defense attorney is expected to forgo any action or challenge any treatment, the process of adjudication, or interaction between the judge and defendant. This is true even when that interaction treads upon important constitutional rights, such as the right against self-incrimination. The defense attorney stands idly by, as part of the team, while the specialty court process takes effect. The only affirmative conduct expected of the defense attorney is to encourage the defendant to follow through with the treatment and any other requirements of the specialty court modality.[170]

Advocates of specialty courts argue that the team-player defense attorney model is superior to other models because of the beneficial results which come from treatment courts. They further state that the apprehension of defense attorneys is "unfounded." They argue that defense attorneys "should view treatment courts as being in their clients' best interest" and as "the best method for "ending the cycle of drugs and crime.'"[171]

While the "good" that can come from specialty courts, i.e., getting needed treatment for criminal defendants, is important and necessary, questions still remain as to whether the specialty court model is sufficient to meet ethical and practice standards,[172]

---

167. Daniel Richman, Professional Identity: Comment on Simon, 40 Am. Crim. L. Rev. 1609, 1610 (2001).

168. See Simon, supra note 5, at 1601.

169. McCoy, supra note 5, at 1524 (citing ABA CJ Section 1996 Monograph on drug courts and due process).

170. For example, regardless of the potential for sanctions, defense attorneys are expected to encourage clients to admit violations of court orders because this recognition is considered a therapeutic step in support of treatment. See Hora, supra note 77, at 479 (arguing defense attorneys forgo "motions to suppress evidence, which might delay the process or prevent the defendant from accepting responsibility for drug use" or "counseling a defendant to disclose continued drug use in order to foster honesty and reduce the barriers to effective drug treatment").

171. See Nolan, supra note 57, at 1557 n.79 (quoting Hora & Schma, Therapeutic Jurisprudence, 82 Judicature 8, 10 (1998)).

172. Hora & Schma, supra note 77, at 508–11.

and whether the loss of constitutional and other protected rights will deprive the specialty court defendant of procedural justice. Indeed, practicing lawyers and some commentators continue to raise several issues and voice their apprehension about the legal representation that is provided in specialty courts. Their comments continue to raise the specter of diluted due process and procedural justice. Unfortunately, the danger inherent in these concerns is heightened if the emergence of specialty courts has shifted the paradigm upon which our criminal justice system operates.

A. Greater Concerns than Realized at First Review

In an important article that reinvigorated the debate on representation in drug courts, and by extension other specialized courts, Public Defender Mae Quinn advocated "pulling back on the reigns of the present high speed drug court movement."[173] Quinn reviewed one of the seminal articles written on the drug treatment court movement and evaluated several role markers of defense attorneys working in the therapeutic justice model.[174] She noted substantial concerns with each noted area of defense attorney action in specialty courts and argued that such concerns could not be dismissed. Quinn found that greater discussion was needed about the ethical and legal issues surrounding these new role markers for defense attorneys practicing in drug treatment courts.[175] Quinn's analysis yields more implications when considering whether the concerns regarding defense attorney practice in specialty courts are magnified or enhanced given the widespread acceptance of such a mode of court administrations.

For example, Quinn showed great concern for the notion that in order to enter a specialty treatment court, a defense attorney must counsel her client to waive important constitutional rights without knowing what the final outcome might be for the defendant.[176] Unlike a plea bargain, where the defendant knows what will happen because there has been a negotiated sentence, or where there are clear boundaries that limit a judge's options in sentencing the client, the defendant and defense attorney in a specialty court scenario do not know the results if the defendant fails treatment.[177] Looking through the results lens, therefore, the advice to the client about whether to enter the treatment court program is meaningless, or at the very least, uninformed.

The magnitude of this issue cannot be measured solely through an analysis of results. In the fictional scenario at the beginning of this article, the defense lawyer is in the same position: counseling a client to enter a specialized court program without having any idea as to the potential results for the client. The lawyer, however, is also counseling the client on this important decision without having adequate information about the client, the case, or the extent of the defendant's so-called problem. In this post-adjudication specialty court scenario, the attorney is incapable of fully explaining the rights that are waived when a defendant enters the specialty court.[178] From the interaction between this client and his attorney, it is clear the trepidation upon which the

---

173. Quinn, supra note 22, at 74.
174. Hora & Schma, supra note 77, at 38.
175. Quinn, supra note 22, at 73–74.
176. Quinn, supra note 22, at 73–74.
177. While jurisdictional differences exist in plea bargaining practices, in almost all situations when a defendant elects to waive his or her rights to trial and to remain silent, he or she knows what sentence will be handed down, or knows the range that the sentence might entail. This range results in a bargained for outcome, which is usually lower than the time that the defendant faces if she elects to proceed to trial.
178. See supra notes 119–121 and accompanying text (discussing pre-versus post-adjudication specialty courts).

decision to enter a treatment court rests. Many of a defendant's basic questions do not get answered because the decision to enter the treatment court must be made very quickly, often on the day of the first appearance in court or very shortly thereafter. At other times, the questions do not get answered because the attorney has developed a mode of practice in the specialty court that does not lend itself to further attorney-client interaction.

Some commentators theorize that the answer to this quandary is to allow for additional time before the defendant makes a decision to accept or deny the specialty court program.[179] Even allowing the additional time that some commentators believe sufficient — up to a couple of weeks — within which to make the decision, does not cure all the problems inherent in this scenario.[180] Looking at the need for more time, one to two weeks additional is just not enough time to: allow the attorney to make informed decisions about the strength of the case through investigating the facts, obtaining discovery, and filing motions; foster a strong relationship between attorney and client that rests upon a sense of trust; or permit the attorney to find out information about the client's background to determine the appropriateness of treatment. Undoubtedly, specialty court advocates, including judges and prosecutors, would balk at expanding the time even more, since immediate treatment is one of the main foundational principles behind therapeutic justice.[181]

Consequently, the defense attorney either has to leave the decision entirely to the client or counsel the client without any basis, as in our scenario.[182] Both courses of action create serious implications for the attorney-client relationship. The transactional trust that underlies the traditional adversarial defense attorney-client relationship may never develop, or where there was at least some predisposition by the defendant to trust the defense attorney by virtue of her position, it may be lost. The trust is replaced by a kind of indifference when a client enters a specialty court. The attorney may not ascertain the extent of the rights the defendant forfeits or may neglect to fully explain them to the defendant either out of a belief that it is not needed given the treatment focus of the specialty court, or that other professionals who are looking out for the defendant's best interests, such as case managers, will explain this and other important aspects to the defendant. Such a course is neither competent nor effective, and may violate ethical rules and render the assistance of counsel ineffective.[183]

---

179. See Jim Neuhard & Scott Wallace, National Legal Aid & Defender Association, Ten Tenets of Fair and Effective Problem Solving Courts (Jan. 1, 2002), available at http://www.nlada.org/DMS/Documents/1019501190.93/documentinfo. See generally Berman & Feinblatt, supra note 113.
180. See Berman & Feinblatt, supra note 113, at 12. Some specialty courts that are in operation, such as those in Seattle and Portland, give "defendants several weeks to test out treatment while their cases are still pending." Id. The client-defendants are then in a position to make an informed decision regarding the waiver of important rights after full consultation with and review of the case by their attorney. The defense attorney is able to investigate the case, evaluate the merits of any potential evidentiary challenges, and engage in some discovery before advising the client on entering the specialty court.
181. See supra note 69 and accompanying text.
182. See supra notes 4–11 and accompanying text.
183. Strickland v. Washington, 466 U.S. 668 (1984), sets the baseline standard for effective representation by defense counsel in criminal cases. Rule 1.4 of the Model Rules of Professional Conduct requires that a lawyer explain court matters to a client in order to permit the client to make informed decisions about their case and to consult with the client about the objects of the representation. This would include consultation about the merits of the case and the need and desire for treatment.

This very real danger cannot be explained away as an isolated example of the "shoddy practice effect," namely that negligent defense attorney practice is not endemic to the specialty court, but rather, is a response to specific poorly structured courts that can be cured by the use of best practices.[184] Several of Washington, D.C.'s specialty courts are concerned with the institution of best practices, although examples of such issues can be seen regularly in its Drug Court. For example, the Drug Court sets aside one to two days each week for new defendants to enter the program. On these days, the judge addresses all program entrants only after the court's case managers have found them to be eligible and the entrants have signed the appropriate waiver forms. Case managers ensure the entrant's eligibility to obtain waivers while interviewing the entrant outside the courtroom. However, no designated time exists for the court to call cases and because the court will often call cases without the defense attorney being present, the defense attorneys often do not attend the interview or court hearing.[185] During the interview, the defendant is asked to sign legal documents which may have constitutional implications, and is asked about the extent of their drug use.[186] Truthful answers to such questions may implicate Fifth Amendment protections against compelled self-incrimination. Such action may violate ethical rules because the attorney is not counseling the client as to a critical decision in the case. The decision is akin to determining whether to accept a guilty plea, to waive a trial by jury, or to testify; decisions, which under the rules, are exclusively left to the defendant.[187] It is one of the most important decisions a defendant can make in a criminal case and should be undertaken only upon full advice and consultation with counsel.

By allowing this practice to continue, and by silently approving unethical behavior by defense attorneys, judges, prosecutors, and court officials in Washington D.C.'s Drug Court and other specialty courts in that jurisdiction and around the country, we may be unwittingly approving a standard of practice that is unacceptable and which may set the standard for ineffective and unethical practice.[188]

---

184. Many specialty court advocates also point to the notion that best practices in these courts will be developed as a result of experiential learning, as more data and experience are gathered with these courts; then issues can be addressed by instituting new practices. This response is troubling because it lends credence to the position that specialty courts are an experiment in which human subjects' life and liberty depend upon untested, theoretical methods. Simon, supra note 5, at 1596; see also Spinak, supra note 51, 1620–21. As an additional matter, the crisis in indigent defense has been documented in many articles and a growing number of cases challenging the ability of defender systems to provide competent and adequate representation given excessive caseloads, nonexistent defender quality controls, and inadequate funding and remuneration for defenders. Bruce Green calls it a "national epidemic of neglect," that carries with it a real danger that economic disincentives exist resulting in indigent representation falling short of ethical and practice standards. See Bruce A. Green, Criminal Neglect: Indigent Defense from a Legal Ethics Perspective, 52 Emory L.J. 1169, 1184 (2003); see also Lisa J. McIntyre, The Public Defender: The Practice of Law in the Shadows of Repute (1987); Robert L. Spangenberg & Marea L. Beeman, Indigent Defense Systems in the United States, 58 Law & Contemp. Probs. 31, 35 (1995); The Southern Center for Human Rights, "If You Cannot Afford a Lawyer ...": A Report on Georgia's Indigent Defense System (Jan. 2003), available at http://www.schr.org/reports/docs/jan.%202003.%20report.pdf.

185. See Quinn, supra note 22, at 64–67 (criticizing Bronx Treatment Court's practice of going forward with status hearings without defense counsel's presence).

186. Among the constitutional rights that may be implicated include the right to a speedy trial and a jury, which a client may waive by agreeing to enter the treatment court program.

187. See Model Rules of Prof'l Conduct 1.2(a) & Cmts.

188. See Virginia Indigent Defense Commission, 2005 Annual Report Executive Summary, available at http://www.indigentdefense.virginia.gov/VaIDC%202005%20Annu al%20Report%20 Executive%20Summary.pdf; Indigent Defense Reports, Report of Chief Justice's Commission on Indigent Defense, Part 1, available at http://www.georgiacourts.org/aoc/press/idc/idchearings/idcrepor

Quinn also notes concern with the notion of collaboration and the team-player model in treatment courts.[189] Specialty court advocates equate the role of the defense attorney in specialty courts with that of the judge, prosecutor, and drug treatment professional. The defense lawyers, however, have no real power in the process. The defense lawyer does not make charging decisions, has no power to dismiss an unjust charge, and has no power to dismiss a charge after successful completion of treatment. The prosecutors retain these decisions and have a large role in system-wide decisions. These are decisions retained by the prosecutor, who has a greater role in decisions in the treatment court on a macro, or system-wide, and micro, or individual case, level.

One of the biggest decisions in the design and initial implementation of a specialty court is whether the court will employ a pre- or post-adjudication model.[190] Prosecutors have been particularly powerful in their ability to "persuade" judges and court officials that the new specialty court should only allow treatment after a defendant has entered a guilty plea. The prosecutors often argue that their ability to go forward on a case when a defendant fails in treatment after many months is compromised without a guilty plea. Their persuasion in this design process often amounts to a veto. Since the prosecutor has charging authority and is an independent branch of government, the court cannot force the prosecutor to allow a case to be dismissed, diverted, or held in abeyance until treatment or restitution is completed.

The veto power by the prosecution is just one example of the fallacy of the team-player mantra in specialty courts. The notion of a team, at least in this example, is one in which all players have an equally important role, voice, and input into the pursuit of a particular goal. This is not the case for the defender in the specialty court; the defender has no veto power during the design phase or thereafter.[191]

Even in those instances where an institutional defender is present at the design and implementation table, the concerns, suggestions, and questions that are brought forth may be weighed down against the momentum that drives the establishment of the specialty court. In other words, the driving forces behind these courts, or their initial laudable or other goals, sometimes do not include defenders and defender organizations in the coalitions of stakeholder groups that have substantial input in the design, formulation, and initial implementation of specialty courts.[192] Perhaps this phenomenon is a recognition by some judges, prosecutors, and other court officials of the very nature of

---

t.doc; see also Green, supra note 184, at 1178–85.

189. Quinn, supra note 22, at 56.

190. See supra note 75 and accompanying text.

191. Professor Spinak notes that defenders often feel as though their role in the creation and execution of specialty courts is unequal to other stakeholders in the system because they do not have the financial control that judges and prosecutors have, are less likely to speak with one voice concerning the specialty court, are skeptical that a cultural transformation is taking place in the way their clients' social issues are viewed, and are apprehensive that the specialty court will devolve into a more unjust system for their clients. See Spinak, supra note 51, at 1618–20.

192. See Jim Neuhard & Scott Wallace, National Legal Aid & Defender Association, Ten Tenets of Fair and Effective Problem Solving Courts intro.(Jan. 1, 2002), available at http://www.nlada.org/DMS/Documents/1019501190.93/document info. It appears, however, that some institutional defender organizations have influenced the design of drug treatment courts. See Nat'l Ass'n of Drug Court Professionals, A Level of Teamwork Not Often Seen: An Interview with Jeffrey S. Tauber (Nov.–Dec. 1997), available at http://www.nlada.org/DMS/Documents/998934264.745/Defenders%20in%20Drug%20Courts.doc#pitfalls. The same cannot be said for other types of specialty courts. See infra Part II.C.

the defense function in the criminal justice system, which is to defend and advocate on behalf of the individual and champion the accused's traditional rights. Under the traditional adversarial model, defending and advocating takes the form of resistance to government-imposed restrictions on liberty, way of life, or any part of self-determination. Some tension might appear when a defender is asked to take part in designing a system that institutionalizes automatic sanctions for defendants who violate conditions of treatment and does not allow defendants to challenge the sanctions or the parameters of the treatment. The extent to which the defenders' powerlessness leads to feelings of inadequacy of purpose and role is an interesting and compelling issue that specialty court advocates should study.[193]

Additionally, Quinn is concerned about the possibility that prosecutors will "dump" non-meritorious cases into treatment courts.[194] That is, cases that would not survive the normal adversarial process, like those vulnerable to a dismissal or motion to suppress, would be charged because in all likelihood the defendant would accept entry into the specialty court. Quinn argues that defense lawyers have little or no power to ensure that case dumping does not occur in jurisdictions using specialty courts.[195]

The case dumping issue that Quinn describes has further ramifications. Even before a prosecutor charges a non-meritorious case, the police may arrest an inordinate number of defendants simply because the specialty court exists. In other words, police discretion may send many defendants into the court adjudication process who normally may be diverted to other systems or not be arrested at all. For example, defendants who exhibit mental health issues when confronted by police officers may more likely be arrested and jailed, on the theory that they will end up in mental health court, than be sent to a locality's mental health system with its overwhelming delay and red tape that officers might have to endure.[196]

Judge Hoffman calls this phenomenon the "popcorn effect," whereby the existence of the specialty courts, specifically drug courts, cause "police to make arrests in" the types of cases that they would normally "not have bothered with."[197] Hoffman focuses on how the increased number of cases funneled through drug courts strains court staff and the docket, and theorizes that this strain on resources leads to "demoralized and ineffective drug courts."[198] Hoffman does not, however, address the issues raised by this problem for the delivery of defense services and the quality of defense representation.

Institutional defender services organizations have been inundated by an increase in the number of cases, particularly those with little to no merit. Caseloads will undoubtedly increase for institutional defender organizations and for individual attorneys who represent defendants through a court appointed voucher system. Institutional defender

---

193. Some Scholars have written about the various issues that might lead to defender burnout and disillusionment. See supra notes 4–11 and accompanying text; Abbe Smith, Too Much Heart and Not Enough Heat: The Short Life and Fractured Ego of the Empathic, Heroic Public Defender, 37 U.C. Davis L. Rev. 1203, 1211 (2005). See generally McIntyre, supra note 184; Paul B. Wice, Public Defenders and the American Justice System (2005).
194. See Quinn, supra note 22, at 58–59.
195. Quinn, supra note 22, at 58–59.
196. See National Mental Health Assoc., Position Statement: Mental Health Courts (Nov. 17, 2001), available at www.nmha.org/position/mentalhealthcourts.cfm.
197. Morris Hoffman, The Drug Court Scandal, 78 N.C. L. Rev. 1437, 1502–03 (2000). Judge Hoffman notes the major increase in the number of drug case filings after the establishment of the Denver Drug Court.
198. Id. at 1504–05.

organizations should be given additional resources to deal with the increased volume of cases, and court appointed systems should be restructured to allow for higher per-hour payments or additional lawyers to represent the increased number of defendants. Lawyers struggling to deal with the increased caseload may skimp on the quality of representation that they are able to provide.[199]

Mae Quinn notes that defenders may also cross an ethical line by having to "specially prepare" a client for an interview or testing by treatment counselors in order to gain admission into the program. Quinn implies that it is problematic for a defender to counsel a client to omit information that might lead a treatment program to reject a client. I, like many defenders, find no fault with "special" preparation of the client in such a circumstance, as it is similar to other special preparation that is essential to the functioning of the adversary process. Special preparation takes place in the context of plea bargaining and trial witness preparation for either side, as case strategy often requires that emphasis be placed on putting forward the best case possible.

While special preparation causes me no concern, the initial point raised by Judge Hora and others that Quinn finds inapplicable to her practice is compelling.[200] In some specialty courts, a defense attorney has the responsibility to prove that a defendant is in treatment, but at the same time, the defender has no power to prove what treatment is needed or to compel that treatment. Many specialized courts have procedures which require the defense attorney to request that a client be admitted to a specialty court according to specific guidelines. These guidelines can be rigid as they focus on a defendant's prior record, exposure to prior treatment, and need for treatment at the time of arrest or charging. Moreover, these guidelines may be dictated by the treatment services that are available to the specialty court. Some of these programs make defendants ineligible for the specialty court treatment if their problem is not deemed serious enough or if they have additional concurrent social problems, such as mental illness or homelessness. Drug treatment programs are often not equipped to deal with clients who are dually-diagnosed with mental health issues and substance abuse addictions. Without strong defense advocacy, defendants who fall into this category are often automatically rejected from a specialty court program. Strong defense advocacy may entail, among other things, zealous efforts to uncover the extent of the defendant's problem, challenges to the provision of services within the specialty court, and contesting the guidelines by which the specialty court operates.

Additionally, defense concern with the notion that they have to prove that a client needs treatment is justified by other scenarios. For example, in Washington, D.C.'s drug court defendants, who have only tested positive for drugs on one occasion, may not be eligible for entrance into drug court. The guidelines specify that a defendant demonstrate a history of substance abuse, and the drug treatment professionals associated with this particular drug court do not believe that one positive test provides an adequate indication of addiction. The defense lawyer may then find herself in a paradox: either counsel her client to continue the use of drugs again so that the client can test positive on a subsequent drug test and gain admission to the specialty court, or counsel the client to follow the law and conditions set by the judge and forego the treatment that the client might need and want. Even under the "best interests" mantra of specialty

---

199. In recent years much has been written about the effects of underfunding defender services and about the potential ethical problems that arise when defenders have overburdened caseloads. See Green, supra note 184, at 1180; see also supra notes 4–11 and accompanying text.

200. See Quinn, supra note 22, at 60–61.

court jurisprudence, this situation presents problems for a defender and is inconsistent with the stated goals of the specialty court movement.[201]

While this scenario presents a catch-22, it is not fictional. It is a real life situation that illustrates that the theory and rhetoric of specialty court advocates is often inconsistent with reality, especially as it pertains to the role of the defense attorney.

Quinn further points to the quandary in which well-meaning defenders may be placed, such as having to advise a client on whether to voluntarily agree to a treatment regime—one that may or may not be necessary and risky—or to take a shorter sentence in a plea bargain or after a guilty verdict at trial.[202] This very real quandary occurs all too often in specialty courts and places a defender at risk of violating ethical rules against advising clients based on insufficient information or investigation.

Although specialty court advocates argue that the defender is part of the team, such rhetoric if often disputed by reality. An additional concern in specialty courts is the right to status hearings and role of defense counsel at such hearings. As noted above, attorneys often are not present at the many status hearings that can occur during the life of a case in specialty court. Sometimes their absence is attributed to the standard operating procedures of the court as hearings are often called immediately to address violations by defendants. This is a precept of specialty courts: immediate reaction to violations or problems with treatment, with the goal of addressing the treatment issue to insure that a defendant can succeed in treatment. Specialty courts focus more on outcomes and pay less attention to the formality of process and notions of procedural justice, which are central goals of the provision of counsel in criminal proceedings.[203]

While Quinn's article was written almost five years ago, the high speed of the drug court movement that she cautioned against shows no signs of slowing down, and has even broadened its focus to include other courts as set forth above.[204] And while some discussion has focused on the defense role in specialty courts, including the extent and quality of the representation, the widespread nature of these courts raises even more issues regarding the new forced non-adversarial role of defense attorneys practicing in these courts.[205]

B. Treatment at Any Cost? Additional Issues that Plague the Forced Non-Adversarial Role of Defense Attorneys in Specialty Courts

Additional issues exist with respect to the new role of defense attorneys in the different court variations which embody principles of therapeutic and restorative justice. From a review of literature and my practice experience, I believe that questions still re-

---

201. This scenario is based on a case that was handled by the students in the Criminal Justice Clinic at Howard Law School. The client, who had no prior criminal record, was arrested and charged with possession of heroin. During the initial processing before arraignment, the client was drug tested and admitted to a long-term addiction to heroin. Even though the drug test results were positive and the client requested to go into the drug treatment court program, he was denied admission because there was no history of drug abuse. The treatment court had defined a history to include multiple positive drug tests. Although the student attorneys pushed for an exception to the treatment court guidelines, the client was not allowed to enter the program and eventually pled guilty pursuant to a plea bargain.
202. See Quinn, supra note 22, at 60–61.
203. Judith S. Kaye, Making the Case for Hands-On Courts, Newsweek, Oct. 13, 1999, at 13.
204. Hoffman, Therapeutic Jurisprudence, supra note 7, at 2071; see Quinn, supra note 22, at 74 (discussing high speed drug court movement).
205. See National Drug Court Institute, Critical Issues for Defense Attorneys in Drug Court 1 (Apr. 2003), available at http://www.ndci.org/CriticalIssues.pdf.

main on the issue of whether the changed defense attorney role in specialty courts can provide zealous, effective, and competent representation to defendants.

1. Prosecutors Remain Adversarial

Conventional wisdom dictates that the prosecutor's job is to seek justice and not just win cases. The reality is, at times, different. With respect to a host of issues in the criminal justice system, prosecutors "hold the cards" and retain greater power than their counterparts in the defense bar.[206] Some might argue their power exceeds that of judges.[207] This very often holds true in the context of specialized courts.[208] While the mantra of specialized courts is that prosecutors and defenders have to shed their traditional adversarial roles and work together as a team in the best interests of the defendant, the reality is that prosecutors in specialty courts still retain many vestiges of adversarial lawyering. Even though specialty court advocates might insist to the contrary, instances of adversarial prosecuting abound in the various incarnations of specialty courts.

During the initial design and development phase of a specialty court, when prosecution representatives require that pleas of guilty be instituted as a precondition of treatment, i.e., requiring that a jurisdiction embrace a post-adjudication model, they are acting as an adversary protective of its position in the controversy.[209] The prosecutors argue for a post-adjudication model in order to protect their ability to go forward with prosecution should a defendant fail in treatment. As treatment often lasts many months up to a full year, prosecutors are concerned that they will lose witnesses and evidence should a case linger for an extended period of time. They are concerned with winning the case, a concept inconsistent with justice in the therapeutic model. Justice in therapeutic jurisprudence is tied to the defendant's success in the proscribed treatment program. Specialty court advocates, however, overlook the adversarialism that prosecutors espouse even at the initial stage of the process. Defenders are very cognizant of this issue, and their anxiety as to the benefit and longevity of specialty courts seems justified.

Moreover, a good number of these courts will only allow the defendant to enter treatment if the prosecution consents.[210] In determining whether to consent, prosecutors look at more than just the need for treatment or whether the defendant meets the program's previously set guidelines. Prosecutors often take into account prior criminal history (whether charged or uncharged), the desires of people in the community or law enforcement officers familiar with the defendant, factors surrounding the particular factual allegations, such as the crime rate in the neighborhood where the crime took place, and whether denying consent will provide leverage in some other matter, such as encouraging cooperation. With respect to the last factor, the action by the prosecution is both highly adversarial and not the least concerned with the best interests of the defendant. In such an instance, the "teamwork" between the prosecution and defense

---

206. See Margareth Etienne, The Ethics of Cause Lawyering: An Experienced Examination of Criminal Defense Lawyers as Cause Lawyers, 95 Crim. L & Criminology 1195, 1235 (2005) (citing interview with attorney who felt powerless against federal prosecutors).
207. Consider, for example, the relationship with the grand jury, the use of police and other resources, the force of charging decisions, and their political power.
208. Casey, supra note 7, at 1518.
209. See supra note 75 and accompanying text (describing post-adjudication model).
210. Some specialty courts allow the prosecution to designate which treatment options will be available to a defendant.

closely resembles plea bargaining, a classic example of traditional adversarial lawyering.[211]

Defense lawyers may be properly concerned with the notion that they must change their way of doing business, while other actors in specialty courts are still conducting business as usual. This can lead to frustration and the sense that defenders have no voice in the process, or when they do participate, that their voice is not heard. This is similar to the frustration that is often cited as a contributing factor in the movement toward specialty courts.[212] Motivation and job satisfaction are important in maintaining quality defense representation, particularly in the context of indigent criminal defense.[213] However, a very real danger exists that this satisfaction and motivation cannot occur in specialty courts.

2. Getting the Treatment and Bearing the Burden: Poor and Minority Populations in Specialty Courts

Statistics from drug courts indicate that the overwhelming majority of clients in this variation of specialty courts are poor and working class people who belong to minority groups. n[214] This may be explained, in part, by the historical evidence tending to show that law enforcement drug initiatives more frequently target urban areas where larger communities of color and poor people reside.[215] Therefore, since there are more drug arrests among these populations, minorities and poor persons represent a large percentage of the individuals assigned to specialty courts. It is "almost inevitable" that individuals from these groups who have drug problems, or who fit the criteria for adjudication in other specialty courts, will also more acutely face any problems that are inherent in such courts, including the danger of inadequate defense representation.[216] This danger has been recognized by prominent specialty court advocates. In its 2001 Resolution Regarding Indigent Defense in Drug Courts, the Board of Directors of the National Association of Drug Court Professionals noted that "the lack of national guidance regarding the role of defenders in drug court has led to wide disparities in defense services, and hence in the quality of justice, particularly for low income people who have no choice in the lawyer assigned to them...."[217]

For this reason, specialty courts must address the perceived or real danger of inadequate representation. An effective system of criminal adjudication must be measured by the adequacy of justice received by the most powerless in the community.

---

211. In the classic case of plea bargaining, the government attorney will make a plea offer that takes into account, from a partisan perspective, the defendant's record, the strength of the government's case, ramifications for future criminality, and the interests of the victim. The defense will evaluate the offer based upon the strength of the government and defense cases, the client's wishes, and the potential sentence that the client will receive, among other things.

212. The lawyers may feel as if their role in the justice system has no meaning, that they are just a cog in the assembly line of justice. See supra note 10 and accompanying text.

213. Charles Ogletree, Beyond Justifications: Seeking Motivations to Sustain Public Defenders, *106 Harv. L. Rev. 1239, 1240–42 (1993).*

214. See McCoy, supra note 5, at 1531.

215. National Drug Court Institute, Critical Issues for Defense Attorneys in Drug Court 33 (Apr. 2003), available at http://www.ndci.org/CriticalIssues.pdf; see also Nat'l Ass'n of Drug Court Professionals, A Level of Teamwork Not Often Seen: An Interview with Jeffrey S. Tauber (Nov.–Dec. 1997), available at http://www.nlada.org/DMS/Documents/998934264.745/Defenders%20in%20 Drug%20Courts.doc#pitfalls.

216. Supra note 215.

217. Board of Directors of the National Association of Drug Court Professionals, Resolution Regarding Indigent Defense in Drug Courts (Apr. 19, 2002) [hereinaver NADCP Resolution], available at http://www.nlada.org/DMS/Documents/1019595446.68.

3. Economic Disincentives to Zealous Representation

The method of defender appointment in specialty courts impacts the defender role and effects the zealousness and competence of these attorneys. In a significant number of jurisdictions where specialty courts operate and institutional defender agencies are not charged with representation in all indigent cases, individual judges routinely appoint defenders to cases that come before them. These appointments are made for a myriad of reasons. In some instances, there is a list from which the judge can randomly or purposefully choose. In others, the reasoning boils down to a matter of convenience. If the judge is acquainted with a particular lawyer who is present in the courtroom, then she may be appointed because it is the easiest solution. With court appointments, judges, who may be staunch advocates of the specialty court jurisprudence, have an additional level of power over the defender role in specialty courts. The judge, who feels that overzealous representation will bog down the process of treatment and the efficiency of the specialty court, has an additional economic power over a defender's practice.[218] For example, the lawyer that contests a sanction, argues for a different course of treatment, or vocally disagrees with any procedure in the specialty court may not be appointed by the judge on subsequent occasions. In smaller jurisdictions, such economic power can have a substantial effect on the quality of defender representation. This economic disincentive to zealous advocacy could have wide ranging effects on the quality of representation provided in specialty courts.

Part VI. Proposed Solutions For the Provision of Defense Services in Specialty Courts

"The question isn't: Gosh, are courts supposed to be doing this? It's: What are you going to do about it? How does it fit in? It's no longer a question of whether this should have been invented. They're here."[219]

While it remains to be seen whether specialty courts will continue or whether they represent the paradigm shift some have noted, there is a growing sense that the problems and issues that have been noted by many scholars and practitioners, especially with regard to the defense role, must be studied, evaluated, and addressed cautiously.[220] As such, there must be more and more consideration of not only the theoretical foundations of this new system of jurisprudence or the rhetorical statements of what these courts wish to do, but more importantly, the practical issues that are raised every day in these types of courts. Court reformers, judges, lawyers, and scholars have to be concerned with real solutions and modifications to address any inequalities, injustices, and ethical or practice issues. At this juncture in the life of specialty court jurisprudence, some modifications can be implemented to make sure that the real and perceived non-zealous representation does not blossom into a blight on the nation's specialty courts. The following proposals seek to counteract this danger.

A. Institutionalize Adversarialism into the Defender's Role

Many have called for defense attorneys in specialty courts to continue the tradition of zealous advocacy. Some have likened advocacy in these courts to the traditional model of

---

218. See Smith, supra note 2, at 129 n.250. Even in non-specialty courts, the fee maximums and low hourly rates for court appointed attorneys cause a crisis in access to justice and the quality of lawyering.

219. Berman & Feinblatt, supra note 113, at 14 (quoting from Greg Berman, What is a Traditional Judge Anyway?: Problem Solving in the State Courts, Judicature, Sept–Oct. 2000, at 78–85 (quoting John Goldkamp)).

220. See McCoy, supra note 5, at 1515; Quinn, supra note 22, at 73–74.

advocacy at the sentencing stage.[221] It is not sufficient, however, to attempt to provide zealous, effective advocacy within the drug court model as these writers suggest, since the structure and operation of the specialty courts frustrate this notion.[222] Rather, it is necessary to change the model that is in existence in most specialty courts today.

If specialty courts are truly experiential and best practices are developed as experience deepens, then it is time to try something new with respect to the defender's role in specialty courts. The issues that have been raised by defenders show no signs of dissipating. If additional variations on problem solving courts continue to develop, the issues will blossom even more. If not addressed, the movement toward specialty court jurisprudence will never achieve full legitimacy.[223]

If prosecutors retain many vestiges of adversarialism, and the judge is a central figure with the power to direct the treatment provided in the specialty court, then there is no good reason for the defender to remain in this category of "forced non-adversarialism."[224] In fact, such an imbalance of power in the specialty court is troubling and may lead to further issues of defense inadequacy. Moreover, the therapeutic and restorative goals of specialty courts can still be accomplished with the traditional model of adversarial defense representation. Since there would still be the provision of treatment and interaction with the judge regarding treatment, the central principles of the specialty court would be met.[225]

Additionally, an adversarial defender is an untapped resource for therapeutic justice in the specialty court context. In conjunction with treatment, which focuses on a particular problem and restoration of some parties, the adversarial defender, who is seen by his client as insuring the individualized fairness of the process, can have a real impact on satisfaction with the court outcome, acceptance of the result, and empowerment of the client. At the very least, a healthy attorney-client relationship compliments the goal of treating the client's social problems. Empowerment of the client, whether through a sense of procedural fairness or because of a relationship with an attorney, can help to lift self-esteem and self-worth. These traits aid the client in recovery from addiction and other social maladies.[226]

---

221. See Clarke & Neuhard, supra note 20, at 35.
222. See Robert Burke, Reconciling Drug Court Participation with Defender Ethical Standards, Indigent Defense, Nov.–Dec. 1997, available at http://www.nlada.org/DMS/Documents/998934264.745/Defenders%20in%20Drug%20Courts.doc#Reconciling.
223. See Casey, supra note 7, at 1503–04.
224. See supra note 24 and accompanying text (discussing adversarial nature of court system); supra note 100 and accompanying text; Quinn, supra note 22; see also Smith, supra note 2, at 136.
225. Judge Hardcastle notes many practical advantages of the general adversary process which also benefit the specialty court. Judge Hardcastle specifically recognizes that if the court encourages and allows the defender to advocate more for the client, the specialty court process is more likely to reflect the truth because the judge garners more contextual and relevant information regarding the defendant and her treatment issues. In instances where the defendant has limited knowledge about the legal process, an adversarial defender in a specialty court could assist the defendant in effectively completing treatment and complying with court orders. The specialty court itself could realize cost savings by putting in place a systems whereby the defender could investigate a particular form of treatment or action. An adversarial defender also guarantees that the court operates on credible information from outside agencies or team members that make representations to the court. See Hardcastle, supra note 24, at 65–67.
226. Client-centered lawyering as an approach to the attorney-client relationship has been noted to enhance client autonomy, self-esteem, and empowerment. See generally David A. Binder & Susan C. Price, Legal Interviewing and Counseling: A Client-Centered Approach (1977); Katherine R. Kruse, Fortress in the Sand: The Plural Values of Client Centered Representation, *12 Clinical L. Rev.* 369 (2006).

In specialty courts, therefore, the everyday model of a defender should be one who is zealous, competent, and effective. No matter what the guidelines, eligibility requirements, or rules of the specialty court, defenders should be trained always to: ask for more time to determine if the defendant wishes to enter the treatment program; file any appropriate motions while in treatment court, including motions to dismiss or suppress evidence; challenge the level or extent of treatment if seemingly inappropriate or unworkable for the client; file and assert due process challenges against the imposition of sanctions; argue the substantive inappropriateness of sanctions; thoroughly investigate the factual allegations of the case, with no time bar; and intervene when the judge seeks to illicit incriminating or secret and confidential statements from the client. Such zealous advocacy will not frustrate the goals of the specialty court, but will potentially increase its effectiveness because these actions by defenders will have system-wide beneficial implications. For example, if law enforcement groups understand that abusive and illegal police practices are still challenged in the specialty court, then they might abandon the use of the specialty court as a dumping ground for non-meritorious cases. Additionally, prosecutors might be more careful in determining what cases to bring and which cases to divert completely from the criminal justice system, thereby reducing the number of non-meritorious cases on the specialty court docket. Moreover, specialty court stakeholders, including prosecutors, case managers, and judges, should be trained that when a defender is adversarial and advocates for the rights and wishes of her client, it does not detract from the potential benefit of providing treatment, when appropriate, to a client.

B. Additional Training for Defenders in Specialty Courts

Many scholars and practitioners have called for increased financial resources in order to upgrade the level of practice for indigent defenders.[227] In the context of specialty courts, both institutional defender agency attorneys and private bar attorneys should be trained thoroughly on all aspects of the treatment court, including the science of addiction, therapeutic and restorative justice principles, procedural and substantive due process, "available treatment programs and sanctions, client assessment tools, treatment cycles and methodologies, and ... the court's documentation and processes."[228] Additionally, attorneys should receive training in basic ethics and practice standards, trial and courtroom skills, and legal writing. Only with adequate education and training can we expect to elevate the level of practice in specialty courts.

Requiring such additional training will not be cost prohibitive for court systems because it may only require more ingenuity on the part of specialty court administrators to seek out such training resources and to enter into collaborative agreements with outside providers of such training. Treatment providers that have existing contracts with specialty courts, treatment affinity groups—such as the American Psychiatric Association, the National Mental Health Association, or the National Drug Court Institute—as well as local bar associations or law schools, could be utilized to specifically train defense attorneys.

---

227. See Jim Neuhard & Scott Wallace, National Legal Aid & Defender Association, Ten Tenets of Fair and Effective Problem Solving Courts (Jan. 1, 2002), available at http://www.nlada.org/DMS/Documents/1019501190.93/document info; Quinn, supra note 22, at 74.

228. See Burke, supra note 222; NADCP Resolution, supra note 217 (stating "inclusion and training of private counsel appointed to represent indigent defendants in drug court is necessary, particularly in jurisdictions which do not have an institutional public defense entity"); see also, Simon, supra note 5, at 1605.

C. Make Real Changes to the System for Appointment of Counsel

As noted above, judges can assert economic power by controlling the appointments that private attorneys receive in specialty courts. This can chill the zealous advocacy that a lawyer should provide to his client.[229] To combat this possibility or perception, specialty courts should not allow individual judges to appoint lawyers, nor should the court use only a small cadre of attorneys to represent defendants in the particular specialty court. Use of a central lottery appointments process and a system of vertical representation will lessen the impact of economic disincentive to zealous representation.[230]

D. Incorporate a Dual Track System for Specialty Court Cases

Specialty court clients should have the opportunity to contest illegal and abusive police conduct and to assert their innocence at trial without the loss of needed treatment services. In order to accomplish this, cases in which the client wishes to contest the allegations against her should remain on a traditional calendar for normal case adjudication and should, at the same time, proceed on the specialty court calendar where the defendant can receive treatment and services. The specialty court should refrain from any action that will impair the defendant's rights when contesting the case. Court rules should be amended to forbid eliciting incriminatory statements in court and using such statements in any prosecutions.

Many will argue that a dual track is costly for local court systems. This, however, remains to be seen. I suspect that over time, because of less case dumping, smaller numbers of cases in which real, substantive issues are raised will be litigated in the traditional docket and remain on the specialty court docket. The defendant will still be able to receive needed services that may affect her life and potential for life change and benefit.

E. Evaluate and Study the Perception of Defender Role Among Specialty Court Clients

The necessity and value of the criminal defender to our legal system is significant. Even those scholars who question and challenge our current adversarial system and the overzealousness of some advocates recognize the importance of the criminal defender, particularly one who provides indigent defense services.[231] The ability of the attorney-client relationship to transform perceptions about the legal system, improve satisfaction with its outcomes, and boost acceptance of its dispositions is substantial and important in both traditional and specialty courts. To clarify the defender's role in specialty courts, court systems and non-profit agencies require more empirical data. Accordingly, they should study defenders', victims', and witnesses' perceptions of lawyering. Additionally, they should examine the effect defense lawyering roles, strategies, and skills have on client decision-making and satisfaction with the process.

F. Conclusion

I am not the first to call for caution in the entrenchment of the methodology and theory of specialty courts in the criminal justice system. Indeed, several authors have noted that the subject demands more discussion, study, and evaluation. If the recent emergence of variations on the drug court model signals a paradigm shift in our sys-

---

229. See Green, supra note 184, at 1178–81 (discussing fees paid to court appointed attorneys and economic incentive to quickly handle numerous cases).

230. See Lisa Schreiberdorf, The Pitfalls of Defenders as "Team Players", Indigent Defender, Nov.–Dec. 1997, available at http://www.nlada.org/DMS/Documents/998934264.745/Defenders%20in%20Drug%20Courts.doc#Pitfalls.

231. Simon, supra note 5, at 1607–08.

tem's administration of cases, then the way criminal defenders practice may also shift. We must remain aware of how such a change in defender practice might imperil our legal system and the cultural and impact-setting effect of silent approval of ineffective, under-zealous, and unethical practice. Because defenders are crucial to the principle of justice in all judicial settings, courts must be vigilant about the reality of the defender role and the quality of defender services in emerging models of justice.

B. Critique of TJ Lawyering Itself: A Conversation with a Critic

i. Mae C. Quinn,[*] An RSVP to Professor Wexler's Warm Therapeutic Jurisprudence Invitation to the Criminal Defense Bar: Unable to Join You, Already (Somewhat Similarly) Engaged

(Reprinted with permission from
48 Boston College Law Review 539, 2007)

Abstract: This Article responds to Professor David B. Wexler's recent suggestion that adopting Therapeutic Jurisprudence ("TJ") principles to create a new type of "rehabilitative" defense lawyer could improve the criminal defense bar. Contrary to the empirical foundation of the therapeutic justice movement, many of his proposed changes seem unsubstantiated. Others, such as calls for creative plea bargaining, are already part of the practice of quality defense attorneys. The "rehabilitative," TJ defense lawyer may be overly paternalistic, imposing his interpretation of the facts and his standards of appropriate behavior on the accused; such a lawyer also may not comport with express ethical standards. Instead, the tradition of zealous and quality advocacy, whether in a law school clinic or in a public defender's office, best serves the interests of defendants.

---

[*] © 2007, Mae C. Quinn, Associate Professor of Law, University of Tennessee College of Law (*mquinn3@utk.edu*). For offering tremendously helpful comments on this Article, I am most grateful to my colleagues Dwight Aarons, Ben Barton, Jerry Black, Doug Blaze, Joe Cook, Tom Davies, Iris Goodwin, Jennifer Hendricks, Glenn Reynolds, Dean Rivkin, Otis Stephens, and Paula Williams. Monroe Freedman, Kate Kruse, Paul Marcus, Michael Perlin, Jane Spinak, Tony Thompson, and Bruce Winick also were most kind to provide their thoughts and feedback. My deep appreciation is extended to Randy Hertz for organizing the first New York University Law School Clinical Writers Workshop, facilitating the Workshop's Criminal Practice Group, and introducing me to my fellow participants Adele Bernhardt, Lily Camet, and Kimberly Thomas, who, along with Professor Hertz, have provided important insights on earlier drafts. I also wish to thank the Southeastern Association of Law Schools ("SEALS") for allowing me to present an earlier version of this paper as part of the 2006 New Scholars Workshop; my SEALS mentor, Professor Arnold Lowey; fellow SEALS presenters Judith Barger, Adam Gershowitz, and Corinna Lain; and panel attendees, including my colleagues Joan Heminway, George Kuney, Donna Luper, Carol Parker, Tom Plank, and Greg Stein. Nick Zolkowski and Tara Wyllie provided excellent research assistance. Special thanks go to Laura Rosenbury for her ideas on RSVP etiquette, and of course, David Wexler, for offering the invitation in the first place, reading and commenting on a draft of this piece, and offering his continuing support of my work.

Introduction

For nearly two decades, Professors David B. Wexler and Bruce J. Winick have considered, written about, and advocated a particular way to study law—one that explicitly considers the therapeutic impact of legal rules, procedures, and processes on those they affect. This distinct approach to the law, which has garnered significant support over the years, has been called the Therapeutic Jurisprudence ("TJ") movement. Although the movement grew out of the mental health law arena and concern for the law's treatment of the mentally ill, its scope has expanded to other substantive areas. It has also moved from being a school of thought largely rooted in theory to an affirmative reform effort that advocates a particular means of delivering justice in our courts. Most recently, the TJ movement and its reform efforts have turned to criminal law and practice. And most significantly, from this author's perspective, it has set its sights on the unique work of criminal defense lawyers and students in law school criminal defense clinics. As this Article explains, however, this facet of the TJ movement presents serious implications for the modern justice system.

As part of a recent law school symposium entitled *Therapeutic Jurisprudence in Clinical Legal Education and Legal Skills Training*, Professor Wexler extended a "warm invitation" to "several communities," including the criminal defense bar and clinical professors, to join him in the TJ movement.[1] His invitation asks those communities to unite to recognize explicitly a special kind of criminal defense practitioner—the "TJ criminal defense lawyer"—and to contribute to an agenda of research, writing, teaching, and practice to foster this "new" role.[2] As described by Professor Wexler, TJ defense attorneys would serve as therapeutic "change agents" within the justice system to actively encourage clients to rehabilitate themselves, modify behaviors, and ultimately change their lives.[3] As a clinician and former public defender, and in the interest of contributing to the ongoing TJ conversation, I write to respond to Professor Wexler.[4]

I share some of Professor Wexler's concerns about the provision of quality legal representation in this country. I fear, however, that extending TJ principles to criminal defense practice and law school clinic work in the ways he suggests goes too far in pressing the limits of this still very much evolving school of thought. Indeed, doing so may negatively affect our legal system. This new practice-based "dimension" of TJ seems to depart significantly from TJ proponents' prior claim that TJ "is merely a 'lens' designed to shed light on interesting and normative issues relating to the therapeutic impact of the

---

1. David B. Wexler, *Therapeutic Jurisprudence and the Rehabilitative Role of the Criminal Defense Lawyer*, 17 St. Thomas L. Rev. 743, 746 (2005) [hereinafter Wexler, *Rehabilitative Role*]. Professor Wexler's article is an extension of earlier work that sought to expand TJ's application to criminal defense practice. Most notably, it builds upon themes Professor Winick raised in *Redefining the Role of the Criminal Defense Lawyer at Plea Bargaining and Sentencing: A Therapeutic Jurisprudence/Preventative Law Model*, 5 Psychol. Pub. Pol'y & L. 1034 (1999). Professors Wexler and Winick have continued to develop these ideas in further writings. *See generally* David B. Wexler, *Some Reflections on Therapeutic Jurisprudence and the Practice of Criminal Law*, 38 Crim. L. Bull. 205 (2002); Bruce J. Winick & David B. Wexler, *The Use of Therapeutic Jurisprudence in Law School Clinical Education: Transforming the Criminal Law Clinic*, 13 Clinical L. Rev. 605 (2006).
2. *See* Wexler, *Rehabilitative Role*, *supra* note 1, at 746–47.
3. *See id.*
4. Professor Wexler has, in turn, responded to my RSVP. David B. Wexler, *Not Such a Party Pooper: An Attempt to Accommodate (Many of) Professor Quinn's Concerns About Therapeutic Jurisprudence Criminal Defense Lawyering*, 48 B.C. L. Rev. 597 (2007). The Boston College Law Review has been kind enough to permit me a few pages at the end of this Article to offer my thoughts on Professor Wexler's response. See infra notes 252–270 and accompanying text.

law ... [and] does not itself provide any of the answers."[5] In fact, Professor Wexler's invitation clearly offers what is supposed to be a correct answer to the question of how lawyers and law school clinics should deliver criminal defense services—using the TJ criminal defense model.[6] Unfortunately, however, this model not only runs the risk of displacing existing defense and clinical community values, but may well conflict with ethical and legal mandates for defense attorneys.

Part I of this Article recounts the development of the TJ movement by Professors Wexler and Winick, its concern with the law's therapeutic and antitherapeutic consequences, and the movement's expansion from the mental health context and the world of theory to other substantive areas of law and the world of practice.[7] In Part II, I outline Professor Wexler's proposal to extend TJ's application to the field of criminal defense work, and his invitation to practitioners and clinicians to join him in promoting a TJ-focused criminal defense bar, whose members would act as therapeutic "change agents" within the legal system and view client rehabilitation as a core value.[8] In Part III, I consider and examine Professor Wexler's invitation, focusing on the occasion (specifically, the advent of a new kind of defense bar), the menu of best practices it offers, and the list of invitees who have been asked to participate.[9]

As Part III explains, although I am intrigued by Professor Wexler's TJ ideas and agree in several respects with his observations about the criminal justice system, I fear that his current call to action is somewhat misguided.[10] On the one hand, many of the TJ practices Professor Wexler urges are wholly consistent with current conceptions of good defense lawyering.[11] On the other hand, some of the new ideas and practices suggested for TJ defense representation seem to be based upon faulty assumptions about current defense practices, raise serious normative questions, and present a host of legal and ethical concerns for defense attorneys and law clinic students alike.[12] TJ defense representation, then, is no panacea for the problems facing our criminal justice system.

Thus, despite the warmth with which it was extended, and my respect for his well-meaning call to action, I feel the need to decline Professor Wexler's invitation to join him in acknowledging a brand new model of practitioner—the TJ criminal defense lawyer—or to foster development of this special breed of attorney. Rather, as the Conclusion of this Article indicates, I will continue with my prior (somewhat similar) engagement of striving to provide good old-fashioned "zealous" and "quality" criminal defense representation, and encouraging my students to do the same.[13]

---

5. David B. Wexler & Bruce J. Winick, *Patients, Professionals, and the Path of Therapeutic Jurisprudence: A Response to Petrila*, in Law in a Therapeutic Key: Developments in Therapeutic Jurisprudence 707, 708 (David B. Wexler & Bruce J. Winick eds., 1996).
6. *See* Wexler, *Rehabilitative Role*, *supra* note 1, at 773–74.
7. *See infra* notes 14–55 and accompanying text.
8. *See infra* notes 56–133 and accompanying text.
9. *See infra* notes 134–250 and accompanying text.
10. *See infra* notes 134–250 and accompanying text.
11. *See infra* notes 134–149 and accompanying text.
12. *See infra* notes 150–172 and accompanying text.
13. *See* Nat'l Legal Aid & Defender Ass'n, Performance Guidelines for Criminal Defense Representation Guideline 1.1 (1997); *see also infra* note 251 and accompanying text.

I. TJ Theory: Evolution of a Movement[14]

In the 1970s, Professors Wexler and Winick became interested in "the interplay of law and psychology" in "the then nascent field of mental health law."[15] Some of their early work explored the tension between society's interest in controlling the behaviors of those seen as deviant because of mental health problems—for instance by way of civil commitment—and the often conflicting individual interests of mentally ill persons.[16] They expressed concern that the desire to use scientifically based treatments to address mental illness had the potential to eclipse other societal values, such as individual autonomy and personal freedom.[17] Thus, they cautioned against permitting "therapeutic efficacy" to trump all other considerations in mental health law.[18]

Over time, however, Professors Wexler and Winick shifted their focus in the mental health arena.[19] Indeed, they began asking whether mental health law, particularly in light of the expansion of client procedural rights and protections, was doing enough to meet clients' clinical needs.[20] They claimed that they still "applauded" mental health law's "civil libertarian" focus, but wondered if it was now failing to draw sufficiently from the behavioral sciences.[21]

Specifically, Professors Wexler and Winick feared that mental health law potentially harmed clients more than helped them by promoting "psychological dysfunction" rather than psychological wellbeing.[22] Such harm, they opined, could result from the

---

14. Attempting to provide a summary of the TJ movement's teachings is a daunting task. Professors Wexler and Winick's writings on the topic span many years and comprise thousands of pages of books, medical journals, and law reviews. *See infra* note 38 and accompanying text. Moreover, it is always challenging to summarize accurately others' views. This is especially true here because some TJ claims have been described as presenting conceptual dilemmas, and, at least to this reader, appear to conflict in a number of respects. *See* Christopher Slobogin, *Therapeutic Jurisprudence: Five Dilemmas to Ponder*, in Law in a Therapeutic Key, *supra* note 5, at 763, 766. Thus, the reader will note my extensive use of direct quotations in an attempt to convey as accurately as possible Professors Wexler and Winick's proposals and suggestions. I have also done my best throughout this Article to reconcile, for purposes of synopsis, what appear to be competing TJ claims, noting potential significant inconsistencies where relevant. I hope that this overview of TJ, particularly given my genuine attempts to grapple with its various teachings, is accepted in the light in which it is offered and not received as a personal indictment or characterized as a misinterpretation of the work. *See* Wexler & Winick, *supra* note 5, at 707 (arguing that in his review of their book, *Essays in Therapeutic Jurisprudence*, Professor John Petrila "puts words in [their] mouths and critiques [them] for writing a book [they] did not (and would not) write").
15. David B. Wexler & Bruce J. Winick, *Introduction* to Essays in Therapeutic Jurisprudence, at ix, ix (David B. Wexler & Bruce J. Winick eds., 1991).
16. *See* David B. Wexler, Mental Health Law: Major Issues 11–57 (1981).
17. *Id.* at 29–31; *see* David B. Wexler, *Therapeutic Jurisprudence and the Culture of Critique*, in Practicing Therapeutic Jurisprudence: Law as a Helping Profession 449, 452–53 (Dennis P. Stolle, David B. Wexler & Bruce J. Winick eds., 2000).
18. Wexler, *supra* note 16, at 29–31; *see* David B. Wexler, *Therapeutic Justice*, 57 Minn. L. Rev. 289, 313 (1972) (stating that "it should be clear that the eradication of deviance ought not be society's superseding goal").
19. Bruce J. Winick, Therapeutic Jurisprudence Applied: Essays on Mental Health Law 12 (1997) ("What can be called the first stage of mental health law was heavily influenced by the civil rights movement and the Warren Court era's developments in the areas of criminal procedure and prisoners' rights.").
20. David B. Wexler, *An Introduction to Therapeutic Jurisprudence*, in Therapeutic Jurisprudence: The Law as a Therapeutic Agent 3, 3 (David B. Wexler ed., 1990).
21. *Id.* at 3–4.
22. David B. Wexler, *An Introduction to Therapeutic Jurisprudence*, in Essays in Therapeutic Jurisprudence, *supra* note 15, at 17, 19–23.

application of substantive laws, procedures employed in courts, or the very roles played by judges and lawyers in mental health proceedings.[23] For instance, substantive rules that give individuals the right to refuse treatment might inhibit the underlying therapeutic aims of mental health law.[24] Commitment hearings, although intended to ensure that mentally ill clients receive treatment, might exacerbate clients' conditions by subjecting them to stress and embarrassment during the legal process.[25] Judges and lawyers, too, might individually behave in ways that undermine therapy goals.[26] Such consequences might be "antitherapeutic" for the very individuals mental health law was intended to assist.

Thus, Wexler and Winick instructed that we should "be sensitive to those consequences" and "ask whether [they] can be reduced, and [the law's] therapeutic consequences be enhanced, without subordinating due process and other justice values."[27] As they stated elsewhere, the law's "positive and negative consequences [should] be studied with the tools of the behavioral sciences, and ... consistent with considerations of justice and other relevant normative values ... [should] be reformed to minimize anti-therapeutic consequences and to facilitate achievement of therapeutic ones."[28]

This way of thinking formed the basis for "Therapeutic Jurisprudence," or "TJ"—the school of thought that Professors Wexler and Winick established around 1990.[29] Thus, TJ's initial underlying premise was "that mental health law would better serve society if major efforts were undertaken to study, and improve, the role of law as a therapeutic agent."[30] It sought, therefore, "to reorient the field of mental health law to better

---

23. *Id.* at 24–35; *see also* Winick, *supra* note 19, at 4. Winick notes:
   Once it is understood that rules of substantive law, legal procedures, and the roles of various actors in the legal system such as judges and lawyers have either positive or negative effects on the health and mental health of the people they affect, the need to assess these therapeutic consequences ... thus emerges as an important objective in any sensible law reform effort. Winick, *supra* note 19, at 4.
24. *See* Wexler, *supra* note 22, at 24–30; *see also* Winick, *supra* note 19, at 67–91 (examining the therapeutic and antitherapeutic implications of the right to refuse mental health treatment).
25. *See* Wexler, *supra* note 22, at 30–32; *see also* David B. Wexler & Bruce J. Winick, *Therapeutic Jurisprudence as a New Research Tool*, in Essays in Therapeutic Jurisprudence, *supra* note 15, at 303, 307–08 ("[O]ne interested in therapeutic jurisprudence could mine the procedural justice literature with a view to considering how legal proceedings in the mental health area—such as commitment and conditional release hearings—might be modified to increase a litigant-patient's perception of fairness and perhaps to increase treatment compliance and treatment efficacy.").
26. Wexler, *supra* note 22, at 33–35; *see also* Winick, *supra* note 19, at 4; Bruce J. Winick, *Competency to Consent to Voluntary Hospitalization: A Therapeutic Jurisprudence Analysis of* Zinermon v. Burch, *in* Essays in Therapeutic Jurisprudence, *supra* note 15, at 83, 132 (opining that "[f]or too long, lawyers and doctors have been in an adversary posture in the hospitalization process, sometimes with the result that the patient becomes a casualty").
27. David B. Wexler & Bruce J. Winick, *Introduction* to Law in a Therapeutic Key, *supra* note 5, at xvii, xvii.
28. Dennis B. Stolle, David B. Wexler, Bruce J. Winick & Edward A. Dauer, *Integrating Preventive Law and Therapeutic Jurisprudence: A Law and Psychology Based Approach to Lawyering*, in Practicing Therapeutic Jurisprudence, *supra* note 17, at 5, 7.
29. *Id.*; *see also* Winick, *supra* note 19, at 11 (explaining that Wexler and Winick began using the term "Therapeutic Jurisprudence" in conference presentations during the late 1980s, but first wrote about it in 1990); Slobogin, *supra* note 14, at 763 (noting that Wexler and Winick introduced the idea of Therapeutic Jurisprudence in the early 1990s); Dennis P. Stolle, *Introduction* to Practicing Therapeutic Jurisprudence, *supra* note 17, at xv, xv (noting that Wexler and Winick "formally introduced therapeutic jurisprudence as a distinct legal theory, about a decade ago").
30. David B. Wexler, *Preface* to The Law as a Therapeutic Agent, *supra* note 20, at vii, vii.

capitalize on its multidisciplinary potential"[31] and "become more sensitive to insights from the mental health disciplines."[32]

Notably, Wexler and Winick also claimed that "[b]y suggesting the need to identify the therapeutic and antitherapeutic consequences of legal rules and practices," they were not "necessarily suggest[ing] that such rules and practices be recast to accomplish therapeutic ends or avoid antitherapeutic results"[33] or that "therapeutic considerations should trump other considerations."[34] Rather, TJ was merely a tool — one that could be used to identify "questions in need of empirical research" and that "set[s] the stage" for conversations about what might occur when therapeutic values happen to conflict with other societal values, such as "individual autonomy, integrity of the fact-finding process, community safety," or others.[35] Thus, TJ seemed to propose an affirmative agenda for reforming existing nontherapeutic laws and procedures, but also purported to serve as nothing more than a lens through which to examine and analyze such existing elements.

Over time, TJ received significant support, in no small measure due to Professors Wexler and Winick's thoughtful advocacy and genuine enthusiasm for its teachings. Indeed, although they conceded that TJ theory applied most naturally to mental health law, they forecast its eventual spread to a range of legal areas.[36] They themselves began using TJ to examine other legal issues, although at the outset their writings tended to have some connection to the mental health arena.[37]

Professors Wexler and Winick urged others to join them in embracing TJ, resulting in the production of a voluminous body of scholarship that applies TJ principles to a host of concerns.[38] In this way, TJ has shifted its focus from mental health, to dealing

---

31. Id.
32. *Id.*; *see also* Winick, *supra* note 19, at 4 ("Accomplishing positive therapeutic consequences or eliminating or minimizing antitherapeutic consequences thus emerges as an important objective in any sensible law reform effort.").
33. Wexler & Winick, *supra* note 15, at xi.
34. Wexler & Winick, *supra* note 27, at xvii.
35. *Id.*; *see also* Wexler & Winick, *supra* note 5, at 708. Wexler and Winick note:
> We have repeatedly emphasized the fact that therapeutic jurisprudence is merely a "lens" designed to shed light on interesting and important empirical and normative issues relating to the therapeutic impact of the law. The therapeutic jurisprudence perspective sets the stage for the articulation and debate of those questions, and hence has the potential for reinvigorating the field, but it does not itself provide any of the answers. Wexler & Winick, *supra* note 5, at 708.
36. Wexler & Winick, *supra* note 15, at x (predicting TJ's future application to family, juvenile, and criminal law).
37. For instance, Professor Wexler coauthored articles with Robert F. Schopp that examined mental health malpractice litigation and negligence claims against psychotherapists. *See generally* Robert F. Schopp & David B. Wexler, *Shooting Yourself in the Foot with Due Care: Psychotherapists and Crystallized Standards of Tort Liability*, *in* Essays in Therapeutic Jurisprudence, *supra* note 15, at 157; David B. Wexler & Robert F. Schopp, *How and When to Correct for Juror Hindsight Bias in Mental Health Malpractice Litigation: Some Preliminary Observations*, *in* Essays in Therapeutic Jurisprudence, *supra* note 15, at 135.
38. Marjorie A. Silver, Professional Responsibility and the Affective Assistance of Counsel 7 (Oct. 27, 2005) (unpublished manuscript), *available at* http://www.law.ucla.edu/docs/silver_marjorie_profrespaffectiveasstcounsel.pdf. Professor Silver notes:
> A glance at the bibliography of the website of the International Network on Therapeutic Jurisprudence graphically demonstrates the impact and growth of TJ on our legal culture. It lists twenty-five books and monographs, twenty-one symposia and 749 articles, all published over the past fifteen years, the vast majority over the past five or six years.

Id. (citation omitted).

with "quasi" mental health issues,[39] to being an amorphous movement that advocates the application of "therapeutic" principles in a broad range of settings—even those where litigants have not been diagnosed with mental illness.[40] For instance, scholars have applied TJ to everything from duty-to-rescue rules in child abuse matters[41] to policies relating to gays and lesbians in the military.[42] They generally examine the "therapeutic" or "antitherapeutic" consequences of the laws under consideration, based on the extent to which they promote the "psychological well-being" of those affected by them.[43] TJ scholarship has gone so far as to consider the law's therapeutic impact on judges, lawyers, and juries, considering whether their psychological well-being is affected by the law and its processes.[44]

Despite TJ's popularity, it has not been without critics. For instance, in the mid-1990s, at least two scholars examined the tensions and ambiguities in its teachings. They warned that TJ's lack of clear parameters and terminology, if not addressed, would present serious efficacy problems for the movement.[45] Professor John Petrila, perhaps one of the strongest early critics of TJ theory, argued that despite TJ's reported concern for individual autonomy, its focus on therapeutic outcomes was largely paternalistic and could work to disempower individuals who were seen as psychologically impaired.[46] More fundamentally, he argued, Professors Wexler and Winick "fail[ed] to

---

39. See Table of Contents to Law in a Therapeutic Key, supra note 5, at vii, vii (entitling section I.B "'Quasi' Mental Health Law").
40. Winick, supra note 19, at 12 ("[T]herapeutic jurisprudence has now been applied to analyze issues in correctional law, criminal law, family law and juvenile law, sexual orientation law, disability law, health law, evidence law, personal injury law, labor arbitration law, contract and commercial law, workers' compensation law, probate law, and the legal profession.").
41. See generally Daniel W. Shuman, The Duty of the State to Rescue the Vulnerable in the United States, in Law in a Therapeutic Key, supra note 5, at 299.
42. See generally Kay Kavanaugh, Don't Ask, Don't Tell: Deception Required, Disclosure Denied, in Law in a Therapeutic Key, supra note 5, at 343.
43. See Shuman, supra note 41, at 299–300 ("Rescue [of abused children] proceeds on the assumption that it will be therapeutic; we encourage rescue because we think it will be beneficial to the physical or emotional health of the person rescued. If legal intervention on behalf of abused children lacks a therapeutic outcome, then a duty to rescue may leave children worse off than if no intervention had occurred."); see also Kavanaugh, supra note 42, at 343–44 (arguing that rules relating to gays in the military are antitherapeutic both for homosexual service members who feel pressured to conceal their sexual identity, and for heterosexual service members "because [the rules] encourage and perpetuate prejudice that is based on ignorance and deter the development of productive relationships"). See generally Rose Daly-Rooney, Designing Reasonable Accommodations Through Co-Worker Participation: Therapeutic Jurisprudence and the Confidentiality Provision of the Americans with Disabilities Act, 8 J.L. & Health 89 (1994); Ronald J. Rychlack & Corey D. Hinshaw, From the Classroom to the Courtroom: Therapeutic Jurisprudence and the Gaming Industry's Impact on Law, 74 Miss. L.J. 827 (2005).
44. See, e.g., Susan Daicoff, The Role of Therapeutic Jurisprudence Within the Comprehensive Law Movement, in Practicing Therapeutic Jurisprudence, supra note 17, at 465, 467; Daniel W. Shuman et al., The Health Effects of Jury Service, in Law in a Therapeutic Key, supra note 5, at 949, 949; James L. Nolan, Jr., Therapeutic Adjudication, Society, Jan.–Feb. 2002, at 29, 38.
45. See John Petrila, Paternalism and the Unrealized Promise of Essays in Therapeutic Jurisprudence, in Law in a Therapeutic Key, supra note 5, at 685, 685–705; Slobogin, supra note 14, at 763–93. See generally Richard Boldt & Jana Singer, Juristocracy in the Trenches: Problem-Solving Judges and Therapeutic Jurisprudence in Drug Treatment Courts and Unified Family Courts, 65 Md. L. Rev. 82 (2006); Morris B. Hoffman, Therapeutic Jurisprudence, Neo-Rehabilitationism, and Judicial Collectivism: The Least Dangerous Branch Becomes the Most Dangerous, 29 Fordham Urb. L.J. 2063 (2002); Arthur G. Christean, Therapeutic Jurisprudence: Embracing a Tainted Ideal, http://psychrights.org/Articles/TherapeuticJurisprudenceTaintedIdeal.htm (last visited Mar. 12, 2007).
46. Petrila, supra note 45, at 695–700.

articulate clear decision rules for determining ... whether and under what circumstances therapeutic values must yield to other values," or when any given outcome would be considered therapeutic as opposed to anti-therapeutic.[47] Professor Christopher Slobogin, although more sympathetic to TJ than Petrila, agreed that TJ theory presented serious conceptual dilemmas, including how best to define the term "therapeutic," measure the therapeutic value of any given outcome, and balance that value against others.[48]

Professors Wexler and Winick attempted to address these critiques. For instance, in a reply to Professor Petrila's article, they reaffirmed their commitment to the interests of the mentally ill, arguing, in relevant part, that autonomous decision making and individual choice are clearly stated core concerns of TJ.[49] As for the questions raised about the term "therapeutic," in a 1995 article, Professor Wexler offered:

> Therapeutic jurisprudence has been criticized for not offering a clear-cut definition of the term therapeutic. As a mere lens or heuristic for better seeing and understanding the law, however, I think therapeutic jurisprudence has quite rightly opted not to provide a tight definition of the term, thereby allowing commentators to roam within the intuitive and common sense contours of the concept....
>
> Although the definition of the term therapeutic ... needs to be left very flexible for promoting research, it is also probably true that, to preserve the camaraderie (and efficient work) of a common scholarly community, there ought to be some notion about the core concept and its rough bounds. In that connection it is noteworthy that the therapeutic jurisprudence literature to date has overwhelmingly conformed to areas within the ordinary mental health connotation of the term therapeutic: mental health-mental illness and health, illness, injury, disability, treatment, rehabilitation, and habilitation....
>
> Therefore, what is meant by therapeutic far exceeds the reversal of psychosis. On the other hand, the term therapeutic has not yet become (and in my view for research purposes ought not to become) synonymous with simply achieving intended or desirable outcomes.[50]

With regard to the relative weight to be accorded therapeutic outcomes and what to do when therapeutic goals conflict with other normative values, in his 1997 book, Professor Winick claimed that such matters were not intended to be addressed by TJ:

> While therapeutic jurisprudence is premised on the notion that [mental] health is a value that law should seek to foster, it makes no attempt to assign relative values to the various other goals of law. To resolve such conflicts of value, one must go outside therapeutic jurisprudence to some ethical or political theory that establishes a hierarchy of values. In our political system this balancing is often performed by the legislature which, within our democratic traditions, attempts to reflect the will of the citizenry. When fundamental constitutional rights are involved, the task is often performed by the courts, and ultimately by the Supreme Court, the institution in our governmental

---
47. *Id.* at 694–95.
48. Slobogin, *supra* note 14, at 763–93.
49. Wexler & Winick, *supra* note 5, at 711–12.
50. David B. Wexler, *Reflections on the Scope of Therapeutic Jurisprudence, in* Law in a Therapeutic Key, *supra* note 5, at 811, 812–14.

structure that is assigned the role of safeguarding constitutional values and protecting them from erosion by majoritarian pressure.

Therapeutic jurisprudence suggests that legislatures and courts should consider therapeutic values in the balancing of competing interests and concerns [—] that is the essential task of law-making. But although therapeutic jurisprudence is normative in this regard, it is careful to acknowledge the relevance of other normative values and does not suggest that they be subordinated to therapeutic considerations.[51]

Thus, although Professors Wexler and Winick seemed to concede TJ was striving to change the law and its focus, they suggested that TJ itself, as merely a school of thought, was not empowered to effectuate modifications.[52] Rather "true decision makers" like legislators and policymakers would need to reform the law and legal system.[53]

Adding to the layers and complexity of TJ's purpose and identity, in more recent years Professors Wexler and Winick have advanced another "dimension" of TJ—application of its teachings to real-world legal practice.[54] They claim that absent any changes in substantive laws, judges and practicing lawyers can use TJ principles to guide their actions and behaviors, thereby transforming their roles within the court system.[55]

II. Professor Wexler's Invitation to Help Establish a TJ-Oriented Criminal Defense Bar

In his recent article, *Therapeutic Jurisprudence and the Rehabilitative Role of the Criminal Defense Lawyer*, Professor Wexler turns his attention to criminal defense practitioners.[56] He contends that although many criminal court judges have already begun applying TJ principles, for instance in drug and domestic violence cases, and in matters

---

51. Winick, *supra* note 19, at 4–7. In a more recent text, Professors Wexler and Winick explained:
> Therapeutic Jurisprudence is an interdisciplinary approach to law that builds on the basic insight that law is a social force that has inevitable (if unintended) consequences for the mental health and psychological function of those it affects. Therapeutic Jurisprudence suggests that these positive and negative consequences be studied with the tools of the behavioral sciences, and that, *consistent with considerations of justice and other relevant normative values*, law be reformed to minimize anti-therapeutic consequences and to facilitate achievement of therapeutic ones.

Stolle et al., *supra* note 28, at 7 (emphasis added). Likewise, in the introduction to *Essays in Therapeutic Jurisprudence*, Wexler and Winick explained:
> Let us, at the outset, emphasize that therapeutic jurisprudence does not embrace a vision of law ... serving exclusively or primarily therapeutic ends.... The law serves many ends, and our suggestion that the impact on therapeutic values of legal rules and practices should be analyzed does not mean that therapeutic values should predominate over others.

Wexler & Winick, *supra* note 15, at xi.

52. Wexler & Winick, *supra* note 5, at 708.

53. *Id.*

54. *See* David B. Wexler, *Practicing Therapeutic Jurisprudence: Psychological Soft Spots and Strategies*, in Practicing Therapeutic Jurisprudence, *supra* note 17, at 45, 45 (stating that this approach "looks not only at possible law reform, but pays attention, too, to how existing law—whatever it is—may be *applied* in a manner more conducive to the psychological well-being of those it affects"); *see also* David B. Wexler, *The Development of Therapeutic Jurisprudence: From Theory to Practice*, 68 Rev. Jur. U.P.R. 691, 696 (1999).

55. *See generally* Practicing Therapeutic Jurisprudence, *supra* note 17; Judging in a Therapeutic Key: Therapeutic Jurisprudence and the Courts (Bruce J. Winick & David B. Wexler eds., 2003).

56. Wexler, *Rehabilitative Role*, *supra* note 1, at 743.

where defendants suffer from mental illness, few defense attorneys are doing the same.[57] Thus, he suggests defense attorneys should rethink the manner in which they represent clients, in light of TJ and its concern for therapeutic well-being.[58]

A. *TJ Theory: Defense Attorneys as Rehabilitative Change Agents*

Indeed, Professor Wexler has extended a "warm invitation" to "involved practitioners" and what he calls "their academic counterparts"—clinical law professors—to join him in rethinking the role of defense counsel.[59] His invitation calls for "the explicit recognition" of a special breed of defense attorney, the "TJ criminal lawyer."[60] He explains that TJ criminal lawyers would have a far broader role than "traditional"[61] criminal defense attorneys, as they would not only serve as legal representatives, but therapeutic "change agents."[62] For Professor Wexler, this means encouraging "positive change" and transformation in clients by adopting a decidedly rehabilitation-focused stance.[63] And ideally, defense counsel's "rehabilitative role" would continue well after resolution of the charges, extending "beyond sentencing, into corrections, conditional or unconditional release, and to life in the community."[64]

Given this suggested metamorphosis in attorney role, the relationship between counsel and client would change, too.[65] Professor Wexler claims that "the proposed attorney-client relationship bears virtually no resemblance" to many of the attorney-client relationships that currently exist, particularly those involving public defenders.[66] Rather, he seems to envision the attorney-client relationship as being more like what is often seen in drug treatment courts.[67] In these relationships, Professor Wexler posits, attorneys spend time cultivating trust and respect, for instance, by allowing clients to tell their stories "unconstrained by rigid notions of legal relevance."[68] In addition to motivating those they represent to participate actively in rehabilitative efforts, TJ attorneys would also "foster[] client hope and expectancy."[69] What Professor Wexler refers to as "emotional intelligence and cultural competence" are also seen as key to the TJ attorney-client relationship.[70]

---

57. *Id*. Wexler urges defense attorneys to keep pace with TJ's rapid move from the "world of theory to the world of practice." *Id*.

58. *Id*. at 743–44.

59. *Id*. at 746. Professor Wexler seems to count this author, along with defense attorneys Martin Reisig and John V. McShane, among those who are considered "involved practitioners." *See id*. at 746 n.14.

60. *Id*. at 746. Professor Wexler also suggests that "social workers, criminologists, psychologists ... academics working in Therapeutic Jurisprudence and in criminal law ... and their students ... would be highly valuable partners in this enterprise." *Id*.

61. As noted further at *infra* notes 134–149 and accompanying text, using the term "traditional" to describe the practices of defense counsel is somewhat problematic because it erroneously implies an existing monolithic method of providing defense representation.

62. Wexler, *Rehabilitative Role*, *supra* note 1, at 745–46.

63. *Id*. at 747.

64. *Id*. at 772. Notably, Professor Wexler does not provide a definition for the term "re-habilitative" as part of his invitation. *See infra* notes 153–155 and accompanying text.

65. Wexler, *Rehabilitative Role*, *supra* note 1, at 747.

66. *Id*.

67. *Id*. at 748. In such courts, defense counsel is called upon to serve with the judge and prosecutor as part of a treatment "team." Mae C. Quinn, *Whose Team Am I On Anyway? Musings of a Public Defender About Drug Treatment Court Practice*, 26 N.Y.U. Rev. L. & Soc. Change 37, 38 (2000–01).

68. Wexler, *Rehabilitative Role*, *supra* note 1, at 748.

69. *Id*. at 747–48.

70. *Id*. at 748.

B. *TJ Theory in Practice: Suggested Methods*

In inviting criminal defense lawyers and clinicians to recognize and encourage this "new" kind of practice, Professor Wexler urges them to write articles and practice-based materials that not only examine "the rehabilitative potential of applying the current law therapeutically," but also suggest reform of current laws, procedures, and practices to permit greater rehabilitative or therapeutic possibilities.[71] Despite this apparent tension between TJ goals and at least some current norms and rules, Professor Wexler provides a list of proposed "best practices" he suggests attorneys, clinicians, and clinic students can employ now at various "stages" of criminal proceedings to become TJ criminal defense lawyers.[72] These "stages"—none of which include trial—and the suggested model practices are outlined below.[73]

1. Diversion and Problem-Solving Courts

Professor Wexler describes effective TJ-focused attorneys as being aware of all non-adjudicative and plea-based options for resolving cases.[74] For instance, they should know about diversionary schemes available[75] and purported "problem-solving court" options, including eligibility requirements.[76] Professor Wexler concedes, however, that many "problem-solving courts" present efficacy issues. For instance, he notes that one studied court required a guilty plea prior to participation even though nearly one-third of defendants will fail out of the program, thereby resulting in imposition of jail or prison sentences.[77] He implies, however, that lack of knowledge of such shortcomings is what renders an attorney less than stellar by TJ measures. Thus, he urges attorneys to be aware of "the actual functioning of the[se] courts and programs, including rates of successful graduation versus the 'flunk out' rate, and the amount of time an average client might expect to spend in jail (for being sanctioned) under a [drug treatment court] program as compared to expected jail time in the conventional jail system."[78] In this way they can inform clients of the risks of such institutions, ensure "true client consent" in accepting a drug court plea, and protect against antitherapeutic results—like the client feeling "sold out."[79]

Professor Wexler further suggests that potential drug treatment court clients should sit in on a treatment court session with their attorney or the lawyer's staff before deciding to enter a treatment court guilty plea.[80] The attorneys or staff could work to enhance

---

71. *Id.* at 746.
72. *Id.* at 745.
73. *See infra* notes 74–118 and accompanying text.
74. Wexler, *Rehabilitative Role*, *supra* note 1, at 747.
75. *Id.* at 748–49. Professor Wexler suggests that "a worthwhile interdisciplinary research project would be to detail the law and practice of diversion in a particular jurisdiction." *Id.* Many forms of diversion allow a defendant to avoid any penalty whatsoever, for instance by agreeing to remain arrest free for a certain period of time, and also involve no admission of guilt. *See* N.Y. Crim. Proc. Law § 170.55 (McKinney 1999).
76. Wexler, *Rehabilitative Role*, *supra* note 1, at 749.
77. *Id.* at 750. Professor Wexler also notes that some drug treatment programs used in specialty courts lack bona fides and that some clients will spend as much time in jail following a drug court plea, presumably through sanctions, as they would have under a standard guilty plea. *Id.* at 749–50 nn.32–33. Indeed, Wexler seems to favor the use of pre-plea treatment courts over post-plea institutions. *See id.* at 753.
78. 78 *Id.* at 749.
79. *Id.* at 749–50.
80. *Id.* at 751. Professor Wexler suggests that "many" clients are free on bail prior to entering into treatment court programs and can therefore attend such proceedings. *Id.*

the therapeutic nature of this experience by "maximizing ... *vicarious learning* by sitting through the session and explaining to the prospective [drug treatment court] client exactly what is happening and why different clients are receiving different dispositions."[81]

2. Pleas and Sentencing Consideration

Pointing out that most cases are resolved by a guilty plea, Professor Wexler submits that "a TJ criminal lawyer will in appropriate cases try to assemble a rehabilitation-oriented packet to present to the prosecutor in hopes of securing a favorable plea arrangement."[82] If that does not occur, a TJ lawyer could share the information with the judge at sentencing.[83]

In advising a client whether to accept a plea offer, a TJ lawyer will explain how the client's early acceptance of responsibility might be perceived by the court and that the judge might offer sentence leniency where an early admission is seen as genuine rather than strategic.[84] Thus, a TJ lawyer might try "to work with the client to create genuineness even within a strategic legal context."[85] This could be accomplished with a psychological "'perspective-taking' approach," where the defendant is asked to "re-enact the crime, playing the role of the victim," view videotapes of victim statements, or write an apology letter taking into account the ways in which the victim's life has been affected by the crime.[86]

Beyond this, Professor Wexler explains that the TJ lawyer will consider the supposed intrinsic value of an admission of guilt: "A genuine acceptance of responsibility—especially if coupled with an apology—is generally regarded as therapeutically welcome by the victim and as a good first rehabilitative step for the defendant."[87]

3. Deferred Sentencing and Post-Offense Rehabilitation

According to Professor Wexler, even after the plea has been entered, defense attorneys can continue to engage in rehabilitation-focused, TJ practices.[88] For example, defense attorneys may postpone sentencing for as long as possible because "[i]n order to accomplish some meaningful rehabilitation—rather than a mere gesture, however genuine—it is of course important to have time on your side."[89] And even though the federal sentencing guidelines expressly permit the sentencing judge to take into account post-offense rehabilitation, as in the case of *United States v. Flowers*,[90] state courts without such legal authority might also be inclined to consider such conduct favorably at the time of sentencing.[91]

4. Probation

"The sanction of probation," too, Professor Wexler submits "is chock-full of TJ considerations, which can inform and enrich the role of defense counsel."[92] Although the TJ lawyer is not expected to be a therapist or social worker,[93] some psychology-based con-

---

81. Wexler, *Rehabilitative Role, supra* note 1, at 752 (emphasis added). These could serve as therapeutically positive experiences by giving the client "a glimpse of the hard work, but also of the opportunity and hope for real recovery that lies ahead." *Id.*
82. *Id.* at 753.
83. *Id.*
84. *Id.* at 753–54. This advice would be in addition to any information about the potential sentence following an unsuccessful trial.
85. *Id.* at 755.
86. Wexler, *Rehabilitative Role, supra* note 1, at 755.
87. *Id.* at 754.
88. *Id.*
89. *Id.* at 756.
90. 983 F. Supp. 159, 163–65 (E.D.N.Y. 1997).
91. Wexler, *Rehabilitative Role, supra* note 1, at 755–56.
92. *Id.* at 756.
93. *Id.* at 747–48.

cepts like compliance and relapse prevention principles might be part of the tools used by an effective TJ lawyer in the context of a client facing a probationary sentence.[94]

Compliance principles include having the client actively propose the terms of probation.[95] The client, Professor Wexler submits, will be more likely to comply with a plan when it is her own idea.[96] The TJ lawyer should talk about the plan as a "behavioral contract" the client has entered into with the court,[97] and consider having the client's family and friends help to enforce the contract.[98]

Relapse prevention principles can be used to come up with the proposed probationary terms.[99] For example, Professor Wexler suggests the lawyer should have clients "think through the chain of events that lead them to criminality so that they may be aware of patterns and of high risk situations" that may lead them to reoffend.[100] As an example of such a risky situation or pattern, Professor Wexler offers that youths often have car accidents when they have other youths in their vehicles.[101] Thus, a young person who is repeatedly "picked up for driving violations" might be asked by his lawyer: "Well, when do you seem to be picked up … ? Day or night? When you are alone or when you are with others? Which others? Your parents? Your friends?"[102] In this way, the client will come to realize what the risky behavior is, and the lawyer can ask the client how this could be used as part of a probationary plan.

That is, the youth "hopefully" will respond that she will agree to drive only with adults or responsible peers, or alone.[103]

The above exchange, Professor Wexler concedes, looks like "a kind of Socratic dialogue," where the lawyer is leading the client to the desired answer.[104] He suggests, how-

---

94. *Id.* at 757.
95. *Id.*
96. Wexler, *Rehabilitative Role*, *supra* note 1, at 760. Professor Wexler explains that this is because the client will understand the terms fully and not view the plan as merely a matter of "judicial fiat." *Id.*
97. *Id.* For even greater therapeutic benefit, the client should be encouraged to personally present the plan to the court and engage the judge on her own behalf at sentencing. *Id.* at 760–61.
98. *Id.* at 757, 761. This is assuming, Professor Wexler offers, that "the client truly agrees with the idea of [family] involvement." *Id.* at 761.
99. *Id.* at 760. The process of coming up with the proposed terms, Professor Wexler submits, is another TJ moment that can focus on compliance. The lawyer can prepare by pitching counterarguments to the client's claims that he will succeed. *Id.* at 761. According to Professor Wexler, "[o]ne would hope the client would personally come up with a suitable answer" that "this time is different." *Id.*
100. *Id.* at 757. Professor Wexler suggests the TJ attorney might walk the client through potential future high risk situations, and problem-solve ways to avoid such situations. *Id.* In another text, Professors Wexler and Winick state:
> [C]linical law students need to learn … the rewind exercise. It is a good technique both for *teaching clients* about how to avoid future problems and for teaching law students about how to see legal problems from a preventive perspective. The idea is a simple one…. In helping the client avoid a future reoccurrence of the problem, it is helpful for the lawyer to *assist the client to understand why the problem occurred*. Let us "rewind" the situation back in time to prior to the occurrence of the critical acts or omissions that produced the problem. What could the client have done at this point to have avoided the problem? What can he or she do now to avoid its reoccurrence?

Winick & Wexler, *supra* note 1, at 611.
101. Wexler, *Rehabilitative Role*, *supra* note 1, at 759.
102. 102 *Id.* at 760.
103. *Id.*
104. *Id.*

ever, that in the "division of labor," the client must think through alternatives and ultimately "buy into a change of behavior that should reduce the risk of criminality."[105] "[P]roposing a plan for the client's acquiescence" would be inappropriate in a TJ attorney-client relationship.[106]

Professor Wexler also says TJ lawyers should be open to innovative probation term possibilities.[107] For instance, without definitively offering his imprimatur, he raises the possibility of the TJ lawyer asking a client with several children, who has been convicted of failing to pay child support, whether he might consider having a vasectomy to influence the court favorably.[108] Thus, he implies clients might be encouraged to take steps to appease the court, even if the court were prohibited as a matter of law from ordering such steps to be taken.[109]

If probation is going well and it is permitted by law, TJ counsel would also move for early termination of probation.[110] Upon termination, as occurs in problem-solving courts, the TJ attorney should make sure that the court congratulates and acknowledges the client's success.[111]

5. Corrections, Reentry, and Beyond

For clients facing incarceration, Professor Wexler offers that "the TJ criminal lawyer should, at some point, engage the client in a dialogue regarding the sentence and the future," including early release options and "good time" credit possibilities.[112] And although defendants are not constitutionally entitled to counsel at such proceedings, "[i]n Therapeutic Jurisprudence terms, there is much meaningful work for an attorney at the parole grant hearing stage," too.[113] Not only could a TJ lawyer advocate for the client's release before the parole board, but she could work with the client "and others to establish a plan ... for conditional release."[114]

---

105. *Id.* at 759.
106. Wexler, *Rehabilitative Role*, *supra* note 1, at 759.
107. *Id.* at 762.
108. *Id.* at 764–66. As an example, Professor Wexler points to the case of *State v. Oakley*, 629 N.W.2d 200 (Wis. 2001). Wexler, *Rehabilitative Role*, *supra* note 1, at 764; *see also generally* Andrew Horowitz, *Coercion, Pop-Psychology, and Judicial Moralizing: Some Proposals for Curbing Judicial Abuse of Probation Conditions*, 57 Wash. & Lee L. Rev. 75 (2000) (criticizing the case for going too far in trying to control the life of a probationer). In *Oakley*, the defendant, a father of nine children, was convicted for refusing to pay child support. 629 N.W.2d at 202–03. The court ordered, as a condition of probation, that the defendant have no more children, unless he was able to support them—a condition that was upheld on appeal. *Id.*
109. *See* Wexler, *Rehabilitative Role*, *supra* note 1, at 766.
110. Professor Wexler suggests that judges conduct probation review hearings, "taking a page from the apparently successful ongoing judicial supervision practices of drug treatment court." *Id.* at 761. TJ defense counsel can play a role at such hearings by "marshalling, with the client, impressive evidence of success, and presenting it to the court, thereby helping to reinforce desistance from criminal activity." *Id.* at 762.
111. Id.
112. *Id.* at 769.
113. *Id.* at 771.
114. Wexler, *Rehabilitative Role*, *supra* note 1, at 771. Professor Wexler also mentions the recent development of reentry courts, which "borrow from the drug court model" as a means of "reinvigorat[ing] the parole process." *Id.* at 770. He notes that although some of these institutions actually have conditional release authority, like parole boards, others are intended to work with former inmates who are released unconditionally to ensure "smoother reentry." *Id.* Professor Wexler suggests that he is in favor of both kinds of reentry courts. *See id.* at 771 n.117.

Once a client has been released from prison or jail, Professor Wexler submits that a TJ lawyer might continue in her therapeutic efforts by "help[ing the client] in the tremendously difficult task of reentry and readjustment, talking with the client about post-release conditions and collateral consequences that might impede the client's adjustment, and offering to assist the client with restoring her rights and expunging her criminal record."[115]

6. Appeal

The appellate process, Professor Wexler contends, is another stage where TJ criminal lawyering can take place because "TJ considerations abound in the kind of conversations lawyers should have with clients both before an appellate brief is filed and in the aftermath of an appellate determination."[116] For instance, the TJ lawyer should communicate meaningfully with her client, notifying her of the issues to be raised and the law relating to the claims, and giving her a realistic sense of what outcome to expect.[117] TJ lawyers should also consider carefully how to convey an unsuccessful outcome on appeal, trying not to suggest to the client that she did not have a "voice" before the court—especially because that might "affect adversely the client's acceptance of the ruling and adjustment to the situation."[118]

C. *TJ Theory, Criminal Practitioners, and Legal Clinics: Envisioning Lawyers Taking TJ "All the Way"*

Professor Wexler explains that some or all of the techniques outlined above may be used by "traditional" practitioners who wish to make their representation more consistent with TJ's goals and teachings.[119] He suggests, however, that some attorneys may "decide to go 'all the way,' and to limit their criminal practice to a concentration in Therapeutic Jurisprudence."[120] Professor Wexler offers the story of one such TJ criminal defense lawyer, John McShane:

> Application of therapeutic jurisprudence in criminal defense work involves a threshold recognition that most criminal defense attorneys and the criminal justice system generally address the symptoms of the client's legal problem rather than the cause. For example, in the classic case of the habitual driving under the influence (DUI) offender, the symptom is the repeated arrests and the cause is usually alcoholism. It is the long-standing policy of the firm of McShane, Davis and Nance to decline representation of this type of defendant unless he or she contractually agrees to the therapeutic jurisprudence approach. If this approach is declined by the potential client, referral is made to a competent colleague who will then represent the client in the traditional model.[121]

Thus, McShane will take a client's case only if he is "willing to accept responsibility for his actions, submit to an evaluation, treatment, and relapse prevention program, and to use [a TJ] approach in mitigation of the offense in plea bargaining or the sentencing hearing."[122]

---

115. *Id.* at 771.
116. *Id.* at 766.
117. *Id.* at 768.
118. *Id.*
119. 119 Wexler, *Rehabilitative Role*, *supra* note 1, at 744. In this regard, Professor Wexler suggests that TJ practices may serve as mere "add ons" to current defender practices. *Id.*
120. *Id.*
121. *Id.*
122. *Id.* (internal quotations omitted).

Once he has accepted a case, McShane tries to forestall final disposition to "allow the client the maximum opportunity to recover":[123]

John McShane tries to delay the imposition of sentence for as long as possible and urges the client to begin to pick up the pieces and to engage in available rehabilitative efforts, whether they be attendance at Alcoholics Anonymous or a more elaborate treatment program. McShane emphasizes to the client that, up to this point, the existing evidence already, by definition, "exists"; it perhaps can be given a "spin," but cannot be changed. On the other hand, suggests McShane, from here on out the client can build his or her own case, can help create evidence that is favorable and that can work to the client's advantage.[124]

In contrast to McShane, whose practice is wholly private and who can pick and choose his clients, Professor Wexler complains that many court-appointed lawyers and public defenders currently practice in "shameful systems," "where crushing caseloads allow for little client contact and where the only real objective is to secure a decent deal on a plea."[125] Thus, he proposes the possibility of "innovative privately funded organizations, such as the Georgia Justice Project, which is selective in the cases it takes, but which takes them with the objective of working with a defendant, win or lose, in a very broad, encompassing, and extensive way."[126] Such specialized programs may be able to be set up with "private funds" "to take over where the [public defender] leaves off," because publicly funded public defenders generally can only represent a defendant through sentence and appeal.[127]

Alternatively, Professor Wexler posits that public defender offices could establish special intake processes "to assess a defendant's likely interest in pursuing a path that would most likely look to diversion (or participation in a problem solving court such as a drug treatment court, mental health court, domestic violence court), plea negotiation, and sentencing."[128] Thus, cases of clients for whom such dispositions seem "appealing" could be sent down a special TJ path and handled by a special TJ lawyer within the public defender's office.[129] Acknowledging that "some" such "models already exist," he suggests that additional "thought needs to be given ... to integrating other professionals — such as social workers — into the law office context."[130]

Finally, Professor Wexler fears that law school clinics may "succumb to mimicking the structural ineffective assistance of counsel exhibited in many ... public sector de-

---

123. *Id.* (internal quotations omitted).
124. Wexler, *Rehabilitative Role*, *supra* note 1, at 755–56.
125. *Id.* at 747.
126. *Id.* at 772. Professor Penny White describes the Georgia Justice Project as a "nontraditional indigent representation organization" that is "significantly different from the Bronx Defenders" and other "community-based lawyering programs." Penny J. White, *Mourning and Celebrating* Gideon's *Fortieth*, 72 UMKC L. Rev. 515, 553 (2003). Rather, it "is a private, not-for-profit organization that seeks to rehabilitate accused offenders and reduce recidivism." *Id.* Because it is supported by private funds alone, it can be "extremely selective in determining who it will represent and ultimately serve." *Id.* As a result, it generally will not take certain kinds of cases, including those that relate to allegations of family violence or child abuse. *Id.* at 553 n.287.
127. Wexler, *Rehabilitative Role*, *supra* note 1, at 772.
128. *Id.* at 773.
129. *Id.* Professor Wexler urges public defense institutions to "confront questions of relative caseload[s]" and "find ways of avoiding the development of intra-office resentment towards lawyers having [the] less frenzied daily diet" of TJ practice, likening the situation to judges who are resentful of others with greater resources in specialized, boutique "problem-solving" courts. *Id.*
130. *Id.*

fense programs."¹³¹ To help avoid this pitfall, he urges clinicians whose students practice in trial-level criminal courts to assign students TJ-focused projects, like producing manuals and other materials that outline the requirements of diversion programs and problem-solving courts.¹³² He further suggests that clinicians develop and use exercises focused on "problem-solving court" practice. For instance, students might "consider the kind of dialogue a lawyer might have with a client about the pros and cons of opting into a [drug treatment court] or mental health court."¹³³

III. Considering Professor Wexler's Invitation

Obviously, it is always flattering to receive an invitation. But before accepting, it is important to think it through. Even if you truly like the person who extended the request, there are other things to consider. What is the occasion? Is this an event to celebrate? What will be on the menu? Who else is included on the guest list? As tempting as it is to join Professor Wexler in his well-intended movement, as a criminal defense lawyer and clinician, his invitation presents a number of issues that give me pause.

A. *Proposed Change in Defense Counsel Role: The Occasion*

1. Misunderstanding Tradition

Despite the openness and warmth with which it was extended, Professor Wexler's call to establish a specialized TJ criminal defense bar is ultimately unconvincing. First, Professor Wexler's invitation erroneously implies that a single defense attorney model currently exists—which he refers to as "traditional."¹³⁴ He never defines what constitutes "traditional" defense representation, however, or describes the traditional defense attorney in practice.¹³⁵ Thus, it is unclear why the alleged current model of representation needs to be replaced with a new model involving "TJ criminal lawyers."

---

131. *Id.* at 747.
132. Wexler, *Rehabilitative Role*, *supra* note 1, at 746–48.
133. *Id.* at 751. Professor Wexler actually discusses the level of effort used in advising a client about "the collateral consequences of a proposed plea" and "whether enrollment in a treatment option should call for the same or a higher standard." *Id.* at 752.

Criminal appeals clinics, Wexler offers, should also use TJ exercises. *Id.* at 769. Although he does not offer a specific plan of action, Wexler suggests that such clinics should have students think about how to handle an appeal that lacks merit. *Id.* For instance, students might consider whether to file a "dressed up brief" for the benefit of making the client feel good, or to withdraw so as to avoid filing a frivolous appeal with the court. *Id.*

134. *See id.* at 747.
135. Although others have also used the term "traditional" when talking about some kinds of criminal defense and law school clinic representation, this description is somewhat misleading. Indeed, descriptions of "traditional" representation models are not uniform and demonstrate that no singular "traditional" defense bar currently exists. *See, e.g.*, Katherine R. Kruse, *Fortress in the Sand: The Plural Values of Client-Centered Representation*, 12 Clinical L. Rev. 369, 402 (2006) ("The 'traditional model' of legal representation falls in line with th[e] justification for professional paternalism, creating a 'means-objectives' division of decision-making authority in the lawyer-client relationship, in which the client tells the lawyer what objective the client wishes to pursue, and the lawyer applies her legal expertise to decide the strategic means by which to attain the client's objective."); Mark H. Moore, *Alternative Strategies for Public Defenders and Assigned Counsel*, 29 N.Y.U. Rev. L. & Soc. Change 83, 104 (2004–05) (referring to the "radical" concept of "whole client" representation, noting that "those who advocate for and seek to practice" in this way "draw a sharp contrast between this [kind of practice] and the traditional kinds of representation"); Robin Steinberg & David Feige, *Cultural Revolution: Transforming the Public Defender's Office*, 29 N.Y.U. Rev. L. & Soc. Change 123, 123–24 (2004–05) (stating that "[t]he traditional defender office is lawyer-driven and case-oriented," that "[t]raditional defenders address themselves primarily to the client's immediate legal needs believing that removing or reducing the imminent threat of incarceration is their function,"

These failings may be explained, however, by the realities of modern criminal defense practice. In my mind, no single, monolithic, "traditional" means of representation currently exists.[136] Rather, good defense lawyers—no matter where they work or what they are called[137]—know that representation of each defendant calls for a range of skills and approaches in light of defense attorneys' legal and ethical obligations, existing practice standards, and the goals and wants of that individual client.[138]

---

and that "[b]y contrast the more holistic model of representation is client-focused, interdisciplinary, and community-based"); Kim Taylor-Thompson, *Taking It to the Streets*, 29 N.Y.U. Rev. L. & Soc. Change 153, 166 (2004–05) (describing some traditional lawyers as not being willing to "push beyond the comfort zone" of their courtroom role). Moore's description of "traditional" defenders, to paraphrase a former colleague, may unnecessarily denigrate some lawyers by suggesting they represent only some component part of clients, perhaps "half."

136. Some public defender offices now use terms like "community-based," "holistic," or "client-centered" to describe the work they do beyond merely defending clients against crimes alleged. *See* White, *supra* note 126, at 547 (discussing use of these terms by defense organizations that attempt to "coordinate legal services for a client, together with social services and community assistance"). Many lawyers and law school clinics, however, have engaged in such work for decades, some without referring to it by a specific name. *See infra* note 189 and accompanying text.

Beyond this, as Professor Kate Kruse describes, Professors David Binder and Susan Price popularized the "client-centered" lawyering concept nearly three decades ago in their influential book, Legal Interviewing and Counseling: A Client-Centered Approach (1977). *See* Kruse, *supra* note 135, at 369–70 (characterizing the "client-centered" model of representation as having enjoyed "unparalleled success" and serving as the "predominant model for teaching lawyering skills" for over twenty-five years). As Professor Kruse explains, the client-centered approach to representation was intended to supplant "treat[ing] clients impersonally as bundles of legal issues ... without exploring a client's actual values." *Id.* at 382. What is more, as "the client-centered approach has grown from its earliest articulation by Binder and Price to its current status as well-established bedrock of clinical education, it has evolved naturally into what might be called a plurality of approaches, which expand aspects of the original client-centered approach in different directions." *Id.* at 371. One of those directions is the "problem-solving ... holistic lawyering [approach] that reach[es] beyond the boundaries of the client's legal case to address a broader range of connected issues in the client's life." *Id.* Nevertheless, some "[d]efenders of traditional zealous partisan advocacy" also describe themselves as client-centered in that "[t]he traditional model of devotion to a client's legal rights and interests is fundamentally client-centered, in the sense that it places fidelity to clients at the center of the lawyer's professional duties." *Id.* at 397–98 n.126 (recounting Abbe Smith's tribute to Monroe Freedman, whom Smith refers to as the first to use the term "client-centered"); *see also* Abbe Smith, *The Difference in Criminal Defense and the Difference It Makes*, 11 Wash. U. J.L. & Pol'y 83, 88 (2003). Thus, what may be considered "traditional" or "nontraditional" is open to debate.

137. *See* Kim Taylor-Thompson, *Tuning Up* Gideon's Trumpet, 71 Fordham L. Rev. 1461, 1500 (2003) (identifying various public defenders' offices, including the Public Defender Service for the District of Columbia, Neighborhood Defender Services of Harlem, and the Bronx Defenders, as consistently providing high-quality defense services to their clients); White, *supra* note 126, at 549 (recounting that more than half of 900 public defenders whom the Brennan Center for Justice surveyed in 2001 "responded that they were engaging in some community-based lawyering").

138. Professor Kruse also criticizes misleading characterizations of modern lawyering methods:
> [P]erhaps contributing to the gap between practical and theoretical conceptions of client-centered representation, the debates within legal ethics are often carried out in terms that reduce client-centered representation to a kind of caricatured "hired gun" lawyering, in which lawyers are impelled by the pursuit of client objective all the way to the limits of what the law arguably allows. While this simplification assists the elegance of theory, it renders clients and the lawyers who represent them unfamiliar—almost unrecognizeable—to lawyers seeking to engage in thoughtful ethical reflection in the contexts of practice in which they are embedded.

Kruse, *supra* note 135, at 440 (citations omitted); *see* Monroe H. Freedman & Abbe Smith, Understanding Lawyer's Ethics 19 (3d ed. 2004) (discussing "the false metaphor of warfare" that is often used by "those who denigrate the adversary system" and noting "[t]he true picture is rather different

For over a decade, the National Legal Aid and Defender Association (the "NLADA"), which serves as a voice for public defenders and other poverty lawyers,[139] has published criminal defense community standards entitled *Performance Guidelines for Criminal Defense Representation*.[140] The very first NLADA guideline addresses the "Role of Defense Counsel."[141] Rather than describing a single model or method of operating to fulfill that role, it explains that "[t]he paramount obligation of criminal defense counsel is to provide zealous and quality representation to their clients at all stages of the criminal process. Attorneys also have an obligation to abide by ethical norms and act in accordance with the rules of the court."[142] What constitutes "zealousness" or "quality" obviously depends on the particular circumstances,[143] Indeed, in some, but by no means all, instances this might mean attempting to improve a client's circumstances,[144] or assisting in client rehabilitation efforts.[145] Thus, good criminal defense attorneys have long recog-

---

from the physical violence and 'bloodletting' that is conjured up by that rhetoric"); *see also* Taylor-Thompson, *supra* note 135, at 167.

139. Professors Backus and Marcus recently described the NLADA as:

> the nation's leading advocate for legal professionals who work with and represent low-income clients, their families, and communities. Speaking on behalf of legal aid and defender programs, as well as individual advocates, it devotes its resources to serving the broad equal justice community. The NLADA provides a national voice in public policy and legislative debates on the many issues affecting the equal justice community.

Mary Sue Backus & Paul Marcus, The Right to Counsel in Criminal Cases, A National Crisis, 57 Hastings L.J. 1031, 1043–44 (2006); see also White, supra note 126, at 525–31 (describing the history and significance of criminal defense standards and guidelines promulgated by the NLADA and the American Bar Association).

140. The NLADA's Performance Guidelines were first adopted in 1994.

141. *See* Nat'l Legal Aid & Defender Ass'n, *supra* note 13, at Guideline 1.1.

142. *Id.* The commentary to Guideline 1.1 explains:

> All lawyers have a professional, ethical duty to provide "competent" legal representation to their clients, under the *Model Rules of Professional Responsibility* of the American Bar Association. When dealing with the provision of counsel to poor persons accused of crime, the ABA and NLADA have both called for "quality" legal representation, a more progressive standard. These Guidelines advocate the provision of zealous and quality representation to all clients charged with crime.... The duty to provide zealous and quality representation applies to all criminal defense attorneys, regardless of the financial status of their clients, or how (or how much) the lawyer is being paid.

Id. at Guideline 1.1 cmt.; *see also* Model Rules of Prof'l Conduct R. 1.1 (2006) ("Competent representation requires the legal knowledge, skill, thoroughness and preparation reasonably necessary for the representation.").

143. *See* Model Rules of Prof'l Conduct pmbl. (2002) (stating that a lawyer's responsibilities include serving as a legal advisor, legal advocate, negotiator, and evaluator for clients); Am. Bar Ass'n, Standards for Criminal Justice: Prosecution Function and Defense Function, Standard 4.12 cmt. (1993) (stating that the role of defense counsel is "complex, involving multiple obligations ... including furthering the defendant's interest to the fullest extent of the law").

144. *See* Taylor-Thompson, *supra* note 135, at 165 ("Defenders frequently need to locate and put in place treatment regimens for a client during the pre-trial period to provide her with the necessary support to make basic decisions about her case."); *see also* Andrew J. Liese, Note, *We Can Do Better: Anti-Homeless Ordinances as Violations of State Substantive Due Process Law*, 59 Vand. L. Rev. 1413, 1418–21 (2006) (discussing problems of the homeless, including their prosecution for quality of life offenses); Lola Velázquez-Aguilú, Comment, *Not Poor Enough: Why Wisconsin's System for Providing Indigent Defense Is Failing*, 2006 Wis. L. Rev. 193, 195–97 (recounting the difficulties of many indigent criminal defendants, including homelessness and transience).

145. Indeed, thirty-five years ago this question was thoughtfully examined in the very particular situation of representing clients struggling with drug addiction. *See* Thomas Rafalsky, *The Addicted Client: Rehabilitation as a Defense Strategy and the Role of an Attorney in the Rehabilitation Process*, 1 Contemp. Drug Probs. 399, 408–09 (1971–72). Rafalsky explained:

nized their job calls for them to wear any number of hats throughout the course of a given case, not just that of trial lawyer or dogged adversary.[146]

In addition to underestimating the complexity of current criminal defense representation practices, Professor Wexler fails to offer a clear motivation for his proposed change in the defense bar. For instance, no data or statistics are provided to demonstrate that the current and alleged "traditional" model of defense lawyering is responsible for "antitherapeutic" consequences in clients. This is particularly striking given TJ's stated concerns about the need for empirical research to support legal rules, procedures, and actions.[147]

Professor Wexler does say that the concept of TJ is increasing in popularity among some audiences, and that it is "moving rather rapidly from the world of theory to the

---

Attorneys have traditionally defended addicted clients in criminal matters without considering the fact that their clients are addicted. If the attorney is successful in the case by having the charges dismissed or by keeping his client out of jail, then he is returning an untreated addict to commit crimes, be rearrested, and eventually be retuned to the street. The cycle continues relentlessly.

There is, however, the means of avoiding this cycle while at the same time improving the representation which can be given to an addicted client. This can be done by adding the informal defense strategy of rehabilitation to the existing array of formal, legal defenses. A lawyer should acknowledge that a client is addicted, should show that the crime in question is related to the addiction, and should demonstrate that the client is being treated for his addiction and is being rehabilitated. If a favorable disposition of the case cannot be reached in that way, the attorney could then proceed according to his normal defense strategies. *Id.*

146. As Marty Guggenheim, former New York City Legal Aid Society attorney, aptly noted two decades ago:

[L]et me say that in my experience there are two kinds of institutional lawyers who are doomed to be ineffective. First, there are the lawyers who do not care about their clients and do not work very hard to represent them. Second, there are lawyers who never give an inch. They fight over every detail, and are never reasonable and never do favors for the court or their adversaries. Such lawyers may think that they are obeying the injunction to represent each client zealously and with undiluted loyalty, but they are sure to fail. After they have proven who they are to their adversaries and to the judges, nobody makes reasonable deals with them. Their clients always seem to be the losers.

Martin Guggenheim, Divided Loyalties: Musings on Some Ethical Dilemmas for the Institutional Criminal Defense Attorney, 14 N.Y.U. Rev. L. & Soc. Change 13, 21 (1986).

Similarly, social workers have been part of many public defenders' offices for decades. Taylor-Thompson, *supra* note 135, at 181 (noting that the Seattle Defender Association was using social workers in the delivery of services since the 1970s); *see* Mark H. Moore et al., *The Best Defense Is No Offense: Preventing Crime Through Effective Public Defense*, 29 N.Y.U. Rev. L. & Soc. Change 57, 79 (2004–05) (explaining that Mary Hoban, Chief Social Worker in the Connecticut Division of the Public Defender Services, "began many years ago" as the agency's only social work intern and that now the agency employs forty social workers to staff its thirty-nine offices); Charles J. Ogletree, Jr. & Yoav Sapir, *Keeping* Gideon's *Promise: A Comparison of the American and Israeli Public Defender Experiences*, 29 N.Y.U. Rev. L. & Soc. Change 203, 208 (2004–05) (commenting that in the years following *Gideon v. Wainwright*, 372 U.S. 335 (1963), "[i]n order to improve the quality of representation ... public defender offices implemented training programs for new lawyers and allocated resources for investigators and social workers to prepare individualized sentencing proposals to the court"); *see also* Elizabeth Wright, *Diversion of Justice*, Knoxville Voice, Aug. 10, 2006, at 9 (discussing the educational and other services provided by the Community Law Office of Knox County, Tennessee, a public defender office run by Mark Stephens that in 2001 began modeling itself on the earlier efforts of programs like the Neighborhood Defender Services of Harlem—thereby making it a second-generation provider of expanded defense services).

147. *See supra* notes 28, 35 and accompanying text.

world of practice."[148] Certainly, however, in and of itself that does not provide support for the kind of fundamental change he is advocating. That judges might be buying into TJ principles and trying to influence practitioners to do the same is not compelling as a basis for change either. Historically, defense attorneys and clinics have served as a check on the judiciary and its actions with regard to clients.[149] It would be wholly inappropriate to sign on to a supposedly new, "therapeutic" way of representing clients simply because judges might think it is a good idea without first ensuring that modifications of current practices are necessary and appropriate.

2. A New Tradition Without Sufficient Form and Substance

Beyond failing to describe the lawyering model he calls for changing, or to offer clear rationales for the modification, Professor Wexler's proposed TJ alternative lacks clear parameters of its own. Despite the critiques offered nearly a decade ago about the need to clarify its mission and identity, the TJ movement seems to have become even more unwieldy and difficult to pin down, at least to this reader. For instance, it still seems to hold itself out as nothing more than a lens through which to examine laws, procedures, and practices to ascertain whether their consequences are therapeutic or antitherapeutic, but at the same time advocates affirmative legal reform.[150] And although the movement claims that it is not empowered to modify current norms, with this invitation, TJ is offering "new" practices for defense lawyers.[151]

More fundamentally, not only is the term "therapeutic" open to numerous interpretations, as Professors Petrila and Slobogin noted in their earlier critiques, it now seems to have had grafted upon it a primary meaning—"rehabilitative."[152] One could dispute, however, whether rehabilitative goals are truly therapeutic in terms of improving psychological well-being of defendants.[153] And, of course, what counts as truly rehabilita-

---

148. Wexler, *Rehabilitative Role*, *supra* note 1, at 743.
149. Polk Co. v. Dodson, 454 U.S. 312, 320–21 (1981) (acknowledging that defense attorneys must exercise "professional independence," "free of state control," to satisfy the teachings of *Gideon v. Wainwright*); *see* Backus & Marcus, *supra* note 139, at 1069 ("Virtually everyone working in the criminal justice system appears to strongly agree with the notion that the defense function should be independent. It should not be too closely linked with, or controlled by, the legislature, the executive, the judiciary or the prosecution."); Thomas F. Geraghty, *The Criminal/Juvenile Clinic as a Public Interest Law Office: Defense Clinics; The Best Way to Teach Justice*, 75 Miss. L.J. 699, 699–700 (2006) (recounting six client stories from over thirty years of clinical teaching that demonstrate how handling their cases "taught ... students," "informed judicial decision-making," and "supported the cause for reform in the public interest"); *see also* Am. Bar Ass'n, *supra* note 143, at Standard 4-1.2 ("A court properly constituted to hear a criminal case must be viewed as a tripartite entity constituting of the judge (and jury, where appropriate), counsel for the prosecution, and counsel for the accused.").
150. *See* Wexler & Winick, *supra* note 5, at 708.
151. *See* Wexler, *Rehabilitative Role*, *supra* note 1, at 746. To be sure, Professor Wexler's current claims are more than just aspirational in nature, and do not read as a "mere lens or heuristic for better seeing and understanding the law." *See* Wexler & Winick, *supra* note 5, at 708. With the list of suggested practices offered for attorney and law clinic use, there can be little doubt that Professor Wexler is calling for some immediate changes. What is more, despite TJ's repeated assertion that empirical research should be used to determine how the law should be modified to attain more therapeutic outcomes, many of the proposed "new" TJ defense lawyer practices do not appear to be empirically supported. *See supra* note 35 and accompanying text; *infra* note 214.
152. *See* Petrila, *supra* note 45, at 695–700; Slobogin, *supra* note 14, at 763.
153. One can easily imagine a defendant for whom the thought of participating in a rehabilitative plan would be so odious that to do so would have a negative effect on her psychological well-being.

tive itself is open to debate.[154] Thus, the very concept of TJ criminal defense lawyering seems to offer practitioners and clinicians little in the way of concrete guidance.[155]

3. Clash of Traditions and Values

Assuming we could agree on some basic understanding of the terms "therapeutic" and "rehabilitative" for purposes of envisioning Professor Wexler's proposal, the concept of TJ criminal defense lawyering raises additional concerns, given that its seemingly singularly-focused aims have the potential to conflict with important existing values and considerations of modern defense attorneys. Indeed, despite TJ's desire not to "subordinat[e] due process or other justice values," even in theory the new model seems to run the risk of doing just that.[156]

First, as already discussed, current norms indicate the paramount obligation for defense counsel is to provide "zealous" and "quality" representation. Quality representation at a particular time in a particular case might, in fact, involve therapeutic considerations. Therapeutic concerns, however, are not in and of themselves intended to be the paramount considerations for defense attorneys. A narrow focus on client rehabilitation, depending upon the situation, may be incongruent with current requirements.[157]

Beyond this, I fear Professor Wexler's TJ model, with its emphasis on rehabilitation and transforming clients' lives, is laden with assumptions about the criminal defense client population—not the least of which is that they are guilty, likely to offend again, and in need of transformation.[158] These assumptions seem somewhat misguided. First,

---

154. See Thom Brooks, Rethinking Punishment (July 20, 2006) (unpublished manuscript, on file with the Social Science Research Network), available at www.ssrn.com/abstract=918045 (disputing some theorists' claims that rehabilitation involves teaching an offender that her crime was a moral wrong as some "victimless" offenses may not be morally reprehensible); see also Nora V. Demleitner et al., Sentencing Law and Policy 527 (2004) (noting that although nearly four million adults were on probation in 2001, their conditions varied widely across the country). See generally Edgardo Rotman, Do Criminal Offenders Have a Constitutional Right to Rehabilitation?, 77 J. Crim. L. & Criminology 1023 (1986); David Shichor, Following the Penological Pendulum: The Survival of Rehabilitation, 56 Fed. Probation 19 (1992).

155. Perhaps the same could be said of the terms "quality" and "zealous," or even "competent." The defense community, however, has long embraced these defining attributes, and they appear to find their genesis in law and in other detailed standards that provide guidance for defense attorneys. See Nix v. Whiteside, 475 U.S. 157, 175 (1986) (Blackmun, J., concurring) (referring to "the values of zealous and loyal representation embodied in the Sixth Amendment"); Avery v. Alabama, 308 U.S. 444, 450 (1940) (concluding that the petitioner was "afforded the assistance of zealous and earnest counsel"); see also Alaska Stat. § 13.26.111(a) (2004) (stating that the principal duty of an attorney representing a ward or respondent is to represent "zealously"); Cal. R. Ct. § 4.117(d)(7), (f)(2) (West 2006) (stating that to be appointed lead counsel in a capital case, a lawyer must demonstrate the "quality of representation appropriate to capital cases"); Model Rules of Prof'l Conduct R. 1.1 (2006) ("Competent representation requires legal knowledge, skill, thoroughness and preparation reasonably necessary for the representation.").

156. Wexler & Winick, *supra* note 27, at xvii.

157. Interestingly, this tension may be best exemplified by a comparison of American and Cuban criminal defense work offered by Professors Monroe Freedman and Abbe Smith:

> It is not surprising that in totalitarian societies, there is a sharp contrast in the role of the criminal defense lawyer from that in the American adversary system. As expressed by law professors at the University of Havana, "the first job of a revolutionary lawyer is not to argue that his client is innocent, but rather to determine if his client is guilty and, if so, to seek the sanction which will best rehabilitate him."

Freedman & Smith, *supra* note 138, at 15 (citations omitted). See generally Anita Bernstein, *The Zeal Shortage*, 35 Hofstra L. Rev. 1165 (2006).

158. See Wexler, *Rehabilitative Role*, *supra* note 1, at 753–55.

this fails to take into account the many truly innocent clients whom defense attorneys represent. Although it may be true that a large number of criminal defendants have committed the crimes with which they are charged, defense attorneys play an integral role in ensuring that their constitutional right to be presumed innocent is protected. Encouraging lawyers, even indirectly, to undertake representation harboring a different presumption may work to undermine or at least discount this important justice consideration.

Moreover, many criminal defendants who plead guilty simply are not. Innocent clients falsely admit guilt for a variety of reasons—from doing whatever is necessary to assure their immediate release from jail to avoiding the risk that a judge will sentence them to a harsher sentence after an unsuccessful trial.[159] What is more, people who commit crimes do so for any number of reasons, some of which relate to the specific facts and circumstances surrounding the particular offense.

Thus, a client's admission of guilt is not proof positive that the client is at risk for offending in the future, and thus in need of correction or rehabilitation.[160] Nor is a determination of guilt dispositive of a defendant's psychological problems, much less problems that the criminal court system can correct through supposed "rehabilitation" processes.[161]

The therapeutically focused model that Professor Wexler offers also suggests a kind of omniscience on the part of defense lawyers that promotes a hierarchical arrangement between lawyer and client.[162] Unlike many persons involved in the mental health system whose clinical diagnosis may indicate what is most "therapeutically" indicated for that individual, clients in the criminal justice system generally do not arrive on a lawyer's doorstep with a diagnosis other than "accused." As suggested above, a great many defendants deserve no further diagnosis. Yet Professor Wexler's proposal implies that defense lawyers are in a position to, and should, assess the needs of their clients and decide whether they are in need of transformation.[163] Thus, criminal defense lawyers, regardless of their background or training, are given the affirmative duty of flagging those clients—apparently based to some degree on whether they are willing to admit "guilt"—who appear to need life-changing intervention. Not only does this run the risk

---

159. Darryl K. Brown, The Decline of Defense Counsel and the Rise of Accuracy in Criminal Adjudication, 93 Cal. L. Rev. 1585, 1612 n.102 (2005) (citing Abbe Smith, Defending the Innocent, 32 Conn. L. Rev. 435, 494 nn.56–58 (2000)); Andrew D. Leipold, How the Pretrial Process Contributes to Wrongful Convictions, 42 Am. Crim. L. Rev. 1123, 1153 (2005); see also Stephanos Bibas, Transparency and Participation in Criminal Procedure, 81 N.Y.U. L. Rev. 911, 957 (2006) (stating that "[c]harge and fact bargains lie about the crime that actually happened and the facts surrounding it").

160. See Daniel A. Krauss, *Evaluating Science Outside the Trial Box: Applying* Daubert *to the Federal Sentencing Guidelines' Criminal History Score*, 29 Int'l J.L. & Psychiatry 289, 303 (2006) (arguing that defendant Criminal History Score evaluations under the federal sentencing scheme, "at best," function poorly to predict defendant recidivism); see also Barry C. Field, The Constitutional Tension Between Apprendi and McKeiver: Sentence Enhancements Based on Delinquency Convictions and the Quality of Justice in Juvenile Courts, 38 Wake Forest L. Rev. 1111, 1129 (2003).

161. Brooks Holland, *Holistic Advocacy: An Important but Limited Institutional Role*, 30 N.Y.U. Rev. L. & Soc. Change 637, 643 (2006) (noting that "even holistic advocacy proponents estimate that only ten percent of cases" require "holistic" intervention); Abbe Smith, *Too Much Heart and Not Enough Heat: The Short Life and Fractured Ego of the Empathic Heroic Public Defender*, 37 U.C. Davis L. Rev. 1203, 1230–31 (2004) ("Like the 'nonaccused,' the accused come in myriad shapes and sizes, temperaments and tendencies.").

162. *See* Wexler, *Rehabilitative Role*, *supra* note 1, at 759.

163. *See id.* at 747–49.

of having lawyers step beyond their level of professional expertise,[164] it may denigrate the important values of client self-determination and autonomy.[165] Indeed, many respected defense lawyers and clinicians have criticized this kind of best-interest-driven representation as being paternalistic, even if it is well-intended.[166]

The very concept of rehabilitation-centered lawyering also seems to conflict with an accused's right to conflict-free, unbiased representation.[167] Undertaking representation with a prior agenda of rehabilitation and correction would likely taint the attorney-client relationship. A client should be able to confide in his attorney about his alleged crime and any other "wrongdoings" for purposes of receiving zealous legal representation without fear of the lawyer's own personal desires coming into play. Existence of an underlying, potentially undisclosed,[168] TJ agenda would likely engender distrust of the entire defense bar, when trust has long been considered a core component of the relationship between lawyer and client.[169]

The TJ defense lawyering model that Professor Wexler posits also seems overly idealistic, particularly when it comes to representing the poor.[170] He suggests that TJ defense lawyers should assist in client change and transformation by fostering "hope and ex-

---

164. *See* Model Rules of Prof'l Conduct R. 1.1 cmt. 1 (2006) ("In determining whether a lawyer employs the requisite knowledge and skill in a particular matter, relevant factors include ... the lawyer's general experience [and] the lawyer's training and experience in the field in question."). *See generally* Joseph Goldstein et al., In the Best Interests of the Child 21–53 (1986) (discussing the importance of maintaining professional boundaries and cautioning lawyers against making mental health and other assessments beyond their area of expertise and qualification).

165. I suspect Professor Wexler would likely respond that in the TJ model, the client retains the final word and ultimately chooses whether to accept or reject therapeutic interventions. See Wexler, Rehabilitative Role, *supra* note 1, at 744. Thus, the client's autonomy is respected. Nevertheless, as is further explored in the context of the "best practices" offered by Professor Wexler, the TJ model of lawyering seems to encourage a fair amount of heavy-handed guiding on the part of lawyers to help clients to make what the lawyer believes is the "right" decision. See id. at 759–62. To this author, this seems much closer to client manipulation than client autonomy. See Stephen Ellman, Lawyers and Clients, 34 UCLA L. Rev. 717, 718–27 (1987) (noting that lawyers sometimes engage in coercive tactics that work to manipulate clients); see also Freedman & Smith, *supra* note 138, at 62 (stating that "the attorney acts both professionally and morally in assisting clients to maximize their autonomy" and that "the attorney acts unprofessionally and immorally by depriving clients of their autonomy"); Kruse, *supra* note 135, at 400 (noting that "respect for client autonomy has emerged as the most salient argument in favor of the client-centered approach" to representation).

166. See, e.g., Freedman & Smith, *supra* note 138, at 51 (expressing concern that some commentators think lawyers should behave paternalistically towards their clients); Jane M. Spinak, Why Defenders Feel Defensive: The Defender's Role in Problem-Solving Courts, 40 Am. Crim. L. Rev. 1617, 1621 (2003) (warning against defenders engaging in paternalistic practices and client manipulation in problem-solving courts, even if "the client's ultimate autonomy is enhanced" by drug treatment and rehabilitation through the court). *See generally* Kristen Henning, *Loyalty, Paternalism, and Rights: Client Counseling Theory and the Role of Child's Counsel in Delinquency Cases*, 81 Notre Dame L. Rev. 245 (2005).

167. *See* Model Rules of Prof'l Conduct R. 1.7 cmt. 10 ("The lawyer's own interests should not be permitted to have an adverse effect on the representation of a client.").

168. *See id*. R. 1.4 cmt. 7 ("A lawyer may not withhold information to serve the lawyer's own interest or convenience or the interests or convenience of another person.").

169. *See* Peter J. Henning, *Lawyers, Truth, and Honesty in Representing Clients*, 20 Notre Dame J.L. Ethics & Pub. Pol'y 209, 212 (2006) (noting that the "core of the attorney-client relationship is trust"); *see also* Jay Sterling Silver, *Truth, Justice, and the American Way: The Case Against Client Perjury Rules*, 47 Vand. L. Rev. 339, 364 n.91 (1994) (offering four factors that contribute to "greater distrust of court-appointed attorneys" as compared to retained counsel).

170. *See* Wexler, Rehabilitative Role, *supra* note 1, at 747.

pectancy" on the part of criminal defendants.[171] For many indigent criminal defendants, however, this simply is not a realistic possibility. Many of the crimes committed by public defenders' clients stem from their extreme poverty. No rehabilitative plan of service provided through our overworked criminal courts can even begin to address this multifaceted problem.[172] Thus, the overly optimistic sentiments underlying TJ defense theory seem unrealistic and may provide clients with a false sense of what may lie ahead. They, too, run the risk of undermining client confidence in the defense bar in the long term.

Thus, despite TJ's assertion that it does not attempt to subordinate other values to therapeutic considerations, the TJ defense lawyering model—even in theory—may well displace existing rights of defendants and subvert existing values and professional standards of defense practitioners.

B. *Role Change in Practice: The Menu*

Examination of Professor Wexler's proposed "menu" of TJ defense lawyer skills and behaviors vividly demonstrates some of these problems in practice. It reveals that, on the one hand, some of Professor Wexler's assumptions about the present, supposedly monolithic criminal defense model may be off the mark. Indeed, defense lawyers and clinics across the country employ many of the practices he suggests as part of the complex set of tools that quality lawyers use during the course of representation. On the other hand, some of the model TJ criminal defense practices not only conflict with existing practices of quality defense lawyers, thereby trumping those justice system norms, but run afoul of existing ethical and legal rules.

1. The Not-So-New Practices

Professor Wexler repeatedly indicates that TJ criminal defense lawyers must have thorough working knowledge of the criminal justice system and meaningfully communicate with clients.[173] This is nothing new, however. Lawyers who do not possess such awareness or fail to convey important information to those they represent simply are not complying with existing norms.[174] For example, as the NLADA warns:

(a) To provide quality representation, counsel must be familiar with the substantive criminal law and the law of criminal procedure and its application in the particular jurisdiction. Counsel has a continuing obligation to stay abreast of changes and developments in the law. Where appropriate, counsel should also be informed of the practices of the specific judge before whom a case is pending.

(b) Prior to handling a criminal matter, counsel should have sufficient experience or training to provide quality representation.[175]

The guidelines continue that defense attorneys have an obligation to keep their clients informed about developments in the case.[176]

Knowing the jurisdiction's system and sharing information with clients obviously include being familiar with diversionary programs, "problem-solving courts," and the

---

171. Id.
172. Indeed, the complex problem of poverty aside, although "[j]urisdictions have always recognized the importance of rehabilitating criminals ... they rarely [have] devoted sufficient money and energy to the programs most likely to succeed." Demleitner et al., *supra* note 154, at 12.
173. *See* Wexler, *Rehabilitative Role*, *supra* note 1, at 748–49.
174. *See generally* Model Rules of Prof'l Conduct R. 1.1 (2006) (competence); *id.* R. 1.4 (communication).
175. Nat'l Legal Aid & Defender Ass'n, *supra* note 13, at Guideline 1.2.
176. *Id.* at Guideline 1.3.

"going rates" of cases in a given locale.[177] Lawyers are also required to timely convey to clients the specific terms of any proposed plea agreement[178] and the various sentencing implications.[179]

Similarly, on appeal, a lawyer should always inform clients of the various issues that can be raised, as well as the risks that may be involved in raising such issues.[180]

Moreover, despite Professor Wexler's suggestion that such practices are an innovation of TJ, good defense lawyers have long collected mitigating evidence from the inception of the case and presented proof of rehabilitation, when appropriate, in plea negotiations and in seeking leniency at sentencing.[181] Such advocacy has often involved defense

---

177. *Id.*; *see id.* Guideline 1.2 cmt. (emphasizing "the need to become familiar with a particular system before guiding clients through it," including becoming aware of the idiosyncratic practices of individual judges and courts); *see also* Am. Bar Ass'n, *supra* note 143, at Standard 4-6.19(a) ("Whenever the law, nature, and circumstances of the case permit, defense counsel should explore the possibility of an early diversion of the case from the criminal process through the use of other community agencies."); Bibas, *supra* note 159, at 957 ("Repeat defense counsel already know the going rates for particular crimes.").

178. Model Rules of Prof'l Conduct R. 1.4 cmt. 2 ("[A] lawyer who receives from opposing counsel ... a proffered plea bargain in a criminal case must promptly inform the client of its substance unless the client has previously indicated that the proposal will be acceptable or unacceptable or has authorized the lawyer to accept or reject the offer."); Am. Bar Ass'n, *supra* note 143, at Standard 4-6.2(b) ("Defense counsel should promptly communicate and explain to the accused all significant plea proposals made by the prosecutor."); Nat'l Legal Aid & Defender Ass'n, *supra* note 13, at Guideline 6.1(c) ("Counsel should keep the client fully informed of any continued plea discussions and negotiations and convey to the accused any offers made by the prosecution for a negotiated settlement.").

179. Model Rules of Prof'l Conduct R. 1.4 cmt. 5 ("The client should have sufficient information to participate intelligently in decisions concerning the objectives of the representation and the means by which they are to be pursued, to the extent the client is willing and able to do so.... For example, when there is time to explain a proposal made in a negotiation, the lawyer should review all important provisions with the client before proceeding to an agreement."); Am. Bar Ass'n, *supra* note 143, at Standard 4-6.2 cmt. ("[T]he client should be given sufficient information to participate intelligently in the decision whether to accept or reject a plea proposal.... It cannot be emphasized too much that a crucial factor in plea discussions is the duty of counsel to explain fully to the accused the consequences of a guilty plea in terms of the range of sentences the court can and may impose."); Nat'l Legal Aid & Defender Ass'n, *supra* note 13, at Guideline 6.2 (noting that when discussing a proposed plea bargain, counsel should inform clients of the maximum term of imprisonment, fine, or restitution that might be ordered if the offer is not accepted, possible consequences of conviction, including deportation, whether good-time credits might be available, and where the client might be confined).

180. Am. Bar Ass'n, *supra* note 143, at Standard 4-8.2 ("Defense counsel should give the defendant his or her professional judgment as to whether there are meritorious grounds for appeal and as to the probable results of an appeal. Defense counsel should also explain to the defendant the advantages and disadvantages of an appeal."); Am. Bar Ass'n, Standards of Criminal Justice: Criminal Appeals, at Standard 21-2.2 (1980) ("Defense counsel should advise a defendant on the meaning of the court's judgment, of defendant's right to appeal, on the possible grounds for appeal, and of the probable outcome of appealing. Counsel should also advise of any posttrial proceedings that might be pursued before or concurrent with an appeal."); Nat'l Legal Aid & Defender Ass'n, *supra* note 13, at Guideline 9.2 ("Counsel's advice to the defendant should include an explanation of the right to appeal the judgment of guilty and, in those jurisdictions where it is permitted, the right to appeal the sentence imposed by the court.").

181. *See* Am. Bar Ass'n, *supra* note 143, at Standard 4-8.1; Nat'l Legal Aid & Defender Ass'n, *supra* note 13, at Guideline 8.1; *id.* at Guideline 8.6. Indeed, such practices were a basic part of my own training during the 1990s as a clinical law student at the University of Texas and as an E. Barrett Prettyman clinical teaching fellow at Georgetown University's Criminal Justice Clinic. It was also encouraged while I was a trial-level public defender at The Bronx Defenders in New York City. My professors and supervisors, it was my understanding, had engaged in such practices for years. *See*

lawyers working with social workers and other mental health professionals to help a client access desired treatment.[182] Similarly, good lawyers also represent clients in seeking modification of sentencing terms where appropriate. Although Professor Wexler suggests that TJ defense attorneys would move to have a client's probation terminated early if it seems appropriate, this is something that any zealous and quality defense attorney should do.[183]

To the extent that defense attorneys are failing to do the things outlined above, regardless of TJ considerations, their performance should be considered substandard. And although it is true, unfortunately, that some individual attorneys and institutional providers are not able to engage in such practices consistently, I do not think this is because defenders generally wish to provide less than adequate representation for their clients.[184] Rather, their inability to satisfy practice standards stems primarily from a lack of resources.[185] Underfunded defender systems have resulted in a lack of training,[186] overwhelming caseloads,[187] and other problems that undermine individual attorneys' ability to do the job they would like to do for their clients.[188] Thus, where lawyers are

---

Rafalsky, *supra* note 145, at 403–05 (discussing various "practical applications" of the "rehabilitative defense strategy" when representing a drug-addicted client in the 1970s, including using proof of rehabilitation during plea discussions and sentencing proceedings).

182. *See generally* Jack B. Weinstein, *When Is a Social Worker as Well as a Lawyer* Needed?, 2 J. Inst. Stud. Legal Ethics 391 (1999).

183. For instance, last semester as a standard part of effective representation, one of my clinic students at the University of Tennessee made a successful motion to have a client moved from supervised to unsupervised probation.

184. See Joan W. Howarth, Women Defenders on Television: Representing Suspects and the Racial Politics of Retribution, 3 J. Gender Race & Just. 475, 485 (2000) (noting that although "feminist women defenders derive great satisfaction from their work," many are frustrated and fear they are not able to represent clients adequately given the constraints under which they operate); Silver, supra note 169, at 364 n.91 (explaining that although public defenders often are viewed as less devoted to clients than private counsel, "[i]n reality ... many public defender offices employ enthusiastic, capable young attorneys who, to the extent their oppressive caseloads and limited investigative resources permit, ably defend their clients").

185. As Professors Charles Ogletree and Yoav Sapir note:
   The growth of the public defense system after the Gideon decision was never matched by sufficient increases in funding, and the situation has grown even worse in recent years.... Largely due to the lack of financial resources, the public defense system lacks a sufficient number of lawyers. The understaffing and lack of funding result in a situation in which the small number of lawyers who are willing to do the work are burdened with high caseloads, tremendous responsibility and pressure, a widely held presumption that public defenders are overworked and unqualified, a sense of isolation, and the frustration of doing work that includes a large bureaucratic, non-legal component.
Ogletree & Sapir, *supra* note 146, at 214–15 (footnotes omitted); *see also* Backus & Marcus *supra* note 139, at 1036 (stating that "we have known for decades" the only remedy for the deplorable "state of affairs" in public defense services is "decent financial support from the government for indigent defense, and the presence of well-prepared, reasonably paid, resourceful lawyers"); White, *supra* note 126, at 553 (discussing the history of the lack of resources provided to public defenders' offices).

186. *See* Backus & Marcus, *supra* note 139, at 1093–96.

187. *Id.* at 1053–59 (describing public defender caseloads as frequently far exceeding the recommended numbers of 150 felonies or 400 misdemeanors in one year). Indeed, in my own experience, New York City trial-level public defenders often represent approximately 100 clients at any one time. *See also* David Feige, Indefensible 30 (2006) (indicating that as an entry level public defender in New York City the author carried between 100 and 125 cases at a time).

188. *See* Backus & Marcus, *supra* note 139, at 1080–87 (noting, for instance, that overburdened public defenders often do "not have the time or the resources to investigate, prepare, or communi-

falling short in the level of representation they are providing, generally it is not as a result of adhering to a "traditional" lawyering model. Converting to TJ defense lawyering would not, therefore, correct this problem.

Professor Wexler's assertion that TJ lawyers attempt to assist clients beyond the confines of the specific legal case also fails to advance his agenda of recasting the role of defense counsel. As he seems to acknowledge, many private defense attorneys, public defenders' offices, and legal clinics currently assist clients with matters that extend beyond the parameters of the criminal prosecution, and they have done so for quite some time.[189] Such lawyers have helped clients, when appropriate, with parole applications,[190] housing issues, accessing government services, addressing civil disabilities that may stem from conviction, and more.[191] Most defense lawyers, however, offer such ancillary assistance[192] only as time, resources, and other obligations permit.[193] Thus, there is

---

cate adequately with the client so that the client can make an informed decision and the attorney can advocate zealously for his client's best interests"); *see also* White, *supra* note 126, at 553.

189. *See* Wexler, *Rehabilitative Role*, *supra* note 1, at 744.

190. For instance, Professor Hastings Jones of Florida A&M University College of Law previously ran a very successful parole hearing representation program at the Public Defender Service for the District of Columbia, which he took over after it was founded by Kirby Howlett, an attorney and professor at Georgetown Law Center. Interview with Professor Hastings Jones, Fla. A&M Univ. Coll. of Law (Feb. 19, 2007). Georgetown Law Center's Criminal Justice Clinic students help provide representation to inmates and parolees through the program that Jones developed and ran. *See* Georgetown Law Ctr., Criminal Justice Clinic, www.law.georgetown.edu/clinics/cjc (last visited Mar. 12, 2007) (noting that participants in the clinic engage in post-conviction representation of incarcerated persons).

191. In New York City, The Bronx Defenders, Brooklyn Defenders, Neighborhood Defender Service of Harlem and The Legal Aid Society currently provide a wide range of ancillary services to clients, including representation on immigration and other noncriminal matters, and have been doing so for several years. *See, e.g.*, The Bronx Defenders, The Civil Action Project, http://www.bronxdefenders.org/?page=content& param=the_civil_action_project (last visited Mar. 12, 2007) (describing the work of the lawyers with The Bronx Defenders' Civil Action Project); Brooklyn Defender Servs., Client Resources, http://www.bds. org/client_resources.htm (last visited Mar. 12, 2007) (providing referral and contact information for a variety of social service providers); Legal Aid Soc'y, http://www.legal-aid.org/(last visited Mar. 12, 2007) (explaining the array of services it provides, including representation in criminal, housing, immigration, and other matters); Neighborhood Defender Serv. of Harlem, NDS Programs, http://www.ndsny.org/programs.htm (last visited Mar. 12, 2007) (explaining that since 1990 the Neighborhood Defender Service of Harlem office has provided not just criminal defense representation but other services, like community education workshops).

192. As will be discussed further *infra* notes 196–216 and accompanying text, providing ancillary "therapeutic" assistance to clients is a delicate matter. It is not appropriate in every case. Some clients might wish to access such services; others might not. Client boundaries and decisions must be respected. Certainly, defense attorneys are not in a position to decide how their clients should live their lives and should not assume such a paternalistic position.

Moreover, unlike TJ's seemingly unmitigated acceptance of judicial oversight and involvement in treatment and rehabilitation, many of the offices listed above try to offer services to clients outside of criminal court proceedings, in part to protect against the risk of punishment if the client fails in treatment or other rehabilitative efforts. *See* Steinberg & Feige, *supra* note 135, at 124–25 (stating that "much client-centered work occurs outside the hallways and stairwells of the courthouse" and "does not interfere with courtroom advocacy"); *see also* Spinak, *supra* note 166, at 1619 (noting that "defenders raise serious questions about funding the courts to provide services to their clients that may be more appropriately funded through other treatment and social services systems").

193. Cait Clarke & James Neuhard, *"From Day One": Who's in Control as Problem Solving and Client-Centered Sentencing Take Center Stage?*, 29 N.Y.U. Rev. L. & Soc. Change 11, 21 (2004–05) (quoting an unnamed public defender as indicating that "[w]ithout the resources needed to free up time, people object that the time they have must be dedicated to direct client advocacy").

nothing inherent in the current role of defense counsel—"traditional" or otherwise—that precludes such assistance or requires modification to allow for it. In fact, if there were more resources available for such expanded and continuing services, there is little doubt that they would be offered more regularly. Again, the real problem is one of funding. For these reasons, Professor Wexler's apparent discontent with the current defense bar seems somewhat misplaced, and his proposed solution of expanding its role with "new" proposed practices likely will not resolve the problem.

2. The New but Not at All Improved Practices

Although many of the "new" practices that Professor Wexler outlines are already very much a part of what quality defense attorneys do, a number of the suggested actions present ethical and professional responsibility concerns. TJ defense lawyering concepts, as applied, may well displace important normative principles that the criminal defense community has embraced for decades.

First and foremost, Professor Wexler's menu of TJ lawyering practices covers a number of stages of the criminal process, but fails to address the possibility of trial—the constitutional "main course" of criminal defense work. This omission seems to suggest that Professor Wexler would accept two tiers of lawyers—those who try cases and those who do not. This kind of separation fails to acknowledge the complexities of criminal practice. A lawyer cannot always know how a case is going to be resolved.[194] A client always has the final word on whether he or she wishes to plead guilty or demand a trial, and is always entitled to change his or her mind.[195] In fact, experienced lawyers know that after spending endless hours preparing for trial, a case may be resolved by plea bargain on the eve thereof. And, conversely, many potential guilty pleas break down at the last minute, requiring a case to be tried on the merits. Thus, zealous and quality representation means keeping all options in mind and being prepared to provide the best representation possible no matter how things unfold. Quickly transferring a case when trial rears its head generally is not a sound option. Thus, both in theory and practice, TJ defense lawyering seems to subordinate zeal to therapeutic considerations.

Various other TJ scenarios that Professor Wexler has outlined drive home the tension between lawyers serving as change agents and zealous defenders. For instance, Professor Wexler makes clear that he is in favor of purported "problem-solving" courts and suggests that TJ defense attorneys should embrace such institutions, including drug treatment and reentry courts.[196] He concedes, however, that some of these institutions may harm defendants by requiring a guilty plea to obtain treatment, by setting them up for failure, or by placing them under supervision when they would not otherwise be subjected to such observation.[197] Even if such courts claim to be concerned with rehabilita-

---

194. As will be addressed further, *infra* notes 238–248 and accompanying text, the tensions of assuming otherwise are borne out by examining John McShane's practice—the paradigmatic TJ lawyer who, according to Wexler, has taken TJ "all the way."

195. *See* Jones v. Barnes, 463 U.S. 745, 751 (1983); Model Rules of Prof'l Conduct R. 1.2 (2006) (Scope of Representation); Am. Bar Ass'n, *supra* note 143, at Standard 4-5.2 (Control and Direction of the Case).

196. Wexler, *Rehabilitative Role*, *supra* note 1, at 749.

197. *Id.* at 750–51; *see also* Mae C. Quinn, *Revisiting Anna Moscowitz Kross's Critique of New York City's Women's Court: The Continued Problem of Solving the "Problem" of Prostitution with Specialized Criminal Courts,* 33 Fordham Urb. L.J. 665, 710–26 (2006) (discussing problems that specialized criminal courts present); Quinn, supra note 67, at 61–63; cf. U.S. Gen. Accounting Office, Drug Courts: Better DOJ Data Collection and Evaluation Efforts Needed to Measure Impact of Drug Court Programs 15 (2002), available at http://www.gao.gov/new.items/d02434.pdf (reporting

tion and the psychological well-being of defendants, encouraging clients to participate in such institutions could subject them to harsher sanctions or penalties. Indeed, if a particular drug court is known for sending a third of its participants to prison after making a good faith effort at treatment, defense counsel would do well to challenge the court's existence rather than merely advise clients that entering the court's program presents a risk.[198]

Professor Wexler's recommendations that clients propose conditions of probation they believe appropriate and that lawyers keep an open mind to being "innovative" leaves room for less-than-zealous representation as well.[199] Indeed, Professor Wexler goes so far as to imply that in some cases it might be appropriate for a lawyer to encourage a client to take preemptive steps to appease a court—as in the matter of a defendant with several children having a vasectomy—when it would be illegal for a court to order that such steps be taken as a term of probation. These suggested practices fail, however, to draw adequately upon a lawyer's legal expertise to attempt to protect the client from legal risks. Accordingly, such suggested practices underscore the likely conflict between TJ considerations in practice and current standards.

Some of the practices that Professor Wexler proposes also demonstrate the ways in which TJ defense lawyering might undermine the presumption of innocence, replacing it with a presumption of guilt and recidivist potential. The TJ lawyer apparently presses a client who has pleaded guilty to accept genuine responsibility for his actions by considering the perspective of his alleged victim, for instance by "reenact[ing] the crime, playing the role of the victim," or watching videotapes of victims' statements.[200] Such actions are suggested, not only to convince the judge that leniency is warranted, but because it "is generally regarded as therapeutically welcome by the victim and a good first rehabilitative step for the defendant," especially if accompanied by an apology to the victim.[201] This set of TJ considerations, however, fails to acknowledge that many defendants plead guilty even though they are not,[202] and that many "guilty" defendants are forced by courts and prosecutors to allocute[203] to wrongdoings they did not commit as a condition of receiving the plea "bargain."[204] In such scenarios, it would be disingenuous

---

that "[the Department of Justice] continues to lack vital information that the Congress, the public, and other program stakeholders may need to determine the overall impact of federally funded drug court programs and to assess whether drug court programs are an effective use of federal funds" and that such information will not be available until at least 2007).

198. *See* Am. Bar Ass'n, *supra* note 143, at Standard 4-1.2(d) ("Defense counsel should seek to reform and improve the administration of justice. When inadequacies or injustices in the substantive and procedural law come to defense counsel's attention he or she should stimulate efforts for remedial actions.").

199. *See* Wexler, *Rehabilitative Role*, *supra* note 1, at 761–63.

200. *Id.* at 755.

201. Id.

202. *See supra* note 159 and accompanying text. As noted *supra* notes 147 and 150–151, advocacy for these proposed new practices has not been accompanied by strong empirical evidence or other convincing social science proof.

203. By "allocute" I am referring to the statement of facts that the defendant offers at the time of her guilty plea, which generally must satisfy the elements of the crime of conviction. This differs from the more traditional understanding of the term that Kimberly Thomas thoughtfully considers in her recent comprehensive history. *See* Kimberly Thomas, Beyond Mitigation: Towards a Theory of Allocution (Feb. 10, 2007) (unpublished manuscript, on file with author).

204. *Cf.* Bibas, *supra* note 159, at 924 (noting that "[c]harge bargaining divorces convictions from actual crimes so that, in court, murder becomes manslaughter and burglary becomes breaking and entering").

to accept responsibility in the manner contemplated, and disrespectful for the lawyer to suggest that the client do so. In addition, these suggestions leave no room for the possibility that a defendant who has committed the crime charged may not ever reoffend and, therefore, does not need to be reformed.[205]

This example also drives home the extent to which the TJ criminal defense model may suggest erroneously a level of inherent wisdom on the part of defense attorneys that allows them to enjoy a position superior to their clients. There is, however, seldom any way for defense attorneys to "know" when clients are truly innocent or guilty, much less to "know" if they are feeling remorseful or "know" what would assist in rehabilitating them. Assuming such superior knowledge, and then trying to "teach[] clients about how to avoid future problems"[206] or offering advice based upon such supposed insights, seems potentially paternalistic and misguided. Professor Wexler underscores this impression that defense lawyers "know" more than their clients in his description of the model exchange between a TJ lawyer and client on the topic of probation compliance, which Professor Wexler concedes sounds like "a kind of Socratic dialogue" to get the client to agree with counsel about proposed probation conditions and future behaviors that would be most rehabilitative.[207]

This paternalistic approach also colors the attorney-client relationship in the other TJ vignettes that Professor Wexler sketches. Again, looking at the "Socratic dialogue" example, it is clear that the lawyer has personal beliefs about the kinds of behaviors the client should avoid in the future, which he would like to offer to the court as proposed probation terms.[208] Thus, this agenda, coupled with the hierarchical attorney-client arrangement, appears to result in client manipulation.[209] Indeed, Professor Wexler is clear about his hope that the client will concur with defense counsel's suggestions about how he should live his life[210] and "buy into a change of behavior that should reduce the

---

205. *See supra* notes 159–161 and accompanying text. Similarly, considering the intrinsic value of a plea of guilty—that is, its effect on the victim's therapeutic needs and on the defendant's rehabilitation—may be inconsistent with providing zealous representation. Indeed, it would be wholly inappropriate under present norms for a lawyer to advise a client to accept or reject a plea offer based upon the lawyer's concern for the victim's psychological well-being or his desire to reform the client. Thus, Professor Wexler's suggestion that TJ lawyers should consider such matters, if such consideration is for purposes of advancing substantive advice, is troubling. *See* Wexler, *Rehabilitative Role*, *supra* note 1, at 754–55. *See generally* Jeffrie G. Murphy, *Well Excuse Me!—Remorse, Apology, and Criminal Sentencing*, 38 Ariz. St. L.J. 371 (2006) (challenging the current "culture of apology" and expressing skepticism about the appropriateness of integrating apologies into criminal sentencing schemes).

206. *See supra* note 100 and accompanying text; *see also supra* note 81 and accompanying text (discussing the encouragement of "vicarious learning" for the client through observation of drug court practices).

207. Wexler, *Rehabilitative Role*, *supra* note 1, at 759–60.

208. *Id.*

209. *See id.*

210. Although Professor Wexler's desire to have criminal defense clients live "good lives" seems wholly well-intended, *see id.* at 757 n.73, over the years well-respected poverty lawyers and clinicians have examined and rejected such misguided good intentions to "fix" clients and the way they live. *See* Lucie E. White, *Subordination, Rhetorical Survival Skills, and Sunday Shoes: Notes on the Hearing of Mrs. G.*, 38 Buff. L. Rev. 1, 4 (1990). Professor Laurie A. Morin offers a particularly relevant description of such critiques:

> It is not sufficient for legal service providers to identify clients who represent the community; in order to provide "client-centered" legal services, they must develop relationships of mutual trust and responsibility rather than lawyer domination and client subordination. Perhaps the best-known critic of the predominant form of lawyering for poor people is Gerald Lopez, whose book *Rebellious Lawyering* admonishes that good inten-

risk of criminality."²¹¹ This hardly seems consistent with respect for autonomous decision making and individual choice, which TJ has steadfastly claimed to support.²¹²

Not only may the TJ practice proposals encourage defense lawyers to assume that they know better than their clients, such proposals may invite lawyers to assume expertise they do not have. Although Professor Wexler contends that defense attorneys do not have to be psychologists or social workers to do TJ work,²¹³ his menu of best practices suggests such role enhancements. Both of the scenarios discussed earlier—pressing a client to feel remorse genuinely through the "perspective taking approach" and purporting to know what kinds of behaviors a client should avoid if he wants not to offend—to some degree involve lawyers making assumptions about areas well beyond the law. More to the point, however, are the suggestions that Professor Wexler offers for helping clients to rehabilitate while on probation. Although he offers only a brief outline of such teachings, Professor Wexler recommends that defense lawyers employ relatively complex psychological concepts like compliance and relapse principles to help clients successfully complete a probated sentence.²¹⁴ Although thinking outside the legal

---

tions do not necessarily prevent poverty lawyers from perpetuating patterns of injustice in their relationships with poor clients. His tales of "regnant" lawyers describe the perils of treating clients like objects to fix rather than like human beings.

Laurie A. Morin, Legal Services Attorneys as Partners in Community Economic Development: Creating Wealth for Poor Communities Through Cooperative Economics, 5 D.C. L. Rev. 125, 168 (2000). See generally Gerald P. Lopez, Rebellious Lawyering: One Chicano's Vision of Progressive Law Practice (1992); Anthony V. Alfieri, Disabled Clients, Disabling Lawyers, 43 Hastings L.J. 769 (1992).

211. *See* Wexler, *Rehabilitative Role*, *supra* note 1, at 759–60.

212. As Professor Kruse aptly notes in her examination of client-centered representation: "There is a real difference—an important difference—between helping someone achieve what she really wants or values, and imposing what you think she should really want or value on her. This distinction marks off the boundary between enhancing her autonomy and paternalistically intervening into her decision-making." Kruse, *supra* note 135, at 410–11. Kruse goes on to note that "in practice" it is "often hard to tell the difference" between a client's desires and values, and the desires and values of counsel. *Id.* When the TJ lawyer comes to the table with a pre-set agenda of advancing client change and rehabilitation, however, and "hopes" that the client will change his or her mind to see things from the lawyer's perspective, there seems to be little question about whose values are superior in the attorney-client relationship. *See also supra* notes 103–106 and accompanying text.

It should be noted that Kruse also recognizes the value of challenging a client's stated desires in some situations. For instance, she suggests that the "client-empowerment approach" might be necessary to "move the client in the direction of self-sufficiency and self-actualization." Kruse, *supra* note 135, at 423–24. This approach is based on the notion "that a client's stated wishes may not accurately reflect the client's true desires, and that lawyers who too quickly accept the client's stated wishes as 'marching orders' will end up working in ways that are at odds with the client's real needs and interests." *Id.* She is careful to point out that this kind of client-centered lawyering seems appropriate in limited circumstances, for instance when representing a battered woman who "face[s] internal obstacles to self-actualization" and may not have the present "capacity to make truly autonomous choices" based upon her history of abuse and oppression. *Id.* Although this author believes such an approach may be problematic as it can run the risk of client essentializing, it at least suggests narrowly drawn exceptions to accepting a client's life choices from which TJ defense lawyering theory might benefit. *See id.*

213. Wexler, *Rehabilitative Role*, *supra* note 1, at 747–48.

214. *Id.* at 757. Here, again, these suggestions seem to be made without strong behavioral science and empirical data to support their adoption. *See* Wexler & Winick, *supra* note 5, at 708. For instance, Professor Wexler suggests, without any real social scientific evidence, that a client is more likely to comply with a probation plan if he has assisted in proposing it. *See* Wexler, *Rehabilitative Role*, *supra* note 1, at 761, 763; *see also* Winick & Wexler, *supra* note 1, at 621–22 (claiming, without any scientific support, that "[t]he direct involvement of the youth[ful offender] in preparation of

box might be useful to good defense lawyering, it would be wholly inappropriate for a lawyer to offer professional advice that he is not qualified to offer.[215] Lawyers who do so run the risk not only of undermining client confidence in their work, but also of running afoul of ethical rules.[216]

Perhaps most problematic is the extent to which the proposed TJ practices fail to account adequately for some of the real challenges that poverty lawyers and their clients face.[217] For example, Professor Wexler strongly suggests that defense lawyers delay sentencing for as long as possible to enable the lawyer to work with clients on post-offense rehabilitation, as in the case of *United States v. Flowers*[218] Although McShane and others who are privately retained may find that clients are willing and able to work for weeks or months on personal improvement plans to get themselves back "on track," often this is not the overwhelming experience of attorneys who represent those struggling under the burden of poverty. First, many poor clients are forced to live transient lives, from street to shelter to hotel to wherever they might be able to find a safe place to stay.[219] Their day-to-day battle to survive, which is sometimes complicated by addiction or other issues, takes priority over returning to court when required, let alone staying in touch with therapists or attorneys.[220] Beyond this, there are simply not enough services available to poor clients who cannot afford private rehabilitation programs.[221] Thus, for

---

the [deferred probation revocation] plan [offered to avoid immediate revocation of probation] would itself increase the likelihood that he will comply with it and benefit therefrom").

215. *See* Taylor-Thompson, *supra* note 135, at 166 ("Some of the client's needs may reach well beyond the defender's area of expertise."). Take, for instance, the example of the "classic case" of the alleged repeat DUI offender. *See* Wexler, *Rehabilitative Role*, *supra* note 1, at 744. Professor Wexler seems to support attorney McShane's assessment of the "real" nonlegal problem plaguing such a client—alcoholism. *See id.* at 744. However, a recent study by the Pacific Institute for Research and Evaluation (the "PIRE"), a nonprofit public health research group funded largely with federal science grants, has found that a majority of alleged repeat DUI offenders suffer from serious mental health issues in addition to problems with alcoholism. *See Study Finds Repeat DUI Offenders Have High Mental Illness Rates*, Med. News Today, Sept. 22, 2006, www.medicalnewstoday.com/medical-news.php?newsid= 52450. Indeed, the PIRE study's principal investigator, a medical doctor, would seem to reject the simplistic assessment offered of this "classic case," noting that an "offender should be viewed as a unique person with a unique set of issues." Id.

216. *See supra* note 164 and accompanying text.

217. *See* Backus & Marcus, supra note 139, at 1034 ("Poor people account for more than 80% of individuals prosecuted.").

218. 983 F. Supp. 159, 170 (E.D.N.Y. 1997); Wexler, Rehabilitative Role, supra note 1, at 756. Although Professor Wexler points to Flowers as instructive, this federal felony airport drug courier case is rather different from the majority of low-level street crime matters encountered by public defenders in local criminal courts. See Wexler, Rehabilitative Role, supra note 1, at 756. As a mother with a job and significant ties to the community, Flowers was released after arraignment on a $250,000 appearance bond. See Docket Sheet, Flowers, No. 96-CR-01064 (E.D.N.Y. Nov. 26, 1996). At the time of her guilty plea, therefore, she was free on bail and able to demonstrate her commitment to rehabilitative efforts by complying with Pretrial Services conditions. Flowers, 983 F. Supp. at 161. In addition, the opinion of the Honorable Jack B. Weinstein deferring sentence for one year indicates that Flowers was not a drug user or substance abuser, as are many clients represented by public defenders in local criminal courts. Id. Therefore, from a defense lawyer's perspective, the risks of adjourning her case were relatively low.

219. See supra note 144 and accompanying text.

220. As noted by Professor Kim Taylor-Thompson: "Quality-of-life campaigns have swept large numbers of individuals with mental health and substance abuse problems into the criminal justice system. Representing these individuals fairly and effectively often means stabilizing them sufficiently to enable them to make judgments about their cases." Taylor-Thompson, *supra* note 135, at 165.

221. My experience suggests that this problem is even greater for clients outside of urban areas where nonprofit agencies and social services providers seem to focus their attention. Smaller cities

many public defenders and law school clinics, routinely encouraging adjournment to allow elaborate rehabilitation efforts and further court appearances runs the risk of setting up clients for failure—and harsher sanctions from courts when they fail to follow through with promises. Accordingly, pursuing such a course is not as straightforward as Professor Wexler might imply.

Similarly, turning again to the "Socratic dialogue," the tone and content of this suggested conversation simply do not capture the complex realities facing individuals that public defenders and legal clinics represent—many of whom are charged with crimes motivated by poverty.[222] Indeed, talking with a probation-eligible urban, teenage drug dealer about the "chain of events" that led him to sell drugs or about "patterns" that might lead him to want to sell more in the future—a conversation that is laden with judgment and blame—seems futile without offering some meaningful alternative.[223] Such situations differ from those of suburban youths repeatedly getting traffic tickets, and present nuances that are not accounted for in the TJ model. The socioeconomic "patterns" that may lead an individual to sell drugs as a means of support may not be avoided as easily as speeding tickets. And there is little a defense lawyer can "teach" a client about avoiding poverty in the future.[224] Thus, the proposed lawyer behaviors do not seem to be sufficiently in tune with the work of those appointed to represent the indigent accused.[225] Accordingly, in theory and in practice, TJ defense lawyering may contribute to the already difficult issue of distrust on the part of such clients.[226]

C. *Role Change and Practitioners: The Guest List*

1. Public Defenders and Clinics

Turning to those who have been included in the invitation, public defenders and clinicians are high up on the TJ movement's guest list. Unfortunately, Professor Wexler has offered a far less than flattering take on them.[227] Yet, as already noted, many public defenders are already trying to do much of what has been suggested by attempting to

---

and rural areas seem to have the greatest dearth of services for the poor. *See* Debra Lyn Basset, *Distancing Rural Poverty*, 13 Geo. J. on Poverty L. & Pol'y 3, 15–24 (2006); Louise Trubek & Jennifer Farnham, *Social Justice Collaboratives: Multidisciplinary Practice for People*, 7 Clinical L. Rev. 227, 248 (2000); *see also* Diane E. Courselle, *When Clinics Are "Necessities, Not Luxuries": Special Challenges of Running a Criminal Appeals Clinic in a Rural State*, 75 Miss. L.J. 721, 733 (2006); Lisa R. Pruitt, *Toward a Feminist Theory of the Rural*, 2007 Utah L. Rev. (forthcoming), *available at* http://papers.ssrn.com/sol3/papers.cfm?abstract_id=933352 (examining the unique legal and other hardships that women face living in rural areas in the United States).

222. *See* Wexler, Rehabilitative Role, *supra* note 1, at 760.

223. Similarly, one wonders how this kind of interaction would translate in other scenarios—for instance, in dealing with an alleged gang member charged with assault while part of such a group. The somewhat artificial or unnatural tone of the conversation that might follow demonstrates the limits of this kind of client counseling: "When do you find that you get into fights with rival gang members? Is it when you are with others or by yourself?"

224. *See supra* note 206 and accompanying text.

225. This is despite TJ's claim that it is concerned with "cultural competence." Wexler, *Rehabilitative Role*, *supra* note 1, at 748.

226. *See* Taylor-Thompson, *supra* note 135, at 173 (stating that "in too many jurisdictions, clients and their families tend not to view the defender as an aggressive or especially effective voice in the courtroom"); *see also* Marcus T. Boccaccini & Stanley L. Brodsky, *Characteristics of the Ideal Criminal Defense Attorney from the Client's Perspective: Empirical Findings and Implications for Legal Practice*, 25 Law & Psychol. Rev. 81, 87 (2001). *See generally* Kenneth P. Troccoli, "I Want a Black Lawyer to Represent Me": Addressing a Black Defendant's Concerns with Being Assigned a White Court-Appointed Lawyer, 20 Law & Ineq. 1 (2002).

227. *See* Wexler, Rehabilitative Role, *supra* note 1, at 747.

stay abreast of developments in their jurisdiction, properly advising clients about the implications of guilty pleas, diligently preparing for sentencing, and involving clients in the appellate process—despite operating within very limited budgets.[228] Thus, these lawyers should not be vilified for failing to do more. Nor should it be suggested they take on additional tasks without providing meaningful suggestions about how they might be accomplished.

Unfortunately, Professor Wexler's proposal to improve services by using private funds, in part to provide for specialized lawyers to take on an "explicit TJ role," is somewhat unrealistic and potentially unwise. Indeed, many public defenders' offices already engage in significant fundraising and grant request efforts. Some, in fact, fund expanded legal services with such monies.[229] If more funds were out there, I suspect they would have tapped into them.[230] And using only private funds to run a public defenders' office may run the risk of relying upon the will and agenda of the funding entities.[231] Indeed, it is easy to imagine a situation where this kind of power might be abused, particularly if wealthy individuals wished to reform a given community with the use of defense lawyers who would employ only TJ approaches, as is further addressed below.[232]

In contrast to public defenders' offices, law school clinics have a wealth of resources and time to provide high-level services to their criminal clients.[233] As a matter of course, such programs, with their low client case loads frequently staffed with two student attorneys, are able to go the extra mile for clients.[234] In addition to being pushed to provide the best legal defense possible for their clients, student attorneys are able to spend time talking with clients about other problems they may be facing, assisting them to access social services, and helping to expunge their criminal record if possible. Thus, the notion of providing criminal defense services in a manner that is not myopically focused on the resolution of the criminal charge is very much a part of what clinics teach (and have taught) students to prepare them to provide both zealous and quality representation.[235] The real challenge for the clinical community is not to prevent students from merely replicating the practices of overworked public defenders while in clinic, but to prepare them for the differences between clinical practice—where they might handle a handful of cases at a time—and real-world practice with its "crushing case-

---

228. See supra note 185 and accompanying text.
229. See Equal Justice Works, Profiles, http://info.equaljusticeworks.org/fellowships/profiles/02print.asp (last visited Mar. 12, 2007) (announcing that The Bronx Defenders obtained funding from Equal Justice Works to help assign a lawyer to the local drug treatment court both to monitor the workings of the court and to ensure that clients were receiving adequate representation).
230. See Wright, supra note 146, at 9–14 (reporting on the struggles of the Knox County Community Law Office in maintaining its social work and related programs as "the original grants have expired and funding shortfalls have required cuts in services and staff layoffs").
231. See Backus & Marcus, supra note 139, at 1046–53 (discussing various funding schemes for public defender programs, including private contract arrangements).
232. See infra notes 237–248 and accompanying text.
233. See Geraghty, supra note 149, at 717 ("Law school clinical programs have also taken the lead in modeling effective representation in juvenile courts and criminal courts and have provided technical support and training to defender organizations.").
234. See id. at 718 (explaining that in comparison to overworked public defender offices, law school clinics generally have the freedom to pick and choose cases and may decide to take on matters that allow them to make systemic challenges).
235. See id. at 714–15 (noting that students in Northwestern's criminal and juvenile clinic learn the importance of caring for clients and that "[c]aring involves empathy and a demonstration of commitment to advance the client's interests").

load[s]."²³⁶ Nonetheless, I would rather struggle to arm my students with appropriate responses to those less-than-ideal circumstances than suggest that they instead embrace a solely rehabilitative approach when they graduate—by taking "TJ all the way."

2. Lawyers Taking "TJ All the Way"

From my perspective, rather than being held out as a guest of honor, the paradigmatic TJ criminal defense attorney who takes "TJ all the way" presents a host of serious concerns. The description of the wholly TJ practice that Professor Wexler offers seems potentially inconsistent with professional norms. Even Professor Wexler appears to concede that it would be inappropriate for a public defender to adopt the stance of John McShane and turn away clients who refuse to plead guilty in order to engage in rehabilitative efforts.²³⁷ Presumably this is because conditioning representation on an admission of guilt and forfeiture of the right to trial would violate the defendant's Sixth Amendment rights to effective assistance of counsel and trial by jury.²³⁸ It therefore seems inappropriate to celebrate such conduct and to promote it as an exemplar in the defense community. This is particularly true given the difficulty in enlisting lawyers to represent zealously the most reviled in our nation.²³⁹

What is more, the restrictions McShane places on his services, even for paying clients, present somewhat of an ethical quagmire. For instance, although the American Bar Association's Model Rules of Professional Conduct permit limits on representation, such limitations must be reasonable.²⁴⁰ And such limitations do not exempt a lawyer from providing competent representation.²⁴¹ Questions of reasonableness and competence may arise, however, when a lawyer advises a client to plead guilty without first investigating the matter fully, regardless of the client's version of events, and without determining the strength of the prosecution's evidence and other possible weaknesses in the case.²⁴²

---

236. *See* Smith, *supra* note 161, at 1257.
237. Wexler, *Rehabilitative Role*, *supra* note 1, at 772.
238. *See* U.S. Const. amend. VI; *Jones*, 463 U.S. at 753.
239. Backus & Marcus, *supra* note 139, at 1063 (describing the difficulties inherent in attracting attorneys to represent the accused); White, *supra* note 126, at 545 (noting that defense attorneys are unpopular figures in the eyes of the general public and politicians); *see also* Am. Bar Ass'n, *supra* note 143, at Standard 4-1.6(a)-(b) ("Lawyers should be encouraged to qualify themselves for participation in criminal cases both by formal training and through experience as associate counsel. All such qualified lawyers should stand ready to undertake the defense of an accused regardless of public hostility toward the accused or personal distaste for the offense charged or the person of the defendant."); *id.* at cmt. ("Lawyers who unabashedly state that they do not practice in the criminal courts denigrate their role and function as advocates. The bar should discourage lawyers from privately or publicly proclaiming that they disdain criminal practice.").
240. Model Rules of Prof'l Conduct R. 1.2(c) (2006) ("A lawyer may limit the scope of the representation if the limitation is reasonable under the circumstances and the client gives informed consent.").
241. The commentary to Rule 1.2 provides that "an agreement for a limited representation does not exempt a lawyer from the duty to provide competent representation." *Id.* R. 1.2 cmt. 7.
242. Am. Bar Ass'n, *supra* note 143, at Standard 4-6.1(b) ("Under no circumstances should defense counsel recommend to a defendant acceptance of a plea unless appropriate investigation and study of the case has been completed, including an analysis of controlling law and the evidence likely to be introduced at trial."); Nat'l Legal Aid & Defender Ass'n, *supra* note 13, at Guideline 4.1 cmt. ("While the decision to enter a plea of guilty ultimately belongs to the defendant, counsel's duty to investigate is not negated solely by a client's initial stated desire to plead guilty."); *see also* Model Rules of Prof'l Conduct R. 1.3 ("A lawyer shall act with reasonable diligence and promptness in representing a client.").
The commentary to the ABA Model Rules provides that "[a] lawyer should ... take whatever law-

The "TJ all the way" paradigm also fails to take into account the unknowns in criminal practice. As already noted, defendants have the right to decide whether to plead guilty or proceed to trial, and have the right to change their mind on this all-important question. It is easily imaginable that a client who initially agrees with a solely TJ approach might change his mind.[243] If this should happen, presumably the TJ "all the way" lawyer would refer the client to another lawyer who would be willing to try the case. Particularly after the case has been pending for several months, however, important investigative time may be lost.[244] Moreover, TJ criminal defense lawyering raises the specter of a "noisy withdrawal" that could harm the client, especially if the TJ lawyer is known as someone who will only represent clients who initially admit guilt.[245]

What is more, if a prosecutor were dealing with a defense lawyer who is known for refusing to try certain kinds of cases, it is hard to imagine that he would extend favorable offers to the defender because there would be no fear that the client would reject an offer.[246] In light of this apparent lack of leverage, the "all the way" model raises an additional question of effective representation.[247]

One also wonders what the TJ "all the way" lawyer would do if a client relapsed. Is the model sufficiently nuanced to permit the attorney to defend the client fully and attempt to protect him from a judge who might hold the relapse against the client? Or would the limitation on representation, with its affirmative agreement on the part of the client that he will undertake rehabilitative efforts, be read as permitting the lawyer to inform on his client and provide less than zealous representation in the name of TJ?[248] Given these concerns, and the others outlined above, it is clear to me that the par-

---

ful and ethical measures are required to vindicate a client's cause or endeavor." Model Rules of Prof'l Conduct R. 1.3 cmt. 1. Other commentary to the Rules provides that an "advocate has a duty to use legal procedure for the fullest benefit of the client's cause." *Id.* at R. 3.1 cmt. 1; *see also* Guggenheim, *supra* note 146, at 14 ("Lawyers cannot intelligently engage in plea bargaining, for example, until they have conducted an investigation into the facts of the case to determine the strength of the prosecution's case and the potential for mounting a defense.").

243. Clarke & Neuhard, *supra* note 193, at 47 ("A criminal defense lawyer must never abandon the core of the defense function—effective trial advocacy skills—because there are always cases that need to be tried and won in court.").

244. See Model Rules of Prof'l Conduct R. 1.3 ("A lawyer shall act with reasonable diligence and promptness in representing a client."); Am. Bar Ass'n, *supra* note 143, at Standard 4-1.3; Nat'l Legal Aid & Defender Ass'n, *supra* note 13, at Guideline 4.1; see also Clarke & Neuhard, *supra* note 193, at 14 (noting that "[e]ffective representation requires" both trial and sentencing preparation, and that such preparation "should begin as early in the representation process as possible").

245. See Model Rules of Prof'l Conduct R. 1.16(b) ("[A] lawyer may withdraw from representing a client if withdrawal can be accomplished without material adverse effect on the interests of the client."). The commentary provides, however, that "[a] lawyer may withdraw if the client refuses to abide by the terms of an agreement relating to the representation, such as ... an agreement limiting the objectives of the representation." *Id.* R. 1.16 cmt. 8.

246. See Am. Bar Ass'n, *supra* note 143, at Standard 4-6.2 cmt. ("In a criminal case, unless advised to the contrary by his or her client, defense counsel may ordinarily proceed on the assumption, for purposes of discussion with the prosecution only, that the defendant may be willing to enter a plea of guilty to some charge. This does not mean that the lawyer should never yield on the position that the accused can and will, if the accused desires, put the prosecution to its proof.").

247. I would like to thank my colleague Ben Barton for raising this concern.

248. Henning, *supra* note 169, at 212 (arguing that although truth seeking might be the object of the court system, given a lawyer's duty to maintain confidences and protect her client's interests, it should not be the governing principle for lawyers); *see also* Richard Silverman, *Is New Jersey's Heightened Duty of Candor Too Much of a Good Thing?*, 19 Geo. J. Legal Ethics 951, 961 (2006) ("The tension that a lawyer faces in balancing his role as zealous advocate for his client and as an officer of the court is an inherent conflict that is not easily resolved.").

adigmatic TJ defense lawyer is not one whom I wish to celebrate, much less encourage my students to emulate.

3. Those Who Have Not Made the Guest List

Finally, in considering Professor Wexler's invitation and his agenda to change the way defendants live their lives, it is worth noting who has not been included on the guest list,[249] even though defenders and clinicians have been targeted for professional reform.[250] Given Professor Wexler's concern that defendants are not given enough encouragement and support as they attempt to complete probationary terms or transition from prison to the community, it seems that probation and parole agencies should be invited to think more about defendants' therapeutic needs. In light of Professor Wexler's statements about a lack of ancillary, therapeutic services for criminal defendants, it also strikes me that it might make more sense to promote a TJ legislature or executive branch to encourage government actors to better fund social service programs in poor communities and provide sufficient resources to already overworked public defenders' offices.

Conclusion

Although our criminal justice system may be flawed, there likely is no panacea. In our desire for reform, we must be careful not to embrace novel-sounding solutions that may be no fix at all. Indeed, like other modern justice reform movements, I fear that TJ proponents, in their desire to improve the court system, inadvertently may be overselling their proposed solutions and failing to consider all of the implications of their call for "innovation." Indeed, much of what the TJ movement suggests, like the problem-solving court movement, parallels earlier paternalistic social reform efforts that were less than ideal and likely should not be repeated.[251] What is more, despite its claims

---

249. Professor Wexler notes that his invitation does not expressly mention prosecutors and that they are beyond the scope of his article. He suggests, however, that it might be worth considering infusing their role with therapeutic considerations. Wexler, Rehabilitative Role, supra note 1, at 745 n.12. Notably, his focus seems to be on prosecutors' treatment of alleged victims with only passing reference to their "dealings with defendants." Id. at 772 n.122. Instead, and consistent with TJ's stated concern for the therapeutic well-being of accused persons, perhaps prosecutors should be asked to consider the impact of widespread criminal prosecution of indigent persons for poverty-related activity. In my opinion, such charging decisions amount to one of the biggest and, to borrow TJ jargon, most "antitherapeutic" features of our criminal justice system. See generally Donald A. Dripps, Over-criminalization, Discretion, Waiver: A Survey of Possible Exit Strategies, 109 Penn. St. L. Rev. 1155 (2005); Erik Luna, The Overcriminalization Phenomenon, 54 Am. U. L. Rev. 704 (2005); William J. Stuntz, The Political Constitution of Criminal Justice, 119 Harv. L. Rev. 780 (2006). But see Darryl K. Brown, Rethinking Overcriminalization (Wash. & Lee Legal Studies Research Paper Series, Working Paper No. 2006-07, 2006), available at http://papers.ssrn.com/sol3/papers.cfm?abstract_id=932667.

250. As a former public defender who has represented many indigent individuals and a clinician whose teaching focuses on defending the accused, I may have recent personal and professional experiences that Professor Wexler does not share. See Winick & Wexler, supra note 1, at 606 n.2 (indicating that Professor Wexler "teaches a course called 'Practicing Therapeutic Jurisprudence,' at the University of Arizona College of Law," which does not appear to involve direct legal representation as in a live-client clinic). Thus, I must confess a certain level of "defensiveness" about a nondefender focusing on transforming the current work of defenders and defender clinics to the exclusion of other institutional players and suggesting how they should behave and interact with clients. Cf. Spinak, supra note 166, at 1619.

251. See Quinn, supra note 197, at 710; Christean, supra note 45, at 7. See generally Morris B. Hoffman, Therapeutic Jurisprudence, Neo-Rehabilitationism, and Judicial Collectivism: The Least Dangerous Branch Becomes the Most Dangerous, 29 Fordham Urb. L.J. 2063 (2002).

to the contrary, TJ runs the risk of gutting worthwhile core values of our current criminal justice system.

Accordingly, although it is flattering to have received the invitation, and despite my respect for Professor Wexler and his well-intended desire to improve the lives of criminal defendants and the criminal justice system, I must decline his invitation to join him in the TJ movement or assist him in promoting a TJ criminal defense bar. Rather, I will continue with my prior (somewhat similar) engagement of providing zealous and quality criminal defense representation and will encourage my clinic students to do the same.

ii. David B. Wexler, Not Such a Party Pooper: An Attempt to Accommodate (Many of) Professor Quinn's Concerns about Therapeutic Jurisprudence Criminal Defense Lawyering

(Reprinted with permission from
48 Boston College Law Review 597, 2007)

Abstract: This Article responds to Professor Mae C. Quinn's critique of the author's piece, *Therapeutic Jurisprudence and the Rehabilitative Role of the Criminal Defense Lawyer*, published in a 2005 symposium issue of the *St. Thomas Law Review*. This Reply Article suggests that Professor Quinn has badly misread or distorted the author's *St. Thomas* article. This Article takes serious issue with her characterization of the author's work, contends that the author and Professor Quinn are closer on many issues than her critique suggests, and points out areas of agreement and disagreement. Therapeutic Jurisprudence can be incorporated into the role of the criminal defense lawyer and, as a simple "add-on," it can be transformative of criminal law practice.

I have had a very interesting—but, at the same time, frustrating—dialogue with Professor Quinn. It began when she sent a draft of her article to which I am now responding. In an email message, I replied that I thought she had (unintentionally) constructed a "strawperson," and had then proceeded skillfully to tear it down. I tried to explain why what Professor Quinn thought I was saying was not actually what I said or proposed—that, despite some obvious differences, we were, in fact, much closer on many issues than she had suggested. Her response was puzzling to me. Basically, she responded, "Nope, that's not what you're saying!"

My reaction to that reminded me of an incident that happened in San Juan to my friend, Tony, who, accompanied by his mother, attended the funeral of a family friend. Arriving a bit late, not atypical for Tony, he entered during the eulogy. The priest spoke of the deceased's fine character, of what a terrific father and husband he had been, of how he was a hard worker, generous and simpatico. Tony's mother, a close friend of the deceased, was overcome with tears. The priest continued, "We will all be poorer for the loss of Señor Ruiz," whereupon Tony and his mother looked at each other with a blend of shock and amusement: "Señor Ruiz? Who's he? We're at the wrong funeral!"

In my view, Professor Quinn is declining an invitation to the wrong party. It is a psychological truism that we are all inclined to assimilate new information according to our preexisting perspectives.[1] I am sure there are several Wexlerian examples around. To

---

1. RICHARD NISBETT & LEE ROSS, HUMAN INFERENCE: STRATEGIES AND SHORTCOMINGS OF SOCIAL JUDGMENT 170 (1980) (discussing the phenomenon of biased assimilation of new information).

me, however, this is the Quinn-tessential example of the phenomenon at work. But a reply to Professor Quinn's RSVP to the effect of "Return to Sender, Addressee Unknown" would not do much to advance the thinking about Therapeutic Jurisprudence ("TJ") criminal lawyering, something both Professor Quinn and I are interested in doing. It would be better, I think, if I go on record showing her and others that there is greater agreement between us than she has supposed, and trying to clarify areas of disagreement and areas in need of further attention.

Let me capsulize my response in the following ten points:[2]

1. The TJ criminal lawyer is not dismantling or "replacing"[3] the "traditional" (whatever we might mean by that) criminal lawyer, but rather he is the "traditional" lawyer with an important "add-on" component of a TJ lens.[4]

2. The addition of a TJ lens to criminal law practice is both simple (in the sense of an "add-on") and, at the same time, "transformative,"[5] for it will encourage criminal lawyers to practice explicitly and systematically with an "ethic of care" and "psychological sensitivity."[6] My guess is that the transformative effect of that role change will increase client and public trust and confidence in lawyers,[7]

---

2. Professor Quinn is aware that she may be a bit annoyed by the fact that I am proposing changes but am not myself a defender. *See* Mae C. Quinn, *An RSVP to Professor Wexler's Warm Therapeutic Jurisprudence Invitation to the Criminal Defense Bar: Unable to Join You, Already (Somewhat Similarly) Engaged*, 48 B.C. L. REV. 539, 590 n.250 (2007). As a matter of fact, a number of defenders have been very supportive of my *St. Thomas* article, David B. Wexler, *Therapeutic Jurisprudence and the Rehabilitative Role of the Criminal Defense Lawyer*, 17 ST. THOMAS L. REV. 743 (2005) [hereinafter Wexler, *Rehabilitative Role*]. Based on my writing in this area, I was invited to address the North Carolina Public Defenders Conference in May 2006. See David B. Wexler, Address at North Carolina Spring Public Defender Conference: Therapeutic Jurisprudence and the Expanding Professional Responsibilities of the Criminal Defense Lawyer (May 19, 2006); *see also* Joel Parris, *Reinforcing Reform Efforts Through Probation Progress Reports,* International Network on Therapeutic Jurisprudence, Oct. 2006, http://www.therapeuticjurisprudence.org (follow "Guest Column" hyperlink) (applying principles from the *St. Thomas* article). But, in any case, although the similarity of the messenger to the audience is *psychologically* a factor in whether the audience will likely accept the message, EVERETT M. ROGERS, DIFFUSION OF INNOVATIONS 19 (5th ed. 2003) ("[T]he transfer of ideas occurs most frequently between two individuals who are similar or homophilus."), such a fit or the absence of it should not be an important factor in intellectually *evaluating* the merits of a proposal, a proposition that underlies the place of anonymous peer review in academic journals.

3. Quinn, *supra* note 2, at 579.

4. *See* Wexler, *Rehabilitative Role, supra* note 2, at 744 ("Mostly, interested lawyers will likely augment a traditional criminal law practice with the more holistic approach suggested by Therapeutic Jurisprudence, and the present article seeks to point interested practitioners in that direction."). A criminal lawyer interested in a TJ approach can, expressly and up-front, say to a client, "I am here for you and will represent you zealously, and I will keep you informed and will call on you to make many of the crucial decisions. I see my job as maybe involving even more than that, however—often, a criminal charge like the one you're facing can be looked at as an opportunity to think through some stuff about one's life, goals, directions, wrong turns and stuff like that If you're interested in approaching the case that way, I can work with you to try and do some of that" *But see* Quinn, *supra* note 2, at 571 (expressing concern about a potentially "undisclosed" agenda).

5. Bruce J. Winick & David B. Wexler, The Use of Therapeutic Jurisprudence in Law School Clinical Education: Transforming the Criminal Law Clinic, 13 CLINICAL L. REV. 605, 629–30 (2006).

6. Id. at 607, 609.

7. See Mark H. Moore et al., The Best Defense Is No Offense: Preventing Crime Through Effective Public Defense, 29 N.Y.U. REV. L. & SOC. CHANGE 57, 76 (2004). See generally Marcus T. Boccaccini et al., Development and Effects of Client Trust in Criminal Defense Attorneys: Prelimi-

3. Some lawyers may choose to go "all the way" and "limit their criminal law practice to a concentration in Therapeutic Jurisprudence."[9] I regard this not necessarily as ideal,[10] but rather as an attractive practice option for some, and as a model worthy of demonstration projects and of serious discussion. Professor Quinn is correct[11] that I suggest (along the lines of the suggestions made by defenders Cait Clarke and Jim Neuhard)[12] thinking about how such an approach might be incorporated in public defenders' offices.[13]

4. TJ "all the way" does not at all mean that cases should not or will not be investigated for possible defenses.[14] For example, in discussing John McShane's "all the way" TJ practice, I note that "referral to out side counsel is also made if the defendant has a viable defense."[15] In public defenders' offices, though some lawyers may do exclusively or primarily TJ-type work, those lawyers can investigate or work with others who will focus on defenses, and other lawyers can be available to take the case to trial if negotiations or the therapeutic path breaks down.[16] I do believe that all clients are entitled to have counsel exercise due diligence regarding possible defenses.

5. The possibility of zealous trial advocacy needs to be built into the legal defense structure—through a single attorney with both skills, or through cooperating attorneys in a public defenders' or private office (for example, Mutt and Jeff, Attorneys at Law). This, as Professor Quinn correctly notes, is essential to make sure the defendant is in a strong bargaining position with the state.[17] Had I been more explicit about my views regarding zealous advocacy and due diligence in defense, misinterpretation might have been avoided.

6. But unlike Professor Quinn, I do not believe the "single attorney" model is required[18] and that all criminal lawyers must therefore be ready to act as vigorous trial attorneys. I recognize that trial skills as currently practiced by first-rate litigators are crucial (though not necessarily for all lawyers), and, thus, I did not deal directly with that topic in my earlier article.[19] In fact, given its relatively

---

nary Examination of the Congruence Model of Trust Development, 22 BEHAV. SCI. & L. 197 (2004).

8. See Roger K. Warren, Public Trust and Procedural Justice, 37 CT. Rev. 12, 14–16 (2000).
9. Wexler, Rehabilitative Role, supra note 2, at 744.
10. See Quinn, supra note 2, at 587–89 (criticizing the TJ "all the way" paradigm).
11. See id. at 560–61.
12. See Cait Clarke & James Neuhard, "From Day One": Who's in Control as Problem Solving and Client-Centered Sentencing Take Center Stage?, 29 N.Y.U. REV. L. & SOC. CHANGE 11, 47 (2004).
13. Wexler, Rehabilitative Role, supra note 2, at 773.
14. But see Quinn, supra note 2, at 587–89 (expressing concern that TJ "all the way" leads to ineffective representation).
15. Wexler, Rehabilitative Role, supra note 2, at 744.
16. See id.
17. Quinn, supra note 2, at 589.
18. See id. at 577–78.
19. Of course, even with litigators, a TJ lens could and should be an "add-on"—and would systematically and explicitly lead to a number of practices, such as careful debriefings, as well as to lawyers explaining upcoming procedures to clients so as to relieve stress and anxiety. See Bruce Winick, Therapeutic Jurisprudence and the Role of Counsel in Litigation, 37 CAL. W. L. REV. 105,

rare occurrence, the trial is unduly emphasized in legal education (and in the legal culture), to the exclusion of other important material and skills needed in criminal defense work (for example, plea negotiations, diversion, problem-solving courts, sentencing, restoration of rights, restorative justice, therapeutic jurisprudence, and expungement).[20]

One serious consequence of this overemphasis on the trial is that law students who do not want a steady diet of confrontation will likely opt out of criminal law practice, even though those students might have other remarkable skills (such as interpersonal skills, cultural competence, and TJ skills) that could make them exceptional, meaningful, effective, and extremely satisfied criminal law practitioners. As I have written elsewhere, we should teach students critical thinking skills, argumentation, and effective advocacy, but should not elevate such a perspective above other crucial skills.[21] We should, I think, try to chip away at, rather than to perpetuate, a "culture of critique."[22] And, I think we owe it to the legal profession to think creatively about various ways of providing defense services, ways that will be advantageous to clients and fulfilling for the legal professionals involved. Our exploration should also be comparative, looking at how TJ might fit within a continental model or within a system of barristers and solicitors.[23] We need to think of "*Gideon* grown up" rather than a "stuck in the sixties" view of *Gideon* and the role of defense counsel.[24]

7. TJ criminal lawyers in whatever setting should, like drug court lawyers, practice with an ethic of care, psychological sensitivity, and ability to work effectively with treatment and mental health professionals.[25] In that sense, the ideal TJ criminal lawyer will be like the drug court lawyer. Nowhere do I suggest, however, that a TJ lawyer should serve simply as a member of an interdisciplinary team as, apparently, many drug treatment court lawyers do.[26] Instead, the lawyer should work to create, coordinate, and lead a team, all in service of the client. In private practice, an excellent example is Ottawa criminal lawyer Michael Crystal's Crystal Criminal Law Office.[27] And as I noted in my article, *Therapeutic Jurisprudence and the Rehabilitative Role of the Criminal Defense Lawyer*, published in the *St. Thomas Law Review*. "In the [public defenders'] office as well as the other settings of potential TJ criminal law practice, thought

---

117–18 (2000). My *St. Thomas* piece did not explore this in the criminal trial arena, and it is an area that should be attended to in future scholarship.

20. *See* Adam Liptik, *Expunged Criminal Records Live to Tell Tales*, N.Y. TIMES, Oct. 17, 2006, at A1 (discussing how even expungement of records can have a continuing impact).

21. Winick & Wexler, *supra* note 5, at 627.

22. David B. Wexler, *Therapeutic Jurisprudence and the Culture of Critique*, 10 J. CONTEMP. LEGAL ISSUES 263, 277 (1999).

23. *See generally* George Hampel, *Therapeutic Jurisprudence—An Australian Perspective*, 17 ST. THOMAS L. REV. 775 (2005) (discussing how TJ fits into the Australian system of solicitors and barristers).

24. *See generally Gideon v. Wainwright*, 372 U.S. 335 (1963) (holding, for the first time, that indigent defendants in criminal cases are entitled to have counsel appointed by the state).

25. David B. Wexler, A Tripartite Framework far Incorporating Therapeutic Jurisprudence in Criminal Law Education, Research, and Practice, 7 FLA. COASTAL L. REV. 95, 100–02 (2005).

26. *See* Quinn, *supra* note 2, at 552 & n.67.

27. *See* Crystal Criminal Law Office, http://www.accidentaljurist.com (last visited Mar. 19, 2007).

needs to be given ... to integrating other professionals—such as social workers—into the law office context."[28]

8. I am very much in favor, of course, of TJ criminal lawyers looking holistically at clients and their situations. In fact, what TJ might add to holistic criminal lawyering is psychologically sensitive techniques regarding *how* to practice: *how* to reinforce client reform efforts, *how* to enhance compliance with court orders, and *how* to increase problem-solving skills (matters I discuss below). To the extent some holistic practices may be structured to include a lawyer simply as another member of an overall team,[29] however, I would dissent.

9. Professor Quinn notes that many good public defenders already do much of what holistic practice and TJ practice suggest.[30] For example, they may work to connect clients with needed treatments and services.[31] In cases of good client performance, the public defender may petition the court for early termination of probation.[32] Professor Quinn's bottom line, it appears, is that this is all simply good lawyering,[33] and so it seems. Much of TJ seems to be making explicit that which some good, interpersonally sensitive judges and lawyers have long been doing. Indeed, as I have written elsewhere, others and I were doing TJ scholarship before we "knew" it—before it had a label.[34] But, having a definition and a conceptual scheme for thinking about all this adds considerable value to the enterprise; when we start thinking about matters explicitly and systematically with a TJ lens, we see many more potential areas of application—areas that may not occur to us when we are simply engaging in "good lawyering."

A powerful example came to my attention when Joel Parris, an assistant federal public defender in Tucson, prepared a Guest Column for the website of the International Network on Therapeutic Jurisprudence[35] entitled *Reinforcing Reform Efforts Through Probation Progress Reports*.[36] Parris noted his constant frustration in battling for his clients in probation revocation proceedings initiated for technical, noncriminal violations; he noted, too, how probation officers, even when not seeking revocation, sometimes file violation reports with the court, allegations that sometimes are used against the client subsequently if revocation is later sought.[37] Parris decided to use favorable "Probation Progress

---

28. Wexler, *Rehabilitative Role, supra* note 2, at 773. This would include involving social workers in the effort to "create a genuineness even within a strategic legal context," something likely to help in sentencing. *Id.* at 755. These "perspective-taking" and apology approaches are, however, dismissed by Professor Quinn as inappropriate. *See* Quinn, *supra* note 2, at 579–83.

29. See generally Brooks Holland, Holistic Advocacy: An Important but Limited Institutional Role, 30 N.Y.U. REV. L. & SOC. CHANGE 637 (2006) (exploring the practical, professional, and ethical limitations of the holistic approach).

30. Quinn, *supra* note 2, at 565 (recognizing that lawyers wear many "hats" when dealing with a given case).

31. Wexler, *supra* note 25, at 107. Wouldn't these lawyers, applauded by Professor Quinn, fall victim to her attack on TJ lawyers—that they risk stepping beyond their professional expertise? *See* Quinn, *supra* note 2, at 565, 574–75, 582.

32. Quinn, *supra* note 2, at 575.

33. *Id.*

34. See David B. Wexler, The Development of Therapeutic Jurisprudence: From Theory to Practice, 68 REV. JUR. U.P.R. 691, 691 (1999).

35. *See* Int'l Network on Therapeutic Jurisprudence, http://www.therapeuticjurisprudence.org (last visited Mar. 19, 2007).

36. *See* Parris, *supra* note 2.

37. *See id.*

Reports" for his own purposes, and, in his Guest Column, he reproduces a fascinating pleading detailing his client's complete compliance with probation conditions and her personal success in obtaining a cosmetology license, being reunited with her child, and more.[38]

This report was not even filed in pursuit of early probation termination. Instead, "counsel ... submit [ted] the ... report as appropriate supplemental information to complete the official record of [the] matter."[39] Of course, as Parris notes in the Guest Column, this positive information added to the record can, in addition to reinforcing his client's reform efforts and hopefully providing additional motivation to perform well, "help counter a subsequent petition to revoke probation based on non-criminal violations such as ... [a] reporting failure."[40] As such, this is surely "good lawyering." But Parris, who has long been a "good lawyer," explains that "in reading TJ literature about the importance of someone supporting or 'believing in' the offender's ability to reform," he decided to use Probation Progress Reports for his own purposes.[41] Of course, he might have decided to do this even without a TJ lens, but it is much more likely that such important techniques of good lawyering will flow from an explicit identity as a TJ criminal lawyer. If moving for early probation termination in appropriate cases is "something that any zealous and quality defense attorney should do,"[42] is filing a Probation Progress Report also something that should be routine for a zealous advocate? My point is that a good lawyer, keeping abreast of TJ literature and developments, will be especially likely to use, develop, and create what we call "theory-inspired practices," a fancy-sounding term used simply to capture the acronym "TIPS."[43]

10. Professor Quinn seems to have problems with some of these TIPS, either because they are already employed by "good lawyers"[44] or because they seem inappropriate or time-consuming.[45] I will not worry, of course, about the "good" TIPS that are already being used. What about the ones she finds problematic? Again, there may have been some misinterpretation. For example, in terms of the involvement of family members in a client's proposed probationary plan and conditions, Professor Quinn sees the family members as "enforce[rs]."[46] But family awareness and involvement, with client consent, is a matter entirely different from family as "enforce[rs]." Instead, such involvement simply taps into recognized psychological compliance principles which suggest that client compliance is enhanced when family members are aware of a client's agree-

---

38. *See id.*
39. *Id.*
40. *See id.*
41. *See* Parris, *supra* note 2.
42. Quinn, *supra* note 2, at 575.
43. Wexler, *supra* note 25, at 107. These TIPS, as I note above, might profitably be used by holistic lawyers—making these lawyers even more holistic than they are now!—and might lead to an increased dialogue between the two closely related perspectives. These "theory-inspired practices" are indeed typically inspired by psychological or social work theory and often have an empirical base. *See id.* at 107–08. The TJ community is far more interdisciplinary than Professor Quinn concedes. *See* Quinn, *supra* note 2, at 566.
44. Quinn, *supra* note 2, at 574–75.
45. *See id.* at 583–84 (discussing practical issues of time and resources with application of TJ practices); *id.* at 582–83 (discussing potential ethical problems with TJ lawyering).
46. *Id.* at 556.

ment to engage in or to refrain from certain behaviors; compliance is strengthened because the client does not want to let down her family members.⁴⁷

Additionally, most lawyers would likely be troubled by defense lawyers requesting routine follow-up (status) hearings when a client is sentenced to probation. It is important to make clear, however, that TJ work on status hearings does not suggest that *counsel* push for such hearings; the TJ literature simply recommends to courts that, for compliance and related reasons, *the courts* should consider holding such hearings. If such hearings are in fact held, *then* the TJ criminal lawyer should approach those hearings seriously, even when all is going well with the client. Those routine hearings could then serve to reinforce reform efforts, similar to the way Parris reinforces client reform efforts even when hearings are not scheduled.⁴⁸

Thus, my *St. Thomas* article suggested neither family enforcement nor defense-requested status hearings. Note, however, that a TJ lawyer, or a plain old "good lawyer" for that matter, might in some cases actually propose just those approaches. If a client is facing likely incarceration, a lawyer might well propose probation instead, and might suggest that probation should be viewed by the judge as a viable option because counsel and client have proposed certain safeguards: the court will hold periodic follow-up hearings to make sure all is going well, and counsel has secured the promise of certain family, friends, or neighbors who have stated that they have no objection to the client remaining in the community and, if informed of the conditions of the client's release, will be willing to report any misconduct.

Both techniques have in fact been used by the Crystal Criminal Law Office.⁴⁹ In one case, a conditional sentence, rather than incarceration, was sought, and periodic judicial supervision was offered as a possibly attractive option.⁵⁰ In another case, while client X was awaiting sentence, letters were prepared by the law firm and were distributed to neighbors by the client's mother, explaining that X was awaiting sentence; that if he were given a community sentence he would be released to live with his mother; that "I would have no fears for my safety or that of my family should Mr. X be released to live with his mother"; and, most important for present purposes, that "If I were provided with a copy of his sentencing conditions, I would have no hesitation in reporting Mr. X to the police if he were in violation of any of the conditions."⁵¹

Indeed, the entire area of creative probation conditions—and the lawyer/client conversations discussing them—seems to trouble Professor Quinn.⁵² For example, she thinks it less appropriate to engage urban youths than suburban kids with questions about the chain of events that seem to have led to the crime in question.⁵³ I do not know why that should be the case.⁵⁴ And she seems troubled by a lawyer using a Socratic

---

47. *See* Wexler, *Rehabilitative Role*, *supra* note 2, at 757–58 & nn.67–73.
48. *See* Parris, *supra* note 2.
49. *See* Crystal Criminal Law Office, *supra* note 27.
50. *See* Karine Langley, Ph.D., *The Case of Robert Piamonte: A Victory for Therapeutic Jurisprudence*, http://www.accidentaljuristcom/featured_topics/display_e.asp?ID=10 (last visited Mar. 19, 2007).
51. *See* Pleading by Crystal Criminal Law Office on Behalf of Client (on file with author).
52. Quinn, *supra* note 2, at 581.
53. *Id.* at 584–85.
54. Professor Quinn suggests the limits of such an approach when dealing with an alleged gang member. *Id.* at 584 n.223. A creative TJ lawyer would not be so dismissive, however. *See generally* C.D. Placido et al., *Treatment of Gang Members Can Reduce Recidivism and Institutional Misconduct*, 30 LAW & HUM. BEHAV. 93 (2006).

questioning technique to draw the client out with questions such as: "When do you usually get into trouble?" "When you're alone or when you're with your friends?" "At day or at night?" and "Okay, so if you want to avoid some of these fights, what might you do?" I suggest such a dialogue as a way of engaging the client—of having the client come up with some high-risk situations and ways to avoid them, and come up with proposed conditions of probation that the client will have a stake in, will understand, and will, we all hope, comply with. I find it a respectful process; Professor Quinn finds it manipulative.[55]

My question to Professor Quinn would be: What is the alternative? Does the lawyer do all the thinking and talking and tell the client, "Look, if you want probation, you'd better say you won't hang with X, and that you won't go out on weekend nights." Is that less manipulative? Or does the lawyer say nothing, and have the judge unilaterally impose those conditions or, worse, simply impose an incarcerative penalty because no one has thought of or brought to the court's attention some protective measures that may make probation a viable option? In my earlier article, I purposefully put some of this in a very controversial context: a promise not to have more kids, or even an agreement to undergo a vasectomy as a possible probation condition. Professor Quinn grudgingly admits I am not supporting such a result and I am not.[56] My point was that some of this activity is present in lawyering (TJ lawyering and all "good" lawyering) and in the judicial mind, whether we like it or not. None of this is presented in a prescriptive way, and, in fact, I specifically open the door to dialogue:

> These issues are set out as an area worthy of serious discussion. Should lawyers raise these topics? Should they not raise them but discuss them if clients bring them up? If they have a dialogue, can they do so in a way—again, an analogy to the Socratic method—that lessens the lawyer's role in suggesting these controversial procedures ... but instead inches the client personally to think of and raise the point? Are there ethical or therapeutic distinctions between the two approaches?[57]

Instead of simply saying, "I'm against this stuff," I wish Professor Quinn had taken up my offer of discussion or had proposed an alternative method of dealing with these difficult issues. Indeed, her article seems generally to accuse the TJ lawyer of overreaching,[58] even when the TJ literature (such as on the criminal defense lawyer's use of "motivational interviewing" and the like) seems to me far more gentle and appropriate than the techniques often used by lawyers, which range from "heavy-handed" to completely "hands off," or sometimes a combination of the two.[59] Motivational interviewing, by contrast, suggests the professional should "affirm client strengths generously; emphasize [the] client's ultimate control of the change process and control over [behavioral] decisions ... ; and seek explicit or implicit permission to give advice."[60]

---

55. Quinn, *supra* note 2, at 581.
56. *See id.* at 557; Wexler, *Rehabilitative Role, supra* note 2, at 765–66.
57. Wexler, *Rehabilitative Role, supra* note 2, at 766.
58. *See* Quinn, *supra* note 2, at 581.
59. *See* Astrid Birgden, *Dealing with the Resistant Criminal Client: A Psychologically-Minded Strategy for More Effective Legal Counseling*, 38 CRIM. L. BULL. 225, 225–26 (2002) (discussing and critiquing the "hands-off" and "heavy-handed" approaches).
60. Theresa B. Movers & Tim Martin, *Therapist Influence on Client Language During Motivational Interviewing Sessions*, 30 J. SUBSTANCE ABUSE TREATMENT 245, 249–50 (2006) (providing these suggestions in the context of clients dealing with substance abuse problems).

In the end, I am pleased to have prepared this response. It has forced me to be more explicit about some points that were either omitted,[61] implicit, or—evidently—subject to misinterpretation in my original piece. Ultimately, I find this exercise and dialogue valuable, and I am hopeful that Professor Quinn does, too. This time, I hope I have convinced Professor Quinn that I am really advocating for these theories and techniques.[62] If not, I will scream—or cry. After all, it's my party and I'll cry if I want to!

iii. Mae C. Quinn, Postscript to an RSVP[1]
(Reprinted with permission from
48 Boston College Law Review 592, 2007)

Rather than make his invitation more inviting, with his response to my RSVP, Professor Wexler further substantiates my concerns about applying TJ principles to criminal defense practice. His response underscores the problem of TJ's amorphous and ever-shifting claims, its lack of appreciation for modern defense community values, and its potential incompatibility with the important and serious task of delivering constitutionally mandated effective representation to the criminally accused. Thus, despite his insistence that I misapprehend the extent to which I agree with him, I remain unsupportive of modifying the role of defense attorneys with something called a "TJ lens."[2]

A. *TJ's Amorphous, Shifting Positions*

Professor Wexler's response underscores the serious identity crisis that plagues TJ.[3] As I have already suggested, although they enthusiastically press for a new way to approach the law, many TJ writings fail to identify specifically the problems they seek to correct or fail to describe precisely the means by which they may be corrected. TJ may wish to reduce "antitherapeutic" consequences in the law by adopting more "therapeutic" approaches. Pressed on the details, however, TJ equivocates.[4] This is particularly problematic as TJ presses forward with its newest "dimension"—application to real-world legal practice—and downright troubling when extended to constitutionally mandated criminal representation.

For instance, at the outset of the analysis in my RSVP, I make the very simple, yet fundamental, point that Professor Wexler has failed to identify the very issue he seeks to resolve. Although his invitation suggests that "traditional" defense lawyers need to change their ways, Professor Wexler never explains what he means by "traditional" defense attorneys or what problem they currently present to the criminal justice system. Rather than addressing this significant deficiency, Professor Wexler explicitly declines to

---

61. *See supra* note 19 and accompanying text.
62. In addition to the St. *Thomas* piece, I have recently written about TJ criminal lawyering in two other articles. *See generally* David B. Wexler, *Therapeutic Jurisprudence and Readiness for Rehabilitation*, 8 FLA. COASTAL L. REV. 111 (2006); Wexler, *Rehabilitative Role*, *supra* note 2; Wexler, *supra* note 25.
1. *See generally* Wexler, *supra* note 4.
2. I also maintain this position notwithstanding an email exchange of over 3500 words that followed after I sent a draft of my paper to Professor Wexler, and during which we did, indeed, "discuss" my continued misgivings about his TJ proposals. *See id.* at 606–07.
3. *See* Slobogin, *supra* note 14, at 763.
4. This is a point that I have repeatedly made in communications with Professor Wexler which, of course, is quite different from "[n]ope, that's not what you're saying." Wexler, *supra* note 4, at 597.

explain what he is talking about to the very community whose aid he seeks to enlist.[5] Instead, his response persists in calling for improvement of "traditional" criminal lawyers, while leaving readers to grapple with "whatever [he] might mean by that" term.[6]

Similarly, Professor Wexler takes issue with my interpretation of his vision for TJ criminal lawyers, suggesting that I have misread or over-read his proposal.[7] He did not intend for this new breed of specially named defense attorneys to replace the current representation model. TJ criminal lawyers are simply "traditional" attorneys who operate "with an important 'add-on' component of a TJ lens."[8]

Yet, Professor Wexler concedes that adding a "TJ lens" to criminal defense practice would have a "transformative effect" on the profession and result in a "role change."[9] Thus, beyond providing a justification and description of the role change that are, at best, ambiguous, it is impossible to see how a change in role that is admittedly "transformative" would not necessarily result in a new kind of practice that would displace — or replace — the current model.[10] It would appear that Professor Wexler vacillates in his conception of TJ defense lawyering, seeking the benefits of being a criminal justice reformer without bearing the heavy burden of all that is necessary to undertake significant structural change in our legal system.

B. *Defense Community Values and Ideals*

Professor Wexler's response also reflects TJ's continuing disconnection from modern indigent criminal defense community norms and values. He is surprised that I find it disrespectful to routinely ask urban youths about the "chain of events" that led them to engage in a criminal act so that I might suggest what "they" might "do" to avoid such conduct in the future.[11] These statements reflect a failure to appreciate my disdain, and the disdain of countless other defense lawyers, for the justice system's assumptions about, and treatment of, indigent criminal defendants.

Things are not as simple as Professor Wexler would like to believe.[12] Again, when asking about the "chain of events" that leads to the commission of many street crimes, it is often impossible to provide an account without incorporating the role of lifelong

---

5. *Id.* at 598.
6. Id.
7. As the reader will recall, this defense echoes a response to an earlier critique of TJ proposals. *See* Wexler & Winick, *supra* note 5, at 707 (arguing that in his review of their book, *Essays in Therapeutic Jurisprudence*, Professor John Petrila "puts words in [their] mouths and critiques [them] for writing a book [they] did not (and would not) write"); *see also supra* note 14 and accompanying text.
8. Wexler, *supra* note 4, at 598–99.
9. Professor Wexler describes that role change as "encourag[ing] criminal lawyers to practice explicitly and systematically with an 'ethic of care' and 'psychological sensitivity.'" *Id.* at 599. He goes on to explain that "psychologically sensitive techniques" would inform "*how*" defense attorneys would practice, pressing them to think about "*how* to reinforce client reform efforts, *how* to enhance [client] compliance with court orders, and *how* to increase problem-solving skills," also presumably of clients. *Id.* at 602.
10. This is particularly striking given that Professor Wexler elsewhere suggests that defense attorneys might learn from the Restorative Justice ("RJ") model, noting that "[b]oth RJ and TJ ... focus on healing the victim, rehabilitating the offender, and preventing future victimization." David B. Wexler & Bruce J. Winick, *Foreword: Expanding the Role of the Defense Lawyer and Criminal Court Judge Through Therapeutic Jurisprudence*, 38 Crim. L. Bull. 200, 202–03 (2002).
11. *See* Wexler, *supra* note 4, at 605–06.
12. Thus, contrary to Professor Wexler's suggestion, I do not reject his proposals because he is not a defender. *See id.* at 598 n.2. Rather, his lack of understanding of day-to-day defender experiences results in his work reflecting somewhat incongruous and sometimes contrived descriptions of

poverty and oppression in the mix. Poverty, oppression, and their incidents, however, are not easy to change or avoid in the future. Nor can their effect be erased in the course of a conversation. Thus, Professor Wexler's repeated suggestion that defense lawyers should simply help clients figure out how to "avoid" the "high-risk" situations in the future still fails to account for pernicious social ills largely beyond their control. It also continues to ignore that TJ's proposals appear to be built upon a conception of criminality and client pathology that many defenders reject.

C. *TJ's Potential Incompatibility with Delivering Effective Representation*

Finally, despite Professor Wexler's clarification that "[t]he possibility of zealous trial advocacy needs to be built into the legal defense structure," his response belies commitment to seriously thinking through the delivery of quality, zealous representation.[13] For instance, in further contravention of his claim that he does not seek to displace current defense customs, Professor Wexler continues to argue that taking TJ "all the way" is an "attractive practice option" for at least "some" defense lawyers.[14] He clarifies, however, that he did not mean that TJ "all the way" lawyers should not fully investigate cases or prepare for the possibility of trial.[15] Rather, in public defenders' offices, "though some lawyers may do exclusively or primarily TJ-type work, those lawyers can investigate or work with others who will focus on defenses, and other lawyers can be available to take the case to trial if negotiations or the therapeutic path breaks down."[16] He rebukes me for purportedly claiming that "the 'single attorney' model is required" in the delivery of indigent criminal defense services, based on his view that not all criminal defense lawyers should be required to act as vigorous trial attorneys.[17]

Although I did not argue, as Professor Wexler suggests, that assignment of a single lawyer at a time is what is required in cases involving an indigent criminal defendant, this is the dominant model for existing public defenders' offices. I suspect this is so because of efficiency and need.[18] I imagine most public defenders would relish the ability to assign two or more attorneys to handle each case from start to finish. A lack of resources, however, usually precludes this option. Therefore, absent a fundamental change in legal and ethical requirements of assigned counsel, or indigent defense funding, Professor Wexler's support of a relaxed view of trial skill competence is highly troubling. To meet constitutional requirements presently, an assigned lawyer generally should be sufficiently competent to try her client's case. Accordingly, Professor Wexler's blithe suggestion of a "Mutt and Jeff" approach to representation may fail to protect adequately an indigent accused's fundamental right to effective assistance of counsel under our current system.[19]

---

attorney-client interactions, which lead to unrealistic, unworkable, and ultimately objectionable proposals.

13. *Id.* at 600.
14. *Id.* at 599.
15. *Id.* at 600.
16. Wexler, *supra* note 4, at 600.
17. *Id.*
18. There is, of course, the important additional concern with developing and earning client respect and trust throughout the representation process. Professor Wexler's suggestion that any competent trial lawyer could jump in once the "therapeutic path breaks down" to "take the case to trial" obviously precludes development of that kind of relationship between client and trial counsel, which would appear somewhat inconsistent with TJ's alleged support of an "ethic of care" and "psychological sensitivity." *See id.* at 599–600.
19. *See id.* at 600.

Thus, although it is true that we may agree in some respects about what it means to be a good defense attorney, I remain unconvinced of the wisdom of Professor Wexler's TJ proposals for transforming criminal representation in this country. Instead, as indicated in my RSVP, I maintain my prior commitment to delivering quality and zealous criminal defense representation—the professionally responsible and, for me, morally compelled alternative to Professor Wexler's invitation.

iv. David B. Wexler, Author's Closing Comments

Quinn's postscript makes three points. I will dispose of two of them very quickly.

Yes, Quinn has it right: I haven't tried to define a "traditional" criminal lawyer, and have urged criminal lawyers simply to "add" a TJ lens to their approach—which I think can be, at the same time, simple and transformative (rejuvenating, etc.). I don't see how we can get hung up on this, when the real point is merely adding TJ to the mix. If a doctor were to say, "I recommend an exercise regimen for typical middle-aged men," would we profitably beat to death what we mean by "typical middle-aged men" or would we instead focus on the exercise regime?

As to a "single lawyer" possessing all skills, my own proposal does indeed envision most TJ to be practiced by that single criminal lawyer "adding on" a TJ focus.

But yes, I do recommend that we think about models for allowing some lawyers to do "TJ all the way." Since Quinn says she did not argue that "assignment of a single lawyer at a time is what is required in cases involving an indigent criminal defendant," she is apparently willing to discuss when and why a single attorney may not be essential. That is all I am proposing as a topic for discussion. And as I said in my reply, I think we should discuss this in a broad context, even taking into account how divisions of labor operate under other systems, such as with barristers and solicitors.

My biggest concern with Quinn's postscript is her claim that my proposal to engage a client—of course, including poor urban clients—in a discussion of high-risk situations and how they might be avoided is somehow disrespectful. First of all, I do not at all propose that "I might suggest what 'they' might 'do' to avoid such conduct in the future." That is precisely why I called for a type of Socratic dialogue to draw the client out, for the client to think about and suggest certain courses of action—courses that might indeed become proposed probationary conditions and that might indeed lead to a probationary, rather than an incarcerative, sanction.[1]

Quinn seems uninterested in the major advances in rehabilitation and how they may be brought into the legal system and help her clients. That very endeavor is specifically what is of interest to therapeutic jurisprudence. And the impressive body of "what

---

1. Nor will these difficult and controversial issues disappear from the defense lawyer's conversational radar screen simply because Quinn finds them distasteful and refuses to discuss them—or how a lawyer might best discuss them with a client. Indeed, since the publication of my original article, we are if anything beginning to see an upswing in a number of troubling topics that will necessarily engage concerned counsel. E.g., Madeline Baro Diaz, *Woman Gets 8 Years for Killing Daughter*, Ft. Lauderdale Sun-Sentinel 1 B (Aug. 8, 2006) (prosecutor agreed to plea deal for woman who underwent tubal ligation); Ruffin Prevost, *Electronic Anklet Has Potential for Prison System*, Billings Gazette (Aug. 21, 2007) (electronic monitoring might allow non-incarcerative sentences for "meth moms").

works" research[2] is not at all restricted to "what works for the rich suburbanite." Indeed, in my reply I even cited a piece on a successful program geared to gang members.[3]

I am, of course, aware of and offended by the role of lifelong poverty and oppression in the mix. Indeed, those same factors often lead people to pay a relative lack of attention to longer-range consequences of behavior,[4] something the successful rehabilitative techniques seek explicitly to attend to.[5]

If these issues aren't attended to, isn't it really a sign of disrespect to deny or ignore the possibility that a poor urban youth can change? And how in the world does Quinn's approach tackle poverty and oppression in a manner superior to mine?

---

2. Steve Aos et al., *Evidence-Based Adult Corrections Program: What Works and What Does Not* (2006), available at http://www.wsipp.wa.gov/rptfiles/06-01-1201.pdf.
3. Chantal Di Placido et al., *Treatment of Gang Members Can Reduce Recidivism and Institutional Misconduct*, 30 Law & Human Beh. 93 (2006).
4. Michael Gottfredson & Travis Hirschi, *A General Theory of Crime* (1990).
5. L. S. Joy Tong & David P. Farrington, *How Effective is the 'Reasoning and Rehabilitation' Programme in Reducing Reoffending? A Meta-Analysis of Evaluations in Four Countries*, 12 Psychology, Crime and Law (2006).

Part III

Practices and Techniques

Despite my best efforts, my guess is that an impartial observer would conclude that I have not convinced Professor Quinn! But here I take solace in the words of Professor Howard Leznick in his Foreword to Professor Marjorie Silver's book *The Affective Assistance of Law: Practicing Law as a Healing Profession* (Carolina Academic Press 2007).

Leznick, a law professor at the University of Pennsylvania long active in humanistic and clinical components of legal education and lawyering, recently remarked that "it is not necessary to change professional norms to make it possible for those who find them seriously deficient to mark out a different road." "That 90s exhortation, 'Just Do It!'", Leznick continued, "is actually feasible, and does not always entail stepping off alone into an uncharted wilderness."

Speaking specifically of TJ, Leznick observes that "lawyers and students who find the concept of therapeutic jurisprudence valid and relevant now have the resources, in the literature and among professional colleagues, to begin to learn the skills necessary to practice it. Responsive to its opportunities as well as its dangers, they can leave off debating whether the latter should choke off serious pursuit of the former."

In this Part, we hear from some of the critical mass who are already practicing therapeutic jurisprudence or whose practices easily lend themselves to such a characterization. This Part emphasizes and puts some meat on the bones of the "practice tips" component of the tripartite framework explained in Part I.

Just as TJ itself can profit from being characterized as a field of inquiry, so too the notion of "practices and techniques" of TJ criminal lawyering deserves to constitute an explicit subfield of inquiry. In that way, we can encourage the production, collection, discussion, evaluation, modification, and dissemination of those techniques. This entire enterprise can constitute an especially dynamic field of "practical interdisciplinary" legal scholarship, where practices and techniques can multiply and evolve along with pertinent advances in the behavioral sciences. It is time, then, to turn to the many rich selections of this Part.

As Leznick reminds us, our practices must be responsive to potential dangers even as we seek to mine the therapeutic opportunities. So begins Part III.

The opening selection, by Professor Meekins, who in Part II is quite critical of some of the constraints on lawyering imposed by problem-solving courts, is nonetheless enthusiastic about certain therapeutic techniques that can be imported into criminal defense practice generally, and her essay details several of them.

Next, Martin Reisig, with much experience in drug treatment court, emphasizes the crucially important defense counsel role in ensuring—for legal and indeed therapeutic reasons—that a client considering entry into drug treatment court do so in an aware and informed manner. Following that, Orna Alyagon, an Israeli public defender, focuses our attention on certain situations where a TJ criminal lawyer needs to be particularly protective and mindful of client rights. Alyagon also sees the development of TJ practices and techniques as a type of "open source" project profiting from the contributions of many.

My own selection follows in that vein, reproducing some especially interesting documents used by practitioners and urging the "practices and techniques" area as an explicit branch of study. Joel Parris, a seasoned federal assistant public defender in Tucson, rose to the bait, and his "probation progress report" follows. Then Ottawa attorney Michael Crystal talks of using an interdisciplinary team to fashion a therapeutic sentence. Dr. Karine Langley, a counselor in Crystal's law firm, shows in a judicially-filed affidavit how the firm marshalled community support in favor of a non-incarcerative sentence for a client.

David Boulding, from Vancouver, shares his expertise dealing with clients with fetal alcohol syndrome, and illustrates the importance of creating a community support system and drafting appropriate probation conditions. John McShane, a private practitioner in Dallas, explains a practice he has employed in securing "treatment" bonds for jailed clients. Robert Ward, with much experience in a North Carolina defender's office, shows how experience in drug court and in civil commitment hearings can well serve an attorney in general criminal court.

Hamilton, Ontario defense attorney Beth Bromberg explores issues of apology and allocution, and Michael King, a former magistrate in Western Australia who is now at Monash Law School in Victoria, concentrates on the lawyer's role in the plea process but, along the way, provides quite an overview of TJ criminal defense lawyering. Jane Anne Murphy, a private practitioner in New York, writes on the lawyer's role in easing a client's transition to prison.

The Part closes with a creative article by Astrid Birgden, an Australian forensic psychologist, suggesting how behavioral science insights from motivational interviewing and stages of change can inform the lawyer-client relationship. It is my fervent hope that the material in this Part will inspire interdisciplinary and international development of the area of TJ practices and techniques.

i. Tamar M. Meekins,[*] You Can Teach Old Defenders New Tricks: Sentencing Lessons From Specialty Courts

(Reprinted with permission from 21 Criminal Justice 28, 2006)

There are nearly 2,000 specialty courts now operating in the United States, leading judges and lawyers to look closely at both their benefits and their negative factors. Today's specialty or problem-solving courts are touted as new ventures on the criminal justice landscape, but the underlying methodologies of many of these courts are reminiscent of a comprehensive sentencing practice that some conscientious defenders have been doing for years. A number of defender agencies employ social workers, educational consultants, civil litigators, and sentencing specialists to help lawyers craft individualized alternative disposition plans that will be compelling to jurists and prosecutors. These plans focus on the same types of issues—problem solving and attention to

---

[*] Tamar M. Meekins is an associate professor at Howard University School of Law in Washington, D.C., director of its Clinical Law Center, and a supervising attorney in its Criminal Justice Clinic.

community or victim interests—that are notable in specialty court theory. Additionally, comprehensive plans that focus on specific issues in the client's life are attractive to many judges in all parts of the criminal justice system because of renewed opportunities for sentencing advocacy opened up by recent cases. On a greater scale, defense lawyers can now propose creative, holistic, and effective sentencing plans that address important issues in the clients' lives and that are positively received by some judges.

There has been a wealth of writing and discussion in scholarly and judicial circles about the benefit of the specialty court approach, which marries principles of problem-solving, therapeutic jurisprudence, and restorative justice to the judicial administration of criminal cases. Almost every major metropolitan city now has a drug court, which is the most prominent example of the specialty court. The judicial problem solving that takes place in specialty courts is akin to the notion of providing and administering alternatives to incarceration at the sentencing stage. (Phyllis Bamberger, *Specialized Courts: Not a Cure-all*, 30 FORDHAM URB. L.J. 1091 (March 2003).) Utilizing a team approach with the judge as the central figure, a system of quick sanctions for noncompliance, attention to issues normally outside of the criminal justice system, such as housing and counseling, and providing additional resources for case management and monitoring, specialty courts have given a renewed and undeniably invaluable focus on developing alternatives to incarceration for a small segment of the criminal justice population. And despite some well-founded concerns of several commentators that problem-solving courts may sacrifice procedural due process protections and facilitate ethical violations by defense lawyers, our clients may benefit from the bright spotlight that sentencing issues now may enjoy. (*See* Tamar M. Meekins, *Specialized Justice: The Overemergence of Specialty Courts and the Threat of a New Criminal Defense Paradigm*, 40 Suffolk L. Rev. 1 (2006).)

Additionally, more judges may now seek to adapt the methodologies of specialty courts to courts of general jurisdiction. (Bamberger, *supra*, at 1099.) Judges returning from rotations in specialty courts, where their assignments may have lasted up to a year, often can be persuaded to fashion innovative sentences for offenders who have been found guilty of a variety of crimes, including those that are more serious than usually seen in problem-solving courts. These returning judges may also influence their colleagues with no specialty court experience to favorably consider alternative sentencing that uses these methodologies. A greatly reopened window of opportunity now exists for a vigorous defense sentencing practice that is client-centered, creative, comprehensive, and effective. Defense lawyers can now use the best and most beneficial principles of specialty courts to enhance sentencing options and alternatives to incarceration for all defendants before a variety of court.

Enhanced sentencing advocacy

Our highest courts have long recognized the critical nature of the sentencing phase in the adjudication of criminal cases and the necessity for the zealous and effective defender. The Supreme Court in *Mempha v. Rhay*, 389 U.S. 128 (1967), noted that *Gideon v. Wainwright* requires that a defendant in a criminal case be afforded legal representation at the critical stage of sentencing even when the defendant is indigent. Defense counsel is, therefore, required to marshal the facts, introduce evidence of mitigating circumstances, and assist the defendant in presenting his or her sentencing requests.

Likewise, many lower federal courts and state appellate courts have gone farther, noting the weighty role the defense lawyer must play at sentencing. In *Taylor v. State*, 339 S.E.2d 859 (N.C. 1986), the North Carolina Supreme Court, citing the *ABA Standards for Criminal Justice* and the federal case of *Pinkney v. US.*, 551 F.2d 1241 (D.C. Cir.

1976), found that the energies and resources of defense lawyers should be directed as fully to the sentencing phase in a criminal case as to the pretrial preparation phase. (*Taylor*, 339 S.E.2d at 861; *see also Christy v. State*, 731 P.2d 1204 *(Wyo. 1987)* (noting that "sentencing may well be the most important part of the entire" criminal proceeding and that therefore it called for thoroughness and resourcefulness, not just a perfunctory allocation by the defense).)

Although the fundamental notion of a proactive defense involvement in sentencing has been the law in federal and state courts for some time, in the recent past—with the advent of "tough on crime" sentencing policies and a movement to determinate sentencing structures with mandatory guideline ranges and mandatory minimum sentences—defense lawyers have found it difficult to implement a proactive sentencing strategy. However, several key legal changes have opened up the possibility for a renewed sentencing practice even in guidelines jurisdictions. In federal courts the holdings in *Booker* and *Blakely* have again given the green light to defender-initiated alternative sentencing plans.

Because of the 2005 Supreme Court decision in *United States v. Booker*, 125 S. Ct. 738 *(2005)*, the U.S. Sentencing Guidelines are viewed as merely advisory, and federal judges now have more latitude to fashion specific individualized sentences in criminal cases. Judges can now consider the guidelines along with any other relevant information, and are not required to sentence within the guideline ranges. (Alan Ellis, *Litigating in a Post-Booker World*, 20 No. 1 CRIM. JUST. 24 (Spring 2005).) This decision gives judges more discretion in fashioning sentences, and defense lawyers practicing before federal judges can present fuller sentencing plans, which may include treatment, restitution, and any other relevant conditions or problem-solving methodologies. Likewise, state and local court systems that utilize guideline systems are open to more creative sentences that make use of a greater range of alternatives to incarceration.

General specialty court theory

At their foundation, some specialty courts, most notably drug and community courts, use alternative sentencing methodologies proactively to process cases and to address issues that may be relevant to a particular case or type of case. (James Nolan, *Redefining Criminal Courts: Problem Solving and the Meaning of Justice*, 40 AM. CRIM. L. REV. 1541 (Fall 2003).)

These courts seek to change the traditional adjudicative process to allow for a combination of treatment, conditions, sanctions and rewards, or other measures, all in an effort to modify behavior, punish the alleged offender, or address a community problem. The prevailing theoretical model of a specialty court calls initially for the placement of a case on a special docket if eligible based on the case type, the neighborhood in which the offense was allegedly committed, government or defense request, or the rules adopted by the particular jurisdiction. Sometimes the judge assigned to that particular docket has received specific training in some issues related to certain social problems, for example, substance addiction, domestic violence, or homelessness. In the case of community courts, the judge may take part in regular meetings with community leaders and residents relating to the incidence of quality-of-life crimes in the area. Specialty courts also usually have social workers, case managers, victim advocates, or other relevant professionals who interact regularly with the defendant or other parties to the case in order to assess any treatment, restitution, or other issues that may be present. Short- and long-term treatment, behavior modification, and especially punitive sanctions are often required and can be enforced through the power of the court. (Candace McCoy,

The Politics of Problem-Solving: An Overview of the Origins and Development of Therapeutic Courts, 40 AM. CRIM. L. REV.1513 (Fall 2003).)

Although there are many types of specialized courts that focus on different issues, such as domestic violence, quality-of-life offenses, mentally ill defendants, or homelessness, supporters of specialty courts point to several fundamental principles that can emerge to varying degrees in a number of these courts. Some of these principles may lead to procedural due process concerns and potential ethical quandaries for defense counsel. These problematic principles include:

- The courts' requirement that treatment for the defendant be imposed early in the life of a case. Often the decision to enter treatment must be made by the defendant before his or her counsel has adequately investigated, evaluated, or negotiated the case. The defense lawyer often advises clients to give up certain rights to enter treatment without the ability to fairly assess the case.

- In order to coerce compliance with the ordered course of treatment, the specialty court judge assesses and enforces a set of increasingly severe punitive sanctions, including jail time, community service, restitution, and/or the abdication of rights or privileges. (Richard Boldt, *Rehabilitative Punishment and the Drug Treatment Court Movement,* 76 WASH. U. L.Q. 1205, 1216 (1998).) A defendant may have agreed to the imposition of sanctions when he or she first entered the treatment court, at a time when the defendant was not fully aware of the ramifications of the sanctions.

- Regular and frequent interaction between the judge and the defendant is encouraged in specialty courts. Many times hearings are scheduled with no reason other than for the judge to learn the defendant's progress in treatment or to determine compliance with the conditions imposed. Unfortunately, the judge often inquires of the defendant in open court about particular aspects of the defendant's life and/or compliance with treatment. These hearings sometimes occur without the presence of the defense lawyer and the defendant is expected to candidly answer the judge's questions, even those that inquire about the violation of additional criminal laws.

- A central tenet of specialty courts is the use of a team approach. (Key Component # 6, *Defining Drug Courts: The Key Components,* Bureau of Justice Assistance (1997).) The team consists of the judge, the prosecutor, the defense lawyer, and case managers. The lawyers are expected to cast aside their traditional partisan roles and work together toward the goal of the specialty court. Defense lawyers may forgo challenges to the imposition of sanctions or not intercede when a judge asks the defendant to make inculpatory statements in court in the presence of the prosecutor.

- Many of these courts involve nonlegal actors as part of the "team," for example, drug treatment professionals, case managers, and social workers. These professionals often use a scientific or medical approach to treatment or client-relations issues that focuses on the best interests of the defendant, who may have more contact with the professionals than the defense lawyer during court proceedings.

- Also key to the operation of the program is the enhanced and increased role of the judge. The judges in specialty courts direct the course of the case, a role that is distinctly different than in traditional courts, where the lawyers take on a more central role, thereby dictating the course of the litigation.

- Finally, and perhaps most significantly, the new treatment courts explicitly disavow adversarialism. In the specialty court, the team approach dictates that each side's goal is the same—the success of the treatment court's goal, be it that the defendant succeed in the proscribed treatment program or that the community be satisfied based upon sanctions that are levied against the defendant. Even in instances where the treatment is something more than substance abuse treatment, for example, group counseling, punitive community service, or monetary restitution, the defense is required to support the completion of the "treatment." Judges frown upon any challenge or argument against the "treatment" or any type of modification to it.

Even amidst concerns about due process and ethics in specialty courts, a general defense sentencing practice can adapt some of the courts' fundamental justifications and treatment methodology to bolster a defense argument for alternative sentencing.

Specialty court models

Two working models of specialty court practices emerge as predominant and provide lessons and opportunities for an enhanced defense sentencing practice. Either of these models can be adapted by the defense to creatively work to the client's benefit.

The first model allows acceptance into the specialized court or its various treatment or social service programs as a condition of pretrial release without the need for the defendant to enter a guilty plea. Usually the program is offered to the defendant with the prosecution's permission very early in the life of the case, sometimes as early as the day of arraignment or presentment. In many instances it is enticing to a defendant to enter the program because it almost always guarantees that the defendant will be immediately released from jail. Many specialty court proponents contend that early entry into a specialty court treatment program is advantageous because the defendant's addiction or other social issues can be addressed immediately. However, there may be consequences for those defendants who refuse the treatment alternative, for example, those who accept it and later fail to meet any or all of its conditions. (Peggy Hora and William Schma, *The Drug Treatment Court Movement: Revolutionizing the Criminal Justice System's Response to Drug Abuse and Crime in America,* 74 NOTRE DAME L. REV. 439 (1999); *see also* Nolan, 40 AM. CRIM. L. REV. at 1560 (recounting statements of judges who push defendants into the treatment court with the veiled threat of the possibility of jail time).) In such a preadjudication model, the defendant is allowed to enter treatment prior to any substantive disposition of the case. If the defendant is unsuccessful in treatment, the case returns to a pretrial stance, and the defendant can elect to go forward with a trial or challenge the constitutionality of police action. However, should the defendant be found guilty, he or she may face a harsher sentence with no possibility for treatment.

The specialty court notion of introducing treatment early in a case can easily be incorporated into a general sentencing practice and may offer defense lawyers support for proposing traditional type sentencing plans early in a case—prior to conviction—as an alternative to pretrial incarceration or other restrictions on liberty. Defense lawyers should always begin to think about sentencing at the start of a case. (*See Ten Principles of Sentencing Advocacy,* The Sentencing Project (December 2003).) From the first interview with the defendant, the lawyers can begin to collect valuable information and to ascertain the client's objectives with respect to the final disposition of the case. (*12 Steps to Effective Defense Sentencing Advocacy,* The Sentencing Project (1993).) Family background information, prior substance abuse treatment history, employment, and education information are all areas that the lawyer can develop at the beginning and throughout the case. However, it is important that counsel not foreclose preparation of the case in the normal course, including evaluating legal suppression issues and factual investigation. As well, defenders need to reassure the client that the gathering of social information does not signal foreclosure of any positive dispositions of the case, including challenges to the government's allegations at a trial. Rather, the client should be informed completely that the information can be used in a variety of ways that inure to the client's benefit.

A second model for the operation of specialty courts has treatment being made available to the defendant only after a guilty plea is entered or many pretrial due process rights, including the right to a speedy trial, right to a jury trial, and the right to a preliminary hearing, are waived. (*Id. at 1559.*) In the post-adjudication model, which is similar to the process in general jurisdiction cases, a defendant must enter a plea of guilty to the charged offense(s) or to a plea-bargained agreement in order to be eligible for the court treatment program. Sentencing is postponed until the defendant is assessed and completes treatment or other court-imposed conditions. A defendant who fulfills the proscribed conditions is guaranteed probation or dismissal of the case. If not successful in treatment, the defendant is sentenced in the normal manner. The post-adjudication model has garnered support from prosecutors who may worry that their abilities to prosecute a case will be irreparably harmed by a delay due to the defendant's treatment. They point to the loss of witnesses or other evidence as one of the rationales for advocating the post-adjudication model. However, the post-adjudication model seems at odds with specialty court jurisprudence because experts argue that a guilty plea has no therapeutic value in a court system that places a premium on treatment. Moreover, the guilty plea may be solely the product of coercion and the defendant's resulting acceptance of treatment may not be voluntary, rather it may be the only way for the defendant to get out of jail. (*See Tenet # 5 of the Ten Tenets of Fair and Effective Problem Solving Courts,* National Legal Association of District Attorneys (2001).)

Despite the questions that surround the post-adjudication model, its emphasis on securing treatment can be applied in general jurisdiction courts by requesting deferrals of sentencing following a conviction at trial or a guilty plea. During the deferral period, the defendant can be given an opportunity to show the court success in whatever treatment may be appropriate, or to gain access to appropriate programs. Some defense lawyers have used the deferral period to secure public benefits to pay the cost of treatment, as a waiting period for treatment beds, to allow for the completion of job training programs, to influence probation authorities, or to secure housing for their clients. Judges may be receptive to this deferral proposal, as the defendant may remain incarcerated during the deferral period or be supervised by a pretrial services agency that can monitor drug use, compliance with court orders, or can impose treatment. In general jurisdiction courts and, indeed, even in some specialty courts, it may be necessary to educate the judge on the benefits of the deferral period.

Client-centered representation and ethics

So how can a conscientious and committed defense lawyer use this open environment for alternative sentencing plans to their client's advantage? First, it requires that counsel be mindful of the positive lessons and principles from the specialty court movement and incorporate them into a sentencing practice in both general jurisdiction or specialty courts. Counsel must also be mindful of the policies or processes in the specialty court model that may compromise their ability to represent their clients fully and zealously. Several commentators have noted concerns about the erosion of client-centeredness and adversarialism in the specialty courts, principles that are essential to full and quality representation of a criminal defendant.

A client-centered defense practice, which is almost always adversarial, can oftentimes be at odds with specialty court principles and almost certainly with the views of other actors in the process, most notably the judge, the prosecutor, and the case manager or social worker. This is because the "teamwork" principle of specialty courts has every actor working toward the basic goals of the court, be it treatment for the defendant, restitution to the victim or community, or otherwise. However, the defense lawyer's allegiance must always be to the client (*see, e.g.,* Abbe Smith, *The Difference in Criminal Defense and the Difference It Makes,* 11 WASH. U. J. L. & POL'Y 83 (2003)); the client's wishes, expressed or implied must trump other goals. This is why it is difficult to renounce adversarialism as required by specialty court practice or within a sentencing practice that seeks to use specialty court principles. The defense lawyer's allegiance to the client should be primary and must be evident to the client and to all others at the beginning of a case and at every step throughout a case, including the formulation and presentation of an alternative sentencing plan.

Client-centered criminal defense representation is in line with the lawyer's ethical obligations under ABA Model Rule of Professional Conduct 1.2. The rule requires that a lawyer abide by the client's wishes with respect to the objectives of the representation and consult with the client with respect to how those objectives are pursued. Continued consultation and adherence to the client's wishes must occur throughout the case. To be sure, the parameters of the requested defense and the means through which its goals are to be achieved fall within the express purview of Rule 1.2.

Because client-centered defense representation promotes the client's desires and wishes, the defendant's wishes serve to establish the direction that the lawyer takes with respect to sentencing, even in instances where the defendant's wishes appear irrational or idiosyncratic. For example, in a case where it is clear that a defendant needs some form of treatment, such as an inpatient drug program, and the judge is likely to defer sentencing to allow for completion of the program or to sentence the defendant to probation with the condition that he or she enter and complete the program, the defense lawyer should argue against a treatment program if the client would rather take jail time in lieu of a treatment program. In other words, the lessons that come from the specialty court movement—that defense lawyers can be therapeutic agents or problem-solvers—may have to take a back seat to the wishes and desires of our clients.

What can a defense lawyer do?

Defense lawyers can and often do spend a great deal of time putting together a sentencing allocution for their clients. This requires them to go beyond the roles of counselor and advisor, and often demands a foray into unfamiliar areas. However, approaching sentencing holistically—similar to the approaches of some specialty courts—may require lawyers to delve into the client's life, challenges, support systems, and goals, and to develop different practices to ensure the persuasiveness of their advocacy.

Input from other professional disciplines. In adjudicating cases, specialty courts make aggressive use of information, personnel, and theories from other, nonlegal disciplines. For example, it is not uncommon for a drug court to have an addiction counselor or social worker assigned to the court. Likewise, judges in specialty courts have often received special training in other disciplines; for example, in drug courts some judges have received limited medical training in the disease model of addiction, some may have attended training courses in pharmacology to determine the effects of drugs on the human body, and some may have attended limited training courses in mental health diagnosis and treatment. Such nonlegal professional disciplines may have different methods, different ethical guides, and different goals from that of the defense lawyer. They may be guided by a desire to do what is in the client's best interests, defined by the professional's expert evaluation, not the client. As a part of the specialty court team, these professionals may push for an outcome that follows their perceptions of the client's problems. They, along with judges and prosecutors, may not understand that a defense lawyer does not have an allegiance to what is in the best interests of the client but rather to what is the client's wishes. The defense lawyer cannot become the disinterested, neutral, greater-good-seeking professional that is central to other disciplines. The defense lawyer must keep vigilant in advocating for the client's wishes, but, in order to be an effective advocate, must also adapt the skill sets and acquire information from these other professional disciplines.

In order to fully inform and persuade the court not to order a full incarcerative sentence, and to use other community-based alternatives to incarceration, the defense lawyer may have to become immersed in the language and substance of these other professional disciplines. This means learning about the subject matter, as well as the goals and methods of treatment or counseling. For example, in order to persuade a judge to defer sentencing and allow a client to enter a community-based anger management course that is offered through a local holistic counseling center, the defense lawyer must understand and convey to the court the goals of the center, what specific topics will be covered, what techniques or methodologies will be used to uncover and address the anger issues, as well as what professional support the particular program receives. This is required in order to competently and persuasively make the presentation to the court.

The lawyer reconnaissance mission. In order to be an effective advocate at any stage of the process — especially in a specialty court or at sentencing before a general jurisdiction court — the defense lawyer must be aware of the idiosyncrasies of the forum, specifically, what matters to the judge who will make the decision in the client's case and what matters to the prosecutor or other professionals upon whose input the judge might heavily rely in making a sentencing decision. The lawyer might talk to other lawyers who have had experience with the judge or prosecutors. The lawyer should ask what the judge has said in previous cases about the treatment issues that may be apparent. Is the judge partial to educational programs? Has the judge looked in the past to family and community support to keep an offender on track? Will the judge hear from family members at the sentencing? Does the judge often think of a monetary fine as key to having the offender take full responsibility?

Prosecutors in specialty courts often have the power to veto the defendant's admission to a specific program or access to a particular disposition. In general jurisdiction courts, of course, the prosecutor's power is great — the prosecutor has the sole authority to offer a particular plea bargain in the case. Moreover, to achieve pretrial release for a client, it is often important to secure the prosecutor's support. This means that the defense lawyer who is working hard to obtain a particular alternative disposition for the client cannot ignore the prosecutor. The defense lawyer should consider advocating the client's position with the prosecutor at the start of the case. Counsel can sensitize the prosecutor to the issues that are extant in the client's life, including work, education, and treatment prospects. The prosecutor may listen to a plan of action that will take into account real services and treatment from which the client can benefit. Counsel should continue to make the prosecutor aware of the defendant's skills and talents that call for more than punishment.

Moreover, treatment personnel and case managers are often not able to have meaningful one-on-one contact with a defendant and may not have enough time, because of overburdened resources or unwillingness, to fully acquaint themselves with the issues and problems that need to be addressed in a client's life. Additionally, these professionals may be so accustomed to treating an issue in a particular manner that they will not consider the defendant's point of view. Counsel can help to change this mindset by advocating on the client's behalf with these professionals at different points in the case. Counsel must keep the lines of communication open by offering assistance with getting the client to appointments or in obtaining needed information that will ensure treatment or success in a particular program.

Developing the sentencing plan. The supporters of such highly publicized and successful specialty courts as Red Hook Community Justice Center in Brooklyn, New York, often point to their program's focus on developing comprehensive services for a particular offender that will benefit that person and the entire community (GREG BERMAN AND JOHN FEINBLATT, GOOD COURTS: THE CASE FOR PROBLEM SOLVING JUSTICE (2005).) Likewise, many defense agencies with a holistic approach to representation or that have dedicated resources to social work divisions or to employing professional sentencing advocates, have also focused much time and resources to looking comprehensively at an individual or a case. This is a very useful and appropriate approach for lawyers to use whether litigating in the specialty court or preparing for sentencing in a general jurisdiction court. The defense lawyer should look at every aspect of the case and look at many facets of the defendant's life to develop a plan for sentencing to present to the court. By identifying at-risk factors, the need for treatment and social services, and bringing to light the talents and motivations of the defendant, the lawyer may be able to make clear a sentencing strategy that will persuade the court to move beyond a traditional sentence of incarceration.

The defense sentencing theory can be built around a particular need for treatment, or can be developed around the need to build foundational elements in a client's life. It can involve the defendant's family commitments or the client's employment prospects. For example, a young client who resorted to drug dealing as a way of making money may desire a career that allows for advancement, job satisfaction, and a stable income. Defense counsel can then focus the sentencing plan on vocational training or exploitation of the client's talents or prior job history to put together a plan that has as its central theme a new career or work experience.

There are many elements that can be addressed in putting together a comprehensive sentencing plan, and a defender should evaluate what role each of these elements may play in designing and presenting the sentencing plan whether it be before a specialty or general jurisdiction court.

Using community resources. It is often important to a judge to take into consideration the needs of the community, as well as the effect on the community of a nonincarceration sentence for a defendant. A sentencing plan that involves the community in some way can go far in convincing a court to consider alternatives to incarceration. Defense counsel may look for resources in the community with which the client can become involved, including churches, service groups, advocacy organizations, or community leaders. Clients could volunteer with these groups or attend programs, or may even be able to educate themselves or others to the needs of the community.

Involving the defendant's family. Family support for a defendant is important and can be a real indicator of success with a sentencing program. At the beginning of a case, defense counsel must identify those family members who have or could have an impact on the defendant. With the defendant's consent, counsel may contact family members, particularly those with whom the client resides, and involve them in the sentencing plan. Counsel should seek to locate absent family members whose presence in the defendant's life may have a positive effect and can ensure that the defendant has the support and assistance of family to aid in meeting the sentencing goals. Counsel should secure letters from family members or have them attend the court hearings and let the court know specifically what role each will play.

Attending to housing concerns. Secure, safe, comfortable, and affordable housing is essential to anyone's attempts to live productively. Therefore, defense counsel must inform the court about the defendant's housing and how it will provide the client with stability and access to the other parts of a sentencing plan. For those clients who may be homeless, counsel should look into shelters or transitional housing programs that will provide a start to self-sufficiency.

Employment prospects. Many judges want to know about the client's employment, its stability and potential to provide for the defendant. Counsel should present verifications of existing employment or letters from employers who may be able to hire the defendant irrespective of court involvement. It may also be important to provide the court with the details of the employment, including the nature of the position, the hours, and locations where the client will work, and the possibilities for long-term tenure and advancement.

Vocational counseling and assessment. In those instances where a client does not have a stable work history or has had difficulty in finding work, counsel should research and evaluate the possibility of the defendant entering a vocational training program. Some of these programs provide a stipend during the full-time training period and placement at completion. For some clients who don't know what they might be interested in, vocational counselors may be able to provide assessments and other evaluative tools that can predict those areas with the most promise.

Financial responsibility. Some jurisdictions require payments to a victims fund or to the court following a conviction, so it is important to ascertain the client's ability to pay such a fine. Counsel should, prior to development of a sentencing plan, consider the impact and necessity of financial restitution to the victim or to the community. Indeed, many specialty courts, particularly community courts, impose varying forms of restitution to the community or to the victim as part of the requirements of adjudication. Several community courts, including the Midtown Community Court in New York, use principles of restorative justice as a reason to require clients to engage in projects that seek to pay back the community for the offense and to instill in the defendant an investment in the community. (*See* www.courtinnovation.org). For example, in a recent District of Columbia case where the defendant was charged with destroying property for painting graffiti, the judge in a general jurisdictional court ordered that the defendant pay for the restoration of some of the property and perform the work of removing the graffiti. (*See Virginia Teen Jailed in DC for Graffiti Vandalism,* RICHMOND TIMES DISPATCH, Feb. 10, 2006.) Additionally, law school clinic students have proposed that a client convicted of cruelty to animals engage in supervised service and education activities with the local animal advocacy group. Unfortunately, sometimes these requirements are counterproductive and may stigmatize the defendants or create resentment because of the use of a defendant's forced labor to benefit a particular business or group of businesses. Before proposing such action, or any other, as part of a sentencing plan, it is important to discuss with the client the details and ramifications of the activity.

Mentorship, internship, and externship. Many lawyers and sentencing advocates sometimes neglect the benefit that mentorship can afford a defendant. Communities have many organizations that offer a one-on-one or group mentoring program for young adults. Some of these groups focus on particular themes, including assistance with education, training, or success in substance abuse treatment. Additionally, many organizations, even small businesses, might be willing to allow a defendant to work as an intern in order to acquire work skills while benefiting the business.

A defendant's talents. Defenders should never neglect to make the court aware of the defendant's talents and skills that may not have had an opportunity to flourish. Talent in art, writing, poetry, music, and many other areas may inform the court of a defendant's potential. Including these skills in a sentencing plan through specific counseling, education, service, or work may allow the court to focus on positive individual characteristics of the defendant that may form the foundation for later success in the community.

Building an educational plan. Especially in situations where a defendant is of high school or college age, and employment prospects are limited, courts are receptive to plans that detail how the defendant will continue education in order to secure employment in the future or as an outlet for creativity and learning. Counsel should look into tutoring programs, college prep courses, GED classes, and admission to colleges or technical schools. To the extent possible, counsel should have the client begin these programs prior to sentencing or continue them while in the specialty court program. Counsel should inform the court of the specifics of the program and should secure proof of placement.

Securing treatment or counseling. Statistics from social science and from data obtained from specialty courts support the notion that a majority of people who enter the criminal justice system have some need for substance abuse, mental health, or other form of treatment or counseling to address chronic or acute issues that have led in some way to the offense. It is of utmost importance that these types of issues be evaluated and assessed prior to or as part of the specialty court program and prior to sentencing. Because of the probability of privacy issues, it is essential that the client be informed and advised, and makes the final decisions regarding the appropriateness of treatment. As well, counsel must follow through on the client's desires for treatment or counseling because the judge may be informed of noncompliance or nonparticipation if the client is not fully invested in the program. Among the treatment options to evaluate are mental health counseling or medication, physical or medical assessment, anger or conflict management, substance abuse treatment, parenting classes, and disability support programs, including day treatment options and dual-diagnosis programs. Counsel must also look into related issues such as 1) securing government or public benefits to allow acceptance into a course of treatment; 2) whether the treatment is inpatient or community based; 3) the security of the treatment facility; and 4) the length of the program.

Cooperation with law enforcement. The judge should be informed of the client's cooperation with police and prosecutors at any stage of the process, from the time of arrest through a bargain with the government. Such cooperation is often substantial because securing or disseminating information may put the client in danger. Counsel should discuss with the client the manner in which the disclosure should be made to the court in order to safeguard the dissemination of the information at a court proceeding, in court records, to treatment or specialty court personnel, or through the defendant's participation in court-ordered treatment or group counseling.

Prior criminal history. The client's criminal justice history will become part of the record that the judge relies on in sentencing or in adjudicating the specialty court case. The information that the court receives comes primarily from court agencies or law enforcement, and sometimes may be incorrect or incomplete, therefore counsel must be careful to verify and correct the information and must give the court additional explanatory information where appropriate.

Using victim impact evidence. In some form or another during a sentencing hearing, the individual victim, victim's family, or the victimized community will be addressed. A central component of some specialty court jurisprudence is to restore the victim and the community to the extent possible. This is done through treatment, service of the defendant, and other means, as well as the reduced possibility that the defendant will recidivate. Counsel has opportunities, as well, to use victim-impact evidence to support a plan for alternative sentencing. There may be instances where counsel can directly involve the victim in the sentencing plan—by illustrating the changed circumstances in the client's life, or that the client has received needed treatment, or any other information that will allow the victim to buy into the sentencing plan. The victim may address the court in writing or in person. When circumstances are appropriate, defense counsel can meet with the victim prior to the sentencing hearing in order to discuss the disposition of the case. Mediation or conciliation may also be considered.

Presentation to the court. Counsel should always be fully prepared when presenting an alternative sentencing plan to the court or in requesting a particular disposition or treatment plan in a specialty court. This preparation may include submitting the plan to the court in writing prior to the day of the hearing. Counsel should submit supporting and verification documentation to the court along with the plan. These additional documents might include a letter of acceptance from a treatment program, psychological, educational, or other assessments by professionals secured by the defense to evaluate the defendant, and letters from the family and community members. Counsel should also include relevant information and argument when requesting a disposition or treatment plan that differs materially from that recommended by the court case managers or other professionals. These documents need to be submitted to the judge far enough in advance of the hearing so that the court can fully digest the information.

Counsel's oral presentation should not rehash every aspect of the written materials, but should cover the most important and compelling elements of the plan. It should also exhibit candor, but clearly set forth how the plan addresses issues affecting the defendant. Counsel may also have to address why incarceration or other traditional disposition is inconsistent with the goal of addressing the client's issues and factors affecting the client's life.

Additionally, counsel should advise and prepare the defendant for participation in the sentencing hearing. The defendant has the opportunity to speak at the hearing and to offer additional information. The defendant's voice and perspective can be a persuasive and important factor that may lead to the court's acceptance of the sentencing plan. Counsel should meet with the client prior to the hearing and discuss allocution and the compelling information that the client wants to convey to the court—be it remorse, an apology, or a forward-looking statement of the defendant's goals after the case is concluded. (*See, e.g.,* Carrie Petrucci, *Apology in the Criminal Justice Setting: Evidence for In-*

cluding Apology as an Additional Component in the Legal System, 20 BEHAV. SCI. LAW. 337 (2002).)

In sentencing, the defense lawyer has a valuable and formidable task to perform. With a renewed focus on this stage of defense representation, spurred on by recent court rulings and the emergence of thousands of specialty or problem-solving courts in local court systems across the country, many more judges are influenced by the notion that their power to sentence means more than just doling out punishment; some are becoming more open to creative sentencing options that focus on specific alternatives to incarceration designed to provide a benefit to the defendant and to the community. These judges are open to full and complete alternative sentencing requests by the defense that will focus on specific issues in a defendant's life or the circumstances of the case that may, in the long run, lower the possibility of recidivism and improve the defendant's life and our communities.

ii. Martin Reisig,[*] The Difficult Role of the Defense Lawyer in a Post-Adjudication Drug Treatment Court: Accommodating Therapeutic Jurisprudence and Due Process
(Reprinted with permission from 38 Criminal Law Bulletin 216, 2002)

At the heart of the new and exciting therapeutic jurisprudence movement is a focus on whether the actions of those of us involved in the justice system produce therapeutic or anti-therapeutic consequences for individuals caught within the system.[1] Therapeutic consequences can be defined as those which promote an individual's overall well-being. How does therapeutic jurisprudence work within the realm of drug treatment courts? What is the relationship between therapeutic jurisprudence and due process? To what extent can this therapeutic focus coexist with the responsibilities of the criminal defense lawyer?

After 30 years as a practicing lawyer, I find myself with two conflicting passions when trying to answer these questions relating to the role of criminal defense counsel, therapeutic jurisprudence and drug treatment courts.

First is the passion for zealous, caring, dedicated and competent representation. The defense lawyer has to make due process a reality and to let the often indigent client know that somebody cares and will go to battle for him. Too often indigent defendants perceive that appointed counsel's only interest is to obtain a quick plea and move on to the next case. To those who do not understand the importance of due process, zealous representation may sound like immature gun slinging egotism. Yet, letting another individual know that he matters may also be a form of therapeutic jurisprudence. Perhaps zealous and caring representation should be called process oriented therapeutic jurisprudence.

---

[*] Martin Reisig practices in Birmingham, Michigan, and is a member of the Oakland County Drug Treatment Court planning team. He is a former appellate defender, federal defender and chief of the economic crime unit of the U.S. Attorney's office for the Eastern District of Michigan. He has been an adjunct professor of legal ethics, trial practice and evidence. He is currently a full time civil mediator.

1. *See* Peggy F. Hora, William G. Schma and John Rosenthal, *Therapeutic Jurisprudence And The Drug Treatment Court Movement: Revolutionizing The Criminal Justice System's Response To Drug Abuse and Crime In America,* 74 Notre Dame L. Rev. 439 (1999). For an overview of therapeutic jurisprudence, *see* Law in a Therapeutic Key: Developments in Therapeutic Jurisprudence (David B. Wexler & Bruce J. Winick eds., 1996).

A second and equal passion is for healing and restoration. Drug treatment courts are proving to be a great asset in ending the cycle of addiction and crime. Acknowledge your crime and your addiction (disease) and we will work with you in support of your return to a full life. Observing those who, through drug treatment courts, discover their self-worth and dignity after endless years of drug addiction is an uplifting experience. Perhaps this is best described as outcome oriented therapeutic jurisprudence.[2]

> drug treatment courts claim to balance my two passions for due process and for healing. However, my concern is that due process is often not an equal partner, especially prior to entry into a drug treatment court.[3] The early drug treatment courts typically focused on defendants with minimal criminal backgrounds who were charged with less serious offenses. A person entered a treatment program and upon completion the charges were dismissed. This is a pre-adjudication model. Failure to complete the program led to reinstatement of the charges. In some of these courts the first paper signed by the defendant was a waiver of defense counsel. This presumably saves money, avoids delays and allows the healing to begin. In these outcome oriented benevolent drug treatment courts due process simply does not appear to be a value; in fact it is treated as a counter to the court's healing purpose.

At a recent training conference for jurisdictions planning drug treatment courts, a national drug treatment court expert spoke about the stakeholders in forming a drug treatment court and for emphasis put his prepared list of the key stakeholders on a screen for all to observe. A defense lawyer was not listed as a stakeholder! I pointed out this oversight, after which a public defender from another jurisdiction commented to me that his planning team did not seem to value his presence at the planning stage of a drug treatment court.[4]

The drug treatment court diversion or pre-adjudication model emphasizes immediate treatment driven intervention. Due process and adversarial defense lawyer conduct are seen as counter productive. When weighing conflicting values the emphasis on treatment may be understandable when the only consequence of failure is to return to a neutral starting point. For better and for worse, the forms of drug treatment courts have been multiplying and changing. Today some drug treatment courts include defendants accused of felonies. These courts often insist on a guilty plea and may not set aside the plea, hence leaving the defendant with a permanent record. These are among the post-adjudication models.

---

2. Over 76% of adult male arrestees and over 50% of juvenile male arrestees test positive for drug use. The relationship between drug use and crime is clear. Breaking this cycle of drug abuse and crime promotes individual well-being as well as minimizing future contacts with the criminal justice system. *See* National Institute of Justice, ADAM: 1998 Annual Report on Adult and Juvenile Arrestees, (Washington D.C.: U.S. Department of Justice, 1999) 3. *See also* The National Center on Addiction and Substance Abuse at Columbia University, *Behind Bars: Substance Abuse and America's Prison Population* (1998).

3. For a skeptical view of drug treatment courts, *see* Morris B. Hoffman, *The Drug Court Scandal*, 78 N. C. L. Rev. 1437 (2000).

4. The Drug Court Program Office, The Drug Courts Standards Committee and the National Association of Drug Court Professionals have prepared a document "Defining Drug Courts: The Key Components" which states for component 2 "Using a non-adversarial approach, prosecution and defense counsel promote public safety while protecting participants' due process rights."

Generally, 30% of all participants in drug treatment courts fail.[5] In one Mentor Court defendants entered their plea within three days of arrest.[6] In this court failure meant a return for sentencing and 30% of the participants returned for sentencing. This is a model court with a 70% success rate. However, was there adequate representation and due process for the 30% who failed and were then incarcerated? Should the outcome oriented therapeutic jurisprudence trump process oriented therapeutic jurisprudence in the post-adjudication model? I would not want to be the defense lawyer involved in a three-day rush to a guilty plea.

Knowing that 30% of the defendants will fail and in many drug court systems go directly to jail, how much due process should be compromised? For years my complaint with defense counsel has been that they often do not do enough. A quick plea and on to the next matter. The fact that appointed counsel represent well over 90% of criminal defendants generally means that there is no inherent trust by defendants in their counsel. Depending on the jurisdiction, a quick resolution may lead to more appointed cases for the defense lawyer and the lawyer has no intent or need to build a long-term relationship with the client. Many observers have written about the crisis in indigent representation. Drug treatment courts must not be allowed to add to this problem.

I am very uncomfortable with quick resolution for the sake of immediate intervention. At the same time I do not challenge treatment professionals who emphasize the importance of taking advantage of a crisis for immediate intervention. The question is how much are we willing to see sacrificed in due process and in the defense attorney-client relationship for the sake of immediate treatment? The following outlines general standards for defense counsel, which have been compromised in the early pre-adjudication diversion model drug treatment courts for the sake of a therapeutic outcome.[7] This compromise must be re-evaluated as the consequences of failure become more punitive in the plea based post-adjudication drug treatment courts.[8]

---

5. As of February 29, 2000, according to statistics from the OJP Drug Court Clearinghouse and Technical Assistance Project at American University 200,000 individuals have been enrolled in adult drug court programs. Of these, 70% have graduated or remained in the program.

6. The National Association of Drug Court Professionals has designated a select group of drug treatment courts as Mentor Courts. These courts participate in running training programs for jurisdictions forming new drug treatment courts.

7. Criminal defense standards require "zealous and quality representation" at all stages of the criminal process. *See* National Legal Aid & Defender Association, Performance Guidelines for Criminal Defense Representation, Guideline 1.1. *See also* ABA Standard 5-1.1 Standard for the Administration of Assigned Counsel Systems, and ABA Defense Foundation Standard, Standard 4-1.2 which requires "effective, quality representation".

8. For a fuller discussion and various defense perspectives, see National Legal Aid & Defender Association articles at www.NLADA.org/indig/nd/97. Of particular interest among these articles, *see* Robert Burke, *Reconciling Drug Court Participation with Defender Ethical Standards* and Michael P. Judge, *Critical Issues for Defenders in the Design and Operation of a Drug Court. See also* Hora *supra* note 1 at 513–516 (for a discussion of the advantages of a pre-adjudication model over a post-adjudication Drug Treatment Court). *See also* Mae C. Quinn, *Whose Team Am I On Anyway? Musings Of A Public Defender About Drug Treatment Court Practice,* 26 N.Y.U. Rev. L. & Soc. Change 37 (2000/2001). Unlike my article, Quinn focuses on the defense role once a client is in a post-adjudication drug treatment court and raises serious questions about the defense lawyer's ethical and legal obligations. Quinn challenges whether a defense lawyer can be a team player within the ethical and constitutional obligations of providing effective and zealous representation. Quinn argues that sanctions within drug treatment courts are analogous to probation violations and require the same level of adversarial defense representation. On this point I differ and believe that there is a difference between sanctions within the post-adjudication drug treatment court and the probation violation and sentencing process. However like the pre-admission concerns which I raise, Quinn's concerns merit serious consideration.

CLIENT INTERVIEW

What are the facts of the offense, arrest, searches, interrogations and lineups? What about witness statements, physical evidence, and the crime scene? Who should be interviewed; which experts could help? As quickly as possible all prosecution information must be reviewed and analyzed with the defendant.

My experience is that it can take many interviews before a defendant is willing to open up. Trust has to be earned. I am questioning the assumption that adversarial preparation is anti-therapeutic. Not caring is anti-therapeutic. Rushing a defendant into making a decision with the knowledge that he could fail in drug treatment court is anti-therapeutic. From 1970–1972 I worked as an appellate defender. True or false, almost every incarcerated inmate blamed not the cop, judge, or prosecutor, but the defense lawyer for his imprisonment. It was the defense lawyer who let him down, did not try and did not care.[9]

PRELIMINARY REVIEW AND DISCOVERY

Counsel cannot provide adequate advice without doing a thorough review of the evidence and of the applicable law. This often takes time! Are the client's stories verifiable, are there other ways of analyzing the scientific information, was the search justified, what do other witnesses say? When a defense lawyer gives advice it should be based on knowledge not expediency. I like to think that demonstrating care for the people represented by treating them all as valued human beings has a therapeutic effect.

CONDUCTING A PRELIMINARY EXAMINATION

Not often, but sometimes cases are dismissed at this preliminary hearing. More often weaknesses in witness stories can be discovered for later usage. Often a defendant finally recognizes some harsh realities. At times the defense lawyer will explain to the defendant that for strategic reasons it is not in the defendant's best interest to conduct a preliminary examination. The point is that the defendant knows that his lawyer cares about him and that he is not being treated like misplaced luggage on an airport conveyor belt.

Long after the crisis that brought me into their lives, I still have a meaningful relationship with many of my former clients. Most clients know when another person has taken them seriously, put in genuine effort and treated them with respect.

THEY ARE NOT ALL GUILTY

Due process must not be under-valued. Barry Scheck and the Innocence Project remind us of the tragedies of rushed justice. There have now been 92 post-conviction DNA exonerations. When DNA evidence has been available and relevant, more than 50% of the time it has supported the innocent-claiming incarcerated inmate. Unfortunately, DNA is not a factor in most cases. However, according to Scheck the DNA exonerations demonstrate that of these cases: 84% were in part based on mistaken identification (often cross-racial), 23% included bad confessions (often to avoid mandatory sentences), 33% were influenced by bad forensics, 50% involved police misconduct (ev-

---

9. For an excellent discussion of the role of the defense lawyer as a therapeutic agent for positive change and the need for improved defense lawyer counseling skills, see Bruce J. Winick, Redefining The Role Of The Criminal Defense Lawyer At Plea Bargaining And Sentencing, A Therapeutic Jurisprudence/Preventive Law Model, 5 Psychol. Pub. Pol'y & L., 1034 (1999).

idence not disclosed), 42% prosecutor misconduct and 25% testimony from jailhouse snitches (to improve their situation).[10]

At the core of all these causes of false convictions is the question: What was the defense lawyer doing? The ultimate therapeutic tragedy is for an innocent person to be incarcerated. We must not allow the need for treatment to lead innocent people into the criminal justice system.

WHEN TO PLEAD INTO A DRUG TREATMENT COURT

A guilty plea should never be entered until there has been a through investigation of the facts and law. The wonderful potential of the outcome oriented therapeutic models must be balanced against the values of process oriented therapeutic jurisprudence. Due process must not be rushed or under-valued. In the post-adjudication drug treatment courts, which are based on guilty pleas, there must be a knowing and informed plea. The stakes, which include a permanent record and a trip to jail or prison for the 30% who cannot complete the treatment program, are too high to allow for any shortcuts.

Prior to entering a guilty plea a defendant must know the strengths and weaknesses of the case against him. To provide anything less than quality and zealous representation prior to a guilty plea will leave the failed 30% of drug court participants believing that they were sold out.

WAIVERS

The easy answer to all due process questions is having a waiver signed. A guilty plea is the ultimate waiver of all the protections of a trial. Hence, motions, preliminary examinations, and counsel can all be waived. One therapeutic view is that the honest admission of a crime is the beginning of recovery. Without disagreeing, I'd also contend that rushed waivers in post-adjudication drug treatment courts could turn into feelings of betrayal and dehumanization. Of all defendants, the addicted and desperate most need time to make an informed decision. The decision can only be informed if defense counsel has done his job. A decision to waive possible defenses is perfectly acceptable, as long as it is made after counsel and the defendant have analyzed the facts, law, strengths, weaknesses and then balanced the alternative courses of action. While rushed waivers may protect the professionals in the system, they do not serve the defendant.

CLIENT RELATIONSHIP

I am most proud of my file of client thank you letters. Most of these people and I have lost track of each other over time, while with others I still occasionally communicate. I hope none would ever again need the services of a criminal defense lawyer. These are special relationships. Another person has shared with me his worst life situation and trusted me to provide solid legal and personal advice.

When I think about referring a person to another lawyer, my primary concern is that the lawyer exemplifies attributes of caring, is honest and a good communicator. Knowing the law is only a preliminary qualification; the key is being the kind of decent person that I would trust to take care of a friend. I know many lawyers who have been practicing in a therapeutic way without ever thinking about it. They simply are good people who happen to be lawyers. Time spent listening to a client and honestly review-

---

10. Presentation "Wrongful Convictions, Causes and Remedies" by Professor Barry Scheck to Criminal Defense Attorneys of Michigan Practice Conference, March 2, 2001, Novi, Michigan. *See also* Barry Scheck, Peter Neufeld and Jim Dwyer, Actual Innocence, Signet (March, 2001).

ing the situation develops a relationship that allows a person to feel good about the process, no matter what decisions are made.

THE INHERENT THERAPEUTIC VALUE OF DUE PROCESS

I have outlined my observations that caring and thorough representation is more than just a matter of legal ethics[11] and defense lawyer obligation, but can also be a critical aspect of the healing i.e. therapeutic process. This may be a new discussion within the drug court movement, but an analogous discussion has been taking place within the area of mental health civil commitments. Therapeutic Jurisprudence co-founder Bruce Winick's observations of the importance of "process" in mental health commitment cases are equally instructive to Drug Treatment Courts.[12]

Similar to my concern that "due process" is valued but not practiced in some Drug Treatment Courts, Winick observes the wide gulf between the "law on the books and law in action" in civil commitments.[13] Civil commitment "due process" can be a sham which can "have severe anti-therapeutic consequences ..." as the shallow process undermines the participants "trust and confidence."[14] Winick cites the work of social psychologists that a participant's perception of being treated with "respect," "politeness" and "dignity" "enhance treatment efficacy."[15] Winick's further observation that "promoting the clients legal rights can be good for his or her mental health" and that the attorney "... should never act in ways that suggest betrayal of the client" are equally important to the structuring of drug treatment courts.[16]

DRUG TREATMENT COURTS AND THERAPEUTIC JURISPRUDENCE

Today 50% to 60% of addicted offenders commit further crimes after their release from jail or prison.[17] The approach of locking them up and then dropping them back into society is a costly and inhumane failure. Within the drug treatment courts supportive judges, prosecutors, defense lawyers and treatment professionals strive cooperatively to help the addict break a life cycle of addiction and crime. The overall well-being of the individual is of paramount value. The potential outcome is so good that it is easy to forget the setting. When the setting includes a guilty plea and a felony as the cost of admission to a drug treatment court the process becomes as important as the potential outcome. A defendant must fully participate in the decision to enter a drug treatment court, trust that he has been provided with full information and perceive

---

11. For an excellent review of the interplay between drug courts and canons of ethics, *see Ethical Considerations for Judges and Attorneys in Drug Courts,* prepared by the National Drug Court Institute (May, 2001), distributed through the U.S. Department of Justice, Office of Justice Programs, Drug Court Programs Office, available at www.ojp.usdoj.gov and at www.ndci.org. *See also* Quinn *supra* note 8.

12. *See* Winick, *"Therapeutic Jurisprudence and the Civil Commitment Hearing,"* 10 J. Contemp. Legal Issues 37 (1999).

13. *ID* at 40.

14. *ID* at 58.

15. *See* Tom R Tyler, *"The Psychological Consequences of Judicial Procedures: Implications for Civil Commitment Hearings,"* 46 SMU L. Rev. 433 (1992), Alexander Greer *et al., "Therapeutic Jurisprudence and Patients' Perceptions of Procedural Due Process of Civil Commitment Hearings," in* Law in a Therapeutic Key: Developments in Therapeutic Jurisprudence 923 (David B. Wexler & Bruce J. Winick eds. 1996).

16. *supra* note12, at 54.

17. A startling 75% of those in drug treatment courts for committing a crime have previously been incarcerated. *See* Drug Court Activity Update: Composite Summary Information, February 29, 2000, OJP Drug Court Clearinghouse and Technical Assistance Project, American University, www.american.edu/justice.

that his views have been fully heard.[18] The therapeutic or anti-therapeutic aspects of the process deserve attention, so as not to undermine the potential good of drug treatment courts.[19]

CONCLUSION

I hope these thoughts challenge the scholars and practitioners of therapeutic jurisprudence and drug treatment courts to focus on the importance of due process and even to recognize that due process can also have a therapeutic value. Most would agree that the best result is a drug-free client. However, this is not just a treatment program, but a program within the criminal justice system often resulting in serious consequences for the defendants. Failures will occur among those suffering from the disease of addiction. When these people are incarcerated after a rushed process, it will be the inadequate defense lawyer who will be blamed. With a greater appreciation for the therapeutic values involved in a caring and thorough representation, this need not be the case. Especially in the post-adjudication drug treatment court model, what constitutes therapeutic jurisprudence is not an easy question. However, there is a tremendous value in constantly asking ourselves about the therapeutic or anti-therapeutic consequences of our actions. It is the right question and the right focus. Drug treatment courts should be able to provide both a therapeutic process and a therapeutic outcome.

iii. Orna Alyagon Darr,[*] TJ and Zealous Advocacy: Tension and Opportunity

What is the difference between a therapeutic jurisprudence lawyer and the good old criminal defense lawyer? A recent debate between David Wexler and Mae Quinn highlights this question.[1] In response to Wexler's proposal that therapeutic jurisprudence ("TJ") should be applied by criminal defense lawyers, Quinn argued that the concept of therapeutic defense practice undermines basic ethical principles. She maintained that having rehabilitation as an overriding consideration comes at the expense of a zealous and quality defense. Addressing this criticism, Wexler clarified that therapeutic considerations do not replace existing principles of criminal defense, but are rather 'add-ons' which enrich and improve the standard practice. Quinn remained unconvinced, contending that these 'add-ons' are practices that good criminal lawyers would employ anyway, and that there is no justification for a separate criminal bar of therapeutic jurisprudence lawyers.

---

18. For a fuller analysis of the importance of "participation, dignity and trust" see Tyler, *supra* note 15.

19. This article has not focussed on the therapeutic, ethical, defense lawyer and due process issues once an individual is admitted to a drug treatment court. My primary concern has been the pre-admission process. For further information, *see* Hora *et al.*, *supra* note 1; Hoffman, *supra* note 3; National Legal Aid and Defender Association articles cited in *supra* note 8; and Quinn, *supra* note 8.

 * Ph.D. The author is a member of the Haifa Public Defender Office, and teaches as an adjunct professor in Haifa University.

1. Mae C. Quinn, "An Rsvp to Professor Wexler's Warm Therapeutic Jurisprudence Invitation to the Criminal Defense Bar: Unable to Join You Already (Somewhat Similarly) Engaged," *Boston College Law Review* 48 (2007), David B. Wexler, "Not Such a Party Pooper: An Attempt to Accommodate (Many of) Professor Quinn's Concerns About Therapeutic Jurisprudence Criminal Defense Lawyering," *Boston College Law Review* 48 (2007), David B. Wexler, "Therapeutic Jurisprudence and the Rehabilitative Role of the Criminal Defense Lawyer," *St. Thomas Law Review* 17 (2005).

Is TJ indeed a practice-module that we simply 'add-on' to fit conveniently with the other aspects of representation? In this essay I explore the inherent tension between therapeutic considerations and zealous representation of the client's defense. I claim that any attempt to treat them as entirely complementing each other runs contrary to practical experience. In the following pages I will try to illustrate the nature of this tension using examples from real cases I have encountered in working as a public defender in Israel. I will further try to understand whether a good-old defense lawyer and a TJ lawyer would make different choices in critical junctures in which a conflict arises between treatment and zealous defense.

Timing

If TJ is merely an 'add-on', should it be applied only after exhausting other options of defense available under the law? The answer is clearly negative. Practicing lawyers are aware that the decision to take the therapeutic course is often made at the beginning of the case. A conditional discharge is an option which appeals to many defendants. Rather than being sentenced to a likely prison term, they are held under probation, during which time they need to cooperate with a designated rehabilitative program. However, if they failed to successfully comply with their rehabilitative program, the case would be brought back to court, and they would be sentenced, possibly more severely. The criminal defense attorney should be able, from the start, to counsel the defendant about the different options, the risks and chances contained in each, and help the client make an informed decision. Even lawyers who do not consider themselves belonging to the TJ school present these options to their clients. Furthermore, a diligent criminal attorney should inquire whether there is mental illness, substance abuse, domestic violence, poverty or other problems at the client's background, and whether therapy or rehabilitation are appropriate options, even when the facts of the case do not imply such unfortunate circumstances. The option of avoiding a harsh sentence in favor of a therapeutic program can also attract those lawyers who are dismayed by the suggestion that they act as 'social-workers'.

The decision whether to seek conditional discharge should be made at an early stage of the case if this line of action is to be realized. After a full blown fact finding hearing or a verdict judges are less likely to allow defendants to seek therapeutic alternatives. Israeli judges are burdened by heavy case loads and haunted by monthly reports measuring their "statistics", that is the number of cases they have brought to completion and the total number of their pending cases. Therefore, judges are more prone to hold hearings for therapeutic purposes when it may save them precious time. In addition, a motion for conditional discharge coming after the defendant has already been found guilty might not strike the judge as a genuine desire for rehabilitation on the defendant's part, but rather as a desperate attempt to save his neck.

About one sixth of Israeli defendants are arrested pending their trial.[2] The prospect of spending long months in custody pending trial motivates many defendants to seek a therapeutic alternative at an early stage of the proceeding. A drug-rehabilitation program is often deemed a suitable alternative to incarceration. Participation in such a pro-

---

2. For example, 72,059 criminal cases were filed in the Israeli courts in 2005. 12,160 defendants were arrested pending their trial that year. The data were taken from official reports published by the Israel Judiciary and the Israel Police. Since a single indictment may include several defendants, and lacking the yearly figure of defendants, it is not possible to calculate the exact percentage of those arrested pending their trial. http://elyon1.court.gov.il/heb/info/DochRashut2005.pdf, http://www.police.gov.il/statistica_umipui/statistica/xx012005bbd_stat.asp#.

gram is the first step towards the goal of conditional discharge. If the defendant was already participating in a rehabilitative program, the court would be reluctant to terminate it by imposing incarceration.

The need to pursue the rehabilitative options from an early stage clashes with the possibility of utilizing the substantive defenses and procedural rights of the client. If the client insists on her innocence, if the evidence is flawed or inadmissible for some reason, she must know that taking advantage of her legal rights might make the therapeutic option at a later stage unfeasible. Theoretically there should be no contradiction between the utilization of legal rights and of an opportunity for rehabilitation. In practice, one often needs to choose between the two.

It is not surprising, therefore, that much of the writing about TJ inspired practices concentrates on the stages of sentencing and post-adjudication or around the plea-bargaining process, which does not involve the contesting of the charges.[3] At these stages TJ is indeed a complementary practice, which does not jeopardize due process. However, at the initial stages of the case a tension does exist.[4]

Treatment v. liberty

The choice between therapeutic and legal interests might be problematic regardless of the question of timing. Mandating therapeutic means through a court order might infringe on the liberty and autonomy of the defendant even more than the likely sentence. A conspicuous example is the dilemma whether to pursue the insanity defense or to argue for incompetence to stand trial. A successful motion for insanity or incompetence typically results in forced hospitalization in a psychiatric hospital. While many mentally ill defendants might prefer hospitalization to incarceration, this is not always the case. The less severe the offence, the less there is to gain by an insanity defense. Under Israeli law the period of psychiatric hospitalization is not limited in time. As long as the patient is hospitalized under a decree of the criminal court, a special committee reviews the case at least once every six months, and determines whether the medical condition of the patient warrants a release from forced hospitalization.[5] As a consequence, a defendant charged with a minor offence which would have resulted in a fine or a suspended sentence and who successfully avoided criminal conviction by reason of incompetence or insanity might stay hospitalized for an indefinite number of years. The need of the mentally ill defendant for therapy is evident. But should the aspiration to promote the health and wellbeing of the mentally ill client take priority over the need to

---

3. e.g. Stephanos Bibas, "Using Plea Procedures to Combat Denial and Minimization," in *Judging in a Therapeutic Key*, ed. Bruce J. Winick and David B. Wexler (Durham, NC: Carolina Academic Press, 2003), James McGuire, "Can the Criminal Law Ever Be Therapeutic?," *Behavioral sciences and the law* 16 (2000), Bruce J. Winick and David B. Wexler, "The Use of Therapeutic Jurisprudence in Law School Clinical Education: Transforming the Criminal Law Clinic," *Clinical Law Review* 13 (2006).

4. Reisig, who writes about the pre-adjudication model drug courts, describes how the balance is tilted towards healing at the expense of due process. Reisig also emphasizes the therapeutic function of zealous representation, and the dangers inherent in rushed therapeutic interventions. Martin Reisig, *The Difficult Role of the Defense Lawyer in a Post-Adjudication Drug Treatment Court: Accommodating Therapeutic Jurisprudence and Due Proces* (2002).

5. Section 28 of the Treatment of Mentally Ill Act, 1991. In a ground-breaking decision of the Israel Supreme Court, it was held that when the period of forced hospitalization disproportionately exceeds the period of maximum penalty, the criminal hospitalization order should be terminated. CrimA 3548/02, John Doe v. District Psychiatric Board for Adults, held 22/1/2003. An English translation is available at: http://elyon1.court.gov.il/eng/verdict/search_eng/verdict_by_case_rslt.aspx?case_nbr=3854&case_year=02.

protect her liberty? Would a TJ attorney and a traditional criminal defense attorney handle this dilemma differently? Would the TJ attorney lean more towards treatment as opposed to protection of liberty? I believe that even TJ lawyers would not pursue therapy at the cost of an indefinite loss of liberty, even if the client needs an immediate psychiatric help.

Minimizing paternalism

The choice between exhausting the legal rights and pursuing treatment is guided by personal preferences and values. However, much of the burden is often on the shoulders of the attorney, when the criminal defendant (be it a juvenile, a mentally impaired or ill individual) lacks the experience, discretion and knowledge to make an informed decision. Wexler emphasizes that the criminal lawyer is better situated than many of his clients to advise them about possible solutions to their problems. He further portrays the image of an attorney who is wiser and more focused than the client, and who can guide the bewildered client to a better understanding of his situation and needs. Being a "respected member of the community", Wexler believes, the lawyer can be effective as an agent of social change.[6] But where exactly does one draw the line between helping clients to carry out their wishes, and matching them with available community resources and a paternalistic attempt to change their values and personal preferences and convert them to middle class values?

To illustrate this point I shall describe the case of Sergei, who has been represented by the public defender's office in a number of cases over the years. Sergei, now 27, was taken from the custody of his alcoholic parents as an infant, and spent his first years in an orphanage. He was later raised by his grandmother and emigrated with her from Ukraine to Israel when he was 18. Sergei grew up in poverty and neglect. He did not go to school and never had a job and is totally dependent on his grandmother, who still takes care of him. She loves him dearly, but is a very limited woman herself, and is unable to attend to his special needs. Sergei's cognitive capabilities are very low (the experts' opinions diverge on whether the problem is organic or developmental and whether or not he suffers from mental retardation). He has not been diagnosed as mentally ill, but suffers from behavior disorder, and occasionally receives psychiatric medication to pacify him. Once in a while Sergei runs into trouble with the law. He was caught a few times driving a car without a license; he was also charged once with breaking into a car, and twice with unlawful possession of a knife. Although it is not a clear-cut case of insanity or mental retardation, his lawyer was able to convince the court that Sergei was incompetent to stand trial. The court ordered therapeutic measures.[7] A team of welfare experts recommended removing Sergei from his grandmother's home, and placing him in a hostel where he could get therapy and instruction that would allow him to develop mentally, learn new skills, and hopefully prepare him to hold a job one day. Sergei and his grandmother were horrified by the idea. Emotionally, Sergei resembles a very young boy, and he cannot bear the thought of being torn away from home and his grandmother, even if this is for his own good. In addition, if Sergei leaves home, his poverty-stricken elderly grandmother would no longer receive his social security payments, and could hardly survive. What should the defense attorney do? What should a TJ lawyer do? Sergei has a great chance of not only avoiding criminal conviction but

---

6. Wexler, "Rehabilitative Role," 758.
7. Under section 19b of the Welfare (Treatment of Retarded Persons) Act, 1951, when the defendant suffers from mental incapacity the court may order that therapeutic measures shall be employed.

also getting an opportunity to develop after many years of neglect, and becoming more independent. Sergei is cognitively deprived (noticeably, trying to engage him in a 'Socratic dialogue', as Wexler suggests, is an impossible mission) but he undoubtedly knows that he will be miserable if taken away from his grandmother. The team of experts which evaluated Sergei was aware of the special bond between him and his grandmother, yet, they concluded, her love and devotion were not enough to affect Sergei's development. Under her care he would remain in neglect and ignorance. Sergei was not swayed by his attorney's advice to consider the therapeutic solution, and at least visit the hostel to see how he liked it. Sergei's preference was unequivocal. A loyal implementation of the client's instruction would go against his therapeutic needs. However, it seems that even TJ attorneys would have to respect Sergei's choice, and refuse the much needed therapeutic course.

Inconsistencies between treatment and legal rights

The above example demonstrates that the best interest of the client is not always easy to define. The defendant has a complex array of interests—legal, financial, familial, medical, therapeutic, etc. The prism of therapeutic jurisprudence focuses on therapeutic considerations, but other preferences are not necessarily inferior.

Although he stresses the importance of the therapeutic approach, Wexler neither proposes a new kind of professional ethics, nor does he undermine in any way the duty of the defense attorney to pursue available lines of defense. If we apply this principle to actual situations of conflict between therapeutic and legal interests, we will find no difference between a TJ lawyer and a traditional criminal lawyer. Nevertheless, a basic discrepancy between therapeutic and legal interest does occur when the need to cooperate with therapy infringes on legal rights. For example, when, for a successful treatment or evaluation, the client needs to disclose to the therapist information regarding his participation in the offence. Whenever the client has to make an admission to the therapist, his right to refrain from self incrimination is violated. Another type of conflict arises when the management of the defense interferes with therapy. For example, Rachel, a defendant charged with possession of heroin, admitted to her attorney that she had committed the offence. Yet the evidence against her was flawed, since the state would not be able to establish the drug's chain of custody. Due to this technical defect, caused by the negligence of the police, she would definitely be acquitted should the case go to trial. The social worker informed her lawyer that unless Rachel admitted guilt in open court and assumed full responsibility for her wrongdoing, she would continue to be in denial of her drug problem, and any treatment would probably fail. The social worker further stressed that if she was acquitted due to a technicality, a significant chance of taking her off drugs would be lost forever.

According to the tenet that TJ considerations should not diminish the rights and protections available to the defendant, in both of the situations above, a TJ attorney would have to recommend to the client to take advantage of the procedural rights, despite the clear damage to the therapeutic process. It should also be remembered that while the client's legal interests may be defended only by the attorney handling the case, her therapeutic interests can be catered to by the social services or other community agents.

Too big a problem

The offence of the criminal defendant is commonly only a small part of a broader picture including poverty, abuse, alcoholism, drug addiction and mental problems. These are not merely personal problems, but often the consequence of wider social problems, determined by where and to whom one is born and in what kind of environment the person was socialized. It would be naive to expect the defense attorney to solve his client's problems single-handedly or to be able to overcome his client's refusal to be helped.

Ana, a defendant in an assault case, needed as much help as she could get. She was homeless, hungry and weak. Kissing the mezuzah with great deliberation and marking the sign of the cross incessantly she attracted much attention wherever she went.[8] In the hot Israeli summer, she always wore her thick wool sweater, long winter skirt and a woolen cap, apparently the only set of clothes she had. Trying to maintain her dignity she denied being homeless, and refused to take the groceries she was offered (although she eventually relented). She was intelligent, but highly suspicious, not to say paranoid. She refused to give access to documents which proved she had been battered by the complainant. She rejected the proposal that she undergo a psychiatric evaluation, although there was a good chance that a psychiatric report could establish a good defense against the criminal charges. All the therapeutic suggestions made by her attorney were turned down. Ana declined any kind of therapy, although she acknowledged her need for counseling and support. Ana also declined the help of social services workers, refrained from contacting the municipality homeless unit, which could have arranged housing for her, and did not go to the NGO where she could get free clothing. Ana was not indifferent. She frequently came to confer with her lawyer. She simply refused to be helped.

One conclusion rising from this discussion and the practical examples given above is that therapeutic and legal interests do clash on occasion. This conflict seems to be inherent in the epistemological dissonance between the non-adversarial therapeutic approach which demands acknowledging wrongdoing as a starting point, and the basic principles of the common law adversary criminal trial, such as the presumption of innocence and placing the burden of proof on the prosecution, which are bolstered by many procedural protections.[9] A second conclusion is that when therapeutic interests conflict with legal rights, the duty of loyalty and the standard of zealous quality representation demand that the defense attorney respect the client's instructions and exhaust the legal defenses and rights available. Writing generally about the conflict between therapeutic jurisprudence and other values, Winick, who co-founded the doctrine of TJ with Wexler, maintained that TJ "is careful to acknowledge the relevance of other normative values and does not suggest that they be subordinated to therapeutic considerations".[10]

Applying this general theoretical principle to particular situations of conflict between the therapeutic interests and a zealous protection of the criminal defendant's substantial and procedural rights, it becomes evident that in practice the good-old de-

---

8. The mezuzah is made of cased verses inscribed on parchment and affixed to the doorpost of Jewish homes. There is a custom of kissing the fingers and touching the Mezuzah upon entering the door.

9. This gap is most crudely manifested when the criminal defendant is required to waive representation or basic legal rights in order to be allowed to pursue the therapeutic course. Reisig points out that some treatment courts demand the defendant to waive the right to a defense counsel. Quinn gives Bronx as an example of jurisdictions where defendants are required to waive their right to appeal in order to accept a drug court plea offer. Mae C. Quinn, "Whose Team Am I on Anyway? Musings of a Public Defender About Drug Treatment Court Practice," *New York University Review of Law & Social Change* 26 (2000–2001): fn 89, Reisig, *The Difficult Role of the Defense Lawyer in a Post-Adjudication Drug Treatment Court: Accommodating Therapeutic Jurisprudence and Due Proces*.

10. Bruce J. Winick, *Therapeutic Jurisprudence Applied: Essays on Mental Health Law* (Durham, NC: Carolina Academic Press Studies in Law and Psychology, 1997), 7.

fense lawyer and the TJ lawyer would make similar choices. It seems that both Wexler and Quinn agree that there should not be a different set of ethical rules for each school of defense work. The discussion above also demonstrates that traditional criminal lawyers also engage in therapeutic practices. There are several reasons for this. Therapeutic measures and procedures are embedded in the law itself. Probation, conditional discharge, drug rehabilitation programs, forced psychiatric hospitalization — these are all sections of the criminal law. In addition, consideration of rehabilitation and therapeutic progress is built into proceedings where the dangerousness and character of the client are examined. Sentencing hearings, committees deciding early release from prison, motions for pardon — these are all proceedings which require the attorney to be familiar with the personal circumstances of the client. This is all the more true for legal systems which include special problem solving courts such as drug courts or mental health courts. Furthermore, the more committed to their client and to the success of the case, the less criminal defenders are likely to be mere presenters of the client's circumstances and therapeutic program, and the more prone they are to play an active role. So if the social workers, carrying their heavy burden of case load, drag their feet, zealous defense attorneys will come with their own suggestions for rehabilitative programs. Not because they believe they are TJ lawyers, but because they are good advocates.

The perspective of therapeutic jurisprudence encourages criminal defenders to reconsider their role, and give their clients more meaningful help — not only coping with the current case, but helping them change their life. A sense of enthusiasm at such a prospect clearly exists. Yet, immediate intervention is not always possible. Although TJ is a theory driven by a preventive rationale, its application at the preliminary stages of the case is problematic.

Sometimes, criminal defenders desperately want their clients to improve, to stop being so destructive of their own lives. However, significant as it may be, this mission should be performed with a sense of modesty and an awareness of the various limitations. Criminal defenders who suggest a rehabilitative program to their clients should disclose the failure rates in these programs, and the legal consequences in case the client does not succeed. In addition, although the criminal defender is more educated and better socially positioned than most of his clients, the client's instructions and choices should be respected, even if the advocate considers them wrong. The defense lawyer should help the client to explore whether the criminal proceeding may be used as leverage for treatment and a better life, and to find alternative therapeutic courses, but not to act as missionaries, who impose their own values and preferences on the client. Avoiding paternalism becomes more difficult when the client's ability to make his own decisions is significantly impaired. When the client is a minor, mentally ill or mentally impaired the dilemmas between therapy and other values are particularly excruciating. Finally, therapeutic jurisprudence may be perceived by the other players in the justice system to being a holistic concept, which takes into consideration not only the interests of the defendant but also those of his family members, the victim and, perhaps, society at large. Nevertheless, therapeutic criminal defense attorneys, zealous as they may be, should remember that it is only the client to whom they owe loyalty.

So if in practice both traditional and TJ lawyers make use of therapeutic measures, if the ethical duties are identical, how can the doctrine of therapeutic jurisprudence contribute to the practice of criminal defense? The answer lies mostly in the enhancement of awareness to therapeutic considerations and the formation of a common body of knowledge, an "open source code" practice, based on the shared experience of a vast number of practitioners.[11] Sharing ideas and techniques would help to expand the scope of therapeutic advocacy. The contribution of therapeutic jurisprudence to existing practice can also be accomplished through further empirical and theoretical studies. Different jurisdictions adopted different alternatives to the traditional adversary criminal trial. Hence, a comparative study of these diverse TJ practices could also develop the formation of such a widely shared body of knowledge.

Law and parallel branches of learning such as criminology, social work and psychology are all intertwined in the TJ practice. Thus, the vision of therapeutic jurisprudence draws on knowledge and practices developed within a wide array of disciplines. The interdisciplinary nature of therapeutic jurisprudence is inspiring and stimulating, yet it carries the risk of theoretical inconsistencies, as the different disciplines diverge in their understanding of the best interest of the client, and have different ethical commitments. The interdisciplinary nature of TJ calls for studies which will explore areas of compatibility and discrepancy between law and the other disciplines. Moreover, the legal theory should further address the ethical implications of the TJ practice.

Much of the TJ oriented literature concentrates on the integration of advocacy and therapy. It investigates the ways in which therapy and law enhance and complement each other. I believe that shedding light on situations of tension between TJ and traditional advocacy would help to improve the theoretical understanding of the relationship between treatment and zealous representation. This theoretical angle, which identifies areas of conflict rather than of harmony, might also lead to restructuring TJ inspired proceedings in a manner which would eliminate or reduce existing tensions.

iv. David B. Wexler, Therapeutic Jurisprudence and Readiness for Rehabilitation
(Reprinted with permission from
8 Florida Coastal Law Review 111, 2006)

After about a quarter of a century, we seem finally to have turned the correctional corner, leaving behind a "nothing works" mentality,[1] and finally embarking upon a more promising path. Indeed, it is now common to see references to what in the correctional context has become known as the "What Works" research.[2]

Researchers—such as those working with the Washington State Institute for Public Policy[3]—are marshalling empirical evidence and are urging correctional authorities to

---

11. The open-source code is a collaborative method of developing software. It permits users to use, improve and redistribute the software, and it is freely distributed to private individual users.

1. The "nothing works" era of criminological thought can be traced to the 1974 piece by Robert Martinson, *What Works?—Questions and Answers About Prison Reform*, 10 PUB. INT. 22 (1974).

2. WHAT WORKS: REDUCING REOFFENDING (James McGuire ed. 1995); David B. Wexler, *How the Law Can Use What Works: A Therapeutic Jurisprudence Look at Recent Research on Rehabilitation*, 15 BEHAV. SCI. & L. 368 (1998) (reviewing WHAT WORKS: REDUCING REOFFENDING (James McGuire ed. 1995)).

3. The Institute is a creation of the Washington Legislature. Washington State Institute for Public Policy, http://www.wsipp.wa.gov (last visited Sept. 27, 2006).

use limited resources to introduce and implement successful evidence-based programs and to eschew programs that have been found wanting.[4] Among the failures, according to the Institute's 2006 report, are adult boot camps and psychotherapy for sex offenders.[5] Programs with demonstrated promise, on the other hand, include educational and vocational programs,[6] prison-based therapeutic communities for drug offenders,[7] and cognitive-behavioral treatment programs (programs that focus on thinking or problem-solving)[8] such as the "reasoning and rehabilitation" model,[9] of demonstrated efficacy for the general offender population as well as for drug offenders and sex offenders.

I. Readiness

Even if such programs are put in place, however, maximum successful results will likely follow only if incarcerated persons are motivated to participate and engage fully in the enterprise. What makes motivated inmates? There is a general body of social science research on determinants of help-seeking behavior, complete with policy recommendations on how such behavior might be increased.[10] The concept at issue is often known as "responsivity" to treatment,[11] or more recently as "readiness" for rehabilitation.[12] This essay looks through a therapeutic jurisprudence[13] lens at how the *law*—more precisely, how the behavior of lawyers and judges[14]—may impact help-seeking behavior and willingness to undertake rehabilitative efforts.

Of course, there are some legal arrangements that can themselves operate as motivating forces—such as, under the right circumstances, the prospect of parole or conditional release.[15] But the question raised here is how the behavior of lawyers and judges may increase an offender's readiness for rehabilitation. Moreover, this essay goes not to the crucially important task of crafting proposed non-incarcerative dispositions,[16] but

---

4. Steve Aos et al., Wash. State Inst. For Pub. Pol'y, Evidence-Based Adult Corrections Programs: What Works and What Does Not (2006), *available at* http://www.wsipp.wa.gov/rptfiles/06-01-1201.pdf (preliminary report; final report to be published in Oct. 2006).

5. *Id.* at 5–6. Even some "failures," however, such as adult boot camps, might be "economically attractive if they cost less to run than the alternative." *Id.* at 6.

6. *Id.*

7. *Id.* at 4.

8. *Id.* at 4–5 (relating effects on drug offenders, general population, and sex offenders).

9. *Id.* at 5; *see also* L. S. Joy Tong & David P. Farrington, *How Effective is the "Reasoning and Rehabilitation" Programme in Reducing Reoffending? A Meta-Analysis of Evaluations in Four Countries*, 12 Psychol. Crime & L. 3 (2006).

10. *See, e.g.*, Philip Skogstad et al., *Social-Cognitive Determinants of Help-Seeking for Mental Health Problems Among Prison Inmates*, 16 Crim. Beh. & Mental Health 43 (2006).

11. Astrid Birgden, *Therapeutic Jurisprudence and Responsivity: Finding the Will and the Way in Offender Rehabilitation*, 10 Psychol. Crime & L. 283 (2004).

12. Tony Ward et al., *The Multifactor Offender Readiness Model*, 9 Aggression & Violent Behav. 645 (2004).

13. *See generally* International Network on Therapeutic Jurisprudence, http://www.therapeuticjurisprudence.org (last visited Sept. 27, 2006) [hereinafter INTJ].

14. Therapeutic jurisprudence looks at the law in action, and is concerned with legal rules, legal procedures, and with the roles of legal actors, such as lawyers and judges. David B. Wexler, Therapeutic Jurisprudence: The Law as a Therapeutic Agent (1990). The emphasis in the present essay is upon the roles of lawyers and judges, specifically.

15. David B. Wexler, *Spain's JVP ('Juez de Vigilancia Penitenciaria') Legal Structure as a Potential Model for a Re-Entry Court*, 7 Contemp. Issues in L. 1 (2003/2004) (emphasizing, among other things, the virtue of "constrained discretion").

16. *See, e.g.*, David B. Wexler, *Therapeutic Jurisprudence and the Rehabilitative Role of the Criminal Defense Lawyer*, 17 St. Thomas L. Rev. 743, 756–66 (2005) [hereinafter *TJ and the Rehabilitative*

rather to how lawyers and judges might be able to contribute to the motivation of *incarcerated* individuals.

This piece follows the direction taken by Australian correctional psychologist Astrid Birgden (a co-author of the "readiness" model noted above),[17] who has explored the use of "motivational interviewing" by criminal defense attorneys,[18] and who has written about harnessing correctional staff as legal actors and potential therapeutic agents.[19]

II. Procedural Justice

Prior work in therapeutic jurisprudence has underscored the importance of procedural justice elements on an offender's judgment as to whether the process was fair and on his or her acceptance of and compliance with even adverse judgments.[20] Treating an offender with respect, imparting to the offender a sense of voice, and genuinely attending to ("validating") that voice are key elements.[21] Offenders are accordingly more likely to be primed for undertaking rehabilitative efforts if those elements are in place. If they are not—meaning the offender feels he or she was mistreated, ignored, or got a raw deal—the rehabilitative prospects may be dramatically lessened. Indeed, for the latter group, criminologists have even posited a "defiance" effect of persistent, more frequent, or even more serious violations.[22]

Judges operating in so-called problem-solving (drug treatment, mental health, community) courts have been particularly sensitive to considerations of respect, and are aware of how they themselves may function as positive change agents.[23] Such judges are typically adept at communicative and interpersonal skills. They will take pains to listen as well as to explain their decisions.

Role]; Karine Langley, *The Case of Robert Piamonte: A Victory for Therapeutic Jurisprudence*, http://www.accidentaljurist.com/featured_topics/display_e.asp?ID=10 (last visited Sept. 27, 2006).

17. Ward et al., *supra* note 12.

18. Astrid Birgden, *Dealing with the Resistant Criminal Client: A Psychologically-Minded Strategy for More Effective Legal Counseling*, 38 Crim. L. Bull. 225 (2002). For important similar work relating to probation officers, see Michael D. Clark, *Motivational Interviewing for Probation Staff: Increasing the Readiness to Change*, 69 Fed. Probation 22 (Dec. 2005); Risdon N. Slate et al., *Training Federal Probation Officers as Mental Health Specialists*, 68 Fed. Probation 9 (Dec. 2004). For techniques to elicit client "change talk," see Theresa B. Moyers & Tim Martin, *Therapist Influence on Client Language During Motivational Interviewing Sessions*, 30 J. Substance Abuse Treatment 245 (2006).

19. Birgden, *supra* note 11, at 290–93.

20. *See generally* Judging in a Therapeutic Key: Therapeutic Jurisprudence and the Courts (Bruce J. Winick & David B. Wexler eds., 2003) [hereinafter TJ and the Courts].

21. *Id.* at 129–64; *see also* Susan Goldberg, Nat'l Judicial Inst., Judging for the 21st Century: A Problem-Solving Approach 8 (2005), *available at* http://www.nji.ca/nji/Public/documents/Judgingfor21scenturyDe.pdf. The judicial manual produced by the National Judicial Institute of Canada is available in English and French on the website: in English under "education" and then "publications;" and in French under "Francais," then "formation" and then "publications".

22. The original piece is Lawrence W. Sherman, *Defiance, Deterrence and Irrelevance: A Theory of the Criminal Sanction*, 30 J. Res. Crime & Delinq. 445 (1993). Later works include Alex R. Piquero et al., *Discerning Unfairness Where Others May Not: Low Self-Control and Unfair Sanction Perceptions*, 42 Criminology 699 (2004), and Raymond R. Corrado et al., *Serious and Violent Young Offenders' Decisions to Recidivate: An Assessment of Five Sentencing Models*, 49 Crime & Delinq. 179 (2003). The criminological concept of "defiance" seems similar to the psychological concept of "reactance." *See* Sharon S. Brehm & Jack W. Brehm, Psychological Reactance: A Theory of Freedom and Control 12 (1981).

23. TJ & the Courts, *supra* note 20, at 129–64.

III. A Judicial Example

Judge David Fletcher of the Community Court in Liverpool, England, probes beneath a client's criminality to uncover problems and to ascertain a client's need for and willingness to accept treatment and other social services. These are discussed with the client at sentencing. Sometimes, an incarcerative penalty is deemed warranted. Even in these instances, however, the court's concern is conveyed in a follow-up letter delivered and explained to the offender, in a matter of days after sentencing, at the correctional institution. The letter is tailored to the prior in-court discussion. For example, in a letter dated February 3, 2006, Judge Fletcher communicated the following to a prisoner sentenced by him only two days earlier:

Mr. X:

You received a ten-week sentence at the North Liverpool Community Justice Centre on Wednesday, 1st February 2006.

At that hearing it was indicated you needed help with a number of issues that contribute to your offending.

As part of the Community Justice Centre approach you will be visited in the very near future by a member of my team who will link you into appropriate services, including Drug Initiatives Team.

Throughout your sentence they will monitor your progress and prior to release give the Court a progress report.

I hope you take advantage of the services whilst in prison.

Yours sincerely,

His Honour Judge David Fletcher[24]

Judge Fletcher's technique of follow-up, respect, and motivation could, of course, be extended beyond a community court to a general criminal court. Moreover, the underlying principles of respect and explanatory communication suggest that, in a general criminal case, a full-blown statement of reasons for a sentence should be written so that it could be read by the defendant personally and could form the basis of an important conversation between counsel and client.

Properly prepared, such a statement of reasons could contribute to a defendant's sense of fair treatment—even in the face of an incarcerative penalty. To do so, the sentencing judge should take pains basically to condemn the act, rather than the actor;[25] to

---

24. Letter from Judge David Fletcher to recently sentenced inmate (name omitted) (Feb. 3, 2006) (on file with author).

25. A judge sensitive to this point is unlikely to tell a woman that she is simply "no good as a mother." And, even when imposing a severe sentence, such a judge is not going to say, "You are a menace and a danger to society. Society should be protected from the likes of you." David B. Wexler, *Robes and Rehabilitation: How Judges Can Help Offenders "Make Good"*, 38 Ct. Rev. 18, 22 (Spring 2001) [hereinafter *Robes and Rehabilitation*].

The general principle of condemning the act rather than the actor is in line with John Braithwaite's notion of "reintegrative shame" rather than "stigmatization." With reintegrative shaming, "the offender is treated as a good person who has done a bad deed," whereas with stigmatization, "the offender is treated as a bad person." John Braithwaite, *Restorative Justice and Therapeutic Jurisprudence*, 38 Crim. L. Bull. 244, 258 (2002). Brathwaite, however, now realizes his point should be modified and made more subtle:

If a man rapes a child or is repeatedly convicted for serious assaults, is it enough for him to feel that he has done a bad act(s) but there is nothing wrong with him as a person? It would seem more morally satisfactory for him to feel that he has done a bad act and

point out strengths that can serve as building blocks for a reconstructed self-image;[26] and should strive to elaborate on the various purposes of sentencing, some of which—such as general deterrence—may better support a period of incarceration even if other factors are favorable to the defense.[27]

IV. CRIMINAL DEFENSE EXAMPLE

The defendant will presumably best understand the sentencing factors if he or she is given a real role in grappling with them. This is precisely what is done by Paul Antonio (Tony) Lacy, an Assistant Federal Defender in the Western District of Oklahoma, in

---

therefore feels he must change the kind of person he is in some important ways (while still on the whole believing he is basically a good person). That is, we do not want the rapist to believe he is an irretrievably evil person; but we do want aspects of the self to be transformed.

Id. at 259. A judge interested in promoting offenders' efforts at positive behavior change should try, as best as possible, to capture this "halfway house of an ethical ideal." Id. Indeed, an interesting continuing judicial education exercise might be to discuss how situations such as the above could best be handled and communicated. For an interesting case—and controversy—regarding the crafting of oral and written sentencing remarks, see United States v. Collington, No. 05-4054, 2006 WL 2506471 (6th Cir. Aug. 31, 2006). For a well-reasoned plea for carefully crafted sentencing opinions—but one that does not explicitly mention their value to criminal defendants themselves—see Steven L. Chanenson, *Write On!*, 115 YALE L.J. POCKET PART 146 (2006), http://www.thepocketpart.org/2006/07/chanenson.html.

26. Criminologist Shadd Maruna notes the importance of helping an offender use his or her strengths to create a future narrative of one who will desist from crime. SHADD MARUNA, MAKING GOOD: HOW EX-INMATES REFORM AND REBUILD THEIR LIVES 86–88 (2001). Lawyers and judges can play an important role in this effort. Consider the following sentencing remarks, drawn from *Robes and Rehabilitation*:

You and your friends were involved in some pretty serious business here, and I am going to impose a sentence that reflects just how serious it is. I want to add one thing, however. There's been some testimony here about how you showed some real concern for the victim. I'm going to take that into consideration in your case. You know, according to some of the letters that were submitted, it looks like that sensitive nature is something you displayed way back in grade school. Nowadays, it seems to peek out only now and then. But if I could peel away a few layers, I'll bet I could get a glimpse of a pretty caring person way down there. In any case, under the law in this state, I'm able to reduce your sentence by a year for what you did when that caring quality came peeking out last March.

Sometimes, a search for and discovery of a favorable feature or quality may not influence the disposition at all, but it may nonetheless plant a helpful seed, like this:

I don't really know what went wrong here. I do know you committed a robbery and someone was hurt. And I know that it is only right that I impose a sentence of such-and-such. What I don't understand is why this all happened. You are obviously very intelligent and were always a good student. Your former wife says that, until a few years ago, you were a very good, caring and responsible father. You obviously have a real talent for woodworking, but it's been years since you spent time on a real woodworking project. Beneath all this, I see a good person who has gotten on the wrong path. I hope you'll think about this and change that path. With your intelligence, personality and talent, I think you can do it if you decide you really want to.

27. *Robes and Rehabilitation*, *supra* note 25, at 22–23.

In R. v. Rachid, 93-4567, [1994] O.J. 4228 QUICKLAW (O.C.J. Feb. 17, 1994), the Provincial Division of the Ontario Court of Justice imposed a custodial sentence of five months, followed by twelve months probation, on a twenty-six-year-old first offender convicted of possessing and passing counterfeit U.S. currency in the City of Niagara Falls, Ontario. The Court noted the prevalence of this activity in this community close to the U.S. border, which adds to the gravity of the offense and justifies a more serious sentence. The court balanced the various sentencing factors and tried to tailor the sentence to this individual accused, "while bearing in mind that the most important factor is general deterrence." *Id.* at ¶ 6.

preparing his clients for meaningful allocution. Lacy's allocution approach can work well in a post-*Booker* world[28] which allows some flexibility in federal sentencing.[29]

United States v. Booker rendered the strict and mechanical federal sentencing guidelines of advisory import only.[30] Moreover, it revivified the federal statute that looks at "the nature and circumstances of the offense and the history and characteristics of the defendant"[31] and directs a sentencing judge to "impose a sentence sufficient, but not greater than necessary"[32] in order to comply with the purposes of § 3553(a)(2), which are:

A. [T]o reflect the seriousness of the offense, to promote respect for the law, and to provide just punishment for the offense;

B. [T]o afford adequate deterrence to criminal conduct;

C. [T]o protect the public from further crimes of the defendant; and

D. [T]o provide the defendant with needed educational or vocational training, medical care, or other correctional treatment in the most effective manner.[33]

When Lacy meets his client to go over a draft of the Pre-Sentence Investigation Report, Lacy asks the client to answer, within two weeks time and usually in handwritten form, a list of questions drawn from the revived statutory scheme.[34] Most allocution statements are one to three pages in length, and are filed as an independent allocution pleading or, sometimes, as a combined sentencing memorandum[35] and allocution statement. The exercise, according to Lacy, "makes the defendant think about the sentencing process and provide insight that would never be reflected in the Pre-Sentence Investigation Report."[36] The allocution statement also keeps the defendant from "freezing up and having nothing to say" when addressed by the court.[37]

---

28. *See generally* United States v. Booker, 543 U.S. 220 (2005) (majority holding federal sentencing guidelines were violative of the Sixth Amendment unless used merely in an advisory capacity).

29. In this essay, however, the author's interest goes not at all to the intricacies of federal sentencing, but rather to the potential roles of lawyer and judges operating under sentencing schemes—in the United States and elsewhere—with a decent dose of judicial discretion.

30. *See Booker* at 249–50 (Breyer, J., delivering the opinion of the Court in part).

31. 18 U.S.C. § 3553(a)(1) (2000).

32. *Id.* § 3553(a).

33. *Id.* § 3553(a)(2)(A)-(D).

34. *See id.* Lacy has prepared and shared with the author an undated memo entitled "The Story Behind the Allocution Pleading," from which the factual information in this section has been derived. Paul Antonio (Tony) Lacy, The Story Behind the Allocution Pleading (undated) (unpublished memo, on file with author, *available at* http://www.nynd-fpd.org/pleadings/allocution%20pleading%20with%20notes%20and%20examples.pdf (last visited January 11, 2007)) [hereinafter Lacy Memo]. Handwritten statements are common and important because the defendant is often detained pending sentencing and lacks access to a typewriter or computer. Moreover, Lacy believes the handwritten form to be more potent. I asked in an email correspondence about illiteracy and language problems and Lacy noted he was working to have his questionnaire translated to Spanish. Beyond that, he has not encountered situations of full-fledged illiteracy. Indeed, he feels handwritten statements, even laden with grammatical and spelling errors, serve their function and bring home the fact that the judge is hearing from a real person.

35. The preparation by counsel of a sentencing memorandum is important, and ideally "should provide a ready foundation for the court's statement of reasons in adopting it." LUCIEN B. CAMPBELL & HENRY J. BEMPORAD, OFFICE OF FED. PUB. DEFENDER W. DIST. OF TEX., AN INTRODUCTION TO FEDERAL SENTENCING 14 (9th ed. 2006), *available at* http://www.ussc.gov/training/intro9.pdf.

36. Lacy Memo, *supra* note 34, at 3.

37. *Id.*

Here is a model statement, provided to me by Lacy, with questions to the defendant tailored to the § 3553(a) factors:[38]

IN THE UNITED STATES DISTRICT COURT

UNITED STATES OF AMERICA	)	
	)	
Plaintiff,	)	
	)	
v.	)	Case No. 06-0000
	)	
ABOUT TOBE SENTENCED,	)	
	)	
Defendant	)	

ALLOCUTION STATEMENT

Rule 32(i)(4) of the FEDERAL RULES OF CRIMINAL PROCEDURE permits a defendant the opportunity to speak or present any information to mitigate the sentence. Counsel for About Tobe Sentenced, gave *him/her* a list of questions relating to reasons *he/she* should be given leniency. The Allocution Statement is provided for the Court's consideration in determining what type and length of sentence is sufficient, but not greater than necessary, to comply with the statutory directives set forth in Title 18, United States Code, § 3553(a).

About Tobe Sentenced's verbatim handwritten (or typed) Allocution Statement addresses the following Section 3553(a) factors:

What are your best accomplishments?[A]

What are your best attributes?[A]

What have you done that you are most proud of?[A]

What are your short-term goals?[A]

What are your long-term goals?[A]

Why are you a better person now?[A]

How does giving you leniency reflect the seriousness of your offense?[B]

---

38. The statement can be easily adapted to other sentencing schemes with similar relevant factors, such as Section 718 of the Criminal Code of Canada, which states:
    The fundamental purpose of sentencing is to contribute, along with crime prevention initiatives, to respect for the law and the maintenance of a just, peaceful and safe society by imposing just sanctions that have one or more of the following objectives:
    a. to denounce unlawful conduct;
    b. to deter the offender and other persons from committing offences;
    c. to separate offenders from society, where necessary;
    d. to assist in rehabilitating offenders;
    e. to provide reparations for harm done to victims or to the community; and
    f. to promote a sense of responsibility in offenders, and acknowledgement of the harm done to victims and to the community.
Canada Criminal Code, R.S.C. 1985, c. C-46, s. 718 (2006).
    A. "[T]he nature and circumstances of the offense and the history and characteristics of the defendant." 18 U.S.C. § 3553(a)(1) (2000).
    B. "[T]he need for the sentence imposed ... to reflect the seriousness of the offense, to promote respect for the law, and to provide just punishment for the offense." *Id.* § 3553(a)(2)(A).

How would leniency promote your respect for the law?[B]

How will giving you leniency promote other people's respect for the law?[B]

What is a just punishment for your offense and why?[B]

Will giving you leniency cause other people not to break the law as you did?[C]

Why will giving you leniency protect the public from further crimes by you?[D]

Do you need educational or vocational training?[E] How would leniency provide you educational or vocational training?[E]

Do you need medical care?[E]

How would leniency provide you with medical care?[E]

What, if anything would you say to your family?[A]

What, if anything, would you say to your victims?[A]

Why should the Judge give YOU a break?[A–E]
Respectfully submitted,
    s/ Defense Counsel
    DEFENSE COUNSEL
    Attorney for Defendant, About Tobe Sentenced
    OFFICE OF THE FEDERAL PUBLIC DEFENDER
    Address, City, State, ZIP
    Telephone: Facsimile:
    E-Mail[39]

V. A Defendant's Allocution Statement

Below is one allocution statement[40] shared with me by Lacy. It was submitted by twenty-year-old Mr. X in a case involving escape from a halfway house. Mr. X will have to return to Bureau of Prisons custody to complete the sentence he would otherwise have served in the halfway house, and his allocution statement seeks leniency in sentencing on the subsequent escape charge:

1) What are your best accomplishments?
   — Being sober over a year, completing my drug Class in prison,

2) What are your best attributes?
   — Carring, People Person, Good work ethics, determination

3) What have you done that you are most Proud of?
   — I was Proud of Myself for working on a Job longer then two months. I set a Goal to work my Second Job ever for six months, but it turned out to be nine months.

4) What are your Short term Goals?

C. "[T]o afford adequate deterrence to criminal conduct." *Id.* § 3553(a)(2)(B).

D. "[T]o protect the public from further crimes of the defendant...." *Id.* § 3553(a)(2)(C).

E. "[T]o provide the defendant with needed educational or vocational training, medical care, or other correctional treatment in the most effective manner." *Id.* § 3553(a)(2)(D).

39. Lacy Memo, *supra* note 34, at 16–17.

40. The allocution statement is reprinted as originally written by the defendant, with no alterations.

—To achieve my G.E.D. with in the next year. I would also like to inroll in a small college to take up Business and Realestate Classes. Plus seek help with my drug, and anger Problem as well as my higher Power.

5) What are your long term Goals?
—Having my G.E.D. While working toward a degree in Something major. Plus living a life with Sobriety. Raise me a family and introduce my kids into a life I never had. Also having a relationship with my higher power.

6) Why are you a better person now?
—After being incarcerated for almost 2 year's now I realize what I had taken for granted. Because this is just as hard on my family as it is for me. I guess it took this situation to happen again for me to open my eyes and get myself together before it's to late for me.

7) How does giving you leniency reflect the Seriousness of your offense?
—my time is reflective of the seriousness of my offense, leniency reflects your ability to see the person behind the paper.

8) How would leniency Promote your respect for the law?
—It would show me that the law system is Capable of seeing all aspects of the crime and the people involved. I was a kid who got out of hand and made the biggest mistakes in my life, but not dangerous or Crimminaly minded. I realize you can get Punished for breaking the law and if shown leniency I will have the up most respect for the law for being able to see I do have something to offer. I can still be successful if giving the change to.

9) What is a Just Punishment for your offense and why?
—I think by me sitting in this county was a big Punishment. Because I still had 5 months left on my sentence and could have Just got a Violation and sent back to Prison. I don't feel that I should be sentenced to any more time, yes I made a really big mistake and realize the seriousness of my decision, Plus I don't want to spend the best years of my life behind bars.

10) Will giving you leniency cause other people not to break the law as you did?
—yes, because all my friends, family, and acquaintence see how serious the law is about the rules and the Consequences it can impose on you if given the Opportunity.

11) Why will giving you leniency protect the Public from further crimes by you?
—The Sooner I can get out the sooner I can get my life together so that the Public can be shown that they need no protection when it comes to me. I also feel that I can live and act civiliz like your average citizen.

12) Do you need educational or vocational training? How would leniency Provide you educetional or vocational traing?
—yes, I still need to get my G.E.D. and will work on that regardless of what happens or where I'll be incarcerated or in the streets. Because that's something I'm going to accomplish for myself. see lenieacy would help to Provide the option to finish my education, because I would be doing it in the right Place to help me be successful.

13) What, if anything, would you say to your family?
—That Im Sorry for taking even my family for granted and putting myself in this situation again and not finishing it the first go around. I'd tell them that I will make up for this time I have been away from them and let them know that I'd spend the rest of my life behind bars if it would take away the Pain of ever having

to go through this again with me. Plus I promise this will be the last time we have to be apart from each other anymore.

14) *Why should the Judge give you a BREAK?*
   —Because I really didn't have the chance to try and make it in the real world. I was only out for two weeks and came back to jail with a new Escape case. I feel like a loser to the one's who had faith in me and supported me while incarcerated the last time. Their willing to help in anyway they can for me to stop using drugs. Plus I'm willing to Participate in any Program to deal with my substance abuse Problem. I also feel like sending me back to Prison doesn't really help. yes, I know theirs Consequences that I've got to face for my mistake I made and Im ready to get it over with. So I can get back out to my family and love one's who need me out their. I have two little brother's who looks up at me as a roll model. I would like to try and help them before it's to late. Because I wouldn't wish this type of Punishment on anybody, and if I can help a person from going threw this situation I will. See I look at this as a blessing for me and a second chance to be successful the right way. Because I've only let my mother and family down once again and this is hard on them as it is for me.

15) *I do realize that their going threw this with me. That's another stress I'm putting on my mother for my mess up. It's really a trip because my mother drove me to Prison on Oct. 4, 2004 to turn myself in. Plus she also came and got me from Prison on Dec. 24, 2005 to make sure I made it to the halfway house safe with out an Escape. But I let her down and still haven't been man enough to talk to her and tell her I'm Sorry for the stupid choice I made that day. See, I'm willing to make a chance for the best of me, but most of all my family. I Just Pray and hope that you give me a Break when that time comes. Plus I would like the chance to prove to the law and everyone else I have learn from my mistake, and I do want to be someone in life not just an inmate to the system. I feel by me only being 20 years old I still have a chance to learn and grow. So no matter what happen's one of my goals are to be successful with in the next 10 years. yes, I can only live and learn from my mistake and I know for a fact not to make this one again. So if you can Mrs. Vicki Miles-LaGrange, would you give me a Break, and another chance to work toward being successful in the world. Thanks.*[41]

VI. Therapeutic Jurisprudence Implications

The Allocution Statement technique brims with therapeutic jurisprudence potential for maximizing an offender's "readiness" for rehabilitation.[42] It educates the defendant regarding the sentencing factors,[43] wholeheartedly solicits the defendant's voice, and induces an optimistic and forward-looking orientation by focusing on the defendant's strengths, goals, and educational, vocational, and treatment needs. Counsel can reinforce and validate the defendant's voice by submitting a sentencing memorandum that, in part, quotes or summarizes the defendant's views, and a sensitive sentencing judge can do the same in a statement of reasons[44] accompanying the judgment and commitment order.

---

41. Lacy Memo, *supra* note 34, at 18–23.
42. *See* discussion *supra* Part I.
43. §3553(a).
44. *Id.* §3553(c).

Counsel will have the delicate task of advocating for the client and, in private conversations, explaining to the client counsel's concerns. For example, in a hypothetical case (not related factually to Mr. X's case) counsel might say: "You're asking for leniency in your allocution statement, and, as you can see, in my sentencing memorandum, I'm pushing for probation. We're doing our best, and I hope we get it. But remember, it's kind of iffy. As I mentioned to you before, what I'm most worried about is how the judge will feel about whether giving you leniency will cause other people to break the law. You passed some counterfeit money, and, although it wasn't much, the courts have treated that very seriously, especially in a tourist town like this one.[45] In counterfeit money cases, the courts emphasize the importance of incarceration for the purpose of 'general deterrence'—to keep others from breaking the law."

Such a conversation sets the stage for a later one that needs to be had if incarceration is indeed ordered. "Yeah, as I feared, the judge gave you some prison time because she wanted to send a message to others that passing counterfeit bills won't be tolerated. As you can see from the statement of reasons, the judge was really impressed by lots of what you said and about your recent behavior, like getting your GED. But because she wanted to send a strong message about the risk of passing counterfeit money, especially in a tourist area, she just didn't buy our plea for probation."[46]

The delicacy of counsel's task is analogous to the task of the appellate lawyer in explaining to a client an appellate affirmance—an explanation which can also impact an offender's "readiness" for rehabilitation:

> The appellate lawyer's task is a highly sensitive one. On the one hand, it is important for counsel to convey the message of voice and validation. On the other hand, it is crucial that counsel not simply serve as an apologist for an appellate affirmance; that appellant know that counsel is truly on the appellant's side, giving the case the best possible shot.[47]

Further, the following advice, again originally addressed to matters in the appellate arena, seems fully applicable to attorneys and courts at the sentencing stage:

> Unless counsel truly believes the [sentencing] court was muddled, inattentive, or outright stupid, it would seem to be without much purpose so to characterize the ruling. Such a characterization suggests that the client was not accorded "voice" and "validation," even with a professional advocate speaking for the client, which would be likely to affect adversely the client's acceptance of the ruling and adjustment to the situation. In the great majority of cases, one would

---

45. *See* R. v. Rachid, 93-4567, [1994] O.J. 4228 QUICKLAW (O.C.J. Feb. 17, 1994).

46. One would hope the combined behavior of the judge (in sentencing and in the accompanying statement of reasons) and the lawyer (in advocating for the defendant but also clearly explaining the various sentencing factors and predicting what might happen) would lead the client to believe the imposed sentence is not unfair in the sense of being seriously disproportionate to the sentence expected or deserved. Of course, excessive sentences are only one source—though a very major one—of defendant perceptions of unfairness. One may also experience unfairness in the manner in which a sentence is communicated, but sensitive sentencing judges should be able to deal well with that concern. More troubling sources of perceived unfairness occur when one is or feels "singled out" for prosecution (selective enforcement) and when the penalty itself seems substantively unfair (stiff mandatory sentences). How courts and lawyers might best deal with these evils is beyond the scope of this essay but well worth future thought.

47. *TJ and the Rehabilitative Role, supra* note 16, at 768.

hope the [statement of reasons for sentence] would reflect the fact that the [defendant]—and thus the attorney as well—was accorded voice and validation.[48]

VII. Conclusion and Future Directions

These, then, are some thoughts on how lawyers and courts can perhaps actually help—and at least not hinder—efforts of rehabilitation. The fact that key points were supported using concrete illustrations from practice—Tony Lacy's Allocution Statement and Judge Fletcher's follow-up letters—leads me to close this commentary with an observation and a proposal.

I've not yet had the pleasure of meeting Tony Lacy in person. He and his important work came to my attention fortuitously, during a conversation with a former student, Joel Parris, who is now an experienced Assistant Federal Defender in Tucson, Arizona with an interest in therapeutic jurisprudence. During this discussion Parris noted, too, that he was also preparing a document to give to his clients on "Why I Deserve Probation."

Judge Fletcher's work came to my attention when he presented, in June 2006, at the Third International Conference on Therapeutic Jurisprudence, held in Perth, Western Australia.[49] On that same panel, Western Australia Judge, Julie Wager, who previously served on the Perth Drug Court, also caught my attention when she spoke of some of her practices. For instance, when a number of family members attend a drug court hearing—particularly prevalent in cases involving aboriginal defendants—she adjusts the seating arrangements so as to maximize hearing and comprehension for all concerned. Furthermore, she insures that the entire court staff is educated in matters such as HIV and Hepatitis C virus transmission. This is done largely to reduce misunderstandings and to improve the interpersonal courtroom atmosphere. Now, staff are less likely than before to distance themselves from drug court clients because of erroneous fears of the risk of virus transmission.

My final point is that a great deal of the most important therapeutic jurisprudence work is now occurring in practice and is "disseminated" to the broader community only sporadically and unsystematically—almost accidentally. In my view, a crucial future direction for therapeutic jurisprudence scholarship, teaching, and practice is to collect this material, share it, comment on it, modify it, use it, and disseminate it further.[50] This is, in any case, a new project of the International Network on Therapeutic Jurisprudence (INTJ),[51] working in conjunction with Ottawa attorney Michael Crystal and the interdisciplinary team-oriented Crystal Criminal Law Office.[52] The Crystal Law Office is a criminal defense firm specifically dedicated to therapeutic jurisprudence, and it hopes, through its website and otherwise, to work with the INTJ and to serve as a

---

48. *TJ and the Rehabilitative Role*, *supra* note 16, at 768.

49. Australian Inst. of Judicial Admin., Inc., Transforming Legal Processes in Court and Beyond (2006), *available at* http://www.aija.org.au/TJ/TJBrochure.pdf (brochure from the Conference).

50. On the judicial front, this practice has been started by social worker Dr. Carrie Petrucci, who has gathered valuable information internationally (US, Canada, Australia, UK, New Zealand) on practices that judges actually use when they engage in a therapeutic jurisprudence approach. *See* Goldberg, *supra* note 21, at 18, 53 n.51.

51. The INTJ website is a resource with an extensive bibliography, announcements of upcoming activities, a listserv, a mailing list, and relevant links. INTJ, *supra* note 13.

52. The website for the Crystal Criminal Law Office notes the problem-solving and interdisciplinary team approach taken by the firm. Crystal Criminal Law Office, http://www.accidentaljurist.com (last visited Sept. 27, 2006).

major resource for this international endeavor.[53] For this project to really work, we of course will need many creative participants. If you are interested in playing a part in collecting, commenting, or critiquing, please contact the author by email.[54]

v. Joel Parris,[*] Reinforcing Reform Efforts through Probation Progress Reports

(From October 2006 Guest Column at
www.therapeuticjurisprudence.org)

Many of my clients have problems with drug or alcohol abuse. Many relapse and face revocation of probation or supervised release. (All offenders sentenced to prison in US federal courts receive a period of supervised release to follow incarceration; it is functionally identical to probation.) Others end up re-offending for reasons related to their addiction. In fact, most of my clients face revocation of supervised release before the period of their supervision ends.

I have become frustrated recently with revocations based on non-criminal violations of probation conditions. This is often failure to comply with reporting or drug counseling conditions. For example, a recent client was re-incarcerated for failure to attend three counseling sessions and failure to show up for three UA tests. (Urine analysis tests are scheduled randomly by having client call a phone number each week; the answering machine announces a color name, and if the color is the one assigned to the defendant, she must report and submit a urine sample within 48 hours.) This client had been attending counseling sessions twice weekly, and had submitted clean urine tests at least twice monthly, for over a year. She has no vehicle and lives in a rural area. The judge responded to my argument that the client had made good effort and substantially complied for a long time by telling me I was minimizing the non-compliant behavior. Back to prison.

Quite often, in revocation proceedings, I learn for the first time that the Probation Officer has submitted prior reports to the judge regarding the client.s lack of compliance with probation conditions. These reports, titled "Probation Progress Report" or "Violation Report," always provide negative information to the court about the client.s unsatisfactory performance, and they are evidence used against the client in subsequent revocation proceedings if violations continue. In reading TJ literature about the importance of someone supporting or "believing in" the offender's ability to reform, I decided to use "Probation Progress Reports" for my own purposes:

1. By checking in with a client who has been released under supervision, I demonstrate my personal support and belief that the client can succeed;

2. By inquiring about the client's progress I give the client a friend they may need, and hopefully provide additional motivation to perform well;

---

53. The law firm's website already contains a number of relevant essays, written by Michael Crystal or his associate, Dr. Karine Langley, a counselor and drug treatment specialist, on their cases (e.g., *The Reena Virk Case, the Felon as Phoenix and the Transforming Power of Forgiveness*; *The Best Case I Never Had: Lessons in Solicitor-Client Communications*; *Catching Criminals One Hug at a Time: The Case of Curtis Dagenais*; *The Case of Robert Piamonte: A Victory for Therapeutic Jurisprudence*; *The Therapeutic Sentence: Chicken Soup for an Ailing Criminal Court*). There are now plans to create a webpage where relevant documents (their own and others, such as the ones noted in this commentary) can be linked to or archived.

54. Author's e-mail address is: davidBwexler@yahoo.com.

[*] Assistant Federal Public Defender, Tucson, Arizona.

3. By filing a positive progress report, I add positive information to the record which can help counter a subsequent petition to revoke probation based on non-criminal violations such as the reporting failure described above.

Clients have responded happily to this defense attorney's post-case inquiries about their welfare. Prosecutors and one judge have expressed genuine confusion as to why a defense attorney would want to supplement the record with positive information when no litigation is pending. Most importantly, I believe this idea may prevent an ex-client from being my future client, and that's good for everyone. I include a sample of a "Probation Progress Report" below:

JON M. SANDS
Federal Public Defender
JOEL C. PARRIS, A.F.P.D.
State Bar No. 014587
email: Joel_Parris@fd.org
407 W. Congress, Suite 501
Tucson, AZ 85701-1355
Telephone: (520)879-7500
Attorneys for Defendant

IN THE UNITED STATES DISTRICT COURT

FOR THE DISTRICT OF ARIZONA

UNITED STATES OF AMERICA,	)	
	)	CR05-XXXXX-TUC-XXX
Plaintiff,	)	
	)	
vs.	)	PROBATION PROGRESS REPORT
	)	
Jane XYZ,	)	
	)	
Defendant.	)	
	)	
	)	

Counsel for Defendant XYZ, submits the following report of her successful progress during the probationary period.

XYZ was arrested on July 10, 2005. She was released to a treatment center on August 3, 2005. A sentence of probation for one year was imposed on December 13, 2005. Ms. XYZ remained in the treatment center until December 17, 2005, and then moved into a residential community of recovering substance abusers.

Counsel recently met with Ms. XYZ to discuss her progress in recovering from substance abuse and spoke to her Probation Officer about compliance with probation conditions. United States Probation Officer _____ has advised counsel that Ms. XYZ is in complete compliance with her conditions of probation and has done "very well" overall. Ms. XYZ has been working in a restaurant and pursuing her education at _____ Beauty College. The restaurant has promoted Ms. XYZ to an acting assistant manager position. Ms. XYZ has declined manager training, but has agreed to assist her employer by filling the position until the business can find another suitable person for that job.

On August 2, 2006, Ms. XYZ graduated from _____ Beauty College. She has successfully completed the required three hundred (300) hours of classes, plus and additional thirteen hundred (1300!) hours of "floor training" (i.e., cutting hair, coloring and tinting, and other numerous other cosmetic procedures). Ms. XYZ subsequently passed her Arizona state written and practical examinations and has been granted a license of cosmetology by the State of Arizona.

Ms. XYZ has continues personal counseling, substance abuse counseling, and specific counseling to help her deal with issues involving her minor child who suffers lingering emotional difficulties from an unrelated prior trauma. In August, 2006, Ms. XYZ was reunited with her daughter, and the they now reside together. Counsel spoke with a case manager and therapist, who both expressed admiration for Ms. XYZ's positive attitude and hard work.

Ms. XYZ has complied with probation conditions, remained consistently employed, completed her educational goals, and now looks forward to a new career. She is healthy and proud to declare that she is "one year and two months clean." Counsel is proud of Ms. XYZ; her determination to recover from extraordinary personal hardships and substance abuse issues have overcome extreme odds and her future looks bright for the first time in many years. Counsel thanks AUSA _____ for permitting resolution of the case in a manner that supported successful rehabilitative efforts. Counsel does not move for early termination of probation, but submits the foregoing report as appropriate supplemental information to complete the official record of this matter.

RESPECTFULLY SUBMITTED: September 21, 2006.
JON M. SANDS
Federal Public Defender
s/ JOEL C. PARRIS
Assistant Federal Public Defender

copy to:
_____, AUSA
_____, USPO
_____ Ms. XYZ

vi. Michael Crystal,[*] The Therapeutic Sentence: Chicken Soup for an Ailing Criminal Court

(Reprinted with permission from the website of the Crystal Criminal Law Office at www.accidentaljurist.com)

Like many public defenders, I laboured in search of ways to mitigate my client's sentence and, like many public defenders, I quickly learned that the resources needed for such a task were severely limited, if existent at all. When I switched to private practice, my first hire was neither a secretary nor a junior lawyer but rather a former prison chaplain and drug and alcohol counselor.

---

[*] Crystal Criminal Law Office, Ottawa, Ontario, Canada.

This was an idea born out of a recognition that for many of our disenfranchised clients we required a wholistic and therapeutic approach. Together we coaxed, coerced and cajoled a merry band of community leaders and health professionals to join us (largely on a volunteer basis) in developing what we termed a 'therapeutic sentence'. While the concept of therapeutic jurisprudence (TJ) and its application in criminal law has been the subject of recent scholarship precious little has been written about the manner in which TJ manifests itself in the day to day life of the courtroom.

This article proposes to address this deficit by outlining how the principles of TJ are utilized by referencing case studies and to note the response to the remedies afforded by the judiciary. At the heart of the TJ sentence exists the notion that a therapeutic remedy can be crafted and partially served prior to the actual sentencing hearing. The benefit of having the client serve this unofficial sentence is that the proposed remedy is allowed to accumulate inertia thereby generating results which can then be employed at the actual sentencing hearing. In cases where a positive track record is produced by the client, counsel is placed in the enviable position of inviting the court to join him in supporting a workable disposition.

The requisites stages of construction of a TJ sentence are as follows: (1) the assembly of a team of professionals, community workers, etc., who will work with counsel and the client to develop a plan. Such a plan could include but is not limited to a course of community service or a treatment regime; (2) structuring a plan—while this may be no more than compiling a finite series activities that the client will participate in prior to his actual sentencing hearing, counsel must ensure that the proposed plan is infused with all the relevant principles of sentencing; (3) executing the plan, what is essential at this point is that there is enough time for the client to accumulate a "track record" and by doing so showcase his commitment to the plan; and finally, (4) The final stage takes place at the sentencing hearing itself, and is where counsel seeks validation by the Court for the TJ sentence.

By this time counsel has transitioned from his traditional role as advocate into shareholder: counsel is not simply advocating a proposed sentence but an actual sentence of which he himself is the architect. Typically, this approach receives a warm reception from the courts, as members of the judiciary are keenly aware that they are disadvantaged by the lack of state resources and programs which would allow them the opportunity to craft therapeutic sentences. Here lies the greatest argument for counsel to adopt a TJ approach to sentencing: the resources embedded in the TJ sentence crafted by counsel and tailored to the specific therapeutic needs of the client far surpasses any remedy the Court could design and is therefore more likely to receive validation from the court.

vii. Karine Langley,* Affidavit

ONTARIO SUPERIOR COURT OF JUSTICE
(EAST REGION)

BETWEEN:

HER MAJESTY THE QUEEN

-and-

JOHN XYZ

DEFENDANT'S SENTENCING BRIEF

AFFIDAVIT OF KARINE LANGLEY

I, Karine Langley of the City of Ottawa in the Province of Ontario, **MAKE OATH AND SAY AS FOLLOWS:**

1. I am a legal assistant with Crystal Criminal Law Office and as such have knowledge of the matters herein deposed to.

2. On September 25th 2003, Justice Chadwick of the Ontario Superior Court of Justice found John XYZ guilty of the following offences arising out of charges from February 3rd 2001:

   a. Assault with a weapon, namely bear repellent contrary to section 267(a) of the Criminal Code of Canada.

   b. Possession of a weapon for a purpose dangerous to the public peace, namely bear repellent.

   c. Possession of a weapon for a purpose dangerous to the public peace, namely a flare gun.

   d. Failure to stop at the scene of an accident.

   e. Possession of incendiary materials for the purpose of committing an offence.

   f. Break and enter.

   g. Arson.

3. I understand that if John XYZ were to be sentenced to serve a conditional sentence in the community that he would be living with his mother Mrs. Sophie XYZ in Ingleside Ontario.

4. I have prepared a letter which I have asked Mrs. XYZ to circulate to her neighbours who have known John XYZ for many years. Attached to this my Affidavit as Exhibit "A" is a true copy of the form letter which I prepared.

5. During the first week of November 2003, Mrs. XYZ delivered the signed letters to our office on 309 Cooper street in Ottawa. Attached to this my Affidavit as Exhibit "B" is a true copy of the letters which Mrs. XYZ circulated. (tabs 18–34 of the defendant's sentencing brief)

6. Those who signed the letters have indicated their willingness to report John XYZ should he be in violation of his conditions, if they are given a copy of the conditions of his sentence.

---

* Karine Langley, Ph.D., is Coordinator of Therapeutic Projects at the Crystal Criminal Law Office in Ottawa, Ontario, Canada.

7. I swear this Affidavit in support of the defendant's sentencing brief and for no other improper purpose.

SWORN before me at the City)
Of Ottawa, in the East Region,)
This 10th day of November, 2003)

_____

KARINE LANGLEY

A. Commissioner, etc.

Exhibit A

TO WHOM IT MAY CONCERN

I ……………………………………… of…………………………………………

Have known JOHN XYZ for …………………………………………………

In the capacity of ………………………………… It is my understanding that on September 25th 2003, Mr. XYZ was found guilty on the following charges arising out of an incident that took place on February 3rd 2001:

1. Assault with a weapon, namely bear repellent contrary to section 267(a) of the Criminal Code of Canada.

2. Possession of a weapon for a purpose dangerous to the public peace, namely bear repellent.

3. Possession of a weapon for a purpose dangerous to the public peace, namely a flare gun.

4. Failure to stop at the scene of an accident.

5. Possession of incendiary materials for the purpose of committing an offence.

6. Break and enter.

7. Arson.

I understand that Mr. XYZ is awaiting sentencing on these charges. Should Mr. XYZ be released to serve his sentence in the community, I understand that Mr. XYZ would be released to live with his mother Mrs. Sophie XYZ in Ingleside.

I would have no fears for my safety or that of my family, should Mr. XYZ be released to live with his mother.

Further, if I were provided with a copy of his sentencing conditions, I would have no hesitation in reporting Mr. John XYZ to the police if he were in violation of any of the conditions.

SIGNED:

DATE:

WITNESS:

viii. David Boulding,* Fetal Alcohol and the Law

What is fetal alcohol?

Fetal alcohol is a permanent physical disability, largely invisible, caused by the consumption of alcohol during pregnancy. The alcohol acts like a solvent on the baby's de-

---

* David Boulding has been a criminal law and family law trial lawyer in Vancouver, B.C., Canada since 1987.

veloping brain much like paint stripper acts on layers of paint on old furniture. The alcohol dissolves brain cells working much like nail polish remover. It is a physical disability because the body is missing parts called brain cells. Missing brain cells means brain functions are missing or impaired. The child will have lifelong problems because of cognitive impairment, and much difficulty because of the resulting chronic poor fit in society.

Defence counsel immediately understand that no jail sentence, no prescription drug, no cognitive therapy, and even the best of probation orders will restore the brain cells and repair the missing brain functions. However we can do something about the chronic "poor fit". As counsel, we have a duty to our clients to create accommodations so they can have successful lives.

How prevalent is fetal alcohol in our jails?

While new studies are underway, there is only one peer reviewed science paper that exists today. Drs Conry et al found that 24% of young offenders in custody had some diagnosis on the fetal alcohol spectrum disorder. Over a cup of tea the authors will tell you it might be as high as 40%. The Canadian prison authorities, for some years now, have been doing quick and dirty studies, not peer reviewed science. The prison research is coming back at 50 to 80 % of the penitentiary population have some diagnosis of fetal alcohol depending on the institution. The prison authorities are concerned because they see that their expensive training programs are not working and they fear the programs are not pitched at the correct cognitive speed for inmates.

Fetal alcohol is often undetected, or called something else. Court documents are full of the following diagnoses from the DSM-IV:

- Pervasive developmental delay
- Attention deficit disorder
- Reactive attachment disorder
- Autism Spectrum Disorder
- Asperger's syndrome
- Learning disabled
- Developmental receptive language disorder
- Sensory integration disorder
- Conduct disorder
- Seriously emotionally disturbed
- Oppositional defiant disorder
- Bipolar
- Antisocial personality disorder

Many of our clients have professional reports to Court which contain several of these diagnoses in one report. If so consider that there might be missing brain functions. Consider fetal alcohol spectrum disorder. Collect enough information on fetal alcohol and send to your report writer and have the court appointed expert re-do the assessment asking the Court appointed expert to consider fetal alcohol. As counsel, getting the correct diagnosis is the greatest service you can do for your client. You would never leave your F-250 Ford truck at your mechanic without telling him what is wrong. Even your dentist does x-rays before he drills. Yet we send people to jail without accurately diagnosing their brains, **and** we expect them to learn complex social lessons from the loss of liberty.

What new thinking is required?

Lawyers need to change how they think about clients who may have brain damage and the research suggests it is a huge slice of our customers (Conry 24%).

Dr. Sterling Clarren has some good news. He advocates using the "external brain concept". This means finding people to stand in and help do the work for those missing brain functions. As a concept the "external brain" is our "duty of care". The law requires accommodation and by using the external brain, mostly in the context of probation orders, we can create successful accommodations for our clients.

Dr. Anne Streissguth of University of Washington (Seattle) and Diane Malbin from FASCETS in Oregon have written helpful books on how to create successful interventions. Malbin suggests a four step process that will guide counsel to re-think our strategies. She says:

1. match the brain to the task
2. adjust your expectations stretching your definition of success
3. change their environment
4. examine your assumptions

She further says if we try to see the brain in its dysfunction, then the behaviours we focus on become cues to try something different, rather than trying harder and harder using the methods that have not worked in the past. Instead of using bad behaviour as a rationale for intervention, use the behaviour as a glimpse at a brain that is not working like yours does. Lawyers can be held to a higher standard of behaviour because our brains are fully functional. Our clients who are missing brain functions are not excused from criminal behaviour because of their disability. Fetal Alcohol is not an acceptable excuse for crime—it's an explanation.

The research divides the behaviours of our fetal alcohol clients into two types: primary behaviours resulting from brain cells missing due to exposure to alcohol in the womb which caused the brain function to be missing or impaired (no fix or repair is possible). Secondary behaviours resulting from a chronic poor fit in society are preventable and resolvable with appropriate interventions and lifelong support. Here defence counsel can create positive outcomes—but only if they change their thinking about their clients. They must consider brain dysfunction and stop focusing on the negative behaviour.

Primary behaviour includes, but is not limited to:

- Memory problems … to retrieve memories appropriate to the situation
- Slow cognitive/auditory processing pace, much slower than yours
- Cognitive gaps … disconnects from hearing to action
- Difficulty making connections, generalizing
- Difficulty weighing, evaluating, making situation appropriate decisions
- Perseveration
- Rigid thinking
- Difficulty in adapting to social cues
- Unable to hold multiple thoughts
- Unable to weigh alternative views or opinions
- Need more time to do tasks

- Literal concrete thinkers and speakers.... do not understand sarcasm, puns, or complex language and legalisms used by lawyers
- Difficulty abstracting, predicting, and anticipating
- Stuck in the "now'
- Cannot take information from Tuesday and use it appropriately on Friday
- Halting speech, slow to develop speech
- Speaking above their learning ... quantity more than appropriate depth, often off topic
- Inexplicable anger, irritability, tantrums
- Suggestibility (peer driven)
- Impulsivity
- Failing to demonstrate remorse
- Unable to understand value, time worth and abstract notions
- Failing to understand consequences
- Distractibility
- Listening but not hearing
- Easily overwhelmed unable to prioritize stimuli
- Easily led into criminal behaviour, a follower, not an initiator
- Sensory input issues under sensitive to temperature, oversensitive to noise, lights
- Developmental dysmaturity (not immature rather functioning at a lower age: 22 years old acts like a 11 year old)

Secondary behaviours include, but are not limited to:
- Fatigue
- Frustration
- Anxiety, fearful
- Feelings of failure
- Depression
- Shame, grandiosity
- Disruptive tantrums, resistant
- May shut down, sullen, non communicative
- Isolated, few friends, picked on
- Sexual acting out
- Suicide
- A variety of mental health issues springing from chronic poor fit

Defence counsel will normally advise the Court about the primary behaviour (because that's what the police report describes) and make submissions on a fix. This has historically has not created positive outcomes for our clients—they keep re-offending. Everyone knows our repeat customers equals future guaranteed work for all in the criminal justice system. Malbin suggests counsel design interventions by acknowledging and then relying on both primary and secondary behaviours. Unless counsel explicitly confronts the secondary behaviours such as shame, depression and anxiety, any intervention focused solely on the primary behaviours will fail.

Success by any measure will depend on first focusing on the secondary behaviour because we can do something there and then design a structure that can accommodate the primary behaviour. The primary behaviours result from the missing brain cells and this is NOT going to change.

The secondary behaviours, because they result from a chronic poor fit in society can be ameliorated if we choose to deal with these difficult topics such as shame and failure. The shame and failure comes from a lifetime of rejection, mistakes and failing to make the grade. So if we adjust our definition of success, match the brain to the task and change the environment of the client, we necessarily will be forced to examine our assumptions.

All too often judges, lawyers, police and probation officers expect those clients who do not have fully functional brains to behave like judges and lawyers. Rarely do judges and lawyers get arrested. There are two simple reasons. Judges and lawyers have a little voice in the back of their head that says 'don't do this—the consequences, if you do will be drastic'. Judges and lawyers also have friends who tell them 'don't do this—the consequences will be drastic if you do'. Our clients who have fetal alcohol do not have this little voice because of the brain damage nor do they have friends who will help them out of possible trouble, because their primary behaviours push away anyone who is likely to become a good friend.

Diane Malbin (2006, p. 106) describes and then charts the new thinking. Her book is a must for every defence counsel and pages of the book can be copied and submitted to the courts as an excellent source for supporting counsel's submissions.

Identification

No one expects Defence Counsel to diagnose fetal alcohol. This disorder properly diagnosed requires a multi disciplinary team including:

- Pediatrician
- Neuro-psychologist
- Speech pathologist
- Occupational therapist
- Physical therapist
- General practitioner
- Psychologist, and other specialists

However doctors Conry, Fast and Loock have developed a quick check mnemonic for police officers. It is called ALARM.

- A   Adaptive behaviours—those are the daily life skills we use in problem solving
- L   Learning
- A   Attention
- R   Reasoning
- M   Memory

Over time by asking your clients questions in these discrete areas, counsel will get a very good picture of what brain function is missing. The key is memory. As Malbin says, these are ten second kids in a one second world. Memory is a sophisticated cognitive skill.

It involves retrieval of memories, prioritizing of memories and being able to abstract, generalize and predict all of which are compromised by prenatal exposure to alcohol. Malbin also advises, think younger.... much younger. Your client may be chronologically twenty-six but twelve cognitively. Each one of the ALARM type of questions may produce some red flags. If you see difficulties in say, reasoning or memory, ask more questions. You ask more questions so you can give more information to the expert who is writing your court report who knows nothing about fetal alcohol. This technique has been taught to the Royal Canadian Mounted Police since 2003. Police officers uniformly tell us the mnemonic is an excellent tool and assists them in dealing with these clients.

Guilty or Not Guilty?

Competent Defence Counsel recognize their daily dilemma.

Do they work hard legally using all their persuasive skills, and hope to secure an acquittal, or do they plead guilty and with the assistance of the court, probation and the prosecutor and various community elements design an external brain?

Defence Counsel know that between 80 and 90 percent of accused plead or are found guilty. I say for Fetal Alcohol clients the number is more like 99%. We also know that this population already has several convictions on their record, so we know that none of the past interventions have worked. So now the challenge is to think differently rather than trying harder with your considerable legal skills. By using Dr Clarren's concept of the external brain and Malbin's suggestions, we are thinking differently rather than trying harder and our interventions, because they are designed with primary and secondary behaviours in mind, can create positive outcomes.

Different outcomes require different thinking. This means that the language of the probation order, the content of the probation order, and the people involved in the external brain of the client must learn and know about Fetal Alcohol and must understand Malbin's suggestions. This means that defence counsel must educate prosecutors, judges, probation and the community because all elements of the legal system, the public included, must be part of the solution. It is a great mistake to think one agency or one person can create a positive outcome for a person who has been prenatally exposed to alcohol. Because there are brain cells missing and brain functions are missing or impaired, we need to think like the math teacher who gives the blind student a Braille text book or the physical education teacher who gives the legless student a wheelchair. This physical disability is a lifelong burden for society. Our clients will not have new brain cells the day their probation order expires.

1. Probation orders must be made to fit on the back of the probation officer's business card—keep it simple using as few words as possible in concrete language. For example: 'you must be home by 7pm every night'.
2. Use the language of the home. This means using language your client understands. Avoid any legalisms.
3. List positive alternatives. Instead of saying 'do not ... do not.... do not', include positive possibilities—for example 'you cannot go to the 7-11: you can go to the Quick Stop'
4. Ask family and community members for help: This requires lawyers to understand the difference between non compliance and non comprehension. Often our clients mask not comprehending with bluster, grandiosity and sullen behaviour because they don't understand what is happening. We talk too fast, we use jargon, we have all kinds of assumptions that do not fit a brain that is miss-

ing parts. Family and community members are part of Dr Clarren's 'external brain'. An external brain is people standing in for missing brain cells. They can help support clients:

i. make appointments

ii. stay away from persons and places of trouble

iii. build in the required daily reminders

iv. help with banking and shopping

v. help with job interviews and job attendance

vi. help in social situations so that people do not take advantage of them

It is crucial that as many members as possible of the community know of the brain injury, know the probation order and understand how to make appropriate interventions. It is probably a good idea in most communities that police, social services and other helping agencies involved with your client have a picture of him or her and on the back a description of the disability, a list of contacts and that your client has a brain based birth defect and **does not give up any legal rights** and needs to contact his or her lawyer—now. In some jurisdictions agencies and parents have made cards for their clients with legal wording on the back to be given to every police officer they encounter. The cards say for example: 'Bob has a brain disability. Please contact _____. Please be advised that Bob is not giving up any legal rights no matter what he says, because he does not understand this situation'. As a defence lawyer, I can advise that my clients who use this card have had very positive results.

Selected references and resources:

1. Diane Malbin—Trying Differently Rather Than Harder, second edition, 2002, FASCETS, Oregon.

2. Diane Malbin—Fetal Alcohol Spectrum Disorders: a collection of information for parents and professionals. Second edition, 2006, FASCETS, Oregon.

3. www.asantecentre.org—website of Dr. K. Asante, Canadian pediatrician, assessment expert.

4. google 'fadu' takes you to the website of Dr Ann Streissguth University of Washington Fetal Drug and Alcohol Unit (Seattle), large website with many pages for lawyers.

5. www.fasdconnections.ca—website of Jan Lutke, Canadian expert, foster parent par excellence!

6. www.fasstar.com—website of Teresa Kellerman foster parent, FASD trainer for parentr.

7. www.davidboulding.com—website of a lawyer writing and training legal professionals see: Lawyer's Brief.

8. Diane Malbin—FASD and The Role Of Family Court Judges In Improving Outcomes For Children And Families—Juvenile And Family Court Journal Spring 2004.

9. The Northwest Partnership—Dr Sterling Clarren's research group of world's leading thinkers on Fetal Alcohol (based in Vancouver, B.C. paid for by provinces of British Columbia, Alberta, Saskatchewan, and Manitoba).

10. google: "Health Canada fetal alcohol".

11. Dr. Julianne Conry et al: Identifying Fetal Alcohol Syndrome Among Youth in the Criminal Justice System. Developmental and Behavioural Pediatrics: vol20, no.5, October 1999. (The only peer reviewed science on prevalence in our jails.)

12. Dr. Kathy Sulik. University of North Carolina. Embryologist who has been feeding pregnant mice drops of alcohol for 25 years and has the photographic proof on line of the damage alcohol as a solvent has on fetal development. She has an online tutorial.

ix. John V. McShane,* Jailhouse Interventions, Treatment Bonds, and the So-Called "Recovery Defense"

I have passionately and zealously practiced law in Texas for forty years. My practice includes criminal defense, family law, and representing professionals in license discipline matters. In my criminal defense practice, I limit my activities to therapeutic jurisprudence. In this regard, I practice criminal defense law as a healer and peacemaker.

I have had great success which is much more the grace of God and lucky timing than any personal merit on my part. My rehabilitative approach to the practice of criminal defense law has been chronicled in the *Dallas Morning News*, *The Wall Street Journal*, and *USA Today*. It has also been featured in two articles in the *American Bar Association Journal*. I am consistently selected for "best lists" including "Best Lawyers in Dallas" (resulting from a yearly poll conducted by *D Magazine*), named as a "Texas Super Lawyer" (resulting from a yearly poll conducted by *Texas Monthly Magazine*), and named in the prestigious publication "Best Lawyers in America". I've also served as chairman of the Grievance Committee of the State Bar of Texas and have been a member of numerous other committees on ethics and professionalism including the Grievance Oversight Committee of the Supreme Court of Texas. If all of the recitations appear to be self-aggrandizing, they unashamedly are. I am very proud of my career and never thought I would need to defend my law practice at this stage of my life. Unfortunately, it is necessary to do so.

Professor Mae Quinn has suggested that I somehow compromise the quality of advocacy and have questionable ethics by the way I limit my criminal defense practice to therapeutic jurisprudence and limit the cases I take. She states (in Part II of this volume):

> "What is more, the restrictions McShane places on his services, even for paying clients, present somewhat of an ethical quagmire. For instance, although the American Bar Association's Model Rules of Professional Conduct permit limits on representation, such limitations must be reasonable. And such limitations do not exempt a lawyer from providing competent representation. Questions of reasonableness and competence may arise, however, when a lawyer advises a client to plead guilty without first investigating the matter fully, regardless of the client's version of events, and without determining the strength of the prosecution's evidence and other possible weaknesses in the case."

Never in my career have I advised "a client to plead guilty without first investigating the matter fully, regardless of the client's version of events, and without determining the strength of the prosecution's evidence and other possible weaknesses in the case". In fact, I always make sure the case is investigated fully and all viable factual and legal defenses are explored. For example, if the client's case raises a search and seizure question, I bring in a lawyer who is highly sophisticated in the law of search and seizure. If necessary, this lawyer files a motion to suppress the evidence, files a supporting brief with the motion, and argues the motion to the Court. The fact that I am not interested in performing these services for my clients does not mean that they don't get done. They *always* do! To suggest otherwise is idiotic.

---

* John McShane is a trial lawyer with the firm McShane & Davis, L.L.P. in Dallas, Texas.

Professor Quinn also suggests there may be something ethically questionable about limiting my criminal defense practice to therapeutic jurisprudence. As stated above, I have extensive background in lawyer ethics and have served the State Bar of Texas in many capacities in the lawyer disciplinary system. I am very knowledgeable about the disciplinary rules which govern my profession and am often retained as an expert witness for trials and hearings in which a lawyer's conduct is being scrutinized. Under Disciplinary Rule 1.02(b) of the *Texas Rules of Disciplinary Conduct*, "a lawyer may limit the scope of the representation if the limitation is reasonable under the circumstances and the client gives informed consent." Many lawyers are now limiting the scope of their services. For example, many divorce lawyers are limiting the cases they take to those in which the collaborative family law model is used. If the client does not wish to use the collaborative law model, they simply cannot hire these lawyers. They have to go elsewhere. By the same token, clients who are not interested in my therapeutic jurisprudence services are free to go elsewhere. Of course, those clients who retain me always receive the full spectrum of criminal defense services that they should have based on their circumstances. It never occurred to me that anyone would misunderstand the way I work and imply that there is less than total zealous, effective, and ethical advocacy. The misunderstanding leads me to believe that I should explain my method.

My method will be best understood by a case history from one of my files. To use a Perry Mason-esque introduction, I call this the case of the "agitated arsonist." The defendant was acutely addicted to daily ingestion of large quantities of cocaine and also suffered acute clinical depression. He suffered from drug-induced delusions. One night he started hearing voices in his mother's house and burned it to the ground. At the Dallas County Jail, he perceived the deputies as forces of evil and tried to fight them. As is always the case in such circumstances, he lost the fight when the deputies gleefully pounced on him and pummeled him into submission. Now battered, bruised, and continuing to hallucinate, he was placed in a cell. He was later taken before a night magistrate who set his bond at $10,000.00 because he had no prior criminal record. This bond was later overturned by the presiding judge who found "extreme dangerousness" based on the arson and the fight with the deputies. The presiding judge ordered the defendant held without bond. The defendant's family hired a well-known Dallas criminal defense attorney who promptly filed a flurry of motions including a Motion for an Examining Trial (preliminary discovery hearing) and a Motion for Bond which he set for a hearing. The defendant's family heard of my reputation as a therapeutic jurisprudence defense attorney and added me to the defense team. My job was to intervene with the defendant, convince him to go to treatment, and then persuade the judge at the bond hearing to release him on a conditional bond so he could attend treatment. The defendant had no resources of his own and any bond would have to be paid for by his family. They had resolved only to pay for his bond if it was a "going to treatment" bond as opposed to a "getting back on the street" bond.[1]

---

1. As I note in the appended Brief in Support of Bond and Treatment, I actively discourage family members from posting bond that would allow the defendant's release from jail and return to home and the street. This is perhaps the luxury of having a private practice with my services being limited to therapeutic goals. When the family approaches me to become a lawyer for the accused, I can decide if I will do so and under what conditions. Of course, I always make sure the defendant has a traditional defense lawyer in place who can seek all appropriate avenues of jail release separate and apart from my therapeutic efforts. When I visit a jailed defendant such as the defendant in this case, I tell him the family has hired me and I will vigorously represent him in a therapeutic context, but only on the condition that "street bail" is off the table. He or she is free to reject my offer and be represented only by his other defense counsel. I acknowledge that, in an indigent defense practice, I

It was clear that the defense team had a rough road ahead because the judge is a former prosecutor and right wing Republican who is known to have no sympathy with drug addicts and who also has an inordinate fear of releasing someone on bond who may then commit another crime thus resulting in bad publicity and political consequences. The prosecutor made it clear that he would vigorously oppose bond based on the demonstrated dangerousness of the defendant.

In the days leading up to the bond hearing, I conducted a series of conferences with the defendant at the Dallas County Jail. At the first interview he was clearly in distressed circumstances. He had suffered a drug withdrawal seizure and had been placed in the jail infirmary. He was toxic and delusional. Although he seemed to have some comprehension of what I was saying, he was clearly unable to process most of it. I waited three days and returned for another interview. The defendant did not even remember me being there three days before. However, his condition was much improved and he was able to process information during this visit. Over the course of my visits, I gradually bonded with the defendant, gained his confidence, used some nonjudgmental therapeutic and informational interviewing techniques to learn about the agonies he had suffered from his drug addiction and depression. I eventually suggested that there was another way to live and it could be possible for him if he would agree to go to treatment if I could get him out of jail on bond. After some feeble attempts at negotiating with me, the defendant agreed to my conditions. We would attempt to secure a conditional bond which allowed him to go to the best available treatment center. It was understood that his family would only post this bond and stay committed to it if he remained in the treatment center. Leaving the treatment center against medical advice or being expelled from the treatment center would result in revocation of the bond and re-arrest. The defendant accepted these conditions.

I also retained a psychiatrist to go to the jail and do a psychiatric evaluation of the defendant. It is important to pick a highly credible expert in this type of situation. The psychiatrist I engaged is one of the few psychiatrists in Dallas who is board-certified in both psychiatry and addiction medicine. He is well-known by the judges in Dallas County because he has frequently been court-appointed to do psychiatric and competency evaluations. I instructed the psychiatrist to do the following:

1. Take a complete history of the defendant;
2. Evaluate the defendant for addiction and mental illness;
3. Make a diagnosis of the defendant based on the DSM-IV;
4. Recommend the most viable treatment facility for the defendant's condition;
5. Be prepared to comment on the dangerousness of the defendant; and
6. Write a report that could be admitted into evidence which contained all of his findings.

The doctor performed his evaluation and indicated that the defendant suffered from a duel diagnosis, to-wit: acute cocaine addiction and clinical depression. The doctor recommended that the client be treated at COPAC in Jackson, Mississippi which he believed to be the most efficacious treatment for the combination of disorders afflicting the defendant. Of course this raised another problem. We were fearful that the judge would not let

---

would not always have the luxury of conditioning my representation on the defendant entering a treatment program. However, in my *pro bono* cases, I am sometimes able to negotiate a scholarship bed for my client in a treatment center. Then I can use the approach described in this article.

the defendant out on bond but, if she did, we felt she certainly would not allow him to go out of state for treatment. When I mentioned the doctor's suggestion at a conference in chambers, the judge's reaction was predictable: "Mr. McShane, I just can't do that. What if he burns down another house in Mississippi? I don't want some judge in Mississippi wondering why I let him out on bond!" However, the judge reluctantly agreed to hear all of my evidence but she predicted that my success was highly improbable.

I next filed a brief with the Court in which I outlined my role and the theoretical underpinnings of therapeutic jurisprudence. A copy of such brief is attached as an Appendix. In the brief, I made it clear that the defendant's substantive and procedural legal rights would be protected by my co-counsel who was part of the defense team. I explained my role as therapeutic jurisprudence counsel and gave the judge an overview of the relief that would be sought at the bond hearing. I attached the psychiatrist report to the brief and included as much advocacy as possible for our position.

We then learned that the prosecutor was cleverly going to agree with our request that the defendant receive treatment. However, he was going to argue that the defendant could receive all the treatment he needed at a local state-operated "lock-down" treatment center. We knew the services at this locked facility were very limited and totally inadequate for our client. At a subsequent conference in chambers with the judge, it appeared that she was going to buy the prosecutor's argument. As she said: "Mr. McShane, this solves both of our problems. You get treatment for your client and I get the assurance that he's not going to be out on bond and causing me any problems." When I protested, the judge again assured me that she would listen to all of my evidence but pretty well had her mind made up.

This turn of events required that our growing defense team add two members. First we needed a drug and alcohol addiction professional who could research the efficacy of the state treatment center for people with a dual diagnosis. This professional could present to the judge that the treatment suggested by the prosecutor would be virtually worthless because the acute depression would not be dealt with. Fortunately, this expert was able to do some quick research and determine that the facility suggested by the prosecutor (and almost agreed to by the judge) had received significant criticism and negative evaluations by a commission charged with investigating such facilities. We then included in our brief the criticisms that had been made of this facility — especially the lack of effectiveness for people with a dual diagnosis.

The next person we needed to add to the team was a specialist in appeals because it appeared almost sure that the judge was going to deny bond or deny bond and remand the defendant to the state-operated treatment center which was just another form of incarceration with very ineffective treatment. We also needed to file a supplemental brief which reminded the Court of the law relating to bond and sent a clear message that we would be appealing if bond was denied inappropriately. This supplemental brief is also in the Appendix. Much of this supplemental brief was prepared by our appellate specialist.

The components of this team illustrate the necessity of having multi-disciplinary resources available on quick notice. Also, the addition of the appellate specialist shows that no procedural or substantive rights of the accused were being overlooked as Professor Quinn suggests may happen. The defense team now had an expert in traditional criminal practice, an expert in appellate law, and a seasoned therapeutic jurisprudence practitioner. It would have been unthinkable to deny the defendant any of these components.

On the morning of the bond hearing, the judge called me into chambers and again told me that I was probably wasting my time—that she was "not inclined" to grant bail and further told me that even if she did grant bail, she would not allow the defendant to go out of state for treatment. (Note: this is an intimidation tactic I have encountered with many judges who try to bully you into not even putting on your therapeutic jurisprudence evidence by implying that you are wasting your time and theirs.) I skated dangerously close to contempt by suggesting the judge was not being fair and open-minded. I begged her to listen to my evidence with an open mind. She finally assured me that she would do so.

At the commencement of the bail hearing, I made an impassioned opening statement about the defendant, his family, and his desperate need for treatment. Several members of the defendant's family were present in the courtroom. I talked about how he suffered from two potentially fatal diseases which were the root of his problem. I talked about the excellent treatment program that had been selected by the psychiatrist and the efficacy of that program. I also promised the judge that our evidence would show that the state treatment program was totally inadequate to address the needs of the defendant and that it would be anti-therapeutic to send him there.

The first witness at the sentencing hearing was the psychiatrist. His report was introduced into evidence. He testified that the defendant suffered from acute cocaine addiction and major depression. He testified that, based on his experience with other patients, the COPAC facility in Jackson, Mississippi was the best fit for the defendant. He said that the defendant was cooperative during the evaluation and professed a sincere desire to be healed. He assured the Court that there was nothing in his evaluation or the defendant's history to suggest future dangerousness.

Our second witness was a drug and alcohol counselor who had been the Executive Director of the Dallas Council on Alcoholism and Drug Addiction. She had extensive experience in researching various treatment programs and placing substance abusers in the most appropriate program. She completely debunked the state treatment facility as having received very poor marks in its last evaluation and as having

absolutely no efficacy for the treatment of someone suffering from both drug addiction and depression. She also described the program at COPAC and echoed the opinion of the psychiatrist that it would be the most appropriate placement for the defendant.

Although these witnesses were cross-examined aggressively, the prosecutor was unable to make any significant dent in their testimony. After vigorous closing arguments on both sides, the judge surprised everybody in the courtroom by reversing herself and releasing the defendant on a conditional bond to allow him to go to COPAC in Mississippi. She set $25,000.00 bail bonds on the arson case and the cocaine case and ordered that the defendant go directly from jail to COPAC. It was estimated that the defendant would remain in treatment for four to six months. The judge told me that she wanted detailed monthly reports from me as to his progress. She also sternly admonished the defendant that if he made one misstep while in Mississippi or left treatment for any reason, she would promptly put him in jail.

The story has a happy ending. The defendant did well in treatment. I used the opportunity to send glowing monthly reports to the judge with copies to the prosecutor. Although this prosecutor was extremely angry at the conclusion of the bail hearing (he even refused to shake my extended hand when the hearing was adjourned), he softened progressively as he got the reports from the treatment center which were sent to him and the judge. By the time the defendant returned from treatment, the prosecutor was amenable to negotiating a very lenient plea bargain. Negotiations were conducted by myself and the traditional criminal defense attorney with the prosecutor. Ultimately, the prosecutor agreed to dismiss the arson charge and allow the defendant to plead to a deferred adjudication to possession of cocaine which would result in him having no record if he lived out his period of probation. The defendant accepted this plea bargain and the case was successfully concluded along these lines. As of this writing, the defendant has been clean and sober for over three years, has been reunited with the estranged members of his family, holds a good job, and is a model citizen. I call this approach the so-called "Recovery Defense." I respectfully submit that this outcome would have been unlikely in the traditional defense model—a therapeutic jurisprudence intervention was required. However, it is also important to note that nowhere in the process were the client's procedural and substantive rights compromised. I had extremely competent defense counsel and an extremely competent appellate counsel with me every step of the way.

I hope this vignette is illustrative of the way a therapeutic jurisprudence practitioner operates. He or she is part of a team which delivers the best possible representation to the defendant. I only wish Professor Quinn had asked me how I practice therapeutic jurisprudence before she impugned my methods.

Appendix

CAUSE NO. F03-71424

THE STATE OF TEXAS	§	IN THE 291ST DISTRICT COURT
	§	
VS.	§	OF
	§	
XYZ	§	DALLAS COUNTY, TEXAS

DEFENDANT'S BRIEF IN SUPPORT OF

BOND AND TREATMENT

TO THE HONORABLE JUDGE OF SAID COURT:

NOW COMES XYZ, Defendant in the above numbered cause, by and through his undersigned attorney of record, and submits this, his Brief in Support of Bond and Treatment, and would inform the Court as follows:

I.
Introduction

The undersigned attorney limits his criminal defense practice to Therapeutic Jurisprudence and Preventive Law. Therapeutic Jurisprudence sees the law and the way it is applied by various legal actors as having inevitable therapeutic or anti-therapeutic consequences for the people affected. It is a holistic approach to the law and the way it is applied. Preventive Law is an approach to legal practice that attempts to avoid recidivism through evaluation, planning, and relapse prevention techniques. Preventive Law is the legal analog of preventive medicine. An emerging legal literature and practice seeks to integrate Therapeutic Jurisprudence and Preventive Law to provide a law and psychology-based approach to the role of criminal defense attorneys.[1]

---

1. *See*, generally, *Law in a Therapeutic Key: Developments in Therapeutic Jurisprudence* (David B. Wexler & Bruce J. Winick, eds., 1996).

Therapeutic Jurisprudence/Preventive Law criminal defense attorneys see themselves as healers and peacemakers.[2] They view pending criminal charges as opportunities for therapeutic intervention and as catalysts for healing. This approach is particularly appropriate when (as in this case) the defendant has no prior criminal involvement other than as a direct consequence of the diseases of drug dependency and major depression. In such cases, the typical Therapeutic Jurisprudence/Preventive Law model involves nonjudgmental initial interviews of the defendant by the attorney, evaluation by an appropriate mental health professional (preferably a physician board certified in both psychiatry and addiction medicine), implementation of the treatment plan recommended by the evaluator, designing of a post treatment relapse prevention program for the defendant, and a monitoring protocol to provide accountability and ensure compliance.

In this model, criminal defense attorneys also refer clients to programs which make them aware of self-defeating behavior patterns and of alternative problem solving methods. These approaches are designed to develop in the offender an internal self-management system that allows the individual to identify those situations and events which lead to criminal behavior and to develop and utilize strategies for avoiding high risk situations. If high risk situations are encountered, these strategies minimize the likelihood that they will trigger the individual's customary behavior patterns. These cognitive self change, evaluation, intervention, treatment and relapse prevention methods are basic tools used by the undersigned attorney in facilitating healing for his clients. Of course, it is also vital to protect the substantive and procedural rights of the accused during this process. For this reason, a traditional criminal defense attorney should also be assisting the defendant. This is the role of Mr. Bob Frisch in this case.

II.
The Jailhouse Intervention

For the past twenty-six years, the undersigned attorney has been utilizing a technique that has come to be known as "the jailhouse intervention" as a part of his Therapeutic Jurisprudence/Preventive Law practice. The optimal circumstance for the jailhouse intervention is when a substance addicted client is incarcerated and charged with a relatively serious crime. The first step is to take aggressive prophylactic measures to prevent any well-meaning family members or friends from posting the bond and causing the defendant's release from jail. Although such people are always acting in good faith and think they are helping, they are actually hurting the defendant in the long term if they assist him or her in jail release. For example, in the instant case, any number of the defendant's family members or friends could have posted the $10,000.00 bond which was originally set by the magistrate. However, they were all strongly admonished by the undersigned attorney that XYZ should remain in jail as an adjunct to the jailhouse intervention.

After a defendant has had sufficient time to detox and suffer the harsh realities of incarceration (also known as "jail therapy"), the undersigned attorney has a series of visits with him or her wherein nonjudgmental interviewing and legal counseling techniques are utilized. The undersigned attorney tells his personal story to the defendant (the undersigned attorney is a recovering alcoholic who has been clean and

---

2. For a discussion of the "healer/peacemaker" orientation of a holistic lawyer, *see Transforming Practices: Finding Joy and Satisfaction in the Legal Life* (an *ABA Journal* book by Keeva, Steven, Contemporary Books, a division of NTC/Contemporary Publishing Groups, Inc., Lincolnwood [Chicago], IL, 1999), pp. 97–109.

sober for over 26 years). The undersigned attorney tells the defendant how the attorney's life was almost destroyed by alcohol and drugs, the availability of treatment for addiction, and the promise of a rich, full, and joyful life if recovery is embraced. The undersigned attorney attempts to create a vision for the defendant of the type of extraordinary life which is possible if alcohol and drugs are forsaken and recovery is achieved.

The undersigned attorney then tells the defendant that this new life is available to him or her but only under certain conditions. The defendant must agree that, if released on bond, he or she will go directly to the treatment center recommended by the evaluator and will remain there in full compliance until discharge is recommended by the staff. The defendant is warned that if he or she should fail to cooperate with treatment or leave the treatment center, the family member or friend making his or her bond will go off the bond and an arrest warrant will ensue. The defendant must also agree to comply with all aftercare treatment recommendations and relapse prevention protocols. Upon securing the defendant's agreement to this program, the undersigned attorney causes an evaluation to be done by a physician who is board certified in psychiatry and addiction medicine.

Upon receipt of the physician's evaluation and recommended treatment, the presiding judge is approached if Court permission is needed for the treatment plan (the most common scenario is when the physician recommends that the defendant be treated out of state). Upon receiving permission of the Court, bond is posted, the defendant is released from jail, and he or she is taken directly to the treatment center. He or she will be escorted by a responsible family member, friend, mental health professional, the undersigned attorney, or a member of his staff. Although virtually every alcoholic or drug addict begs for some free time between jail release and treatment, the undersigned attorney has a zero tolerance policy in this regard. As the undersigned attorney jokingly states to his clients, "This is not a 'getting on the street' bail bond. It is a 'going directly to the treatment center' bail bond. You do not pass go, you do not collect $200.00, you go directly to treatment." Although this approach may seem harsh, experience has proven that it is very effective "tough love". Since the undersigned attorney is himself a recovering substance abuser and has himself been incarcerated in various jails, the clients are able to accept his approach because they know at some level that he has been where they are and that he acts with love and compassion for them.

III.
The "Recovery Defense"

After treatment is completed and the defendant has embarked on the relapse prevention program, the undersigned attorney assembles all available documentary and testimonial evidence of the client's healing to be used as mitigation evidence if the defendant is found guilty or pleads guilty. Although this approach is not technically a legal defense, it has become known in some legal circles as the "recovery defense". Over the last twenty-six years, the recovery defense has been highly successful and has been taught by the undersigned attorney to thousands of other lawyers nationally and internationally. Favorable articles about this approach have appeared in many periodicals including *The Wall Street Journal*, *USA Today*, *The Dallas Morning News*, and *The American Bar Journal*. The success of the recovery defense and its multiple benefits to society have also been the subject of a number of radio and television programs.

IV.
Assurances to the Court

The evaluating psychiatrist, Dr. Louis E. Deere, has recommended that the defendant be treated at COPAC, an excellent inpatient facility located near Jackson, Mississippi. It is not a locked unit. It is quite reasonable and understandable that, under the current circumstances of this case, this Honorable Court would have concerns about releasing the defendant on bond to be treated at an out-of-state facility which is not locked. While still suffering from his drug-induced psychosis (see Psychiatric Evaluation of Dr. Deere attached hereto as Exhibit "A" and incorporated herein for all purposes), XYZ became extremely agitated and struggled with the deputies when they were attempting to bring him to Court on the jail chain. Further, he is charged with a serious crime and has a history of drug addiction. Without having any more information, it is easy to understand the Court's caution. Notwithstanding the Court's appropriate reservations at this time, Dr. Deere's report and his testimony will verify that XYZ's drug-induced psychosis is in remission, he is generally passive and non-dangerous, and is an excellent candidate for treatment. As further assurance to the Court, the undersigned attorney hereby represents as an officer of the court that he has handled hundreds of "recovery defense" cases over the last twenty-six years, that he has done the "jailhouse intervention" dozens of times. Not every case was successful and a *very small* minority of the clients continued to abuse substances. Each of these failures is grieved for since substance dependency is a fatal disease and most of these unfortunates are now dead or institutionalized. However, the undersigned attorney is unaware of any of his clients ever having committed another crime while free on a "going to the treatment center" bond. Although in most cases over the last twenty-six years it has not been necessary to seek judicial approval for this approach (it is usually necessary only when an out-of-state treatment center is being proposed), no judge who has been approached has ever denied the request for out-of-state treatment or lived to regret the decision allowing same. Upon request, the undersigned attorney will supply a list of judges who will confirm the efficacy of this approach and their positive experiences with it.

WHEREFORE, PREMISES CONSIDERED, XYZ respectfully requests that the Court set his bond at a reasonable amount and allow him to embark on the recommended course of treatment which will give him a new life in accordance with the program outlined above.

Respectfully submitted,

JOHN V. McSHANE
Co-counsel for XYZ
Bar Card No. 13859000
McShane & Davis, L.L.P.
A Registered Limited Liability Partnership
Including Professional Corporations
The Rolex Building, Suite 350
2651 North Harwood Street
Dallas, Texas 75201
Telephone No. 214/969-7300
Facsimile No. 214/969-7531

CERTIFICATE OF SERVICE

This is to certify that a true and correct copy of the foregoing Defendant's Brief in Support of Bond and Treatment was hand delivered to Mr. Bill Wirskye, Prosecuting

Attorney for the 291st District Court, at the Frank Crowley Courts Building, 133 N. Industrial Blvd., 7th Floor, on this the 13th day of March, 2003.

JOHN V. MCSHANE

CAUSE NO. F03-71424

THE STATE OF TEXAS	' '	IN THE ___ST DISTRICT COURT
VS.	' '	OF
_____	'	DALLAS COUNTY, TEXAS

DEFENDANT'S SUPPLEMENTAL BRIEF
IN SUPPORT OF BOND AND TREATMENT

TO THE HONORABLE JUDGE OF SAID COURT:

NOW COMES _____, Defendant (also referred to as "_____" herein) in the above numbered cause, by and through his undersigned attorney of record, and submits this, his Supplemental Brief in Support of Bond and Treatment, and would inform the Court as follows:

I.
Incorporation of Original Brief

This brief is filed as a supplement to Defendant's Brief in Support of Bond and Treatment which was filed with this Honorable Court on March 13, 2003. In the interest of efficiency and judicial economy, all attempts will be made to not restate the arguments made on behalf of _____ in that brief. However, _____'s original Brief In Support of Bond and Treatment is hereby incorporated herein by reference.

II.
Applicable Law

Code of Criminal Procedure Article 17.15 is a legislative effort to implement the constitutional right to bail. The court's discretion in setting the amount of bail is governed by the following rules:

1. The bail shall be sufficiently high to give reasonable assurance that the undertaking will be complied with.
2. The power to require bail is not to be used as an instrument of oppression.
3. The nature of the offense and the circumstances under which it was committed are to be considered.
4. The ability to make bail is to be regarded, and proof may be taken upon this point.
5. The future safety of a victim of the alleged offense and the community shall be considered.

TEX. CODE CRIM. PROC. ANN. ART. 17.15 (Vernon Supp. 2001).

The following factors should also be weighed in determining the amount of bond:

6. The accused's work record;

7. The accused's family and community ties;

8. The accused's length of residency;

9. The accused's prior criminal record, if any;

10. The accused's conformity with the conditions of any previous bond;

11. The existence of outstanding bonds, if any; and

12. Aggravating circumstances alleged to have been involved in the charged offense.

See, Ex parte Rubac, 611 S.W.2d 848, 849-50 (Tex.Crim.App. [Panel Op.] 1981); *Brown v. State,* 11 S.W.3d 501 (Tex.App.-Houston [14th Dist.] 2000).

III.
Facts Which Overwhelmingly Support a Reasonable Bond

When the facts of this case are examined in the context of the applicable law, such facts literally cry out for the immediate release of the Defendant on a conditional bond so he can be treated at COPAC as recommended by Dr. Louis Deere and requested in Defendant's Brief in Support of Bond and Treatment filed March 13, 2003. These facts will be proven at the bond hearing set for Friday, March 21, 2003 at 9:00 a.m. These favorable facts include, but are not limited, to the following:

13. _____ is charged by indictment with burning the house of his mother _____. _____ does not want _____ to be prosecuted and urgently requests that he be released on a conditional bond to be treated at COPAC. Her Affidavit of Non-Prosecution and Request for Treatment is attached hereto and incorporated herein as Exhibit "A."

14. _____ has no prior criminal record.

15. _____ has extensive family ties and the members of his family are uniformly supportive of treatment at COPAC. Members of _____'s family will testify to this effect at the bond hearing.

16. _____ is not subject to other bonds. He has not failed to comply with the conditions of a bond, and the only type of bond being sought here is a conditional bond which would require full cooperation with the treatment personnel at COPAC.

17. As will be discussed in detail below and proven at the bond hearing, there are numerous inadequacies with the SAFP program. _____ is desirous of being treated for his life-threatening diseases at the most efficacious facility and will promise the court that he will give the treatment staff at COPAC his full cooperation. He will testify to this effect at the bond hearing.

18. Although this brief is not to be construed as an admission of guilt, the circumstances under which _____ is alleged to have committed the offense are highly mitigating (e.g., alleged to have committed the offense while in the grips of a fatal and progressive disease which temporarily impaired his cognitive functioning).

19. Dr. Deere has assured the court in chambers and will assure the court during his sworn testimony that it is highly remote that, after the period of extended detox in the Dallas County jail, _____ would be dangerous to himself or others.

20. Dr. Deere will testify that the best way to predict whether someone will engage in violent behavior in the future is to carefully examine their entire life and de-

termine whether or not they have a history of violence. Dr. Deere will also testify that _____ is extremely passive and has no history of violence. Clearly, the offense with which he is charged (even if the allegation is true) would be an aberration and it was not an act of violence.

IV.
The SAFP Treatment Program is Not Appropriate for _____

At the meeting in chambers on March 14, 2003, this Honorable Court instructed the undersigned counsel to investigate whether or not SAFP treatment programs were available to individuals with _____'s diagnosis. Pursuant to the Court's instructions, the investigation was immediately commenced. The undersigned counsel retained Vicki Johnson, M.S., to conduct this research. Ms. Johnson is a Licensed Chemical Dependency Counselor and was Assistant Executive Director of the Greater Dallas Council on Alcoholism and Drug Abuse. She is intimately familiar with most drug treatment programs but has had limited experience with SAFP. Accordingly, it was necessary for her to conduct research, review documents, interview SAFP personnel, and make other collateral investigations. Ms. Johnson's resume is attached hereto as Exhibit "B" and incorporated herein. Ms. Johnson's findings form the basis for most of this section. Ms. Johnson will testify on her findings in detail during the bond hearing.

There are two locked units in the State of Texas which treat special populations technically described as individuals who have "co-occurring disorders" (also referred to as "dual-diagnosis"). These units are part of the penitentiary system and are located in Huntsville (the Estelle Unit) and in Richmond (the Jester Unit). The treatment program within the penitentiary is referred to as SAFP—Substance Abuse Felony Punishment Program.

Pursuant to Vicki Johnson's telephone conversation on March 17, 2003 with SAFP admissions manager Linda Bosby, there are 153 males on the waiting list for these units. The waiting time for a bed is estimated to range from 18–20 weeks. Ms. Bosby may be reached at 936-437-2845.

According to the *Report to Congress on the Prevention and Treatment of Co-Occurring Substance Abuse Disorders and Mental Disorders*,[1] effective interventions for defendants/offenders with co-occurring disorders (dual diagnosis) include ... "individualized, flexible treatment provided by well trained staff; a long term focus; and integrated services ..." (See page 91 of Report attached hereto as Exhibit "C" and incorporated herein by reference).

When evaluated by this criteria, SAFP fails miserably. According to *The Substance Abuse Felony Punishment Program; Evaluation and Recommendations*,[2] the problems with all SAFP treatment programs include the following:

- *Quality of Treatment*—Due to inadequate reimbursement rates that have led to pay scales too low to attract and retain qualified staff, less experienced and qualified staff are utilized. This report also cited problems with the reduction of individual and group counseling and limited training for staff.

---

1. Issued by the Substance Abuse and Mental Health Services Administration, U.S. Department of Health and Human Services, December 2, 2002, www.samhsa.gov/news/cl_congress2002.html.
2. Prepared by the Criminal Justice Policy Counsel for the 77th Texas Legislature, February, 2001, www.cjpc.state.tx.us/reports/adltrehab/SAFPinDepth.pdf.

- *Relapse Options*—This report cited the need for additional training and education regarding response to relapse and relapse prevention.
- *Treatment Team Meeting/Coordination*—This report cited the need to properly structure and consistently use team meetings to facilitate the client's success and monitor progress.
- *Information Flow*—This report cited the need for information regarding client's problems/needs to consistently flow between the levels of services.

The efficacy of SAFP as a viable treatment program (especially for unfortunates with a dual-diagnosis) is widely criticized by people who understand the program and its limitations. For example, Criminal District Judge John Creuzot recently sent shockwaves through the Texas Legislature when he testified that state funded and sponsored inpatient drug treatment programs are ineffective and often "a joke." The undersigned attorney applauds Judge Creuzot for his courage in confronting this problem which is compounded by the institutional denial of the criminal justice system and the Texas Legislature. Judge Creuzot is considered one of the most knowledgeable jurists in the nation with reference to state implemented drug treatment. His drug treatment diversion court became a prototype of excellence and received national awards. Judge Creuzot's drug treatment diversion court also was a "mentor court" for other judges and their staffs. The undersigned attorney invites this Honorable Court to confer with her colleague, the Honorable John Creuzot, on this issue.

V.
Application of Applicable Law

As stated above, the power to require bail is not to be used as an instrument of oppression. The undersigned attorney respectfully submits that continued denial of bail at a reasonable amount and the opportunity for treatment at COPAC would be oppressive. Additionally, the undersigned attorney believes that continued denial of bail under the circumstances of this case would be cruel and unusual punishment. The applicable law also requires the Court to consider the future safety of the community. The most responsible decision to maximize the safety of the community would be to select the option which is most likely to result in _____'s recovery. From everything presented in this brief and Defendant's original brief, it is clear that private treatment under the conditions outlined is more likely to achieve this result.

VI.
Conclusion

_____ urgently requests that he not be forced to languish in jail suffering from two fatal and progressive diseases another day. It is respectfully requested that the Court not wait for the bond hearing but order a reasonable bond for _____ *instanter!* A copy of this brief is also being submitted to prosecutor Bill Wirskye. It is respectfully requested that Mr. Wirskye recommend release on a conditional treatment bond in a reasonable amount. This is the responsible thing to do to optimize the protection of the people Mr. Wirskye is charged with protecting—the citizens of Dallas County and the State of Texas.

Prayer

WHEREFORE, PREMISES CONSIDERED, _____ respectfully requests that the Court set his bond at a reasonable amount and allow him to embark on the recommended course of treatment which will give him a new life and freedom from the horrors of his addiction.

                              Respectfully submitted,

                              JOHN V. McSHANE
                              Co-counsel for _____
                              Bar Card No. 13859000
                              McShane & Davis, L.L.P.
                              A Registered Limited Liability Partnership
                              Including Professional Corporations
                              The Rolex Building, Suite 350
                              2651 North Harwood Street
                              Dallas, Texas 75201
                              Telephone No. 214/969-7300
                              Facsimile No. 214/969-7531

CERTIFICATE OF SERVICE

    This is to certify that a true and correct copy of the foregoing Defendant's Supplemental Brief in Support of Bond and Treatment was hand delivered to_____, Assistant District Attorney for the ___st District Court, at the Frank Crowley Courts Building, 133 N. Industrial Blvd., 7th Floor, on this the 20th day of March, 2003.

                              JOHN V. McSHANE

x. Robert Ward,[*] Criminal Defense Practice and Therapeutic Jurisprudence: Zealous Advocacy through Zealous Counseling: Perspectives, Plans and Policy

Representing people charged with crimes can be difficult. Our clients frequently face a fearful, angry and disapproving public and court system. They face people who are looking for retribution. They face people who are skeptical of meeting the burden of proof beyond a reasonable doubt. There are those who are cynical about a viable alternative explanation or interpretation of events. Some victims and jurists have high expectations for remorse and repentance, and are leery about plans to restore faith in the client's future safe conduct. In this environment, defense attorneys need the law but also

---

[*] Robert L. Ward has experience in civil and criminal trial (including capital defense) and appellate advocacy and currently works in and manages the defense attorney component of the S.T.E.P drug treatment court (criminal division) in Charlotte. He has worked continuously on criminal justice management, technology and policy issues since 1987 at the local, state and national level. He served on the Justice Fellowship Task Force in North Carolina, which helped to establish substantial reforms in conjunction with the Structured Sentencing Act in 1993 and with the reform of the Juvenile system in 1998. He helped to create the Charlotte S.T.E.P. Drug Treatment Court and the North Carolina Drug Treatment Court Program, and served on the North Carolina State Advisory Committee on Drug Treatment Courts from 1995 to 2005. He has served as President of the North Carolina Public Defender Association (1991–1992). He has been a member of the Mecklenburg County Criminal Justice Partnership Board since it began in 1994, the Charlotte-Mecklenburg Drug Free Coalition since 2003, and the Justice and Mental Health Collaboration Committee since 2006. He taught in the Criminal Justice Department at the University of North Carolina at Charlotte.

facts and reliable theories behind both. Then they are more likely to obtain dismissals or reduced charges from prosecutors, not guilty verdicts or verdicts of guilty of lesser-included offenses, or treatment and probation from judges and the system. To achieve these results, the defense benefits from having the theoretical construct of therapeutic jurisprudence.

Attorneys have always had the professional duty to be *both* advocates *and* counselors. As expected, the focus of much initial and continuing legal education has been on knowing the law itself and on traditional advocacy—such as courtroom or boardroom victories. In this context, the attorney's role as counselor is to advise primarily about the law and the likely legal result of available choices within the client's circumstances and stated intent. Frequently that takes the form of accepting the client's interests at face value and then delivering the legal product or option.

Zealous counseling is about the human side of the practice of law. It is about being reasonably comprehensive about understanding the people one represents. It is about being empathetic (not just sympathetic), and about assessing the case in a behavioral context, and then helping the client assess and decide what course to take. Armed with such information and a good attorney-client relationship, zealous counseling creates the ability and opportunity to be a zealous advocate in the criminal justice system.

There are those who think that clients are not very interested in mitigation or therapeutic expertise. Yet I have heard harsh criticism of defense attorneys from former defendants who were resentful that they were not even made aware of alternative sentencing options or who were never asked if they wanted or needed treatment. Before they can open up to their attorney, clients need to know that it is safe to talk about their addiction or mental illness and that it may be relevant to their case. Unfortunately, the justice system can follow the dysfunctional family system motto which is: "don't talk, don't trust, don't feel". Perhaps this is why many feel so at home in the criminal justice system.

I began my work at the Public Defender's Office by representing clients facing civil involuntary commitments and regular misdemeanors. Knowledge gained there later helped me with the more serious cases. I learned much from clients and the hospital staff, particularly how to identify the symptoms of common illnesses such as schizophrenia and bipolar disorder. I learned how to speak with them as I would any other client. Essentially, the key was to be aware of their condition and then work with them to develop an action plan. I saw some clients in both the hospital and the court setting. This is not surprising, since much of criminal work involves representing people who have psychological, learning and sociological issues.

It is troubling that there are many cases where the same statement of wrongdoing can result in either a petition for a mental health commitment or a criminal charge. It just depends on the knowledge and disposition of the community, family, officers or victims. It also depends on the availability of services or the bureaucratic difficulties of a strained mental health system. A mentally ill client can either be treated as a patient and get medical help at a psychiatric hospital or can be charged as a criminal and sent to jail. It is almost like the Middle Ages where if you made it to the cathedral or monastery, you found sanctuary and redemption. If not, you found jail or the hangman's noose.

Knowing that people in "the system" have much discretion with their power, I have found value in welcoming the perspective of therapeutic jurisprudence in mitigation and sentencing advocacy. I have seen remarkable results by gaining a client's trust through showing awareness and understanding of his condition and by providing the prosecution or judiciary with reasonable alternative explanations for behavior. Experienced prosecutors and judges appreciate suggestions for ways to provide stability and public safety while minimizing charge levels or restraints on liberty.

Most people do not come in neat packages of being either mentally ill or not mentally ill. Human behavior is a dynamic continuum of skill sets, thoughts, moods, perspectives, habits and choices. In areas of the law dealing with crime and other social behavior, identifying what happened, why it happened, and how to explain or rectify it is crucial to representing clients and constructing workable solutions or alternative explanations.

There are many criminal lawyers who are able to target clients with special needs. They strategically assess and guide clients with everyday problems. Most lawyers go into the practice of law to help people. To give that help, it is just common sense that we must learn about our clients, what they want, and what options are available to them. Therapeutic jurisprudence is simply a broader, deeper and more refined approach to do that work. Not surprisingly, the very "therapeutic" knowledge I learned through representing people in commitment hearings, serious felony cases, DWI cases, drug treatment court, sentencing advocacy generally, and other settings also helped me in client counseling, trial work, working with witnesses and family members, negotiating with prosecutors and probation officers, and presenting cases in court.

It is important to recognize the basic signs and behaviors of mental illness or condition and then to apply them to the facts and theory and of the case. Does the client report having a history of mental illness and addiction (e.g., bipolar disorder with mood swings involving anger and violence, where medication and substance abuse treatment could prevent further problems), developmental disability (e.g., attention deficit disorder that is undiagnosed or not medicated, resulting in failure to maintain probation responsibilities), mental retardation (e.g., where the client is being used by drug dealers to sell drugs—the last time to a vice officer), traumatic brain injury (e.g., where the client may need special treatment if probation is to be successful), or addiction (e.g., where a young man in his twenties stabs his mother's boyfriend over eighty times in a blind rage brought on by cocaine and mental illness and the jury returns a verdict of life)?

Clients and others can be hurt by not understanding, respecting or appreciating a therapeutic context or "moment". The "moment" has to do with the attorney being both cognitively and emotionally aware of the client's need and desires, expressed or unexpressed. It most likely will be at the initial interview and then at any key decision point during the course of the case. It certainly has to do with choices such as going to trial or pleading guilty, and about how the client can save or repair their life or liberty.

I had been practicing law for a few years when I heard a story from a reliable source about a domestic violence case where the senior partner of a law firm was contacted by the Sheriff's department late one evening. A woman was in custody for shooting and killing her ex-husband. She told the deputies that she did it because she feared for her life and because her lawyer said killing her ex-husband was her only option to protect herself. The young, bright, legally knowledgeable lawyer had in fact seen her a few days prior to the killing.

At the earlier scheduled appointment with her young attorney, the woman pleaded for help and was very upset and fearful because her very violent ex-husband was disregarding the protective order. When asked what she should do about this, he said she should call the police if he violated the order. Distraught, she implored him for other ways to help, since she feared the police would not arrive in time, and exclaimed, "What else can I do?!"

Confounded, the young attorney reportedly replied, "Other than shooting him, not much …" When her ex-husband appeared on the property a few days later, that's what she did. I never heard what happened afterward. Perhaps if the lawyer had allowed her to further express her fears or directed her to a counseling resource, she could have seen that she had other avenues of support. However, the story reflects just how ill equipped lawyers can be at the interpersonal level to help clients with emotionally charged or complex matters—sometimes with dire consequences.

Lawyers can use other information to help clients make those choices every day—or even to create additional choices. This is particularly true in criminal practice. However, few attorneys are genuinely skilled at recognizing and assisting clients with addiction problems, brain diseases or cognitive, emotional or family dysfunctions that can weigh heavily on the real interests of the client and the value and outcome of the case. At best most lawyers rely on natural ability or on-the-job training.

In my own practice I have seen the positive results of being intentional about a therapeutic perspective. Several years ago I was substituting for an attorney at a bond hearing for a young client in a routine probation violation case. Some clients would rather get probation behind them and serve their time. At the hearing he told me that he just wanted to get off of probation and to just "do his time." This was his prerogative so perhaps no more questions were necessary. The speed with which the system handles cases would have made it easy for me to accept his request and move the case along. However, there was something in his demeanor that was not right. He appeared just slightly naïve, and a bit too eager to please his cellmates, and a bit too tough talking to be really tough. I urged him to wait for his probation violation hearing and allow me to discuss his decision with him.

He insisted on waiving his right to a probation violation hearing and he asked the judge to activate his sentence at the bond hearing. The judge proceeded with the usual list of questions to determine if his choice was knowingly, willfully and understandably made. After finding that it had been, the sentence was activated. Troubled by the situation, I asked my investigator (who had social work experience) to visit him for a more comprehensive interview, specifically to look for signs of mental retardation. It is common for those with mental retardation to hide their condition, to blend in with those around them, and for others to ignore the potential difficulty in working with a person with that condition. I discovered a history of traumatic victimization. The investigator agreed, indicating that "something was going on there", but unsure of an explanation.

After discussing the case further with the client (and making it safe to talk about the tough issues), I was able to pull the matter back into court that same week, set aside the decision to terminate probation and reset the case for a revocation hearing. I was then able to obtain a defense expert through an "Ake" motion. *Ake v. Oklahoma*, 470 U.S. 68, 84 L. Ed. 2d 53 (1985), where the U.S. Supreme Court ruled that the defense could obtain an Order for a defense expert through an *ex parte* motion before the trial judge. I subsequently discovered that the client was in fact mentally retarded. The plea transcript for the underlying felony conviction indicated that the defendant could read and write at the ninth grade level. In fact, it was more like second grade.

After presenting this information to one of the chief prosecutors, he informed me that the discovery in the underlying case had information showing behavior consistent with mental retardation. Had the client's condition been made available earlier, the prosecution would most likely have exercised discretion and either dismissed the charges or arranged for some form of deferred prosecution or misdemeanor conviction. In the end, the state consented to setting aside the conviction. With outside help our office put together the best available treatment and case management plan for this young man.

Some lawyers view this kind of work as social work and "nice" but not really "what lawyers do." Yet our explicit duty and challenge is with understanding and explaining our client's behavior to prosecutors, judges, the client, probation officers, and family members. It is still surprising to me that some science is accepted—such as DNA—while other science—such as addiction or learning disabilities—is ignored and even dismissed as inconsequential to the client or case. A probation officer that I once cross-examined testified that it was not necessary for him to have even a basic understanding of mental illness or addiction to adequately supervise a probationer. Sadly, there are lawyers, prosecutors and judges who have the same opinion towards representation, prosecution and sentencing.

In most cases it does matter whether the client has a mental health issue. The three basic types of mental illness are personality disorders, thought disorders and mood disorders. The latter two are more treatable than the first, but the symptoms may overlap. It also matters if the client is addicted. Nearly 70% of any felony caseload is dependent or at risk for dependency. One of the less recognized mental conditions has to do with learning disabilities and traumatic brain injury.

Many women and a significant percentage of men have a history of being sexually abused, which is why they may fail treatment (and probation). People use drugs and alcohol to self medicate. If they successfully complete treatment but do not get appropriate counseling for the sexual abuse, they will most likely return to addiction because the underlying condition was never treated. As recent tragedy within the Catholic Church revealed, there is much shame, pain and guilt associated with that affliction. It takes patience and expertise to reach genuine recovery.

Clients with mental retardation make up a smaller population we see in the court system. Many clients who have at least one of these problems may have others. They have a dual or multiple diagnoses and are in need of integrated treatment and case management services. Integrated services can be difficult to access in the community. That is also why we get them as clients—many communities have limited funding or support structures to assist such individuals.

While attorneys debate the value of understanding psychology or social work in their practice, other professions, in contrast, face legal obligations to acknowledge and work with such disabilities. For example, in the education system, an eighteen-year-old with ADD (Attention Deficit Disorder) and depression is entitled by law to have certain accommodations in the school and classroom. While the teacher is not expected to be a counselor or to be an expert in a particular field, a basic understanding of the child's condition is necessary for the student and the school to reach their goals.

If that same child (or adult) is arrested and placed in the criminal justice system in most places there are essentially no such protections. While national and state criminal practice guidelines may require investigation and consideration of mental health and other disabilities, the admonitions are difficult to apply and enforce except in cases of gross negligence. If attorneys are unable or unwilling to put forth such a defense (such as competency, insanity, or mitigation) or if judges or prosecutors do not properly exercise their discretion, injustice prevails.

For those of us who work in the system, we know that accountability for discretionary matters is arbitrary at best. This is especially true where the police, prosecutors, probation officers and judges have much discretion and essentially little true accountability. The depth and breadth of prosecutorial discretion to bring charges (such as seriousness of the charge, the number of charges, and recommendations for sentencing) and judicial discretion (more with probation revocation decisions and less with sentencing guidelines) is deep and wide. The only real standard for judges is "abuse of discretion," which is hard to define and even harder to establish. There virtually is no such standard for prosecutors.

In much of criminal practice where the apparent facts or law are against your client, the best negotiation practice is usually from principle-based negotiation rather than a position-based approach. The former method focuses on persuading the other on taking right action, regardless of technical rights or power, and the latter focuses on your actual or perceived power and rights. Armed with therapeutic theories and facts, it is easier to appeal to a prosecutor's desire or duty to do justice than it is to go to trial and hope the jury will nullify a case (where technical guilt exists but broader discernment and mercy is the better course). But even if you have to go to trial, you potentially have more evidence or alternative theories available for the jury and the judge.

There are those who take the view that a therapeutic approach requires the attorney to take on a parental, caregiver or priestly role and direct or urge the client to take a course of action (such as confession, waiver of trial rights, or participation in unwanted treatment) that is not the expressed desire of the client. That has not been my understanding of adopting a therapeutic approach. However, if an attorney is not knowledgeable enough to suggest a possible expert or sentencing alternative as an option, then perhaps that attorney has not zealously represented the client. Arguably, if an attorney intentionally avoids knowing about or presenting this information, perhaps that attorney is the one making the decision for the client.

There is article on the ABA Model Ethics Rule 2.1 that addresses the lawyer's duty to counsel clients concerning non-legal advice: *More than Lawyers: The Legal and Ethical Implications on Counseling Clients on Non-Legal Considerations*, Georgetown Journal of Legal Ethics, Spring 2005, by Larry O. Natt Gantt II. The *DSM IV-TR*, American Psychiatric Association, 2000, has comprehensive technical information about the disorders and afflictions of many of our clients.

In the Appendix to this article are client expectations of defense counsel as set out by the New York Public Defender Association, relevant sections from the Performance Standards for the North Carolina Indigent Defense Program, a sample "Ake" Motion and Order for a Defense Expert, and a Motion and Order for Appropriate Relief to set aside a conviction. One can infer from the selected Performance Standards that there is a professional expectation in North Carolina that mitigation, or therapeutic, information from a broad-based perspective, is important. There are no explicit expectations about using sentencing information at the charge or even plea stage. However, a thoughtful reading of the standards would lead one to conclude that disposition, or sentencing information, is important at all stages of the criminal process.

For further background there are some insightful books to read on the value and need for a therapeutic perspective. Two true stories, both illustrative of the problem, are *The Innocent Man*, Doubleday, 2006, by John Grisham, and *Crazy*, Putnam, 2006, by Pete Earley. Both write about the truly insane "system" (medical, legal, housing, etc.) that we have for treating or responding to people and families suffering from mental illness.

Another good resource is *A Lawyers Guide to Healing*, by W. Donald Carroll, Jr. Mr. Carroll is the Director of the Lawyers Assistance Program for the State Bar in North Carolina and has published this compilation of his writings over the years on issues concerning mental illness, addiction, lawyers and the practice of law. This book is helpful not only for better understanding lawyers (which would also include prosecutors and judges) and their afflictions, but also for understanding by negative implication the double standard the system has for professionals with mental illness (treatment and assistance) and the poor who are frequently written off until they come to us labeled as criminals unworthy of care.

Lastly, *Downsizing Prisons*, by Michael Jacobson, presents the policy arguments and flaws in the system that can assist the creative defense attorney persuade the prosecution or judiciary to justify deferral to the treatment system and to remember that correctional resources are not endless, and that further investment in them takes resources from the very services that could be provided to those who end up in our courts. *Perspectives, plans and policy*. Unless the client has a clear choice for suppression, trial or not guilty, those three words all are we really have to offer our clients, the system, the public, and each other.

Appendix

Client Advisory Board of the New York State Defenders Association
CLIENT-CENTERED REPRESENTATION STANDARDS July 25, 2005

Clients Want A Lawyer Who—

1. Represents a person, not a case file; represents a client, not a defendant.

2. Listens to them and represents them with compassion, dignity and respect.

3. Makes sure the client's privacy is respected and that communications take place in a space and by means that protect the confidential nature of the client-attorney relationship.

4. Refrains from displays of affection and other behavior with the prosecution that might project the image of a conflict of interest.

5. Meets with them and visits them when incarcerated, accepts phone calls, answers letters, and takes time to counsel and explain in a manner that communicates understanding and respect.

6. Listens to the client's family and with permission of the client shares and exchanges information so that the client, lawyer, and client's family remain informed.

7. Uses language in court, legal writing, and conversation that is clear and understandable to the client.

8. Pursues an investigation of the facts of the case, is culturally sensitive, appreciates the dimensions of the client's life, and becomes familiar with the communities from which his or her clients come.

9. Acknowledges personal cultural values, beliefs, and prejudices that might affect his or her ability to effectively represent a client and takes appropriate steps to shield the client from resulting harm.

10. Thoroughly and carefully reads all documents, discusses them with his or her client, and provides the client with copies.

11. Knows the law and investigates the facts, and applies the knowledge of both creatively, competently, and expeditiously.

12. Aggressively seeks resources, such as interpreters, experts and investigators, necessary for effective representation.
13. Works and strategizes in collaboration with his or her client.
14. Is committed to obtaining the best outcome for the client, zealously advocating on the client's behalf.
15. Identifies disabilities of his or her client, and obtains assessments and services to address needs.
16. Informs the client about plea negotiations, tells the client when a plea has been offered, explains the importance of the client's decision whether or not to plead guilty, advises the client on the appropriateness of any plea and all of its consequences and, acting in the best interest of the client, helps the client reach an informed decision.
17. Aggressively pursues alternatives to incarceration, assesses immigration and collateral consequences of a client's criminal conviction, acts to prevent such consequences, and explains the reason for any fines or penalties.
18. Relays to the client what criminal history information is being relied upon, makes sure the information is accurate, and sees that errors are corrected.
19. Accurately informs the client about sentencing, reviews the presentence report with the client, makes sure the court removes any errors in the report, ensures that the client has a copy of the report, and files where appropriate a comprehensive defense presentence memorandum.
20. Accurately informs the client who may be incarcerated about the incarceration process, including jail and prison programs, and works with the client to plan the future in terms of treatment while incarcerated, transitional issues, and reentry.

(Also approved and endorsed by the Board of Directors of the New York State Defenders Association, October 7, 2005.)

North Carolina Commission on Indigent Defense Services
Performance Guidelines for Indigent Defense Representation in Non-Capital Criminal Cases at the Trial Level
Adopted November 12, 2004

SECTION 1:
Guideline 1.1 Function of Performance Guidelines

(a) The Commission on Indigent Defense Services hereby adopts these performance guidelines to promote one of the purposes of the Indigent Defense Services Act of 2000—improving the quality of indigent defense representation in North Carolina—and pursuant to G.S. 7A-498.5(c)(4).

(b) These guidelines are intended to serve as a guide for attorney performance in non-capital

criminal cases at the trial level, and contain a set of considerations and recommendations to assist counsel in providing quality representation for indigent criminal defendants. The guidelines also may be used as a training tool.

(c) These are performance guidelines, not standards. The steps covered in these guidelines are not to be undertaken automatically in every case. Instead, the steps actually taken should be tailored to the requirements of a particular case. In deciding what steps are appropriate, counsel should use his or her best professional judgment.

Guideline 1.2 Role of Defense Counsel

(a) The paramount obligations of criminal defense counsel are to provide zealous and quality representation to their clients at all stages of the criminal process, and to preserve, protect, and promote their clients' rights and interests throughout the criminal proceedings. Attorneys also have an obligation to conduct themselves professionally, abide by the Revised Rules of Professional Conduct of the North Carolina State Bar and other ethical norms, and act in accordance with all rules of court.

(b) Defense counsel are the professional representatives of their clients. Counsel should candidly advise clients regarding the probable success and consequences of adopting any posture in the proceedings, and provide clients with all information necessary to make informed decisions. Counsel does not have an obligation to execute any directive of a client that does not comport with law or standards of ethics or professional conduct

Guideline 2.2 Initial Interview

(2) Information that should be acquired during the initial interview includes, but is not limited to:

(A) the client's ties to the community, including the length of time he or she has lived at the current and former addresses, family relationships, employment record and history, and immigration status (if applicable);

(B) the client's physical and mental health, including any impairing conditions such as substance abuse or learning disabilities, and educational and armed services history;

(C) the client's immediate medical and/or mental health needs;

(H) the names of individuals or other sources that counsel can contact to verify the information provided by the client, and the permission of the client to contact those individuals.

(3) Information to be provided to the client during the initial interview includes, but is not limited to:

(H) what arrangements will be made or attempted for the satisfaction of the client's most pressing needs, such as medical or mental health attention, and contact with family members.

(d) *Additional Information*

Whenever possible, counsel should use the initial interview to gather additional information relevant to preparation of the defense. Such information may include, but is not limited to:

(5) where appropriate, evidence of the client's competence to stand trial and/or mental state at the time of the offense.

Guideline 2.3 Pretrial Release Proceedings in Misdemeanor and Felony Cases

(f) Where the client is incarcerated and unable to obtain pretrial release, counsel should alert the jail, and if appropriate the court, to any special medical or psychiatric and security needs of the client that are known to counsel.

Guideline 3.2 Client's Competence and Capacity to Proceed

(a) When defense counsel has a good faith doubt as to the client's capacity to proceed in a criminal case, counsel may:

(1) file an *ex parte* motion to obtain the services of a mental health expert and thereby determine whether to raise the client's competency before the court; or

(2) file a motion questioning the client's competence to stand trial or enter a plea under G.S. 15A-1001(a) and applicable case law, in which case the court may order a mental health examination at a state mental health facility or by the appropriate local forensic examiner.

(b) While the client's wishes ordinarily control, counsel may question competency without the client's assent or over the client's objection if necessary.

(c) After counsel receives and reviews the report from any court-ordered competency examination, counsel should consider whether to file a motion requesting a formal hearing on the client's capacity to proceed.

(d) Whenever competency is at issue, counsel still has a continuing duty to prepare the case for all anticipated court proceedings.

(e) If the court enters an order finding the client incompetent and orders involuntary commitment proceedings to be initiated, defense counsel ordinarily will not represent the client at those proceedings, but should cooperate with the commitment attorney upon request.

SECTION 4:
Guideline 4.1 Case Review, Investigation, and Preparation

(b) Sources of review and investigative information may include the following:

(2) *The Client*

An in-depth interview or interviews of the client should be used to:

(A) seek information concerning the incident or events giving rise to the charge(s);

(B) elicit information concerning possible improper police investigative practices or prosecutorial conduct that may affect the client's rights;

(C) explore the existence of other potential sources of information relating to the offense or client, including school, work, jail, probation, and prison records;

(D) collect information relevant to sentencing; and

(E) continue to assess the client's medical and/or mental health needs.

Guideline 4.3 Theory of the Case

During case review, investigation, and trial preparation, counsel should develop and continually reassess a theory of the case. A theory of the case is one central theory that organizes the facts, emotions, and legal basis for the client's acquittal or conviction of a lesser offense, while also telling the defense story of innocence, reduced culpability, or unfairness. The theory of the case furnishes the basic position from which counsel determines all actions in a case.

Guideline 6.2 The Contents of the Negotiations

(c) In developing a negotiation strategy, counsel should be completely familiar with:

(3) information favorable to the client concerning such matters as the offense, mitigating factors and relative culpability, prior offenses, personal background, employment record and opportunities, educational background, and family and financial status;

(4) information that would support a sentencing disposition other than incarceration, such as the potential for rehabilitation or the nonviolent nature of the crime; and

(5) information concerning the availability of treatment programs, community treatment facilities, and community service work opportunities.

Guideline 6.3 The Decision to Enter a Plea of Guilty

(a) Counsel shall inform the client of any tentative negotiated agreement reached with the prosecution, and explain to the client the full content of the agreement, including its advantages, disadvantages, and potential consequences.

(b) When counsel reasonably believes that acceptance of a plea offer is in the client's best interests, counsel should attempt to persuade the client to accept the plea offer. However, the decision to enter a plea of guilty ultimately rests with the client.

Guideline 7.1 General Trial Preparation

(c) In advance of trial, counsel should take all steps necessary to complete thorough investigation, discovery, and research. Among the steps counsel should consider in preparation are:

(1) interviewing and subpoenaing all potentially helpful witnesses;

(2) examining and subpoenaing all potentially helpful physical or documentary evidence;

(3) obtaining funds for defense investigators and experts, and arranging for defense experts to consult and/or testify on issues that are potentially helpful;

Guideline 8.1 Obligations of Counsel in Sentencing

Counsel's obligations in the sentencing process include:

(a) where a defendant chooses not to proceed to trial, to attempt to negotiate a plea agreement with consideration of the sentencing, correctional, and financial implications;

(b) to try to ensure the client is not harmed by inaccurate information or information that is not properly before the court in determining the sentence to be imposed;

(c) to ensure that all reasonably available mitigating and favorable evidence, which is likely to benefit the client, is presented to the court;

(d) to develop a plan that seeks to achieve the sentencing alternative most favorable to the client, and that reasonably can be obtained based on the facts and circumstances of the offense, the defendant's background, the applicable sentencing provisions, and other information pertinent to the sentencing decision;

(e) to try to ensure that all information presented to the court which may harm the client, if inaccurate, untruthful, or otherwise improper, is stricken from the text of any sentencing services plan or presentence report;

(f) to consider the need for and availability of sentencing specialists, or mental health or mental retardation professionals; and

(g) to identify and preserve potential issues for appeal.

Guideline 8.2 Sentencing Options, Consequences, and Procedures

(a) Counsel should be familiar with and advise the client of the sentencing provisions and options applicable to the case, including:

(1) the applicable sentencing laws, including any habitual offender statutes, sentencing enhancements, mandatory minimum sentence requirements, mandatory consecutive sentence requirements, and constitutional limits on sentences;

(2) deferred prosecution, prayer for judgment continued, probation without a conviction, and diversionary programs;

(3) probation or suspension of sentence, and mandatory and permissible conditions of probation;

(4) confinement in a mental institution;

(5) forfeiture of assets seized in connection with the case;

(6) any mandatory registration requirements, including sex offender registration, or mandatory DNA testing; and

(7) the possibility of expungement and sealing of records.

(b) Counsel should be familiar with and advise the client of the direct and collateral consequences of the judgment and sentence, including:

(1) credit for pretrial detention;

(2) the likelihood that the conviction could be used for sentence enhancement in the event of future criminal cases, such as sentencing in the aggravated range, habitual offender status, or felon in possession of a firearm;

(3) the possibility of earned-time credits;

(4) the availability of correctional programs and work release;

(5) the availability of drug rehabilitation programs, psychiatric treatment, and health care; and

(6) the likelihood of the court imposing financial obligations on the client, including the payment of attorney fees, court costs, fines, and restitution. Counsel should also discuss with the client that there may be other potential collateral consequences of the judgment and sentence, such as deportation or other effects on immigration status; motor vehicle or other licensing; parental rights; possession of firearms; voting rights; employment, military, and government service considerations; and the potential exposure to or impact on any federal charges.

(c) Counsel should be familiar with the sentencing procedures, including:

(1) the effect that plea negotiations may have upon the sentencing discretion of the court;

(2) the procedural operation of the applicable sentencing system, including concurrent and consecutive sentencing;

(3) the practices of those who prepare the sentencing services plan or presentence report, and the defendant's rights in that process;

(4) access to the sentencing services plan or presentence report by counsel and the defendant;

(5) the defense sentencing presentation and/or sentencing memorandum;

(6) the opportunity to challenge information presented to the court for sentencing purposes;

(7) the availability of an evidentiary hearing to challenge information, and the applicable rules of evidence and burdens of proof at such a hearing; and

(8) the participation that victims and prosecution or defense witnesses may have in the sentencing proceedings.

Guideline 8.3 Preparation for Sentencing

In preparing for sentencing, counsel should consider the need to:

(a) inform the client of the applicable sentencing requirements, options, and alternatives, and the sentencing judge's practices and procedures if known;

(b) maintain regular contact with the client prior to the sentencing hearing, and inform the client of the steps being taken in preparation for sentencing;

(c) obtain from the client relevant information concerning such subjects as his or her background and personal history, prior criminal record, employment history and skills, education, medical and mental health history and condition, and financial status, and obtain from the client sources through which the information provided can be corroborated;

(d) inform the client of his or her right to speak at the sentencing proceeding and assist the client in preparing the statement, if any, to be made to the court, after considering the possible consequences that any admission of guilt may have on an appeal, subsequent retrial, or trial on other offenses;

(e) inform the client of the effects that admissions and other statements may have on an appeal, retrial, or other judicial proceedings, such as collateral or restitution proceedings;

(f) inform the client if counsel will ask the court to consider a particular sentence or range of sentences; and

(g) collect and present documents and affidavits to support the defense position and, where relevant, prepare and present witnesses to testify at the sentencing hearing.

Guideline 8.4 The Sentencing Services Plan or Presentence Report

(a) Counsel should be familiar with the procedures concerning the preparation and submission of a sentencing services plan or presentence report, and should consider the tactical implications of requesting that a plan be prepared.

(b) If a plan is prepared, counsel should:

(1) provide to the official preparing the plan relevant information favorable to the client, including, where appropriate, the client's version of the offense;

(2) prepare the client to be interviewed by the person preparing the plan;

(3) review the completed plan and discuss it with the client;

(4) try to ensure the client has adequate time to examine the completed plan; and

(5) take appropriate steps to ensure that erroneous or misleading information that may harm the client is challenged or deleted from the plan.

Guideline 8.5 The Prosecution's Sentencing Position

Unless there is a sound tactical reason for not doing so, counsel should attempt to determine whether the prosecution will advocate that a particular type or length of sentence be imposed, including the factual basis for any sentence in the aggravated range.

Guideline 8.6 The Defense Sentencing Theory

Counsel should prepare a defense sentencing presentation and, where appropriate, a defense sentencing memorandum. Among the topics counsel may wish to include in the sentencing presentation or memorandum are:

(a) information favorable to the defendant concerning such matters as the offense, mitigating factors and relative culpability, prior offenses, personal background, employment record and opportunities, educational background, and family and financial status;

(b) information that would support a sentencing disposition other than incarceration, such as the potential for rehabilitation or the nonviolent nature of the crime;

(c) information concerning the availability of treatment programs, community treatment facilities, and community service work opportunities;

(d) challenges to incorrect or incomplete information, and inappropriate inferences and characterizations that are before the court; and

(e) a defense sentencing proposal.

Guideline 8.7 The Sentencing Process

(a) Counsel should be prepared at the sentencing proceeding to take the steps necessary to advocate fully for the requested sentence and to protect the client's legal rights and interests.

(b) Where appropriate, counsel should be prepared to present supporting evidence, including testimony of witnesses, affidavits, letters, and public records, to establish the facts favorable to the defendant.

(c) Where the court has the authority to do so, counsel should request specific orders or recommendations from the court concerning the place of confinement and psychiatric treatment or drug rehabilitation, and against deportation or exclusion of the defendant.

(d) Where appropriate, counsel should prepare the client to personally address the court. In addition, counsel should prepare any expert and other witnesses to address the court.

(e) After the sentencing hearing is complete, counsel should fully explain to the client the terms of the sentence, including any conditions of probation.

STATE OF NORTH CAROLINA   IN THE GENERAL COURT OF JUSTICE
                                                      SUPERIOR COURT DIVISION

COUNTY OF MECKLENBURG

STATE OF NORTH CAROLINA)
)   **EX PARTE MOTION FOR**
          VS   )   **FUNDS FOR PSYCHOLOGIST**
)
)
          Defendant.   )

NOW COMES Robert L. Ward, attorney for the defendant, and makes this *ex parte* Motion to the Court for allocation of funds to assist in the evaluation and preparation of the defense of the defendant. This Motion is made pursuant to the authority of *Ake v. Oklahoma* 470 U.S. 68, 84 L. Ed. 2d 53 (1985), *State v. Ballard*, 333 N.C. 515 (1993), *State v. Bates*, 333 N.C. 523 (1993), and North Carolina Gen. Stat. 7A-450(b), 451 and 454.

In support of this Motion, the undersigned shows the Court as follows:

1.   The defendant is an indigent citizen who is charged in these cases with violation of probation and he faces three consecutive sentences of _____.

2.   The defendant is currently incarcerated at the Mecklenburg County Jail.

3.   The defendant is to have a forensic exam for competency and is need of further examination for purposes of his defense and disposition of the probation cases.

4.   Based upon interviews with the defendant and upon information gathered in investigation of his prior history, the undersigned attorney for the defendant has determined that an evaluation of the defendant by an expert in the field of psychology is necessary to determine competency to stand trial and to conform his conduct to the requirements of law, whether his capacity to conform his conduct to the requirements of law was impaired, and to identify and provide expert testimony as to statutory and non-statutory mitigating factors at any probation revocation hearing.

5.   The defendant's attorney lacks the necessary expertise to sufficiently determine the extent of any defendant's social, mental health status or history. Counsel is in need of the assistance of a psychologist to assist him in defending the defendant against the charge or in sentencing.

Accordingly, the undersigned requests that the Court grant the following relief:

1.   That this Motion be treated as a verified affidavit in the cause.

2.   Authorize counsel for the defendant to retain the services of a psychiatrist for the purpose of assisting in evaluating mitigating circumstances and in placing the defendant in appropriate mental health treatment, in an initial amount not to exceed $1500.00, without further authorization of this Court.

3.   Require the State of North Carolina to pay the costs and assessments in accordance with the order of this Court.

4.   That this Motion and any orders resulting there from be sealed and preserved for appellate review.

5. For such other relief as the Court deems just and proper.

Respectfully submitted this the _____

_____
Robert L. Ward
Assistant Public Defender
720 E. Fourth St., Suite 308
Charlotte, North Carolina 28202
(704) 347-7870

Sworn to an subscribed before me
On this the ____ day of _____.

_____
Notary Public

My Commission Expires: _____

STATE OF NORTH CAROLINA	IN THE GENERAL COURT OF JUSTICE
	SUPERIOR COURT DIVISION

COUNTY OF MECKLENBURG

STATE OF NORTH CAROLINA	)	
	)	**EX PARTE ORDER FOR**
VS	)	**FUNDS FOR PSYCHOLOGIST**
	)	
	)	
Defendant.	)	

THIS MATTER came on before the undersigned Judge presiding in the Superior Court for Mecklenburg County on the written *ex parte* Motion of the defendant for funds for a psychologist to assist in the defense of this case. Based upon matters of record and upon the Motion, the Court finds as fact:

1. The defendant is indigent and entitled to assistance of an expert at the expense of the State in this case.

2. Based upon the information available to the Court at this time, the defense should not spend in excess of $1500.00 for a psychologist without further authorization of the Court.

The Court further finds as fact and concludes, as a matter of law [pursuant to the authority of *Ake v Oklahoma*, 470 U.S. 68, 84 L. Ed. 2d 53 (1985), *State v. Ballard*, 333 N.C. 515 (1993), *State v Bates*, 333 N.C. 523 (1993), and North Carolina Gen. Stat. 7A-450(b) 451 and 454], that the defendant is entitled to the assistance of a psychologist at the expense of the State of North Carolina, in an amount not to exceed $1500.00 without further authorization of the Court.

It is therefore ORDERED, ADJUDGED and DECREED that:

1. The defendant, through counsel, may retain the services of a psychologist to assist in preparation of the defense of this case, in an amount not to exceed $1500.00 without further authorization of the Court.

2. The State of North Carolina, through its Administrative Office of the Courts, will pay the expert retained by the defendant pursuant to this authorization.

3. The defendant's *ex parte* Motion for funds and this Order will be sealed in the Court file and retained for appellate review.

This the _____ day of _____.

_____
The Honorable
Superior Court Judge Presiding

This document is sealed by order of this Court and is not to be opened without further order of this Court.

This the _____ day of February, 2001.

_____
The Honorable

| STATE OF NORTH CAROLINA | IN THE GENERAL COURT OF JUSTICE |
| | SUPERIOR COURT DIVISION |

COUNTY OF MECKLENBURG

STATE OF NORTH CAROLINA)
)
)
VS)   MOTION FOR APPROPRIATE
)   RELIEF
)
)
Defendant.)

NOW COMES the defendant, _____, by and through his undersigned counsel, and moves the court pursuant to N.C.G.S. Section 15A-1415(b)(3) and (c) to set aside the conviction and pleas in the above cases and reset the case for hearing, and in support of this motion the defendant states as follows:

1. That on ____ the defendant appeared in Mecklenburg County Courtroom for a probable cause hearing pursuant to a pending probation violation. Against advice of counsel and after court admonishment, the defendant elected to admit the violations and sought to have his sentence activated, and the Court accepted the admission of willful violation, and the sentences were revoked (two were consolidated).

2. Upon subsequent information and further investigation by undersigned counsel, a hearing was scheduled during the same term of court to raise issues of a knowing and voluntary admission of a probation violation, and to reschedule the matter for a violation hearing.

3. That based on that investigation and upon inquiry of the defendant by the Court in open court _____, Superior Court Judge presiding, pursuant to undersigned counsel's oral motion for appropriate relief, set aside the revocation of probation and ordered that a competency evaluation be conducted. The signed Order is attached as Exhibit A and incorporated by reference.

4. That pursuant to that Order, two evaluations were conducted concerning the defendant's mental capacity. Reports from those evaluations would indicate that the defendant is currently in the borderline to mild mental retardation range, with a vocabulary level of a seven year old. That at the time these charges appeared in court for plea and conviction, there had been no evaluation or assessment of the defendant.

5. Given the defendant's social and academic history and the reports from the evaluations, the defendant's mental capacity was highly likely that of a seven-year-old when the pleas and convictions in the above cases were made.

6. That at the time the plea was taken and Judgment was entered on _____, the transcript of plea indicated the defendant could read and write at the ninth grade level. This was not correct.

7. That because the defendant, at the time of plea and conviction, was treated and communicated to as though he were a person of at least below average to average intelligence and education, it is highly unlikely that he understood and comprehended the information conveyed and the rights waived on the plea transcript. As a result, the defendant did not knowingly and understandingly waive his rights to trial.

8. That subsequent to the defense disclosure of the report to the District Attorney's Office, it was reported that in the defendant's confession, the defendant stated that he broke into the house because his life was threatened if he did not do so.

9. That if the new information concerning the defendant's mental capacity were to have been available prior to the plea and conviction, the defense of duress should have been pursued. This would likely have resulted in a different outcome.

WHEREFORE, the defendant prays the Court to grant this motion and set aside the _____ Judgment and pleas of guilty in these cases.

This the ___ day of _____.

Robert L. Ward
Assistant Public Defender
720 E. Fourth St., Suite 308
Charlotte, North Carolina 28202
(704) 347-7870

Sworn to an subscribed before me
On this the ____ day of, _____.

_____

Notary Public

My Commission Expires: _____

This is to certify that the foregoing Motion for Appropriate Relief was served upon _____, Assistant District Attorney by hand delivery.

This the ____ day of _____.

Robert L. Ward
Assistant Public Defender

STATE OF NORTH CAROLINA   IN THE GENERAL COURT OF JUSTICE
                                 SUPERIOR COURT DIVISION

COUNTY OF MECKLENBURG

STATE OF NORTH CAROLINA)
)   ORDER GRANTING
              VS   )   MOTION FOR APPROPRIATE
)   RELIEF
)
      Defendant.   )

THIS MATTER came on to be heard on _____ in Courtroom _____ before the undersigned Judge presiding in the Superior Court for Mecklenburg County on Defendant's Written Motion For Appropriate Relief pursuant to N.C.G.S. Section 15A-1414(b)(3) and (c) to set aside the Judgments in the above cases.

Based upon the hearing in open court, the Court makes the following FINDINGS OF FACT:

1. That on _____ the defendant appeared in Mecklenburg County Courtroom _____ for a probable cause hearing pursuant to a pending probation violation.

2. That on _____, the Honorable _____ set aside the Judgment of revocation entered on _____ and ordered an evaluation of the defendant.

3. That pursuant to that Order, two evaluations were conducted concerning the defendant's mental capacity. Reports from those evaluations would indicate that the defendant is currently in the borderline to mild mental retardation range, with a vocabulary level of a seven year old. That at the time these charges appeared in court for plea and conviction, there had been no evaluation or assessment of the defendant.

4. Given the defendant's social and academic history and the reports from the evaluations, the defendant's mental capacity was highly likely that of a seven-year-old when the pleas and convictions in the above cases were made.

5. That at the time the plea was taken and Judgment was entered on _____, the transcript of plea indicated the defendant could read and write at the ninth grade level. This was not correct.

6. That because the defendant, at the time of plea and conviction, was treated and communicated to as though he were a person of at least below average to average intelligence and education, it is highly unlikely that he understood and comprehended the information conveyed and the rights waived on the plea transcript. As a result, the defendant did not knowingly and understandingly waive his rights to trial.

7. That subsequent to the defense disclosure of the report to the District Attorney's Office, it was reported that in the defendant's confession, the defendant stated that he broke into the house because his life was threatened if he did not do so.

8. That if the new information concerning the defendant's mental capacity were to have been available prior to the plea and conviction, the defense of duress should have been pursued. This would likely have resulted in a different outcome.

9. That defense counsel has furnished to Assistant District Attorney _____ copies of defendant's evaluations and has discussed with him opportunities for counseling and supervision that have been explored on behalf of the defendant. Based upon the unique facts and circumstances of this case the District Attorney's Office consents to the entry of an order setting aside the original conviction in this case and to then dismiss this charge against the defendant.

Based on the foregoing FINDINGS OF FACT, the Court makes the following CONCLUSIONS OF LAW:

1. That based on N.C.G.S. Sections 15A-1414 (b)(3) and (c) the Judgments should be set aside and the matter rescheduled for arraignment or other disposition.

Based upon the foregoing FINDINGS OF FACT AND CONCLUSIONS OF LAW it is therefore ORDERED, ADJUDGED AND DECREED:

1. That the Judgment and Sentence entered in open court on _____ be set aside and the pleas of guilty withdrawn.

This the ___ day of _____

By consent:

_____
The Honorable _____
Superior Court Judge Presiding

_____
Assistant District Attorney

_____
Robert L. Ward
Assistant Public Defender

xi. Beth Bromberg,[*] A Defense Lawyer's Perspective on the Use of Apology

Conventional wisdom teaches defense lawyers not to allow their clients to speak in any significant way at their sentencing hearings even when the judge asks whether the accused has anything to say before being sentenced. While this may be the opportune time for the client to apologize, the dangers can be significant. Assuming that the sentencing submissions have gone well, and counsel has indicated that their client is remorseful, the client's own words have the potential to make things much worse. What if the client says something to indicate that they no longer admit that the alleged facts are true, and the plea has to be struck? What if they apologize, but try to cast some of the blame on the complainant/victim? What if they ramble inarticulately? What if they do not seem genuine? What if they do not have an appropriate demeanor, or have an unappealing personality? What if they clearly do not understand the issues, or they just apologize for wasting the judge's time, as if that is what really matters? What if there has been a sentencing agreement made that has been reviewed ahead of time with the Judge, and the sentence is a certainty in any event? Is there any point to having the client say something, thereby taking up valuable court time, maybe even making the Judge impatient that time is being wasted?

Because of these concerns, it was my practice, for many years, to have the client say nothing most of the time. If the sentence had already been cleared with the Judge, I

_____

[*] Beth Bromberg is a criminal defense lawyer from Hamilton, Ontario, Canada. She has over 20 years of experience, and a very busy defense practice, representing adults and youth on all kinds of charges from the most minor property offences, to the most serious offences, including murder. Because of the nature of the legal aid system in Canada, she can be retained by clients privately, as well as through legal aid, and her practice consists of both types of retainers approximately equally. She is past president of the Hamilton Criminal Lawyers' Association, and a director or the Ontario Criminal Lawyers' Association. She is also retained on an occasional basis by the Crown Attorney's office and the Federal Department of Justice to prosecute Criminal Code and Narcotics offences.

would not have the client speak. If there was a reasonable joint submission (an agreement between defense counsel and prosecutor) being suggested, I would usually have my client remain silent because I knew that the Judge was almost certain to accede to the joint submission, and I would not want my client to do or say anything that could make things more uncertain. If an apology seemed expected or appropriate, I would coach my client to state simply, "I am very sorry. This will never happen again." Or, "I am very sorry. I will take all of my counseling to make sure this will never happen again." I would instruct my client in the strongest terms to SAY NOTHING ELSE! From a traditional defense perspective, this approach is very sound. Because of the inherent risk, it is usually prudent to advise the client to decline the opportunity to speak freely.

However, in appropriate cases, with a bit of time and care taken to help the client genuinely understand how their actions have harmed another person, and to genuinely express their remorse, defense lawyers can do a great deal to make the sentencing experience much more therapeutic for both the client and the complainant by facilitating an apology.

The Victim Impact Statement

The traditional belief is that the victim impact statement is prepared for the Judge's consideration in deciding an appropriate sentence. While this is true in many cases, there is often a joint submission on sentencing, or an agreement that has already been approved by the judge. In these situations, the victim impact statement will have little, if any, effect on the length of the sentence ordered. One is left to wonder: what is the point of waiting for the victim impact statement, or reviewing it with the Judge or the accused, when it has no real potential of affecting the length of the sentence imposed?

In my view, however, the most significant benefit of the victim impact statement lies in what the accused can learn from it. If the client is able to offer an apology based on a genuine understanding of the harm caused to the victim, the sentencing experience will be more beneficial, and may motivate the client toward rehabilitation. Additionally, the dangers of the client's own words adversely affecting the sentence are diminished if the client understands the issues, and is properly prepared.

Example 1

Some time ago I had an interesting experience with the use of a victim impact statement. My client (who had a criminal record for sexual assault and the criminal harassment of a number of women) was being sentenced for sexually assaulting a female acquaintance in her own living room, in the presence of her young son. The victim did not scream or overtly demonstrate her extreme level of distress and alarm when she was trying to resist the sexual assault, because she did not want to frighten her child. My client also had a mild acquired brain injury which affected his ability to empathize and read social cues. I was quite concerned that my client would continue to commit sexual assaults once he completed his sentence because he had absolutely no insight into his issues. Obviously, I could not express my concerns to anyone, although I ensured that my client would have appropriate counseling upon his release from custody. I tried to explain the typical impact of a sexual assault to my client, and I talked to him about the need to make absolutely certain that any potential sex partner is consenting freely. He still had absolutely no insight into the harm he had caused. I told my client that I could ask the Judge for a recommendation that he serve his sentence at a correctional facility that specialized in rehabilitating sex offenders. He refused, indicating that he did not want to go any place where there would be "diddlers".

I had negotiated a reasonably lenient sentence with the prosecutor, and I had met with the judge in chambers for a pretrial, so I knew exactly what the sentence would be. There was no need for my client to say anything at the sentencing hearing, and given his lack of remorse and insight, I believed it would be best for him to say nothing.

Immediately before the sentencing hearing, the prosecutor handed me a victim impact statement. The case had been called, and there was no time for me to review the statement with my client. Initially, I thought it would not matter if my client never saw the victim impact statement. He had no empathy anyway, and there was no potential for the victim impact statement to change the sentence previously agreed upon by the Judge. I read the statement to check it for any content that was not appropriate. The statement was extremely articulate, and it detailed clearly and graphically, the profound impact that the sexual assault had on the victim. Among other things, she felt unsafe in her own home—the place where she should feel most secure. She worried about being able to protect her son, and she suffered from depression. She had become unable to be intimate with her husband, and her marriage had suffered. The victim wanted to read her statement out loud in court, and I was concerned that my client might react inappropriately and loudly, so I asked for a brief recess to review the statement with my client. Even then, my client seemed angry at the victim for reporting him, and causing him to go to jail. I told my client to be quiet in court, and to say absolutely nothing when the statement was being read, and when the Judge asked if he had anything to say.

My client listened intently while the victim read her very powerful, personal, and heartfelt victim impact statement to the court. I was surprised by how moving it was. I was even more surprised to find that my client was profoundly affected. He stood and cried as he listened. When the judge finally asked him if he wished to say anything before sentencing, he made an obviously sincere apology directly to the victim. He clearly understood the impact of his actions, and he asked the judge to recommend that he serve his sentence at a facility where he could get help so he would never harm anyone like that again.

Example 2

On another occasion, I was representing a client on a robbery of a female taxi driver. The allegations could be proved, and my client agreed it would be best to plead guilty. The facts were egregious. My client had forced the woman to drive while he was holding a gun to her head. After terrifying her, my client robbed the woman of her money, and finally allowed her to run away while he stole the taxi. I had negotiated a penitentiary sentence that I considered fair in the circumstances, and I had pretried it with the Judge. There was no question of what the sentence would be. I took the victim impact statement with me to the court cells and reviewed it with my client. I made sure he understood it completely. We had already talked about his drug addiction, the root causes of his behavior, and what steps he would need to take to rehabilitate himself. I told my client that the victim would be in the body of the court and that he might want to make an apology. I told him that the apology would not affect the sentence, and that it was his choice.

When my client said that he would like to apologize, I asked him to tell me what he wanted to say so that I could ensure that he understood the issues properly, and that the apology would be appropriate. When he was given his opportunity to speak, he apologized very sincerely to the victim for the terror he had caused her, and to his mother 'who had not raised him to behave that way'. I cannot say for sure what impact the apology had on my client, and specifically on his ability to turn his life around, although I believe it sent him off with the right attitude, and motivation. However, I can say that the apology had a significant positive effect on the victim and on my client's mother.

Outside of the courtroom the victim explained to my client's mother that she had come to court that day, because she wanted to know more about the young man who had robbed her. She needed to understand how something so disturbing and terrifying could have happened. She said that the apology meant the world to her, and she believed she would now be able to get over the fear that she had been experiencing since the robbery. She told my client's mother that she hoped her son would be able to get help for his drug addiction, and move forward to have a good life. The two women hugged and cried together, and I am certain that my client's apology, which led to this surprising connection between the two women, had a significant healing effect on both of them.

Example 3

Recently, I represented a client on a charge of Criminal Negligence Causing Death. My client was driving an old car that had never been insured or registered because it could not be certified to be safe. My client knew the car needed brake work, but he was driving with the repairs only half completed, because he could not afford any more, and he needed transportation for work. One day, on his way home from work, he was blinded by sunlight. Instead of stopping the car immediately, my client continued driving, assuming that he would be able to see the road again in a few seconds. At that moment he struck and killed a pedestrian who was crossing the road.

My client had never been in any kind of trouble before. He was mortified. He was paralyzed by guilt and depression. He began counseling to help him cope with his guilty conscience and remorse. Ultimately, I was able to use an accident reconstruction expert to prove that the outcome of the accident was not affected by the faulty brakes, and that the fatality was caused only by my client's decision to continue driving while he was blinded by sunlight. I was able to negotiate a guilty plea to the lesser charge of Dangerous Driving, with a conditional sentence (house arrest, except for work and counseling).

My client's guilty conscience was worsened when I reviewed the victim impact statement with him. The man he had killed had left behind a twin brother. Neither of the men had ever married, and they had always lived together, sharing everything, including expenses. The twin brother had suffered a terrible emotional loss, and was in financial difficulty.

In preparation for the sentencing hearing, I asked my client if he would like me to help him write an apology. I told him that it would not affect the sentence that I had already negotiated, but I believed that it might help him feel better and move forward. I told him that I knew he would be emotional, but that we could write it together and he could simply read it in court. He said that he genuinely wanted to apologize, but that he felt too traumatized by the court process, and his own guilt, and he thought he was not capable of apologizing in court. I asked if he would like me to apologize on his behalf to the victim's brother, and he said that he would like me to do that. At the recess I asked the police officer in charge of the case to join me so that I could talk to the victim's brother without fear of being accused of saying anything inappropriate. I told him that my client wished me to express his apology, but that he did not want to disturb him at this difficult time. I told him that my client was filled with regret and remorse, to the extent that he feared he could not articulate his own apology. When I made my sentencing submissions I repeated this theme.

After my client had been sentenced, he left the courtroom at the same time as the victim's brother. I asked my client one last time if he would like to say anything to the brother. (The brother had been clear that he would be happy to talk to my client.) Once the stress of the court proceeding was over, my client was able to apologize to the twin brother. The brother said that he forgave my client, and that he saw the incident as a terrible accident that could have happened to anyone. The two men hugged and cried together, as they had both been terribly affected by the same tragedy.

When I ran into my client on the street a few months later, I asked him how he was doing. He said that he was on his way home from a counseling appointment, and the house arrest was fine. He said that he felt better, and more able to move forward with his life, because he had apologized, and the victim's brother had forgiven him.

Example 4

On another occasion I represented a seventeen year old girl on charges of Break and Enter, Theft, and Mischief. She was accused of breaking into a house with a number of other youths, and stealing various items, as well as spray painting, and breaking things in the house, causing about $50,000 in damage. One of the youths was the daughter of the homeowner, and as a result, the insurance policy would not cover the loss. Since my client did not personally participate in causing the damage, and since she may not have known at the outset that the homeowner's daughter was not permitted in the home (and probably because of her sympathetic circumstances), I was able to negotiate that my client would plead guilty only to Theft Under $5000.00, and Being Unlawfully in a Dwelling. The sentence would certainly be probation since my client was a youthful first offender, but the restrictiveness of the probation conditions was in issue as the offence had caused a great deal of harm to the victim.

At the sentencing hearing, I explained that my client had been living at a youth shelter because her stepfather had assaulted her, and he was placed on probation conditions to have no contact with her, for her protection. Since my client's mother wanted to maintain her relationship with the stepfather, she had taken my client to a youth shelter so that her husband could live at home without breaching the probation order. My client, who had never been in trouble before, had committed the offence with other youths from the shelter in order to have companionship.

Because of these circumstances, I helped my client prepare for the sentencing hearing by following a plan that involved getting counseling, stable housing, schooling, and a part time job. I asked her to save $100.00 from her wages to contribute to restitution, even though the value was insignificant compared to the amount of the loss. I also suggested that my client take the opportunity in court to make a very simple apology when asked if she had anything to say before sentencing.

The complainant was not in court for the sentencing hearing, but the details were reported in the newspaper. After court I mailed the restitution check to the complainant on behalf of my client. A few weeks later I received a note from the complainant, asking me to forward a letter to my client. The letter read:

> Dear L.,
>
> Thank-you for your considerate check, which is a gesture we appreciate. Our biggest hope is that you will move forward with your life in positive ways after

this incident. Be of good courage, have integrity and do things that make you proud of yourself. God bless you.

Sincerely,

The B. family

I do not know what impact that letter had on my client. I do know that she is still in school and working part time, and staying out of trouble.

Conclusion/Other Considerations

A properly prepared apology can have a very positive impact in the right circumstances. However, defense counsel must, above all else, protect their client's interests. There are times when an apology is not appropriate or advisable. Normally, the client is under conditions not to have any contact with the victim. When the client asks in the early stages of the proceedings if they can call the victim to apologize, or if they can send a letter of apology, the answer must be: absolutely not—yet. The client must be cautioned against breaching bail conditions. Additionally, an apology can be used by the prosecutor as an admission of guilt to strengthen the case against the client. As a result, an apology cannot be considered until the decision has been made that there will definitely be a guilty plea, and usually until the plea negotiations have been completed. Then, the apology should normally be made in court at the time of sentencing so there is no possibility of an accusation of impropriety. An appropriate apology can sometimes help the client achieve a better sentence. However, more often, the benefit of the apology is in its therapeutic value to the people involved. Without ever compromising the client's legal interests, defense counsel can, and should, always be alert to possible therapeutic opportunities that may promote healing and rehabilitation, and give their clients the skills and confidence to move forward with their lives, and avoid making the same mistakes again.

xii. Michael S. King,* Therapeutic Jurisprudence, Criminal Law Practice and the Plea of Guilty

The traditional role of a lawyer is to secure the best outcome for the client. In criminal proceedings this is commonly regarded as an acquittal or upon conviction the least possible sentence in the circumstances. Once the broad parameters of the client's instructions have been defined—which are generally determined by the nature of the intended plea—the strategy of how this is to be secured is largely in the hands of the lawyer. Apart from certain formalities such as confirming identity and a plea to charges and the client's giving of evidence at trial—if he elects to give evidence—the talking in court and interaction with the bench is carried out by the lawyer.

With the emergence of problem solving courts and the emergence of different vectors in what Daicoff has called "the comprehensive law movement"—such as therapeutic jurisprudence, preventive law, collaborative law, holistic law, and restorative justice—lawyers are questioning the very nature of their role and the processes they use in interacting with clients, courts, justice system agencies and the community.[1]

---

* Michael King is a senior research fellow in the Faculty of Law at Monash University. He previously served as magistrate at Geraldton, Western Australia and in the Perth Drug Court, where he applied Therapeutic Jurisprudence in his work.

1. Susan Daicoff, *The Role of Therapeutic Jurisprudence Within the Comprehensive Law Movement,* in PRACTICING THERAPEUTIC JURISPRUDENCE 465 (Dennis P Stolle, David B. Wexler & Bruce J. Winick eds., 2000).

Therapeutic jurisprudence suggests there are good reasons for a more active and involved client in all court and tribunal proceedings.[2] These reasons have their basis in procedural justice research and findings from the behavioral sciences as to what works in motivating behavioral change that are highly relevant to securing client and justice system goals.

Procedural justice research emphasizes the importance litigants place in being able to tell their story to an attentive court or tribunal who is genuinely concerned about the litigant's situation, treats the litigant with respect, is interested in hearing the litigant's story and demonstrates that that story has been taken into account in the court or tribunal's decision-making process.[3]

In other words, litigants value courts that apply an ethic of care. People see social institutions and people in authority with whom they interact as important in valuing their identity and status in the community; treating them with an ethic of care confirms their status as a valued member of society worthy of respect.[4] As a result, people respect the institution of the court—or other justice system instrumentality or professional—and obey its orders. The opposite can be expected when the court or other institution's procedures denigrate the individual and fail to demonstrate an understanding of or interest in the individual's story or wellbeing.

Tyler points out that these factors are also valued by people who encounter other justice system professionals such as the police.[5] Lawyers, as officers of the court, are justice system professionals who assist clients to negotiate the system to achieve beneficial outcomes within the boundaries of the law. It is suggested that these aspects of communication are also important in the lawyer-client relationship. The importance of narrative —of telling one's story to an attentive and concerned professional in promoting trust— and the setting and promotion of client goals is also recognized in the health professions, such as medicine.[6]

A recurring theme through legal, behavioral science, economic, political, social and spiritual literature is the value people place on self-determination.[7] Self-determination is seen to be important for motivation and achievement. It can inspire a person to engage more fully in a course of conduct. In contrast, people often resent being told how to live their lives. By taking a coercive or paternalistic approach a judicial officer, lawyer or other professional is at risk of implying that those who are the subject of this approach are incompetent to make adequate decisions concerning their wellbeing. Few are willing to accept such a message. If they are, the approach may simply be counterproductive by reinforcing doubts they have in their own ability to lead a constructive and law-abiding life.

From this perspective, a court that involves a party in decision making in matters intimately concerned with the party's wellbeing is more likely to earn the party's respect,

---

2. JUDGING IN A THERAPEUTIC KEY (Bruce J. Winick & David B. Wexler eds., 2003).

3. Tom R. Tyler, The Psychological Consequences of Judicial Procedures: Implications for Civil Commitment Hearings, in LAW IN A THERAPEUTIC KEY, 3 (David B. Wexler & Bruce Winick eds. 1996).

4. *Id.* at 10.

5. Tom R. Tyler, *Trust and Law-Abidingness: A Proactive Model of Social Regulation* 81 B. U. L. REV. 361 (2001).

6. Warren Brookbanks, *Narrative Medical Competence and Therapeutic Jurisprudence: Moving Towards a Synthesis*, (2003) 20 LAW IN CONTEXT 74.

7. Bruce J Winick, *On Autonomy: Legal and Psychological Perspectives*, 37 VILL. L. REV. 1705 (1992); Michael S King, *What can Mainstream Courts Learn from Problem Solving Courts?* ALT. L. J. (2007).

trust and compliance with court orders than a court that takes a coercive approach.[8] That is why a problem solving court such as a drug court may ask a person to set goals and strategies for their time in a court program and support the person in the implementation of the plan rather than ordering them to do what the judicial officer thinks is best for them.[9]

Lawyers can also adopt therapeutic principles in their practice—such as voice, validation and respect and self-determination—to promote a more constructive and less traumatic court experience for clients and the achievement of client goals.[10] This article uses a case involving a plea of guilty to illustrate how lawyers can take a therapeutic approach to legal practice.

The degree to which therapeutic strategies need to be applied will vary. Most criminal cases are relatively minor and will be disposed of quickly upon a plea of guilty by way of fine with little need for follow-up in relation to the defendant. Here all that may be required is for the lawyer to listen to the client, show that she has listened, express empathy for the client's situation, to present the client with the options open and upon the client's instructions to appear in court and present a simple and short plea in mitigation that covers the critical issues including relevant issues raised by the client.

More serious criminal cases—particularly where there are entrenched patterns of offending and significant offending related problems such as substance abuse or domestic violence—provide a greater scope for the application of therapeutic principles. The approach described in this article assumes cases involving more serious offending and entrenched problems.

Therapeutic Lawyering from Taking Instructions to Sentencing in Court

Therapeutic lawyering does not derogate from basic aspects of legal practice such as the taking of adequate instructions, giving of advice, preparation of the case, negotiation, and courtroom advocacy. But it does highlight the importance of the lawyer's exercise of proper communication skills and client involvement at each stage.

For example, in the taking of instructions, the lawyer seeks to promote the client telling their story. Sensitivity as to environment and to personal issues relating to the client impacting upon communication—such as illness, mental health problems, language or cultural issues—is important in promoting open communication. Some environments where instructions are taken in criminal cases are not ideal in terms of promoting comfortable communication—such as a prison or court detention facilities. Here it is particularly important for the lawyer to try to allay client concerns so as to promote sound communication.

The lawyer should take note of both the factual and emotive content of the client's instructions. The lawyer uses strategies to show that he or she is listening such as repeating key aspects of the instructions back to the client, acknowledging emotive content—"It seems from what you are saying you were angry with your wife, were you?"—and asking other clarifying questions where necessary. Expressing empathy for the client's situation where appropriate is important in promoting an ethic of care and promoting client trust in the lawyer.

---

8. Winick, *supra* n 7.
9. Michael S King, *Problem-Solving Court Judging, Therapeutic Jurisprudence and Transformational Leadership*, 17 JJA 115 (2008).
10. David B. Wexler, *Therapeutic Jurisprudence and the Rehabilitative Role of the Criminal Defense Lawyer,* 17 ST. THOMAS L. REV. 743.

Ascertaining a client's feelings in relation to a matter may give the lawyer a critical insight into what a client is seeking from the case. For example, in a domestic violence case, the client may be filled with guilt for his actions and concerned about the wellbeing of his partner. This may suggest the client's openness to engage in rehabilitation programs and provide a convenient stepping stone in the conversation to the client's desired outcome.

In any case, taking an approach that promotes self-determination, the lawyer should ask the client what outcome the client seeks from the case. Sometimes client outcomes are clearly not feasible — such as an acquittal in the presence of overwhelming evidence of guilt. Instead of being dismissive of the client's wishes — with its potential to make the client resistant to further communication and/or advice from the lawyer, the lawyer could draw the client's attention to the evidence and ask the client what he or she thinks a court would find in such a case. If the client considers an acquittal is open, then the lawyer is of course under a duty to convey the lawyer's opinion as to the likely outcome. It is the client's choice whether to proceed to trial or not.

In most cases, a client will wish to plead guilty without any prompting from the lawyer. The client is often keen to act to address underlying issues. A time of personal crisis can prompt people to consider their situation, the reasons for the crisis and to undertake remedial action, including behavioral change.[11] In a criminal case this can include the client returning stolen property, paying restitution to a victim, participating in victim offender mediation and engaging in rehabilitation programs.

However, there are a small core of hard cases where a client will plead guilty but not acknowledge the existence of underlying problems that has resulted in a cycle of offending. Birgden suggests that lawyers can adapt principles and practices commonly used in counseling to assist in such cases.[12] She suggests that the Transtheoretical Stages of Change Model can be used to identify the stage the client is at in relation to behavioral change. She proposes that lawyers use motivational interviewing techniques that could encourage clients to move from a stage where they do not acknowledge the existence of a problem to a stage where they not only acknowledge the problem but take active steps to change. It is important that criminal lawyers are familiar with these principles not only to assist in interacting with clients but also to assist in advising them, as the principles may well be used by a therapeutically minded judge or magistrate in interacting with the lawyers' clients in court.[13]

There will also be cases where the client's instructions raise a legitimate defense to charges before the court but where the client insists on pleading guilty or decides not to contest the charges so as to avoid prolonged engagement in the court or justice process or for other reasons. Voice, validation, respect and promoting self-determination are as important here as at any other stage of criminal law practice. Indeed, a coercive approach: telling the client forcefully to "get real" may promote resistance and impede the lawyer-client relationship. Here the lawyer would explore the client's reasons for the proposed action fully, acknowledge the reasons and express empathy concerning the client's situation.

---

11. See generally: JUDGING IN A THERAPEUTIC KEY, *supra* n 2, at 177–180.
12. Astrid Birgden, *Dealing with the Resistant Criminal Client: A Psychologically-Minded Strategy for More Effective Legal Counseling*, 38 CRIM. L. B. 225 (2002).
13. Michael S. King, *The Therapeutic Dimension of Judging: The Example of Sentencing* 16 JOURNAL OF JUDICIAL ADMINISTRATION 92(2006) http://spa.american.edu/justice/pubcats.php?subnumber=72.

Naturally the lawyer would explore with the client his or her understanding of the legal and other consequences of the proposed course of action. For example, the lawyer could ask the client to state its advantages and disadvantages. This would help to ensure that the client has carefully thought through all aspects of the proposed action. This process may result in the client reconsidering his instructions to the lawyer. If the clients instructions do not change, then the lawyer would advise the client as to alternative options available at law and ask the client to consider their advantages and disadvantages. The lawyer would also advise the client as to any limitations placed upon the lawyer's ability to represent the client upon non contest or a plea of guilty, including limitations as to what could be presented to the court in relation to penalty. For example, if the client instructs the lawyer to raise with the court the matter that discloses the client's possible defense, then a court may well refuse to accept the plea and set the matter for trial.

However, the bulk of criminal cases will be relatively straightforward: the client wishes to plead guilty, knows there is a problem and is keen to address it—either to avoid a prison term or to create a constructive, happy and law-abiding life or both.

A lawyer taking a therapeutic approach will take instructions as to the client's understanding of his or her offending related problems and what steps the client needs to take to address these problems. It is important that both client and lawyer are clear as to the nature of the problems and their resolution. A client may downplay the significance of a problem or refer to one problem but ignore others. If there is evidence of other problems, then naturally the lawyer will gently raise that evidence with the client and ask for the client's comment. If the client is resistant and the approach suggested by Birgden or a similar strategy does not yield results, then it is advisable not to probe further; that is the role of the appropriate health professionals.

It is an area that can be particularly sensitive for a client and the lawyer needs to tread carefully. A confrontational approach is fraught with risk. A client may have a long-standing substance abuse problem and be willing to discuss its effects on her life. But the trigger for that problem may have been the abuse she experienced as a child. The client may not feel comfortable in discussing such underlying issues and raising them may be cause her trauma and aggravate substance abuse issues. Sometimes the lawyer will be aware of these issues from past contact with the client or from court or other materials; with a new client, the lawyer may not be aware of issues such as past trauma.

Having the client state the problems and suggest their solution is a means of respecting the client's integrity and promoting their self-determination. It becomes the basis for taking an approach used by Dallas lawyer John McShane of having the client formulate a rehabilitation plan.[14] The plan sets out the client's strategies for addressing underlying issues in relation to the client's offending. In jurisdictions where plea-bargaining is possible, it provides evidence in support of the plea bargain. In jurisdictions where plea bargains are rarely or never used, it can be presented ahead of time to the prosecution in an endeavour to persuade the prosecution to present a united front to the court that a rehabilitation-based sentencing disposition should be used. In any jurisdiction it becomes a basis for persuading a court to use such a disposition. It is not so much a matter of convincing a court to be lenient as persuading the court that in the particular case greater weight should be apportioned to the factor of rehabilitation rather than deterrence or other factors that would lead to a term of imprisonment.

---

14. John V. McShane, *The Need for Healing* 89(5) A.B.A. J 59 (2003).

It is important that the plan be well-thought out, realistic and properly presented. An ill-conceived plan is likely to produce a result opposite to the one sought by the client. Naturally clients should consider rehabilitation programs appropriate to their needs. A comprehensive approach whereby all factors impacting upon offending — including substance abuse issues, accommodation, education, employment and relationships — is ideal but may not be possible given the availability of programs and the level of client motivation. It should also be considered whether the client should apply to be referred to a problem solving court program or a diversion program or whether the plan should be tailored for approval and a sentencing disposition in a general criminal list.

The situation of the victim should also be considered. The lawyer should raise issues of victim safety, payment of restitution and restorative justice approaches such as victim offender mediation with the client and seek instructions for the purposes of the preparation of the plan. If the client lacks genuine remorse or motivation to compensate the victim, then the client's motivation and commitment to reform may be in issue and require further exploration by the lawyer. In any event, if the client is equivocal in this area, it is best left out of the rehabilitation plan to prevent the possibility of non-compliance with the plan.

If the matter is to remain in a general criminal list, it is advisable for the rehabilitation plan to be presented with a submission as to the sentencing disposition to be used to facilitate the implementation of the plan. Most jurisdictions allow for probation or similar community based supervision. For example, in Western Australia the law allows a court to impose a presentence order where a term of imprisonment is warranted but the court considers an offender should have the opportunity of participating in rehabilitation programs for up to two years before the court finally determines the issue of sentence.[15] Many jurisdictions have a mechanism for adjournment of sentencing for good cause. The proposal could also suggest regular reports to the court from the offender's probation or community corrections officer and regular court reviews, where they are possible at law.

Wexler has described how a rehabilitation plan can be used in the form of an allocution statement in jurisdictions which provide for such statements.[16] In Australia and other jurisdictions where allocution statements are not used, the rehabilitation plan could be included in a letter from the defendant to the judicial officer and submitted by defense counsel to the court.

It is also preferable that the client, if possible, begin to implement the plan as soon as it has been formulated. Judicial officers are often faced with defendants in court professing their eagerness to reform but with little evidence of any commitment to the process. Judicial officers in such situations can often be skeptical of defendants' motives. On the other hand, a clear rehabilitation strategy with evidence of implementation by a defendant and with results achieved — as evidenced by supporting documents from treatment agencies, family members, employers etc — can be highly persuasive in achieving a rehabilitation oriented sentencing outcome. Where there has been no opportunity for the client to implement the plan, then the lawyer should explain to the court why this is the case.

By scheduling regular appointments with the client between the formulation of the rehabilitation plan and the client's appearance in court for the sentencing hearing the lawyer can monitor the client's progress, help the client fine tune the plan where

---

15. Sentencing Act 1995 Part 3A (Western Australia).
16. David B. Wexler, *Therapeutic Jurisprudence and Readiness for Rehabilitation* 8 FLA COASTAL L. REV. 111 (2006).

needed, engage in problem solving with the client where problems have arisen and praise and support any progress made by the client.

The next step is for the client, with the assistance of the lawyer, to determine the strategy for presenting the case to the court. Is the lawyer to do all the talking? Are the speaking duties in court to be shared? What documents are to be tendered? Are there to be written submissions as well as oral submissions? Is the client to write a letter to the court to accompany the rehabilitation plan?

As noted above, previously the involvement of a represented offender in court proceedings, depending on the jurisdiction, was limited. The emergence of therapeutic jurisprudence and problem solving courts has seen more represented offenders actively involved in court proceedings. Judicial officers who have been involved in problem solving court programs have found it to be valuable to communicate directly with the offender for several reasons: the judicial officer can gain a more comprehensive insight into the offender, develop a rapport with an offender and promote therapeutic and justice system goals such as rehabilitation and respect for the justice system. When these judicial officers return to general criminal lists, they will often bring their problem solving skills and approach with them. More judicial officers are becoming open to taking this approach.[17]

Advocacy on behalf of parties by professionals—lawyers—though an indispensable part of our justice system has its limitations. Skilled advocates do use affective content and method to good effect in court, but in method it is the affect of counsel rather than that conveyed by the client. The power of the emotive content of a client's story can be diminished when conveyed through a third party rather than directly. When the offender is genuine, it can be far more moving for a judge or magistrate to hear directly from an offender that the offender is remorseful and about the life problems that precipitated the offending behavior—taking in the offender's tone of voice, appearance, body language and words—than when the message is conveyed through counsel. It can add to the strength of the client's case that a rehabilitation based approach be taken by the court. It may be the factor that tips the balance in favor of a therapeutic sentencing outcome. Naturally, counsel would not advise a client to address the court where there are doubts as to the client's veracity.

The involvement of the client in speaking to the judicial officer does not displace the role of the lawyer. Instead, the client becomes a useful resource in advocacy. Together, the client and lawyer can present a powerful argument. While matters of law, outlining differences as to the facts between prosecution and defense, outlining key personal factors relating to the client and submissions as to sentence are properly the role of the lawyer, the lawyer could suggest that the client to speak in relation to why the offense was committed, any offending related problems and their impact and steps to reform both planned and undertaken.

There are a number of factors that will influence whether the lawyer will advise the client to take this approach. Many judicial officers will be open to hearing from the offender, while some may not wish to do so. Being rebuffed by the court may well be a difficult experience for a client. Knowing the judicial officer and the approach that judicial officer is likely to take is important.

Clients can be anxious, fearful, despondent, angry, or upset about a court appearance. They may not be accustomed to public speaking, much less so to speaking about

---

17. King, *supra* n 12.

personally sensitive matters in open court. There is a risk they may raise matters that could aggravate their case. There may be cultural or language issues impacting upon the ability to communicate in court. Many of these issues can be resolved with the assistance of a lawyer sensitive to the client's issues and who is properly prepared and by a judicial officer who is patient and sensitive in dealing with the client in court. Having the client prepare some notes to assist in speaking to the court could help to allay concerns. If actually speaking to the court is inadvisable, then having the client write a letter to the court will be an acceptable substitute. However the author's experience as a judicial officer is that in the vast majority of cases, when an offender does address the court directly the offender performs well and assists the court to understand the offender's case more fully.

In many cases, clients will wish to make a personal contribution, particularly if they see that the judicial officer is likely to treat them with respect, express an interest in what they have to say and listen to them. In the author's experience, often offenders are eager to add something to what has been presented to the court by their lawyer or correct any perceived miscommunication of the client's case. If the lawyer knows that a therapeutic jurisprudence oriented judicial officer is to preside in the client's case, then having the client wait in the public gallery of the court prior to the client's case being called on and watching the judicial officer as she or he handles other cases can help the client relax and be more comfortable with and confident in the process of engaging with the court.

However, even if the client decides not to say anything to the court, the lawyer should warn the client that the judge or magistrate may ask the client questions directly. As has been noted, judicial officers applying therapeutic jurisprudence promote dialogue with offenders in court in order to promote therapeutic outcomes. The judicial officer will seek to establish a rapport with the offender, ascertain whether the offender understands the causes of his or her offending and whether the offender has realistic rehabilitation goals and strategies, and seek to support the offender's confidence in his or her ability to implement the goals and strategies. The lawyer can advise the client as to the likely questions a judge or magistrate may ask. Again, knowledge of the approach of the relevant judge or magistrate can assist the lawyer in giving this advice. If there are unique factors relating to the client that will affect communication between the Bench and offender, then the lawyer should alert the court to this fact.

Some court lists are very busy and the time that a court can spend in a case may be limited—particularly in lower court matters. If a therapeutic approach to sentencing is proposed by the lawyer on instructions from the client and the matter is to take some time, an application for an adjournment to a suitable time would be advisable.

If a court takes up the option of adjourning sentencing while the offender implements the rehabilitation plan, then the role of the lawyer is to support the client through the process—including advocacy at any review hearings before the court—and to provide particular assistance when the client encounters problems. Each client will have a unique path to tread, with its own challenges and its own ups and downs.[18] A lawyer's sensitivity to where the client is at and the application of appropriate communication skills is a significant aspect of the support process.

---

18. Michael S King, *Therapeutic Jurisprudence and Criminal Law Practice: A Judicial Perspective* 31 CRIM. L. J. 12, at 16; Deen Potter, *Lawyer, Social Worker, Psychologist and More: The Role of the Defense Lawyer in Therapeutic Jurisprudence* 1 eLAW J. (SPECIAL SERIES) 95 (2006) https://elaw.murdoch.edu.au/special_series.html.

The first step in the follow-up process is to ensure that the client understands what the court has ordered and the effect of any additional comments made by the judge or magistrate to the client. In the context of a court experience—which can be personally overwhelming—it is natural that the client may not recall or understand crucial aspects of the proceedings.

There are ethical issues that can arise in the follow-up process. For example, traditionally the client is not obliged to disclose to the court matters adverse to his or her case—such as a relapse into substance abuse. The lawyer generally must also follow this obligation not to disclose but is also under a higher duty not to mislead the court. On the other hand, from a therapeutic perspective, the client's recognition of relapse is vital for the healing process. If a client has relapsed, the lawyer may well advise the client to admit the relapse to the court and at the same time to present the court with the reasons for the relapse and a relapse prevention strategy. At a time of a relapse, the client may be particularly distressed, have self-doubts and have related life problems such as relationship breakdown, loss of a loved one or loss of employment. The lawyer's skills in promoting the telling of the story by the client, listening, empathy and promoting the client's self-determination are particularly important is assisting the client to handle the legal consequences of his or her actions.

If the relapse has been accompanied by serious offending, then the lawyer needs to prepare the client for the likely outcome of termination of the program and sentencing. If the sole problem is relapse and there is evidence that the offender has been making a genuine effort in relation to implementing the rehabilitation plan, then a therapeutically minded judicial officer is unlikely to terminate the program and immediately impose a sentence. The judicial officer will be primarily concerned with problem solving and will seek information as to the circumstances of the relapse and ways to resolve the situation from the offender.[19] The judicial officer will also seek to support the offender's ability to implement the relapse prevention strategy. If such a strategy is not presented in court, then the judge or magistrate will engage in a dialogue with the offender to facilitate the formulation of a strategy.

Not all clients will have problems in the course of implementing their rehabilitation plan and many of those who do will also have made some significant progress along the way. Problem solving court judges and magistrates are learning about the power of praise in encouraging offenders and reinforcing the progress that has been made. It is an approach that can readily be used by criminal lawyers in supporting their clients in their progress through a court sanctioned rehabilitation plan.

Conclusion

A therapeutic approach to court practice is changing the dynamics of courtrooms, particularly in the context of sentencing. These dynamics include more active judges and magistrates and more involved offenders. Criminal law practice needs to adapt to the new dynamics. Taking a therapeutic approach to criminal law advocacy in cases involving a plea of guilty is more of a partnership between client and lawyer than a client delegating all responsibility for the advocacy to the lawyer. At the same time, lawyers need to be aware where the court practice of a judicial officer who is to hear the client's case is closer to the conventional model so as to prepare a client and the courtroom strategy accordingly.

A therapeutic approach to criminal law practice has the potential to empower clients, to provide a more satisfying courtroom experience and to facilitate them breaking long-

---

19. King, *supra* n 12.

standing cycles of offending. It uses strategies based on findings as to "what works" in promoting compliance with counseling and treatment programs. It also offers the potential for a more rewarding criminal law practice: satisfied clients bring satisfaction to their lawyers for a job well-done. Therapeutic criminal law practice also challenges lawyers to expand their skill set, to think more deeply about how they interact with clients and how they prepare matters for hearing in a way that produces a better experience for clients in terms of process and outcome. In that regard, it mirrors the experience of judicial officers applying therapeutic jurisprudence who enjoy greater satisfaction from their work than other judicial officers.[20]

As problem solving courts continue to grow in number and as more judicial officers seek to apply therapeutic jurisprudence in general court lists, the demand for lawyers conversant with a therapeutic jurisprudence approach to criminal law practice is likely to increase.

xiii. JaneAnne Murray,[*] Easing Your Client's Experience of Federal Prison

(Reprinted with permission from
New York Law Journal, December 17, 2006)

The lengthy sentence imposed on former Enron CEO Jeffrey Skilling recently is a stark reminder that the U.S. Sentencing Guidelines have made federal prison a reality for many first-time offenders. In fact, one third of all federal inmates are first-time, nonviolent offenders. Moreover, because of the length of their sentences, many of these individuals, like Skilling and WorldCom founder Bernie Ebbers, are denied placement in camp facilities.

But whether an inmate is assigned to a camp without wires and fences or a locked two-person cell, few would disagree that prison life is a profoundly dehumanizing experience.

How then can a prospective inmate obtain the most favorable placement in federal prison? Some hire sentencing consultants, the best of whom—if hired early enough in the case—can position and prepare their client for the least onerous experience the Bureau of Prisons (BOP) offers. But defense lawyers can readily develop expertise in this area and exert a positive impact on the quality of prison time their clients serve.

This article will focus on the various ways before, during and after sentencing, in which attorneys can ease their client's passage through federal prison. While a defense lawyer's primary objective will always be to avoid or reduce a prison sentence, surprisingly minimal effort can substantially improve the client's experience of prison life—from securing a coveted lower-bunk pass, to entry into a program that makes participants eligible for early release.

Before the Sentencing

The groundwork for ameliorating a federal prison sentence is laid between the plea (or trial) and the sentence. During this time the Probation Department conducts the

---

20. Peggy Fulton Hora and Deborah J Chase, *Judicial Satisfaction when Judging in a Therapeutic Key* 7 CIL 8 (2003/2004).

* JaneAnne Murray is a criminal defense lawyer in New York City. She was previously an assistant federal public defender is the Eastern District of New York.

pre-sentence investigation and prepares the critical pre-sentence investigation report (PSR), a detailed portrait of the client's personal and criminal history. Akin to an academic transcript, the PSR accompanies a federal inmate throughout her prison experience and is used by the BOP to make several critical determinations about the inmate, including:

- *Designation:* Generally, an inmate will be designated to a facility matching her security level, within 500 miles of the inmate's home. BOP facilities are classified into one of five security levels, ranging from minimum (dormitory-style accommodations, limited or no perimeter fence and the lowest staff to inmate ratio) to high (locked single and two-person cells, tightly controlled movement and the highest staff to inmate ratio). An inmate's security level is calculated using an elaborate scoring system based on the inmate's current offense behavior and prior criminal conduct, age, education, substance abuse history and whether she was permitted to surrender to prison voluntarily.[1] In this process, the BOP primarily utilizes information from the PSR, unless superseded by the sentencing court's Judgment in a Criminal Case" and accompanying "Statement of Reasons" (collectively, the Judgment). Critically, in scoring the inmate's current and prior criminal conduct, the BOP will look beyond the actual finding of guilt and consider the often more serious underlying description of the offense, as set forth in the PSR. Certain factors, known as Public Safety Factors—such as a client's alien status, sex offender status or the length of the sentence—can preclude minimum security (camp) placement. In addition, the BOP may in its discretion apply "Management variables" to increase or lower an inmate's security level, based on such factors as the inmate's program needs or a finding that the inmate's scored security level is inconsistent with her security requirements.

- *Program Eligibility:* The BOP will use the PSR to determine an inmate's eligibility for a variety of educational and vocational programs. Of particular note is the Residential Drug Abuse Treatment Program (RDAP), a 500hour, six-to 12-month intensive substance abuse treatment program, which qualifies eligible graduates for a six-month halfway house placement and a sentence reduction of up to one year.[2] Candidates for the program must volunteer for it, have a documented substance abuse disorder (i.e., usually corroborated in the PSR), and 36 months or less remaining on their sentences. The sentence reduction is not available to deportable aliens, inmates previously convicted of certain violent offenses, or those whose current offense involved violence or the possession of a dangerous weapon.[3]

- *Medical Treatment:* The BOP will use the PSR, as supplemented by the Judgment, to determine any medical or mental health treatment appropriate for the

---

1. See BOP Program Statement 5100.08, Security Designation and Custody Classification Manual, Chapters. 3, 4 (available at www.bop.gov/policy/progstat/5100_008.pdf).

2. The sentence reduction is authorized by statute. See 18 USC §3621(e)(2).

3. The policies and procedures of RDAP are set forth in BOP Program Statement 5330.10, Drug Abuse Programs Manual, Inmate, available at www.bop.gov/policy/progstat/5330_010.pdf. Further information on early release eligibility can be found in BOP Program Statement 5331.01, Early Release Procedures Under 18 USC §3621(e), available at www.bop.gov/policy/progstat/5331_001.pdf; see also Ellis & Henderson, "Getting Out Early: BOP Drug Program," Criminal Justice 20, no. 2 (A.B.A. 2005). The other sentence-reducing program at the BOP (the boot-camp program for nonviolent, first-time offenders) was phased out last year.

inmate. The BOP will generally continue to provide the inmate's medical prescriptions (or their equivalent) listed in the PSR. Documented medical issues may entitle the inmate to certain exemptions. For example, back problems may secure the client a lower-bunk pass — a not insignificant privilege when the sleeping arrangements are dormitory-style.

- *Other:* The PSR is used to establish, among other items, visitation lists, religious affiliations, dietary restrictions and appropriate work assignments, as well as to assist in pre-release planning.

Given the preeminence of the PSR, it is critical that the defense lawyer play an active role during the pre-sentence investigation stage to influence this process to the client's advantage. The investigation is an opportunity for the lawyer to frame the PSR, not merely serve witness to it.

As part of the investigation, the assigned probation officer will schedule an interview with the client. In advance of that interview, the lawyer should fully debrief the client and family members on all matters pertinent to the PSR, from allergies to prescription medications to substance abuse history, in order to select the issues that need to be emphasized (or conversely downplayed) with the probation officer. A failure to mention alcohol or drug abuse problems could ruin the client's chances of getting into RDAP; an overemphasis on medical issues could cause the client to be designated unnecessarily to a facility with specialized medical care.

A cooperative relationship with the probation officer at this stage will usually be more productive than an adversarial one. At the interview, the lawyer should not hesitate to prompt the client to give more expansive answers or interject to provide additional relevant information. It is also helpful to provide the officer with all available corroborating documents. Detailed notes should be taken, in the event there is a dispute later about what was said After the PSR is issued, the lawyer should review it carefully with the client for any inaccuracies or omissions and communicate any objections to the probation officer in a timely manner. See FedRCrimP 32(f)(1) (requiring objections to be made within 14 days of receipt). While no inaccuracy is too small or immaterial to correct, particular attention should be paid to the descriptions of the client's role in the current offense and any alleged past criminal conduct. An improper application of a firearm enhancement in the sentencing calculation for the current case could render the client ineligible for the RDAP sentence reduction; an erroneous description of a prior domestic violence incident could negatively impact the client's security classification.

At the Sentencing

There are several applications that can be made to the sentencing judge, either orally or in writing, with the aim of enhancing the client's prison experience.

Most importantly, the lawyer should move for any amendments to the PSR that have not already been made by the Probation Department in response to the lawyer's previous objections.[4] The lawyer may also request judicial recommendations for designation to a particular facility or class of facilities, and admittance to a particular BOP pro-

---

4. Such amendments cannot be made after the sentencing. See, e.g., *United States v. Giaimo*, 880 F2d 1561, 1563 (2d Cir.1989) (no jurisdiction under FedRCrimP 32 to correct inaccuracies in PSR after a defendant has been sentenced).

gram, such as the RDAP. While not binding on the BOP, such recommendations have persuasive power, assuming the client meets the requisite eligibility criteria. In fact, the BOP must explain in writing to the court why it rejected the court's recommendation.[5]

Specific medical or mental health treatment may be requested for the client, mindful, of course, of the potential impact this application can have on the client's ultimate designation. If the judge imposed a fine or restitution, the lawyer can move for payment to commence after the completion of the prison sentence.[6] Finally, the lawyer should always request permission for the client to self-surrender (not just to spare the client the hospitality on "Con Air," but to improve the client's security score) and sufficient time for the client to get his or her affairs in order.[7]

Surprisingly minimal effort can substantially improve a client's experience of prison life—from getting a coveted lower-bunk pass, to entry in a program that makes early release more likely.

After the Sentencing

By the time the sentencing is over, most of the foundations of the client's federal prison experience are already set in stone. There are, nonetheless, several constructive steps the lawyer can take at this stage.

It is important to follow up with the probation officer to make sure the PSR is corrected according to the sentencing judge's instructions and that the corrected version is forwarded to the BOP. In addition, the Judgment should be reviewed to confirm it accurately reflects the rulings made at sentencing, and the court immediately petitioned for amendments if it does not. In certain situations, it might be helpful for the defense lawyer to write directly to the BOP on the issue of the client's designation, for example, where the lawyer believes the client's likely security level will overstate her security needs. If so, this letter should be written as soon as possible after the sentencing, as it is much harder to change a designation decision once it has been made. The lawyer should make sure the client is designated before the surrender date, or move for an adjournment of the surrender date to permit completion of the designation process.

Finally, the lawyer can help the client prepare practically and psychologically for the transition to prison life. The client can be introduced to the wealth of Internet re-

---

5. See BOP Program Statement 5070.10, Responses to Judicial Recommendations and U.S. Attorney Reports, available at www.bop.gov/policy/progstat/5070_010.pdf. In the U.S. Court of Appeals for the Second Circuit, the BOP might, but not necessarily will, honor recommendations that an inmate with a sentence of 12 months or less be designated to a community confinement center (halfway house), as a result of the Court's decision in *Levine v. Apker*, 455 F.3d 71 (2d Cir. 2006) (holding that the BOP's rule limiting inmate's placement in a halfway house to the lesser of the last 10 percent or six months of the sentence was an improper exercise of the BOP's rulemaking authority). Such a designation would be guaranteed, however, through a sentence of probation with a condition of community confinement. In addition, the BOP might not necessarily honor recommendations of camp placement for eligible offenders with sentences of 15 months or less, since such inmates may be required to man the work cadres of pretrial detention centers.

6. If the court grants this application, the inmate will usually not be required to participate in the Inmate Financial Responsibility Program (the program by which the BOP assists in the collection of court-ordered financial obligations), which can result in substantial deductions from the inmate's commissary account every month.

7. A discussion of the interplay between state and federal sentences is outside the scope of this article. If the client is primarily subject to state jurisdiction, the lawyer should review "Interaction of State and Federal Sentences," available at www.bop.gov/news/publications.jsp.

sources[8] and literature[9] on the subject. A meeting with a former inmate, if it can be arranged, can also be a valuable way of dispelling unnecessary fears. The client should also be encouraged to schedule full medical and dental check-ups prior to surrender.

Conclusion

For many prison inmates, the quality of the time they serve is as important as the length of the sentence. Time will certainly pass faster for most, for example, if one is in the relatively freer and less volatile environment of a camp facility. Thus, in federal criminal cases, once the client has pleaded guilty or has been convicted after trial, it is in the client's interest for the defense lawyer to adopt the dual strategy of mitigating the sentencing exposure and simultaneously positioning the client for a favorable prison placement. This is true even if the likelihood of incarceration appears to be remote. Once a prison sentence has been pronounced, it is often too late to take the measures that can make that sentence more palatable.

xiv. Astrid Birgden,[*] Dealing with the Resistant Criminal Client: A Psychologically-Minded Strategy for More Effective Legal Counseling

(Reprinted with permission from
38 Criminal law Bulletin 225, 2002)

Criminal defense attorneys routinely face a difficult and hostile situation where a criminal defendant denies and minimizes a serious offence even in light of overwhelming evidence of guilt. This situation is a difficult one in terms of the attorney mounting a defense and the mental health professional providing rehabilitation after conviction. This article proposes a psychologically-minded strategy for the defense attorney to use with so-called "defensive" clients. The attorney is to use motivational techniques determined by what stage of change the client is experiencing. If the client is then prepared to change offending behavior, the mental health professional can effectively provide rehabilitation with ongoing motivational support from the attorney. The strategy respects client autonomy in increasing client decision-making, sets the scene for possible client change and takes into consideration the possibility of client innocence. The approach is persuasive and supportive, rather than coercive and argumentative. The proposed strategy is particularly relevant for attorneys who wish to practice therapeutic jurisprudence in the criminal law context.

Introduction

Criminal defense lawyers routinely face a difficult and frustrating situation when a criminal defendant denies and minimizes criminal involvement in a serious offense

---

8. See, e.g., www.bop.gov (downloadable copies of all BOP program statements as well as other information on BOP facilities, rules and procedures); www.prisontalk.com (message board on federal prisons with up to date information provided by former inmates and the families of current inmates); www.michaelsantos.net (Web site of long-term federal prisoner, with articles on prison life and advice to the newly sentenced); www.fedcure.org (advocacy group for federal inmate population, with news, publications and links).

9. See, e.g., Alan Ellis, "Federal Prison Guidebook" (2005); David novak, "Down Time: A Guide to Federal Incarceration" (2005); Michael Santos, "What if I Go to Prison?" (2003); Clare Hanrahan, "Jailed for Justice: A Woman's Guide to Federal Prison Camp" (2002).

* Forensic Psychologist in Australia. Contact: astrid99@hotmail.com.

even in light of overwhelming evidence of guilt. A defense attorney may be challenged by a Mr. X who vehemently denies that the assault against his daughter was sexually motivated; a Ms. Y whose repeated drink driving charges are merely "bad luck"; or a Mr. Z who says that his wife is equally to blame for the domestic violence he perpetrates. How should the attorney respond? The standard attorney strategy is likely to use one, or even both, of two approaches.

One attorney strategy may be to take a "hands-off approach" and accept the client's position at face value and simply not challenge him or her. After all, given client autonomy and a client-centered approach to legal counseling,[1] a client is entitled to have whatever is his or her position vigorously advocated. The client-centered approach to legal counseling is designed to enhance client decision-making. However, such an approach may lead to attorney frustration, which in turn may then lead to the second attorney strategy.

The second traditional attorney strategy may be to take a "heavy-handed approach" resulting from knowledge of likely judicial and jury reaction to the defendant's position. The lawyer may emphasize in harsh terMs. the force of the prosecution's evidence:[2] "What about this fact? Is it going to go away? How the hell would you vote if you were a juror in your case?" It may sometimes be a lawyer's duty to say bluntly, "I cannot possibly beat this case. You are going to spend a lot of time in jail, and the only question is how long". This approach reflects the traditional attorney-client relationship where the attorney can expect to be assertive and controlling.[3] Such an approach does not encourage decision-making in the client and is likely to increase client resistance.

This article proposes a third strategy for the criminal defense attorney. Stages of change and motivational interviewing are psychological techniques designed to encourage behavior change using a non-confrontational approach. They provide a psychologically-minded strategy for attorneys to enhance decision-making and autonomy in the resistant criminal defendant. These psychologically-based techniques enhance the client-centered approach as espoused by the American Bar Association.[4] The proposed

---

1. Client-centered counseling aims to motivate clients to reveal salient legal and non-legal information and make choices that best meet their individual needs (Binder D. *et al.*, Lawyers As Counselors: A Client-Centered Approach (1991)).

2. Alschuler A., *The Defense Attorney's Role in Plea Bargaining*, 84 Yale L. J. 1179, 1309 (1975).

3. The traditional attorney relationship is one where the client is passive and merely chooses the goals and objectives of representation while the attorneys selects the defense strategies and tactics as a means to achieve the ends (Shaffer T. L. & Elkins J. R., Legal Interviewing And Counseling In A Nutshell (1978); Uphoff R. J., *Strategic Decisions in the Criminal Case: Who's Really Calling the Shots*, 14 Criminal Justice 4 (1999)). The traditional approach has been criticized for establishing an overly controlling relationship focused upon legal analysis and doctrinal categories (Smith L. F., *Interviewing Clients: A Linguistic Comparison of the Traditional Interview and the Client-Centered Interview*, 1 Clin. L. Rev. 542 (1995)). The traditional approach is therefore considered inconsistent with client dignity and rules of professional responsibility regarding inclusion in decision-making (Cochrane R. F. *et al.*, The Counselor-At-Law: A Collaborative Approach to Client Interviewing and Counseling (1999)).

4. The fundamental skills required for attorney competence in communication and interpersonal interactions are considered by the American Bar Association to be interviewing, counseling, problem-solving and negotiating (Strutin K. R., *Client Communication: An Essential Element of Criminal Defense Practice* 68 N. Y. ST. B. J. 24 (1996); Zeidman S., *Sacrificial Lambs or the Chosen Few? The Impact of Student Defenders on the Rights of the Accused*, 62 Brook. L. Rev. 853 (1996)).

strategy provides the defense attorney with an approach that is persuasive and supportive, rather than coercive and argumentative.[5]

According to psychological theory, many individuals contemplate change when they move into a new developmental stage of life or experience distress.[6] While some individuals will respond to environmental pressure to change, others will become defensive.[7] In the criminal justice system a "teachable moment" may therefore occur in conviction and sentencing. It is assumed that an individual is more receptive to those who have authority if s/he is treated with dignity, offered participation and trust has been instilled.[8] A criminal defendant, who has been charged and consequently is in a psychologically distressed state, may become either amenable or resistant to change. Considering this, the strategy assists mental health professionals in their rehabilitative efforts to address serious offending such as sexual, violent and drug crimes. Currently the most effective psychological interventions for offenders are considered to be cognitive-behavioral techniques followed by relapse prevention;[9] psychological interventions target the offending behavior and relapse prevention plans manage high risk situations in the community. In the case of the resistant criminal defendant, assisting the client to understand his or her emotions, cognitions and behavior may take several months.

Recently it has been proposed that defense attorneys can also contribute to rehabilitative efforts[10] and therefore play a vital role in encouraging offenders to engage in such

---

5. Miller W. R. & Rollnick, S., Motivational Interviewing (1991).
6. A number of psychological theories underpin motivation to change. *Cognitive dissonance* occurs when contradictory behavior and attitudes create an unpleasant state. The individual therefore seeks to reduce this state by changing attitude, removing and replacing inconsistent attitudes or trivializing the dissonant element (Draycott S. & Dabbs A., *Cognitive Dissonance 1: An Overview of the Literature and Its Integration Into Theory and Practice in Clinical Psychology*, 37 Brit. J. of Clin. Psychol. 341 (1998)). Free choice is important as it improves the efficacy of the outcome. *Self-efficacy* (or self-appraisal about how well one can perform actions to deal with a situation) influences emotions, cognitions and behavior (Bandura A., Self-Efficacy: The Exercise Of Control (1997)). Self-efficacy increases as individuals gain new skills to manage threatening situations. *Decisional balance* is also required when individuals weigh the gains and losses associated with a particular course of action when making decisions (Janis I. L. & Mann L., Decision-Making: A Psychological Analysis of Conflict, Choice and Commitment (1977)).
7. Miller W. R., *Motivation For Treatment: A Review With Special Emphasis on Alcoholism*, 98 Psychol. Bull. 84 (1985); Prochaska, J. & DiClemente C. C., *Transtheoretical Therapy: Toward a More Integrative Model of Change*, 19 Psychotherapy: Theory, Research & Practice 276 (1982).
8. Casey P. & Rottman D. B., *Therapeutic Jurisprudence in the Courts*, 18 Behav. Sciences & Law, 445 (1998); Sydeman S. J. et al, *Procedural Justice in the Context of Civil Commitment: A Critique of Tyler's Analysis*, 3 Psychol. Pub. Pol'y & L. 207 (1997).
9. For example, What Works: Reducing Offending (J. McGuire, ed., 1995).
10. Recent examples of restructuring the role of the defense attorney have been made. McShane has provided an example of a legal practice in the US based upon a therapeutic jurisprudence approach (McShane J. V., *The How and Why of Therapeutic Jurisprudence in Criminal Defense Work*, Paper presented at the 2nd International Conference on Therapeutic Jurisprudence, Cincinnati, May, 2001). The legal firm of McShane, Davis and Hance address the underlying cause of criminal behavior (e.g. alcoholism) rather than the symptom alone (e.g., repeated arrests for drink driving). The criminal defendant has to contractually agree to this therapeutic jurisprudence approach or seek legal assistance elsewhere. The legal practice focuses on rehabilitation and does so by: (1) interviewing, counseling and contracting the client, (2) obtaining a mental health professional evaluation with a recommended treatment and relapse prevention plan, (3) pleading to both protect the community and provide rehabilitation opportunities, and (4) advocacy by the attorney to postpone disposition to allow the defendant to address the offending behavior. Winick also suggests that reha-

interventions. These approaches for effective legal counseling assume client cooperation with little proactive intervention by the defense attorney. Therefore, attorneys require a strategy to assist them in dealing with the resistant client.

Criminal defense attorneys and law students currently receive no specific instruction in dealing with the resistant client.[11] I believe that to train defense attorneys in the client-centered approach alone is inadequate for enhancing decision-making and coop-

---

bilitation needs should be addressed (Winick B J., *Redefining The Role of the Criminal Defense Lawyer At Plea Bargaining and Sentencing: A Therapeutic Jurisprudence/Preventive Law Model*, 245 in Practicing Therapeutic Jurisprudence: Law as a Helping Profession (D. P. Stolle, D. B. Wexler & B. J. Winick, eds., 2000) [*hereinafter Redefining the Role*]). For example, in domestic violence cases, Winick argues that it is in the client's best interests to deal with repetitive abuse both legally and therapeutically where there is no genuine or technical defense and the client appears overwhelmingly likely to be convicted upon the basis of evidence (Winick B. J., *Applying the Law Therapeutically in Domestic Violence Cases*, 69 U. M. K. C. L. Rev. 33 (2000)). Defense attorneys are in a unique position to explore with the client diversion prograMs. or acceptance of negotiated pleas that include treatment conditions. Specifically in relation to sex offenders, Wexler has indicated that nolo pleas (permitting the offender to accept the consequences of a conviction without going to trial and without admitting guilt) and Alford pleas (permitting the offender to both plead guilty and protest innocence) serve to reinforce denial and minimisation. If jurisdiction were to refuse to accept such pleas, the role of the lawyer would be restructured as she or he would need to "... coax more actively those clients who lack plausible defenses to admit guilt and accept the bargain" p. 160 (Wexler D. B., *Therapeutic Jurisprudence and the Criminal Courts*, 157 in Law in a Therapeutic Key: Developments in Therapeutic Jurisprudence (D. B. Wexler & B. J. Winick, eds., 1996). Similarly, Wexler has proposed that defense attorneys become more actively involved in developing relapse prevention plans together with both the adult and juvenile client, correctional staff and significant others (Wexler D. B., *Some Reflections on Therapeutic Jurisprudence and the Practice of Criminal Law*, Crim. L. Bull. (forthcoming 2001); Wexler D. B., *Relapse Prevention Principles For Criminal Law Practice*, 237 in Practicing Therapeutic Jurisprudence: Law as a Helping Profession (D. P. Stolle, D. B. Wexler & B. J. Winick, eds., 2000); Wexler D. B., *Just Some Juvenile Thinking About Delinquent Behavior: A Therapeutic Jurisprudence Approach to Relapse Prevention Planning and Youth Advisory Juries*, 69 U. M. K. C. L. Rev. 93 (2000)). This approach assists in obtaining plausible community-based dispositions with a realistic plan which is "owned" by the client.

11. Methods for coping with the resistant client is rarely addressed in the law-based literature. Client-centered counseling is taught in the majority of law schools in the US and numerous texts have been written for attorneys listing the skills required such as open-ended questioning and reflective listening. Such a client-centered approach assumes client cooperation. A few authors have presented strategies for the client described as reluctant, inhibited, angry, negative, bullying, seductive, withdrawn and pathological liars (Binder D. *et al*, *supra* note 1; Nelson, N. C., *Connecting With Your Client: Success Through Improved Client Communications Techniques* (1996)). However, the strategies are broad and not based on a theoretical framework. In addition, they do not recognize the strong emotions triggered in attorneys by such a client or how these reactions should be managed. For an exception see Mills L. G., *Affective Lawyering: The Emotional Dimensions Of The Lawyer-Client Relation*, 419 in Practicing Therapeutic Jurisprudence: Law as a Helping Profession (D. P. Stolle, D. B. Wexler & B. J. Winick, eds., 2000); Silver M. A., *Love, Hate and Other Emotional Interference in the Lawyer/Client Relationship*, 357 Practicing Therapeutic Jurisprudence: Law as a Helping Profession (D. P. Stolle, D. B. Wexler & B. J. Winick, eds., 2000). Winick has addressed client denial and resistance in relation to legal planning regarding future incapacity/illness and engagement in rehabilitation to address offending behavior (Winick B. J., *Client Denial and Resistance in the Advanced Directive Context: Reflections On How Attorneys Can Identify and Deal With a Psycholegal Soft Spot*, 327 in Practicing Therapeutic Jurisprudence: Law as a Helping Profession (D. P. Stolle, D. B. Wexler & B. J. Winick, eds., 2000) [*hereinafter Client Denial and Resistance*]; *Redefining the Role*, *supra* note 10). Winick suggests that attorneys should understand the underlying psychological mechanisMs. of denial and the techniques used to manage it, understand the social psychology of persuasion, be sensitive to clients' emotional needs and demonstrate empathy. This is achieved through improved interviewing, counseling and interpersonal skills. However, Winick warns that some more sophisticated clinical methods may require referral to mental health professionals.

eration in the resistant criminal defendant. Training by an experienced mental health professional in continuing legal education prograMs. and law school curriculum requires consideration. This approach is important for all criminal attorneys and should be particularly stimulating for those who wish to practice therapeutic jurisprudence in the criminal law context.

Psychological Approaches to Dealing with the Resistant Client

As in lawyering, the mental health professional needs to enhance motivation to change and maximize appropriate decision-making in the resistant client.

Stages and Processes of Change

Based upon the comparison of 18 leading psychological therapies, Prochaska developed a general explanatory model in order to determine how individuals change health-related behaviors, particularly addiction. The model involves emotions, cognitions and behavior and incorporates psychological theories to explain how individuals deal with unpleasant states and threatening situations, make free choices and make informed decisions.[12] The transtheoretical (or across theories) model can be described as a cognitive-behavioral approach integrating verbal processes (i.e. verbal therapies) and environmental management (i.e. behavioral therapies). Processes of change are the activities the client uses to change emotions, cognitions and behavior as s/he moves through stages of change readiness.

Therefore, mental health professionals need to match the right thing (process) at the right time (stage) in order to assist individuals to change. The integration of stage and process for the client with addictive behaviors is as follows (see Table 1):[13]

Motivational Interviewing Techniques

Motivational interventions increase the likelihood of individuals entering, continuing and complying within an active change strategy.[14] Motivational interviewing is a brief, practically-oriented intervention that arose out of the counseling style of Miller. It is described as a directive-client centered counseling style for eliciting behavior change by helping the client explore and resolve ambivalence[15] about health-related behavioral change such as polydrug use, domestic violence and risky sexual activity. It is a technique founded on motivational psychology and client-centered therapy and complements the stages and processes of change model previously outlined.[16] In essence, motivational interviewing involves a therapeutic relationship; it relies upon client articulation of goals and motives for present or potential probleMs. and emphasizes freedom of choice.

---

12. *Supra* note 5.
13. Prochaska J. & DiClemente C. C., *www.med.usf.edu* (2001); Prochaska J. & DiClemente C. C., *Transtheoretical Therapy: Toward A More Integrative Model Of Change*, 19 Psychotherapy: Theory, Research & Practice 276 (1982); Prochaska J. et al, *In Search of How People Change: Applications to Addictive Behaviors*, 47 Am. Psychol. 1102 (1992); Prochaska, J. & Norcross, J. C., SysteMs. Of Psychotherapy: A Transtheoretical Analysis (1994); Prochaska, J.O. & Prochaska, J. M., *Why Don't Continents Move? Why Don't People Change?*, 9 J. Psychotherapy. Integ. 83 (1999).
14. Miller W. R., *Motivation For Treatment: A Review With Special Emphasis on Alcoholism*, 98 Psychol. Bull. 84 (1985); Miller W. R. & Rollnick S., *supra* note 5; Wagner C. & Connors W., *www.motivationalinterview.org* (2001).
15. Rollnick S. & Miller W. R., *What Is Motivational Interviewing?*, 23 Behav. & Cog. Psychotherapy 325 (1995).
16. Lawendowski L. A., *Motivational Intervention for Adolescent Smokers*, 27(5, Pt 3) Prev. Med. A39–A46. (1998).

Table 1 Stages and Processes of Change Model

STAGE OF CHANGE	BEHAVIOUR	UNDERLYING PROCESSES
1. Pre-contemplation	The clients has no intention to change in the near future and may be unaware of any problems. The client is resistant to recognising or modifying the problem behavior. Alternatively, the client may wish to change but does not seriously consider change in the near future. The client may be uninformed about consequences of behavior.	Consciousness-raising Expressing feeling about problems and solutions Assessing the consequences of behavior
2. Contemplation	The client is aware that the problem exists and is seriously thinking about overcoming it but is not yet committed to action. The costs and benefits are being weighed i.e., a decisional balance is made. The ambivalence created by the decisional balance may keep the client "stuck" in this stage for some time.	Consciousness-raising Expressing feeling about problems and solutions Assessing the consequences of behavior
3. Preparation	Client intentions are combined with small behavioral changes but have not yet reached a criterion such as absence from substance abuse. At this stage, decision-making is evidenced and there is a plan of action.	Self-reevaluation by assessing core values
4. Action	The client modifies his/her behavior, experiences or environment to overcome problems i.e., reach an acceptable criterion. Modification involves overt behavioral changes and considerable commitment. Professionals often erroneously equate action with change. Vigilance against relapse is critical.	Client belief in the ability to change—greater self-efficacy Use rehabilitation to make a public commitment to change Change the consequences in the environment Change responses to stimuli Change the environment
5. Maintenance	The client works to prevent relapse and consolidate gains made during the Action phase. The client is less tempted to relapse and is increasingly more confident that change can occur. Relapse is effected by self-efficacy and maintenance may be required for a lifetime.	Change the consequences in the environment Change responses to stimuli Change the environment

In this form of intervention, client resistance or denial is seen as a defense mechanism or normal response to mental health professional behavior of diagnostic labeling, threatening, coercing, confronting and arguing with the client. In motivational interviewing, resistance can be defused by enhancing client control or self-esteem.

Miller and Rollnick list five principles of motivational interviewing to be delivered by mental health professionals:[17]

Table 2 Principles of Motivational Interviewing

1. Express empathy	Acceptance facilitates change and ambivalence is normal. Reflective listening through rephrasing client statements and a problem-solving approach assists. Allow client to explore probleMs. in an atmosphere of trust and avoid argument.
2. Develop discrepancy	Highlight discrepancy between present behavior and important goals to motivate change and confront attempts to resolve them in the absence of behavior change. An awareness of consequences is important and the client should present arguments for change.
3. Avoid argumentation	Arguments are counterproductive, labeling is unnecessary and defending produces defensiveness. Resistance is a signal to change strategies. Confront client but do not engage in aggressive argument as clients will attribute discomfort to personal conflict.
4. Roll with resistance	The client is a valuable resource in finding solutions to problems and momentum can be used positively. Perceptions can be shifted and new perspectives invited but not imposed. If the client is resistant, the therapist has attempted to force a topic too soon.
5. Support self-efficacy	Belief in the possibility of change is an important motivator and the client is responsible for choosing from a range of alternatives. If the client feels that intentions to change can be translated into action, s/he is more likely to have a good outcome and so experience mastery.

The goal for motivational interviewing is for the client to take responsibility for decision-making and change. The task is to facilitate self-motivational statements that tip the balance towards the direction of change: (1) problem recognition, (2) expression of concern, (3) intention to change, and (4) optimism about change.[18]

Stages of Change and Motivational Interviewing Combined

Motivational interviewing provides a practical technique and the stages of change model the theoretical underpinning. Prochaska and Norcross recommend that initially problem behaviors should be addressed at the Precontemplation and Contemplation stages using motivational interviewing techniques and at the Action and Maintenance

---

17. Miller W. R. & Rollnick S., *supra* note 5.
18. *Id.*

stages using behavioral methods.[19] The application of motivational interviewing and stages of change by mental health professionals, before cognitive-behavioral techniques and relapse prevention plans, should enhance behaviour change in the serious offender. A proposed combination of stages of change and motivational interviewing is outlined in the table below.[20]

Table 3   Combined Stages of Change and Motivational Interviewing Approach

STAGE OF CHANGE	INTERVENTIONS	MENTAL HEALTH PROFESSIONAL ROLE
1. *Precontemplation* No acknowledgment Unmotivated In denial	Motivational interviewing to elicit problem recognition: • Raise awareness and doubt • Create dissonance	*Nurturing parent* Join with resistance and defensiveness
2. *Contemplation* Acknowledges problem but minimizes Ambivalent Seesaws, "yes, but ..." Decisional balance	Motivational interviewing to elicit expression of concern: • Evoke reasons to change • Strengthen confidence in change	*Nurturing parent* Join with resistance and defensiveness
3. *Preparation* Recognizes problem Seeks help Committed to action Decision-making	Motivational interviewing to elicit intention to change: • Determine best course of action • Determine barriers to success	*Socratic teacher* Encourage insight
4. *Action* Adheres to program plan	Motivational interviewing to elicit optimism about change, apply cognitive-behavioral interventions and develop a relapse prevention plan: • Assist to take achievable steps towards change • Create external monitors of activity	*Experienced coach* Provide or review strategies
5. Maintenance Applies strategies consistently	Monitor the relapse prevention plan: • Assist to use strategies to avoid lapse and relapse	*Consultant* Provide expert advice and support when action is not progressing smoothly and reduce towards termination

Applying the Integrated Approach

As already noted, the defense attorney plays a major role when faced with a resistant client in relation to the "teachable moment" triggered by initial contact with the criminal justice system. The psychological techniques outlined above have been designed for mental health professionals to apply. However, the role of defense attorney in enhancing decision-making and choices in the client places the attorney in an excellent position to increase cooperation in the resistant criminal defendant. Stages of change and motiva-

---

19. Prochaska J. & Norcross J. C., SysteMs. Of Psychotherapy: A Transtheoretical Analysis (1994).
20. *Id.*; Prochaska J. et al., *supra* note 13; Prochaska, J. O. & Prochaska J. M., *supra* note 13.

tional interviewing have primarily been applied to changing health-related rather than criminal behaviors. Furthermore, the application of stages of change and motivational interviewing by the defense attorney to enhance cooperation in the resistant client has not previously been postulated in the literature.[21]

A joint defense attorney and mental health professional strategy is proposed to maximize cooperation in the resistant client; the attorney applies motivational techniques at the Precontemplation, Contemplation and Preparation stages while the mental health professional applies cognitive-behavioural intervention and relapse prevention at the Action and Maintenance stages. While receiving rehabilitative intervention from the mental health professional, ongoing motivational intervention by the defense attorney or a correctional case manager is required.

Table 4 outlines the strategy.

Table 4 An Integrated Defense Attorney and Mental Health Professional Approach

STAGE OF CHANGE	DEFENSE ATTORNEY ROLE	MENTAL HEALTH PROFESSIONAL ROLE
1. Precontemplation	*Educator or coach* Motivational interviewing to elicit problem recognition	
2. Contemplation	*Educator or coach* Motivational interviewing to elicit expression of concern	
3. Preparation	*Socratic teacher* Motivational interviewing to elicit intention to change	
4. Action	*Case manager* Motivational interviewing to elicit optimism about change	*Experienced coach* Apply cognitive-behavioral intervention and develop relapse prevention plan
5. Maintenance	*Case manager* Motivational interviewing to elicit optimism about change	*Consultant* Monitor relapse prevention plan

The following examples indicate how the defense attorney may apply motivational interviewing at the Precontemplation, Contemplation and Preparation stages of change with a resistant criminal defendant. Techniques previously designed for the mental

---

21. Recommendations for brief interventions regarding addictive behaviors by non-specialists such as general practitioners and undergraduate psychology students have been made (Lawendowski L.A., *supra* note 16). These interventions may be three or less sessions and can be between 5 to 30 minutes duration. Lawendowski warns that although motivational interviewing appears simple, it is a sophisticated research-based clinical therapy. A training program for non-specialists would require micro counseling skills—open-ended questioning, reflective listening, forming a balanced summary while being non-authoritarian, and being empathic and client-centered; skills currently being taught to law students. In addition, defense attorneys and students would need to be able to determine at what stage of change the client is. A review of a number of instruments devised to assess stages of change has been conducted (Carey K. B. *et al*, Assessing Readiness to Change Substance Abuse: A Critical Review of Instruments, 6 Clin. Psychol. 245 (1999)). However, these questionaires are designed for health-related behaviors. Whether such instruments could be appropriately applied by defense attorneys in a criminal justice context is currently untested.

health professional regarding motivating change[22] and techniques for the defense attorney regarding enhanced decision-making[23] are combined. Concerns may be raised that the defense attorney is presuming that the client has committed the offense as charged. In the examples below, it is understood that there is overwhelming evidence that the client has committed the offense; the aim is not have the client "confess" guilt but to harness any indications of motivation to change determined by the stage of change the client is experiencing. The essence of the client-centered approach is that defense attorneys are agents of the client.[24] Ultimately decisions lie with the client who may still decide that the state is obliged to prove guilt.

Example 1: Precontemplation Stage

Mr. X comes to the attorney's office for the initial interview and indicates that he has been charged with sexual offenses against his seven-year-old daughter. He hotly denies the charges and states that he was merely providing her sex education because his wife had failed to do so. The attorney ascertains that at present Mr. X has no intention to change in the near future. Any suggestions regarding change will be met with resistance. The benefits of Mr. X denying the behavior clearly outweigh the cost of being labeled a sex offender. However, resistance to change is the problem for the attorney rather than Mr. X to deal with.

How should the attorney respond? The attorney needs to gently elicit from Mr. X recognition that there is a problem so that Mr. X may start to contemplate behavior change.

An empathic approach is required for Mr. X to explore his legal problem in an atmosphere of trust. At this stage, raising doubt and creating dissonance is important. *Reframing statements* are loaded in favor of change: "You're saying that you didn't have sexual thoughts at the time and are not a pervert, but others see your behavior as sexual and so illegal". If Mr. X is resistant to discussing the discrepancy between his stated aim of sex education and the assumed sexual assault, then the attorney should *invite a new*

---

22. For example, Draycott S. & Dabbs A., *Cognitive Dissonance 2: A Theoretical Grounding of Motivational Interviewing*, 37 Brit. J. Clin. Psych. 355 (1998); Miller W. R., *supra* note 14; Mann, R., Motivational Interviewing With Sex Offenders: A Practice Manual (1996); Miller, W. R. & Rollnick S., *supra* note 5; Lawendowski L.A., *supra* note 16.

23. Intervention for attorneys to enhance communication and decision-making (Shaffer T. L. & Elkins J. R., *supra* note 3):

Discrepancy: Call attention to a contradiction in attitude or action to remind the client of the hard choices and keeps decisions in line with choices.

Psychological theory: Draw upon theory to highlight the connection between underlying assumptions and present behavior or to predict consequences for a particular course of action.

Procedure and consequences: Put events into sequence and relate them logically as clients may not understand cause-effect relationships.

Relationship: Focus attention on personal feelings, particularly negative ones that hinder coordinated effort, and provide feedback.

Experimentation: Test and compare two courses of action before a final decision is made.

Dilemma: Identify a point where decisions are being made unwittingly or implicitly and ask client to re-examine assumptions and seek alternatives.

Perspective: Evaluate present actions by providing a broader historical perspective.

Structure: Examine the familial, organizational and personal structures within which clients habitually function.

Culture: Examine tradition, precedents and established practice.

Logic: Determine the logic being used to increase client options.

Morals: Describe the moral issues involved to reduce conflict of morals.

24. *Client Denial and Resistance, supra* note 11.

perspective: "What do you think your wife thought when she found out that you were giving your daughter sex education?". After Mr. X states the wife's perception then *use the momentum positively*: "So, your wife thought you were teaching her too much too soon. What's another way your daughter could be taught sex education while keeping both you and your wife happy?".

Initially strategies are required to build motivation. Capturing any self-motivating statements Mr. X may make, will assist him to begin to recognize that there is a problem. *Elaboration* takes any statement with an element of motivation and asks Mr. X to expand on it: "So, you say that your wife had a problem with what you were doing— tell me more about that".

Emphasizing *personal choice and control* is important for Mr. X: "I'm not here to tell you which way to plead. All I'm here to do is go through the evidence and the pros and cons of pleading guilty or not guilty. That is, if you plead not guilty, the state is obliged to prove that you were sexually assaulting your daughter. The evidence is pretty strong— your wife saw you. If you go before a jury, what do you think ordinary members of the community would think about that sort of behavior? If you plead not guilty, the sentence may be a lot tougher if you're then found guilty".

In this example, Mr. X presents with no acknowledgment of sexually motivated behavior, he is in denial and unmotivated to change. The role of the attorney is to raise doubt and create dissonance about the appropriateness of sex education with his daughter. At this stage, discussion regarding treatment of sexually offending behavior is not yet appropriate. Even if raising doubt is the only task of the attorney, it may encourage a move towards contemplation of change. The alternatives are increasing client resistance to change (the traditional approach) or the client remaining at pre-contemplation (the client-centered approach).

Example 2: Contemplation Stage

Ms. Y has been referred again for drink driving charges. She has previous convictions for driving under the influence of alcohol. Ms. Y states that she had been at a lunch with friends. She gives several reasons why she had been caught—she is unlucky that the police always apprehend her, she could not find a taxi on that day and she did not realise she was over the alcohol limit. Ms. Y agrees that she has previous convictions and that she needs to do something about this. The attorney ascertains that although she is thinking that a problem exists and beginning to think about how to solve it, Ms. Y has not yet made any commitment to change. Therefore, there is serious contemplation of change and a decisional balance is being made.

How should the attorney respond? Ms. Y understands the legal issue at hand. The attorney needs to elicit from Ms. Y concerns regarding her behavior to prepare her in addressing excessive alcohol use.

If Ms. Y becomes resistant to discussion, this is a signal for the attorney to roll with the resistance and *shift focus*: "I agree that the label drink driver is not useful. Let's get away from that and talk about your particular situation".

Because Ms. Y is ambivalent, *double-sided reflection* acknowledges what she is saying but adds the unspoken side of her ambivalence: "You don't think you have a drinking problem but you're worried about what your friends must be thinking by now". Engaging Ms. Y in *decisional balance* lists the costs and benefits of continuing as she has been: "What are the good things you get out of drinking and what are the downsides of drinking".

Self-motivating statements to change should be elicited from Ms. Y. *Expressing concern about the need to change* can assist this: "What worries you about your drinking and driving?". Alternatively, *using extremes* can elicit thinking about the consequences: "What are your worst fears about what might happen if you keep drink driving?".

Emphasizing *personal choice and control* is important in having Ms. Y feel she has a right to choose: "I'm not here to tell you what you should do in relation to drinking and driving. All I'm here to do is go through the evidence regarding this particular charge and help you to work out what the best plea is. You have a record of drink driving convictions and if you indicate that you'll do something about your drinking, that could help with your sentence".

In this example, Ms. Y has presented to you with the acknowledgment of a problem but she minimizes its impact. The attorney task is to evoke reasons to change and strengthen confidence in change. At this stage, discussion regarding treatment for alcohol abuse is not yet appropriate but Ms. Y has begun to think about alternative strategies.

Example 3: Preparation Stage

Mr. Z comes to your office indicating that he has been charged with physically assaulting his wife resulting in significant injury. He reports that his violence towards her has been increasing over time. This is the first time she has called the police however. Mr. Z says that although he has been charged it is "unfair" as his wife is equally to be blamed and he did not mean to hurt her. Since the police were called to the house, Mr. Z has agreed to seek psychological counseling with his wife. Therefore, the attorney ascertains that Mr. Z is determined to change his behavior and has taken small steps towards doing so. However, Mr. Z has not yet ceased to be violent or address the problem directly.

How should the attorney respond? The attorney needs to elicit from Mr. Z intentions regarding change and ensure that any treatment Mr. Z engages in actually targets the violent behavior.

Mr. Z requires assistance in determining the best course of action. *Double-sided reflection* addresses both sides of Mr. Z's ambivalence but this time with a greater emphasis on the perceived problem: "What you're saying is that you want to deal with your violence and that you're getting help through counseling with your wife about your relationship. You may also need some specialized help to control your temper".

If Mr. Z feels that his intentions to change can be translated into action, he is more likely to *experience mastery* which can be reinforced: "So, you agree that you'll find out more about the local domestic violence group that you doctor has recommended and then we'll put this to the court to consider in sentencing".

Self-motivating statements should be elicited from him so Mr. Z can express *intention to change*: "What reasons are there besides having come to see me for making a change?"

The attorney emphasizes *personal choice and control* with Mr. Z: "I'm not here to tell you what kind of treatment you should do to address violent behavior but, once you've decided, we can put it to the court to consider in your sentencing. Even better, if you start treatment straight away, we could ask the court to postpone sentencing until we see how you're progressing and maybe get a community-based disposition so you can keep attending the group".

In this example, Mr. Z has presented with recognition of the problem and is seeking help. The attorney task is to determine the best course of action. Discussion regarding treatment of violent behavior is now appropriate and a referral to a mental health professional to assist in the Action and Maintenance stages can be made.

In the proposed strategy, the defense attorney has initial contact with the criminal defendant who is more likely to be at the Precontemplation or Contemplation stage of change. Through a client-centered approach, the defense attorney applies motivational interviewing techniques with an emphasis on autonomous decision-making. Once the client has moved to the Preparation stage of change and is willing to engage with a mental health professional, the defense attorney may refer for intervention. The mental health professional can then provide the cognitive-behavioral intervention and develop the relapse prevention plan at the Action stage and monitor the relapse prevention plan at the Maintenance stage together with ongoing case management support.

Conclusion

The stages of change are derived from a theoretical psychologically-based model and conceptualize individuals proceeding through stages as they modify their behaviors. Motivational interviewing is a non-confrontional technique that uses the stage of change to enhance the likelihood of behavior change. The stages of change model and the motivational interviewing technique both utlize psychological concepts. These concepts should be applicable to the criminal justice context and can enhance the client-centered approach currently advocated for defense attorneys.

Psychological distress or the "teachable moment" caused by the legal process can be harnessed to encourage cooperation in rehabilitative efforts. The proposed joint defense attorney and mental health professional strategy allows proactive client-counseling utilizing the skills of both professions within the criminal justice context; the defense attorney enhances autonomous decision-making and cooperation while the mental health professional provides cognitive-behavioural interventions and maintains relapse prevention plans. An interdisciplinary approach is essential in teaching these techniques to attorneys and law students.

Part IV

Practice Settings and Clinical Opportunities

As we saw in Part III, TJ criminal law practice is available to the private practitioner as well as to public defenders and assigned counsel. Some law school clinical programs offer TJ educational opportunities to law students, and others are now being proposed in the literature.

This Part looks at some of that scholarship, and tries to pave the way for more TJ opportunities in criminal law and juvenile delinquency settings. Cait Clarke and Jim Neuhard open the Part with a selection written from the vantage point of public defenders. Gregory Baker and Jennifer Zawid follow, describing TJ clinics operating in drug treatment court settings at William & Mary and the University of Miami Law Schools. Bruce Winick and I explore and propose other clinical opportunities, and in a subsequent short essay, I suggest that law school programs counseling crime victims can constitute an excellent experience for students who may wish later to serve as TJ criminal defense lawyers. The Part closes with important work by Kristin Henning, exploring the ethics of TJ practice in a juvenile setting, and presenting a concrete exercise she has used in continuing legal education training sessions.

i. Cait Clarke & James Neuhard,[1] Making the Case: Therapeutic Jurisprudence and Problem Solving Practices Positively Impact Clients, Justice Systems and Communities They Serve

(Reprinted with permission from
17 St. Thomas Law Review 781, 2005)

I. INTRODUCTION

Therapeutic Jurisprudence, which stems from the legal academy, and problem solving lawyering, which stems from practitioners, are two fields benefiting from assimila-

---

1. James Neuhard is the Executive Director of the State Appellate Defender Office in Michigan. Cait Clarke is the Director of the National Defender Leadership Institute at the National Legal Aid and Defender Association in Washington, D.C. The authors would like to express their sincere appreciation for research assistance provided by Maureen James, NLADA associate attorney, and Jennifer Osborne, intern for the Defender Legal Services Division of NLADA. We are most grateful to David Wexler and Bruce Winick for not only discovering but actually reading our first joint article, *"From Day One": Who's in Control as Problem-Solving and Client-Centered Sentencing Take Center Stage?*, 29 N.Y.U. REV. L. & SOC. CHANGE 11 (2004). We are so thankful that they tracked us down

tion.[2] Increasingly, criminal defense advocates engage in interdisciplinary outreach, team-based advocacy, integrated service models of lawyering and creative arraignment advocacy to achieve diversion or alternatives to incarceration. The most effective sentencing work in the defender community incorporates the expertise and problem solving approaches from other professions such as mental health, social work, and criminology.[3] Defense practitioners and civil legal aid lawyers[4] who integrate other professional expertise into their advocacy work have been moving towards an expanded notion of what it means to "provide the assistance of counsel."[5] Within the criminal justice context, these expanded approaches to law practice share the underlying values of using the legal process to address problems in people's lives and reduce recidivism by helping individuals become healthy, peaceful and productive members of a community. These practices focused on providing integrated professional services to accused persons are called "problem solving lawyering," "holistic advocacy," or "integrated service models." An acceptable umbrella term for these practices is "whole client representa-

---

and invited us to participate in this important Symposium. Our hope is that this article will be the first of many collaborative efforts between practitioners/advocates who embrace whole-client representation and the founding fathers of the Therapeutic Jurisprudence movement. By uniting our perspectives, commitment and problem solving skills, we can bring these important approaches to more equal justice advocates nationwide, which will ultimately help more individuals, families and communities thrive within and through our justice systems rather than being damaged by those systems.

2. David Wexler, one of the founding fathers of Therapeutic Jurisprudence, has written an excellent essay in this special issue exploring how the theory has moved into the world of practice for criminal defense lawyers. David B. Wexler, *Therapeutic Jurisprudence and the Rehabilitative Role of the Criminal Defense Lawyer*, 17 St. Thomas L. Rev. 741 (2005). As public defenders, we see that there are many ideas to embrace and develop in Professor Wexler's article that can improve the work of problem solving, community-oriented defenders. The authors work with institutional public defense programs including assigned counsel, contract attorneys and public defenders. It will be important to think strategically to develop training and mentoring opportunities so that Therapeutic Jurisprudence theories infuse defense practices, particularly to benefit socio-economically deprived individuals and communities.

3. "Problem solving lawyering" in this essay will be used as an umbrella term that includes lawyers who think and practice law in a way that is more expansive than traditional case representation. These lawyers provide integrated services to clients; they promote collaboration between civil legal aid and public defense practitioners to help clients and communities; and they rely on other professionals such as social workers, mental health experts and mitigation specialists to address accused person's underlying problems. The theories of Therapeutic Jurisprudence and problem solving lawyering are also closely linked to the underlying values of restorative justice. As a threshold matter, however, terms like "problem solving" and "therapeutic" make a significant portion of the defense bar uncomfortable. There are pockets of innovative defender leaders across the country rethinking their program structures and redefining the scope of their representation towards team-based representation models. Some defenders prefer to call these wrap-around services or problem solving approaches an "integrated services" model or "whole-client representation" model.

4. *See, e.g.*, Penda Hair, *Louder Than Words; Lawyers, Communities and the Struggle for Justice*, (March 2001), *available at* www.rockfound.org (monograph produced for the Rockefeller Foundation) (last visited Mar. 7, 2005). This report highlights several community and problem solving lawyering approaches in the civil legal aid community. Projects include: racial diversity in Texas; client-centered lawyering for garment workers in Los Angeles; redistricting campaign in Mississippi; Los Angeles community members' effort to secure bus service; and community lawyering as a way to deal effectively with labor disputes, land disputes. *Id.* at 17, 41, 63, 85, 105, 123.

5. U.S. Const. amend. VI. Most defense attorneys embrace some or all of the goals of these problem solving approaches and Therapeutic Jurisprudence because these approaches provide access to resources and professional help that normally would not be available to indigent accused persons, guilty defendants, prisoners reentering society, poor communities, and state justice systems as a whole.

tion," which is broader than Therapeutic Jurisprudence. Regardless of what one calls these practices, all lawyers, especially indigent defense practitioners and leaders of public defense institutions, should know about Therapeutic Jurisprudence because it is an important component of whole-client representation.[6]

Various client-based practices that began as defense strategies to gain lower bonds, secure probation, or avoid the death sentence are congealing into a new philosophy of sentencing. For some programs, these expanded notions of providing 'counsel' are fundamentally changing the focus of some defender programs and expanding attorneys' scope of representation. Sentencing advocates in capital cases, social worker divisions in defender programs, diversion programs, conditional bonds, and other team-based representation models (once individual efforts for select clients) have become an integral part of a growing number of defender organizations. Many programs have internal procedures designed to release clients from jail on bond or secure lower sentences. The goal is to impact the client beyond the criminal case facts and potentially increase the client's ability to avoid future criminal conduct. From bond through sentencing, creative public defense programs are trying to effectively meet the interests and needs of those they represent. To sustain and broaden this movement, it is essential that law schools do a better job of training students in the skills that will be needed. One effective approach is through a law school criminal defense clinical program that teaches students the Therapeutic Jurisprudence and problem solving skills that increasingly are becoming essential for quality criminal lawyering.

From the perspective of criminal defense lawyers, there are shared values between the world of Therapeutic Jurisprudence and problem solving lawyering practices.[7] Similar to the values of the restorative justice movement,[8] the aim is to provide resources

---

6. Despite the initially jarring sound of 'therapeutic,' the term does remind lawyers to cling to an ethic of care and to be sensitive to disciplines and professions such as mental health, social work, and criminology. The Therapeutic Jurisprudence literature tries to suggest ways on *how* one can provide 'whole client representation' in many contexts including: how the law can increase compliance with release conditions; how clients can develop an appreciation of their high risk situations; and how the law can reinforce client efforts at desisting from criminal behavior. In other words, Therapeutic Jurisprudence, and its extensive and growing literature, should be an essential ingredient of the education and continuing education of whole client representation lawyers. Lawyers need, therefore, to be 'desensitized' to the use of the term, rather than shocked by it. The job of academics and leaders in the public defense field is to recognize the importance of the literature, which is kept more or less up to date in the Therapeutic Jurisprudence bibliography of the International Therapeutic Jurisprudence Network website: http://www.therapeuticjurisprudence.org, and also at the Cumulative Bibliography, *at* (last visited Mar. 8, 2005).

7. We write this essay from the perspective of one group of criminal justice stakeholders—that of criminal defense providers. For a more comprehensive explanation of problem solving defense lawyering *see, e.g.*, Cait Clarke, *Problem-Solving Defenders in the Community: Expanding the Conceptual and Institutional Boundaries of Providing Counsel to the Poor*, 14 GEO. J. LEGAL ETHICS 401 (2001); Mark Moore, Michael Judge, Carlos Martinez, & Leonard Noisette, *The Best Defense is No Offense: Preventing Crime Through Effective Public Defense*, 29 N.Y.U. REV. L. & SOC. CHANGE 57 (2004) (conveying a published collection of papers from Harvard University and BJA's Executive Session on Public Defense, which explored the theoretical and practical impact of problem solving lawyering, community justice initiatives, and ways that defender practitioners can impact public policymaking and law reform more effectively).

8. Akin to community problem solving and Therapeutic Jurisprudence theories, restorative justice involves the victim, offender and community reaching reconciliation. Often defined as the opposite of retributive justice, restorative justice defines crime as a violation of people and relationships as opposed to a violation of the state. *See* http://www.websterdictionary.org/definition/Restorative%20justice (last visited Mar. 8, 2005); Jeffrey Fagan & Victoria Malkin, *Theorizing Com-*

and expertise beyond traditional legal advocacy skills in order to address a person's recurring problems such as addiction, joblessness, family crises, education needs and mental illness. Ultimately, the goal is to stabilize communities using the legal process as opposed to destabilizing communities caused by recurring social ills, increased arrests, and high incarceration rates even when crime rates are dropping.[9]

These approaches will spread most effectively through the ongoing education of clinicians, academicians, law students and criminal defense practitioners. To achieve the largest impact, it is important to focus on institutional defenders. These defender programs include public defender offices, conflict counsel programs and assigned counsel programs. Defender programs provide the most fertile ground for Therapeutic Jurisprudence and problem solving or whole client representation approaches to take root inside our local, state and federal justice systems. Two primary hurdles, however, must be overcome, which are: 1) the need to change the culture inside public defense programs towards client-centered advocacy so that traditional zealous trial warriors understand the benefit of these practices to their individual clients; and 2) the need for data collection to show these approaches have a measurable impact on individuals and on a community. This article discusses a few defender offices that are now practicing client-centered representation. It explores how the mission and design of the office attempts not only to provide zealous traditional advocacy for their client's cases, but also provide programs that impact their client's lives.

What is becoming known as Therapeutic Jurisprudence or client-centered representation is new to most line-lawyers or leaders of traditional public defense programs. However, many of these practices have been incorporated into the daily practices within defender offices for decades. Strategies that secure better bonds or sentences lead many public defense programs to seek early entry into the jails and to verify client information. Efforts to learn about "beds" for their clients that were unknown to swamped probation programs have lead offices and individual defenders to actively participate and create alternative treatment programs. Overworked offices hire less expensive sentencing specialists or have their investigators develop "plans" for their clients at sentencing.

We will discuss one office that has been doing just this for some time and has a track record on the more traditional statistics used by policy makers to measure what they believe is the test of whether a program is working. We look at data gathered by the Michigan Department of Corrections, which tracks how many defendants are sent to prison, how many receive jail sentences, and from those who would have gone to prison, how many failed on probation. Before looking more closely at this data, it is important to consider briefly a few components of defender programs that engage in problem solving lawyering and embrace the fundamentals of Therapeutic Jurisprudence.

THERAPEUTIC JURISPRUDENCE AS A PART OF PROBLEM SOLVING DEFENDER ORGANIZATIONS

The Neighborhood Defender Service of Harlem ("NDS"), one of the first integrated service public defender programs, has a mission that makes theories of Therapeutic Jurisprudence into reality;

---

munity Justice Through Community Courts, 30 FORDHAM URB. L.J. 897 (2003).

9. Fox Butterfield, *Despite Drop in Crime, an Increase in Inmates*, N.Y. TIMES, Nov. 8, 2004, at A14.

> We are committed to eliminating crime in our community by addressing the problems that bring our clients into court in the first place. This is made possible by an innovation created by NDS—holistic team defense. We involve civil and criminal attorneys, social workers, investigators, paralegals, and college and law school interns in the aggressive defense of our clients. We are dedicated to our mission—to make our constitutional promise of justice a reality for those farthest from its reach. NDS is organized differently from traditional defender offices, which reflects its broadened role in the community it serves. Its services go beyond direct legal representation, to helping clients avoid future contact with the criminal justice system.[10]

Key structural factors that make NDS a highly successful public defense program that protects each client's rights through zealous advocacy and problem solving is its location in the Harlem community, early intervention, team defense, and civil representation and education programs offered in the community.[11]

Similarly, the Georgia Justice Project provides public defense using a therapeutic model. New clients sign a contract with their defense lawyer outlining their obligations, which may include attending counseling, enrolling in a drug rehabilitation clinic or pursuing their GED.[12] For those clients who are incarcerated, members of the Georgia Justice Project visit them in the penitentiary and are available when they return home. The GJP provides many with jobs working at the project's New Horizons Landscaping Company. Innovative public defense practitioners hope to see problem solving approaches like this thrive *so long as each accused person's right to zealous representation remains a fundamental tenet of what it means to provide the assistance of counsel.*[13]

Although this "movement" began in the academy, by linking legal practices to mental health approaches, there are an increasing number of criminal defense lawyers who conceive of their role as counsel more broadly. The Bronx Defenders, one such example, offers their clients a team of staff support that includes an attorney, investigators, a social worker, and if necessary, a civil attorney, administrative support and community developers. The Bronx Defenders "is committed to working with [its] clients, their fam-

---

10. NDS, *Mission Statemement, at* http://www.ndsny.org/mission.htm (providing the NDS mission statement in full) (last visited Apr. 29, 2005).

11. *Id.*

12. Bill Rankin, Unusual Legal Aid Group Helps Turn Lives Around, ATLANTA JOURNAL AND CONSTITUTION, Dec. 2, 2002, at AI; Douglas Ammar, *Georgia Justice Project Turns Lives Around Through Aggressive Defense, Holistic Relationships*, 28 CHAMPION 50 (Jan./Feb. 2004). Contracting with clients is practiced by individual defense lawyers and promoted by Therapeutic Jurisprudence experts. *See* Symposium, *Therapeutic Jurisprudence and Criminal Law*, 38 CRIM. L. BULL. 199 et seq. (Mar.–Apr. 2002).

13. Legitimate theories and innovative practices are always important to explore, but what really counts is whether they take hold in professional practice to improve justice for all. The approaches advocated in Therapeutic Jurisprudence, problem solving justice, and community-oriented lawyering generally make sense to criminal defense lawyers, but most are legitimately concerned that the protections of the adversarial system will be lost if too much emphasis is placed on problem solving rather than zealous advocacy. One of the consensus points articulated at the end of the BJA/Harvard Executive Session on Public Defense (ESPD) was that in defining the role of defenders "[z]ealous representation to individual clients is an essential base or threshold, but expanding the role is also necessary." Cait Clarke, *Introduction* to The Executive Session on Public Defense, 29 N.Y.U. REV. L. & SOC. CHANGE 3, 5 (2004). ESPD members defined this expanded role to include public education, holistic advocacy, and interdisciplinary outreach. *Id.*

ilies, and their communities to address the problems that drive many of [its] clients into the criminal justice system."[14]

On a practical level, retained criminal defense attorneys began the practice of Therapeutic Jurisprudence long ago. They aggressively used treatment for their client as grounds for obtaining favorable release conditions, getting charges dismissed or getting their client diverted out of the system. As a tactical strategy, they used it to make their client more appealing, more alert and "better looking" at trial. When necessary, this treatment often significantly mitigated the sentence. Public defender programs came to holistic sentencing along a slightly different path. Early on they began to use social workers and sentencing specialists in capital cases to ease the pressure of large caseloads and to secure better sentencing plans for their clients. With the growth of problem solving courts,[15] particularly drug courts,[16] and increased attention to sentencing, defenders began to recognize the role effective treatment could play in helping a client's whole life, not just in getting this client a lower sentence in one case.

Effective treatment could stop the cycle of failure and their offices could play a significant role in making these programs work far better than they ever had before. Some leaders of public defense programs realized that community connections are essential to obtaining non-legal services for their clients.[17] They understand that increased community involvement and leadership connections serve three purposes: 1) to access more

---

14. The Bronx Defenders' official website provides the following information:
   Created and staffed by advocates with a broad vision of public defense work, The Bronx Defenders views clients not as "cases," but as whole people: caring parents, hard workers, recent immigrants, native New Yorkers, and students with hope for the future. Our staff of attorneys, social workers, investigators, administrative support, and community developers is committed to working with our clients, their families, and their communities to address the problems that drive many of our clients into the criminal justice system—challenges like addiction, mental illness, inadequate education, lack of access to social support services, and severe family conflict.

The Bronx Defenders, *Welcome to the Bronx Defenders: Introducing Ourselves to the Community*, at http://www.bronxdefenders.org/home (last visited Mar. 14, 2005).

15. The American Counsel of Chief Defenders (ACCD) proposes crucial protections for both accused persons and attorneys against malpractice. For example, the "Ten Tenets" of the ACCD mandate that the accused individual's participation in the program be voluntary, that guilty pleas not operate as prerequisites to participation in treatment court, and that the accused shall be able to withdraw from a program at any time. *See* National Legal Aid & Defenders Assoc., *American Council of Chief Defenders (ACCD) Ten Tenets of Fair and Effective Problem-Solving Courts*, available at http://www.nlada.org/DMS/Documents/1001792198.75/Ten%20Tenets%20of%20 Fair%20and%20Effective%20Problem%20Solving%20Courts-Final%20Version.doc (last visited Mar. 14, 2005).

16. In 22 states at least half of the counties have drug courts in the planning or operational stages. American University School of Public Affairs, *OJP Drug Court Clearinghouse and Technical Assistance Project: Summary of Drug Court Activity by State and County* (Sept. 2, 2004), *available at* http://spa.american.edu/justice/publications/us_drugcourts.pdf (last visited April 29, 2005) [hereinafter *OJP*].

17. *See generally* Cait Clarke, *Community Defenders in the 21st Century: Building on a Tradition of Problem-Solving for Clients, Families and Needy Communities*, 49(1) CMTY. PROSECUTION JAN. 2001, at 20, *available at* http://www.usdoj.gov/usao/eousa/foia_reading_ room/usab4901.pdf (last visited April 29, 2005) (providing a brief overview of the many innovative community defense programs nationwide). Innovative public defense leaders build relationships with an array of community leaders and program because these community resources can provide assistance to their clients beyond what a traditional public defender office can provide. Those who cultivate community relationships outside of the courts recognize how important it is to be tapped into community concerns such as racial profiling or mandatory minimum sentences as well as the need to educate the community about the important role of public defense in justice systems.

community-based social services and other resources; 2) to educate the public about what public defenders do; and 3) to build greater 'good will' with communities to assist with political support when needed. Full-time public defenders in particular are positioned well to embrace problem solving lawyering and therapeutic approaches.

II. Public Defense Programs are Well-Situated to Provide Problem Solving Services and Engage Therapeutic Jurisprudence

There are innovative public defense offices that hire social workers or sentencing advocates as integral team members for representing clients in need of services beyond a criminal case. These lawyers try to problem-solve on behalf of their clients in such areas such as finding substance abuse programs, mental health treatment, job counseling, and community support groups. Professor Bruce Winick, a "founding father" of Therapeutic Jurisprudence, has spelled out how defense lawyers can use advances in offender rehabilitation to design post-offense rehabilitative programs for their clients and use their progress in such programs as grounds for a better plea deal, probation, or a lighter sentence.[18]

Therapeutic Jurisprudence assists defense lawyers in preparing for sensitive conversations with their clients about the need for and value of participating in rehabilitative programs.[19] Overwhelming numbers of cases make these sensitive conversations difficult, but more importantly, defenders are generally not trained to deal with psychological resistance and denial on the part of the client. Therapeutic Jurisprudence approaches can and should be a part of any criminal justice clinics' curriculum as well as public defense training programs nationwide. Particularly with the recent Supreme Court's decision in *Wiggins*, affirming the role of mitigation specialists in capital cases, it is important to note that sentencing and mitigation trainings offered nationwide by the National Association of Sentencing Advocates ("NASA") are grounded in core principles of Therapeutic Jurisprudence.[20] The same applies for non-capital cases. The lead mitigation specialist in the Federal Defender program in Chicago and active NASA board member, James Tibensky, writes that in non-capital cases:

> [o]ne of the ways in which a sentencing advocate differs from a traditional investigator is our emphasis on holistic and clinical interviews with problem-solving recommendations. A clinical interview uses open-ended questions that lead to more questions and to the type of information that a standard informational interview never reaches.... Problem-solving advocacy uses the perspective that the offense represents a problem for society, for the community, for the victim, for the court and for the defendant. The more of those constituencies that can benefit from the sentence, the better the chances that the mitigation work will succeed and the judge will follow the sentence recommendation

---

18. Bruce J. Winick, *Therapeutic Jurisprudence and Preventive Law's Transformative Potential for Particular Areas of Legal Practice: Criminal Law: Redefining the Role of the Criminal Defense Lawyer at Plea Bargaining and Sentencing: A Therapeutic Jurisprudence/Preventive Law Model*, 5 Psychol. Pub. Pol'y & L. 1034, 1082 (1999) ("reconceptualiz[ing] the role of the defense lawyer at plea bargaining and sentencing," exploring how "post-offense rehabilitation [should be] a ground for a downward departure under [the Federal] [S]entencing [G]uidelines" and how, when insufficient time exists to demonstrate substantial progress in rehabilitation, defense lawyers can seek—and judges can grant—deferred sentencing or postponment of a sentencing decision to enable a defendant to demonstrate rehabilitation).
19. *Id.* at 1037–38.
20. *See generally* Wiggins v. Smith, 539 U.S. 510 (2003).

of the defense.... The advocate often must explain to the court the effects of prejudice, poverty, mental illness and family influences on the client. This requires a wide range of experience and training on the part of the advocate. He or she needs to know about mental health, substance abuse, family systems, physiology, community and professional resources, interviewing techniques, persuasive writing, testifying in court, record finding and how to find the necessary experts for evaluations.[21]

Many sentencing advocates and leaders within the NASA have used and trained on motivational interviewing techniques for criminal defense social workers, investigators, mitigation specialists, therapists, paralegals and defense lawyers.[22] Institutional public defenders are perhaps the best place to ensure that whole-client representation and Therapeutic Jurisprudence principles are practiced and improved upon over time with an effective evaluation process in place. One public defense program has moved from a very traditional public defense office to an integrated services model. The Knox County Tennessee Public Defender Community Law Office ("CLO") offers zealous trial advocacy in cases ranging from misdemeanors to death penalty cases; however, an entire wing of the defender offices is dedicated to therapeutic social services that clients can voluntarily join.[23] The CLO provides volunteer services that are said to benefit the community and instill a sense of belonging for their clients.[24] In a therapeutic mode, clients have access to mental health services, behavioral health, alcohol and drug treatment, job counseling, literacy, and even life skills classes, including budgeting and parenting skills.[25] The CLO also provides a unique "Communications Through Art" program for youth from age 11–19 that includes watercolor, painting, pottery, and creative writing

---

21. James Tibensky, *What a Sentencing Advocate Can Do in a Non-Capital Case*, CORNERSTONE, Fall 2004, at 11. James Tibensky, the mitigation specialist in the Federal Defender program in Chicago has been a leader in promoting motivational interviewing techniques in the sentencing advocate and public defense communities for years.

22. *See* Astrid Birgden, *Dealing with the Resistant Criminal Client: A Psychologically-Minded Strategy for More Effective Legal Counseling*, 38 CRIM L. BULL. 225, PINPOINT (2002) (discussing how motivational interviewing explores the kinds of skills that defense lawyers need in these new roles and that clinical programs can help to teach them); *see also* Motivational Interviewing Network of Trainers (MINT), *Motivational Interviewing*, *at* http://motivationalinterview.org (last visited Mar. 14, 2005). *See generally* WILLIAM R. MILLER ET AL., MOTIVATIONAL INTERVIEWING: PREPARING PEOPLE FOR CHANGE (The Guilford Press 2d ed. 2002); JAMES O. PROCHASKA ET AL., CHANGING FOR GOOD: THE REVOLUTIONARY PROGRAM THAT EXPLAINS THE SIX STAGES OF CHANGE AND TEACHES YOU HOW TO FREE YOURSELF FROM BAD HABITS (William Morrow & Co. 1994).

23. The Knox County Public Defender Community Law Office ("CLO") has a mission of providing zealous trial representation, but also a social service mission to promote Therapeutic Jurisprudence principles to help clients and the Tennessee community they serve.

The CLO's Social Service Component is dedicated to working directly with the client to design a life skills plan of action. This plan offers clients the opportunity to address individual needs and to utilize their skills and talents to generate personal and community value. Rather than dictating a direction for the future, the CLO empowers the client to play an active role in shaping his or her own personal goals.

Knox County Public Defender Community Law Office, *Social Services: Providing a Framework to Build Upon, at* http://www.pdknox.org/2Social.htm (last visited Mar. 14, 2005) [*Providing a Framework*].

24. Knox County Public Defender Community Law Office, *Community Outreach: Developing a Sense of Belonging, at* http://www.pdknox.org/3community.htm (last visited Mar. 14, 2005).

25. *Providing a Framework*, *supra* note 23 (including information on social services provided by the Knox County Public Defender Community Law Office).

classes along with field trips to museums and live performances.[26] From a civil legal services approach, the CLO assists their public defense clients with issues such as employment, immigration, domestic relations, social security claims, on-the-job injuries and aid in obtaining valid identification, such as Social Security cards, drivers' licenses, or birth certificates.

Other public defense providers are perhaps unknowingly promoting Therapeutic Jurisprudence by working more closely with sentencing advocate professionals, community corrections programs, and empowering lawyers, family members and community members to become active in progressive sentencing advocacy.[27] Defenders who think in terms of problem solving observe that a criminal case can provide an opportunity, with the client's permission, to address underlying problems that brought the person into the criminal courts. This mirrors the thinking of some judicial leaders of the Therapeutic Jurisprudence movement like Judge Peggy Fulton and Judge William G. Schma who explain that "[t]he idea behind Therapeutic Jurisprudence is that since the experience of coming before our courts is having therapeutic consequences for defendants, our courts should capitalize on the moment when a person is brought before us and use it as a starting point for improving the defendant's overall lifestyle."[28] Creative defenders and public defense leaders understand the importance of early case entry then using the post-arrest interviews and plea negotiations as opportunities to encourage clients to engage in problem solving activities or rehabilitation.[29]

A. DEFENDERS HAVE A SPECIAL CONNECTION TO CLIENTS AND COMMUNITIES FOR THERAPEUTIC JURISPRUDENCE

Public defense programs play a critical role in advancing the problem solving, therapeutic movement because they have special connections to their clients and the indigent communities they serve. The attorney-client privilege means that defense lawyers are uniquely situated for special communications and information-sharing opportunities. They bring an entirely different and crucial perspective to the problem solving, Therapeutic Jurisprudence movements. Public defenders' daily work brings them into close proximity with the jails, court personnel, probation and parole, and most importantly, constant access to their clients and their families who often live in socio-economically deprived communities. Professional public defenders have experience at creatively leveraging and allocating social service resources, which generally private attorneys or

---

26. Knox County Public Defender Community Law Office, *Communication Through Art*, at http://www.pdknox.org/calendar/ArtsProgram.htm (last visited Mar. 14, 2005).
27. Therapeutic Jurisprudence and restorative justice scholarship explores attributes of a good treatment court from a more global perspective. Restorative justice explains the need for the changes in the criminal justice system. Innovative programs that promote the community's role in case adjudication are the best place to explore the need for convergence between Therapeutic Jurisprudence, community problem-solving, and restorative justice. For example, Community Leadership for Justice, a new collaboration between The Center for Community Alternatives, The Sentencing Project, and the National Association of Sentencing Advocates (NASA), seeks to transform the framework that governs sentencing advocacy. Much like the theories of Therapeutic Jurisprudence, community problem-solving, and restorative justice, this program plans to empower family members and neighbors to become active participants in progressive sentencing advocacy.
28. The Honorable Peggy Fulton Hora & the Honorable William G. Schma, *Therapeutic Jurisprudence*, JUDICATURE, July–Aug. 1998, at 8, 9.
29. Winick, *supra* note 18, at 1049, 1059 (discussing that pretrial release and attempts to defer sentence can be valuable problem solving opportunities and that defenders can use this time to encourage the client to engage in post-arrest rehabilitation).

contractors cannot perform on a larger scale. Thus, defenders need to be full and equal partners in any court reform effort (such as the creation of problem solving courts) or innovative justice programs like those of Therapeutic Jurisprudence or problem solving justice initiatives.

A cultural shift towards Therapeutic Jurisprudence and problem solving has already occurred in one area—the spread of problem solving or specialized courts.[30] Data collection and analysis has been critical in shifting cultural attitudes about these specialized courts. Drug courts now number over 1100 and mental health courts are increasing in numbers.[31] The data, although not conclusive for all analysts, has been generally persuasive—persuasive enough to cause a cultural shift among judges, prosecutors, a growing number of defender offices and the U.S. Department of Justice, which promotes problem solving court development nationwide. Data has been a crucial link to the spread of these courts. The National Drug Court Institute's data collection efforts support findings that drug courts decrease recidivism, save money and provide affordable treatment.[32] A number of state and local studies have found that drug courts are more cost effective than conventional adjudication.[33] On the other hand, a 2000 study by the Vera Institute reports that the effect of drug courts on jail and prison costs are unclear. The authors suggest that a more accurate picture of bed savings would require more research into whether drug courts are enrolling offenders actually bound for jail or prison and the effect of using detention to punish noncompliant program participants. Even if the outcomes are unclear, positive signs reported from data gathered by Institutes, the academy and non-profit centers like the Center for Court Innovation feed the movement.

B. WHAT IS NEEDED FOR DEFENDERS TO ENGAGE THERAPEUTIC JURISPRUDENCE AND ADOPT PROBLEM SOLVING PRACTICES?

There are cultural barriers to an expanded notion of what it means to provide counsel in a therapeutic mode inside defender programs; and, perhaps most importantly, there is simply not enough data to show it works. Without the data, there is not enough financial or political support to expand the role of indigent defense providers to engage in creative problem solving or therapeutic approaches that reach beyond providing a zealous defense to treating the whole client in a way that benefits the client, the system,

---

30. For a more thorough discussion of these emerging problem solving court models, *see generally* JUDGING IN A THERAPEUTIC KEY: THERAPEUTIC JURISPRUDENCE AND THE COURTS (Bruce J. Winick & David B. Wexler eds., Carolina Acad. Press 2003).

31. The National Drug Court Institute ("NDCI") reports that there are "1,183 drug courts currently in operation ... [with] 414 actively involved in the planning process in 2003 ... and another 184 jurisdictions accepted into the ... BJA[.]" C. WEST HUDDLETON, III ET AL., 1(1) NAT'L DRUG COURT INST., *PAINTING THE CURRENT PICTURE: A NATIONAL REPORT CARD ON DRUG COURTS AND OTHER PROBLEM-SOLVING COURT PROGRAMS IN THE UNITED STATES* 1 (National Drug Court Institute May 2004), *available at* http://www.ndci.org/publications/paintingcurrentpicture.pdf (last visited April 29, 2005). The BJA has a Mental Health Courts Program that assists states through grants and technical assistance to develop mental health courts nationally. *See* Bureau of Justice Assistance, *Mental Health Courts, at* http://www.ojp.usdoj.gov/BJA/grant/mentalhealth.html (last visited Mar. 14, 2005). BJA selected the Council of State Governments (CSG), coordinator of the Consensus Project, as the technical assistance provider for the BJA Mental Health Courts Grant Program. *See* Criminal Justice/Mental Health Consensus Project, *BJA Mental Health Courts Program, at* http://www.consensusproject.org/projects/BJA-MHCP/(last visited Mar. 14, 2005).

32. Huddleton, III et al., *supra* note 31, at 2.

33. Id.

and the community. Proponents need a strategy to use this data to educate and promote a cultural shift among all the stakeholders in a criminal justice system.[34] Community-oriented, problem solving defenders, such as the Bronx Defenders, are keenly aware of the need for cultural shifts both inside a defender program and in the community, and have written about ways to shift that culture.[35] Educating future lawyers, judges, and lawmakers about problem solving approaches to defense practice and Therapeutic Jurisprudence, particularly through law clinics, is also an important part of this strategy to cause a cultural shift.

Data showing reduced recidivism, lower probation, and parole failure rates, greater access to bond, shorter sentences, and less jail and prison time will be necessary to engage defenders and other stakeholders in these approaches that make sense, but are hard to execute.

Defender programs need a commitment that shifts resources away from incarceration and towards the front end to further these therapeutic approaches on behalf of their clients. Measuring success and cost-savings, therefore, is as important as implementing a broader education campaign. There is some work underway to measure outcomes for defender programs that provide holistic representation. For example, the Georgia Justice Project reports that their,

> lawyers and social workers have been using this approach for over 17 years and it works. The recidivism rate for GJP clients is 18.8% compared to a national average of over 60%. The incarceration rate for GJP clients is 7.30% compared to an average of 71.30% in a study of urban public defender offices.[36]

The National Legal Aid and Defender Association ("NLADA") is currently engaged in a pilot project to collect and analyze data from a holistic defender program in Atlanta, Georgia. The Holistic and Community-Oriented Defender ("HCOD") project is working with the Fulton County Conflict Defender ("FCCD") to study the impact of their publicly-licensed clinical social worker staff that works with clients on substance abuse, mental disability, and homelessness. The data collection is underway and the report will be published in 2005.[37] The goal of HCOD is to study whether FCCD's therapeutic services and structural approaches to indigent defense will achieve both signifi-

---

34. By a "cultural shift" we mean changing the knowledge, skills, attitudes and beliefs of public defense practitioners, other criminal justice stakeholders, legislators, funding agents and community leaders so that they embrace problem solving approaches and Therapeutic Jurisprudence theories.

35. *See* Robin Steinberg & David Feige, *Cultural Revolution: Transforming the Public Defender Office*, 29 N.Y.U. REV. L. & SOC. CHANGE 123 (2004).
> Changing the culture of a public defender office is nothing more than privileging the values of those who care and making them universal. It takes commitment and it takes time, but it is good for clients, and underserved communities, and even good for public defenders. Creating a client-centered public defender office can change the way you see the work, and ultimately, in some little way, perhaps the world.

Id. at 133.

36. Georgia Justice Project, *GJP Approach*, at http://www.gjp.org/about (last visited Mar. 29, 2005). It is worth noting, however, they "do not take the following cases except under exceptional circumstances: drug trafficking, domestic violence, sex crimes, federal cases, child abuse, cases outside Fulton or Dekalb Counties, vehicle violations, civil cases." *Id.*

37. The HCOD report will be published on the NLADA web site *at* http://www.nlada.org. (forthcoming) (on file with authors). Dr. David Meyer, of the University of Southern California, and David Carroll, director of Research and Evaluation at NLADA will author the much-awaited HCOD report.

cantly better case outcomes for clients and significant savings of public funding compared to traditional case dispositions (i.e., incarceration).

Another program, the Rhode Island Public Defender office, began a holistic community outreach program called the Defender Community Advocacy Program ("DCAP"), which focuses primarily on court intervention at the arraignment stage. The Rhode Island public defenders work with social workers, investigators, intake specialists, the office's Community Outreach Liaison and administrative support staff to provide assessments and alternatives to incarceration at the arraignment stage. The Rhode Island program has begun to see dramatic results for their clients and have begun measuring the cost savings. Data collected from March 2004 through September 2004 shows that due to reduced prison time, they believe it has saved the taxpayers over four million dollars in prison costs along with court days saved that would have been held for pretrial hearings and violations of probation.[38]

It is critical to the successful integration of these ideas into traditional criminal defense practices to gather data demonstrating positive outcomes and convincing the key players that it is worth the time and energy to pursue problem solving or Therapeutic Jurisprudence practices.

C. Defenders Can Adopt Procedures to Impact Client Outcomes

Positive data may promote a cultural shift inside different justice sectors so that more professionals and community members favor these approaches—and eventually become advocates for increased financial and political support for implementing problem solving practices.[39] For example, good defense lawyers understand the value of getting one's client out of jail as fast as possible because of the impact incarceration has on case outcomes—not to mention the social impact such as employment, family life demands, collateral consequences, and community pressures. In a 1992 study of the Nation's seventy-five most populous counties, the Bureau of Justice Statistics found that defendants who were released before trial had lower conviction rates (61%) than those who were detained (79%).[40] Detained convicted defendants "were more than twice as likely as released defendants to receive a state prison sentence."[41] Traditional defender program leaders who are aware of these statistics can restructure their office procedures to ensure that pre-trial release is a priority. It does not have to fall entirely on lawyers' shoulders either. Systems can be developed or vastly improved through working with

---

38. DCAP's preliminary data for this time period shows 4.4 million in prison dollars saved along with 1,027 dates in court saved. Peter Wells, Presentation at the National Legal Aid and Defender Association's Annual Conference in Wash., D.C., *Taking Public Defense to the Streets: Working with Client Communities Outside the Courtroom* (Dec. 2, 2004) (the Rhode Island Public Defender Program's Community Outreach Liaison Statistical breakdown of data is on file with author, Cait Clarke).

39. Sectors ripe for this cultural shift include public defense, prosecution, judiciary, court administration, legislators, policymakers, parole and probation, pretrial services, corrections and funding agents.

40. Brian J. Reeves & Jacob Perez, *National Pretrial Reporting Program: Pretrial Release of Felony Defendants, 1992*, Bureau of Justice Statistics Bull., Nov. 1994, at 14, Table 18, *available at* http://www.ojp.usdoj.gov/bjs/pub/pdf/nprp92.pdf (last visited Mar. 30, 2005). This disparity widens in the context of felony defendants. Detained felony defendants were convicted at a rate of 70%, compared to 45% for released defendants. *Id.*

41. *Id.* at Table 19. Upon conviction, 87% of detained defendants were sentenced to incarceration while only 51% of the convicted released defendants were sentenced to incarceration. Among detained defendants, 67% were convicted and sentenced to incarceration. Only 29% of released defendants were convicted and sentenced to incarceration. *Id.* (Statistics summarized in Figure 4).

the locals criminal justice system to ensure that accurate, client based information is gathered, by the defender office, or through other system agents and presented to magistrates, diversion programs, and pre-trial services from the day of arrest forward. Early intervention of social workers, paralegals, investigators, mental health experts or mitigation specialists, for example, can assist trial lawyers in getting their clients out of jail pre-trial thereby having a direct impact on the likelihood of a sentence of imprisonment. This also increases the likelihood that the client may be open to social services in a therapeutic environment.

Examples of defense practices more aligned with Therapeutic Jurisprudence values are those whose defenders are provided with the opportunity for early case entry, adequate time to meet with and counsel their clients privately, access to pre-trial services or diversion alternatives early-on, and entrée to treatment programs so they can encourage their clients to take advantage of these resources. All these defender-related factors can have a positive impact on the way accused persons are treated, (i.e., fairly and with dignity) while fostering efficiency and cost-savings for a justice system.

III. Can Traditional Defender Programs Take Steps to Improve Client Outcomes?

The real challenge is that most public defense programs cannot become wholly integrated service providers like the Georgia Justice Project, the Neighborhood Defender Service of Harlem, the Bronx Defenders, the Community Law Office in Knox County, highlighted above, or the Washtenaw Public Defender Office, discussed below. Legitimate theories of Therapeutic Jurisprudence and innovative problem solving practices should be explored, but what will really count is whether they take hold in professional practice to improve justice for those in need. These approaches generally make sense to criminal defense lawyers. In reality, however, overwhelming caseloads and diminishing resources to support the fundamentals of criminal defense representation make these ideas and practices unattainable for most public defense practitioners.

Problem solving approaches and Therapeutic Jurisprudence practices demand more resources to be practiced effectively. Most line-lawyer defenders do not have the time or resources to do the basic job of representing individual clients competently from start to finish in each and every case.[42] There may, however, be some incremental ways that defender programs can be set up and provide effective representation that produces: 1)

---

42. *See generally* The National Legal Aid and Defender Association, *Evaluation of the Public Defender Office: Clark County, Nevada* (March 2003) (reporting on the state of indigent defense in Las Vegas, NV) *available at* http://www.nlada.org/Defender/Defender_ Evaluation/old_index_html (last visited Mar. 17, 2005). Though Clark County policymakers must balance other demands on the County's resources, the Constitution does not allow for justice to be rationed to the poor due to limited funding. The issues raised in this report serve to underscore the failure on the part of the state of Nevada to adhere to the *Gideon* decision. *Id* at 76. Though *Gideon* vests the responsibility for funding indigent defense services with the state, the County continues to near the brunt of providing adequate defender services until such time as the State accepts its constitutional responsibilities. *Id.*; The National Legal Aid and Defender Association, NATIONAL ASSOCIATION OF CRIMINAL DEFENSE LAWYERS, *In Defense of Public Access to Justice: An Assessment of Trial-Level Indigent Defense Services in Louisiana 40 Years after Gideon* (March 2004) *available at* http://www.nlada.org/Defender/Defender_Evaluation/la_evaluation (last visited Mar. 30, 2005) (describing in detail how the indigent defense system in Louisiana is in violation of the Louisiana Constitution, the U.S. Constitution, and the ABA Ten Principles of a Public Defense Delivery System adopted by the ABA in 2002).

better case outcomes; 2) opportunities to infuse problem solving approaches early in each case; and 3) cost savings and efficiencies for the system.

The following section is a case study that shows positive signs of how a traditional public defender office can achieve these three goals. We are not social scientists, but the data set forth in the next section from an Ann Arbor Michigan study is quite promising for public defender leaders who are interested in these more therapeutic outcomes for clients, reduced incarceration rates and systemic efficiencies. Moreover, it provides measures that are extremely persuasive with policymakers such as lower use of prison jails and lower probation violation rates. It is persuasive because the analysis and conclusions were developed, not by the defender office, but by researchers in the Washtenaw Community Corrections Program and in the Michigan Department of Corrections.

IV. THE WASHTENAW COUNTY CASE STUDY

The Defender Office in Ann Arbor Michigan, the Washtenaw County Public Defender Office, illustrates how more data analysis of public defense roles can promote better results for their clients, a more efficient criminal justice system and reduce the costs to the system they serve. Washtenaw County makes the case for the practical impact of such an approach. Demonstrating lower prison commitment rates, lower use of the jail and lower probation violation rates creates support for such an approach that will reach out to policy makers across a wide spectrum of values. Further, the results in Washtenaw are not the result of a new program begun in the last few years. Over thirty years ago, the Defender Office became a full partner in the criminal justice system. They fully participated in the design of new programs systems and procedures. Their attorneys sit on the boards of local mental health centers, the local judicial council, juvenile treatment programs, shelters and drug treatment programs. There are no drug courts or even pretrial release services. Problems were identified, tasks delegated and efficiencies obtained within their resources. For example, within 48 hours of arrest, the client is interviewed and assessed for mental illness. Client histories are taken by community corrections and the defender office is notified of their appointment. Magistrates grant personal bonds if the accused is "scored" as likely to not receive prisoner jail time if convicted. They also know that the defender will see their client before the preliminary examination, take even more detailed client histories and file a motion for bond reduction at the preliminary examination. If denied, and the defendant remains incarcerated, they will file another motion before the trial judge.

This intense involvement by the office assures a significantly lower number of client sitting jail awaiting trial. It is this information that is relied upon at bond hearings, for diversion planning and in plea negotiations. Further, when bonds were thought to be creeping higher than their clients could post, the defense community appeared before the judicial council and raised their concern. This action not only reined in the bonds, but it helped establish a climate of dialogue, trust and cooperation among all the participants in the system and relieved growing tensions.

Coping with Washtenaw County's undersized jail gives rise to another example of the impact they have by being part of the process. First, the Washtenaw County jail is the smallest per capita in Michigan. County growth and changes in the states sentencing policies designed to lower prison commitments, created pressures for innovative change. Long ago, authorities developed a broad array of processes and programs that, up to now, have successfully avoided overcrowding. The county recently released a report[43] calling for a larger jail. The Task Force, on which the Defender Office sat, called not only for a larger jail, but for a study on what kind of beds to add, for more treatment programs and for procedural reforms in the court processes to decrease the length of time that pretrial detainees spend in jail when they cannot make bond.

A. Lower Prison Commitment Rates and Lower Probation Violation Rates

From 1998 through 2002, Washtenaw County Michigan had the lowest prison commitment rate among the 13 largest Michigan counties when judges had the discretion to give a non-prison sentence. In many cases the low prison commitment rate is off-set by higher use of local jails. However, in Washtenaw County this is not the case. In fact, it has one of the smallest jails in Michigan. Finally, perhaps to achieve these results, probation was "overused." However, even this is not the case. Washtenaw's probation violation rate was significantly below the state average. In 2003, Joseph DeGraff, the Community Corrections Manager for Washtenaw County, spoke to the Michigan Legislature[44] on the role that the Washtenaw County Public Defender Office had in keeping their counties commitment rate so far below the state average. He first acknowledged that isolating the impact of one component in the system is difficult to do. But he noted several factors that made the case that their presence and activities where the major factor that separated their county from the rest in Michigan.

First, the public defender plays a significant role in case processing in Washtenaw County. The office represents 85–87% of the felony defendants in the County. In addition, they represent significant numbers of misdemeanants, probation violators and juvenile offenders. Second, Degraff analyzed the data for measurable outcomes that made the case for the impact of the office. Michigan is a mandatory sentencing guideline state, and there are many felonies that carry mandatory sentences. Degraff isolated the data where judges have discretion to impose prison or non-prison sentences. This occurs in "straddle cell" cases and probation violations. Straddle cells are those cases that when scored under the guidelines, fall in cells that allow the judge to sentence to probation, jail, or prison. Degraff additionally found that in the thirteen mid-size counties with populations between 150,000 and 600,000, Washtenaw County had the lowest straddle cell commitment rate. In fact, it was not even close. Washtenaw was the only county below 30% on the commitment rate. More impressive was the data that Washtenaw County's return rate for probation violators was 6% below the state average—even though they had more straddle cell "risks" out on probation.[45]

Percentage of Probationer Intakes to Prison CY 2001[46]

The low prison commitment and return rate translated to 68 fewer annual prison commitments. Using a conservative cost of incarceration rate, this translates to over

---

43. *See generally* Washtenaw County Jail Overcrowding Task Force, *Final Report and Recommendations: A New Criminal Justice System*, March 31, 2004 [hereinafter Washentaw Task Force].

44. Joseph DeGraff, *Reducing the Corrections Budget Through Effective Public Defense*, Michigan State University, Institute for Public Policy and Social Research, Public Policy Forum (Oct. 15, 2003) (on file with author). Joseph DeGraff is the Community Corrections Manager for Washtenaw County in Michigan.

45. Michigan Department of Corrections, *2002 Annual Report*, available at http://www.state.mi.us/mdoc/jobs/pdfs/2002AnnualReport.pdf.

46. *Id.*

$2,000,000 annually plus additional money returned to the county by the state for using alternative sanctions.

County	1998	1999	2000	2001
Bay	56.5	46.0	41.1	44.3
Calhoun	46.3	49.6	46.4	35.9
Genesee	50.9	56.7	54.2	43.6
Ingham	41.5.	34.5	32.2	39.2
Kalamazoo	36.4	36.3	44.8	36.9
Kent	46.4	40.1	40.7	27.6
Macomb	33.7	44.0	44.9	29.7
Muskegon	64.3	62.7	63.1	38.2
Oakland	31.8	31.6	33.5	
Ottawa	35.2	33.3	34.7	
Saginaw	61.8	46.3	32.8	
Washtenaw	23.3	29.5	24.1	
Wayne	25.9	35.8	41.8	
State Average	39.0%	41.0%	43.0%	

Other possible contributors to the low prison commitment rate, such as a higher use of the jail, need to be eliminated. However, this could only be true if Washtenaw had a larger than average jail. In fact, the Washtenaw jail is 40% smaller than the state average. It has 332 beds for a population of 334,000. It is the only jurisdiction in Michigan that has less than 1 bed per thousand of population. Since the county pays for the jail and the state pays for the prison, it would seem there would be an incentive to send inmates to the prison rather than the jail, particularly since it is so small. Finally, one would expect to see a widened net of alternative sanctions if the jail and prison commitment rates are low. However, of the 13 mid-size counties, Washtenaw ranks eighth in alternative program funding. The existence of a well-funded public defender office cannot be the sole factor contributing to these low rates of incarceration and use of alternative sanctions.

The question arises whether the existence of *any* public defender office or other assigned counsel system or contract private practitioner would have a similar effect. The answer is clearly "no." Of the 13 counties compared in this study, Bay, Kent and Washtenaw had public defender offices. However, the prison commitment rates and probation violation commitment rates were significantly higher than Washtenaw's—among the highest in the state. In fact, as noted below, while the Washtenaw office comes fairly close to meeting the American Bar Association's *10 Principles of a Public Defense System*,[47] the Bay County office is woefully under-funded. Even cursory comparisons reveal important differences. The caseloads in Bay City are 4–5 times higher than in Washtenaw. There are four characteristics of the Washtenaw Public Defender office that the Community Corrections office believes supports the case for the impact of this defender office and which none of the other offices meet:

---

47. *See generally* ABA, STANDING COMMITTEE ON LEGAL AID AND INDIGENT DEFENDERS, *Ten Principles of a Public Defense Delivery System*, *available at* http://www.nlada.org/Defender/Defender_Kit/principles (last visited Mar. 30, 2005).

Proximity and Presence. The office is located adjacent to the county courts and provides attorneys for a wide array of services from Personal Protection Order's, line-ups and probation violations to murder trials and felony sentencing and diversion programs.

Continuity and experience. The office has been a fixture in the County of decades. They have salary parity with the prosecutor, have career defenders and are required to attend training. The experience of the staff and office contributes to community trust and the competency of the services delivered.

Partner in the System. The public defender is a full and equal partner in the justice system in the County. They are represented in virtually every programming, policy or procedural committee. For example, they are represented on the community corrections advisory board, the judicial oversight committee, the domestic violence initiative, the jail overcrowding task force, the jail mental health work group, the executive sessions of the judicial counsel, the restorative justice committee, the foster care abuse and neglect board, the racial profiling committee, and the attorney appointment board. *The public defender influences policy, educates justice, and advocates for alternative dispositions.*

Economy in the system. The public defender creatively leverages and allocates resources and provides services not readily available from the private sector appointees or contractors. They also generate hidden efficiencies in docket management and other cooperative programs to increase efficiencies or reduce costs at no additional county expense. In the midst of a budget crisis in 1995, they looked at eliminating the defender office to use cheaper methods. They found that while the office cost more than six other similarly sized counties' defense systems, they needed to look at the impact on the entire system.

Besides a comparison of dollars, quality of services should also be taken into consideration. The office of the public defender provides a great deal of flexibility in the county's court system and offers other programs and services that a contracted attorney or firm would not, such as the extensive use of college interns.

B. Early Case Entry

There is one more factor that separates this office from all other public defense systems in Michigan and greatly contributes to its success: The office has worked with the local community corrections department to design a system that collects accurate information early in the process and get it to key custody decision makers. In addition, the office meets with all of their clients and the prosecutor before the day of the preliminary examination and collects even more data on the client. The information is then used at the first arraignment when bond is set through all the possible pretrial release decisions and plea discussions. Further, if the client remains in custody, at least two bond reduction motions are made — one before the preliminary examination judge and one before the trial judge. As discussed above, national statistics show that whether a client is incarcerated pretrial has a significant impact on whether he or she ultimately receives a sentence of incarceration.[48] Reduced incarceration rates of accused persons pretrial can mean significant cost savings.

Unlike anywhere else in the state, this information identifies every potential option for the client. Unlike data scraped together by the defendant or overworked impersonal pretrial released services or court personnel, Washtenaw's accused have the information

---

48. This disparity widens in the context of felony defendants. Detained felony defendants were convicted at a rate of 70%, compared to 45% for released defendants.

screened and verified by professionals in the defender's office. Moreover, they have the ability to obtain additional supporting information at every step of the pretrial process. This early entry, coupled with the office's contacts throughout the system and community, produces the profound and predictable impacts noted above. This significantly benefits not only the county, but also the budgets of their county and state. Finally, if the defendant violates probation or bond, they meet with the community corrections department before the hearing, which develops programs in order to keep the client out of jail. They appear at the probation violation hearing and jointly present their proposal.

As a result of the above factors, the office has an even more significant impact on the local justice system. The office advocates effectively for pre-trial alternatives, such as supervised release to financial bail for non-violent offenders. These advocacy opportunities can further Therapeutic Jurisprudence opportunities resulting in better client outcomes and system savings. These pre-trial programs are typically designed for, and populated by, drug or alcohol addicted clients, many of whom cannot afford retained legal counsel.

In FY 2001–02, *only half of 200 felonies enrolled in pre-trial supervised release were ultimately convicted of a felony charge*, with charges actually dismissed for 7% of these defendants.

In FY 2001–02, *the prison commitment rate for these defendants was less than half* that of all non-violent offenders county-wide.

Since FY 1998–99, *the percentage of inmates lodged in jail for alcohol-related offenses has decreased from 11% of the total jail population to less than 7%* through the use of electronic alcohol monitoring as a condition of pre-trial release. The reduction translates to twelve fewer defendants in jail on any given day. Approximately 90% of the clients completed the average 70-day period of round-the-clock alcohol monitoring without evidence of further alcohol use. According to County Jail Reimbursement Program Data, Washtenaw County's average length of stay for OUIL three defendant's in jail is among the state's lowest, because offenders are efficiently placed into treatment programs.[49]

This is an office that not only provides a zealous defense on the merits of the case, but profoundly reduces incarceration and recidivism. Good defense is good business—for everyone.

C. Collaboration with Defenders and Other Stakeholders

With all this, Washtenaw County leaders believe they can and must do better. The above results came about not through a new vision or commitment to drug courts. They do not have one. Rather, the above is the result of years of collaborative effort. The Jail Overcrowding Task Force Final Report of 2004 recognizes the need for a larger jail due to county growth and truth in sentencing laws passed by the legislature.[50] This Overcrowding Task Force report however calls for even more reforms and a commitment to further enhance community corrections programs. County leaders want to know what kind of beds to add, how many and how they can further reduce the total need. They want to not only "resolve the questions about the jail, but the mission is to manage the system."[51] The particularly good news from Washtenaw County is that collaborative efforts, good structural design and early defense involvement can have signif-

---

49. Degraff, *supra* note 44.
50. Washtenaw Task Force, *supra* note 43.
51. *Id.*

icant impacts on the clients, on the system's efficiency and citizen support. Coalitions like the one in Washtenaw County, where public defender participation is valued, will promote more Therapeutic Jurisprudence practices and provide data that problem solving early on in a criminal case will benefit clients, communities, and the county coffers.

V. Another Way to Promote a Culture Shift Among Public Defender Leaders — Education

The cultural shift towards problem solving lawyering and holistic advocacy is taking place among innovative leaders in the indigent defense community. Public defender and assigned counsel leaders are attending Executive leadership seminars in NLADA's National Defender Leadership Institute ("NDLI"). Through trainings, networking, mentoring opportunities and publications, the NDLI promotes ideas on problem solving lawyering and the value of strengthening an array of community connections to support indigent defense programs. NDLI messages to public defense leaders and their allies emphasize the importance of community outreach in order to provide more social service resources for indigent clients and political support.

Although NDLI faculty do not use the terminology "Therapeutic Jurisprudence," much of the curriculum and leadership initiatives further Therapeutic Jurisprudence theories. Problem solving on behalf of individual clients seems to be more acceptable among defense practitioners. In 2002–2004 the U.S. Department of Justice, Bureau of Justice Assistance ("BJA"), funded only one program designed for public defenders. This discretionary grant funded a public defense leadership seminar series called "Impact Leadership." The seminars taught public defense leaders to develop innovative leadership initiatives, all of which were geared towards an expanded role for public defenders in their communities and new ways to help their individual clients. These initiatives ranged from prisoner reentry programs to problem solving for foster children moving out of foster homes so that they did not enter the criminal justice system.

The NDLI is working on promoting a cultural shift that favors problem solving, community-oriented representation. Funding and grass-roots support for this work is critical to its success. The cultural shift needs to take place inside defender programs as well as funding agencies and governing bodies, such as state legislators and city governments. The NDLI has trained public defense leaders on how to build coalitions with both likely and unlikely allies. These leadership-training events promote problem solving through communications training, political outreach training, networking skills and strategic thinking about more technical assistance, research and evaluation of public defense programs.

This much-needed cultural shift inside defender programs and other justice sectors will not happen unless there is evidence that Therapeutic Jurisprudence and problem solving lawyering is cost-effective, efficient, and creates improved justice systems. Innovative defense lawyers recognize that public defense leaders need to be more open to evaluation and data collection. We need other professionals like social scientists and academics to evaluate the impact of their representation models. With the help of academics in law schools and other schools, defenders who support problem solving models can demonstrate the value of these integrated services and holistic practices. Academics are in good positions to help practitioners and policymakers gather data, engage in critical analyses of data, develop strategies and assist in the dissemination and education so that these innovative ideas take root.[52] Those interested in seeing problem solving ap-

---

52. *See generally* Bruce J. Winick, *Redefining the Role of the Criminal Defense Lawyer at Plea Bargaining and Sentencing: A Therapeutic Jurisprudence/Preventive Law Model*, in Practicing Thera-

proaches and Therapeutic Jurisprudence become grounded in criminal proceedings and public defense practices will need to demonstrate the practical benefits. Law schools are not the only allies for public defense leaders espousing these therapeutic practices. Other parts of universities can provide invaluable expertise and can be unlikely allies of institutional public defense reform. For example, defender leader, James M. Hingeley, the Public Defender of the Charlottesville—County of Albemarle Indigent Defense Commission regional office, reached out to the Engineering Department at the University of Virginia to seek assistance with mental health diversion alternatives for the public defender clients. The University's engineering department produced the report *An Analysis of Mental Health Diversion Options in the City of Charlottesville Criminal Justice System*[53] which was a cutting edge approach to analyzing data and practices that would further practices consistent with Therapeutic Jurisprudence theories. Leadership is about relationship-building. The more innovative public defender leaders understand the value of building relationships with likely—and unlikely allies.

A. LEGAL CLINICS CAN SUPPORT PROBLEM SOLVING PUBLIC DEFENSE

Clinicians, academics and practitioners in the field need to collaborate to gain a more accurate sense of how the entire justice system works. Legal clinics could be a critical component in this effort. Clinics not only teach Therapeutic Jurisprudence theories, and train future lawyers how to engage in problem solving for individual clients, but also how to advocate for systemic support for these approaches to practicing law. Larger systemic analysis of the impact of these innovative practices on individual cases is where clinical legal education can teach law students and other justice system players that it is not only affordable for lawyers to practice law with an expanded role, but that it is cost effective for state and local judicial systems.

Clinics provide a unique opportunity for professors and students interested in justice systems to study how different sectors impact one another as well as the political context for decision-making. These data can be used to play a different and possibly more important advocacy role. Future lawyers interested in equal justice need to be taught how to advocate before legislators, policymakers and community members who may want to cut funding or limit the role of public defense lawyers in a justice system.

Clinical legal education generally focuses on individual case representation. Few criminal clinical supervisors gather empirical data and justice system "big picture" analyses for use in teaching. Likewise, few defense lawyers who lead programs have access to real numbers showing how different approaches to criminal defense practices can impact the outcome of cases either pre-trial, during trial or at disposition hearings. Clinical training for future defense lawyers, for example, could provide this informa-

---

PEUTIC JURISPRUDENCE: LAW AS A HELPING PROFESSION 245 (2000); David Wexler, *Therapeutic Jurisprudence and Preventative Law's Transformative Potential For Particular Areas of Legal Practice: Criminal Law: Relapse Prevention Planning Principles for Criminal Law Practice*, 5 PSYCHOL. PUB. POL'Y & LAW 1028, 1032 (1999) (suggesting a strategy for proposing client-centered—and client generated—release conditions, a process that encourages a client to think through his/her high risk situations and how to avoid them).

53. RYAN BOULAIS, ET. AL., *An Analysis of Mental Health Diversion: Options in the City of Charlottesville Criminal Justice System*, UNIV. OF VA. SYSTEMS AND INFORMATION ENGINEERING DEPT' ed., April 23, 2004 (Corporate participants in this collaborative effort to analyze the therapeutic diversion options included: Northrop Grumman, MITRE Corp., Directed Technologies, Lockheed Martin Corp., Oracle Corp., and BAE Systems) (on file with author).

tion. Clinicians could not only teach about systemic operations but they could publish studies of state and local justice systems including the inefficiencies and innovations like Therapeutic Jurisprudence. Clinical legal educators could provide law students, as well as practitioners focused on individual cases, with a birds-eye view of their local criminal justice systems.

B. The Role of Criminal Justice Clinics

Criminal defense clinics present a unique opportunity for future lawyers to take a reduced caseload and learn how to practice defense the correct way. Clinics teach law students how to prepare a case fully from start to finish—from initial client interviews, investigations, developing a theory of defense, creating a trial notebook, preparing and practicing each element of a trial and then developing a sentencing plan the way it should be done. In the real world of public defense, it is universal that in state courts there are too many cases and too little time for public defense practitioners to do it this way.

It would be most beneficial if Therapeutic Jurisprudence and problem solving lawyering could be an integral part of clinical legal education in two respects. First, train future lawyers to practice zealous advocacy and think about a broader more therapeutic role for lawyers, particularly for those who represent indigent people moving through the system. Second, teach students how to have a broader sensitivity to larger justice systems and how they can be reformed to provide better representation. The first goal is the most common approach to clinical legal education in American law clinics. The focus is on individual case representation.

The second goal is much less common. In traditional classrooms, law schools focus on reading and analyzing appellate cases. In law clinics, they focus on cases with real clients. It is more unusual in either the traditional law classroom or clinic for students to spend time analyzing larger systemic issues. It is imperative as justice systems become more complex—and more therapeutic or provide integrated services alongside social service providers—that lawyers learn how to analyze structures and data to see the efficiencies and inefficiencies of a system and the impact on their clients.

Finally, criminal justice clinics are an excellent platform to address the myriad of ethical issues that are involved with problem solving coalitions with communities or other criminal justice stakeholders. In the criminal justice context, criminal defense clinics allow for the opportunity to delve deeper into the lives of clients to better understand the problems that contributed to the client's criminal charges, and perhaps more importantly, what keeps them in the system, unable to break the cycle of recidivist conduct. In a therapeutic, problem solving approach, a defense lawyer will face many ethical crossroads as she meets with a client, prepares a case from a holistic perspective, plans for bond hearings, seeks out diversion or treatment plans all the while preparing for a trial or plea negotiation. For example, how far should an attorney go in encouraging client participation in a diversion or treatment program? In a problem solving defender context, these ethical boundaries remain largely unexplored.

Criminal defense clinics, where the defense lawyers generally have reduced caseloads, provide opportunities to thresh out the ethical issues, especially those arising for defense lawyers who practice in problem solving courts. A starting point for this education lies within the pages of this special issue. Professor David Wexler's article explains how legal clinics can explore, with students, the ethical and related issues about how far an attorney should go in suggesting that a client engage in diversion or treatment programs.[54] Wexler's article poses just such questions that can be used, not only in clinic discussions but also in training programs, for defense attorneys that are offered by institutional defender offices and national associations.[55]

Another area where law clinics can provide a valuable role is in the effort for lawyers to build stronger connections with community leaders. For example, public defense lawyers across the county, particularly in preparation for sentencing hearings following a plea or trial conviction, are reaching out to the communities they serve to better understand the array of problems they face. Public defense leaders are engaging in dialogues with community members on issues beyond a traditional criminal case such as racial disparity in the criminal courts,[56] prisoner reentry into communities,[57] how to provide mental health or special education services,[58] and law reform efforts.[59] Sentencing advocates are also reaching out to communities and defense lawyers suggesting they seek a more problem solving approach to sentencing advocacy. For example, the *Twelve Steps to Effective Sentencing Advocacy*, by the Sentencing Project,[60] suggests ways to prepare for sentencing from day one, seek alternatives to incarceration, to problem solve

---

54. *See* David Wexler, *Therapeutic Jurisprudence and the Rehabilitative Role of the Criminal Defense Lawyer*, 17 ST. THOMAS L. REV. 741 (2005).

55. Several national associations provide interactive training programs for defenders, investigators, sentencing advocates and chief defenders. The following are associations that offer the best platform upon which Therapeutic Jurisprudence advocates can reach a large number of leaders in the public defense community: The National Legal Aid and Defender Association ("NLADA"), *available at* http://www.nlada.org (last visited Mar. 16, 2005); the National Association of Criminal Defense Lawyers ("NACDL"), *available at* http://www.nacdl.org (last visited Mar. 16, 2005); the National Association of Sentencing Advocates ("NASA"), *available at* http://www.sentencingproject.org/nasa/ (last visited Mar. 16, 2005); and the Brennan Center for Justice at NYU School of Law (Community Oriented Defender Network or what defenders call the COD network), *available at* http://www.brennancenter.org/ (last visited Mar. 16, 2005).

56. The Charlottesville-Albemarle Public Defense Program has a Community Advisory Board, which has sponsored several public discussions on racial discrimination and disparate treatment in the Virginia criminal justice system. *See* Tobey Fey, NATIONAL DEFENDER LEADERSHIP INSTITUTE, *Working With the Community, For the Community: The Citizens Advisory Committee, Charlottesville, Virginia*, available at http://www.nlada.org/Defender/Defender_NDLI/Defender_NDLI_Success/Virginia (describing the work of Jim Hingeley) (last visited Mar. 16, 2005).

57. *See* NEIGHBORHOOD DEFENDER SERVICE OF HARLEM, *Mission & Organization: Making our Constitutional Promise of Justice a Reality for Those Farthest from its Reach available at* http://www.ndsny.org/mission.htm (last visited Mar. 16, 2005) (providing a holistic model of defense practice and a new prisoner reentry program); *see also* REENTRY RESOURCE NETWORK, *available at* http://www.reentry.net (last visited Mar. 16, 2005) (part of the online non-profit legal services and information portal, Probono.net, *at* http://www.probono.net).

58. The Community Law Center in Knoxville, TN is a public defender office that provides an array of social services to clients on a voluntary basis such as counseling, treatment programs, art programs and community service opportunities. *See* COMMUNITY LAW OFFIC OF THE PUBLIC DEFENDERS OFFICE FOR THE SIXTH JUDICIAL CIRCUIT, TN, *Community Law Office*, *available at* http://www.pdknox.org/title.htm (last visited Mar. 16, 2005).

59. Virginia Indigent Defense Commission ("VIDC") out of Richmond, VA has participated in several law reform efforts with a coalition of other stakeholders in the community. These efforts include a recent reform of eyewitness identification laws to the more reliable sequential and double blind show-up and line-ups. The Minnesota Public Defender statewide system has a full-time legislative liaison on staff with extensive political experience. The Public Defender, John Stuart, and all the chief defenders from each of the districts throughout Minnesota are experienced at rallying their defender staff and broad community support for legislative or policy reform efforts.

60. THE SENTENCING PROJECT, *Twelve Steps to Effective Sentencing Advocacy*, 1, 1–3 (1993), *available at* http://www.sentencingproject.org/pdfs/2065.pdf (last visited Mar. 16, 2005); NAT'L ASS'N OF SENTENCING ADVOCATES, CODE OF ETHICS AND PROFESSIONAL STANDARDS 1–6 (1997), *available at* http://www.sentencingproject.org/nasa/pdf/CodeofEthics.pdf (last visited Mar. 16, 2005).

for clients when asked by clients, and consider the social implications of sentencing.[61] Clinics can assist in exploring these important connections from a broader systemic perspective as well as explore the ethical conundrums that arise with these expanded models of providing assistance of counsel.

VI. Conclusion

This essay advocates that Therapeutic Jurisprudence and problem solving lawyering will not be sustainable unless proponents cultivate and educate advocates who understand how these approaches improve the efficiency, fairness and outcomes in justice systems. Advocates, researchers and clinical legal educators need to partner in order to gather data and explain how important these approaches are impacting towards the courts, the prisons, and socio-economically deprived communities, where the right to counsel can have a real impact on improving lives. Developing the yardsticks to measure outcomes, collecting data and presenting it effectively will bring partners to the process from all parts of the system to produce a truly fundamental shift in the goals of the justice community and confidence in politicians and policymakers that this "new" approach will work—not only by defense measures but also by their measures.

ii. Gregory Baker[1] & Jennifer Zawid,[2] The Birth of a Therapeutic Courts Externship Program: Hard Labor but Worth the Effort

(Reprinted with permission from
17 St. Thomas Law Review 711, 2005)

I. Introduction

In this article, we focus on the use of externships to introduce law students to the concepts of Therapeutic Jurisprudence and problem solving courts (also referred to herein as therapeutic courts). We begin with an examination of the birth of William & Mary Law

---

61. See THE SENTENCING PROJECT, supra note 60.

1. Director, Therapeutic Jurisprudence and Interdisciplinary Studies, William & Mary Law School. Founder of juvenile drug court during tenure as Chief Judge for the Thirtieth Judicial District of Virginia. B.A., University of Virginia's College at Wise 1982; J.D., Samford University, Cumberland School of Law 1985; Certificate in Comparative Law, University of Heidelberg, Germany 1984. I would be remiss if I did not mention the expert guidance and unwavering encouragement I have received from Therapeutic Jurisprudence's co-founders Professor Bruce J. Winick, of the University of Miami Law School, and Professor David B. Wexler of the University of Puerto Rico and University of Arizona School of Law. A special debt of gratitude goes to Paul Marcus, Haynes Professor of Law at William & Mary for bringing David Wexler and me together. Lastly, I wish to recognize Andrew L. Teel, my Graduate Research Fellow, for his work on this article.

2. Assistant Clinical Professor of Law, University of Miami School of Law since 1993. B.A., University of Wisconsin-Madison 1991; J.D., University of Miami School of Law 1994. I would like to thank the following individuals: Assistant Clinical Professor Sarah Calli of the University of Miami, School of Law for her support and friendship and for comments on earlier drafts; Carolina Garcia for her expert research assistance; Professor Laurence Rose of the University of Miami, School of Law for his support and mentoring; and Professor Bruce Winick of the University of Miami, School of Law, of course, for among many other things, inspiring me. I am also extremely grateful for the support and assistance I received from Broward County Public Defender Howard Finkelstein, Chief Assistant Public Defender Douglas Brawley, and the Honorable Gisele Pollock, all of whom truly represent the best in their fields. Their combined talents have helped countless individuals recover from the ravishing effects of addiction and mental illness.

School's therapeutic courts practice externship, arguably the most comprehensive externship of its kind. Next, we will focus on an alternative model of a therapeutic court externship clinic, still in its infancy, at the University of Miami School of Law.

Our goals are both simple and lofty. We want as many law students as possible to be exposed to the field of Therapeutic Jurisprudence and the concept of therapeutic courts. We have seen first hand that the benefits of such exposure are tremendous. Thus, we hope that by sharing our "birth stories" we will encourage other law schools to contemplate ways in which these paradigms can be incorporated into their own clinical curriculum. Finally, we hope to contribute to the growing scholarship about externship pedagogy by using our own experiences as text.

II. Therapeutic Jurisprudence and Clinical Education

Those of us in the trenches know that Therapeutic Jurisprudence[3] has the potential to revolutionize clinical teaching. Therapeutic Jurisprudence and clinical education have been described as a "natural 'fit.'"[4] Law school clinics and externships provide an "experiential setting that is a natural laboratory for applying therapeutic jurisprudence."[5] In considering the integration of Therapeutic Jurisprudence into clinical teaching, Professor Mary Berkheiser writes:

> As a theory in search of application, therapeutic jurisprudence can derive much from clinical legal education. Clinicians also have a tradition of welcoming new viewpoints that can provide fresh insights into the educational and lawyering process. The perspective of therapeutic jurisprudence could enhance both individual client representation and law reform efforts. The questions that therapeutic jurisprudence poses would encourage exploration of clients'

---

3. Therapeutic Jurisprudence has been defined by its co-creator Bruce Winick as:
[A]n interdisciplinary field of legal scholarship and approach to law reform that focuses attention upon law's impact on the mental health and psychological functioning of those it affects. The scholarly agenda of therapeutic jurisprudence is to study the therapeutic and antitherapeutic consequences of law with the tools of the behavioral sciences, and its law reform agenda is to reshape law so as to minimize its antitherapeutic consequences and maximize its therapeutic potential when to do so is consistent with constitutional, justice, and other normative values served by law. The focus is not only on the therapeutic dimensions of substantive legal rules and legal procedures, but also on how such rules and procedures are applied by legal actors such as judges and attorneys.
Bruce J. Winick, *Therapeutic Jurisprudence and the Civil Commitment Hearing*, 10 J. Contemp. Legal Issues 37, 38 (1999) [hereinafter *Civil Commitment Hearing*]. Therapeutic Jurisprudence scholarship has exploded over the past decade. "Must reads" include Bruce J. Winick & David B. Wexler, Essays In Therapeutic Jurisprudence (Carolina Acad. Press 1991); Bruce J. Winick, Therapeutic Jurisprudence Applied: Essays on Mental Health Law (Carolina Acad. Press 1997); and Bruce J. Winick & David B. Wexler, Judging in a Therapeutic Key: Therapeutic Jurisprudence And The Courts (Carolina Acad. Press 2003) [hereinafter Judging]. In addition, new Therapeutic Jurisprudence enthusiasts should familiarize themselves with the International Network of Therapeutic Jurisprudence's website, www.therapeuticjurisprudence.org, which maintains an up-to-date bibliography and serves as a clearinghouse and resource center for reporting the developments of Therapeutic Jurisprudence.

4. Keri K. Gould & Michael L. Perlin, *"Johnny's in the Basement/Mixing Up His Medicine": Therapeutic Jurisprudence and Clinical Teaching*, 24 Seattle Univ. L. Rev. 339, 341 (2000).

5. Mary Berkheiser, *Frasier Meets CLEA: Therapeutic Jurisprudence and Law School Clinics*, 5 Psychol. Pub. Pol'y & L. 1147, 1171 (1999).

needs in ways that could enhance their well being and that of student lawyers. In short, both therapeutic jurisprudence and clinical legal education could profit from integration.[6]

Additionally, critics contend that law schools are not doing enough to provide students with a "moral framework" for conceptualizing legal issues, a concept key to Therapeutic Jurisprudence.[7] Instead students are taught to follow the "black letter law" and not to factor "emotion, imagination, or sentiments of affection and trust" into their analysis of legal problems.[8] Therapeutic Jurisprudence, by contrast, values these intangibles and teaches lawyers to view their roles in a different light. Lawyers become counselors, and for our purposes, will be inclined to embrace programs "centered on treatment and recovery, as opposed to the rote application of the law."[9] Law students and attorneys with a "traditional legal education," would have a much harder time making such a conceptual leap.

In sum, Therapeutic Jurisprudence has much to offer clinical teaching.[10] By incorporating Therapeutic Jurisprudence principles in both the classroom and out of classroom components of clinic courses, law professors can give students new and important insights into some of the most difficult problems regularly raised in practice settings, including therapeutic courts.[11]

III. Therapeutic Jurisprudence and Problem solving Courts

Problem solving courts, also called therapeutic courts, have become an important feature of the American court landscape.[12] "Developed in response to frustration by both the court system and the public to the large numbers of cases that seemed to be disposed of repeatedly but not resolved, problem solving courts offer the promise of a more meaningful resolution of court cases involving individuals with psychosocial problems as well as legal issues."[13] The dockets are used to address a variety of needs facing juveniles, adults, and families whose mental health or substance abuse problems

---

6. *Id.* at 1155.
7. Paul G. Haskell, *Teaching Moral Analysis in Law School*, 66 Notre Dame L. Rev. 1025 (1991); *see also* Jane Harris Aiken, *Striving to Teach "Justice, Fairness, and Morality"*, 4 Clinical L. Rev. 1, 4 (1997), *cited in* Pamela L. Simmons, *Solving the Nations Drug Problem: Drug Courts*, 35 Gonz. L. Rev. 237, 238 n.10 (1999–2000).
8. Simmons, *supra* note 7, at 261.
9. *Id.* at 262.
10. Professors Gould and Perlin, in their collaborative article on Therapeutic Jurisprudence and clinical teaching, suggest at least four applications for using Therapeutic Jurisprudence to enrich clinical teaching: "(1) to improve our teaching of skills, (2) to provide a better understanding of the dynamics of clinical relationship, (3) to investigate ethical concerns and the effect on lawyering roles, and (4) to invigorate the way we as teachers and students question accepted legal practices." Gould & Perlin, *supra* note 4, at 355.
11. *Id.* at 341.
12. In recent years, there has been a tremendous amount of scholarship devoted to problem solving courts. In particular, in March 2003, the Fordham University Urban Law Journal published a symposium devoted to problem solving courts and Therapeutic Jurisprudence. A much anticipated symposium on mental health courts is also forthcoming: Symposium, *Mental Health Courts*, 11 Psychol. Pub. Pol'y (Bruce J. Winick & Susan Stefan, guest eds.) (forthcoming 2005). For a comprehensive list of current citations to literature surrounding mental health courts, interested scholars should consult Bruce J. Winick, *Outpatient Commitment: A Therapeutic Jurisprudence Analysis*, 9 Psychol. Pub. Pol'y & L. 107, 135–43 (2003) [hereinafter *Outpatient Commitment*]. Of course, any scholar with an interest in this field should also read judging, *supra* note 3.
13. *See* Pamela M. Casey & David B. Rottman, *Overview of Problem-Solving Courts: Models and Trends*, in Nat'l Center for St. Cts. (2003) [hereinafter *Models and Trends*].

contribute significantly to their legal problems. A common thread that runs through these specialized courts includes an individualized approach to justice with effective case management and a "closer collaboration with the service communities in their jurisdictions."[14] Additionally, the new problem solving courts are all characterized by active judicial involvement. "Not only is the judge a leading actor in the therapeutic drama, but also the courtroom itself becomes a stage for the acting out of many crucial scenes."[15]

A close relationship exists between Therapeutic Jurisprudence and problem solving courts. Indeed, it is hard to imagine one without the other. Therapeutic Jurisprudence is one of the major "vectors" of a growing movement in the law towards a common goal of a more comprehensive, humane, and psychologically optimal way of handling legal matters.[16] Problem solving courts are also one of these "vectors," and thus, share many common aims with Therapeutic Jurisprudence.[17] Problem solving courts often use principles of Therapeutic Jurisprudence to enhance their function.[18] These principles include integration of treatment services with judicial case processing, ongoing judicial intervention, close monitoring and/or immediate response to behavior, multidisciplinary involvement, and collaboration with community-based and governmental organizations.[19]

In sum, both Therapeutic Jurisprudence and problem solving courts see the law as an instrument for helping people, particularly those with a variety of psychological and emotional problems. A clinical program that exposes students to both vectors will place students at the forefront of these exciting movements and can ultimately help transform clinical education.[20]

---

14. *Id.*

15. Bruce J. Winick, *Therapeutic Jurisprudence and Problem Solving Courts*, 2003 FORDHAM. URB. L.J. 1055, 1060 (2003) [hereinafter *Problem Solving Courts*].

16. Susan Daicoff, *The Role of Therapeutic Jurisprudence within the Comprehensive Law Movement*, in PRACTICING THERAPEUTIC JURISPRUDENCE: LAW AS A HELPING PROFESSION 466 (Dennis P. Stolle et al. eds., 2000).

17. *See* Pamela Casey & David B. Rottman, *Therapeutic Jurisprudence in the Courts*, 18 BEHAV. SCI. & L. 445, 454 (2000) (stating that "therapeutic jurisprudence principles are consistent with court performance goals."); *see generally* David B. Rottman & Pamela Casey, *Therapeutic Jurisprudence and the Emergence of Problem Solving Courts*, in NAT'L INST. JUST. J. 12 (1999); Leonore M. J. Simon, *Proactive Judges: Solving Problems and Transforming Communities*, in THE HANDBOOK OF PSYCHOLOGY IN LEGAL CONTEXTS (Ray Bull & David Carson eds., John Wiley & Sons LTD 1995) (forthcoming) (manuscript at 2–7); Bruce J. Winick & David B. Wexler, *Therapeutic Jurisprudence and Drug Treatment Courts: A Symbiotic Relationship*, in PRINCIPLES OF ADDICTION MEDICINE (Allan W. Graham & Terry K. Schultz eds., 3d ed.) (forthcoming) (manuscript at 1).

18. *Problem Solving Courts*, *supra* note 15, at 1064.

19. CONFERENCE OF STATE COURT ADM'RS, *COSCA Resolution 4: In Support of Problem-Solving Courts*, *at* http://cosca.ncsc.dni.us/Resolutions/resolutionproblemsolvingcts.html (last visited Mar. 15, 2002).

20. Efforts to incorporate discussion and analysis of problem solving courts into the clinical curriculum have been bolstered by the recent Conference of Chief Justices (CCJ) and the Conference of State Court Administrators (COSCA) whose resolutions specifically urge law schools to educate their students on these issues:

> Resolution 22
> In Support of Problem Solving Court Principles and Methods
> WHEREAS, the Conference of Chief Justices (CCJ) and the Conference of State Court Administrators (COSCA) appointed a Joint Problem Solving Courts Committee to continue the work of the previous Task Force on Therapeutic Jurisprudence; and
> WHEREAS, the Joint Problem Solving Courts Committee found that:
> There is evidence of broad support for the principles and methods commonly used in problem solving courts, including, ongoing judicial leadership, integration of treatment

services with judicial case processing, close monitoring of and immediate response to behavior, multidisciplinary involvement, and collaboration with community-based and government organizations;

These principles and methods have demonstrated great success in addressing certain complex social problems, such as recidivism, that are not effectively addressed by the traditional legal process; and

The application of these principles advance the trust and confidence of the public; and WHEREAS, CCJ and COSCA adopted CCJ Resolution 22 and COSCA Resolution 4 on August 3, 2000 that agreed to:

1. Call these new courts and calendars "Problem Solving Courts," recognizing that courts have always been involved in attempting to resolve disputes and problems in society, but understanding that the collaborative nature of these new efforts deserves recognition.
2. Take steps, nationally and locally, to expand and better integrate the principles and methods of well-functioning drug courts into ongoing court operations.
3. Advance the careful study and evaluation of the principles and methods employed in problem solving courts and their application to other significant issues facing state courts.
4. Encourage, where appropriate, the broad integration over the next decade of the principles and methods employed in the problem solving courts into the administration of justice to improve court processes and outcomes while preserving the rule of law, enhancing judicial effectiveness, and meeting the needs and expectations of litigants, victims and the community.
5. Support national and local education and training on the principles and methods employed in problem solving courts and on collaboration with other community and government agencies and organizations.
6. Advocate for the resources necessary to advance and apply the principles and methods of problem solving courts in the general court systems of the various states.
7. Establish a national agenda consistent with this resolution that includes the following actions:
    a. Request that the CCJ/COSCA Government Affairs Committee work with the United States Department of Health and Human Services to direct treatment funds to the state courts.
    b. Request that the National Center for State Courts initiate with other organizations and associations a collaborative process to develop principles and methods for other types of courts and calendars similar to the *10 Key Drug Court Components*, published by the Drug Courts Program Office, which define effective drug courts.
    c. Encourage the National Center for State Courts Best Practices Institute to examine the principles and methods of these problem solving courts.
    d. Convene a national conference or regional conferences to educate Conference members and other appropriate policy leaders on the issues raised by the growing problem solving court movement.

NOW, THEREFORE, BE IT RESOLVED that CCJ and COSCA reaffirm their commitment to these action items; and

BE IT FURTHER RESOLVED that CCJ and COSCA agree to develop a national agenda that includes the following actions:

a. Encourage each state to develop and implement an individual state plan to expand the use of the principles and methods of problem solving courts into their courts;
b. Support the development and delivery of national and local judicial and staff education curricula based on the principles and methods of problem solving courts;
c. Encourage the attendance by judicial officers and staff at national and local courses based on the principles and methods of problem solving courts;
d. Encourage the development in each state of at least one "demonstration" jurisdiction to serve as a laboratory in the use of problem solving court principles and methods within a traditional court setting;
e. Support the identification and promulgation of national best practices in the

IV. The William & Mary Externship: The First Born[21]

William & Mary Law School celebrates its 225th anniversary this year. At the urging of Thomas Jefferson, William & Mary became the first academic institution in America to teach law in a university setting and the school has been a pioneer in legal education ever since. Thus, it is not surprising that in August 2003, William & Mary birthed the first therapeutic courts externship program in the country.[22] The externship is part of the law school's new and promising Program for Therapeutic Jurisprudence and Interdisciplinary Studies. The overall impetus for the externship program was a belief on the part of the law school's administration and Virginia Drug Court experts that problem solving courts were cutting edge, both in the academic community and in the profession. Thus, their objectives were to: (1) combine a cutting edge academic experience with research and scholarship opportunities; and (2) to provide a public service to the

---

        use of problem solving court principles and methods within a traditional court setting;
- f. Request the National Center for State Courts' Problem Solving Court Community of Practice to seek funding to document best practices in "demonstration" jurisdictions and other jurisdictions and widely promulgate this information;
- g. Request that the National Judicial College, the National Center for State Courts and the National Association of State Judicial Educators update their existing training curricula to include the principles and methods of problem solving courts;
- h. *Ask CCJ and COSCA members to request of the law schools in their states that they, as appropriate, include the principles and methods of problem solving courts in their curricula*;
- i. *Request that the Association of American Law Schools support expanded education by their members on the principles and methods of problem solving courts*;
- j. *Request that Legal Education and Admission to the Bar Section of the American Bar Association support the efforts of CCJ and COSCA in pursuing the initiatives included in this Resolution*; and
- k. Advocate for necessary financial resources for treatment and services that are integral to a successful problem solving court.

Adopted as proposed by the CCJ/COSCA Problem solving Courts Committee at the 56th Annual Meeting on July 29, 2004 (emphasis added). *Id.*

21. As will hopefully be apparent to the reader, although much of this paper has been written together, the authors write separately to describe their respective programs.

22. The program's conception can be traced to the thoughtful ideas, steadfast support and nurturing of several key people: James E. Moliterno, Director of William & Mary's Legal Skills and Clinical Programs; John Levy, Emeritus Professor; Patricia E. Roberts, Director, Externship Programs; and Donna L. Boone, Director of the Therapeutic Courts Program, all significantly contributed to the founding of the Externship. As the Therapeutic Jurisprudence Program gains traction at William & Mary Law School, the highest of praise is reserved for the law school's Dean, W. Taylor Reveley, III and Vice-Dean, Lynda L. Butler. Without their wisdom, foresight, and commitment to deliver creative and innovative programs to law students and the legal community, the program would not exist.

    The desire to cultivate fresh ideas in legal education is as alive today at William & Mary as it was in the 18th century. The study and application of managing partners' Winick and Wexler's Therapeutic Jurisprudence has taken roots at a law school, where teaching students to be skilled legal craftsmen includes the understanding that the law has a distinct human dimension that deserves careful study and reflection.

    To date, the Externship has been funded through the generosity of private donors giving via the law school's foundation. The law school also continues to pursue federal and state grants and appropriations for the program, along with corporate and private sponsorship. In addition, in September 2004, the law school was gratified to learn the program would receive funds from the United States Department of Justice to develop curriculum and distance learning training modules for drug court judges.

courts and to legal professionals in the field. The externship was designed to work in conjunction with the adult and juvenile drug treatment courts in Virginia.

The Commonwealth of Virginia Drug Court Program

Virginia's first drug treatment court was established for adults in September 1995 in Roanoke, Virginia. Since then, twenty-two (22) drug courts have become operational and fourteen (14) more are in the planning phase. Juvenile drug treatment courts make up ten (10) of the courts now operating in the Commonwealth, with four (4) additional juvenile courts in the planning stage.

Like most drug treatment courts, Virginia's drug treatment courts were a response to the recognition that processing nonviolent drug possession charges in the criminal courts and then sentencing the offender to prison did not succeed in changing the offender's addictive behavior.[23] Thus, Virginia's drug court programs all share three basic components: (1) strict and frequent probation supervision with random weekly drug tests, (2) intensive drug treatment and counseling, and (3) regular reporting to the court with immediate sanctions for relapse or program noncompliance.

According to the Virginia Department of Criminal Justice Services Statistics, 32% of all convicted felons are drug offenders, 50% of all convicted felons have evidence of prior drug abuse, and 31% are alcohol abusers. By anyone's standards, Virginia's drug courts have had a positive impact in both preventing crime and providing appropriate treatment for defendants with drug and alcohol problems. An examination of the agency's records reveal a 5.9% recidivism rate for drug treatment court offenders compared to a 50% felony recidivism rate for other Virginia drug offenders handled in traditional court programs such as probation and incarceration. Further, drug court costs an average of $6,000 per year for an offender, while the Virginia Department of Corrections reports average incarceration costs range from $22,000 to $38,000 per offender per year.[24]

Objectives

The objectives of the externship are multifold. First, the externship is the perfect vehicle to introduce students to the principles of Therapeutic Jurisprudence. Students are challenged by the instructor to think "outside the box" and view legal rules and legal processes through a different lens. Seeing a court respond to a significant societal prob-

---

23. *Problem Solving Courts*, supra note 18, at 1056; *see* Winick & Wexler, supra note 17 (manuscript at 2). More than 1,183 drug courts operate in all 50 states with an additional 414 courts in the planning stages. The White House Office of National Drug Control Strategy, *National Drug Control Strategy Update 2004*, at http://www.whitehousedrugpolicy. gov/publications/policy/ndcs04/healing_amer.html (last visited Oct. 29, 2004). Ironically, however, while today *every state* has a drug court to address the needs of nonviolent offenders, there is not a single drug court in the *federal* system. In his recent New York Times editorial on this issue, *Rehab Justice*, Donald P. Lay states that "our federal justice system has a great deal to learn from our state court system" and advocates for the creation of federal drug courts. Donald P. Lay, *Rehab Justice*, N.Y. Times, Nov. 18, 2004, at A31. Hopefully Lay's commentary will encourage additional discussion and reflection on this pressing issue.

24. For additional reading on the drug court movement, *see, e.g.*, Pamela L. Simmons, *Solving the Nation's Drug Problem: Drug Courts Signal a Move Toward Therapeutic Jurisprudence*, 35 Gonz. L. Rev. 237 (1999); LeRoy L. Kondo, *Advocacy of the Establishment of Mental Health Specialty Courts in the Provision of Therapeutic Justice for Mentally Ill Offenders*, 28 Am. J. Crim. L. 255 (2001); James R. Brown, *Drug Diversion Courts: Are They Needed and Will They Succeed in Breaking the Cycle of Drug-Related Crime*, 23 New Eng. J. on Crim. & Civ. Confinement 63 (1997); Cait Clarke & James Neuhard, *"From Day One": Who's in Control as Problem Solving and Client Centered Sentencing Take Center Stage?*, 29 N.Y.U. Rev. L. & Soc. Change 11 (2004).

lem, by utilizing Therapeutic Jurisprudence principles and a problem solving approach, opens wide the Therapeutic Jurisprudence lens and can give instant credibility to this innovative and creative way of thinking. The hope is that students will come away from the experience with the belief that Therapeutic Jurisprudence is worthy of further consideration in their future endeavors with people and the law.

At the same time, the externship attempts to stimulate thinking by students about the new and innovative strategies of therapeutic courts. Therapeutic courtrooms seem like "foreign countries" to most law students who, unfortunately, only have a traditional understanding of the criminal justice system.[25] The externship is an attempt to bridge this gap by pointing out to students why such vast differences exist. For example, early in their legal training, students become familiar with the constitutional rights afforded to criminal defendants who have been accused of a crime. They are initially concerned when they learn that, in drug courts, defendants often sign these rights away as a prerequisite for participation in the drug court program.[26] While an argument inevitably breaks out over this controversial issue, students learn that the theory behind this requirement is to aid the client in the rehabilitative process by implementing greater court control over the offender.[27] Thus, while some aspects of the therapeutic courts are at odds with the traditional courts, there is a purpose behind these differences. In demonstrating these purposes, the externship is designed to address common fears and criticisms that many unfamiliar with Therapeutic Jurisprudence and the problem solving courts movement may have.

NUTS AND BOLTS

The William & Mary externship has two components. First, there is a classroom component, which consists of at least four classroom sessions. In many cases, the externship will be a student's first encounter with Therapeutic Jurisprudence. Thus, the first classroom session is devoted to exposing students to the basic principles of Therapeutic Jurisprudence and problem solving courts. William & Mary also use this class to introduce students to the mechanics of Virginia's drug treatment court program in which they will be participating. The second and third classroom sessions provide a forum for students to reflect on what they have seen and experienced while participating in the externship and to compare the practices employed by the different placements. Students find this particularly instructive, in that, by discussing the different approaches employed by the courts, they discover that certain techniques and strategies are more effective than others. As students discuss their placements, everything from philosophy to style is reflected upon. Much of the discussion centers on the personal attention that externs see given to drug court participants and how this interaction is essential to the success of the process. Students are also required to maintain a journal, providing another opportunity for reflection and critique.

In the final session, students discuss how they plan on carrying the knowledge they have gained forward into their careers. What is always striking during this last session is

---

25. For example, while sentences in a traditional criminal court context are generally of a fixed nature and signal closure of the legal process; in therapeutic courts, the imposition of a sentence is not the primary goal and, to some, will seem wildly indeterminate. While traditional criminal courts are generally thought of as being populated solely by those with a legal background, therapeutic courts often introduce treatment providers and other non-legal actors into the proceedings. Finally, while criminal courts are generally thought of as having a retributive purpose, one purpose of therapeutic courts is clearly to be rehabilitative. Instead of an adversarial setting, therapeutic courts promote cooperation and alternative dispute mechanisms. *See Models and Trends*, *supra* note 13.

26. JAMES L. NOLAN, JR., REINVENTING JUSTICE 198–99 (Princeton Univ. Press 2001).

27. *Id.* at 154.

how many students express a commitment to utilize Therapeutic Jurisprudence in their legal careers, even students not previously predisposed to Therapeutic Jurisprudence and like-minded legal endeavors.

The professor of the course also meets with students on a regular basis throughout the semester to discuss the externship. During these meetings, students are given an opportunity to discuss any problems or concerns and to reflect on their performance. Students also are required to meet periodically with their field instructor, who in most cases, as discussed below, is a drug court judge. As we know, supervisors in the field are vital to the success of all externships. Because of the unique nature of the therapeutic courts practice externship, dedicated field instructors play an invaluable role. Upon completion, field instructors are required to submit an evaluation of the extern's performance which is given substantial consideration in determining satisfactory completion.

In addition to a journal, students are required to write a final paper. Topics that must be addressed include: (1) whether the course objectives have been met; (2) an explanation of their basic understanding of Therapeutic Jurisprudence; (3) how this externship has enhanced their learning; (4) future uses of the principles learned; (5) any change in attitudes or philosophy as a result of the course; and (6) strengths and weaknesses of the program.

The classroom aspect, while helpful, is only part of the externship. It is the on-site learning in the trenches (the courts) where students see, feel, and learn about Therapeutic Jurisprudence and its application in the real world. Each student is assigned to work with a drug treatment court judge and act as "therapeutic court law clerks." Like all law clerks, they perform tasks at the request of the judge. For example, one judge recently had a student research a constitutional issue related to the waiver drug court clients sign upon entering the program. Another judge asked for a legal memorandum on drug testing.

While the judges act as the intern's "field supervisors," students also are required to meet with other members of the drug court team (the drug court treatment team is normally comprised of the judge, the prosecutor, the defense counsel, the probation officer, the substance abuse counselor, and the drug court coordinator) to interview them and get their perspective on therapeutic courts. In addition, each student is required to spend some time shadowing the public defender or other defense counsel as they meet with drug court clients. This is done to further develop the students' advocacy and communication skills.

By setting up the externship in this fashion, students witness how *all* members of the drug court team work together to maximize therapeutic benefits. Rather than make the Therapeutic Jurisprudence courts an adversarial proceeding, each actor attempts to make the clients feel as if the court is a *partner* in their recovery. Students who have participated in the externship comment on how transformative it was to see this vastly different side of the judiciary.

Care is taken to ensure that students are able to witness how the drug team operates at every stage, from a client's entrance into the program to (hopefully) the client's successful completion of a rehabilitation plan. Students also get to see the bumps that often occur along the way. Most students remark that this comprehensive approach allows them to witness how the criminal justice system can be used in a way they never imagined.

Of course, students also see offenders who are unsuccessful in this effort and are then reassigned to traditional courts. While discouraging, these "failures" provide for some of the best learning opportunities of the externship. For example, when a client fails a drug test and is placed in detention, students who witness this sad turn of events often comment on how "emotional" the courtroom becomes and how much they empathize, not only with the client, but with the judge and prosecutor who have to put back on their "punitive cap." Students often walk away from these experiences shaken.

Perhaps the most important component of the externship, however, is the human interaction (crucial to Therapeutic Jurisprudence) between the students and the offenders in the drug treatment courts. This is encouraged in various ways. Careful observation of the drug court treatment docket is required as students follow the progress of selected offenders. Students participate in interviews with drug court clients as they go through the program and upon graduation to obtain their views on the process. Participation with court professionals as they work with offenders on many different fronts, such as employment and education considerations, is vital to student understanding and satisfaction.

In addition, students have opportunities to interact with clients outside the mahogany walls of a courthouse. For example, students can fulfill some of their required hours by assisting in community outreach programs that are frequented by therapeutic court participants. In the past, students have worked at housing projects, community centers, homeless shelters, and a domestic violence "safe haven."

One particularly creative student extern combined her enthusiasm and skill with the artistic talent of a drug court participant to design a "logo" for the drug court, to the delight of the judge and drug treatment court team. Other students assisted court participants, who reside in a housing project, to hold a rummage sale with its proceeds used for playground equipment. Yet another student worked as a mentor with a drug-abusing teenager in an effort to improve the offender's education and disciplinary record.

This high level of client interaction is important to the pedagogical goals of the program for a number of reasons. First, it works to show the favorable outcomes of the therapeutic courts and thereby favorably distinguish them from the regular criminal and civil courts. With recidivism high in the normal criminal courts and the public generally skeptical of the judicial system, displaying the positive outcomes of therapeutic courts helps to promote a positive view of the Therapeutic Jurisprudence movement.

Second, such interaction helps to highlight the client-centered approach that is vital to Therapeutic Jurisprudence. Too often, the adversarial nature of the traditional court system puts a premium on winning for the sake of winning, and not for the sake of the client. Interaction ensures that a "real face" is placed onto a person generally known simply as "the client." This shift in focus is beneficial not only in the therapeutic courts setting, but also for the future of the legal profession, producing better and more responsive advocates.

EVALUATION AND FUTURE PLANS

Early indicators of the externship program are very encouraging. In evaluating any course or program, however, one must always check to see if the pedagogical goals and objectives set forth for the program are being achieved.[28] From all indications, the goal of introducing Therapeutic Jurisprudence to law students through the use of drug treat-

---

28. In the world of law school externships, we look to things such as the variety and challenge of the work; quality of the work environment; consideration of professionalism and ethical issues; and strengths and weaknesses of feedback and supervision, and the skills and values sought to be developed. These seem like reasonable components to assess any externship, not to mention that they represent a general summary of the required legal education standards promulgated by the American Bar Association for externship programs at American law schools. ABA, *American Bar Association Standard 305*, at www.abanet.org/legaled/standards/chapter3 (last visited Mar. 25, 2005).

ment courts is being met and exceeded. When evaluating the externship, students generally conclude that the experience was a positive one that offered a unique focus on the practice of law. Students comment on how much they appreciated the opportunity to interact with judges and other members of the drug court team. In some cases, students write that such exposure has "a life changing" effect on them.

As their teacher, it is very rewarding to see how everything from their attitudes about the criminal justice system to their overall philosophy about the law and legal process is subject to new thinking. Even students who were generally predisposed to the more traditional brand of justice concluded that there was a place in legal education and the legal community for this approach. In almost all cases, students who complete the externship concede that Therapeutic Jurisprudence is worthy of further study and thought.

Looking at student logs and journals, one common theme is evident. Students regret not being exposed to Therapeutic Jurisprudence earlier in their legal education, which makes the case for such introduction most compelling. In addition, some students feel a sense of frustration, in that, upon conclusion of the externship, they lose contacts with team members and participants. Not knowing the final outcome for a drug court participant, with whom they worked closely, can be viewed as a process lacking closure. The course professor can offer suggestions as to how students might stay in contact with a team member or even participants to track progress. The mere fact that students come away from an externship with this kind of response is telling.

As with any new endeavor that inevitably involves change, however, the sculpting and delivery of the therapeutic courts externship at William & Mary Law School is a work in progress. In an effort to build upon the program's successes, brainstorming continues on new initiatives. A clinic that devotes itself to the practice of law from a Therapeutic Jurisprudence standpoint is at the top of the list. Utilizing existing clinics, such as the Domestic Violence Clinic and Legal Aid Clinic to promote a better understanding of Therapeutic Jurisprudence for our students is also a logical expansion. An effort to promote other therapeutic courts or related programs in Virginia, such as mental health courts, teen tobacco courts, teen truancy courts, and others would provide additional learning opportunities for our students. Further, I believe that it is essential that Therapeutic Jurisprudence be introduced to first year law students at least on a limited basis.

V. The University of Miami Therapeutic Courts Externship: A Sibling

Clinical Education has always played a seminal role at the University of Miami. The law school's Litigation Skills Program,[29] under the helm of Professor Laurence Rose, is a model for other programs nationwide and is widely lauded by both faculty and students. Up to 90% of the law school's students enroll in "Litigation Skills" in a given year and course evaluations indicate that many regard the program as their "best law school experience" or, at the very least, the "most practical."

Students who successfully complete Litigation Skills have the option of signing up for a six-credit externship the following semester.[30] Students are placed in up to forty

---

29. This comprehensive and rigorous trial training program offers students a unique opportunity to develop fundamental skills for trial practice. This is achieved through intensive classroom exercises and simulated courtroom exercises under adjunct faculty members who are experienced trial lawyers and judges.
30. The University requires that each student devote not less than 220 hours per semester, an average of sixteen (16) hours per week in the fall and spring semesters, or thirty-two (32) hours per week during the summer session, while working in the placement in which he or she is enrolled.

(40) participating civil and criminal agencies and they practice under the supervision of agency attorneys. Despite the wide range of placements available, however, the majority of students each semester choose criminal placements because of the perception that such placements provide the most "trial experience."

As is the case in most large externship programs of this kind, there is a "classroom component" of the program that groups together students from all the different civil and criminal placements, including students from the prosecutor and defender's offices. The fact that students from "opposing sides" are housed together in the same class makes the class a fertile breeding ground for debate and reflection.

What has been so surprising, however, is that although my "criminal students" consistently report a very high level of satisfaction regarding the externship experience as a whole, they finish the externship feeling very disillusioned and discouraged about their role in the criminal justice system. In other words, while students in criminal placements almost without exception report in their journals and end-of-semester evaluations that they are "extremely satisfied" with their "skill development" and feel that they received much needed "practical training," it is much more rare for a student to report that they did "good work" or "public service." I was particularly troubled by this reality because it is very important to my own pedagogical goals as a teacher to promote the social justice and public service instincts of my students.

Professor Mary Jo Eyster, in her article "Designing and Teaching the Large Externship Clinic," also noted the importance of incorporating "justice and service goals" into the classroom component of a large externship clinic. Eyster's observations over her many years of clinical teaching were that many students choose particular types of externships *precisely because* "they want to do good, to help people in need, or to promote a worthy cause."[31] Thus, she urges law schools to design externship opportunities for students whose justice and service goals are the "main force that drives them."[32] She posits that for these students, "there is little enough in the traditional curriculum to sustain them while they are in law school."[33] "It is usually their passion that brings them to law school, and in the three or four years of law school they have limited opportunities to express that passion, or to discuss it with others."[34] Thus, by offering a "forum for these students to explore the social justice concerns that they care about most deeply, the extern clinic may provide them with the energy and inspiration to continue to pursue their ultimate objectives."[35] Moreover, Eyster notes that even students that do not identify serving the public or social justice concerns as their primary goals when they begin an externship, most are receptive to discussing these issues as they evolve from their externship experiences.[36]

When searching for reasons why these justice and service goals were being perverted I discovered no easy or obvious answers. When probed, students did not point to the judges, their supervisors, their co-workers, or even their clients as the problem, it was simply that the criminal justice system as a whole was broken and there was nobody to fix it. One particular student's journal entry summed it up for the others: "Working at

---

31. Mary Jo Eyster, *Designing and Teaching the Large Externship Clinic*, 5 CLINICAL L. REV. 347, 358 (1999).
  32. *Id.*
  33. *Id.*
  34. *Id.*
  35. *Id.*
  36. *Id.*

the PD's office was like working for FORD, it was assembly line justice, defendants come in, defendants come out...."

Equally troubling to me as a new clinical teacher was how jaded I saw some of my criminal students becoming *very early on* in their externship (perhaps mirroring what they were witnessing from the other professionals in the criminal justice system).[37]

Desperate to find a way to expose my students to alternative models of justice and lawyering, and already a convert of Therapeutic Jurisprudence, it was natural to begin to slowly incorporate the concepts of Therapeutic Jurisprudence and problem solving courts into my curriculum. I was also extremely fortunate that Bruce Winick, the "co-guru" of the Therapeutic Jurisprudence movement and a member of the law school's faculty, was extremely supportive of my work. Thus, I gradually began assigning readings on Therapeutic Jurisprudence and later, as discussed *infra*, on therapeutic courts. Students were asked to write about Therapeutic Jurisprudence in their journals and to reflect on the therapeutic and anti-therapeutic consequences of the choices they were making as legal externs. I designed classroom exercises in which students would analyze the Therapeutic Jurisprudence implications of various high profile cases.[38] In later semesters, I invited attorneys who practiced in the local drug court and mental health

---

37. For example, at some point during the first few weeks of each semester it is my practice to devote at least one class to legal ethics. This semester, I used a particular hypothetical adopted from Lisa Lerman's article, *Professional and Ethical Issues in Legal Externships: Fostering Commitment to Public Service*, 67 FORDHAM L. REV. 2295 (1999), to flesh out ethical issues surrounding supervisor misconduct:

> I'm working at the prosecutor's office, and mainly working for this one guy named "Steven Charney" (not his real name). Yesterday I went with him to court to see him try a case involving charges of possession of cocaine. It was a pretty straightforward felony case, except for one thing.
> The arresting officer got on the stand and testified that when he searched the suspect, he found a large bag of white powder (which later turned out to be cocaine) in the suspect's right jacket pocket. Well, of course the defendant was convicted, and that was that. Steve stayed in the courtroom to deal with another case, but I left to go back to the office to work on a memo I was writing. I stopped at the water fountain, and then noticed that the cop who had testified was chatting with another officer a few feet away. So I took a long drink and listened.
> The arresting officer was boasting to his friend about how this poor slob was going away for years, for sure, and that it was about time, because everyone knew he was a dealer. He said: "Of course I didn't really find anything when I searched him, but no one will ever know that now. It's about time that guy got taken off the street." I felt like I had just stumbled onto the set of "Law and Order." I couldn't believe it. When Steve got back to the office, I went in to see him and told him what I had heard. He said: "Well, Isaiah, welcome to the real world. These things happen all the time. It's just part of law enforcement." I tried to argue with him, but he became incredibly patronizing, as if I was some sort of Polyanna.

Id. at 2299–2300. When discussing the journal, at least half the class believed that Isaiah satisfied his ethical obligations by informing Steve of the conversation he overheard. The fact that Steve was not planning to act on the information did not seem to trouble them. When pressed, they told me "that's how things work" and "cops lie all the time." When I continued to express outrage that an innocent man was going to jail, I was reminded by my "seasoned" students that "these things happen everyday and the judges all know about it."

38. For example, one semester, I had students study the case of Omar Paisley, a 14-year-old boy who died from a burst appendix while locked up in a youth facility in Miami-Dade County. The case commanded tremendous media attention after it became known that Omar suffered in excruciating pain for a number of days and the staff at the detention facility refused to provide any medical treatment. *See* Editorial, *Paisley Case is Sickening*, SUN-SENTINEL, Sept. 13, 2003, at 18A.

court to make presentations to the class. Professor Bruce Winick also gave a particularly well-received presentation.

The reaction of my students was explosive. Once exposed to Therapeutic Jurisprudence, my students had a whole new perspective from which to view their clinical experience. They became increasingly reflective. One student wrote:

> When I got this assignment, I thought I would just write a short response about Therapeutic Jurisprudence and the importance of it in general. But after thinking about it for a couple of days I started to examine the environment I was working in (the state criminal court system) to see what aspects of Therapeutic Jurisprudence were present, and if it seemed to be effective.

Another student, reflecting on her experience through Therapeutic Jurisprudence filters, stated:

> Today, I experienced "restitution" for the second time, and while the first time was extremely boring, I have different views now that I've visited the proceedings again. That may be because of the fact that I just reread the article you handed out to us about Therapeutic Jurisprudence that really made me think.

Therapeutic Jurisprudence also empowered them. The following journal entry was typical:

> I began thinking about the many possible aspects of Therapeutic Jurisprudence. So many people just yo-yo in and out of the system and I think that the fact that Therapeutic Jurisprudence attempts to go beyond and cure some of these issues that bring hope back into the system.

Finally, Therapeutic Jurisprudence provided the necessary tools for my students to engage in institutional critique. Some clinical education scholars contend that such institutional critique is actually the *primary function* of clinical placements.[39] Professors Stephen Wizner and Dennis Curtis describe a clinical classroom that effectively engages in institutional critique as "a laboratory in which students and faculty study, in depth, particular substantive areas of law ... to develop a profound understanding of the legal theory, economic implications and social dynamics of a given segment of the legal system."[40] I was pleased to say that I was beginning to create such a laboratory. One student wrote:

---

39. See Robert J. Condlin, *"Tastes Great, Less Filling": The Law School Clinic and Political Critique*, 36 J. LEGAL EDUC. 45 (1986); *see also* Kenney Hegland, *Condlin's Critiques of Conventional Clinics: The Case of the Missing Case*, 36 J. LEGAL EDUC. 427 (1986) (responding to Condlin's contentions). *But see* Erica M. Eisinger, *The Externship Class Requirement: An Idea Whose Time Has Passed*, 10 CLINICAL L. REV. 659 (2004) (arguing that the imposition of the externship seminar class as a vehicle to provide institutional critique is flawed as reflecting an anti-practitioner and anti-externship bias). Even though Eisinger questions the role of the externship class in promoting institutional critique, however, she does acknowledge a "valuable role" for such critique in certain externship classes such as when the seminar class is structured to bring together students from opposite sides such as prospectors and defenders. "Often these students become socialized early in the workplace to demonize their opponents or to see issues simplistically, which diminishes their abilities to represent clients effectively or to work cooperatively to improve the system." *Id.* at 668.

40. See Stephen Wizner & Dennis Curtis, *"Here's What We Do": Some Notes About Clinical Legal Education*, 29 CLEV. ST. L. REV. 673, 678–79 (1980); *see also* Henry Rose, *Legal Externships: Can They Be Valuable Clinical Experiences for Law Students?*, 12 NOVA L. REV. 95 (1987) (arguing that lawyers and law students who are committed to meeting their ethical obligations should constantly question whether the legal system and the lawyers who function within it are meeting the needs of the public in a fair and efficient manner and that "clinical experiences" should be structured to allow these questions to be raised explicitly by students and supervisors).

> I thought about the whole Therapeutic Jurisprudence thing, and realized that my judge's courtroom was no place for that. He seems to care more about locking people up for trivial things rather than Therapeutic Jurisprudence. My heart ached this week more than once.

As the semester progressed, more and more students recognized the value of Therapeutic Jurisprudence but were frustrated that traditional court models did not allow for implementation. The following journal entries were typical:

> Last Friday, our judge had 108 cases scheduled for an hour time period. This makes it very difficult, if not impossible, to give any case the individualized attention necessary for Therapeutic Jurisprudence. (from a student at the public defender's office).

> I have recognized a need for Therapeutic Jurisprudence. Here an attorney fresh out of law school has a caseload of close to a hundred clients. With this, I can imagine that the clients leave the experience feeling insignificant. The lawyer spends little to no time healing ... but this is not any one person's fault. It is the system. (from a student at the prosecutor's office).

Interestingly, Therapeutic Jurisprudence also made the students question *their own* complicity in a stressed out criminal justice system. A student wrote:

> It is mind boggling to see the common case of a person that is arrested for DUI come into court stoned or drunk. I want to shake them and ask what's going on but time doesn't allow.

Late in the semester, I had students actually observe drug court and mental health court for an afternoon and reflect on the experience. The students were intrigued. Even though their experience in the traditional criminal justice system was limited, they instantly recognized the benefits of the alternative approach of the therapeutic courts. One student wrote:

> Therapeutic courts are one of the best examples of where the legal system is not just giving a tranquilizer pill to stop the pain, but instead is reaching out and removing the problem.[41]

While I believe that these various exercises and assignments were useful, I felt that some students were not as fully engaged as they could have been, as evidenced by their lack of class participation. This was, in part, because there was a disconnect between the theory I was teaching and the practice they were engaged in while working in the traditional court system. Similarly, I was sensitive to the fact that the externship pedagogy at our law school provided great emphasis on *experiential* learning and I did not want to develop a curriculum that did not complement these goals.

Despite these issues, I was convinced that the benefits of Therapeutic Jurisprudence were too important not to teach and was still anxious to continue introducing my hard-

---

41. Professor Perlin wrote about a similar transformation he noted in his students when they were exposed to Therapeutic Jurisprudence's principles:
> When students present on their placement experiences ... they regularly apply [therapeutic jurisprudence] principles.... They assess the role and behavior of the lawyer with whom they are working, the opposite lawyer, the judge and, often, other court personnel. They focus on the critical moment of their case (perhaps a bench ruling on the admissibility of hearsay evidence ... or an interaction with a hospital doctor about a patient's responsiveness to a certain medication), and apply [therapeutic jurisprudence] principles in deconstructing that moment.

Gould & Perlin, *supra* note 4, at 366.

ened students to alternative models of justice and lawyering. I realized, however, that to be true to the externship pedagogy I subscribed to, I had to design a program where students could actually practice Therapeutic Jurisprudence in therapeutic courts. It was with these concerns in mind that I decided to craft a therapeutic courts externship program at the University of Miami.

CURRENT PROPOSAL

The proposal for a therapeutic court externship program currently being contemplated at the University of Miami allows students to be placed in Broward County's misdemeanor and felony mental health courts under the supervision of the Broward County Public Defender's Office.

The Broward County Mental Health Court[42]

The Broward County Mental Heath Division was established in 1997 as a special division of the Criminal Courts in Broward County (Fort Lauderdale), the first program in the country to separate mentally ill defendants from the criminal justice system and route them to treatment programs.[43] The court received national attention from the day it opened its doors and has been the model for other mental health courts as far away as Seattle.[44] Some of the goals of the courts are to create effective interactions between the criminal justice and mental health systems, ensure legal advocacy for the mentally ill defendants, and monitor the delivery and receipt of mental health services and treatments. The court has been a success by anyone's standards. Currently, the division operates two courts; one for misdemeanors and one for felonies.

Unlike the William & Mary model, the Miami students would be integrated into the law school's generic civil and criminal externship program. Obviously this model has the benefit of ease of implementation because the program is, in essence, already operational and does not require any additional resources in terms of staffing or funding.[45]

---

42. Publications about the Broward County Mental Health Court include: *Court Review*, 37 J. OF AM. JUDGES ASSOC., *in* NAT'L CENTER FOR ST. CTS (Winter 2001) and *Emerging Judicial Strategies for the Mentally Ill in the Criminal Caseload: Mental Health Courts*, U.S. DEPARTMENT OF JUSTICE (Apr. 2000).

43. The court was the "outgrowth of three converging perceptions." There was a perception in the community that was seeing the "criminalization of the mentally ill," where individuals were increasingly arrested for non-violent psychiatric acting-out. In the past, these individuals may have sought refuge in state psychiatric hospitals or other such programs. These resources have largely disappeared due to shrinking resources. There was also a law enforcement perception that it was easier and quicker to arrest and book individuals than to have them evaluated at a local crisis or mental health center. Finally, the overall lack of an adequate community-based health system of care led to a highly fragmented system that is difficult to access and navigate. *Mental Health Court Progress Report, 17th Judicial Circuit, Broward County, Florida*, (July 2000–June 2001). The Honorable Ginger Lerner-Wren, who presides over the court, has repeatedly described mental health courts as based on principles of Therapeutic Jurisprudence and, along with other members of the Court team, gives community presentations on issues of mental illness and Therapeutic Jurisprudence.

44. Primarily as a result of recent federal funding, there are now at least one hundred mental health courts in the country.

45. Robert F. Seibel & Linda H. Morton, *Field Placement Programs: Practices, Problems and Possibilities*, 2 CLINICAL L. REV. 413, 420–21 (1996) (discussing that field placement programs have historically provided a financially viable solution to the problem that staffing a sufficiently wide variety of doctrinal courses in response to the full range of student interests, is probably economically unfeasible. At their best, externship programs provide students an opportunity to "learn the substantive law and the application of lawyering in a particular area without law schools' having to create several different courses and specialized departments." *Id.* at 421.

Ultimately, however, none of these factors were the driving force behind my decision to structure the program this way. Rather, the decision was based on my belief that this model would impact the largest number of students. Therapeutic interns would be required to enroll and participate in the same weekly seminar as students in the traditional placements. The seminar would provide a space for students to open up their field experiences to discussion and analysis by the entire class, thus enabling all its members to learn from each other's perspectives. The seminar would be the "centerpiece" of the program and would be a "primary" site of learning along with student's work in the field.[46] Thus, I reasoned that mixing therapeutic court externs with traditional externs would allow the traditional extern students to learn about Therapeutic Jurisprudence and therapeutic courts *via* osmosis.[47]

In addition, I believed that by housing traditional externs and therapeutic externs in the same classroom, the opportunities for institutional critique, discussed *supra*, would be greatly enhanced. Students in traditional placements would be forced to compare the services they were providing with these alternative models. By the same token, however, I expected students in traditional criminal placements to challenge and engage the therapeutic court externs and provide periodic reality checks.[48]

In fashioning the seminar's curriculum, I plan to introduce the concept of Therapeutic Jurisprudence early on by using a combination of some of the same lectures, simulations, class presentations, and writing assignments, discussed *supra*, that I used in the past.[49] I plan to continue to use Therapeutic Jurisprudence throughout the semester as a

---

46. This program model mirrors the model in place at American University as described in Peter Jaszi et al., *Experience as Text: The History of Externship Pedagogy at the Washington College of Law, American University*, 5 CLINICAL L. REV. 403, 404 (1999) [hereinafter *Experience as Text*]. As discussed in *Experience as Text*, this model differs in perspective from other "ecological" learning models which emphasize the placement as the primary site of learning (*see, e.g.*, Brook K. Baker, *Beyond MacCrate: The Role of Context, Experience, Theory, and Reflection in Ecological Learning*, 36 ARIZ. L. REV. 287 (1994)), and differs from models that view the field supervisors as the students' primary teachers. See, *e.g.*, Liz Ryan Cole, *Training the Mentor: Improving the Ability of Legal Experts to Teach Students and New Lawyers*, 19 N.M. L. REV. 163 (1989).

47. Professor Jaszi and others in *Experience as Text*, supra note 46, at 421, describe the give-and-take that takes place at these externship seminars as crucial to externship pedagogy. Jaszi gives the example of a student planning for a career in International Law (and doing a related field placement) being so intrigued by another student's description of his externship working with domestic violence victims that she considers a change in her own career focus or at least plan to investigate the new area further.

48. Also unlike the William & Mary model, Miami students will not be law clerks but will instead be acting as "defense lawyers" under the supervision of the Broward County public defender's office. I made this tactical decision in light of the fact that the therapeutic externs will be integrated with the generic extern class. Thus, I wanted *all* the students to share a common denominator. In addition, I felt that by allowing the students to work at the public defenders office it would give them more of a chance to hone their oral advocacy skills than if they were acting as law clerks. Finally, I believed that the supervision at the Broward County Public Defender's office was particularly effective, and I knew that the office could absorb a large number of students.

49. Although the externship seminar at the University of Miami is currently graded pass/fail, the University's clinical committee is seeking to have the course graded in the near future. In the event that change takes place, I will likely assign more complex writing assignments, perhaps even a final paper. *See, e.g.*, David B. Wexler, *Some Thoughts and Observations on the Teaching of Therapeutic Jurisprudence*, 35 REV. DER. P.R. 273 (1996). Professor Wexler assigned students in his Therapeutic Jurisprudence seminar to complete final papers applying the Therapeutic Jurisprudence lens to the legal area or issue of their choice. He noted that that these papers have been "richly diverse and inventive and can sometimes contribute to the literature and constitute part of the assigned reading in future semesters."

unifying theme to shape classroom discussion, and to give students new insights into the practice of law. I expect these discussions to take on an added dimension because students, actually practicing Therapeutic Jurisprudence in therapeutic courts, will have real life experiences to bring into the classroom to be used as the "text" for critical analysis.[50]

Finally, I plan to use Therapeutic Jurisprudence to supplement the students' skills training. It is here that I think Therapeutic Jurisprudence may have the greatest impact. Although all students in the externship will have had the benefit of taking our law school's Litigation Skills course (a prerequisite) and were (hopefully) receiving additional training "on the job," Therapeutic Jurisprudence has much to offer in skills education. Thus, I will design exercises to enhance student's interviewing and counseling skills by perhaps having students conduct mock interviews and counseling sessions with "clients" using Therapeutic Jurisprudence as a framework. Alternatively, I plan to have students use Therapeutic Jurisprudence to deconstruct the real life client interactions they experience at work. I believe that these exercises will make students more focused and empathetic advocates.[51]

As a complement to the classroom seminar, I will meet with students individually throughout the semester. While in the past I have used these meetings to discuss students' personal learning objectives, career issue, and other issues that students were hesitant to raise in a large group, I will now make time during the course of these one-on-one meetings to engage students in discussions regarding the relevance of Therapeutic Jurisprudence to the students' work.[52]

Other logical extensions to the program that I contemplate might include having students assigned as a "law clerk" to a therapeutic judge, similar to the William & Mary

---

50. While there does not appear to be any hard data on this issue, the "externship community" is small and discussions with our colleagues reveal that, as the number of specialty courts continue to increase, such integration is *already happening* at many law schools, although somewhat unconsciously. For example, at the University of Washington School of Law's Children and Youth Advocacy Clinic, directed by Professor Lisa Kelly, students sometimes have the opportunity to practice in both dependency drug court and mental health court. While it is not the focus of the clinic, it does happen on occasion. In addition, Professor Kelly periodically invites members of the drug court team and/or mental health court team to come and speak with all of the clinic's students about the operation of the courts and she encourages clinic students in traditional placements to at least visit the specialty courts to observe the proceedings. At Brooklyn Law School's criminal practice clinic, under the direction of Professor Lisa Smith, each semester, approximately 4–5 students out of the 40 or so in the generic externship class act as externs for prosecutors or defense attorneys practicing exclusively in drug and mental health courts. In addition, students in the law school's judicial clinic, on occasion, act as interns for the presiding drug and mental health court judges. Consequently, Professor Smith incorporates discussion of problem solving courts into her seminar and has found that such discussion has tremendous curricular value. It is our hope that this article provides additional inspiration and ideas for our colleagues who are already finding new and creative ways to teach this new crop of externship students.

51. Many of these ideas stem from a curriculum developed by Bruce Winick in his groundbreaking class titled "New Directions in Lawyering: Interviewing, Counseling, and Attorney-Client Relational Skills."

52. Of course, one of the first question that must be considered in the creation of any clinical program is how can said program be evaluated. What are the criteria for "success?" While this question requires further study, preliminary questions will likely include: Do students who complete the program come away from the say with an enhanced understanding and appreciation of therapeutic practice? Are students who complete the program, as compared to students in traditional placements, more effective advocates? Is the classroom experience for all students enhanced by having students in therapeutic placements participate?

Model. I would also like to expand the program to Dade and Broward County's drug courts, Dade County's domestic violence court, and Broward County's future DUI court (currently under development).

VII. ALTERNATIVE MODELS

As discussed, in writing this article we hope that other clinical educators are encouraged to contemplate ways in which therapeutic externships could fit into their own clinical curriculum. The time is ripe for the development of these programs because, with new ABA requirements on the horizon mandating that *all* law students take clinical coursework, law schools across the country will be contemplating new ways expand and enhance their current clinical offerings.

Clinical educators have always rejected one-size fits all approach when designing clinical programs.[53] Similarly, there are many options other than those described herein for exposing students to Therapeutic Jurisprudence and therapeutic courts. The possible variations in design and content are extensive and similar objectives can be achieved through a variety of methods.

We are realists, however, and are cognizant of the fact that often institutional realities related to funding and faculty politics play as strong a role in dictating design choices, as do teaching objectives. Thus, we want to provide interested clinical educators with as many options as possible to get these programs off the ground.

One viable alternative not yet discussed is the more traditional "individual tutorial" model in which an individual student would take the initiative to obtain a placement in a therapeutic court and then canvass a faculty members to provide supervision for academic credit. Another version of this model involves a faculty-initiated placement wherein faculty members with preexisting relationships with particular courts would recruit students to extern in these settings.[54]

Although individual tutorials vary dramatically based on the individual faculty member's (and in some cases University's) requirements, such programs have a lot of appeal for new Therapeutic Jurisprudence enthusiasts: the most obvious being flexibility and low cost. In addition, individual tutorials allow for tremendous interaction between (in most cases a full-time) faculty member and the student. Individual tutorials have the added benefit of giving the faculty member the opportunity to get some exposure to the "real world" in a very controlled way and keep their skills fresh without having to make the commitment to teach in a traditional clinical program. In addition, an individually supervised externship may be preferable when a student's externship is in an area within the personal expertise of a particular faculty member who is not also a clinical education.

The most obvious problem with this model of course is that only a limited number of students could benefit. Most faculty members would probably not want to take on more than a couple students a semester. In most cases, only students predisposed to the idea of Therapeutic Jurisprudence or therapeutic courts would seek faculty sponsors out or, in the case of faculty initiated externships, be solicited to participate. Finally,

---

53. *See, e.g.*, Eyster, *supra* note 31, at 358; Peter A. Joy, *Evolution of ABA Standards Relating to Externships: Steps in the Right Direction?*, 10 CLINICAL L. REV. 681 (2004); Linda F. Smith, *Designing an Extern Clinical Program: Or As You Sow, So Shall You Reap*, 5 CLINICAL L. REV. 527 (1999).

54. For further discussion of the efficacy of this model, *see Experience as Text*, *supra* note 46, at 403, 407, 416 n.17.

there is the added concern that non-clinical faculty who are not schooled in clinical methodology may not take the initiative to engage "tutorial students" in reflective learning through such tools as journaling.[55]

A variation of the individual tutorial model would combine an externship opportunity with a doctrinal classroom course[56] that, for our purposes, has relevance to the study of Therapeutic Jurisprudence. An obvious example would include a doctrinal course in mental health law. Under this model, a student would have the opportunity to earn credit hours for participating in an externship approved by a faculty member who teaches the related course.[57] This model shares many of the same practical benefits as the individual tutorial model discussed above. Additionally, it has the added benefit of giving students in the doctrinal class a context to assimilate otherwise abstract information. It gives them "real world" examples of issues addressed in the classroom. Clinicians who have studied this model, however, note that the danger of combining an externship with a substantive course is that, too often, insufficient attention is given to supervision. In addition, as discussed above in regards to the individual tutorial model, there is no guarantee that the teacher will be schooled in externship pedagogy.[58] Moreover, even if the teaches expresses an interest in focusing on reflective learning, there may simply not be enough time to do so while teaching the substantive course.

Despite these issues, we believe that this model has a lot of promise especially for schools that do not have a preexisting generic externship seminar in which to place students who express an interest in externing in therapeutic courts. However, more attention needs to be paid to the design of these programs in order to mitigate some of the recognized drawbacks.

Finally, therapeutic court externship programs are ripe for collaborative efforts with other fields of study such as social work, psychology, medicine, and criminal justice. Personally, we would love to see such cross-fertilization between, for example, law students and graduate students schooled in mental health. Mental health students would have unique insights into interviewing and counseling skills that would complement a law student's legal training. David Wexler listed additional advantages to a course enrolled in by both law students and graduate behavioral science students including: the richness of class discussion, the opportunities for observing each other in professionally related work environments (e.g., a law student working in juvenile court, a psychology

---

55. This model may also be less appealing in light of new American Bar Association requirements that do not allow "independent study" to count towards core credits.

56. This model derives from; a program called Advanced Clinical Experience (ACE) at American University, and was the subject of a paper presented by Avis Sanders and Mary Wolf at the 2003 Externship Conference, *Learning From Practice*, at Catholic University in Washington, DC. I want to thank Avis Sanders, in particular, for sharing all her materials and work product with me and for supporting me in my work.

57. In one variation of this model, the student would enroll in a substantive class in which all or some of the students participate in a related externship but where the focus of the class is entirely on conveying the substantive law, and there is little or no supervision of the externship by a faculty member. In another variation, supervision would be provided by the faculty member who has expertise in the practice area, i.e., the faculty member acts as both teacher and field supervisor.

58. In fact, when evaluating the success of this model at American University, this was the biggest danger that clinical professors saw with relating externships to doctrinal courses—that conveying substantive law tended to take precedence over spending time on reflection of the externship within the seminar. This problem was further exacerbated when externships were optional, and only some students enrolled in the substantive course were participating.

student externing in a shelter for battered women), and the possibility of collaborating on class papers or projects.[59]

While each academic discipline is understandably protective of its own turf, we view collaboration as a logical extension of the underlying foundation of the externships discussed, namely, the therapeutic, problem solving courts. In fact, David Wexler writes that such interdisciplinary teaching is crucial to law reform: "if therapeutic jurisprudence is to reach its objective of transcending academic lecture halls and influencing law reform and clinical practice, we must constantly chip away at existing professional provincialism, which often leads each profession to regard the other with suspiciousness and, on occasion, even antipathy."

Admittedly, the complexities involved in implementing interdisciplinary programs are formidable. However, as scholars and the legal community begin to recognize Therapeutic Jurisprudence as a brand name, cross-training in the related and varied disciplines will be inevitable.

VI. THERAPEUTIC EXTERNSHIPS PROVIDE VALUABLE SKILLS TRAINING

One of the issues that we confronted when talking with others about the design of a therapeutic courts externship program was whether or not it would be an appropriate and valuable educational opportunity for all clinical students. While we believe the answer to this question is a resounding YES, others have questioned whether such programs provide enough skills training. In other words, according to the conventional wisdom, students sign up for an externship precisely because they want to be in court arguing motions and, if they are lucky, conducting trials. The concern is that they will not get the same opportunities to hone these oral advocacy skills in therapeutic courts.[60]

These are valid issues and must be addressed. Certainly, students considering such placements must be fully informed of the differences between a traditional courtroom and a therapeutic courtroom and what their roles would be in each. It is probably not enough to relegate the task of explaining these differences to the University's placement coordinator. Instead, students should be encouraged to flesh out these issues with a member of the clinical faculty before signing up for an externship in a therapeutic court. Similarly, clinical staff must recognize that not all students are cut out for this experience. While a background in mental health or medicine would be ideal, an open mind and compassion should be a prerequisite.

---

59. David B. Wexler, *Some Thoughts and Observations on the Teaching of Therapeutic Jurisprudence*, 35 REV. DER. P.R. 273 (1996). Wexler writes that one of the most exciting teaching possibilities would be to offer a University wide graduate level course in Therapeutic Jurisprudence, open to law students, psych residents, and graduate students of psychology, social work, criminology, public health, nursing, and other behavioral science or health related fields. *Id.* at 286. He notes that the "only real downside to such an offering, is that given the "diversity of background, the class discussion may at times sink to the level of the lowest common denominator." *Id.* Such a problem could likely be prevented if the course is "jointly taught by, say, a law professor and professor of psychology." *Id.* For our purposes, a University-wide graduate level course in therapeutic courts would probably have as much or more appeal that a course in Therapeutic Jurisprudence because of the more immediate and obvious career implications of the later.

60. Of course, there are certainly going to be student who will prefer to go to court if the type of work they would be doing would be therapeutic rather than traditional. Thus, a therapeutic court's externship program may actually recruit some student who otherwise might opt completely out of a courtroom-orientated skills training program.

Ultimately, however, we strongly believe that while a student's experience in a therapeutic courtroom will certainly be *different* than the experience they would receive in a traditional courtroom, the experience will be of *at least* equal value.[61] A therapeutic courts externship gives students an opportunity to test and fine-tune their advocacy skills while dealing with people in crisis. Instead of standing before a judge arguing the finer pointes of evidence, however, students will be encouraged to view their roles as advocates in a different way. For example, while so much emphasis in traditional skills training is placed on speaking, the emphasis in Therapeutic Jurisprudence is on listening. By placing a focus on listening, students are better able to understand the opinions and concerns of other team members and client.[62] Since so much emphasis is placed on team meetings, advocacy skills are honed in this setting. Albeit different from courtroom arguments, students learn to espouse their views and recommendations in a manner that focuses on consensus building. In some cases students excitedly report in class or in their journals that their opinions became the catalyst for what was the recommendation of the entire team. Part of making these recommendations, of course, requires that students familiarize themselves with therapeutic services available to defendants. Students interning at Broward's mental health courts, for example, would be expected to develop a relationship with a range of different players in the county's mental health delivery system. Students actually conduct on-site visits to these provider programs so that they can advocate in regards to them in court. While a variety of opinions abound regarding a particular case, students learn to see themselves as part of a "helping process," where professionals from various disciplines work together to solve a client's problems. It is our belief that these skills are crucial to the lawyering process and have a place in any well-rounded clinical curriculum.

Moreover, contrary to popular belief, therapeutic externships would provide for opportunities to engage in traditional advocacy activities, albeit to a different extent. In the typical drug court externship, for example, a student working for a public defender's office would need to be familiar with all the possible defenses a client might have *before* they could advise that client whether to waive their right to assert those defenses in order to participate in drug court. This requires sophisticated interviewing and counseling skills on the part of the student. On a typical day, a drug court extern may also have the opportunity to argue before a judge that a client who tested positive for a controlled substance, or otherwise failed to satisfy a condition of his or her treatment plan, should be allowed to remain in the program, albeit with more intense treatment or frequent monitoring, i.e., make an argument that there are "mitigating factors."

---

61. In addition, the students' roles in both settings should not be seen *in conflict*. Professor Winick writes that, "in addition to training attorneys in their legal responsibilities in the representation of clients ... [potential] lawyers need more guidance on *reconciling the interest in protecting their clients' legal rights with that of promoting their clients' therapeutic needs.* The attorney-client relationship in this context needs to be reconceptualized in ways that augment its potential therapeutic effects." *Civil Commitment Hearing, supra* note 3, at 54 (emphasis added). Although Winick, in this instance, is referring specifically to the role of counsel in *civil commitment hearings*, his comments have a much broader application.

62. In fact, in many therapeutic courts, the client is encouraged and expected to speak directly to the judge as part of the healing process. This lawyer plays a less prominent role. *See Outpatient Commitment, supra* note 12, at 135–43. This may be a hard but necessary adjustment for the student who has been trained to believe that the lawyer is the "mouth piece" for the client.

In Broward's mental health court, for example, students would use their advocacy skills to argue for the "least restrictive placement" for their client. At the felony level, this may mean arguing to a judge that a defendant should not be committed to a state psychiatric hospital, and should, instead, receive outpatient therapy. Students would also have the opportunity to participate in contested competency hearings that require substantial fact investigation, direct examination of clients, experts and family members, and the cross-examination of expert witnesses (most often the psychiatrist). In fact, while it is rare for a student to have the opportunity to examine an expert witness in traditional criminal externships, expert testimony is common in mental health courts.

In some cases, students may even have the opportunity to participate in "downward departure" hearings; arguing in essence, that a client's mental illness justifies a downward departure from harsh sentencing guidelines. The outcomes of these proceedings can be dramatic. A defendant facing thirty years in jail could, with the right advocate, be given probation with appropriate treatment as an alternative. Involvement in this type of proceeding would be a tremendous learning opportunity for the clinical student.

On occasion, students in the Broward program would also have the opportunity to appear in *civil court* in Baker Act Litigation, i.e., a civil proceeding that could result in the involuntary hospitalization or involuntary mediation of a client.[63] Insofar as the Broward public defender's office provides representation for indigent defendants in these matters, therapeutic interns could participate in these proceedings as well.

Finally, any criminal attorney who practices in the trenches knows that you are missing the boat if you are going to do criminal defense work for a living and you do not have training in mental health issues. In Broward County, for example, 25% of the incarcerated adult population and 45% of the incarcerated juvenile population are on psychotropic medications. Nearly 10% of all criminal defendants have a diagnosed mental illness. Virtually every capital case requires extensive psychological testing. Thus, students who choose to practice in this area would be very well served to get mental health advocacy training and exposure early on. They will be more marketable and effective advocates. Indeed, administrators responsible for filling these positions remark on how difficult it is to find attorneys with a mental health background. In general, large offices such as the Broward County State Attorneys Office have specific attorneys (usually one or two) assigned to each of the county's various drug and mental health courts. Administrators note how difficult it is to staff these positions because so few attorneys have the requisite background in mental health law.[64] The administrators that we spoke with have all been extremely encouraging about Miami's Therapeutic Courts Externship proposal because, as well as recognizing the educational benefits, they have very real gaps in hiring that these programs could help ameliorate. For example, on average the Broward County Public Defender's office has several hundred applicants for

---

63. For a discussion of the evolving therapeutic role of lawyers in civil commitment hearings *see Civil Commitment Hearing supra* note 3 at 37. Civil commitments are also extensively discussed in Professor Winick's forthcoming book, BRUCE J. WINICK, CIVIL COMMITMENT: A THERAPEUTIC JURISPRUDENCE MODEL (forthcoming 2005).

64. Similarly, state bar associations are also beginning to recognize the brain drain in this area. In Florida, for example, a committee under the Florida Bar has recently been established to help educate members of the bar about the mental heath and substance abuse issues that many of their clients face.

less than 20 spots each year.[65] Students who have a background in mental health would go a very long way in distinguishing themselves from the scores of other applicants.

Finally, a traditional criticism of externship programs in general, is that the quality of field supervision is often inconsistent.[66] By contrast, students in therapeutic court externships will have the benefit of working with lawyers and judges who are usually "hand picked" because of the breath of their experience and superior advocacy skills. In addition, because of the "team concept" employed in most problem solving courts, students will have the benefit of working with high caliber professionals in other fields. Finally, while in traditional internship, many field supervisors may not be "sufficiently open to allow students to question freely the strategy and techniques utilized to provide results in a given cases,"[67] field supervisors in problem solving courts will likely be much more willing to allow students to engage in this type of institutional critique that helps make the externship experience such a valuable learning tool.

In sum, as long as participating students are willing to embrace the different philosophy of problem solving courts, a therapeutic court externship is an extremely valuable educational opportunity that represents a significant new direction for clinical education.

IX. Conclusion

We hope that our enthusiasm is contagious and that this article encourages other Therapeutic Jurisprudence enthusiasts to begin the process of crafting externship programs that give students the opportunity to practice Therapeutic Jurisprudence in therapeutic courts. With new ABA requirements on the horizon, we know that clinic directors are going to be looking for ways to enhance and expand their current menu of clinical offerings. We hope this article gives them food for thought. There is nothing like a baby's birth to focus our minds on the limitless hopes, dreams, and possibilities for the future. Along that future path, lots of dedicated nurturing will be required. Obstacles will abound, and the labor will often be difficult. However, the rewards shall be compelling. We can think of no better analogy in describing the past, present and future of therapeutic courts externship programs.

---

65. Information provided by Broward County Public Defender Howard Finkelstein.
66. *See, e.g.,* Barbara A. Blanco & Sande L. Buhai, *Externship Field Supervision: Effective Techniques For Training Supervisors And Students*, 10 Clinical L. Rev. 611, 612 (2004). In their article on the topic, professors Blanco and Buhai state that monitoring effective and motivated supervision of off-campus law externs in a structured field placement program has traditionally been the "chimera" of law school curriculum. This is because, among other things, in an off-campus filed placement, the primary concern of the supervising attorney must be the work of the agency or judicial chambers, while the concern for the education of the field extern must by nature be a secondary goal. *See also* Rose, *supra* note 40, at 104 (Professor Rose argues that law schools often "lack leverage" with site supervisors to guarantee that the supervision provided to students is adequate. Since most site supervisors are not compensated for their work with students, the incentives for them to supervise closely and evaluate carefully the work of their students are minimal. In addition, although a site supervisory might be a competent attorney, this does not guarantee that they are effective teachers). *But see* Eyster, *supra* note 31, at 389 (arguing that the fact that supervisor may have varying levels of lawyering skills, teaching abilities and supervising abilities actually facilitates the goal of self-directed learning).
67. Rose, *supra* note 40, at 104.

iii. Bruce J. Winick* & David B. Wexler,**
The Use of Therapeutic Jurisprudence in Law School Clinical Education: Transforming the Criminal Law Clinic

(Reprinted with permission from
13 Clinical Law Review 605, 2006)

Abstract

This article describes how therapeutic jurisprudence, and the therapeutic jurisprudence/preventive law model, can be imported into legal education and practice. Although the approach can (and does) find application in a broad spectrum of legal areas, the present article focuses on the criminal law clinic and on training future criminal lawyers with an expanded professional role: one that explicitly adds an ethic of care and considerations of rehabilitation. As such, it brings an interdisciplinary perspective into clinics and law practice, with particular emphasis on insights and techniques drawn from psychology, criminology, and social work. The article explores a therapeutic jurisprudence framework for thinking about criminal law competencies, and illustrates the explicit use of the expanded professional role in the area of sentencing, in juvenile parole revocation proceedings, and in a tribal reentry court project.

Introduction

Recent years have seen the emergence of the therapeutic jurisprudence/preventive law model of lawyering.[1] This model contemplates lawyers practicing with an ethic of care and heightened interpersonal skills, who seek to prevent legal difficulties or repetitive legal problems for their clients through sensitive counseling, advance planning, creative problem solving, careful drafting, and the use of alternative dispute resolution techniques. In recent years, this emerging model has begun to penetrate legal education, notably in courses on lawyering and in interviewing and counseling[2]

---

* Professor of Law and Professor of Psychiatry and Behavioral Sciences, University of Miami.
** Professor of Law and Director, International Network on Therapeutic Jurisprudence, University of Puerto Rico School of Law and Distinguished Research Professor of Law and Professor of Psychology, University of Arizona.

1. E.g., Practicing Therapeutic Jurisprudence: Law as a Helping Profession (Dennis P. Stolle, David B. Wexler & Bruce J. Winick, eds. 2000) [hereinafter, Practicing Therapeutic Jurisprudence]; Symposium, Therapeutic Jurisprudence and Preventive Law: Transforming Legal Practice and Education, 5 Psychol. Pub. Pol'y & L. 793–1210 (Bruce J. Winick, David B. Wexler & Edward A. Dauer, guest eds 1999); David B. Wexler & Bruce J. Winick, *Putting Therapeutic Jurisprudence to Work*, 89 A. B. A. J. 54 (May 2003). See also Judging in a Therapeutic Key: Therapeutic Jurisprudence and the Courts (Bruce J. Winick & David B. Wexler eds. 2003) [hereinafter, Judging in a Therapeutic Key](applying approach to judging).

2. The co-authors teach the model at their respective law schools. Wexler teaches a course called "Practicing Therapeutic Jurisprudence," at the University of Arizona College of Law. Winick uses this model in a skills training course at the University of Miami School of Law called "New Directions in Lawyering: Interviewing, Counseling, and Attorney/Client Relational Skills." For a detailed description of how therapeutic jurisprudence is used to teach these skills, see Bruce J. Winick, *Using Therapeutic Jurisprudence in Teaching Lawyering Skills: Meeting the Challenge of the New ABA Standards, 17 St. Thomas L. Rev. 429 (2005).* The model also is taught in sixteen other law schools in courses and seminars dealing with therapeutic jurisprudence more generally, lawyering, and judg-

It has much to offer clinical legal education, in particular.[3]

This model can be seen as a reconceptualization of an approach to skills training that previously has been used in clinical legal education. But the model, by explicitly valuing the psychological wellbeing of the client, by calling for enhanced interpersonal skills, through creative application of behavioral science research to the legal context, and by emphasizing the prevention of legal problems, adds a new dimension to clinical law teaching. The model, by bringing insights from psychology and social work into our understanding of the role of counsel, also brings a much needed interdisciplinary perspective to clinical legal education. Moreover, although much of clinical legal education has focused on litigation skills, this model includes law office counseling skills in a variety of non-litigation contexts.

This article describes the therapeutic jurisprudence/preventive law model, and demonstrates its value in the area of clinical legal education and skills training. While, in our view, this approach can fruitfully be used in all clinical settings, this article illustrates the model by offering some suggestions on how it can be applied to transform criminal law clinics. This article focuses on the criminal context in order to provide a detailed example of how the model can restructure and revitalize clinical legal education.

Part I describes the therapeutic jurisprudence/preventive law model. After offering some general considerations, Part II then provides three illustrations of how the model can be used to transform criminal practice—one drawn from criminal sentencing, one from juvenile parole revocation, and the final one from a proposed tribal reentry court. We also use these three illustrations to introduce a new tripartite analytical framework for how lawyers can creatively use behavioral science theory and research in their lawyering. Part III offers some concluding thoughts on how the model can bring new skills and techniques to the criminal law clinic.

I. The Therapeutic Jurisprudence/Preventive Law Model

In the last fifteen years, a number of new conceptions of the lawyer's role have emerged. All seem to have in common a more humanistic orientation, seeking to lessen the excessive adversarialness of lawyering, trying to improve client wellbeing generally, and psychological wellbeing in particular. Law professor Susan Daicoff calls these the "vectors" of the "comprehensive law movement"—therapeutic jurisprudence, preventive law, creative problem-solving, holistic law, restorative justice, the increasing array of alternative dispute resolution mechanisms, including collaborative law, and the emergence of problem-solving courts.[4] These models all seek to go beyond an exclusive focus on clients' legal rights or interests, to value as well their human needs and emotional wellbeing. This broadened conception of the lawyer's role calls for an interdisciplinary, psychologically-oriented perspective and enhanced interpersonal skills.

---

ing. For information on such courses, see http://www.therapeuticjurisprudence.org/ (last accessed on August 8, 2006).

3. Symposium, *Therapeutic Jurisprudence and Clinical Legal Education and Skills Training*, 17 St. Thomas L. Rev. 403–896 (2005).

4. Susan S. Daicoff, Lawyer, Know Thyself: A Psychological Analysis of Personality Strengths and Weaknesses 169–202 (2004); Susan Daicoff, *Law as a Healing Profession: The "Comprehensive Law Movement,"* 6 Pepp. Disp. Resol. L. J. 1 (2006); Susan Daicoff, The Role of Therapeutic Jurisprudence within the Comprehensive Law Movement, in Practicing Therapeutic Jurisprudence, *supra* note 1, at 465.

As a more theoretical and interdisciplinary perspective therapeutic jurisprudence can function as an academic organizing framework for all of these emerging movements. Therapeutic jurisprudence explicitly values the psychological wellbeing of the client, and recognizes that the legal interaction will produce inevitable psychological consequences for him or her. In the ways they deal with their clients, lawyers thus inevitably are therapeutic agents. Once this insight is absorbed, it is transformative for both lawyer and client alike. Lawyers embracing this broadened conception of the professional role must strive to avoid or minimize imposing psychologically damaging effects on their clients. They explicitly value their clients' psychological wellbeing, and in their problem analysis, problem-solving, and counseling efforts on behalf of their clients, seek not only to protect and promote their clients' rights and economic interests, but also to improve their emotional lives. Lawyers applying a therapeutic jurisprudence approach thus explicitly practice law with an ethic of care. Although the model stresses practicing with an ethic of care, it is not paternalistic.[5] Therapeutic jurisprudence work often has stressed the psychological value of self-determination and has criticized paternalism as antitherapeutic.[6] Therapeutic jurisprudence is committed to client-centered counseling.[7] The lawyer may have her own views about the client's best interests, and certainly should discuss them with the client when appropriate. However, in doing so, she should avoid being paternalistic or manipulative, and always remember that it is the client who makes the ultimate decision.

In its application to the lawyering process, the therapeutic jurisprudence paradigm has been enlarged as a result of its integration with preventive law.[8] Preventive law, originated in the early 1950s by Professor Lewis Brown of the University of Southern California Law Center, started out as an approach designed to minimize the risk of litigation and other legal problems and to bring about greater certainty for clients concerning their legal affairs.[9] It is a proactive approach to lawyering, emphasizing the lawyer's role as planner.[10]

Preventive law has much in common with the concept of preventive medicine. Indeed, the lawyer/client relationship has much in common with the doctor/patient rela-

---

5. David B. Wexler & Bruce J. Winick, Patients, Professionals, and the Path of Therapeutic Jurisprudence: A Response to Petrila, 10 N.Y.L. Sch. J. Hum. Rts. 407 (1993).

6. E.g., Bruce J. Winick, *On Autonomy: Legal and Psychological Perspectives*, 37 Vill. L. Rev. 1705 (1992). For applications in the area of mental health law, where the individuals involved may have reduced decision-making competence as a result of their mental illness, see Bruce J. Winick, Civil Commitment: A Therapeutic Jurisprudence Model (2005); Bruce J. Winick, The Right to Refuse Mental Health Treatment (1997). In contexts involving clients who are not mentally ill in a clinical sense, the psychological value of self-determination and the potentially negative effects of paternalism may be even more pronounced.

7. E.g., Bruce J. Winick, Redefining the Role of the Criminal Defense Lawyer in Plea Bargaining and Sentencing: A Therapeutic Jurisprudence/Preventive Law Model, in Practicing Therapeutic Jurisprudence, *supra* note 1, at 245, 286–87.

8. See generally Dennis P. Stolle, David B. Wexler, Bruce J. Winick &Edward A. Dauer, *Integrating Preventive Law and Therapeutic Jurisprudence: A Law and Psychology Based Approach to Lawyering*, 34 Cal. W. L. Rev. 15 (1997), reprinted in Practicing Therapeutic Jurisprudence, *supra* note 1, at 5; Wexler & Winick, *supra* note 1.

9. Louis M. Brown, *The Law Office—A Preventive Law Laboratory*, 104 U. Pa. L. Rev. 940, 948 (1956). See also Louis M. Brown & Edward A. Dauer, Perspectives on the Lawyer as Planner (1978) (text designed for law students and lawyers that further conceptualizes and illustrates the preventive law model).

10. See Brown & Dauer, *supra* note 9; Robert M. Hardaway, Preventive Law: Materials on a Non Adversarial Legal Process (1997).

tionship. Preventive medicine is premised on the concept that keeping people healthy is better and more cost effective than providing treatment for them once they become ill. Analogously, preventive law is based on the idea that avoiding legal disputes is inevitably better for the client than costly, time-consuming, and stressful litigation.[11] Just as physicians and other health care professionals can prevent future illness through periodic health checkups, testing and screening, inoculations against infectious disease, and the provision of counseling about nutrition and exercise, attorneys can use a variety of mechanisms to identify and avoid future legal difficulties.

The preventive lawyer, working in collaboration with a client, seeks to identify the client's long-term goals and interests, and to accomplish them through means that minimize exposure to legal difficulties. Through creative problem-solving, creative drafting, and the use of alternative dispute resolution techniques, the lawyer seeks to accomplish the client's objectives and to avoid legal problems. The preventive lawyer sees the client periodically, conducting "legal check-ups" to receive updates on the client's business and family affairs, to keep the client out of trouble, to reduce conflict, and to increase the client's life opportunities.

Moreover, just as for physicians and other health care professionals to play their preventive medicine roles effectively requires a degree of "bedside manner,"[12] preventive lawyers need to develop what might be called their "desk side manner" in order to function effectively as preventive lawyers. Therapeutic jurisprudence has much to offer lawyers in this connection. It calls for an increased psychological sensitivity in the attorney/client relationship, an awareness of some basic principles and techniques of psychology, enhanced interpersonal skills, interviewing and counseling techniques, and approaches for dealing with the emotional issues that are likely to come up in the legal encounter.

The integration of therapeutic jurisprudence and preventive law has broadened and reconceptualized both approaches. Taken together it constitutes a new model of lawyering that brings insights from the behavioral sciences into the law office, seeking to improve the psychological wellbeing of clients as well as to achieve their legal interests and avoid legal difficulties. It embraces both a therapeutic and a preventive orientation, and sees law as a helping profession.[13] The therapeutic jurisprudence/preventive law model of lawyering involves both practical law office procedures and client counseling approaches, and an analytical framework for justifying emotional wellbeing as an important priority in legal planning and prevention.

What can this new model contribute to clinical legal education? The model brings to clinical legal education and law practice a much needed interdisciplinary perspective grounded in an already rich body of social science and law research.[14] This integrated

---

11. Hardaway, *supra* note 10, at xxxvii; Stolle et al., *supra*, note 8, at 16; Bruce J. Winick, *The Expanding Scope of Preventive Law*, 3 Fla. Coastal L. J. 189 (2002) [hereinafter, Expanding the Scope]. Even in the context in which litigation has already commenced or seems likely to do so, lawyers applying the therapeutic jurisprudence/preventive law model strive to avoid litigation through the use of creative approaches to plea bargaining (in the criminal process) or to negotiation and settlement (in the civil context). E.g., Winick, *supra* note 7; Bruce J. Winick, Overcoming Psychological Barriers to Settlement: Challenges for the TJ Lawyer, in The Affective Assistance of Counsel: Practicing Law as a Healing Profession (Marjorie A. Silver ed. forthcoming 2007) [hereinafter, Psychological Barriers to Settlement].

12. See Francis Peabody, The Care of the Patient, 88 JAMA 887 (1927).

13. Indeed, the subtitle of our 2000 book applying therapeutic jurisprudence to law practice is "Law as a Helping Profession." Practicing Therapeutic Jurisprudence, *supra* note 1.

14. Although therapeutic jurisprudence started in the area of mental health law, see generally David B. Wexler & Bruce J. Winick, Essays in Therapeutic Jurisprudence (1991), it soon spread to

approach has given lawyering a more human face and provided lawyers with the enhanced interpersonal skills needed to be more effective interviewers, counselors, and problem-solvers. It is time that we taught this approach to law students, both in skills training courses and in the clinics themselves.

Two concepts drawn from the therapeutic jurisprudence/preventive law model are particularly helpful in training clinical law students. The first is the psycholegal soft spot. This concept refers to any aspect of the legal relationship or legal process that is likely to produce in the client a strongly negative emotional reaction.[15] Sometimes the legal problem faced by the client, or even the process of discussing it in the attorney's office, produces anger, stress, hard or hurt feelings, anxiety, fear, or depression. These feelings may get in the way of the attorney/client dialogue, preventing the lawyer from eliciting the entire story, understanding the client's real needs and interests, devising an appropriate strategy to solve the problem, or counseling the client in ways that the client is able to understand and follow. Sometimes the anxiety produced by the legal encounter or by facing a problem produces in the client a form of psychological resistance, denial, minimization, rationalization, or another psychological defense mechanism.[16] Clinical law students need to be taught how to identify these psycholegal soft spots, and various strategies for dealing with them.

Another important therapeutic jurisprudence/preventive law technique that clinical law students need to learn is the rewind exercise.[17] It is a good technique both for teaching clients about how to avoid future problems and for teaching law students about how to see legal problems from a preventive perspective. The idea is a simple one. Once a legal problem has become manifest, the task at hand is to solve it. This calls for the usual lawyering skills—negotiation or re-negotiation, settlement, and sometimes litigation. At this stage, the preventive lawyer is interested both in ending the controversy and in preventing its reoccurrence. In helping the client avoid a future reoccurrence of the problem, it is helpful for the lawyer to assist the client to understand why the problem occurred. Let us "rewind" the situation back in time to the period prior to the occurrence of the critical acts or omissions that produced the problem. What could the client have done at this point to have avoided the problem? What can he or she do now to avoid its reoccurrence?

Thinking about the problem in this way is a little like the performance of an autopsy after the patient has died. Once the cause of death has been identified, the doctors may

---

other areas of law, becoming a mental health approach to law generally. See generally Law in a Therapeutic Key, Developments in Therapeutic Jurisprudence (David B. Wexler & Bruce J. Winick eds. 1996). The approach not only brings insights from the behavioral sciences into legal studies, but also has itself spawned a body of empirical work testing therapeutic jurisprudence hypotheses. See id. at 843–994 (containing chapters reporting on empirical studies); Charles L. Kennedy, Judicial Behavior and the Civil Commitment Petitioner in Judging in a Therapeutic Key, *supra* note 1, at 158; Carrie J. Petrucci, The Judge-Defendant Interaction: Toward a Shared Respect Process, in Judging in a Therapeutic Key, *supra* note 1, at 148; Deborah J. Chase & Peggy F. Hora, The Implications of Therapeutic Jurisprudence for Judicial Satisfaction, 37 Ct. Rev. 12 (2000); Peggy F. Hora & Deborah J. Chase, Judicial Satisfaction When Judging in a Therapeutic Key, 7 Contemp. Issues L. 8 (2003/2004).

15. See, e.g., Mark W. Patry, David B. Wexler, Dennis P. Stolle, & Alan J. Tomkins, Better Legal Counseling Through Empirical Research: Identifying Psycholegal Soft Spots and Strategies, in Practicing Therapeutic Jurisprudence, *supra* note 1, at 69; David B. Wexler, Practicing Therapeutic Jurisprudence: Psycholegal Soft Spots and Strategies, in id. at 45; Bruce J. Winick, Client Denial and Resistance in the Advance Directive Context: Reflections on How Attorneys Can Identify and Deal with a Psycholegal Soft Spot, in id. at 327.

16. Winick, *supra* note 15.

17. Patry, *supra* note 15, at 71; Wexler, *supra* note 15, at 64–5.

learn something about how to avoid similar problems for their other patients, or how to avoid the mistake that may have contributed to the patient's death. Rewinding the legal problem can provide both lawyer and client with important insights about how to avoid future problems. For similar reasons, the rewind exercise is an important teaching tool that can help clinical students to think preventively. Moreover, the rewind technique is empowering for students because it allows them to see how creative lawyering can be. Rewinding also is a technique that allows students to improve their interviewing and counseling skills because it provides an opportunity for them to see how the interviewing and counseling approach used by an attorney in a particular case or hypothetical failed to succeed and also allows them to think about what alternative approaches could have brought about better results.

II. Illustrating Application of the Therapeutic Jurisprudence/Preventive Law Model: The Criminal Law Clinic

A. Some general thoughts

The therapeutic jurisprudence/preventive law model can be applied in all clinical settings. It is particularly useful in contexts involving the interviewing and counseling of clients who are confronting stressful situations or suffering from various psychosocial problems. A recently published symposium illustrates application of the approach in a variety of clinical contexts, including child dependency, elder law, criminal law, immigration law, and bankruptcy.[18] The model has considerable value even in contexts involving traditional litigation.[19] In this section, the model will be illustrated by applying it to the criminal law clinic, a context involving both interviewing and counseling and litigation skills.

We usually think of criminal lawyers—defense attorneys and prosecutors—as litigators. However, because such a high percentage of criminal cases are resolved by guilty pleas, an important aspect of criminal law practice is negotiation and settlement.[20] Another increasingly important part of the practice involves representation of the defendant or the state at sentencing.[21] The increasing use of sentencing guidelines has spawned litigation about the contours of the various guideline categories, and disputes are common about the defendant's correct characterization within the structure of the guidelines. One area that allows for creative lawyering is post-offense rehabilitation, which constitutes a ground for a downward departure under Federal Sentencing Guidelines, as well as under parallel state guidelines, or as grounds for mitigation in states that do not have sentencing guidelines and leave more discretion in the hands of the sentencing judge.[22] Even under the Federal Sentencing Guidelines, the Supreme Court's recent decision in United States v. Booker[23] has given sentencing judges considerably more discretion to depart from the guidelines.

---

18. *Supra* note 3.
19. Bruce J. Winick, Therapeutic Jurisprudence and the Role of Counsel in Litigation, in Practicing Therapeutic Jurisprudence, *supra* note 1, at 309; Winick, Expanding the Scope, *supra* note 11; Winick, Psychological Barriers to Settlement, *supra* note 11.
20. Winick, *supra* note 7. See also Catherine Clarke & Jim Neuhard, *Making the Case: Therapeutic Jurisprudence and Problem Solving Practices Positively Impact Clients, the Justice System and the Communities They Serve,* 17 St. Thomas. L. Rev. 781 (2005); Robin G. Steinberg, *Beyond Lawyering: How Holistic Representation Makes for Good Policy, Better Lawyers, and More Satisfied Clients,* 30 N.Y.U. Rev. L. & Soc. Change 625 (2006); David B. Wexler, *Therapeutic Jurisprudence and the Rehabilitative Role of the Criminal Defense Lawyer,* 17 St. Thomas. L. Rev. 743 (2005).
21. Practicing Therapeutic Jurisprudence, *supra* note 1.
22. Id. at 254–66.
23. *543 U.S. 220 (2005).*

Such post-offense rehabilitation is also an important factor in plea bargaining or in persuading the sentencing judge to grant probation in lieu of a prison sentence.[24] In addition, it often is a basis for pretrial diversion from the criminal process to an appropriate treatment program, with charges dismissed upon its successful completion, or for a withholding of adjudication, also with charges dismissed if rehabilitation is successfully completed. The concept of diversion has also been expanded in recent years with the emergence of a variety of "problem-solving" courts—including drug treatment court, mental health court, and domestic violence court—all designed to facilitate the offender's rehabilitation.[25]

Criminal defense attorneys thus need to understand the rehabilitative options that may be open to their clients, and how to have what often are sensitive conversations with them about these rehabilitative alternatives.[26] The criminal defense lawyer therefore must possess the psychological skills necessary to understand when the client's problem is the product of alcoholism or substance abuse, mental illness, or some behavioral disorder, all of which may respond to treatment or rehabilitation in an appropriate community program. But is the client ready to acknowledge the existence of a problem and willing to participate voluntarily in treatment designed to end it? Not all clients will be. Some will be plagued with denial, rationalization, or minimization—psychological defense mechanisms that will make it difficult to acknowledge that they have a problem or see the appropriateness of engaging in treatment.[27]

Interviewing and counseling such a client can be a real challenge. While it clearly may be in the client's best interests to participate in a rehabilitative alternative to criminal conviction and punishment, the decision is up to the client.[28] The criminal defense attorney's task thus becomes one of informing clients of their options and attempting to persuade them to consider the rehabilitative possibilities. Sometimes the criminal charges and pending trial alone are a sufficient catalyst for the defendant to face his or her prob-

---

24. See David B. Wexler, Relapse Prevention Planning Principles for Criminal Law Practice, in Practicing Therapeutic Jurisprudence, *supra* note 1, at 237 (discussing how criminal defense lawyers can make effective use of several emerging technologies of rehabilitation in attempting to obtain a term of probation for their clients); Winick, *supra* note 7 (discussing how criminal defense attorneys can use rehabilitative options in plea bargaining and sentencing).

25. See, e.g., Judging in a Therapeutic Key, *supra* note 1; Symposium, *Mental Health Courts*, 11 Psychol. Pub. Pol'y & L. 507–632 (Bruce J. Winick & Susan Stefan, guest eds., 2005); Bruce J. Winick, *Applying the Law Therapeutically in Domestic Violence Cases*, 69 UMKC L. Rev. 33 (2000); Bruce J. Winick & David B. Wexler, *Drug Treatment Court: Therapeutic Jurisprudence Applied*, 18 Touro L. Rev. 479 (2002). For a discussion of law school clinical programs explicitly involving the representation of defendants in problem-solving courts, see Gregory Baker & Jennifer Zawid, *The Birth of a Therapeutic Courts Externship Program: Hard Labor but Worth the Effort*, 17 St. Thomas. L. Rev. 711 (2005). For a discussion of the role of the criminal defense attorney in representing a client in drug treatment court, see Martin L. Reisig, The Difficult Role of the Defense Lawyer in a Post-Adjudication Drug Treatment Court: Accommodating Therapeutic Jurisprudence and Due Process, 38 Crim. L. Bull. 216 (2002).

26. Winick, *supra* note 7, at 283–98.

27. See Winick, *supra* note 15; Winick, *supra* note 7, at 285.

28. This is true under principles of client-centered counseling. See Robert M. Bastress & Joseph D. Harbaugh, Interviewing, Counseling, & Negotiating: Skills for Effective Representation 334–38 (1990); David A. Binder et al., Lawyers as Counselors: A Client-Centered Approach 2–13 (2d ed. 2004); Robert D. Dinerstein, *Client-Centered Counseling: Reappraisal and Refinement*, 32 Ariz. L. Rev. 501 (1990); Winick, *supra* note 7, at 286–87. It also is true under constitutional requirements. A defendant opting for a rehabilitative diversion alternative is forgoing a whole range of constitutional protections should he contest the charges, and therefore must make a personal, voluntary relinquishment of these rights. *Boykin v. Alabama*, 395 U.S. 238 (1969).

lem. When this occurs, a real rehabilitative or educational opportunity may be present, and the way in which the attorney talks to his or her client about these issues may be all important. In this connection, attorneys should understand the technique of motivational interviewing, originally developed in the context of alcoholism and drug abuse counseling, and which psychologist Astrid Birgden has adapted for criminal defense lawyers.[29] Frequently, for these conversations to be successful, the attorney needs to possess some psychological insights to deal effectively with the client's resistance and denial.[30] The attorney, conveying empathy and avoiding paternalism, uses open-ended questioning to elicit the client's long-range objectives and the extent to which his behavior problem has frustrated goal achievement. The objective is to allow the client himself to understand the relationship between his behavior pattern (substance abuse, for example) and the frustration of his goals (holding a job or maintaining a relationship, for example). The client may not be prepared to deal with his problems, of course, but sometimes the criminal charge can provoke a readiness for change, and when this is so, allowing the client to see for himself the negative effects of his behavior pattern may produce a willingness to change and the degree of intrinsic motivation that probably is necessary to achieve it. In such cases, the attorney can help the client to find an appropriate rehabilitative program or to fashion a relapse prevention plan that then can be used to argue for a more lenient plea agreement or sentence or for diversion or probation.

Playing such an active part in their client's rehabilitation is a new and expanded role for the criminal defense attorney. It is an entirely appropriate role, one through which the attorney can both prevent or minimize the client's loss of liberty and maximize the chances that the client will achieve rehabilitation, avoid a repetition of criminal behavior, and stay out of trouble in the future. Properly understood, this is a preventive law role.

Law students need to understand how to engage in these inherently delicate conversations with their clients in a non-judgmental way and without being paternalistic. The student should avoid telling the client what he "should" do, instead letting the client reach his own decision through motivational interviewing or by asking him whether his current course of conduct "is working for you?" Sometimes the victim's agreement may be necessary for persuading the judge to accept a rehabilitative option instead of a more traditional sentence of imprisonment. In this connection, students should learn about the value of an apology by the defendant to the victim.[31] Several law school clinical programs may already teach techniques such as these,[32] as do some courses in interviewing and counseling.[33] However, a criminal clinic based on principles of therapeutic ju-

---

29. Astrid Birgden, Dealing with the Resistant Criminal Client: A Psychologically-minded Strategy for More Effective Legal Counseling, 38 Crim. L. Bull. 225 (2002).
30. See Winick, *supra* note 11.
31. See, e.g., Jonathan R. Cohen, *Advising Clients to Apologize*, 72 S. Cal. L. Rev. 1009 (1999); Carrie J. Petrucci, Apology in the Criminal Justice Setting: Evidence for Including Apology as an Additional Component in the Legal System, 20 Behav. Sci. & L. 1 (2002). Obtaining an apology is an important aspect of restorative justice, an emerging approach that is used with increasing frequency in Australia, New Zealand, the United Kingdom, and Canada. See, e.g., John Braithwaite, Crime, Shame and Reintegration (1989); John Braithwaite, Restorative Justice and Therapeutic Jurisprudence, 38 Crim. L. Bull. 244 (2002). This approach makes use of victim/offender conferencing occurring in the presence of all interested parties, including the victims' and offenders' families and support networks, in an effort to restore the equilibrium to the parties and the community that the crime has disturbed.
32. For descriptions of clinical programs that use therapeutic jurisprudence, see Symposium, *supra* note 3.
33. See, e.g., Winick, *supra* note 2. For analyses of the interpersonal skills needed for therapeutic jurisprudence lawyering, see Silver, *supra* note 11; Practicing Therapeutic Jurisprudence, *supra* note 1.

risprudence would provide more systematic training in the interpersonal skills needed in the criminal context, and more opportunities for students to apply these skills.

These somewhat general therapeutic jurisprudence considerations apply in representation of clients throughout the criminal process. We next offer more concrete illustrations of how therapeutic jurisprudence can function in a criminal practice and in law school criminal law clinical programs. The first is drawn from the sentencing context, and shows how therapeutic jurisprudence can be used at a sentencing hearing and in designing a rehabilitative sentence. The second is drawn from the context of parole revocation. It describes an innovative approach being used in Arizona that provides an excellent opportunity for therapeutic jurisprudence lawyering and for the use of law students functioning in a law school clinical program. The third comes from a work-in-progress of creating a tribal reentry court.

B. An Illustration drawn from Sentencing

Much of the skills training suggested for lawyers and law students is inspired by literature in counseling and social work. Recently, we have been thinking through the various components of a therapeutic jurisprudence criminal lawyer's role. We have found it instructive to use an actual case to explore these components, and we offer it here by way of illustration of how therapeutic jurisprudence can be used to think about transforming criminal lawyering. The case we have selected is an 'ordinary' case, not unlike the steady diet of cases handled by criminal defense attorneys. The case is United States v. Riggs,[34] involving a federal firearm violation by one formerly convicted of a felony. [The Riggs discussion appears in the "Tripartite Framework" of Part I of this volume, and is accordingly omitted here. Subsequent footnotes have been renumbered and thus do not conform to the numbering in the original Clinical Law Review article from which this essay is drawn.]

C. An Illustration drawn from Juvenile Parole Revocation

Another potential context for clinic involvement in criminal law-type therapeutic jurisprudence work lies in the juvenile parole revocation/reinstatement area. One of us (Wexler) is currently working with the Arizona Department of Juvenile Corrections to bring a therapeutic jurisprudence perspective to center stage in the department's parole revocation process.[35] The Department has recently issued a policy dealing with deferred parole revocation for juvenile offenders previously released on parole who are found to have violated a parole condition.[36]

Although as presently drafted the procedure does not involve legal or law student representation, some thought is being given to the involvement of law students at a later date. In our judgment, such involvement would be an excellent vehicle for providing high level representation for the juvenile involved and for exposing law students to the use of therapeutic jurisprudence in a practical and important context. In brief, under the policy, once juveniles are released on parole, they may come before a departmental hearing officer if violations of parole conditions are alleged by the parole officer. A hearing on revocation may then be held, with the Department being represented by a parole

---

34. *370 F.3d 382 (4th Cir. 2004)*, vacated and remanded, *543 U.S. 1110 (2005)*. We use Riggs as a general sentencing example, and thus will not get bogged down in the intricacies of the federal guidelines and the impact of the Booker case, *supra* note 23.

35. C. Jennifer M. Sanchez, *Therapeutic Jurisprudence and Due Process in the Juvenile Parole Revocation Process: An Arizona Illustration*, 7 Fla. Coastal L. Rev. 111 (2005).

36. Ariz. Dep't of Juvenile Corrections, Deferred Revocation Process (July 30, 2007 Administrative Memorandum #104-06), (Attached as Appendix to this article).

officer and the youth being represented by a departmental employee known (at the moment) as a youth ombudsman. In the traditional functioning of the revocation process, if a violation is found parole will either be revoked or reinstated; if it is reinstated, the youth simply resumes status as a parolee.

Using therapeutic jurisprudence insights, the Department, in a pilot program, is now allowing for a third disposition, a deferred revocation, where the youth and his or her ombudsman propose giving the youth a second chance through deferred revocation in lieu of immediate revocation. The burden would be on the offender to persuade the Department to defer parole revocation based on a rehabilitative plan that he or she would propose. The youth, working with the ombudsman, would be heavily involved in preparing such a conditional liberty success plan, proposing conditions that should better the youth's chances for success in the community. The direct involvement of the youth in preparation of the plan would itself increase the likelihood that he will comply with it and benefit therefrom. If approved by the hearing officer, revocation will be deferred, and periodic review hearings will be held to assess and reinforce the youth's compliance, to ascertain whether needed services have been forthcoming and the like. If the youth successfully completes this stage, his or her ordinary parole will be reinstated.

In working with the youth, the youth ombudsman will be using skills augmented by therapeutic jurisprudence considerations,[37] and will receive some additional training along the lines of guiding a youth to "rewind" his or her situation to uncover high risk problem areas that need to be avoided, and to incorporating those concerns in a proposed conditional liberty success plan. The youth ombudsman will also learn to reinforce and present positive reform and compliance efforts to the hearing officer at review hearings. In short, this is advocacy enhanced by a therapeutic jurisprudence spin.

In its initial implementation, the youth will be represented by a youth ombudsman at the hearings and the department will be represented by the parole officer. There are, however, some concerns. One of them is extra workload. Another is that as non-lawyer state employees, youth ombudsman cannot guarantee the same sort of confidentiality to the youth as could a lawyer. Such a limitation might compromise the development of trust that would facilitate positive therapeutic outcomes. Accordingly, the Department is contemplating the possible use of lawyers to represent the youth at the revocation and follow up hearings. One thought is to recruit lawyers for pro bono work in this connection. But that resolution may not be well received by the parole officers, who would function as the state representatives in hearings with the professional lawyers.

Another possibility is to bring law students into the representation, both of the youth and of the Department. Such an approach would have two immediate advantages. First, the law students, closer in age to their clients, could be seen as excellent role models for the youth. Second, the involvement of law students representing the state would provide a new opportunity for discussion and reflection about the role of therapeutic jurisprudence from the perspective of the prosecution, an area thus far virtually un-

---

37. See, e.g., Wexler, *supra* note 24; David B. Wexler, *Just Some Juvenile Thinking About Delinquent Behavior: A Therapeutic Jurisprudence Approach to Relapse Prevention Planning and Youth Advisory Juries*, 69 UMKC L. Rev. 93 (2000).

touched.[38] In our view, this context provides an excellent opportunity for a law school clinical program.[39] Indeed, this context is illustrative of others in which, although representation is needed, lawyers may be unavailable or undesirable. With some creativity, we should be able to bring a therapeutic jurisprudence perspective into criminal law/juvenile law clinics, and may be able to do so in some context where lawyers themselves are appropriate but are not currently involved.

D. An Illustration Drawn from a Proposed Tribal Court Re-Entry Project

Our final illustration is drawn from ongoing discussions that one of us (Wexler) is engaged in to create a re-entry program in the Tohono O'odham Tribal Court. Moreover, as we will see below, the re-entry court is more likely to reach fruition if it contains, and is in essence fueled by, a clinical component.

Like many tribes, the Tohono O'odham Nation, with a governmental seat in Sells, Arizona (approximately 60 miles from Tucson), has a Law and Order Code and retains jurisdiction over many criminal offenses. Under the Indian Civil Rights Act, tribally-imposed punishments cannot exceed a year of imprisonment.[40] Nonetheless, under consecutive sentencing options, tribal courts often "stack" sentences, resulting in a number of offenders serving sentences of several years. The offenders are incarcerated in a tribal jail situated in Sells.

The "re-entry" into the community of confined offenders is, of course, a major current concern across the country, and "Indian country"[41] is surely no exception. Indeed, in one sense, the notion of a "re-entry court" patterned along the lines of drug treatment courts and other problem-solving courts might have a legal leg-up in tribal courts as opposed to state courts. That is because a number of tribal codes, including the Tohono O'odham Law and Order Code, contain an interesting and important provision not typically contained in state criminal codes: They allow the tribal court to "parole" offenders after successfully serving a portion (typically, one-half) of the imposed sentence.[42]

Under current practice in the Tohono O'odham Nation, prisoners are not typically represented at the post-sentence stage, and whether they know about, and petition for, "parole" is very much a hit-or-miss matter. Further, typically a tribal judge presented with a parole petition either grants or denies it. The imposition of creative conditions of release—or for that matter of conditions of release of any type—seem to be a real rarity.

---

38. See Wexler, *supra* note 55, at 745, (citing Ulf Holmberg, Police Interviews with Victims and Suspects of Violent and Sexual Crimes: Interviewees' Experiences and Interview Outcomes (2004)) (unpublished doctoral dissertation, Stockholm University) (on file with the Stockholm University Department of Psychology); Carolyn C. Hartley, A Therapeutic Jurisprudence Approach to the Trial Process in Domestic Violence Felony Trials, 9 Violence Against Women 410 (2003).

39. A concern with a law school clinical program representing both the youth and the parole officer is the potential for conflict of interest. In our view, this concern could adequately be avoided by insuring that the students representing each side be supervised by a different supervising attorney and that a firewall be used to protect confidentiality. Another possibility would be to have law school clinical programs from separate law schools represent each side.

40. Indian Civil Rights Act, *25 U.S.C.A. §1302 (2006)*.

41. The term "Indian country" comes from federal law. See *18 U.S.C. §1151 (1948)*.

42. E.g., Tohono O'odham Law and Order Code § 1.15 (5) (1994) ("a person convicted of an offense and sentenced to jail may be paroled after he or she has served at least half of the particular sentence with good behavior"). For a concise history of the Tohono O'odham Nation, see Winston P. Erickson, The Tohono O'odham in History (2003).

Recently, however, the Tohono O'odham judiciary has been discussing re-entry concerns and therapeutic jurisprudence, and is contemplating the use of the tribal code "parole" provision as a legal cornerstone to facilitate prisoner re-entry and to create a re-entry court in which the judges will play a reasonably active role. The tribal court judges are considering holding hearings on early release petitions (especially of longer-term inmates), soliciting petitioner, victim and community input, imposing tailored release conditions, requiring periodic review hearings, and celebrating the successful termination of parole:

> Issues for future discussion will relate to the kinds of cases with which a re-entry court might best begin, as well as issues such as the nature of a judicial parole eligibility hearing, the type of preparation that an offender should engage in prior to the hearing, the kind of parole conditions that might be imposed, the role of the community and the victim in the process, the type of representation the offender might have before, during and after the hearing, the type of follow up hearings that might be held, and many other questions.[43]

While the tribal judges are thus considering adopting a more active, problem-solving approach using relevant TJ principles, they recognize the difficulty of carrying out such a program when so much of the burden will fall on the court itself. In other words, this proposed project underscores the importance of additional legal and social services components—where offenders would know about the possibility of parole, could benefit from correctional programming, could plan for release, could work with counsel and others to propose a plan and release conditions, and so forth. These additional legal and social services components is where clinical programs can profitably and prominently enter the mix.

The tribal court will be best served to play a facilitating re-entry role if confined persons make the most of their time in jail,[44] and if they plan properly for discharge and re-entry. In turn, the confined persons will be best able to plan if they are provided professional assistance in doing so.

The discussions to date have accordingly led to a proposal to establish an Interprofessional Parole and Reentry Clinic. This seems logistically feasible for the Tohono O'odham Nation because persons convicted in the tribal court serve incarcerative sentences locally (which is not always the case with other tribes), because there is a nearby law school clinical program which is enthusiastic (the University of Arizona—UA—in Tucson), and because there is a local community college (the Tohono O'odham Com-

---

43. Judge Betsy Norris, Julia Corty and David Wexler, Therapeutic Jurisprudence and Tribal Justice: Steps of Creation, 4(2) Tribal Just. Today 17 (2005) (newsletter of National Tribal Justice Resource Center), also available at http://www.tribalresourcecenter.org/aboutus/newsletter_053005.pdf.

44. One would hope that correctional programming would take into account the mounting "what works" evidence. See Steve Aos, Marna Miller and Elizabeth Drake, Evidence-Based Adult Corrections Programs: What Works and What Does Not (monograph of Washington State Institute for Public Policy, 2006), available at http://www.wsipp.wa.gov (proposing use of cognitive-behavioral programs, drug treatment programs, and programs with an educational and vocational focus).

The "reasoning and rehabilitation" program of cognitive-behavioral change has consistently held up to empirical scrutiny. L.S. Joy Tong and David P. Farrington, How Effective is the "Reasoning and Rehabilitation" Programme in Reducing Reoffending? A Meta-Analysis of Evaluations in Four Countries, 12 Psych. Crime & L. 3 (2006). Such a program can lead an offender to develop a relapse prevention plan that can in turn be useful in formulating a proposed parole plan with conditions tailored to the situation of the particular offender. Wexler, *supra* note 20, at 771. Of course, all of the correctional programming will need to take careful account of the cultural and geographical context.

munity College—TOCC—in Sells) with social welfare and criminal practice expertise and with a mission of and genuine interest in community service.

The notion is to fuel and facilitate the parole and re-entry process with the services of a small number of supervised UA law students and a small number of supervised TOCC students. Working together, the students could help prepare inmates for discharge and return to the community, and could help prepare proposed parole plans for inmates to present to the court. TOCC students could work with the inmates on discharge planning and on relapse prevention planning, and the law students could help develop a proposed parole plan with conditions that would tie into effective relapse prevention and successful discharge.

There are, of course, many more issues to iron out, some of them before the clinic is launched and

others as we begin to feel our way. For instance, there is now some good clinical scholarship on "interprofessional practice,"[45] and on integrating law and social work in clinical settings,[46] and these issues now need to be tweaked in the context of re-entry. We need, too, to profit from the re-entry clinic experience of other law schools, notably the programs at New York University and Maryland.[47]

For a variety of reasons, there is now discussion regarding the question whether law students should provide in-court representation, or whether the law student role should be restricted to providing legal information and pre-hearing preparation. These discussions are of both a legal and of a therapeutic nature.

Legally, what are the limits and constraints of providing information about the law and the legal process in contrast to an advocacy or representational role? Some of these issues have been dealt with by lawyers employed by court-operated self-help legal centers, though typically not in criminal cases, and will make for interesting and educational discussions.[48]

Therapeutically, there is much to be said for legal representation at a parole-eligibility hearing, as well as at later periodic review hearings.[49] But might there be a therapeutic silver lining even in self-help legal information clinics where the client needs to go it alone at the tribal court hearing? Under such circumstances, wouldn't the pre-hearing job of a "self-help" interprofessional clinic be to ready the client for self-representation and to facilitate a role for the client in creating and buying into a workable—and defensible—conditional release plan?

We have spent some time in this essay reviewing the thought process, to date, regarding the proposed re-entry court for the Tohono O'odham Nation. We do so in part, however, because we think tribal justice programs generally—and perhaps tribal "heal-

---

45. Jennifer L. Wright, *Therapeutic Jurisprudence in anInterprofessional Practice at the University of St. Thomas Interprofessional Center for Counseling and Legal Services*, 17 St. Thomas L. Rev. 501 (2005).

46. Susan L. Brooks, *Practicing (and Teaching) Therapeutic Jurisprudence: Importing Social Work Principles and Techniques into Clinical Legal Education*, 17 St. Thomas L. Rev. 513 (2005); Christina Zawisza & Adela Beckerman, Two Heads are Better than One: The Case-Based Rationale for Dual Disciplinary Teaching in Child Advocacy Clinics, 7 Fla. Coastal L. Rev. 631 (2006).

47. E.g., Anthony C. Thompson, *Navigating the Hidden Obstacles to Ex-Offender Reentry*, 45 B.C.L. Rev. 255, 299–306 (2004) (describing New York University School of Law's Offender Reentry Clinic); http://www.law.umayland.cdu/course_info.asp?coursenum=598D (discussing the University of Maryland School of Law's Reentry of Ex-offenders clinic).

48. For helpful online materials from the California judicial library regarding self-help legal information programs, see http://www.courtinfo.ca.gov/programs/equalaccess.

49. Wexler *supra* note 20, at 756–62, 770–71.

ing to wellness courts"⁵⁰ and re-entry programs in particular—are very worthy of greater consideration by law school clinical programs.

In fact, there is a real connection between therapeutic jurisprudence and the interest in healing traditionally endorsed by many systems of tribal justice,⁵¹ and a two-way sharing of insights may prove extremely valuable. Accordingly, tribal courts are excellent venues for learning and honing holistic legal skills. Moreover, crime and related social problems are a devastating reality on many reservations, and the complex jurisdictional maze of the criminal justice system, with distant, unfamiliar and feared federal courts looming large, is in disarray and is greatly in need of more responsive and culturally compatible initiatives.⁵² Clinical programs can provide a desperately needed service and can provide a wonderful training ground for developing the legal skills essential in practicing therapeutic jurisprudence.

III. Conclusion: How Therapeutic Jurisprudence Can Bring New Skills and Techniques to the Criminal Law Clinic

The criminal law clinic traditionally has focused on representation of the defendant at trial, including pretrial suppression motion practice. As such, it has been a good vehicle for teaching interviewing, trial preparation, and litigation skills. Bringing therapeutic jurisprudence to the criminal law clinic would broaden the role that clinical law students play, in the process teaching them skills in addition to litigation. Because therapeutic jurisprudence focuses on ways of enhancing the client's psychological wellbeing, an important component of the clinic would be to focus on the client's potential for rehabilitation. Of course, some clients are not guilty or would like to plead not guilty and vigorously contest their charges. Others, however, are guilty of the offense and will enter a guilty plea. These constitute the overwhelming majority of clients, and the criminal law clinic should include teaching students the skills they will need to be effective lawyers in this process.

Increasingly, representing clients in plea bargaining involves the creation of rehabilitative options and alternatives to incarceration. At the outset, is the client prepared to accept responsibility for the offense and willing to undergo rehabilitation? The criminal charge can function as a catalyst for change, creating an opportunity for the attorney to assist the client to understand the need for attitudinal and behavioral change. Persuading clients to accept rehabilitation in appropriate cases can provide a significant opportunity both to preserve the client's liberty and to promote his or her psychological wellbeing. Judges and prosecutors increasingly are willing to offer probation or reduced sentences to offenders willing to accept rehabilitation and to participate meaningfully in it. While the rehabilitative ideal has fallen into decline since the mid-1970s, the pendulum has begun to swing back in the direction of rehabilitation as a significant goal of the criminal process.⁵³

---

50. Laura Mirsky, *Restorative Justice Practices of Native American, First Nation and Other Indigenous Peoples of North America, Part One*, available at http://www.realjustice.org/library/notjust1.html.

51. Id. See generally John M. Ptacin, Jeremy Worley and Keith Richotte, *The Bethel Therapeutic Court: A Study of How Therapeutic Courts Align with Yup'ik and Community Based Justice*, 30 Am. Indian L. Rev. 133 (2005); Ronald Eagleye Johnny, *The Duckwater Shoshone Drug Court: 1997–2000: Melding Traditional Dispute Resolution with Due Process*, 26 Am. Indian L. Rev. 261 (2001); James W. Zion, *Navajo Therapeutic Jurisprudence*, 18 Touro L. Rev. 563 (2002).

52. Kevin K. Washburn, *Federal Criminal law and Tribal Self-Determination*, 84 N.C. L. Rev. 779 (2006); Kevin K. Washburn, *American Indians, Crime and the Law*, 104 Mich. L. Rev. 709 (2006).

53. Fox Butterfield, Repaving the Long Road Out of Prison, N.Y. Times, May 4, 2004, at A25. For a discussion of emerging techniques of offender rehabilitation that empirical research is show-

Helping the client to understand the value of entering into rehabilitation presents exciting opportunities for law students to learn and practice the subtleties of interviewing and counseling. Moreover, it presents opportunities to engage in interdisciplinary work and to work with professionals from other fields—social workers, psychologists, and clinicians and paraprofessionals working in substance abuse and other types of offender rehabilitation programs. Creating rehabilitative options is itself an exercise in creative lawyering. Presenting these options to prosecutors and courts provides an important context for the teaching of negotiation and advocacy skills. These are important skills that every criminal defense attorney needs to possess, and that every prosecutor needs to understand.

Therapeutic jurisprudence brings much to the table concerning the development and improvement of these needed skills. The attorney/client dialogue concerning plea options and rehabilitative alternatives is one that requires heightened interpersonal skills on the part of the attorney. In therapeutic jurisprudence/preventive law terms, this context is filled with psycholegal soft spots. Bringing therapeutic jurisprudence to the criminal law clinic can teach students how to have these sensitive conversations and to deal with psychological defense mechanisms like denial, minimization, and rationalization, in ways that can help to keep them out of serious trouble in the future. Once a client has decided to accept a rehabilitative option—in diversion, by entering drug treatment court or another specialized problem-solving court program, or as a condition of probation—additional counseling concerning the client's compliance with program requirements is of increased importance. A considerable number of clients in these programs will fail to meet program requirements, often resulting in severe 629 consequences for the client, some of which will be worse than had the client not entered the program in the first place. Clients need to understand these consequences and to make informed and voluntary choices concerning their criminal justice options. These are difficult decisions for the client, and ones that require the guiding hand of counsel possessing emotional sensitivity, heightened interpersonal skills, and a familiarity with behavioral science theory.

In addition to persuading the client concerning the value of undergoing rehabilitation and helping the client to forge an appropriate rehabilitative plan, the attorney needs to be able to persuade the prosecutor and/or the judge that the proposed plan should be accepted and serve as a basis for a more advantageous plea bargain, a sentence of probation, a downward departure, or some other sentence reduction. This provides the clinical law student with an opportunity to practice advocacy skills, but in a way that departs from the typical clinical experience. A clinical program emphasizing a therapeutic jurisprudence approach would teach students about how to use insights drawn from the behavioral science literature to help craft rehabilitative proposals and arguments that will be persuasive to prosecutors and judges. This interdisciplinary component, inherent to therapeutic jurisprudence scholarship and practice, is what we previously refer to as "Theory-Inspired Practices" or TIPs. Moreover, because the need may exist to produce expert behavioral science testimony concerning the client's rehabilitative plan, potential for rehabilitation, or success in rehabilitation, the TJ criminal clinic can provide law students with the opportunity to deal with expert witnesses and to put on expert testimony.

---

ing to be effective, see James McGuire, What Works?: Reducing Reoffending (James McGuire ed., 1995); Tong and Farrington, *supra* note 70; David B. Wexler, How The Law Can Use What Works: A Therapeutic Jurisprudence Look at Recent Research on Rehabilitation, 15 Behav. Sci. & L. 365 (1997) (book review).

Should law students be involved in representing clients in these non-litigation contexts? We think so. Teaching law students these skills does not derogate from the traditional role of the criminal defense lawyer in contesting the client's guilt in cases in which the client wishes to plead not guilty.[54] We believe that the criminal clinic should continue to teach these skills and provide pretrial motion and trial experience. But modern criminal practice requires an expanded array of skills, including the interviewing, counseling, and negotiating skills in which a TJ-oriented criminal clinic will provide training. This is an important aspect of criminal practice, and one that is growing increasingly more important with the reemergence of the rehabilitative ideal. We believe that law school criminal clinics should include this aspect of criminal representation, and that therapeutic jurisprudence can provide a significant set of skills, interdisciplinary insights, and creative opportunities for interdisciplinary work and interdisciplinary collaboration.

We therefore suggest the development of therapeutic jurisprudence-oriented criminal clinical programs. Such clinics should focus on the representation of clients at diversion, plea bargaining, sentencing hearings, in drug treatment court, domestic violence court, or mental health court, and hearings involving probation or parole revocation.[55] A recently published article proposes a therapeutic jurisprudence clinical program involving drug treatment courts.[56] In this article, we have sketched how such a program could apply in the sentencing context, in the context of deferred parole revocation for juveniles, and in a tribal court reentry setting. It is time to expand our concept of the criminal law clinic in this direction, and to train a new generation of criminal lawyers to represent their clients more effectively and to play a major role in their rehabilitation.

---

54. See Brooks Holland, *Holistic Advocacy: An Important But Limited Institutional Role*, 30 N.Y.U. Rev. L. & Soc. Change 637, 651–52 (2006) (defending a holistic advocacy model for public defender offices as a complement to the traditional trial practice model, but cautioning that holistic advocacy should not be overemphasized institutionally).

55. In some of these contexts, it may be that having law students represent the defendant, but having the state represented by an experienced prosecutor, would be considered objectionable as a result of the imbalance it may create. If this concern is considered serious in one or more of these contexts—plea bargaining comes to mind—the problem could be remedied by having the supervising attorney at the clinic "second chair" the student in the conduct of negotiations with the prosecutor. In any case, there would seem to be less concern with having the student interview and counsel the client, consult with a social worker or other professionals, help the defendant to create a rehabilitative plan, and represent the defendant at the plea colloquy.

56. Baker & Zawid, *supra* note 25.

Appendix

Administrative Memorandum #104-06

DATE:	July 30, 2007
DISTRIBUTION:	Agency
FROM:	Charles Adornetto, Chief Hearing Officer
THROUGH:	Louis A. Goodman, Assistant Director, Legal Systems Division
SUBJECT:	Deferred Revocation Process

Please be advised that, effective August 1, 2007, the following procedure will be used as an alternative to Procedure 2302.06, Conditional Liberty Revocation Hearing and available for qualified juveniles.

Qualified juveniles are limited to those juveniles who are pending revocation for technical allegations only; do not have pending criminal charges; and who are assigned to the Northwest Parole Office.

A Parole Officer (PO), in accordance with Procedure 2302.06.4.c, may choose to allow a juvenile to remain in the community while considering revocation after one or more technical violations. The PO shall follow this process for a Deferred Revocation:

- The PO shall first hold a Cite In with the juvenile, parents, and CPS and provider, if applicable;
- At a second Cite In, the PO and the Parole Supervisor may recommend Deferred Revocation. The juvenile, parents, Ombuds and providers will be notified. A staffing shall be held with those individuals to develop a plan;
- The PO shall issue a Citation rather than an Apprehension Warrant, and the PO shall indicate on the Citation that a deferred revocation is being pursued.

The Due Process Proceedings Office (DPPO) shall schedule the deferred revocation hearing at the most convenient parole office or placement. The PO shall arrange for the presence of law enforcement or the Warrant Team at the hearing if the PO deems it advisable. Participants may appear telephonically or via videoconferencing. POs shall strongly encourage parents and guardians to attend.

If a juvenile does not appear at the hearing, the hearing shall proceed without the presence of the juvenile. If any allegation is found proven, the PO shall request that an Apprehension Warrant be issued. The juvenile shall be revoked for a minimum of 30 days without further due process upon apprehension.

The fact-finding phase of the revocation hearing is unchanged. If a technical allegation is found proven, the Youth Hearing Officer (YHO) will proceed to the disposition phase.

At the disposition phase, the YHO has the following choices:

- Reinstate to existing home or placement;
- Reinstate to other (home or placement);
- Revoke to secure care;
- Revoke but defer the revocation (only for qualified youth).

For a deferred revocation, the YHO would first conclude that revocation is appropriate rather than reinstatement. Then, either the Parole Officer (PO) or the Juvenile Ombuds (JO) may request that a deferred revocation be considered. The YHO may deny this request or may agree to consider it.

A deferred revocation will require a Conditional Liberty Success Plan (CLSP). The CLSP shall be a contract developed by the juvenile with the assistance of the JO and PO which will describe what happened to cause the juvenile to violate the earlier terms of conditional liberty, and what the juvenile will do to prevent another failure.

The CLSP shall be drafted and agreed upon prior to the hearing. The juvenile must play an active part in developing the CLSP and the parents and guardians will also be encouraged to participate and sign the CLSP.

If the juvenile, JO, PO and YHO all approve the CLSP, the YHO shall order a deferred revocation. The YHO will write a Hearing Report and attach the CLSP. The CLSP will also be incorporated into the Continuous Case Plan. In addition to the standard conditions, the CLSP will include that the juvenile shall attend Status Reviews with the YHO (the revoking YHO if possible), JO, PO, victims or representatives, and parents/guardians, if possible. The Status Reviews will occur twice-monthly for at least the first six weeks, and then may be held less frequently if the juvenile is performing well. The Status Reviews will most likely be scheduled at the Parole Office or at a placement, and while in-person appearances are preferable, parties may attend telephonically or via videoconferencing. The Status Reviews will continue for at least 3 months if the juvenile remains compliant. The CLSP may provide for a period longer than 3 months, but not shorter (unless the juvenile will age-out). If the juvenile completes the CLSP period in substantial compliance, the juvenile shall be reinstated to conditional liberty status.

The Status Reviews will be an opportunity for a frank and open discussion about how the juvenile is progressing and will provide for positive reinforcement when appropriate and will not be recorded except as noted below. Juveniles will be advised that they have the right to remain silent, but also that the juvenile has the burden of establishing that the juvenile should remain on deferred revocation status.

If the juvenile has not been compliant with the CLSP, the YHO shall go on the record at a Status Conference and re-open and complete the disposition phase of the earlier proceeding which led to the deferred revocation. The CLSP may be amended or the YHO may revoke the juvenile's conditional liberty. The only due process required for a revocation would be for the YHO to write a supplemental report on the changed disposition. (The juvenile does have a paper appeal right for the supplemental report, in accordance with Procedure 2302.06.) The juvenile's conditional liberty would then be revoked for a minimum of 30 days.

If a juvenile does not appear for a Status Review, an Apprehension Warrant may be issued. If an Apprehension Warrant is issued by a YHO while a juvenile is on deferred revocation, the juvenile's conditional liberty will be revoked without any further hearings. The juvenile will have a paper appeal right for the revocation based on an Apprehension Warrant, in accordance with Procedure 2302.06.

If a PO suspects that a juvenile's conditional liberty may be revoked at a Status Review, the PO may request an Apprehension Warrant prior to the Status Review and then arrange for law enforcement or the Warrant Team to take the juvenile into custody if the juvenile appears for the Status Review.

The information above has been sent to the Policy and Procedure Unit (PPU) to review and to post on the Intranet. The process owner for the procedure shall ensure that the PPU receives changes and modifications to the policy/procedure noted above within five business days from the original date of the Memo's issuance.

YOUTH RIGHTS/HEARING NOTICE
(DEFERRED REVOCATION)

Juvenile's Name: _____ K#: _____

Re: Allegation(s) of Violation of Conditional Liberty

You must appear at a Revocation Hearing on _____, 2007

At _____ ☐ a.m ☐ p.m.

at Northwest Phoenix Community Resource Center
<u>2802 North 37th Avenue, Phoenix, AZ 85009</u>

FAILURE TO APPEAR MAY RESULT IN A WARRANT FOR YOUR ARREST

At this hearing, a Youth Hearing Officer will decide whether you have violated the terms of your Conditional Liberty as specified in the attached Citation. You are protected by rights that begin with this notice and continue to protect you throughout your hearing and possible appeal:

> You should telephone the Youth Rights Ombuds Administrator immediately at 602-542-7050 to obtain the name and phone number of your Juvenile Ombuds (JO). Then you may contact your JO immediately to prepare for your hearing.
>
> You have the right to remain silent. You may decline to answer any questions by any person about the allegations against you now and throughout your hearing
>
> You have the right to bring your parent/guardian to the hearing.
>
> You have the right to receive a copy of the allegations being brought against you.
>
> You have the right to defend yourself against these allegations at your Conditional Liberty Revocation Hearing.
>
> You have the right to question every witness who testifies against you and to call witnesses in your own behalf at the Conditional Liberty Revocation Hearing.
>
> You have the right to receive a written copy of the decision(s) made at the Conditional Liberty Revocation Hearing.
>
> You have the right to appeal the decision(s) and to have the assistance of a JO to prepare the appeal.

Juvenile's Signature _____ Date _____

Parole Officer's Signature _____ Date _____

NOTE: Title II of the Americans with Disabilities Act prohibits ADJC from discriminating on the basis of disability. Individuals with disabilities, who need a reasonable accommodation to attend or participate in this hearing or require this material in an alternate format, may contact the Due Process Proceedings Office at 602.364.3510.

Distribution: Juvenile, JO, Field File, Due Process Proceedings Office

PROMISE TO APPEAR
(DEFERRED REVOCATION
STATUS CONFERENCE)

Juvenile's Name: _____ K#: _____

Re: Deferred Revocation Status Conference

You must appear at a Deferred Revocation
Status Conference on _____, 2007

At _____ ☐ a.m ☐ p.m

at Northwest Phoenix Community Resource Center
    2802 North 37th Avenue, Phoenix, AZ 85009

FAILURE TO APPEAR MAY RESULT IN A WARRANT FOR YOUR ARREST

I understand that my Conditional Liberty has been revoked and that I may remain in the community only as long as I am in compliance with the terms of my Conditional Liberty Success Plan.

I understand that if I fail to appear at the Status Conference at the date and time listed above, a Warrant may be issued for my arrest and I may be returned to secure care for a 30-day minimum revocation.

I understand that if an Apprehension Warrant is issued for any reason during my deferred revocation, I may be returned to secure care for a 30-day minimum revocation.

Juvenile's Signature _____ Date _____

Parole Officer's Signature _____ Date _____

NOTE: Title II of the Americans with Disabilities Act prohibits ADJC from discriminating on the basis of disability. Individuals with disabilities, who need a reasonable accommodation to attend or participate in this hearing or require this material in an alternate format, may contact the Due Process Proceedings Office at 602.364.3510.

Distribution: Juvenile, JO, Field File, Due Process Proceedings Office

iv. David B. Wexler, Crime Victims, Law Students, and Therapeutic Jurisprudence Training

INTRODUCTION

In March, 2007, the Oñati International Institute for the Sociology of Law, in Oñati, Gipuzkoa, Spain, sponsored a workshop entitled "Victim Participation in Justice and Therapeutic Jurisprudence: A Comparative Analysis." As a workshop participant, I presented and submitted a paper for that conference. The present essay is a revised version of that paper, adapted to the needs and purposes of this volume.

The present volume, of course, is devoted to a discussion of therapeutic jurisprudence and criminal defense practice in general judicial settings. Yet, in this part of the book, I draw on the rich educational opportunities for students to learn therapeutic jurisprudence principles and techniques in intensive problem-solving court contexts, such as in drug treatment court clinics attached to the law schools of William & Mary and of the University of Miami. And here, I propose student participation in a victim-centered clinic as a stepping stone to TJ criminal defense lawyering. Indeed, in the final section of this book—dedicated to opening a discussion of therapeutic jurisprudence in a comparative law context—University of Stockholm law professor Christian Diesen discusses the situation in Sweden, where victims receive actual legal representation in criminal cases. He notes that, especially in smaller cities, the same lawyer may sometimes serve as defense counsel and, at other times, may be called upon to represent a victim. Consistent with the educational philosophy I propose here, Professor Diesen notes that "a lawyer who one days represents a suspect and the next day a victim should be able to see the need of less short-sighted solutions than the ones that the trial can offer."

It is time, then to turn to the proposal: a Victim Legal Advisor Clinic (VLAC) attached to a law school and, ideally, affiliated with an existing Victim Witness Assistance Program operative in the jurisdiction.

I. VICTIM LEGAL ADVISOR CLINIC

My thinking about this topic is preliminary and evolving, and is presented in outline form, intended to serve as a springboard for further discussion:

1. Law school clinical programs are plentiful, at least in the U.S., and therapeutic jurisprudence (TJ) is of growing interest to law school clinics.[1]

2. Legal clinics have traditionally emphasized litigation, but are increasingly interested in imparting interviewing and counseling skills.[2]

3. Law students could offer to provide support and legal information to victims of crime in pending criminal cases. In fact, a handful of victim legal clinics already exist, assisting victims in state courts and in one case in federal court as well.[3] Some of those clinics seem to emphasize litigation issues. The kind of clinic I have in mind, however, would focus on providing legal information, advice, and counseling. In jurisdictions with well-staffed Victim Witness Assistance programs, many of the functions described

---

1. Bruce J. Winick and David B. Wexler, The Use of Therapeutic Jurisprudence in Law School Clinical Education: Transforming the Criminal Law Clinic, 13 Clinical Law Review 605 (2006); Symposium on Therapeutic Jurisprudence in Clinical Legal Education and Legal Skills Training, 13 St. Thomas Law Review 403 (2005).

2. Bruce J. Winick and David B. Wexler, The Use of Therapeutic Jurisprudence in Law School Clinical Education: Transforming the Criminal Law Clinic, 13 Clinical Law Review 605 (2006).

3. National Crime Victim Law Institute website, at (www.ncvli.org).

here are in fact already offered by the program. But law student involvement can provide additional cost-free resources to such programs, and law students may add their developing professional expertise and knowledge of criminal procedure to the mix of talents. Of equal importance, these programs offer a superb TJ training opportunity for law students to improve their interpersonal communication skills in sensitive settings, to enhance their ability to work with allied professionals, and to improve their knowledge of legal and courtroom procedures.

4. The proposed clinic would allow students to observe courtroom proceedings (itself an important educational objective) and, at the same time, would provide the students with actual client contact in an interviewing and counseling context.

5. Since such a clinic would involve counseling but would not technically involve actual in-court client representation, such a clinic could be open to students who are not yet in their final year of law school (in the U.S., a typical requirement for engaging in limited, supervised, in-court representation).

6. Such clinics could seemingly operate in any jurisdiction, although they would provide students a more robust role in jurisdictions—like the U.S. federal jurisdiction[4] and many states[5]—that basically permit victim presence throughout the proceedings, as opposed to those that may treat the victim as a mere "witness," subject to rules governing witness sequestration during trial.

7. The precise role of the clinic will need to be fleshed out, and will also depend somewhat on the local legal landscape, but some functions might include:

(a) Explaining to the victim the legal proceedings and legal terminology (e.g., no contest plea, not guilty by reason of insanity, allocution): what just happened, what is happening, what is supposed to happen next?

This function might also include a discussion whether the victim would desire to be present or absent from an upcoming portion of the proceedings, e.g., one that might be disturbing or one that might be dry, technical, and deadly dull.

(b) Accompanying the victim when the prosecution interviews and prepares the victim for direct and cross examination. The presence of a familiar figure—the clinic student—should render the meeting with the prosecutor less frightening for the victim, and the observational opportunity should provide an excellent educational experience for the law student.

(c) Working with a victim support service to hook the victim up with available, appropriate services—a function that will be of obvious value to the victim and will be valuable to the law student by providing an opportunity to learn about social services and to work with social service professionals, matters of increasing importance in the work of today's criminal and poverty lawyers.[6]

(d) Supporting the victim in the preparation of a written or oral Victim Impact Statement, explaining the substance and procedure of sentencing, and generally preparing the victim for allocution.[7]

---

4. United States Code, 18 U.S.C. 3117 (a) (3).
5. D. Beloof and P. Cassell, The Victim's Right to Attend Trials: The Reascendant Consensus, 9 Lewis and Clark Law Review 481 (2005).
6. David B. Wexler, A Tripartite Framework for Incorporating Therapeutic Jurisprudence in Criminal Law Education, Research and, Practice, 7 Florida Coastal Law Review 95 (2005).
7. David B. Wexler, Therapeutic Jurisprudence and Readiness for Rehabilitation', 8 Florida Coastal Law Review 111 (2006).

(e) Explaining the judges' sentencing decision and underlying reasons.[8]

(f) Helping the victim prepare a Legal System Victim Impact Statement (as described more fully in Section II infra).

8. A Victim Legal Advisor Clinic could, of course, provide its services in criminal cases generally. But, especially if the law school clinic operates in affiliation with an established and broad-based Victim Witness Assistance Program, the law school clinic might limit its participation to certain categories of cases.

For example, one excellent opportunity for learning and service might be a victim clinic limited to the specialized area of federal Indian law cases. These are serious criminal cases that, had they occurred outside the boundaries of Indian nations, would be heard in state court. But because of their special status, these cases are prosecuted in federal court, a forum often regarded—by defendants and victims alike—as distant, foreign and frightening.[9] Students participating in a Federal Indian Victim Legal Advisor Clinic could bring to their work (and further develop) a heightened cultural competence, an attribute that ought to be much appreciated by the clinic clients.[10]

II. LEGAL SYSTEM VICTIM IMPACT STATEMENT

The proposal for a Legal System Victim Impact Statement (LSVIS) is sufficiently important to warrant separate attention. The traditional Victim Impact Statement speaks to the impact of the *crime* on the victim. The victim is given "voice" and that voice might influence the court's sentencing decision.

But a major concern in victimology concerns "secondary victimization" and the often anti therapeutic impact of the legal system itself. Why, then, should we not also have a *Legal System Victim Impact Statement,* told from the victim's perspective? Such a statement can serve an important expressive function, and can provide the victim with further "voice". Some might argue, however, that, since, in contrast to the traditional Victim Impact Statement, a Legal System Victim Impact Statement would have no possibility of influencing the outcome of the victim's case, it might be "patently unfair" to "solicit an opinion from someone who has *no* potential to affect the outcome".[11]

But a Legal System Victim Impact Statement may "pacify the need to speak and participate"[12] *and* have real world impact, albeit in the *future*. A Legal System Victim Impact Statement might indeed serve a legal system reform function, and many victims would no doubt be interested in providing their feedback if such might yield value to others in time to come. So long as the victim is made aware that the preparation of a LSVIS is not intended to influence his or her *own* case, the ethical issue evaporates.

---

8. Id.
9. Kevin K. Washburn, Federal Criminal Law and Tribal Self-Determination, 84 North Carolina Law Review 779 (2006).
10. Carolyn C. Hartley and Carrie J. Petrucci), Practicing Culturally Competent Therapeutic Jurisprudence: A Collaboration Between Social Work and Law, 14 Washington University Journal of Law and Policy 133 (2004). Another specialized area in federal court practice—one typically (but incorrectly) thought of as only a state court matter—is domestic violence. Myrna Raeder, Domestic Violence in Federal Court: Abused Women as Victims, Survivors and Offenders, Federal Sentencing Reporter (2006). Of course, specialized knowledge and sensitivity would be crucially important to those clients as well, and a law school clinic might limit itself to such federal cases.
11. Kevin Burke and Steven Leben, Procedural Fairness: A Key Ingredient in Public Satisfaction 12 (a White Paper of the American Judge Association) (2007), available at http://aja.ncsc.dni.w/htdocs/AJAWhitePaper9-26-07.pdf.
12. Id.

Ideally, a LSVIS could be prepared in stages—following police interviews, after cross-examination, following the imposition of sentence, and the like. But the ideal may not always prove to be logistically feasible. In any case, a LSVIS could be prepared *after* the case, perhaps as a component of a detailed exit interview with a Victim Witness Program and its affiliated law school Victim Legal Advisor Clinic.

In that connection, note that therapeutic jurisprudence has, in a number of contexts, made effective use of the preventive law pedagogical "rewind" technique, where a scenario is re-wound to a time in the past and consideration is given to what might have been done differently to have avoided the eruption of a troublesome legal issue or the accompanying emotional turmoil.[13] The LSVIS can be looked at as a type of rewind exercise, one we might learn from so as not to repeat mistakes in the future.

Of course, some difficulties encountered by victims inhere in the adversary process itself (e.g., cross examination). But many others do not. Consider an actual example given by Erez and Downs[14] of how disrespected victims might feel when, before or after a formal court session, but in the courtroom and in the presence of the victim, informal conversations take place among defense attorneys, judges, and prosecutors about such mundane matters as family vacation plans and the like. The actual case documented by Erez and Downs involved just such a casual conversation in the presence of parents awaiting the adjudication of a case involving the murder of their child.

Such conversations likely occur without any disrespect intended. But if the offensiveness of such conduct is later called to the attention of those individuals, perhaps in the form of a LSVIS, my guess is those legal actors would think twice before having a similar conversation in the future.

A LSVIS could be prepared by a victim with the support and assistance of a student legal advisor. Involvement of a law student in the statement preparation should serve to increase the future lawyer's sensitivity to the emotional and interpersonal consequences of the legal system and to the behavior of its functionaries—a matter of utmost importance but traditionally neglected by legal education.

The LSVIS should emphasize both good and bad behaviors by various actors, beginning with the police and continuing throughout the process. It is indeed important to include the good in order to reinforce that type of behavior by system participants and to move toward the eventual development of "best practices" in the area.

A completed LSVIS could be distributed by the clinic student to the relevant actors. Indeed, a legal clinic might even collect and compile LSVISs and prepare a year-end report summarizing victim views of proper and improper behaviors. Such a report might lead to reforms of practice or even of the law itself, and the report and underlying statements can constitute a rich resource for researchers, educators and reformers.

A preliminary form for a LSVIS could profitably be drafted by a team of Victim Witness Assistance Program professionals working with researchers in the field. Such a team would be ideally suited to draft a document based on their considerable combined

---

13. M. W. Patry, et al, Better Legal Counseling Through Empirical Research, 34 California Western Law Review 440 (1998); Bruce J. Winick, A Legal Autopsy of the Lawyering in Schiavo: A Therapeutic Jurisprudence/Preventive Law Rewind Exercise, 61 University of Miami Law Review 595 (2007).

14. Erez, E and Downs, D. (2007), Victim Participation in Justice and Therapeutic Jurisprudence: The American Perspective (2007) (paper presented at Oñati workshop on victim participation and therapeutic jurisprudence).

knowledge of the types of behaviors and processes of importance and concern to crime victims.

CONCLUSION

A Victim Legal Advisor Clinic has the advantage of bringing resources into the system without appreciable cost to the system itself. Of course, law school clinics will cost something to run, but law schools are always looking for good, interesting, and effective ways of educating their students, and a victim legal clinic could do so while serving an important social function. Students exposed to such a clinic—ideally augmented by the preparation of Legal System Victim Impact Statements—will take enhanced interpersonal skills and a TJ perspective with them into practice. And that practice may be in criminal law—leading to prosecutors with greater interpersonal understanding and sensitivity (a matter of considerable interest and concern in TJ circles) and to criminal defense attorneys who employ a TJ lens. Indeed, if students participate in a Victim Legal Advisor Clinic before their final year, they might indeed cap off their clinical experience with a final year stint in a prosecutor or defense clinic.

v. Kristin Henning,[*] Defining the Lawyer-Self: Using Therapeutic Jurisprudence to Define the Lawyer's Role and Build Alliances that Aid the Child Client

(Reprinted with permission from
The Affective Assistance of Counsel: Practicing Law as a Healing
Profession 411, Marjorie A. Silver, ed. Carolina Academic Press, 2007)

Introduction

The application of therapeutic jurisprudence to juvenile court is not new. In fact, juvenile courts were designed to meet an explicit rehabilitative agenda and have historically relied on paternalistic judges to dole out an array of therapeutic services to youth charged with crime.[1] Today, therapeutic outcomes are not limited to judicial paternalism and rehabilitative programming, but may also be achieved or hindered through the child's daily interaction with lawyers, probation officers, the police, and even his own family. The child's interactions with key players in the juvenile justice system will inevitably shape the child's perceptions of justice, authority, and morality and may alter or reinforce the path the child has set for his own future. Because the attorney-client relationship may be the sole means by which the child may participate in the process of justice and earn credibility and respect with others in the system, the attorney-client relationship warrants special care and attention in the juvenile court.

This chapter considers ways in which therapeutic jurisprudence may inform and improve attorney-child relationships in the juvenile justice system. Therapeutic jurisprudence recognizes that there is considerable therapeutic value to attorney-client relation-

---

[*] Copyright © 2005 by Kristin Henning. Associate Professor of Law, Georgetown University Law Center. J.D., Yale Law School, L.L.M., Georgetown Law Center; A.B., Duke University. The author has represented juveniles in the District of Columbia for the last ten years. She previously served as lead attorney for the juvenile unit of the D.C. Public Defender Service and is currently the Deputy Director of the Juvenile Justice Clinic at Georgetown.

[1]. Josine Junger-Tas, *The Juvenile Justice System: Past and Present Trends in Western Society*, in PUNISHING JUVENILES: PRINCIPLE AND CRITIQUE 30 (Ido Weijers & Antony Duff eds., 2002) [hereinafter *Juvenile Justice System*].

ships that educate, empower, and validate the client. Attorneys who validate clients are neither patronizing nor paternalistic, but instead seek and respect the client's perspective, identify and affirm the client's strengths, and convey empathy for the client's plight. Attorneys who empower clients give voice to the client's views and attempt to understand the client from the client's own cultural, ethnic, gendered, and socioeconomic perspective. Therapeutically inspired attorney-client relationships not only yield immediate benefits of client-satisfaction and positive self-esteem, but may also promote effective long-term rehabilitation for children accused of crime.

The attorney-child relationship is also influenced by a myriad of external factors that may impede or enhance the attorney-client dynamic. Notwithstanding the child's independent legal interests, the child always exists within the context of family and community and is generally dependent on parents, teachers, and other significant adults for basic necessities and guidance. Thus, successful lawyering on behalf of children may require the lawyer to build alliances and forge partnerships that will inform and improve attorney-child interactions and aid the lawyer in representing the whole child. In a delinquency case, alliances with family members, teachers, social workers, psychologists, public benefits attorneys, and special education advocates may facilitate a more informed choice among case-related alternatives, empower the child to participate more effectively in the juvenile justice system, and increase the child's

opportunity for favorable outcomes. The second half of this chapter explores the value of interdisciplinary partnerships.

I. Defining the Lawyer-Self

A. *Selecting the Appropriate Attorney-Client Paradigm*

The selection of an appropriate attorney-child paradigm cannot be taken lightly in the juvenile justice system. The attorney-client relationship is the primary means by which an accused child may exercise or waive important constitutional rights; it is the lens through which the child views, understands, and evaluates the juvenile court system; and it is the relationship through which the child comes to understand broader notions of law, liberty, justice, and fairness. The attorney-client relationship is also the means by which the child will develop positive or negative responses to the rehabilitative goals of the court.

Lawyers interested in the study of effective attorney-client relations will find a wealth of literature on the theories and practice of client counseling, client interviewing, "affective" advocacy, and moral responsibility.[2] In the literature, the lawyer is left to choose from among a variety of attorney-client paradigms creatively named: the hired gun, the guru, the godfather, the authoritarian, the friend, the best interest or guardian advocate, and the client-centered or collaborative lawyer among others.[3] The lawyer's choice of paradigms often depends more on the lawyer's values, experience, and ego

---

2. For a representative sampling, see DAVID A. BINDER ET AL., LAWYERS AS COUNSELORS: A CLIENT-CENTERED APPROACH (2d ed. 2004); Robert F. Cochran et al., *Client Counseling and Moral Responsibility*, 30 PEPP. L. REV. 591 (2003) [hereinafter *Client Counseling*]; Linda G. Mills, *Affective Lawyering: The Emotional Dimensions of the Lawyer-Client Relation*, in PRACTICING THERAPEUTIC JURISPRUDENCE: LAW AS A HELPING PROFESSION 419 (Dennis P. Stolle et al. eds., 2000); ROBERT F. COCHRAN ET AL., THE COUNSELOR-AT-LAW: A COLLABORATIVE APPROACH TO CLIENT INTERVIEWING AND COUNSELING (1999) [hereinafter COUNSELOR-AT-LAW]; THOMAS L. SHAFFER & ROBERT F. COCHRAN, LAWYERS, CLIENTS AND MORAL RESPONSIBILITY (1994).

3. COCHRAN ET AL., COUNSELOR-AT-LAW, *supra* note 2, at 165–82 (discussion array of client-counseling models).

than on the client's expressed or negotiated preference in the attorney-client relationship. The selection of an appropriate attorney-client framework is especially complicated when the client is a child or an adolescent who has limited life experience, incomplete cognitive and psychosocial development, and limited ability to effectively negotiate roles and responsibilities within the attorney-client dyad.[4] The traditional paternalistic and rehabilitative mission of the juvenile court further complicates the role of the child's lawyer.

Principles of law and ethics are obvious and important means by which the lawyer may select among the various advocacy models. Today, emerging principles of therapeutic jurisprudence provide an additional consideration in the evaluation of lawyering paradigms. This section looks at the therapeutic values and skills that lie at the heart of a successful and satisfactory attorney-client dyad and considers whether therapeutic preferences conflict or converge with other more important values and norms.

1. *Values*

Therapeutic jurisprudence is a study of the ways in which legal rules, legal procedures, and the roles of legal actors—such as lawyers, judges, and probation officers—produce intended or unintended therapeutic or anti-therapeutic consequences for parties in the relevant system of justice.[5] Therapeutic jurisprudence seeks to promote policies, systems, and relationships, consistent with principles of justice and constitutional law, that will secure positive therapeutic outcomes and minimize negative or anti-therapeutic consequences.[6] Modern applications of therapeutic jurisprudence in the juvenile justice system suggest that when children perceive legal rules, procedures, and actors as unfair, they have less respect for the law and legal authorities and are less likely to accept judicial interventions.[7] By contrast, when children believe the legal system has treated them with fairness, respect, and dignity, they are more inclined to accept responsibility for their conduct and engage in the process of reform.[8] Long before the evolution of therapeutic jurisprudence as an organized school of thought, the Supreme Court in *In re Gault*[9] recognized that the appearance and actuality of fairness, impartiality, and orderliness in the juvenile court may be just as, if not more, therapeutic for the child than programming.[10] That is, the child's perception about whether she is being treated fairly in the system is "integral to the child's behavioral and psychological development."[11]

Research suggests that litigants evaluate fairness and impartiality by opportunity for voice, validation, participation, autonomy, choice, accuracy of outcomes, and access to information.[12] In a juvenile case, the child has voice when he is given an opportunity to tell his story and express his own views and opinions before important decisions are

---

4. Melinda G. Schmidt et al., *Effectiveness of Participation as a Defendant: The Attorney-Juvenile Client Relationship*, 21 BEHAV. SCI. & L. 175, 176–78 (2003).
5. Bruce J. Winick, *The Jurisprudence of Therapeutic Jurisprudence*, 3 PSYCHOL. PUB. POL'Y & L. 184, 185 (1997) [hereinafter *Jurisprudence of TJ*].
6. *Id.* at 188.
7. Amy D. Ronner, *Songs of Validation, Voice and Voluntary Participation: Therapeutic Jurisprudence, Miranda and Juveniles*, 71 U. CIN. L. REV. 89, 93 (2002).
8. *Id.* at 94.
9. 387 U.S. 1 (1967).
10. *Id.* at 26.
11. Ronner, *supra* note 7, at 114 (quoting *In re Amendment to Rules of Juvenile Procedure*, 804 So.2d 1206, 1211 (Fla. 2001)).
12. Stephen J. Anderer & David J. Glass, *A Therapeutic Jurisprudence and Preventive Law Approach to Family Law*, in PRACTICING THERAPEUTIC JURISPRUDENCE, *supra* note 2, at 231.

made.[13] Validation goes further by ensuring not only that the child's story is heard, but also that the fact-finder has really listened to and considered his views.[14] Voice and validation have both symbolic and utilitarian value for the accused. Meaningful participation in the process not only allows the respondent to feel like a valued member of society whose opinion is worthy of consideration, but it also gives the respondent confidence in the accuracy of results and allows him to feel more in control of the outcome even if he is not the ultimate fact-finder.[15] In effect, voice and validation provide the accused with a real opportunity to influence the judge's final decision and increase the probability of either a favorable or a more equitable outcome.[16] In the disposition stage of a juvenile case, for example, participation enhances the child's perception that his interests are being considered in determining whether he needs treatment at all and, if so, whether that treatment may be accomplished in the least restrictive placement.

Individual autonomy, self-determination, and choice are other important components of therapeutic jurisprudence that promote the psychological well-being of those who are involved in legal proceedings.[17] Studies in the psychology of choice indicate that people who make choices for themselves function more effectively and have greater satisfaction.[18] Paternalism, by contrast, is anti-therapeutic because it breeds apathy, hinders motivation, and limits the potential for rehabilitation.[19] By facilitating the child's choice and self-determination in the disposition phase of a juvenile case, the system can enhance the child's motivation and increase the efficacy of treatment in which the child chooses or agrees to participate.[20] Children who design or actively participate in the development of their own treatment plans are more likely to follow through and succeed.[21]

Because meaningful choice is virtually impossible without information, children in court are also likely to measure fairness and impartiality by access to information.[22] Information relieves stress, increases the respondent's understanding and acceptance of procedures, and may increase the respondent's expectations for a positive result.[23] Individuals who obtain information about the law and the legal process also perceive that they have greater control within the system.[24] In a juvenile case, the accused child is powerless to make critical decisions in his case without information about basic statu-

---

13. Allen E. Lind et al., *Voice, Control, and Procedural Justice: Instrumental and Noninstrumental Concerns in Fairness Judgments*, 59 J. PERSONALITY & SOC. PSYCHOL. 952, 952 (1990).

14. Juan Ramirez, Jr. & Amy D. Ronner, *Voiceless Billy Budd: Melville's Tribute to the Sixth Amendment*, 41 CAL. W. L. REV. 103, 121 (2004).

15. Lind et al., *supra* note 13, at 952.

16. *Id.* at 952–53 (but also acknowledges potential for "frustration effect" caused by repeated unfavorable outcomes or biased communications of others that may subvert the impact of voice).

17. Winick, *Jurisprudence of TJ*, *supra* note 5, at 192; Bruce J. Winick, *Client Denial and Resistance in the Advance Directive Context: Reflections on How Attorneys Can Identify and Deal with A Psycholegal Soft Spot*, 4 PSYCHOL. PUB. POL'Y & L. 901, 916 (1998) [hereinafter *Client Denial*].

18. Winick, *Client Denial*, *supra* note 17, at 916.

19. Winick, *Jurisprudence of TJ*, *supra* note 5, at 192; Ramirez & Ronner, *supra* note 14, at 120–21; Bruce J. Winick, *Therapeutic Jurisprudence and the Civil Commitment Hearing*, 10 J. CONTEMP. LEGAL ISSUES 37, 45 (1999) [hereinafter *Civil Commitment*].

20. Winick, *Jurisprudence of TJ*, *supra* note 5, at 197.

21. David Wexler, *Problem Solving and Relapse Prevention in Juvenile Court*, in JUDGING IN A THERAPEUTIC KEY: THERAPEUTIC JURISPRUDENCE AND THE COURTS 189, 193 (Bruce J. Winick & David B. Wexler eds., 2003) (excerpted from David B. Wexler, *Just Some Juvenile Thinking About Delinquent Behavior: A Therapeutic Jurisprudence Approach to Relapse Prevention Planning and Youth Advisory Juries*, 69 UMKC L. REV. 93 (2000)).

22. *See* Winick, *Civil Commitment*, *supra* note 19, at 46–47.

23. *Id.* at 46–47.

24. *Id.* at 46–57.

tory and constitutional rights. The child may also feel alienated, anxious, and vulnerable when he does not understand what is happening to him or why he is being evaluated, referred for treatment, or removed from his home.

2. Attorney-Client Paradigms and Values

Proponents of procedural justice and therapeutic jurisprudence recognize the central importance of attorneys in securing therapeutic objectives.[25] In the criminal and juvenile justice systems, the attorney gives voice to the client's story and advances the client's participatory and dignitary interests in the system.[26] The attorney also arms the client with information and makes the proceedings seem less coercive. The selection of an appropriate attorney-client paradigm thus clearly lies at the heart of positive therapeutic outcomes. While some attorney-client paradigms, such as collaborative or client-centered models of advocacy will produce positive therapeutic outcomes for the child, other paradigms, such as authoritarian, best-interest, and parent-directed models of advocacy, will be anti-therapeutic and produce psychologically dysfunctional responses from the child.

a. Authoritarian and Best Interest Models of Advocacy

In authoritarian models of advocacy, the advocates presume that their clients lack the competence or wisdom to make the right legal decisions.[27] In response, the authoritarian lawyer adopts a directive, and sometimes coercive, role in the attorney-client dyad,[28] and expects that his client will passively follow his direction, either by choice or default.[29] Authoritarian lawyers deprive the client of control by manipulating information or controlling the content and sequence of meetings with the client.[30] Attorneys control the content by interrupting the client, limiting topics of conversation, withholding information, or narrowing the alternatives from which the client may choose.[31] Attorneys may also influence client decisions by speaking in legalese, framing issues in a narrow and limiting fashion, or strategically arranging the list of options to exaggerate or emphasize negative or positive outcomes.[32]

The opportunity for coercion is particularly great when the client is a child. Differences in age and experience combined with the child's natural inclinations to defer to adults create inherent power imbalances between the child and the attorney.[33] When the lawyer is concerned about the child's need for psychiatric or psychological treatment, for example, the lawyer may manipulate the options available in order to earn the child's consent to a residential treatment program despite the child's desire to re-

---

25. Ramirez & Rommer, *supra* note 14, at 108.
26. *Id.* at 121.
27. Rodney J. Uphoff, *Relations Between Lawyer and Client in Damages: Model, Typical, or Dysfunctional?*, 2004 J. DISP. RESOL. 145, 152; Robert F. Cochran, *The Rule of Law(yers): The Practice of Justice: A Theory of Lawyers' Ethics by William H. Simon*, 65 MO. L. REV. 571, 589 (2000) (book review).
28. COCHRAN ET AL., COUNSELOR-AT-LAW, *supra* note 2, at 2 (stating that the authoritarian lawyer exercises "predominant control over and responsibility for the problem-solving").
29. Joseph Allegretti, *The Role of a Lawyer's Morals and Religion when Counseling Clients in Bioethics*, 30 FORDHAM URB. L.J. 9, 12 (2002).
30. COCHRAN ET AL., COUNSELOR-AT-LAW, *supra* note 2, at 11, 14–16.
31. *Id.* at 137.
32. *Id.* at 137; Lynn Mather, *What do Clients Want? What do Lawyers Do?*, 52 EMORY L.J. 1065, 1070 (2003) (discussing malleability of legal language).
33. Ellen Marrus, *Best Interests Equals Zealous Advocacy: A Not So Radical View of Holistic Representation for Children Accused of Crime*, 62 MD. L. REV 288, 342 (2003) (stating that "children naturally look to adult authority figures to make decisions for them").

main at home. The client who feels stifled by the control of an authoritarian lawyer will often be dissatisfied with the legal process and unwilling to follow through with recommendations and court orders made by those who have never heard or considered his views.[34]

Like the authoritarian lawyer, the best-interest, or paternalistic, advocate believes that his clients, particularly his child clients, are not able to identify and act in accord with their own best interests. As a result, some more experienced, rational adult must be given authority to make decisions on the child's behalf.[35] By advocating for what they believe to be best for the child, the paternalistic advocate—like others in the juvenile justice system—hopes to divert the child from a life of crime and protect the child from the consequences of his risky behavior. Evidence suggests that paternalistic, best interest advocacy is pervasive on behalf of children in contemporary juvenile courts.[36] Because juvenile court is traditionally committed to rehabilitation in lieu of punishment, many advocates believe that children do not need the vigorous assistance of counsel and view best interest advocacy as an essential tool in the rehabilitative process.[37] In many jurisdictions, lawyers will assume the role of guardian advocate and lobby the court to provide services and treatment that are purportedly best for the child. In other jurisdictions, lawyers will defer to the direction and control of a parent who presumptively knows and desires what is best for the child.

The paternalistic advocate, who is frequently more concerned about the rehabilitative needs of the child and less about the child's guilt or innocence in the delinquency case, will often conduct little or no investigation and decline to challenge facts alleged in the petition. These lawyers may also routinely waive Fourth and Fifth Amendment rights, fail to explore creative alternatives to incarceration, and generally look to probation officers to secure treatment for the child.[38] Because these advocates often have little confidence in the child's views and opinions, they may neglect to meet with their clients before court and instead draw from their own wisdom and experience to evaluate the advantages and disadvantages of the child's case-related options. In some cases, the advocate may coerce the child to plead guilty to expedite the rehabilitative process. In other cases, the paternalistic advocate may defer to the judge or probation officer for a determination of what is best for the child at disposition, or in some instances, actually request more restrictive or longer periods of confinement when the advocate believes

---

34. Allegretti, *supra* note 29, at 13 (stating that an authoritarian model produces less satisfaction for clients); COCHRAN ET AL., COUNSELOR-AT-LAW, *supra* note 2, at 115 (positing that clients who lose trust in their lawyers are less likely to fully disclose important information, less likely to follow through on necessary steps and less likely to comply with any agreement reached by the parties); *cf.* Ronner, *supra* note 7, at 93–96 (arguing that attorneys who give voice to child can increase likelihood that juvenile will have positive response to judicial decisions and rehabilitative objectives).

35. Emily Buss, *"You're My What?" The Problem of Children's Misperceptions of Their Lawyers' Roles*, 64 FORDHAM L. REV. 1699, 1701–02 (1996) (best interest model involves substitution of the lawyer's judgment for the child client's judgment).

36. Kristin N. Henning, *Loyalty, Paternalism and Rights: Client Counseling Theory and the Role of Child's Counsel in Delinquency Cases*, 81 NOTRE DAME L. REV. 101 (2005) (documents history and persistence of paternalistic advocacy in juvenile justice system).

37. *In re* Gault, 387 U.S. 1, 16–17 (1967); Mary Berkheiser, *The Fiction of Juvenile Right to Counsel: Waiver in the Juvenile Courts*, 54 FLA. L. REV. 577, 586 (2002).

38. Henning, *supra* note 36, at 142–43; *cf.* Winick, *Civil Commitment*, *supra* note 19, at 41–43 (describing the conduct of best interests lawyers in the civil commitment process to include deference to expert witnesses, little cross examination, failure to meet with clients, little or no investigation, failure to challenge allegations, failure to explore alternatives to hospitalization and waiver of patient's right to testify).

such penalties are appropriate.[39] Even if the attorney questions his own ability to decide what is best for the child, the paternalistic advocate may look to the child's parent for guidance and direction. Like the advocate who usurps decision-making authority for himself, the parent-directed advocate presumes that the child lacks the judgment, wisdom, and experience to make good decisions on his own behalf, but views the parent as an experienced and responsible adult who has special insights into the needs of the child and the family.

Although the best interest advocate believes that he is advancing the rehabilitative interests of the child, evidence suggests that by usurping voice and autonomy from a child in the juvenile justice system, the paternalistic advocate may actually impede rehabilitation by stifling the child's commitment to and cooperation with the disposition plan.[40] A child who is deprived of a meaningful opportunity to participate in his juvenile case is likely to perceive the system as unfair and likely to resent and resist any efforts to engage him in the rehabilitative process.

b. *Client-Centered and Collaborative Models of Advocacy*

In stark contrast to best interest and authoritarian models of advocacy, client-centered and collaborative models advance therapeutic goals and produce positive therapeutic outcomes. Client-centered advocacy rejects lawyer paternalism and manipulation and recognizes individual autonomy and self-determination as a foundation of the American legal system.[41] Client-centered advocates recognize that client participation in the attorney-client relationship may reduce the anxiety that often accompanies the client's passive or blind role in the legal process.[42] They also believe that clients are more likely to accept and comply with decisions they make for themselves.[43] The client-centered lawyer ultimately respects and validates the client's interests and gives the client voice in the proceedings. When the client seeks advice from the lawyer, the lawyer may provide information about several possible courses of action, but will urge the client to make decisions for himself.

Collaborative models of advocacy seek to refine client-centered paradigms. Critics of client-centered advocacy worry that excessive deference to clients will deprive the client of important insight from the lawyer and produce unnecessarily poor decisions.[44] Critics also believe that clients rarely come to the attorney-client relationship with a preconceived set of goals and interests, but instead shape and construct those goals through interaction with the lawyer.[45] Although collaborative lawyers, like client-centered advocates, value attorney loyalty and client autonomy, the collaborative lawyer will also engage the client in a realistic and objective appraisal of all of the legal and non-legal advantages and disadvantages of a contemplated course of action.[46] The collaborative lawyer will also provide clients with relevant information about available options, help

---

39. Janet E. Ainsworth, *Re-imagining Childhood and Reconstructing the Legal Order: The Case for Abolishing the Juvenile Court*, 69 N.C. L. Rev. 1083, 1127 (1991).
40. *See supra* notes 8–24 and accompanying text.
41. Robert D. Dinerstein, *Client-Centered Counseling: Reappraisal and Refinement*, 32 Ariz. L. Rev. 501, 510–13 (1990); Mather, *supra* note 32, at 1068; Cochran, *supra* note 27, at 590–91.
42. Dinerstein, *supra* note 41, at 548–49; Ronner, *supra* note 7, at 93.
43. Jason J. Kilborn, *Who's in Charge Here? Putting Clients in Their Place*, 37 Ga. L. Rev. 1, 36 (2002); Dinerstein, *supra* note 41, at 547–48.
44. Dinerstein, *supra* note 41, at 505–06.
45. *Id.* at 517.
46. Cochran et al., Counselor-at-Law, *supra* note 2, at 135; Allegretti, *supra* note 29, at 18–19.

clients clarify personal goals and objectives, and give clients emotional and social support for their decisions.[47] Both the collaborative and client-centered lawyer will provide the client with an opportunity for meaningful participation and secure positive therapeutic outcomes by educating, informing, empowering, and validating the client within the system.

3. Conflicting Norms

Notwithstanding its benefit to the mental health of juveniles, therapeutic jurisprudence is not both a means and an end unto itself. The goals and values of therapeutic jurisprudence must be evaluated in light of other potentially competing legal and social norms, values, and principles.[48] In juvenile court, lawyers must weigh the therapeutic benefits of voice and autonomy with normative objections to ceding autonomy to children, societal commitment to producing healthy well-adjusted children, the need for public safety, and the constitutional rights of parents to raise children as they deem appropriate. Reliance on therapeutic principles to promote the child's psychological health is appropriate only if those principles do not abrogate important constitutional mandates or conflict with other more highly valued norms.

In the search for an appropriate attorney-child paradigm, a careful evaluation of competing values suggests that client-centered and collaborative models of advocacy are consistent not only with therapeutic objectives, but also with fundamental principles of constitutional law and justice, public safety, and societal efforts to develop productive, law-abiding children. Even though client-centered models may be inconsistent with the rights of parents to rear children without the interference of others, the child's constitutional right to counsel, as well as rules of professional ethics, support client autonomy and may outweigh the parents' rights in the juvenile justice context.

a. Normative Objections to Ceding Authority to Youth

Opponents of client-directed advocacy in juvenile court argue that children should not be allowed to direct lawyers because they lack the experience, judgment, and cognitive capacity to act in their own best interests.[49] Normative opposition to the allocation of decision-making authority to children is well documented in laws that use age to grant or deny certain rights or privileges to children and adolescents. State statutes that require children to attend school or that deny children the right to contract, marry, vote, drive, or purchase alcohol, tobacco, or pornographic material all seem to reflect a societal presumption that children lack the wisdom, judgment, and cognitive capacity to make good decisions in these areas.[50] Societal norms that guide the legislative allocation of decision-making authority between children and adults are necessarily concerned with balancing competing interests such as respect for parental authority, the need to protect society from the consequences of immature and unwise decisions of children, and the state's obligation to protect certain constitutional rights of the child.[51]

The paternalistic ideology of the traditional juvenile justice system supports and advances best-interest advocacy on behalf of children charged with delinquency. Since the inception of the first juvenile court, the legacy of paternalism has shaped and continues

---

47. COCHRAN ET AL., COUNSELOR-AT-LAW, *supra* note 2, at 113.
48. Winick, *Jurisprudence of TJ, supra* note 5, at 197–98.
49. Marrus, *supra* note 33, at 343.
50. Elizabeth S. Scott, *The Legal Construction of Adolescence*, 29 HOFSTRA L. REV. 547, 547, 557–58 (2000).
51. *Id.* at 557–58 (discussing allocation of children's rights based on a myriad of socio-political factors).

to shape the attitudes of many juvenile defenders who have a sincere desire to aid in the rehabilitation of children.[52] Even when the child's attorney wishes to advocate for the child's expressed interests, the attorney will often face tremendous systemic opposition from judges, prosecutors, and probation officers who expect defense counsel to participate as a part of the juvenile justice team.[53] Prosecutors may resent defenders who seek to vindicate their client's legal rights and interfere with the child's potential for rehabilitation, while judges may chastise attorneys for seeking to litigate legal issues or challenging factual allegations on the merits.

Therapeutic jurisprudence, on the other hand, offers a useful shift from traditional responses to presumed youth and adolescent irresponsibility and dependence. Therapeutic jurisprudence suggests that we may actually enhance the quality of adolescent decision-making and ensure that children become responsible members of society precisely by giving them voice and respect in the juvenile justice system. Attorney-client paradigms that allocate decision-making and choice to the child improve the child's psychological well-being by facilitating self-regulation and responsibility, encouraging positive self-determination, and enhancing the child's appreciation for law and authority.[54] By contrast, authoritarian and paternalistic models of advocacy which deprive the child of a meaningful voice in the attorney-client relationship, and thus in the juvenile justice system as a whole, hinder the public safety and rehabilitative objectives of the court.[55] Likewise, authoritarian and paternalistic models of advocacy, which deprive the child of his own rights and due process, ultimately undermine the child's respect for the rights of others and eventually erode society as a whole.[56]

Authoritarian and paternalistic lawyering also frequently produces poor and unsatisfactory legal outcomes by inhibiting a full exchange of information between the lawyer and the child.[57] When the lawyer controls the client interview, limits free input from the child, and excludes the child's voice from the system, the lawyer deprives both himself and the court of important information and insight. Without critical input from the child, the diagnostic team assigned to develop the child's treatment plan will likely have an inaccurate or incomplete picture of the child's needs.

Moreover, even accepting that many youth and adolescents will have cognitive and psychosocial limitations that affect judgment, lawyering models that give the child voice and validation in the juvenile justice system present minimal risk of harm to the child or the community. Because delinquency cases are adversarial hearings in which the judge makes the final decision about questions of guilt, innocence, detention, and disposition, the child's voice is but one of many that will influence judicial outcomes. Thus, even where the child wisely or unwisely instructs counsel to advocate for his re-

---

52. Janet E. Ainsworth, *Youth Justice in a Unified Court: Response to Critics of Juvenile Court Abolition*, 36 B.C. L. Rev. 927, 1129–30 (1995).

53. *See* Henning, *supra* note 36, at 116–18.

54. Carolyn Copps Hartley & Carrie J. Petrucci, *Practicing Culturally Competent Therapeutic Jurisprudence: A Collaboration Between Social Work and Law*, 14 Wash. U. J.L. & Pol'y 133, 153 (2004); Wexler, *supra* note 21, at 191–93; Ronner, *supra* note 7, at 111–12.

55. *See supra* notes 5–20 and accompanying text; *see also* Rhonda Gay Hartman, *Adolescent Autonomy: Clarifying an Ageless Conundrum*, 51 Hastings L.J. 1265, 1330–31 (2000) (stating that in the civil commitment context, evidence suggests that allowing adolescent to direct his own care enhances the effect of therapy).

56. Ramirez & Ronner, *supra* note 14, at 121.

57. Cochran et al., Counselor-at-Law, *supra* note 2, at 115 (stating that clients who lose trust in their lawyers are less likely to disclose important information); Allegretti, *supra* note 29, at 13–14.

lease back into the community, it is the judge, after hearing arguments from prosecutors, parents, probation officers, and victims, who will decide whether release is consistent with the rehabilitative needs of the child and the safety of the public. Even where there is an adverse ruling, the child who has been given an opportunity to participate in the hearing will, hopefully, still perceive that the process has been fair and learn to respect law and authority.[58]

b. *Rights of the Child's Parent*

In selecting an appropriate attorney-client paradigm for the representation of children, principles of therapeutic jurisprudence must also be weighed against the rights and interests of parents. Given the long legal and social history of paternal control over almost every facet of a child's life, the law is generally reluctant to interfere with the rights of parents to raise and direct their children as they deem appropriate.[59] In some areas of the law, parents may even have a constitutional right to make decisions for the child.[60] In addition, from a therapeutic perspective, the participatory and dignitary interests of an accused child may conflict with the participatory interests of the parent. While parents who feel engaged in the child's decision-making process will be more likely to support the child in juvenile court proceedings, parents who feel excluded from the attorney-client relationship altogether may refuse to help the attorney, the child, or the court in the rehabilitative plan.[61] Attorneys who respect the rights and interests of parents may reject client-centered models of advocacy that challenge the authority of parents within the home and instead look to the parents to determine and articulate the goals and objectives in the juvenile case.

When the rights and norms of different groups conflict, lawyers, judges, and legislators must look to overarching principles of law and ethics as a means by which to weigh and prioritize competing interests.[62] In weighing the therapeutic interests of parents and children in juvenile court, lawyers should recognize that the denial of parental control in the attorney-child relationship does not preclude parental involvement and influence in the juvenile justice system as a whole. In most juvenile courts today, parents generally have an opportunity to communicate directly or indirectly with the judge through probation officers, prosecutors, or other court officials.[63] When the child, however, is denied meaningful participation in the attorney-client relationship, the child generally has no other means by which to be heard in the system.

---

58. Ramirez & Ronner, *supra* note 14, at 120 ("[W]hat influences [individuals] most is not the result, but their own assessment of the fairness of the process itself."); *see also supra* notes 16–17 and accompanying text.

59. Martin Guggenheim, *Minor Rights: The Adolescent Abortion Cases*, 30 Hofstra L. Rev. 589, 593–94 (2002); Scott, *supra* note 50, at 551.

60. *See, e.g.*, Pierce v. Society of Sisters, 268 U.S. 510, 518 (1925) (finding that compulsory public school attendance unreasonably interferes with parental right to direct the upbringing and education of children).

61. Bruce C. Hafen & Jonathan O. Hafen, *Abandoning Children to Their Autonomy: The United Nations Convention on the Rights of the Child*, 37 Harv. Int'l L.J. 449, 483–84 (1996) (discussing fear that denial of parental rights may have long term effect of reducing parental commitment to childrearing); Scott, *supra* note 50, at 551 (recognizing that parental rights and authority might be viewed as legal compensation for the burden of responsibility to provide food, shelter, health care, affection and education).

62. Winick, *Jurisprudence of TJ*, *supra* note 5, at 197–98.

63. In many jurisdictions, the parent will be a formal party to the proceedings. *See, e.g.*, Ala. Code § 12-15-31(5) (1995) (giving court jurisdiction to make parents parties to all juvenile court actions).

The balancing of therapeutic interests, alone, cannot determine the allocation of decision-making authority among parents and their children. The parties must also consider the competing legal interests. Although the constitutional rights of parents are significant, they are not without limits.[64] Recognizing the diversity of circumstances in which children and parents are involved, courts and legislatures have chosen to allocate the rights of children and parents on an issue-by-issue basis, and in each instance, have considered a wide range of sociopolitical variables including the age of the child, the liberty and due process rights of the child, the rights of the parents, and the needs of society.[65] Likewise, in selecting an appropriate attorney-client paradigm in the juvenile justice context, lawyers, too, must weigh the constitutional rights of parents against the liberty and due process interests of the accused child.

c. Constitutional Rights in the Juvenile Justice System

Notwithstanding the history of paternalism in the juvenile justice system, due process is now guaranteed as a fundamental right in the juvenile court.[66] After years of procedural irregularity, unfettered discretion, and the appearance of judicial partiality, the Supreme Court, in *In re Gault* and a series of cases that followed, held that due process and fundamental fairness would no longer be sacrificed in favor of some nominal commitment to rehabilitation.[67] To ensure due process, the Court determined that an accused child would be entitled to adequate notice of the charges, the right to counsel, the right to be free from self-incrimination, the right to confront and cross examine witnesses, and the right to require the government to prove guilt beyond a reasonable doubt.[68] The right to counsel—or more importantly, the right to direct and control counsel—clearly falls at the center of all other rights.[69] As an advocate for the interests of the child, the child's lawyer is the primary means by which the child may effectively assert or waive all other individual legal rights in the system.

The Court's commitment to fundamental fairness also suggests that an accused child has the same interest in fair and accurate fact-finding as an accused adult in a criminal case.[70] Adversarial, client-directed models of advocacy have been identified as essential

---

64. Bellotti v. Baird, 443 U.S. 622 (1979) (striking down requirement of parental consent for abortion).

65. Scott, *supra* note 50, at 557–58.

66. *In re* Gault, 387 U.S. 1 (1967) (defining basic procedural due process requirements owed to an accused juvenile).

67. *Id.* at 33–56; *In re* Winship, 397 U.S. 358, 368 (1970); Breed v. Jones, 421 U.S. 519, 541 (1975).

68. *Gault*, 387 U.S. at 33–56 (requiring adequate notice of charges, right to counsel, privilege against self-incrimination, and rights of confrontation and cross-examination); *Winship*, 397 U.S. at 368 (finding that guilt must be proved beyond a reasonable doubt in delinquency proceedings).

69. Susan D. Hawkins, Note, *Protecting the Rights and Interests of Competent Minors in Litigated Medical Treatment Disputes,* 64 Fordham L. Rev. 2075, 2076 (1996) (arguing that control over the decision-making process lies at the heart of the American legal system when personal legal rights are at stake); Shannan L. Wilber, *Independent Counsel for Children,* 27 Fam. L.Q. 349, 353 (1993) (arguing that our emphasis on individual rights and personal autonomy are furthered by role of attorney which enables litigants to pursue and protect their legal rights); Martin Guggenheim, *The Right to Be Represented But Not Heard: Reflections on Legal Representation for Children,* 59 N.Y.U. L. Rev. 76, 81, 86–87 (1984) (arguing that child's constitutional rights would be meaningless if the attorney were allowed to assert and waive those rights in his own discretion).

70. *Gault*, 387 U.S. at 30 (finding no material different between criminal and juvenile delinquency proceedings when considering the child's need for counsel); *Bellotti*, 443 U.S. at 634 (recognizing the child's right against the deprivation of liberty without due process of law as virtually coextensive with that of an adult).

to fair and accurate fact-finding.[71] As the Supreme Court has recognized, society is better served when the lawyer is advancing the interests of the client rather than joining together and acting in concert with the government.[72] Considering the indispensable role of the attorney in ensuring due process and protecting the constitutional rights of children, client-centered and collaborative paradigms of lawyering are not only therapeutically preferred, but also constitutionally required. By contrast, paternalistic models of advocacy in the juvenile justice system may deprive the child of fundamental rights.

d. *Principles of Professional Ethics*

Principles of professional ethics further promote client-centered and collaborative models of advocacy over paternalistic or parent-directed alternatives. Collectively, the *Model Rules of Professional Conduct* remind lawyers that clients must be treated with respect, that the client's interests are foremost, and that attorneys should intrude on the client's decision-making authority to the least extent possible.[73] Even when the parent hires an attorney for the child, the *Rules* prohibit interference from a third-party payer and prohibit the attorney from communicating about the case with the parent, absent consent of the child.[74] The *Rules* also entitle the child to conflict-free representation by the lawyer.[75] Recent developments in juvenile justice policy challenge the traditional assumption that parents are the best decision-makers for an accused child. Today, parents may be held civilly or criminally liable for the misconduct of their children, forced to pay the cost of treatment and services for a child in the juvenile justice system, and held in contempt for failing to ensure their child's compliance with the conditions of probation.[76] Considering the ever-expanding risk of parental liability, allocating decision-making authority to parents may compromise the child's right to conflict-free advocacy.[77]

The *Model Rules* also require the lawyer to maintain, as far as reasonably possible, a "normal" attorney-client relationship with clients of potentially diminished capacity, including minors.[78] Likewise, therapeutic jurisprudence implicitly assumes that affected parties will have the cognitive capacity to appreciate and value concepts such as voice, participation, and fairness.[79] Even if the youth's cognitive and psychosocial capacities are not fully developed, most adolescents in the juvenile justice system will be able to communicate basic goals and concerns to their lawyers and intuitively grasp notions of

---

71. Strickland v. Washington, 466 U.S. 668 (1984); Polk County v. Dodson, 454 U.S. 312 (1981).
72. *Polk County*, 454 U.S. 312; U.S. v. Cronic, 466 U.S. 648, 655–57 (1984).
73. MODEL RULES OF PROF'L CONDUCT R. 1.2, 1.14 cmt 1 & cmt 3 (2002) [hereinafter MODEL RULES].
74. *Id.* at R. 1.8(f).
75. *Id.* at R. 1.7.
76. For a representative sampling, see S.D. CODIFIED LAWS §26-7A-51 (1999) (parent may be held in contempt for failing to bring child to court when promised); ALA. CODE §12-15-11 (1995) (court may order parent to reimburse state for expense of evaluations, commitment, special schools, detention, counseling or other treatment ordered for juveniles); ALASKA STAT. §47.12.155(b)(3) (2004) (parent may be held jointly or independently responsible for restitution to victims); N.Y. PENAL LAW §260.10 (McKinney 2000) (parent guilty of misdemeanor when parent "refuses to exercise reasonable diligence in the control of the child to prevent his from becoming a juvenile delinquent"); CAL. CIV. CODE §1714.1 (Deering 2005) (parent or guardian may be civilly liability for the willful misconduct of minors).
77. *See* MODEL RULES R. 1.7 (noting that absent the consent of both parties, the lawyer generally cannot advise two parties who have conflicting interests in the same proceedings).
78. *Id.* at R. 1.14.
79. *Cf.* Winick, *Civil Commitment*, *supra* note 19, at 49 (applying therapeutic jurisprudence to civil commitment context and recognizing that some clients may be so impaired that they will not realize procedural justice of a fair, participatory hearing).

fairness.[80] Commentary to the *Model Rules of Professional Conduct* recognizes that "children as young as five or six, and certainly those of ten or twelve" have the ability to "understand, deliberate upon and reach conclusions about matters affecting [their] own well-being."[81] Collaborative models of advocacy, which recognize cognitive reasoning and moral judgment as evolving skills that improve with experience, provide the child with an opportunity to try on and enhance newly acquired cognitive abilities.[82]

The therapeutic value of voice, the guarantee of due process, and ethical considerations that require lawyers to maintain a "normal" relationship with minors all suggest that client-directed and collaborative models of advocacy provide an appropriate framework in which to advance the interests of youth in the juvenile justice system. Client-centered relationships also have benefits for the health and satisfaction of the lawyer.[83] Attorneys often experience high burnout in juvenile court as they attempt to reconcile the internal tension between their legal obligation to advocate for the expressed interests of the child and their own well-meaning, paternalistic desires to advocate in the best interests of the child.[84] The attorney should find solace in therapeutically-inspired relationships that motivate compliance and yield greater rehabilitative outcomes for the child.[85] The lawyer who understands and applies principles of therapeutic jurisprudence need not choose between due process and rehabilitation. Therapeutic, client-centered models of advocacy advance rehabilitative objectives without excluding the child's voice.

4. Skills: The Lawyer as an Agent for Change

Once the lawyer accepts the client-centered or collaborative paradigm as the appropriate model of advocacy, the lawyer must learn and apply relevant skills for effective and affective lawyering.[86] Lawyers who are committed to advancing the participatory interests of their clients and promoting other components of therapeutic jurisprudence will again find guidance in the wealth of literature on collaborative lawyering, client interviewing, and affective counseling.[87]

As a starting point, therapeutic jurisprudence requires the lawyer to relinquish his own ego needs and focus on the client. Client-centered and collaborative lawyers do not assume they know what is best for the client, but instead help the client explore and

---

80. Scott, *supra* note 50, at 555 n.35 (noting that adolescents are close to adulthood and by the age of 14 and 15 generally have cognitive capacity for reasoning and understanding process).

81. MODEL RULES R. 1.14 cmt. 1.

82. COCHRAN ET AL., COUNSELOR-AT-LAW, *supra* note 2, at 170 (stating that individuals develop their own code of personal morality and adopt virtues such as courage, truthfulness, faithfulness and mercy through the trial and error of exercising moral judgment); William A. Kell, *Ties That Bind?: Children's Attorneys, Children's Agency, and the Dilemma of Parental Affiliation*, 29 LOY. U. CHI. L.J. 353, 375 (1998) (discussing the benefits of encouraging children to exercise their own developing decision-making skills with the aid of a "teacher). If the child, however, is so cognitively limited that he cannot articulate and act in his own interests, the Rules permit the attorney to employ alternative, protective measures on the client's behalf and principles of therapeutic jurisprudence may not apply. MODEL RULES R. 1.14 cmt 5 & cmt 7.

83. Hartley & Petrucci, *supra* note 54, at 153.

84. Thomas F. Geraghty, *Justice for Children: How Do We Get There?*, 88 J. CRIM. L. & CRIMINOLOGY 190, 236 (1997); Ainsworth, *supra* note 39, at 1129–30; David A. Harris, *The Criminal Defense Lawyer in the Juvenile Justice System*, 26 U. TOL. L. REV. 751 (1995); *cf.* Winick, *Civil Commitment*, *supra* note 19, at 57 (discussing advocate's internal tension in civil commitment context).

85. Winick, *Civil Commitment*, *supra* note 19, at 57.

86. Mills, *supra* note 2, at 421–22 (recognizing affective lawyering as a psychology-based approach to lawyering that offers emotional ways for lawyers to connect with clients).

87. *See Juvenile Justice System*, *supra* note 1.

clarify his own goals and objectives.[88] Lawyers who are committed to voice and validation will give the client a safe space to speak and express emotions, elicit the client's views through open-ended questions, and offer verbal and nonverbal responses that express interest and sympathy and confirm that the lawyer is listening.[89] The lawyer also understands that good decision-making is predicated on the lawyer's ability to create an appropriate environment for counseling.[90] For children, who demonstrate better cognitive capacity in contexts that are familiar to them and devoid of stress,[91] the collaborative counselor will provide a comfortable physical and emotional environment and allocate sufficient time for questions.[92]

Effective, therapeutic counseling also requires the lawyer to become culturally competent in dealing with clients of different socioeconomic, ethnic, and racial backgrounds. To achieve cultural competence, the lawyer must first be cognizant of and examine his or her own attitudes and beliefs about other groups.[93] The lawyer must also increase his or her knowledge about diverse populations and acquire skills that facilitate healthy cross-cultural communications.[94] Specifically, the lawyer must recognize and acknowledge differences in the communication styles among different racial and ethnic groups, including differences in nonverbal communication such as the use of personal space, body movements, and gestures.[95] Culturally competent lawyers communicate respect to clients by acknowledging the range and validity of diverse perspectives and by providing them with an opportunity to share their views.[96]

While attorneys should not try to be therapists or social workers, therapeutically-inclined lawyers should understand the basic principles of psychology and develop skills necessary to accommodate the psychological dimensions of the attorney-client relationship.[97] Lawyers will need appropriate interpersonal skills to deal with the client's psychological and emotional issues such as denial, anger, frustration, despair, resentment, and even indifference and helplessness which are common among those who enter the legal system.[98] Empathy is thus one essential skill in effective therapeutic lawyering.[99] Empathy involves both an "intellectual response" that suggests that the listener thinks the same way as the speaker and an "emotional response" that suggests that the listener feels

---

88. Kilborn, *supra* note 43, at 36; Dinerstein, *supra* note 41, at 508, 516; COCHRAN ET AL., COUNSELOR-AT-LAW, *supra* note 2, at 113.

89. Winick, *Client Denial*, *supra* note 17, at 912; COCHRAN ET AL., COUNSELOR-AT-LAW, *supra* note 2, at 33–37, 40–48 (discussing array of passive and active listening skills).

90. Uphoff, *supra* note 27, at 155–57; COCHRAN ET AL., COUNSELOR-AT-LAW, *supra* note 2, at 113.

91. *See* Emily Buss, *Confronting Developmental Barriers to the Empowerment of Child Clients*, 84 CORNELL L. REV. 895, 918–19 (1999); Thomas Grisso, *The Competence of Adolescents as Trial Defendants*, 3 PSYCHOL. PUB. POL'Y & L. 3, 16–18 (1997).

92. COCHRAN ET AL., COUNSELOR-AT-LAW, *supra* note 2, at 152–53.

93. Hartley & Petrucci, *supra* note 54, at 170.

94. *Id.*

95. *Id.* at 179.

96. *Id.* at 179–80. *See generally supra* ch. 5: Paul R. Tremblay & Carwina Weng, *Multicultural Lawyering: Heuristics and Biases*; *supra* ch. 6: Susan J. Bryant & Jean Koh Peters, *Six Practices for Connecting with Clients across Culture: Habit Four, Working with Interpreters, and Other Mindful Approaches.*

97. Winick, *Client Denial*, *supra* note 17, at 903–04 (exploring ways in which principles of psychology enhance the effectiveness of lawyers in advance directive and preventive lawyering context); Hartley & Petrucci, *supra* note 54, at 140–41.

98. Winick, *Client Denial*, *supra* note 17, at 903–04, 909.

99. *Id.* at 909–10.

the same way as the speaker.[100] As the lawyer evolves as an empathetic counselor, the lawyer should learn to read nonverbal cues, project himself into the feelings of his clients, and express warmth and understanding.[101]

In juvenile cases, the lawyer should engage the child in one-on-one, age-appropriate dialogue and repeat information as many times as the child needs to hear it.[102] Age-appropriate consultation is essential to empower children who are often unsophisticated and lack knowledge about legal matters.[103] Research also suggests that psychosocial impediments to effective adolescent decision-making, such as lack of trust for adults, limited risk perception, and poor risk preference, are likely to improve as the attorney-client relationship improves.[104] Because youth tend to have higher levels of trust and satisfaction with attorneys who spend more time working with them,[105] the child's lawyer must set aside adequate time for meetings with young clients. The lawyer may ultimately improve the quality of adolescent decisions by encouraging the child to slowly identify and consider all of the long-term implications of any decision.[106] When the lawyer equips the child with all of the relevant information and provides the appropriate environmental and emotional supports, the child may make well-reasoned decisions and appropriately direct counsel in the legal representation.

Therapeutic jurisprudence also recognizes the child's entry into the juvenile justice system as a "teachable moment" that presents the child with an opportunity for change and rehabilitation.[107] It is at this moment that lawyers have a unique role in promoting the child's psychological well-being and assisting in the child's positive development.[108] Therapeutic jurisprudence draws from a variety of psychological tools that increase positive self-motivation and improve psychological functioning.[109] Studies in the social psychology of adolescent delinquent behavior suggest that undesired behavior may be corrected when the child begins to identify personal ambitions and gain confidence in his ability to achieve personal goals.[110] Legal actors, such as lawyers in the juvenile justice system, may motivate the child by challenging negative internal and external messages and helping the child identify a greater range of positive alternatives and positive self-images.[111]

Rather than coercing the child into change through paternalistic advocacy, the therapeutic lawyer must learn to actively engage the child in the design of his own treatment

---

100. *Id.* at 910.
101. *Id.* at 909.
102. Wallace J. Mlyniec, *A Judge's Ethical Dilemma: Assessing a Child's Capacity to Choose*, 64 FORDHAM L. REV. 1873, 1898 (1996); Dinerstein, *supra* note 41, at 556.
103. *See* Cochran, *supra* note 27, at 592 (stating that effective legal counseling may empower politically disadvantaged clients); Uphoff, *supra* note 27, at 768 (same); Dinerstein, *supra* note 41, at 519 (same).
104. Schmidt, *supra* note 4, at 193–94.
105. *Id.* at 180 (discussing study conducted in 2000 finding that youth were more likely to be satisfied with their lawyers, regardless of the ultimate outcome of the case, when the lawyer spent time with them); *see also* Hartley & Petrucci, *supra* note 54, at 159 (reporting that time defendants spent with lawyer had a significant impact on perceived justice in the system).
106. *See* COCHRAN ET AL., COUNSELOR-AT-LAW, *supra* note 2, at 172.
107. Astrid Birgden, *Dealing with the Resistant Criminal Client: A Psychologically-Minded Strategy for More Effective Legal Counseling*, 38 CRIM. L. BULL. 225, 237 (2002).
108. *See* Winick, *Jurisprudence of TJ, supra* note 5, at 202.
109. *Id.* at 194.
110. Georgia Zara, *Therapeutic Jurisprudence as an Integrative Approach to Understanding the Socio-Psychological Reality of Young Offenders*, 71 U. CIN. L. REV. 127, 140–41 (2002).
111. *Id.* at 135–43.

plan.[112] Through a series of probing and directed questions at the disposition phase, the lawyer may help the child identify an array of realistic disposition alternatives, lead the child through a reflection on his own strengths and needs, and encourage the child to consider the likely response of the court, victims, and others impacted by the child's conduct.[113] When the lawyer engages the child in this way, the lawyer becomes an agent in the child's rehabilitation and motivates the child to take responsibility for change.[114]

Collaborative models of advocacy provide a useful framework through which the lawyer can guide the process of self-actualization and change. In the collaborative paradigm, the client controls the decisions, but the lawyer offers advice and structures the counseling process in a way that is likely to foster good decision-making by the client.[115] Collaborative lawyers are "nondirective" as to the client's ultimate decision, but "directive" as to the process to be followed in reaching that decision.[116] The lawyer's responsibility is not just to passively or neutrally list alternatives, but also to ensure that the client will consider and evaluate all of the available options and choose the best alternative. The collaborative lawyer will empower the child to identify the widest range of alternatives through techniques such as brainstorming that encourage the client to think broadly, be creative, and withhold judgment until all options have been discussed.[117] The lawyer will also help the child evaluate alternatives by encouraging the child to identify all consequences that might flow from an identified alternative. With the lawyer's help, the child will decide whether each consequence is positive or negative, consider the relative importance of each consequence, and assess the likelihood that each consequence will occur.[118] In identifying potential consequences, the lawyer will encourage the client to consider not only the impact his choices will have on himself, but also to consider the impact his choices will have on others.[119]

Moreover, because the collaborative lawyer wants his client to avoid mistakes, the lawyer may appropriately advise and persuade the client in the decision-making process.[120] When trust and rapport are well-established in the attorney-client relationship, the lawyer may even tell the client that he is choosing a patently bad alternative and explain why.[121] When the lawyer is not overbearing and delays advice until he has an appropriate rapport with the child, the child retains individual autonomy and is free to reject the lawyer's opinion.[122]

Paternalistic advocacy persists in juvenile courts today not only because the experienced, well-educated lawyer thinks he knows better than his immature client, but also

---

112. Wexler, *supra* note 21, at 192; Ronner, *supra* note 7, at 112.
113. *See* Wexler, *supra* note 21, at 192–93 (in the relapse prevention context, the lawyer will help the child identify specific methods for avoiding and coping with high risk situations and prepare the child to address likely concerns of the court in the disposition hearing).
114. *Id.* at 192–93.
115. COCHRAN ET AL., COUNSELOR-AT-LAW, *supra* note 2, at 6; Cochran et al., *Client Counseling*, *supra* note 2, at 598 ("The client makes the ultimate decision, but the lawyer is actively involved in the process.").
116. COCHRAN ET AL., COUNSELOR-AT-LAW, *supra* note 2, at 131; Allegretti, *supra* note 29, at 16.
117. COCHRAN ET AL., COUNSELOR-AT-LAW, *supra* note 2, at 139–40.
118. *Id.* at 146.
119. COCHRAN ET AL., COUNSELOR-AT-LAW, *supra* note 2, at 147.
120. Dinerstein, *supra* note 41, at 517 (drawing from medical doctrine of informed consent in which persuasion is not only acceptable is necessary).
121. Allegretti, *supra* note 29, at 18–19 (noting that in the collaborative model, as between friends, the lawyer should advise the client when the lawyer believes the client is making a bad decision); COCHRAN ET AL., COUNSELOR-AT-LAW, *supra* note 2, at 132.
122. COCHRAN ET AL., COUNSELOR-AT-LAW, *supra* note 2, at 175.

because the paternalistic model is often less time-consuming for the lawyer. Unlike best-interest models of advocacy, collaborative and client-centered lawyering requires the lawyer to devote an indeterminable amount of time to explaining relevant legal rights and procedures and to engage the client in a process that facilitates good decision-making. Because the collaborative model requires considerable time and training, it may be resisted by those lawyers who have high caseloads or work in resource poor defender offices. Although systemic reform is beyond the scope of this chapter, child advocates committed to a therapeutic agenda need to encourage policymakers to allocate adequate resources to therapeutic processes and procedures that will improve rehabilitative outcomes and enhance public safety.

II. Building the Child's Legal Team

By definition, therapeutic jurisprudence is an interdisciplinary enterprise that looks to psychology, mental health, and other related disciplines to inform and shape the development of law.[123] Collaborations between lawyers, social workers, and mental health experts provide opportunities for training, consultation, and dialogue in legal offices, law school classrooms, and continuing legal education programs. Specifically, mental health professionals bring expertise and skill in the application of psychological tools that may improve the attorney-client relationship. In addition, because therapeutic jurisprudence recognizes that all clients exist in a larger network of familial and communal relations,[124] therapeutic lawyers who represent children will learn to engage the child at multiple levels and may partner with parents, teachers, mentors, and other relevant adults in the child's life.

A. *Interdisciplinary Collaboration: Expanding the Lawyer's Skill Set*

Probably the greatest benefit the lawyer will gain in collaboration with mental health professionals is training. Consistent with the lawyer's potential as a therapeutic agent, lawyers would benefit from training in relapse prevention, adolescent development, theories of cognitive change, and the social psychology of persuasion among others.[125] As but one of many examples, forensic psychologist Astrid Birgden has developed a framework for training criminal defense lawyers in motivational interviewing. In Dr. Birgden's framework, the lawyer will use directive, but client-centered counseling to help clients recognize problem behavior or thinking, articulate concerns about their behavior, and become optimistic about the prospect for change.[126] At varying stages of the relationship, the lawyer will motivate change by inviting the client to consider a new perspective, such as that of the judge or victim, asking the client to elaborate when the client displays some recognition of the problem or desire to change, and shifting focus away from negative aspects of the problem and redirecting attention to the possibility of a positive outcome. Neither the tone nor the content of motivational counseling should be coercive, paternalistic, or judgmental. Consistent with the child's constitutional rights, motivational interviewing may only be appropri-

---

123. Winick, *Jurisprudence of TJ, supra* note 5, at 185; Hartley & Petrucci, *supra* note 54, at 151.

124. Hartley & Petrucci, *supra* note 54, at 140–43 (urging lawyers to adopt generalist approach to social work which includes recognition of organizational context of client interaction).

125. *See* Wexler, *supra* note 21, at 190–93 (encouraging juvenile courts and its lawyers to learn rudimentary principles of relapse prevention and self change); Birgden, *supra* note 107, at 229 (proposing that sophisticated research-based clinical therapy of motivational interviewing can be applied by lawyers); Hartley & Petrucci, *supra* note 54, at 133 (encouraging application of generalist theories of social work); Winick, *Client Denial, supra* note 17, at 914 (arguing that attorneys should acquire basic understanding of the social psychology of persuasion).

126. Birgden, *supra* note 107, at 234.

ate when the child has made a decision to plead or the evidence of guilt is overwhelming.[127] Although motivational interviewing is a sophisticated, research-based clinical therapy designed for mental health professionals, Dr. Birgden argues that lawyering skills such as open-ended questioning, reflective listening, and empathy equip lawyers with the rudimentary foundation they need to apply motivational methods in legal counseling sessions.[128]

When psychological techniques are beyond the ability of lawyers, the lawyer may consult with an expert or refer the client for counseling.[129] External referrals may be appropriate when sophisticated methodologies are necessary to deal with a particularly resistant client or a client with a significant mental health history.[130] In the juvenile justice context, crisis intervention, counseling, or individual therapy may be required to stabilize the youth, diffuse immediate crises within the family, or to decrease anxiety, hostility, or depression among family members.[131] Such referrals should be handled with sensitivity as the client may be offended at the suggestion that he needs counseling and may perceive the lawyer's suggestion as paternalistic.[132]

Therapeutic jurisprudence is concerned not only with individual relations between legal actors and consumers: it is also concerned with broader procedural and organizational features within the relevant system of justice.[133] Thus, in the juvenile justice system, therapeutic jurisprudence recognizes that the very structure of the juvenile court process may produce therapeutic or anti-therapeutic outcomes. One of the most pervasive changes in juvenile justice policy in recent years has involved the implementation of multi-systemic or family-focused therapeutic responses to juvenile crime. Juvenile justice strategies no longer focus on the child alone as the cause of his delinquent behavior, but now reflect a growing recognition of the multidimensional causes of delinquency to include family, peers, schools, neighborhoods, and communities.[134] Juvenile drug courts, truancy courts, Unified Family Courts, and family-focused juvenile justice systems that employ Multisystemic Therapy (MST), Multidimensional Treatment Foster Care (MDTFC), and Functional Family Therapy (FFT), all recognize the need for multidimensional responses to the risk factors associated with delinquency.[135]

---

127. *Id.* at 239 (finding that motivational interviewing by lawyer does not presume that client is guilty).
128. *Id.* at 237.
129. Winick, *Client Denial, supra* note 17, at 907–09.
130. Birgden, *supra* note 107.
131. Janet Gilbert et al., *Applying Therapeutic Principles to a Family-Focused Juvenile Justice Model (Delinquency)*, 52 Ala. L. Rev. 1153, 1180 (2001).
132. Winick, *Client Denial, supra* note 17, at 908.
133. Gilbert, *supra* note 131, at 1201.
134. Scott W. Henggeler & Ashli J. Sheidow, *Conduct Disorder and Delinquency*, 29 J. Marital & Fam. Therapy 505 (2003); Gilbert, *supra* note 131, at 1169.
135. Family-focused strategies such as MST, FFT, and MDTFC recognize the role of family, schools, and community in the onset, prevention, and resolution of adolescent delinquent behavior. Family-focused and multi-systemic interventions thus seek to build supportive intra-family relationships, improve supervision and disciplinary practices among caregivers, monitor school attendance, increase positive collaboration between the family and the school, develop supportive mentoring relationships with adults, and reduce the child's exposure to delinquent peers. For an overview of clinical procedures, policies, and rationale for MST, FFT, and MDTFC, see Henggeler & Sheidow, *supra* note 134; Cindy M. Schaeffer & Charles M. Borduin, *Long-Term Follow-up to a Randomized Clinical Trial of Multisystemic Therapy With Serious and Violent Juvenile Offenders*, 73 J. Consulting & Clinical Psychol. 445 (2005); Barbara J. Burns et al., *Comprehensive Community-Based Interventions for Youth with Severe Emotional Disorders: Multisystemic Therapy and the Wraparound Process*, 9 J. Child & Fam. Stud. 283 (2000); Gilbert, *supra* note 131, at 1156.

The influx of multi-systemic responses to juvenile crime has radically altered the way attorneys interact with and advocate on behalf of children in juvenile court. Because multi-systemic models require extensive collaboration between treatment providers, the state juvenile justice agency, the school system, the court, and various social services agencies,[136] therapeutic lawyers in modern juvenile justice systems must advance the participatory interests of children not only in the juvenile court itself, but also in the public school system, the public housing authority, and the public benefits office among others. The lawyer must arm the child with information, give the child voice, and validate the child's concerns in all of the interrelated systems. Lawyers who are interested in motivating change and facilitating positive self-actualization will necessarily be concerned with reducing negative messages from other systems, generating positive educational, housing, and community-based alternatives, and building positive and supportive relationships within the child's family, peer group, school, and community.[137] Not surprisingly, the shift to multi-systemic models of rehabilitation has led to greater collaboration among attorneys, children, teachers, counselors, social workers, and other relevant adults in the child's life. Interdisciplinary partnerships are also consistent with principles of collaborative and client-centered advocacy, which encourage the child to make use of all available resources and consult with other professionals when necessary.[138]

The collaboration of social workers and attorneys is increasingly common in the domestic relations, family law, and juvenile justice contexts.[139] Social workers have collaborated with lawyers as consultants, resource developers, agents, independent service providers, and co-advocates on behalf of the child.[140] Because the social worker is trained to work with the client at micro (individual), mezzo (familial), and macro (communal) levels,[141] the social worker is well suited to collaborate with lawyers in the contemporary multi-systemic juvenile justice system. In some cases, the social worker may provide direct services to a child with extreme and immediate emotional needs.[142] In other cases, social workers may enhance attorney-client relations by modeling or training in effective interviewing and counseling skills.[143] The social worker may also broaden the lawyer's perspective and help advance the child's participatory interests in the many systems the child will encounter.[144] In the juvenile case, for example, the social worker may educate the attorney and the child on a greater range of positive community-based services and improve the child's opportunity to influence the outcome of his disposition. The social worker may identify creative alternatives to incarceration, make appropriate referrals, provide the client and the lawyer with information to challenge court-ordered diagnostic assessments, and help engage the child's family, school, or neighborhood in the treatment plan. Together, the lawyer, the child, and the social

---

136. Gilbert, *supra* note 131, at 1176.
137. *Id.* at 1172 (discussing the need to foster pro-social relationships for the child).
138. COCHRAN ET AL., COUNSELOR-AT-LAW, *supra* note 2, at 140, 155.
139. Hartley & Petrucci, *supra* note 54, at 133; Jacqueline St. Joan, *Building Bridges, Building Walls: Collaboration Between Lawyers and Social Workers in a Domestic Violence Clinic and Issues of Client Confidentiality,* 7 CLINICAL L. REV. 403 (2001); Louise G. Trubek, *Context and Collaboration: Family Law Innovation and Professional Autonomy,* 67 FORDHAM L. REV. 2533 (1999).
140. St. Joan, *supra* note 139, at 431 (describing various models of social work-attorney collaboration).
141. Hartley & Petrucci, *supra* note 54, at 140.
142. St. Joan, *supra* note 139, at 419 (describing example).
143. *Id.* at 405.
144. *Id.* at 415.

worker may develop a more comprehensive treatment plan and win the support of judges and prosecutors.

Child advocates also have many opportunities to collaborate with special education and public benefits attorneys. Because effective treatment in the juvenile justice system often requires comprehensive intervention to improve educational opportunities for the child and to improve housing conditions and economic sufficiency within the family,[145] the juvenile lawyer must be familiar with an ever-expanding range of legal subjects and interdisciplinary resources. Like the juvenile justice system, both the school system and the public benefits office have daunting administrative procedures that leave the child and his family feeling vulnerable, anxious, and alienated. Like social workers, education advocates and public benefits attorneys provide information, make collateral systems more accessible, and increase the child's opportunity to influence outcomes in both the juvenile case and related fora. The civil legal services lawyer may help the child obtain subsidies for food, clothing, housing, utilities, medical assistance, and childcare. The education advocate may help the child navigate school disciplinary hearings, explore public, private, and charter school options, and obtain auxiliary education equipment and services such as hearing aids, tutors, and transportation. The simultaneous resolution of multiple legal and social issues is therapeutically advantageous as it may provide the child and his family with a sense of completeness and increase the child's hope for an overall positive change.[146]

Notwithstanding the benefits discussed herein, interdisciplinary collaborations among lawyers, social workers, and other professionals must be approached with forethought and care as they may jeopardize both the legal rights and the participatory interests of the child. Therapeutic juvenile justice models such as juvenile drug courts and all-inclusive Unified Family Courts may compromise due process and feel very paternalistic for the accused child.[147] In these models, defense attorneys must be ever vigilant in protecting the child's constitutional rights and be careful not to be co-opted by the best-interest standard of other members of the juvenile justice "team." The lawyer should carefully explain both the advantages and disadvantages of collaboration and clearly secure the child's consent before developing partnerships and sharing confidential information with other professionals.[148] In contemplating collaboration with a social worker, for example, the lawyer should explain that the social worker generally has a different ethical and professional obligation than the lawyer. When the client withholds consent, or when systemic and ethical barriers prohibit full interdisciplinary collaboration, the lawyer may often seek the social worker's advice without disclosing confidential or identifying information about the child.[149]

B. *Ecology of the Family*

The unique interaction between children and their parents merits special attention for lawyers representing youths in the juvenile justice system. Although therapeutic ju-

---

145. Gilbert, *supra* note 131, at 1169.
146. Barbara A. Babb, *Fashioning an Interdisciplinary Framework for Court Reform in Family Law: A Blueprint to Construct a Unified Family Court*, 71 S. Cal. L. Rev. 469 (1998).
147. *See* Mae C. Quinn, *Whose Team Am I On Anyway? Musings of a Public Defender about Drug Treatment Court Practice*, 26 N.Y.U. Rev. L. & Soc. Change 37, 54–55 (2000); Anne H. Geraghty & Wallace J. Mlyniec, *Unified Family Courts: Tempering Enthusiasm with Caution*, 40 Fam. Ct. Rev. 435, 439 (2002).
148. St. Joan, *supra* note 139, at 415.
149. *Id.* at 432 (describing consultant model in which lawyer and social work never share identifying information).

risprudence argues against delegation of the child's participatory rights and interests to the parent, therapeutic jurisprudence would not exclude parents from the attorney-client relationship entirely.[150] In fact, principles of therapeutic jurisprudence recognize that familial support may play an important role in ameliorating the coercive nature of the juvenile court process and may compliment the child's voice in the juvenile hearing. Although I have found no empirical studies on the therapeutic value of parental support, it is widely assumed among judges, legislators, law enforcement officers, and attorneys that moral support from parents may make juvenile defendants more confident in their rights and counterbalance coercive law enforcement practices.[151] In the interrogation context, for example, state legislatures often deem juvenile confessions *per se* involuntary unless a parent or guardian is present at the time of questioning.[152]

In some cases, parents may also help the child exercise his constitutional right to counsel. In introductory attorney-client interactions, the parent may explain the lawyer's obligations to the child, help build trust between the child and the lawyer, and help the child articulate questions and concerns. When the parent is familiar with how the child receives and processes information, the parent may help the lawyer explain legal concepts in terms the child will understand. The parent may also help the lawyer and the child plan meaningful case strategies and choose between various options in the case.[153] Even as adolescents begin to assert their independence from parents, adolescents generally remain emotionally attached and regularly seek guidance, acceptance, and approval from parents and other significant adults.[154] Thus, in the decision-making process, the lawyer may encourage the child to talk to family members who may provide additional information and offer an alternative perspective.[155] Parental support may even enhance the lawyer's own cultural competence and make the lawyer a better advisor, counselor, and advocate for the child.

Collaboration between the lawyer and the child's parent may also improve the child's self-image, enhance the child's opportunity to influence the fact-finder, and increase the likelihood of favorable outcomes. In fact, family-focused responses to juvenile crime are designed to keep families together and avoid the unnecessary placement of youth in out-of-home residential facilities.[156] A prosecutor who is

---

150. *See supra* ch. 2: Susan Brooks, *Using Social Work Constructs in the Practice of Law* at pp. [ ].

151. *See* Ronner, *supra* note 7, at 102–03 (discussing police tactics that deprive suspects of psychological confidence and advantage by secluding them from family and friends who may offer moral support); *but see* Hillary B. Farber, *The Role of the Parent/Guardian in Juvenile Custodial Interrogations: Friend or Foe?*, 41 AM. CRIM. L. REV. 1277 (2004) (arguing that parents may intentionally or unwittingly join in coercive police tactics).

152. *See, e.g.*, COLO. REV. STAT. § 19-2-511 (2003); CONN. GEN. STAT. § 46b-137 (2003). In jurisdictions where voluntariness is determined by a judicial evaluation of the totality of the circumstances, judges generally view the parent's presence as a positive factor ameliorating the threat of coercion. *See, e.g.*, A.M. v. Butler, 360 F.3d 787 (7th Cir. 2004) (court considering failure to contact child's mother as one of factors important to finding that confession was involuntary); State v. Presha, 748 A.2d 1108, 1110 (N.J. 2000) (court should consider absence of parents as highly significant factor in evaluating whether child's waiver was knowing, voluntary and intelligent).

153. Catherine Ross, *Implementing Constitutional Rights for Juveniles: The Parent-Child Privilege in Context*, 14 STAN. L. & POL'Y REV. 85, 107 (2003).

154. Laurence Steinberg, *Autonomy, Conflict and Harmony in the Family Relationship*, *in* AT THE THRESHOLD: THE DEVELOPING ADOLESCENT 257–58 (Shirley Feldman & Glen R. Elliott eds., 1993); RALPH J. GEMELLI, NORMAL CHILD AND ADOLESCENT DEVELOPMENT 467 (1996).

155. COCHRAN ET AL., COUNSELOR-AT-LAW, *supra* note 2, at 155 (suggesting that an attorney might direct the client by asking "Is there anyone else that you would like to talk to about this choice?").

156. Gilbert, *supra* note 131, at 1172.

pleased with pretrial interventions in the child's home, school, or community may be inclined to dismiss charges or divert the child from formal court proceedings.[157] A judge who is satisfied that negative community factors have been corrected may also be more inclined to allow the child to remain in or return to his home at the time of disposition.

Consistent with principles of client autonomy and self-determination, the lawyer should provide the child with information about his right to engage parents in the decision-making process, but should give the child an opportunity to specify the nature, extent, and content of the consultation with parents. Initial attorney-client meetings conducted without parents provide the child a safe space in which to consider his right to confidentiality and understand the limits of parental control over case-related decisions. In jurisdictions where communications between the child and the parent are privileged or where the attorney-client privilege extends to parents of a minor child,[158] the lawyer should inform the child that he may invite his parent to participate in attorney-client interviews and consultations. In jurisdictions where there is uncertainty about the parameters of the attorney-client and parent-child privileges, the lawyer should advise the child not to discuss the details of his factual involvement in the alleged offense, but may offer to speak to the parents on the child's behalf or encourage the child to talk generally with parents about legal options, disposition alternatives, and general fears and concerns.

In negotiating an appropriate framework for the interaction among attorneys, children, and their parents, the child and the lawyer should carefully identify and evaluate all of the benefits and risks of collaborating with parents. The lawyer and the child might consider the child's ability to communicate with counsel and understand important legal issues without the parents' assistance, the potential that parents will provide information or insight not otherwise available to the child or his lawyer, and the existence of unique cultural, ethnic, religious, or moral norms that are shared between the parent and the child but not with the lawyer. The lawyer might also help the child consider strategic advantages that might be gained by including the parents in attorney-client discussions and earning the parents' support for the child's stated objectives such as in-home or other community-based alternatives to detention.[159]

If the child decides to include the parents in an attorney-client consultation, the lawyer is provided with an opportunity to employ motivational strategies that will promote the psychological well-being of the entire family.[160] Like strategies for individual

---

157. *Id.* at 1194.
158. Only three states have enacted statutory parent-child privileges, and only one state has clearly recognized such a privilege at common law. CONN. GEN. STAT. §46b-138a (2003); IDAHO CODE ANN. §9-203(7) (2004); MINN. STAT. §595.02(j) (2002); *In re* Mark G., 410 N.Y.S.2d 464, 464–65 (N.Y. App. Div. 1978). Only one state has explicitly extended the attorney-client privilege to parents by statute, but a few courts have found that the parents' present will not waive the attorney-client privilege when the child looks to the parent as an advisor and clearly intends that the communications remain confidential. WASH. REV. CODE §5.60.060 (2004 & Supp. 2005); State v. Sucharew, 66 P.3d 59 (Ariz. Ct. App. 2003) (noting privilege is generally waived when a third party is present, but finding that parents presence did not waive privilege in that case); Kevlik v. Goldstein, 724 F.2d 844 (1st Cir. 1984) (same); United States v. Bigos, 459 F.2d 639 (1st Cir. 1972) (same). Lawyers will need to thoroughly research the nature and extent of local parent-child and attorney-child privileges to preserve the child's right to be free from self-incrimination.
159. *See* Gilbert, *supra* note 131, at 1189–90 (noting that when child and family participate in services, they may prevent the child's removal from the home).
160. *See* Winick, *Jurisprudence of TJ, supra* note 5, at 202.

relapse prevention, family-focused interventions encourage legal actors to avoid "doing for" the family and stress enabling the family to do for itself.[161] Family-focused juvenile justice models are designed to develop feelings of self-worth and teach families that they are primarily responsible for, and capable of, achieving treatment goals.[162] Together, the family intervention specialist and the family will agree on appropriate goals and methods to achieve those goals.[163] The interventions will identify and draw on strengths within the family and maximize the capacity of family members to effect change in their own lives.[164] Family intervention specialists also teach families to advocate on behalf of children in other systems.[165] In meetings with the attorney, the client, and the client's parents, the lawyer may advance the rehabilitative process by helping to mend relationships within the family and secure the parents' support for the child's stated objectives. When parents are angry, for example, about court fines and missed hours at work, the lawyer may help the child develop a plan to pay parents back, increase household chores, or take greater responsibility for the care and supervision of younger siblings.

Although a lawyer who collaborates in family-focused advocacy may advance significant therapeutic interests, the lawyer must never loose sight of his role as counselor or advisor for the child and may not allow parents to usurp control over the child's legal representation. In the initial interaction with parents, the lawyer must clearly identify the child as his client and advise the parent that the child will be the ultimate arbiter of all key decisions, including those about whether to plead or go to trial.[166] Collaboration with parents also does not relieve the attorney of his duty to educate the child about his constitutional and statutory rights within the juvenile justice system or to provide the child with candid advice about how the child should proceed in the case.

Conclusion

Application of therapeutic jurisprudence to juvenile court has evolved considerably since the inception of the juvenile court movement. While judges in early juvenile courts offered kindly, paternalistic guidance and treatment to children in lieu of punishment, due process has changed the landscape of the modern juvenile court. Today, therapeutic outcomes are not only achieved through rehabilitative programming, but are also deeply intertwined in both the process of justice itself and the legal relationships in which the child will engage. Lawyers, judges, probation officers, parents, and teachers all have a role to play in the therapeutic success of the juvenile justice system. As the primary ally and voice for the child, the child's attorney plays a significant role in advancing therapeutic objectives for the child. By applying basic principles of psychology, the attorney may become a positive therapeutic agent and empower the child to comply with the court's rehabilitative efforts without violating overarching principles of law and justice. By building alliances within the child's family, school, and community, the lawyer may improve the child's self-image and help the child conceive of and pursue a greater range of positive alternatives.

---

161. Gilbert, *supra* note 131, at 1206.
162. *Id.* at 1178, 1180.
163. *Id.* at 1178.
164. *Id.* at 1176, 1178, 1186.
165. *Id.* at 1174.
166. Nancy J. Moore, *Conflicts of Interests in the Representation of Children*, 64 FORDHAM L. REV. 1819, 1824–25, 1830 (1996).

Appendix

PRACTICING THERAPEUTIC JURISPRUDENCE

An Example from Juvenile Court

You represent Mark who has been charged with one count each of burglary and unlawful entry. As you investigate, you learn the following facts: Mark is generally shy and studious, but lately he has been trying to make more friends. Mark was pleasantly surprised when one of the popular kids invited him to a party at 111 Main Street. Mark decided to go. Unbeknownst to Mark, it turns out that a few of the popular kids had discovered that the residents of 111 Main Street were out of town for a month-long vacation. The kids decided to break in and plan a big party for all of their classmates. As you get to know Mark, you realize that he is a really great kid who would never have done something like this knowingly and on purpose. You also think you have a strong defense because all of your investigation and interviews lead you to believe that Mark thought the house belonged to the kid who invited him and had no guilty knowledge that the house had been broken into. Mark is very remorseful, but thinks that it would be unfair for him to plead guilty to a crime he didn't know he was committing. He would like to go to trial.

Mark asks you to speak with his parents. When you do, you learn that Mark's parents are very angry with Mark for going to an unsupervised party with alcohol and for choosing friends who would break into a house. Mark's father is a minister and both of his parents are very strict. Mark's parents are insisting that Mark plead guilty and tell you as much. Mark's parents become very angry with you when you tell them that Mark has a legal defense to the charges. They stop returning your phone calls and don't answer the door when you show up to speak to your client one Saturday morning. What do you do?

Let's say you go to Mark's school and talk to him. He tells you that you are wasting your time because his parents want him to plead and that even if he went to trial no one would believe him because he is just a kid and judges and police don't believe kids. Why do you think Mark feels the way he does?

On some level, you believe that Mark's parents have a right to their opinion about how to raise their son. You see how an adjudication might serve as a "lesson" for Mark about the dangers of drinking and hanging out with the wrong crowd. Furthermore, you realize that Mark has made his own decision to plead—albeit with considerable pressure from his parents. Is there any reason to talk to him more about his decision?

Assume you do decide to talk to Mark further about the plea v. trial decision, how do you help him feel like he is a legitimate and valued participant in the juvenile justice system?

Part V

Therapeutic Jurisprudence in a Comparative Law Context

Virtually since its inception, therapeutic jurisprudence sought international insights and encouraged a comparative law approach, "releasing legal scholarship from the confines of United States constitutional construction, ... regarding law as something more than a domestic discipline, ... enriching our understanding by studying and discussing, in a truly international context, the relationship between legal arrangements and therapeutic outcome." David B. Wexler, The Development of Therapeutic Jurisprudence: From Theory to Practice, 68 Revista Jurídica Universidad de Puerto Rico 691, 695–96 (1999).

Happily, the international involvement has become a reality. TJ writings have appeared in English, Spanish, French, Italian, Dutch, Swedish, Japanese, Hebrew, Portuguese and Urdu. There have thus far been three large full-fledged international TJ conferences (UK, US, Australia), many more TJ streams or mini-conferences as components of larger meetings (Hawaii, Edinburgh, Dublin, Paris, Padua, San Juan). Canada's National Judicial Institute (NJI) has produced an excellent TJ manual for the judiciary that has gained worldwide attention (available online, in English and French, on the NJI website, www.nji.org, as has the Australasian Institute of Judicial Administration's (AIJA www.aija.org.au) impressive and user-friendly Australasian Therapeutic Jurisprudence Clearinghouse (likewise available online on the AIJA website).

Now, writing is beginning to emerge that turns the TJ lens on some distinctive legal arrangements. This Part collects that nascent scholarship, and I hope it will stimulate more analyses in a comparative law context. Here, we have two quite different Australian takes—from Victoria and from Western Australia—on TJ and barristers. The first is by Professor George Hampel, a barrister and former Victoria Supreme Court Justice. The other is by Perth barrister Patrick Mugliston. The volume closes with a selection by University of Stockholm law professor Christian Diesen taking a look at the Swedish inquisitorial system. The comparative law endeavor is a rich and exciting one. It has great potential for bringing practical interdisciplinary scholarship to a new level and dimension and for producing insights that may prove useful for the reform of law and practice on the domestic stage as well.

A. Barristers

i. The Honorable George Hampel QC,[1]
Therapeutic Jurisprudence — An Australian Perspective
(Reprinted with permission from
17 St. Thomas Law Review, 775, 2005)

INTRODUCTION

At a recent conference in Crete on Ethics and Professional Responsibilities, I had the privilege of meeting David B. Wexler and hearing his presentation on Therapeutic Jurisprudence. I also had the advantage of reading his article entitled *Therapeutic Jurisprudence and the Rehabilitative Role of the Criminal Defense Lawyer.*

Over a cup of good Greek coffee, Mr. Wexler asked me about developments in this area in Australia and suggested I might contribute to a forthcoming publication. The short answer is that there has been little development in academic circles compared to the work being done by Mr. Wexler and others in the United States and little development within the Australian legal profession. However, there is real development, particularly in the State of Victoria, at the instigation of our Justice Department headed by the Attorney General, the Honorable Rob Hulls.

DEVELOPMENTS IN VICTORIA

The Victorian Justice Department has initiated a number of programs to address the problems of the vulnerable and disadvantaged people in the community and their relationship with the justice system. Such initiatives include the Aboriginal Justice Agreement, the Women's Safety Strategy, the State Disability Plan and the Cultural Diversity Project. It has improved responses to the needs of victims of crime to assist in their recovery, particularly in the areas of family violence and sexual assault. A victims' support agency has been established, and has provisions for compensation for pain and suffering.

Most significantly, there have been developments in what is more clearly Therapeutic Jurisprudence, namely, the establishment of problem-solving courts. There is now a division of the Magistrates Court to deal with family violence. The age limit in the Children's Court has been increased to 18 years. A drug court has been established, which has special powers to impose treatment orders. Koori courts have been established to deal with special issues which arise in dealing with aboriginal offenders and provide as much understanding and support with these special problems. Although there has been some criticism of the concept of establishing special courts for sections of the community, it seems that the judiciary and the profession have embraced these initiatives and are cooperating with the work being done by the Magistrates Court. Victoria's Chief Magistrate, Ian Gray, presented an interesting paper describing the practice of the Koori court and its early achievements at the Ethics Conference in Crete. In addition, needed funding has been given to the Victoria Legal Aid and community legal centers.

---

1. Professor of Trial Practice and Advocacy at Monash University, President, International Institute of Forensic Studies, Chairman, Australian Advocacy Institute, Former Barrister and Justice of the Supreme Court of Victoria. Contact: George.Hampel@law.monash.edu.au.

All these developments are the work of the government and Magistrates Court, but the profession, while cooperating with these initiatives, has not seriously looked at other aspects of Therapeutic Jurisprudence of the kind described by Mr. Wexler in his paper.

Some Problems for Professional Involvement in Therapeutic Jurisprudence in Australia

In the three most populated States in Australia, that is, New South Wales, Victoria and Queensland, the profession is divided into barristers and solicitors along the British model. Other states have also seen the development of separate referral bars. The solicitor, usually working in firms, is in a sense the general practitioner and advisor to the client. Solicitors have a right of audience in the courts as advocates, but generally do not practice as such. If they do, it is often in country and suburban areas and in the larger cities only in the Magistrates Court. There are some exceptions, but generally the skills, knowledge and experience required of a professional advocate reside in members of the Bar. They practice as individuals and usually act only when briefed by solicitors and when the solicitors' clients become involved in litigation in which higher skills and experience in advocacy is needed.

It follows from these arrangements that the solicitor has the main contact with the client and not the barrister. The barrister is often briefed shortly before the case goes to court, and even if the barrister is briefed earlier, his or her activities are limited to advising on evidence and preparing a case for trial. There has been a long-standing debate about the advantages and disadvantages of this system, compared to the systems in which lawyers are amalgams although they may in fact specialize in trial advocacy. When working with the National Institute for Trial Advocacy in the United States in training of advocates, I learned that one of the problems was that trial lawyers do not get sufficient court experience. One well-known trial lawyer, who was described as a busy one, appeared in about ten trials during the year. A moderately successful barrister in Australia would appear in trials throughout the year, and a successful one would have very few days out of court. This is because the solicitors do much of the preparation and pre-trial activity. A good analogy may be that of the medical general practitioner who looks after the patient, engages a specialist surgeon when an operation is needed and then continues looking after the patient's rehabilitation.

The Australian, like the British system, has imposed, at least on barristers, some ethical obligations that are based on the way a barrister operates as an independent practitioner and an officer of the court. Amongst those ethical obligations is the so-called 'cab rank rule.' The rule requires a barrister to accept a brief from a solicitor in the area the barrister practices. It is a breach of the barrister's duty to choose or refuse cases, except in most exceptional circumstances. The character of the client or the nature of the cause is not a basis for a refusal of a brief. This stems from the traditional duty of a barrister to not make judgments, but to be available to represent clients in court. This duty has been expressed in various ways. Lord Elden[2] said:

> The advocate lends his exertions to all, himself to none. The result of the cause is to him a matter of indifference. It is for the courts to decide. It is for him to argue. He is merely an officer assisting in the administration of justice and acting under the impression that truth is best discovered by powerful statements on both sides of the question.

---

2. This statement is quoted in Ex parte Elsee (1830) MONT 69, at 70N, 72 *available at* http://www.geocities.com/artofadvocacy/about_advocacy_folder/what_is_advocacy_pagetwo.htm (last visited Feb. 22, 2004).

Dr. Johnson,[3] in expressing the same concept, stated that:

> [A] lawyer (advocate) has no business with the justice or injustice of the cause which he undertakes, unless his client asks his opinion, and then he is bound to give it honestly. The justice or injustice of the cause is to be decided by the judge.... A lawyer is to do for his client all that his client might fairly do for himself, if he could.... If lawyers were to undertake no causes until they were sure they were just, a man might be precluded altogether from a trial of his claim, though, were it judicially examined, it might be found a very just claim.

It follows from the peculiar role of a barrister, and the ethical principles which bind barristers, that it would be wrong for a barrister to attempt to become a social reformer by refusing briefs from solicitors because the clients are not willing to participate in rehabilitation programs.

Another factor, which is a relevant and a significant difference in Australia, is that we do not have plea bargaining, as it is known in the United States. There is a limited form of discussion between the defense and prosecution about the nature and number of charges but that is resolved on the basis of the sufficiency of evidence and rarely for other reasons. Such discussions do not involve the Judge. Also, any agreed positions about sentencing considerations put before a judge do not bind the judge. Further, judges infrequently refuse to act on what is jointly submitted by the parties, unless the evidence supports the result which the parties seek.

Consequences of These Differences

Action by government and the judiciary to develop and support Therapeutic Jurisprudence initiatives is underway and should be encouraged, subject to the legitimate concern that the fundamental concepts, rights and protections of litigants are not infringed. The profession should be encouraged to cooperate with such developments, provided that the ethical obligations of professional lawyers in their representation of the clients' interests are not compromised.

The nature of barristers practice and ethics makes it difficult to see how Therapeutic Jurisprudence, in the sense that it is described in Mr. Wexler's article, can be significantly developed. It would be quite unethical for a barrister to refuse to accept a brief, in a criminal matter, at trial or upon sentence, if it were conditional on the client's agreement to participate in prevention or rehabilitation programs. A private solicitors' firm may well be entitled to take this approach, but in my view a solicitor who has a right of audience in the courts and acts in a sense, in the same way as the American trial lawyer, could also be bound by a similar ethical obligation. There are firms in Australia who, for example, do mainly plaintiffs' work and would not appear for a defendant say in a tobacco industry case. They are entitled to do that but a barrister is not.

Having said that, there are some ways in which barristers can and should cooperate fully with the practices of the special needs courts or other Therapeutic Jurisprudence initiatives. It is also possible to attempt to introduce a culture of a more cooperative approach by the bar with trial management and a culture of avoiding behavior that unnecessarily upsets victims and witnesses. This must be within the limits of the right of a barrister to conduct a case in the best interest of the client provided it is within the bounds of ethics, etiquette and his or her position as an officer of the court.

---

3. James Boswell, The Life of Samuel Johnson 342 (David Campbell Publishers 1992).

I have read the article by Bruce Winick which deals with his views about the role of what he calls 'counsel' in Therapeutic Jurisprudence. If by counsel he intends to include barristers in a system like the one which exists in Australia, then I repeat the ethical limitations which bind barristers. Nevertheless, some of the actions by counsel, to which Mr. Winick refers, can properly have a therapeutic approach. I refer to helping the clients with their pre-trial attempts at negotiation and mediation, as well as helping the client with an easier path through the trial process by better informing the client about the process so as to make it more understandable and acceptable. All this can be done by barristers, and many good barristers already do it.

Conclusion

I think the Australian law schools could devote more time to the question of how the Australian profession, given the way it practices, can, consistently with its duties, become involved in the development of Therapeutic Jurisprudence. This could be done in university courses, particularly Criminal Law, Family Law and Trial Practice and Advocacy, as well as Clinical Programs. The same can be said for both barristers and solicitors. Bar Readers' courses, Advocacy Training workshops and Continuing Legal Education programs could be used to develop an understanding of the basic aims and approaches of Therapeutic Jurisprudence. Despite the ethical restrictions, lawyers, solicitors and barristers can be encouraged to understand and apply the principles of Therapeutic Jurisprudence to their work. These developments, designed to introduce a culture of Therapeutic Jurisprudence, should be cautious and considered without dampening the enthusiasm for the idea by David Wexler and his colleagues, who are doing important, interesting and constructive work.

ii. Patrick Mugliston,[*] Should the Role of a Barrister Change to Enable the Adoption of a More Therapeutic Approach to the Practice of Law?

Our justice system has seen significant changes to the traditional adversarial system and we shall examine whether there is today room for barristers to adopt a more therapeutic approach to their work. I have read with much interest the learned article by Judge Hampel on therapeutic Jurisprudence and the role of the barrister. I am profoundly respectful of Judge Hampel's view but wish to state my thoughts on the subject; which are firmly that a barrister can, and at times should, adopt a therapeutic approach to the practice of the law.

There have been changes over the years which have impacted on our justice system, and which I believe calls now for a re-definition of a barrister's role in the context of being more of a therapeutic agent in the justice system. I intend to look at the tradi-

---

[*] Patrick Mugliston B Juris, LLB, LLM, M CRIM JUST. (UWA) has lectured in criminal & contract law, tutored final year law students civil procedure, practised in civil, criminal & family law for 25 years and currently practices as a barrister from Francis Burt Chambers. In 2004 he won the Bar Reader evidence prize. He has written on appeals, bail applications, criminal procedure, and co-wrote a chapter in "The Executive State: WA Inc. and the Constitution" in 1991, which was recommended text for politics 100 students at UWA. He co-authored a legal text on Traffic Law in 2007, and is a reporter for the WA State Reports in Mining Law, State Administrative Tribunal and District Court Decisions. He is doing his PhD on Therapeutic Jurisprudence at Murdoch University. (The author wishes to thank his research assistant Michael Mugliston (paralegal at Francis Burt Chambers and law student at Notre Dame University) for his considerable assistance with this chapter.)

tional definition of how a barrister conducts him/herself and whether there are any limits associated with that definition. We shall also look at the arguments as to why the changing role of a barrister is important and why it may not be enough for a barrister to be 'indifferent' to the plight of their client in a social or psychological sense.

The advocates in support of adopting a therapeutic jurisprudence approach say there are good objective reasons for supporting the use of therapeutic principles and aims because, put simply, they often work. They argue that the courts will be more willing to accept the arguments of both the person charged and, to use an emotive and popular phrase, the 'victim of crime' when they adopt a therapeutic approach, and all parties involved are likely to be more satisfied with the outcome. The question arises, if the legislation, the judges and the courts are adopting therapeutic principles should not the barrister's do like wise?

We shall look at the evidence that suggests today that we have a justice system that positively encourages barristers to become part of a therapeutic process and this may mean that the traditional role of a barrister must now change.

The concept of therapeutic jurisprudence provides useful tools to analyse whether we are getting the most from our justice system. Put another way, therapeutic jurisprudence looks at the problem of regulation of behaviour from a wide perspective. It considers not only the legal consequences but also the social, psychological and personal ones that may be costly results of the court process. In such a light it regards the justice system as a social force that often produces therapeutic or anti-therapeutic consequences.

It suggests that the system's role as a therapeutic agent should be understood. It suggests further, that by understanding that role the community may, more effectively, encourage the behaviours it seeks to promote.

There are times when a justice system creates as many problems as it hopes to solve. In the arena of therapeutic jurisprudence this is known as having an 'anti-therapeutic' effect. For example in the civil jurisdiction there is evidence to suggest that the compensation process may in itself encourage litigants to remain unwell.[1] A recent report has found that people with injuries who seek compensation have a worse long term health outcome than people with similar injuries who don't seek compensation.[2]

As a barrister I see myself as being an agent in the system with a potential to have either a therapeutic, anti-therapeutic or neutral effect. I am certain also that a barrister may have an anti-therapeutic effect on their client, even in circumstances where the client might win the case but really 'lose it' in the sense of the loss of those intangible matters we shall discuss.

The barrister's role here in Western Australia is based on the English model where traditionally barristers were strictly to represent each client in the courtroom. Under the English system a solicitor is charged with the responsibility of maintaining day-to-day contact with clients and with the handling of all pre-trial matters. More specifically, a barrister is an attorney in the British legal system licensed to argue cases in higher courts, as opposed to a solicitor, who may only prepare cases for a barrister and argue in certain lower courts.

---

1. See Daniel W. Shuman, The Psychology of Compensation in Tort Law, in Law in a Therapeutic Key 433 (David B. Wexler & Bruce Winick eds. 1996).
2. Radio National with Damien Carrick On Tuesday 23/10/2001 Does Litigation Harm Your Health?

Here in Perth we have a 'hybrid system', which I think works quite well. I certainly see my role to provide expert, impartial, detached advice and advocacy, but at times I have been asked for a stronger commitment than that. More and more I have been called upon to contribute to the planning and development of a client's case, effectively guiding my instructing solicitor with advice as to the matters which I consider will best advance my client's interests. This is certainly the case with criminal matters where the client must have expert advice at the start as to how he should plead to a charge, in order to decide whether he will avail himself of the discount on sentence which would attach to a plea of guilty but which would not be available if such a plea was entered at the eleventh hour. In civil cases I find a lot of my work is to provide advice and to negotiate. Mediations are often compulsory and barristers are frequently briefed to attend such conferences.

Barristers historically insulated themselves from the client by maintaining a detached approach. Solicitors undertook a more 'hands on' approach to the law as they handled clients' day-to-day concerns, negotiated, drafted documents, interviewed witnesses, prepared cases leaving the trial work for barristers. The solicitor's function was to be accessible, unlike the barrister.

Historically the law has been criticized as being not accessible to many people. For my part I feel I have a role to play by ensuring I am more accessible than what the historical definition of my role might indicate. This suggestion is however very controversial. I think it justified for a number of complex reasons which I shall go into.

The Traditional Role of a Barrister

The role of a barrister is often defined by traditions and attitudes from a bygone era. We will look at the evidence that suggests that it is now timely for barristers to explore new dimensions in their role in the fields of criminal justice, mental health, and working with Aboriginal communities. It is interesting to note that The Hon Judge Sherry Van de Veen commented that in Canada it was precisely those areas of the law in which the traditional system was 'unfair and ineffective'. This is what she had to say on the subject, and I suggest, for reasons we will explore, that her comments have application in Australia and impact on the role of barristers:

> *"The traditional adversarial system is designed to deal with the intentional behavior and in cases involving ill people whose behavior is beyond their control, the traditional system is both ineffective and unfair. In the case of drug dependant individuals, it is clear these individuals will continue to re-offend as long as the underlying cause of their addition is not dealt with. In the case of Aboriginal people the aboriginal culture is not based upon punishment or separation of offenders from society. It is based upon the concept of restoring relationships between the offender and the victim. The aboriginal culture involves a community-based system of sanctions, and therefore the traditional system is often not understood by aboriginal people ... In all of the foregoing areas, there is a growing recognition that the traditional adversarial system, on its own, is often inadequate to bring about justice to offenders, victims, and the community itself."*[3]

This examination will illustrate the changing dimensions to our laws, and why, to be effective, barristers may be wise to move in the same direction as the legislation. In examining these issues we shall look at why our fiduciary relationship with our client may re-

---

3. *Some Canadian Problem Solving Court Processes*, 3rd International Conference on Therapeutic Jurisprudence, 7–9 June 2006, Perth, Western Australia, p 5.

quire us not only to simply view the 'best interests of my client' in terms of a good legal outcome, but also in terms of the client's overall wellbeing. Such an approach requires a barrister to be sensitive to a client's emotional state and to the life problems underlying the legal issue. In this context, we may have to begin to see our role as counsel to motivate a criminal or mental health client to undertake rehabilitation.

At the opening of the Perth Drug Court and Geraldton Magistrates Court Conference on 6 May 2005, the former Chief Justice of the Supreme Court of Western Australia, the Hon David Malcolm AC, raised this issue when he said:

> "The best outcome for a client may not be an acquittal on a technical legal point, but recognition of an ongoing problem that causes chronic offending which needs to be addressed as a priority. It raises issues regarding the approach lawyers take in engaging with their clients and with the court."[4]

Malcolm CJ explained that in Australia therapeutic jurisprudence involves courts focusing less on coercive powers. He said the court would use its authority to motivate litigants, principally offenders, to address not only the legal problem at hand, but also the underlying social problems. This will require a change in approach by the professionals working within the justice system.[5] This is a significant challenge to those barristers who see their role defined by the traditional definition expressed by Lord Elden:

> *The advocate lends his exertions to all, himself to none. The result of the cause is to him a matter of indifference. It is for the courts to decide. It is for him to argue. He is merely an officer assisting in the administration of justice and acting under the impression that truth is best discovered by powerful statements on both sides of the question."*[6]

Lord Eldon, the former Chief Justice of England was a brilliant jurist. He was able to capture the sentiments of his time. However, it is well to remember that Lord Eldon resisted proposals to abolish slavery, end imprisonment for mere civil debt and provide emancipation for Roman Catholics. It is said that he was so resistant to change that he wept while sitting on the woolsack when he learnt that the death penalty would no longer be available for petty larceny[7].

Today lawyers, and indeed judges, often make statements that suggest that they see their role in a very different light. Lawyers often take a broad approach to their role in and outside the court. It is not uncommon to read of judges seeing themselves as participating in the process of developing social changes and social justice. It raises issues regarding the approach lawyers take in engaging with their clients and with the courts. In such a context, they clearly do not regard the result as a matter of 'indifference to them'.

A classic example of such a judge is the former Chief Justice of India, the Hon Mr. Justice PN Bhagwati. His Honour, as the Chairperson of the United Nations Human Rights Committee, delivered a speech in New Delhi on 3 November 2002 on the topic of 'Access to Justice'. On that occasion he said:

> "In the beginning when I started social action litigation in India as a Judge in the Supreme Court of India there was criticism from some quarters that entertaining social action litigation and making orders and giving direction for taking affirma-

---

4. At p 13.
5. Malcolm CJ, op cit, p 13.
6. *Ex parte Lloyd*, 5 November 1822, reported as a note in *Ex parte Elsee* (1830) Mont 69, 70n at p 72.
7. The Right Hon Earl of Birkenhead, *Fourteen English Judges*, Cassell & Co Ltd, 1926, p 237.

tive action to make human rights meaningful and effective was going beyond the traditional judicial function. This criticism was repelled by me as unfounded because the law cannot remain static; it has to adapt itself to the needs of the people and to satisfy their hopes and aspirations."[8]

Many of us engaged in the court system see ourselves as being deeply concerned with the outcome, whether from the perspective of our client's interest, or in the wider sense being referred to by Justice PN Bhagwati. At this level we may even be passionate about the result. Some may well view our passion as being a positive attribute.

Today few people are likely to consider it a sign of judicial weakness if a judge reveals a personal view or emotion in relation to a case, depending of course on the circumstances. Examples abound. To give just one example, I refer to his Honour Justice Kirby's remarks in *The Queen v Taufahema*[9] wherein Kirby J stated that he arrived at his conclusion 'without enthusiasm'. Indeed, his Honour made a point of saying:

> "The impartial application of basic legal principles is the more important in criminal appeals because the circumstances in which such principles are invoked sometimes make it painful to apply the principles with judicial dispassion and complete even-handedness."[10]

Such a statement would have great impact on the widow and children of the deceased police officer allegedly murdered by the appellant. Judges do however become more involved than just making such a remark in their judgments. Some judges, and Kirby J is an example, become involved in 'judicial activism' and see such activity as highly consistent with their role as judges and ensuring the delivery of a 'just' system.

We should note that the concepts of 'rights to justice' are not new. They stretch back as far as the Magna Carta and even further. The Magna Carta tells us that 'no freeman shall be taken or imprisoned or disseised or outlawed or exiled or in any way ruined, nor will we go or send again him, except by the lawful judgment of his peers or by the law of the land. To no one will we sell, to no one will we deny or delay right to justice'.[11]

What such a statement is implying is something more than indifference to the result. Would you wish to be represented by somebody who was indifferent as to whether you succeeded or failed? In this context we may wish to ask ourselves: are we delivering a system worth having if we are seen to be professing it as a worthy attribute in advocates that they are indifferent to the result?

In looking at changes in how a barrister might perceive their role it is useful to look at how judges have changed the perception of their roles. The fact is that 'judges are a fundamental part of the legal profession, and a lawyer's role is a natural extension and outgrowth of their work'.[12] The interplay between the legislative and judicial arms of government has resulted in much debate. On one side are those who support the judiciary adopting a strictly legalistic attitude while on the other side are those who support

---

8. Hon Mr Justice PN Bhagwati, *Democratisation of Remedies and Access to Justice*, First South Asian Regional Judicial Colloquium on Access to Justice, New Delhi, 1–3 November 2002.
9. [2007] HCA 11 (delivered 21 March 2007).
10. ibid., at [180].
11. The Magna Carta, 1215, para. 39.
12. David Hall, *The Spiritual Revitalization of the Legal Profession*, The Edwin Mellen Press, 2005, p 359.

legal activism. As a result of a study[13] on this issue, there has emerged an awareness of just how important in Australia is a judge's perception of his or her role as a judge, as to how they do actually perform as a judge. Jason Pierce, in *Inside the Mason Court Revolution*, points out that it was a change in how judges perceived their role which resulted in the transformation of Australia's High Court in a way which was unparalleled anywhere else in the world. He explains:

> *"When one considers the High Court's role transformation with the role changes that have occurred in the last twenty years or so in other judiciaries, Australia's stand out. Put simply, Australia's transformation was endogenous to the High Court to an extent not true elsewhere. The High Court under Mason's leadership abandoned the orthodoxy not out of statutory or constitutional obligation, not because it was suddenly vested with new judicial review powers, but because the individual judges of the court held role perceptions that compelled them to pursue the politicised role."*[14]

Over the years there has been significant interplay between the legislative and judicial arms with certainly the legislature recognizing the larger issues involved when it legislates in relation to crime and punishment. One can see in our current legislation a therapeutic view being adopted by the legislature towards our criminal justice system. However, increasingly the judiciary is also becoming more active as an agent for change. In such a context the question may be asked whether barristers should also be active, or 'excused' for being active, in delivering therapeutic consequences to their clients. Is there a need for 'barristerial activism'?

The traditional role of the legislature may be stated to be that it enacts laws designed to further the common good. The duty of the judiciary is to uphold those laws, and more generally to uphold the constitutional framework and the rule of law.[15] However, judicial activism goes against this traditional view. *Black's Law Dictionary* defines judicial activism as 'a philosophy of judicial decision-making whereby judges allow their personal views about public policy, among other factors, to guide their decisions, usually with the suggestion that adherents of this philosophy tend to find constitutional violations and are willing to ignore precedent'. The Hon Mr. Justice PN Bhagwati, referred to earlier, sees himself as such a judge:

> *"The law is not an antique to be taken down, dusted, admired and put back on the shelf. It is a dynamic instrument fashioned by society for the purpose of eliminating friction and conflict and unless it secures social justice to the people, it will fail in its purpose and some day people will cast it off. It is therefore the duty of the judges to mould and develop the law in the right direction by creatively interpreting it so that it fulfils its social purpose and economic mission."*[16]

Speaking on the subject of 'judicial activism', the Hon Justice Michael Kirby, Judge of the High Court of Australia, delivered the Bar Association of India Lecture in 1997. He spoke highly of the tradition in India of judicial activism, mentioning that it was because of judicial activism that basic principles were established in India by the judiciary where the legislature had failed to do so. These important decisions were made on is-

---

13. Jason Pierce drew heavily on 80-plus interviews which he conducted with Australia's most senior appellate judges from 1997 to 2000.
14. ibid., p 290.
15. *Collins*, 'Democracy and Adjudication' in *MacCormick and Birks* (eds), *The Legal Mind*, Clarendon Press, 1997, p 67.
16. See above note 7.

sues such as the right to go abroad; the right to privacy; the right to protection against solitary confinement; the right not to be held in fetters; the right of an indigent person to have legal aid; the right to speedy trial; the right against public hanging; the right against custodial violence; the right, in certain circumstances, to medical assistance; and the right in certain circumstances to the provision of physical shelter.[17] Kirby J said:

> "... Although the detail of Indian jurisprudence is no more known in my country than that of Australia is known here, there is a general belief or understanding that the Supreme court of India, and the High Courts under its leadership, have been particularly creative and imaginative in the development of the constitutional and common law of this country. Sometimes in my own decisions, I have drawn upon the jurisprudence of the Indian courts to sustain a small advance in the exposition of the common law."[18]

Proponents of judicial activism are not without their critics. Although there is utility in the approach of judicial activism, how does one determine the common good and desirable end? Padraic McGuinness, editor of *Quadrant* (a conservative magazine), wrote an article entitled 'Under Kirby's Law, We are All Subject to the Whim of Judicial Adventurism'. In it he said:

> "But Kirby does not believe that judicial adventurism is without principle. He relies on another theory. This is unclear, but seems to be essentially that there are principles of human rights and justice which are inherently true, and only judicial authorities can define them. Where do the judges find these principles? Either they make them up as they go along, or they rely on a theory of natural moral law, either as defined by, say, Catholic natural law philosophy or some other external doctrine. Kirby calls this 'legal policy'.
>
> Where does his legal policy derive? From nowhere but the often ill-informed beliefs by the judges about the society and the economy. Thus he refers to the matter of liability, and whether a rule might 'result in intolerable economic burdens on citizens', 'have adverse implications for the availability of liability insurance', 'leave a vulnerable party without recompense reasonable to the circumstances', and so on.
>
> These are all matters for research, which the High Court does not undertake, and judgement which properly lies with parliament and government, not with the courts. His reformation is the triumph of lawyers over the law."[19]

Here in Western Australia, we face embarrassing statistics with regard to the rate of imprisonment of Aboriginal people. Certainly the Chief Justice of our Supreme Court, His Honour Wayne Martin, considers that the legal system imposed on the Aboriginal people has failed them. At the start of Law Week, Martin CJ called for a 'fresh approach' to tackling the high imprisonment rate of Aboriginal people in Western Australia. He stated that there was no easy or short-term solution and conceded that whatever 'we have done in the past does not appear to have worked'.[20] His Honour was addressing the problems in terms of looking at the results of our legal system dealing with the Aboriginal people. He spoke of the recommendations of the WA Law Reform Commission,

---
17. New Delhi Hilton Hotel, 6 January 1997, p 3.
18. ibid., p 2.
19. 9 December 2003, see: <http://www.smh.com.au/articles/2003/12/08/1070732144112.html>.
20. The *West Australian*, 8 May 2007, p 10.

particularly those aimed at enhancing the relevance of the law for Aboriginal people. He made the following observations:

> "The Equal Treatment Benchbook will be developed in conjunction with a revision of the Aboriginal Benchbook, and the two publications will be linked so as to provide a combined resource. Tragically, Aboriginal people are still grossly overrepresented in our criminal justice system. Tonight, Aboriginal people will comprise almost 42% of the prison population, as compared to 3% of the general population of the State. Tonight, about one out of every 16 Aboriginal men in this State will spend the night in prison. Despite the recommendations of the Inquiry into Aboriginal Deaths in Custody, since that inquiry, the Aboriginal imprisonment rate has increased, rather than decreased.
>
> And even more alarmingly, given that 50% of the Aboriginal population is aged 20 years or under, the situation is even worse in the juvenile justice area. Aboriginal youths comprise over 80% of the inmates of the State's two juvenile custodial facilities—Rangeview and Banksia Hill. Viewed by reference only to the Aboriginal population, the imprisonment rate of Aboriginal people in this State is almost double that of the next highest jurisdiction in the country—the Northern Territory. And for most Aboriginal offenders there is an Aboriginal victim. Aboriginal women have a 45 times greater chance of being assaulted than non-Aboriginal women.
>
> These shocking statistics reveal a continuing crisis in the interaction between Aboriginal people and the justice system in this State."[21]

What can be said of the fact that Aboriginals are imprisoned at such a high rate? Let us look at this issue from the perspective of the interface of the dominant white culture towards the Aboriginal sub-culture it has subsumed. It has imposed a justice system on Aboriginals. It may be timely to look at the function of a justice system. The Hon Mr Justice PN Bhagwati said on the topic of justice when Chairman of the United Nations Human Rights Committee:

> "The judges must realise that the law administered by them must become a powerful instrument for ensuring social justice to all and by social justice, I mean justice which is not limited to a fortunate few but which encompasses large sections of have-nots and handicapped, law which brings about equitable distribution of the social material and political resources of the community."[22]

How should we gauge whether a justice system delivers such an objective? Therapeutic jurisprudence may be a useful yardstick. In a presentation on therapeutic jurisprudence, Professor Wexler[23] said:

> "Therapeutic jurisprudence wants us to be aware of [these consequences] and wants us to see whether the law can be made or applied in a more therapeutic way so long as other values, such as justice and due process, can be fully respected."[24]

---

21. The Start of Law Week Address, 7 May 2007, 'The State of Justice'.
22. Hon Mr Justice PN Bhagwati, *Democratisation of Remedies and Access to Justice*, New Delhi, 1–3 November 2002.
23. David Wexler is Professor of Law and Director of the International Network on Therapeutic Jurisprudence at the University of Puerto Rico. The Network maintains a website, which includes comprehensive therapeutic jurisprudence bibliography, at <http://www.law.arizona.edu/upr.intj>.
24. D Wexler, 'Therapeutic Jurisprudence: An Overview' (2000) 17 *Thomas M Cooley Law Review* 125–34, available at <http://www.therapeuticjurisprudence.org>.

In this regard, for instance, Aboriginal people may be justified in questioning whether they have inherited a legal system that has dealt with them or their environment in a therapeutic way. Paul Nichols has suggested that the interface between the Aboriginal and White Australian justice system has been anti-therapeutic.[25] Nichols suggested that it might be possible to observe in the Aboriginal people, as a consequence of this interface, a cluster of symptoms that may be seen as a form of mass post-traumatic stress syndrome that, he explains, most Aboriginal communities are suffering from.

The trauma causing this syndrome has been the debilitation of their culture and their forms of 'government' in the years since the arrival of the white culture into Australia. Nichols explains that anyone who has ever been in a position to control the welfare of a large number of people knows how important 'morale' is. Those people with it retain initiative, optimism, forward thinking. Those without it tend to take to drink and all the other indicia of social unhappiness. People affected by post-traumatic stress syndrome exhibit much the same features. Considered in this way, Nichols sees the following anti-therapeutic consequences of our justice system to the Aboriginal:

- poor self-esteem;
- believing the problems are unsolvable;
- believing they were the cause of the problems;
- reduced legal status;
- being placed at the bottom of the social spectrum.

Nichol explains in his article:

> *"If indeed post-traumatic disorder arises from a severe and prolonged assault on the personality's security, it is at least arguable that reinforcement of this disorder will occur if it comes from more than one direction. The proposition is that military force was little used, but used enough to make submission the only alternative. But that it was reinforced by economic ruin, but most of all it was reinforced by total disregard of the culture and personal qualities of aboriginals. Furthermore that last reinforcement had in it three facts that made it the most influential of reinforcements:*
>
> *a. It was virtually continuous from white settlement; and,*
>
> *b. The disregard was from the class with whom the aborigines mixed most, viz the white working class; and,*
>
> *c. That meant that initiatives to improve conditions tended to be opposed by white working-class political representatives and that the first improvements in aboriginal conditions had to be imposed from above not from below."*[26]

The theory that post-traumatic stress syndrome can infect entire families and conceivably cultures is not novel. Sigmund Freud said: 'If we consider mankind as a whole and

---

25. P Mugliston and P Nichols, 'Does the Legal System Deal with Aboriginal People and Gays/Lesbians in a Therapeutic or Anti-therapeutic Way, and What Lessons May we Learn from History?', Transforming Legal Processes in Court and Beyond: Third International Conference on Therapeutic Jurisprudence, 7 June 2006.

26. ibid., p 7.

substitute for it a single individual we discover it too has developed illusions which are inaccessible to logical criticism and which contradict reality.'[27]

More recently, Richard Heinberg[28] postulated that when hunter-gatherers encounter civilised people, they often remark on how the latter appear generally to be disconnected, alienated, aggressive, easily frustrated, addictive and obsessive. These are the very traits often associated with post-traumatic stress syndrome. So, while it is possible to see the impairment of a culture as a result of its contact with a civilising dominant culture, Heinberg also argues that it is possible to see in those dominant cultures certain traits of psychic distress. He explains that in order to deal with the concept of mass neurosis we can and are compelled to draw analogies with individual manifestations of psychic distress. In this way, it may be possible to see how such distress may be healed.

Heinberg sees that western civilisation is itself suffering from post-traumatic stress syndrome. He asks:

> "Trauma victims frequently suffer from psychic numbing—the decreased ability to feel joy or sorrow, or to empathise with the feelings of others. Native peoples wonder how civilised Europeans can treat other humans, and the animals, trees, and land, with such unfeeling indifference. Of course, the relentless monetisation and compartmentalisation of our society are partly to blame: trees and animals have ceased to be magical beings and have become instead 'economic resources'; people have ceased to be members of a community and have become instead 'workers' or 'consumers', 'national allies' or 'enemies of the state'. Nevertheless, the questions arise: Why is it that people in Western society have failed to put brakes on tendencies to turn empathic relationships into abstract, manipulative ones— even when these tendencies are clearly out of control and acting to the detriment of people's own fundamental interests?"[29]

Heinberg also asks whether the population is already numbed to some extent, and whether this is because of 'some ancient trauma, the destructive energy of which has been passed along from generation through abusive child rearing?'[30] The notion of passing a psychic numbing on from generation to generation is something worth examining in the context of legal education. Is our education system producing a 'numbed' population of barristers and is the acceptance of Lord Eldon's definition of a barrister's role part of the process of psychic numbing?

From a therapeutic jurisprudence point of view it is of considerable interest to examine the state of legal education, and to see what evidence exists to support such numbing taking place there. Professor Hall[31] argues that law professors are themselves therapeutic agents in the classroom, and if in fact they saw themselves in such a light they would be more sensitive to the serious impact that their teaching styles, comments and

---

27. S Freud (1937), 'Constructions in Analysis' in J Strachey (trans, ed), *The Standard Edition of he Complete Psychological Works of Sigmund Freud*, vol 23 (1937–1939), [P: publisher & place of pub'n?] pp 255–70, at p 269.
28. 'Catastrophe, Collective Trauma, and the Origin of Civilisation': <http://www.newdawnmagazine.com.au/Articles/Origin%20of%20CivilisationP1.html>.
29. ibid.
30. ibid.
31. Professor of Law at Northeastern University School of Law. He holds LL M and SJD degrees from Harvard Law School, Master of Human Relations and Juris Doctor degrees from the University of Oklahoma, and a BS in Political Science from Kansas State University.

feedback have on the development of the students[32]. This is, put differently, really part of the educative function of teachers, and those who neglect this are not doing their job. Hall explains that:

> *Humanizing Legal Education is a movement of legal educators who are deeply concerned about the anti-therapeutic effects of law schools on the students who attend these institutions. Through scholarship, empirical research and conferences, various legal educators have been able to persuasively argue that much of the stress, depression, substance abuse and other negative behaviour among law students are, in part, a product of the structure and practice of legal education. This approach attempts to systematically sensitise students and faculty members to the various ways these negative consequences can be prevented and addressed."*[33]

Let us now look more closely at the question of the relationship between the litigant, the justice process and this notion of a mass neurosis. The correlation between the role of the litigant in the process of social justice, and this idea that humanity itself suffers a form of post-traumatic stress disorder, is not transparent, but is worth a closer examination. As advocates, we play a pivotal role in aiding the other components of the legal system to reach a point where they can fairly and reasonable deliver justice to all. In doing this, nothing is lost by us being concerned with the actual results.

We may be able to draw inspiration from Kant's view that a person is right in doing something if they would be happy to have it done to them, and if they would be happy to live in a world where such an action is commonplace.[34] When this thought is applied to a system of justice, it is easy to see why we as lawyers should not be 'indifferent' to the outcomes where such outcomes may impact on human rights and a healthy planet which should, applying Kant's philosophy, be our responsibility and legacy to others.

This and other innovative ways of analysing the role of the advocate is essential for the legal system to progress in the way it deals with issues of social justice. We are all familiar with Alice Minister's book, *For Your Own Good* (Farrar, Straus, Giroux, 1983), in which she examines the attitudes towards child rearing behaviour which she postulates may have led to Nazism being possible. In her text, Minister produces evidence that parents were taught to bring up their children to suppress crying and feelings. Parents were told to reward stoicism and self-control. Childhood excitement was considered a vice, and 'inhibition of life" was extolled as a virtue. In the context of such a childhood, it may be possible to understand why Eichmann SS (head of the Department for Jewish Affairs in the Gestapo from 1941 to 1945 and chief of operations in the deportation of three million Jews to extermination camps) was able to listen to highly emotional testimony at his trial with no feeling whatsoever, yet blushed when it was pointed out to him that he had forgotten to stand when his verdict was read.

In such a context I find the remarks of the former Chief Justice Bhagwati consoling, but they do not sit well with the critics of judicial activism. The criticism against Bhagwati's style of judging was well explained by Jason Pierce in 'Inside the Mason Court Revolution' when he said:

---

32. *The Spiritual Revitalization of the Legal Profession*, The Edwin Mellen Press, 2005, p 308.
33. ibid., p 313.
34. 'Act only on the maxim whereby thou canst and at the same time will that it should become an universal law': I Kant (1785), in JW Ellington (ed, trans), *Grounding for the Metaphysics of Morals,* 3rd ed, Hackett, 1993, p 30.

> "It is also evident that the orthodox model leaves little room for judges who take on the airs of legislators. '[J]udges ought to stay out of legislating—I'm very strong on that!' remarked a Western Australian Supreme Court judge. 'We should not try to legislate. I know when we give a decision the effect of it might be to change the law. Once we start legislating we are in deep trouble. We're not elected. We're supposed to interpret the law, which is made by parliament and the common law ... When we're operating in the common law areas we tend to unwittingly legislate, but the less of that the better.'"[35]

Examples from my experiences of a therapeutic jurisprudence approach to my work as a barrister

My work at the Mental Health Law Centre

For a few months in 2001 I worked as a volunteer as a barrister appearing for clients before the Mental Health Review Board. My experiences there, and the many discussions I subsequently had with Dr Neville Barber, the chairman of the Mental Health Board, helped influence my notions of the role of a barrister in this challenging arena. It also helped to evolve my notion that 'having your say' was in itself a very sanative process, and while it was not likely in the context of mental health to achieve good legal results, very much more important results were going to ensue to the patient/client in a therapeutic jurisprudence sense.

One of the defining characteristics of the work I did before the Board was that my applications were almost certainly bound to fail. The fact that inevitably all of my clients wanted to proceed with their application, even after hearing my advice that their application was certain to fail, began to intrigue me. Before discussing this aspect of my work, let us look first at the mechanics of applications to the Mental Health Review Board and then at four representative examples of applications where I worked as counsel.

The basic parameters of a review are set out in the *Mental Health Act 1996*.[36] In summary, the legislation contained provisions requiring the review body:

- to give each party to proceedings a reasonable opportunity to call or give evidence;
- to examine or cross-examine witnesses;
- to make submissions;
- to be represented; and
- to have closed hearings about which information later cannot be published in any identifying form.

The mental health legislation required[37] that the following criteria be satisfied before a person can be made an involuntary patient:

- The person has a mental illness (as may be defined) that requires treatment.
- The person is shown to be at some risk to him or her self or others.
- The person is unable to or has refused to consent to treatment.
- There is no less restrictive means of treating the person.

The chairman of the Board at that time made a study of the success rates of such applications over the years. This is his summary of the findings:

---
35. op cit, p 68.
36. See sections 4.5 and 4.6.
37. See section 4.4.

> "For example, in Western Australia between 13 November 1997 and 30 June 2002, the Board completed 3,840 reviews. Of those, statistics indicate that there were only three occasions when the Board discharged patients from involuntary status on the basis of it not being satisfied that the person had a mental illness. In the first instance, the psychiatrist sought that the involuntary order be continued on the basis of a 'suspicion' that the person had a mental illness (as defined) and proposed that further tests be conducted on the person. The Board concluded that the patient's order should be discharged on the basis that at the time of the review he did not meet the criteria for involuntary status. On the second occasion, the treating psychiatrist told the Board that her patient's diagnosis was 'up for grabs' and that she could not be certain—or even clearer—that he had a mental illness. Again, the Board concluded in these circumstances that the threshold of the patient having a mental illness had not been met. In the third example, a majority of the Board found that there was insufficient evidence to establish that the patient had a mental illness. The minority found that the patient had a mental illness but agreed that the order should be discharged on the basis of risk not being sufficiently demonstrated. In these examples, the Board reached its decision primarily upon what the psychiatrist told it, rather than the patient.
>
> In contrast to these examples, a much more common occurrence from the observed reviews and my experience is for information to be presented to a review body that a person has a mental illness, but the patient denies this. In these instances, it is both logical and to be expected that the Board will accept the opinion of the psychiatrist (almost always based upon historical as well as more recent information) in preference to the opinion of the patient, which is usually unsupported by medical or other evidence."[38]

Once I started having contact with patients, I saw time and again, that I was not going to be able to persuade them to see that their applications were destined to fail. However, in all instances they wanted to be heard, and instructed me to proceed with their applications. It was clear to me that they were an oppressed minority group that had very few rights and were feeling very much the brunt of everything. Often they would see their caregivers as being hostile people who were imprisoning them and restricting their life choices. The validation of them through a process of adjudication, which was coming from the outside, and was independent, was something that they valued greatly.

After a few cases before the Board I concluded that there were in fact good purposes being served by the process of adjudication before the Board and that they had nothing to do with whether or not my client was going to be successful. I thought the process could be said to be working, as the important thing was that our community values freedom, and the right of people to be heard before that freedom is taken from them.

I thought it wrong to judge the success of the system, then, on the success of the people who appealed successfully against decisions they did not like, because time and time again very intelligent people were doing that, knowing that they most certainly would fail. Also, there is no doubt in my mind that any organisation, no matter what the organisation, has the capacity to make mistakes, to be overworked, to not look at things properly. In the mental health sphere that organisation, being the hospital, is responsible for the treatment of vulnerable patients; over time a lackadaisical attitude may develop. We need some mechanism that puts that possibility to one side. In such a

---

38. Dr Neville Barber, PhD thesis, 6.2.2.

context, reviews, even in hopeless cases, are a useful device. The psychiatrist is aware that their notes will be scrutinised and questions will be asked. Bringing everything out in the open is a good idea.

I therefore left with an appreciation of the importance of the Mental Health Law Centre and the vital role that the Mental Health Review Board had in the scheme of things. As far as the appearances before the Board were concerned, that was always a matter of great privilege and pride for me. The Board treated the clients with dignity and respect, regardless of the merits of what was being said. The Board had the sophistication and knowledge of mental health to know that sometimes people will be saying absurd things, but you don't discount that necessarily. To the Board's credit, I thought it also very important that it wasn't patronising with people by trying to create the appearance of an interest in what was obviously a point that could not go any distance at all and then simply come down against that person. I also applaud the open-door policy of letting family and people in.

Criminal trial

I shall give just one example in a criminal law case of where I considered that I stepped outside the traditional role of a barrister. Peter faced serious charges. The State's case was that his presence during the crimes assisted others to actually commit the crimes. At the time of the alleged offence he was close to 'living on the streets' and had very poor education and would have been very frightened when appearing in Court. I sat through parts of other cases with him. I had him also believe that the jury were going to listen to him. Before I spent time with him he thought he had no chance as no-one would listen to a 'street kid'. He was certain they would not accept that he was only at this terrible place because the alternative was under a bridge where he would be attacked by as he put it 'the low life'. I got him to believe that he had a real chance. I also stressed that Australians believe in giving someone a "fair go" as I knew this would appeal to Peter's sensibilities.

An interesting aspect of this case was that one of the investigating police officers said under oath that in his view Peter should not have been charged. Peter has now got a good job, a young daughter and a lovely wife.

This is what Peter said of the experience:

" ... After being through what I have been through, I am a changed man. Though, I believe, had it not have been for your efforts, I would most likely have not been open to the experience and as such probably wouldn't have been affected.

This is to say, generally I (and I believe most people) by default do not let things emotionally affect me and by doing so I may have missed some important lessons along the way. It has been a very liberating(?) experience in that before I had this 'run-in', I saw very few consequences of my actions to be affecting anyone other than myself. For example when you took the time to visit courts and show me jurors, accused persons, judges, lawyers etc, I had never seen a trial before. I did not know what to expect and certainly would not have kept an active interest in the proceedings as they (quite frankly) were boring as midday tv.

But you showed me I needed to keep an interest in everything. I remember you testing me about what time I might have witnessed an event and explaining to me that the slightest slip up can end up looking very bad in my favour. Was it

2:00, was it 3:00? Had I missed a simple detail like that, I may have been put on the spot by the prosecution and for this I thank you, as I continue to apply this ethos(?) in my life today....

During the trial you conducted yourself excellently, in fact you hardly said anything. I might have been worried had we not spent so much time together previously. I believe this was because you needed to know that I understood our case theory so that I didn't look perplexed if you said something I might not have agreed on. This most likely contributed to the strength of our case."

It would be difficult to see how a barrister working in the field of criminal law could be effective without a knowledge that he/she might be able to make their client confortable when appearing in court.

If a barrister is representing someone who does decide to plead guilty to drug charges, it is difficult for me to see how a barrister equipped with only a 'traditional skill set' will be of much value to the client — except in a very limited sense.

Early plea of guilty

Except in rare cases, an early plea of guilty should result in a recognisable penalty discount. The extent of that discount, however, will vary according to the circumstances of the particular case. Nevertheless it must be recognisable in the sense that the penalty imposed must be objectively seen to be below that which its criminal gravity would otherwise demand. This factor weighs heavily in the changing role of a barrister when advising a client. Prior to this rule of discount, a client could proceed to trial with no threat of further penalty for doing so. A poorly advised client will be disappointed in a barrister who has not been very clear when advising of the practical benefits of a plea of guilty.

Conclusion

In litigation we are having to negotiate, or at least attempt to negotiate, an outcome before commencing proceedings. Even if proceedings are on foot, we must attempt a negotiated settlement before making any interim applications to the court. The Supreme Court rules require this. Mediation is also a requirement in every case. I consider that my role as a barrister requires me to be a good negotiator and to appreciate the importance that a negotiated settlement might have to a client. Often the value of the client's continuing relationship with the other side is worth far more than the amount in dispute. In this context it is also important to appreciate that there does not have to be an adversarial battle. As Moffitt and Bordone[39] explain in their *Handbook of Dispute Resolution*:

> "While negotiation is often assumed to be an adversarial battle focused on conflicting interests, this assumption overlooks two important points. First, some of the most intense conflicts are often fueled by identical interests — both parties want to feel fairly treated. Negotiators are often shocked to discover this, which usually leads them to explore why their perceptions of fairness differ. Second, the potential value inherent in shared or differing interests may be as large or larger than the value in dispute. In one commercial litigation, for example, the parties' anger about some-

---

39. Michael L Moffitt is an Assistant Professor and the associate director of the Appropriate Dispute Resolution Program at the University of Oregon School of Law. Robert C Bordone is the Thaddeus R Beal Lecturer on Law and the deputy director of the Harvard Negotiation Research Project at Harvard Law School.

thing that had happened in the past caused them not to realise that, as circumstances had developed, the potential value of a continuing relationship was more than ten times greater than the amount in dispute. When an outsider pointed this out, the parties suddenly found the motivation to find a settlement."[40]

In recent years we have seen courts redefining themselves—problem-solving courts such as the Drug Court emerging out of the then existing legislation; judges redefining themselves by becoming judicially active, often in the face of much criticism; parties being forced to negotiate and mediate before proceeding to trial; incentives being offered in criminal matters for an offender to plead guilty; legal educators becoming concerned with the dehumanising aspects of traditional legal education; and the growing emphasis on legislation to providing therapeutic results to those engaged in our justice system.

Given these changes it is timely to consider that barristers are also agents in the justice system and that we have a capacity to assist it to bring about a therapeutic result. This may involve us stepping outside the traditional definition of a barrister's role. Should we be criticised for doing so, we can point to all the other changes discussed in this paper to show that the adversarial system is also changing, and if we are to survive me must adapt to the needs of the people and to satisfy their hopes and aspirations. There will undoubtedly be critics of barristers who adopt changes in their traditional roles. As with the issues attached to judges being judicially active, there will be some persuaded by arguments that the traditional orthodox roles should not change. There are merits associated with the arguments on both sides of the debate. However just as with judicial activism, there is now scope for the exploration of new roles. Given the development of the principles of therapeutic jurisprudence and philosophical arguments in support of barristers who adopt wider roles, barristerial activists may point to sound reasons for making such radical changes.

B. Continental Approach

Christian Diesen,[*]
Neither Freedom Fighter Nor Saboteur—
Some Notes on the Role of the Defence Counsel in Sweden

From the Swedish point of view (and as a lawyer) it was interesting to watch the American TV series *The Practice*. The lawyers at the fictional firm of Donnel, Young & Frutt were frequently driven by a moral dilemma: You defend a murderer and get the jury to acquit him. Still you know that the client has not only committed the murder of which he was acquitted, but there is also reason to believe that he will kill again. Is it possible to break the client-attorney privilege or are you forced to live with the insight that the lives of others are in danger?

The series presented variations on the same theme: A person whom the defence attorney knew was guilty of a major crime received a verdict of not guilty due to the fact that the lawyer found some formal errors during the investigation, e.g. violations of the

---

40. A publication of the Program on Negotiation at Harvard Law School; Jossy-Bass 2005 at p 281.

* Christian Diesen is a professor of Procedural Law in Stockholm University.

Miranda formula. Or a person was convicted in spite of the well-founded suspicions of the defence lawyer that the real perpetrator was another person, whose identity could not be revealed because of ethical reasons or the wishes of the defendant.

The question is whether these dramatized ethical issues have more than an academic, theoretical interest, if they have any bearing on a lawyer's professional life in Sweden.[1] Everything is bigger in the USA, even the moral dilemmas.[2]

In this article I will present some ideological aspects of the role of the defence counsel in Swedish law and discuss whether the lawyer could or should act from a proactive or therapeutic perspective. The purpose is not to give the full picture nor to deliver general recommendations, but rather to illustrate the discussion with some situations where the Swedish defence lawyer has good reason to reflect upon the consequences of their work. During this discussion the reader should be aware of the basic facts that Sweden has a procedural system within the continental tradition, with a mixed court (no jury), free production and evaluation of evidence and with the possibility to have a criminal case examined in two instances.[3]

Acquittal at any cost?

When a practicing Swedish lawyer meets students, the most common question they ask is: How can you defend someone who denies the crime but confesses it to you? The lawyer answers that such a situation never happens in real life. If the client has decided to deny his guilt, he will never confess to his lawyer, because he realizes that he will get a poorer defence in that case, and so does the lawyer. The function of the defence counsel is to serve the defendant's wish to be acquitted. It is crucial for a good performance in court not to know the truth—professionalism does not require it either.[4]

Just like in the USA, the focus on the role of the defender in the Swedish debate is on the boundaries—to what limits can the defence counsel expand their efforts to free the suspect? But it happens, occasionally, that the issue of the defender's role is lifted to a higher and broader level. An opinion expressed in that discourse is that the defence counsel can be regarded as a servant of the law in a major concept and that 'the function of the defender is constituted as much for the state as for the defendant'.[5] The rationale behind this reasoning is that the existence of a defender guarantees the upholding of the principles of the procedure—like 'equality of arms' and 'contradiction'—and the truth-finding method through cross-examination, but also, being a manifest expression of the civil rights of the constitution, promotes good justice. In that respect it

---

1. In the USA it is an IRL (= In Real Life) issue; the most famous case probably is the Lake Pleasant murders in 1974, in which the defence lawyers knew where the suspect-client had buried the victims but did not reveal it.

2. The attorney-client privilege is not as absolute in Sweden as it is in the USA, see Patricia Shaughnessy, "The attorney-client privilege. A comparative study of American, Swedish and EU law" (dissertation, Stockholm 2001).

3. A criminal case in the District Court is tried with one professional judge with three lay judges and in the Court of Appeal by three judges and two laymen. (The lay judges are elected for a period of four years by the political parties in the region). It should be noted that all verdicts leading to prison sentence can be taken to the Court of Appeal for a total review.

4. Whether this standard answer is an acquired attitude or not is difficult to say, but no Swedish lawyer will claim that he has to know the truth about the matter to do his job. Compare the statements of American lawyer Elliot Levine in *Utah v. Taylor* (Utah 1997), and see J. Frank, *Courts on Trial*, Princeton 1950, for further discussion about the matter of 'fight versus truth'.

5. Anne Robberstad, "Mellom tvekamp og inkvisisjon", ("Between duel and inquisition", dissertation, Oslo 1999) p. 105.

could be discussed whether the realization of the function could or should be extended towards a social responsibility, in which case the defence lawyer should look upon his or her function as a social reformer.

A crime represents a social conflict and if the grounds of the conflict are not eliminated, the conflict will probably continue and most probably lead to more conflicts, and more crimes will be committed. This statement is valid on a macro as well as on a micro level. If society is not able to diminish poverty, discrimination, drug abuse and other social and economic disadvantages, criminality will remain. The wider the social gaps, the greater the risk of (increased) criminality. If individuals convicted of crime do not receive help to handle the personal and social problems that caused or contributed to their crime, the risk of relapse is evident. The weaker the support, and the more severe the exclusion of criminals and drug addicts, the less is the chance that the individual criminal can be reintegrated (or integrated) into the community.

This means that *the primary interest of the defence counsel—from this social point of view—should not be the short-sighted aim of having the client acquitted at any cost, but to make him a member of the community*. The real target should be to help him to solve his conflicts and problems without committing these destructive, but also self-destructive, acts towards other citizens. In that long-term perspective, the verdict in a criminal case—no matter if it is a conviction or an acquittal—can be of a subordinate importance. An acquittal means that the defendant can return to his normal life situation. But if he was innocent he may feel violated by the system and those living in his environment may regard him as a criminal anyway ('no smoke without a fire'). If he had committed the crime but was given the benefit of the doubt in court, it is possible he learned a lesson, but it is more likely he will continue to commit crimes. Either he concludes that he is untouchable, or he sees no alternative to the life he is living. If the verdict was a conviction, he will not only be labelled as a criminal for the rest of his life, but a longer stay in prison will confirm his criminal identity. And what can be expected in that role is nothing else—as long as the correctional treatment is not based on real treatment and social support—but a continued criminal career after release from prison.

From the defendant's point of view, an impending verdict against him may look like a choice between all or nothing, between heaven or hell; either he will remain in the community or he will be excluded. But, as illustrated above, the effects of a criminal court case cannot be described in such a black and white manner. The solutions offered to someone accused of a serious crime consist of *different degrees of exclusion*. The defendant has often lost something already when he was prosecuted and as a consequence the natural strategy of the defence counsel will be to try to minimize the negative effects. If it is not possible to gain an acquittal, it is important to limit the damage suffered by the (suspected) perpetrator as a consequence of commission of the crime and the accusation. As a representative of the accused, the idea that you are in the middle of a situation made for bargaining seems inevitable. Especially for an American defence counsel, it is often crucial to try to prevent the defendant from losing everything. From a law-economics perspective it is much better to admit a misdemeanor than to risk prison for a felony, far better to admit a second-degree murder and take ten years in prison than to risk life in prison for 'murder one', and so on. But a crime of any importance is connected with personal losses for the accused—in many cases he will suffer loss for the rest of his life (while the defence counsel only has to live with the defeat until next case comes along). Regarding the defence as a struggle to win or lose is too rigid a way to look upon the task of the defence counsel. But regarding 'the second line of defence' only as a strategy to limit the time behind bars is also too rigid a way to look upon the mission.

The short-sighted perspective, the struggle for winning or losing the case, is the evident weakness of the traditional role of the defence counsel. And this is where the ideas of preventive law and therapeutic jurisprudence enter. Thinking proactively, the defence counsel can put his profession in a social context and thereby try to minimize the antitherapeutic effects of the process. Looking upon crimes as social conflicts and upon his own role as a therapeutic agent, the lawyer may accomplish better results and more permanent solutions. This does not mean that the lawyer has to become something of a social worker or psychiatrist. The main task still is to keep watch for the rights of the suspect, to represent his legal and personal interests in the proceedings and to question the evidence and the burden of proof, but more focus on the psycho-social situation and the needs of the defendant promotes more constructive solutions than does incapacitation and/or relapse.

Hired gun or moral agent?

A discussion about a proactive defence is similar—and connected—to the classical question of whether a defence counsel should act as a 'hired gun' or a 'moral agent'.[6] The *hired gun* handles the defence consequently in line with the wishes of the client, and in fulfilling that strategy is prepared to use any means within the law to reach this goal. In practice, this often means counsel making their own investigations to produce evidence in favour of the defendant and using the rules of the proceedings to prevent, delay or divert the course of justice. A *moral agent*, on the other hand, takes a more back-seat position, is more reluctant with his or her own investigation efforts, discusses alternative strategies for the defence with the client and tries to convince him to choose a realistic and ethical road. In court you may note the differences between the two schools in a more fact-based (hired gun) or more principle-based (moral agent) argumentation. A hired gun normally goes at full indignant speed in all his or her deliberations (to make at least the client satisfied), while a judge from the emotions behind the speech can read to what extent the moral agent believes in his or her own arguments.

With some generalization, most American lawyers represent the ideal of the hired gun, while most Swedish lawyers represent the model of the moral agent. But during the last decade the members of the Swedish Bar Association have become more focused on issues of civil rights (such as fair trial and due process) than before, probably as a result of the increasing impact of the European Convention on Human Rights and the precedents of the European Court. During the same period—and probably with some connection—the 'American style' has become more common amongst Swedish lawyers. Alternative investigation efforts and a more categorical rhetoric have become more frequent, and criticism against the work of police and prosecutors has grown.

The reason Swedish defenders have historically felt obliged to accept the role of moral agent (and the reason for the upcoming criticism as well) is to be found in the formation of the criminal procedure in Sweden. The crime investigation phase is inquisitorial and is performed by a prosecutor with the duty to be objective, i.e. with the obligation also to investigate circumstances and collect evidence in favour of the suspect. As a consequence there is (supposed to be) no need for investigative actions by the

---

6. This dichotomy is discussed in a Swedish dissertation; Lena Ebervall, "Försvararens roll" ("The role of the defence counsel"), Lund 2002.

defence, and all expert witnesses in a trial will (normally) be called by the prosecutor.[7] The role of the defence counsel is to question, not to produce, evidence.

A major problem is that even this limited function of scrutiny cannot be fulfilled in most criminal cases. Defence lawyers are appointed by the court, and as the courts are not involved in the investigation phase unless the suspect is taken into custody for more than three days, defence counsel are seldom appointed during the preliminary investigation. In the case of detention, the suspect will always have the support of a lawyer (funded by the state), but in other cases the court has discretion over the need for a public defender.[8] In most cases the decision will be that no defender is needed—even if the case goes to trial[9]—which leads to the fact that a majority of the criminal cases in Sweden are tried without a defence counsel.[10].

Another reason why the role of the defender is limited in Sweden is that *the Swedish criminal procedure prohibits plea bargaining*. As a result of this rule, many trials proceed in spite of the existence of a confession and/or other overwhelming evidence against the defendant.[11] This way of proceeding—or the absence of an alternative—has led to a situation today where more than 94% of all prosecutions lead to conviction. That high a conviction rate might be explained by poor or lacking defence, but the main reason is that in most cases—also in cases with a defence counsel appointed—the evidence against the suspect is so strong that a defender has an impossible mission on the question of guilt. A Swedish prosecutor is obliged to prosecute if he can prove that a crime has been committed, but at the same time he is forbidden to prosecute if he cannot expect criminal liability to be proven beyond reasonable doubt.[12]

This means that prosecutors (as a principle, there are exceptions in practice) only take clear-cut cases to court and that defence counsel often have to set the question of reasonable doubt aside and concentrate on giving arguments against a prison sentence (or to make the time in prison as short as possible). In Swedish practice the difference between the hired gun and the moral agent therefore should not be exaggerated; the former is more active, the latter more passive—but both are focused on avoiding the worst.

What is gain, what is loss?

Considering the actual situation, the criminal trial in Sweden is no longer a duel between two parties, as it was at the time when criminal charges were taken to court by private persons.[13] In fact we are now closer to the feudal situation in Europe before the

---

7. The defence lawyer can make requests to the district attorney (DA) about elements of the investigation or for expert assistance. If the DA refuses, the defender can seek a court order for this investigation.

8. An appointment depends on the severity of the crime, the evidence, the complexity of the matter, the probable sanction and the suspect as a person; a young person denying a crime and who risks prison certainly has better chances of having a defence counsel than a middle-aged person risking a fine for a denied misdemeanor.

9. A suspect can always employ a private defence lawyer, but this is very unusual as it is expensive (and no insurance is available to cover the costs). All Swedish criminal barristers work as public defenders; only occasionally are they are employed privately.

10. If the trial is to be performed without a defence counsel, the role of the prosecutor changes from an adversarial one to a more neutral, objective role.

11. The suspect of a petty crime has the possibility to admit the charges and to be fined by the prosecutor without a trial, but in these cases, defence counsel very seldom appear.

12. If a prosecution is filed and it appears that the prosecutor did not have 'probable cause', he himself can be sentenced to prison for 'unjust prosecution'.

13. Before the seventeenth century there was no public prosecution in Sweden—all trials (civil and criminal) had to be initiated by a plaintiff.

French revolution.[14] The suspect who was brought into the court of the local nobleman knew that he would be convicted. The grounds of this deterministic court justice are no longer, as in the feudal era, that the court serves as a direct instrument of arbitrary repression. The reason is that the resources for crime prevention and crime investigation are not sufficient. Most police reports never lead to an investigation, but only serve as formal fulfilment of conditions for the victim's insurance claim. Most police investigations started will be closed with the justification 'no result', and even in those cases where the investigation has led to an identified suspect, most cases will be closed with the justification, 'crime cannot be proven'.

This case selection process, in which the police force steers its resources towards the most serious criminality, also has the consequence of social selection. In practice, it means that a socially well-adapted citizen can commit a crime without being punished. If the act was not committed *in flagrante*, if the evidence is weak from the start, the case sooner or later will be closed. But if the suspect is an ex-convict the investigation will continue—it is worth using the resources on that case as the police can expect a prosecution and a conviction. The odds can also be favourable if the suspect is an unemployed immigrant or a drug-addict. In short, the criminal procedure in Sweden today works, just as in the feudal times, as a socio-political sorting-mechanism—persons not wanted within the community will be excluded.

The development into this situation has been evident since the beginning of the 1990s and the result is that *the very focus of the criminal procedure has been dislocated from the court trial to the investigation phase.* If a prosecution in most cases (at least when the crime is minor) in reality means conviction, the task of the defence counsel becomes different from the role of the 'dueller'. Only exceptionally can the successful cross-examination of a witness or a rhetorical pleading on reasonable doubt influence the outcome. Certainly there are some types of cases, e.g. financial and sexual offences, where the acquittal rate is as high as 20–25 %, but on the other hand this means (considering the general conviction rate) that the chances that the client will be acquitted are minimal in most other cases, e.g. assault and theft. The obvious risk with these bad odds is that the trial will be a predestined ceremony, as the judges know that the prosecutor only brings clear cases to court, and they will have the prejudice to assume that the verdict will be a conviction. Another, likewise obvious, risk is that the defence lawyers become defeatist.

The result of this development is that a Swedish defence lawyer who wants to do a good job for his client (and not only put up a 'show'), must try to be appointed to the case as soon as possible. Of course, as long as the prosecutors are so extremely restrictive in their probing of the possible charges many suspects will escape punishment without any effort by a defence lawyer, but if winning a criminal case in court is only a remote possibility, a good defence performance often means 'killing the case' at an early stage. By launching an alternative hypothesis as soon as the suspect is brought in for interrogation, the defence counsel can drive the prosecutor to the conclusion that it is better to close the case than to continue the investigation. Here is one more reason—the most important— why many Swedish defenders have started to work in a more American way.

---

14. The courts of Sweden (and Finland, then a part of Sweden) were less influenced by the feudal system than were courts in other European countries (as the farmers of Sweden always had political power strong enough to resist the king and the nobility) and there was no urge for jury reform in the nineteenth century (while all other countries introduced the jury system in criminal cases). See C. Diesen, *Lekmän som domare* (*Lay Judges*), Stockholm 1996.

The problem is that the defence counsel enters the picture too late, when there already is a prosecution decided. In practice this means that it is only in cases concerning major crimes and with the suspect detained, that the defence counsel has a realistic possibility of influencing the police investigation.

The best material result a Swedish defence counsel can accomplish seems to be to have the case closed before prosecution—in cases of petty crime, there will never be a counsel appointed and if a more severe crime is prosecuted, one can count on a conviction. As a professional function it appears a destructive one (or like being a member of an intellectual fire-brigade) and the question is whether it is possible to develop any therapeutic ambitions in that function. There is a risk that the lawyer contributes to the social sorting that the prosecutorial restrictiveness implies. Wealthy people, who realize how much importance the participation of a lawyer can have at an early stage, employ a private defence attorney who enters to 'obstruct' the investigation through objections towards the work of the police, demands towards the prosecutor and instructions towards the client.[15] Most suspects, who do not realize this and/or cannot afford a lawyer, have to rely on hope or confidence that their case still will end up in the growing pile of closed cases.[16]

The issue in this context is *whether it is acceptable that most crimes are never solved, and even if this failure is in the best interests of the suspect.* If the crime-solving process at a macro level works as a social exclusion apparatus, where the main purpose is to exclude persons not wanted in the community (because of what they have done or what they can be expected to do in the future), it should be essential for suspects not to be labelled as criminals, sorted out, and in worst cases, be incapacitated. The threatening punishment is, at least in a country like Sweden where the length of time in prison is fairly short for most crimes,[17] not the primary danger but the ultimate expression of that sorting mechanism.

For a defence counsel it therefore should be important, in the interests of the client, not only to focus on what has happened in the past (the crime), the strength of the evidence (the question of guilt) and the advantages of the defence within the rules of the proceedings (due process), but also upon the consequences of the suspicion and a possible conviction. How is a feeling of being an outsider created and how can it be repaired? When is a criminal identity so stable that it can hardly be altered? When and how is it possible to succeed in rehabilitation?

When the most important part of the defence work is performed during the investigation phase, trying to prevent the case from reaching trial, the defence counsel may also prevent the suspect from being labelled as a criminal—which can be a major gain in itself—but it also implies that the incitement for a positive change in life can be lost. Even if a punishment seldom works as it is supposed to, as a means of improvement for the individual, the lack of consequence could have a negative impact.[18]

In some cases, e.g. concerning crimes like child 'disciplining' and shop-lifting, the police report itself can function as a warning and a starting-point of correction. The

---

15. Introducing a private lawyer at a stage where, according to the police, there is no need for a defender can have a backlash effect and strengthen their suspicions.
16. Approximately 80% of all reported crimes (1.3 million per year) never lead to prosecution (or to imposing a fine).
17. Murder can lead to a life sentence (meaning 16–22 years in practice) but 10–12 years is normal, drug trafficking warrants 12–14 years in prison, but for example for armed robbery or rape the criminal law stipulates 4–6 years as the standard sentence. Parole is given (to all) after serving two-thirds of the sentence period.
18. That a prosecution in itself can have a negative effect has been discussed above.

fact that the offender escaped justice this time does not mean that the same thing will happen next time around. On the contrary there is a notable possibility that he will be prosecuted and punished if reported another time. Other reports, concerning for example, violence against women or other violent crimes, will not have any preventive effects at all. The criminal acts are so closely connected to a certain personality and a certain way of life that the probability is high the offender will repeat his actions. Even higher is the probability if the crime is connected with drugs and the circumstances in which the offender has to commit crime to support his addiction.

The concrete questions for a defence counsel with the ambition to act in a proactive way are: Am I responsible for breaking or not breaking the criminal behaviour of my client? Should I act even if the case is dismissed? *How* can I act and react?

Truth wins in the long run?

A prerequisite for breaking criminal habits normally is that crimes are admitted, at least partly. If the client claims that he is completely innocent it would be difficult for the defence lawyer to get the client to admit that he has a problem. Whether he is convicted or acquitted, the defendant has to admit his responsibility for the crime to give his defender the opportunity to help him from relapsing. Therapeutic and rehabilitating efforts, like cognitive therapy or anti-drug treatment, seldom work unless the person needing help admits his or her problems. Even if it is possible for the lawyer to help their client by pleading for sanctions combined with cure,[19] he or she can seldom give any aid to those who are acquitted. The acquittal (or the lack of prosecution) becomes a 'receipt' that is interpreted as 'no problem' and a 'licence' to go on as before. But if the client does not change his attitudes or life patterns there is a great risk that he will become worse next time around. That is why the lawyer must ask himself if the client would be better served—in the long run—if he confesses.

This issue—the making of a confession—is often linked to procedural advantages, especially to a discount in the punishment tariff. A problem in Swedish law within this aspect is that *a confession does not pay off*. The sanctions of a crime are exclusively decided by its 'punishing value', i.e. its seriousness, severity and consequences according to penal law. No consideration is taken of personal factors, with the exceptions of very young or very old offenders.[20] Furthermore a relapse leads to a more severe punishment than a first time offence. If you report yourself to the police, you can have a small reduction of the punishment, but not if someone else has made the report. Neither is a reduction of the penalty given if you provide the investigation with important information (for example, by giving evidence against your co-offenders), nor is there any immunity for crown-witnesses.

At present a commission at the Swedish Justice Department is working on a report on the possibility of giving a reduction of the penalty if there is a confession,[21] but before such legislation is in force, the defence has nothing to offer the prosecution in a negotiation. Therefore there are no such negotiations—quite the contrary, they are forbidden. In practice some informal talks between the prosecutor and the defence counsel

---

19. See below (under "How to promote a confession?") for examples.
20. The roots of this policy, founded in 1989, is a reaction against the so called 'treatment ideology' tried in the 1970s and 1980s, where the sanction was determined by a prognosis of the chances of social rehabilitation. This in turn led to injustices from a class perspective—offenders from the lower classes received prison sentences while offenders from the upper-classes were paroled.
21. Since the beginning of the twentieth century the confession has had a minor or no influence on determination of punishment in Sweden.

can take place, but most of the time the bidding is unilateral; the prosecutor 'informs' the suspect that he can leave custody or meet his girlfriend if he confesses. It also happens that the prosecutor 'threatens' with a prosecution of a major crime if a minor crime is not admitted and, of course, the defence produces a tactical confession of a minor crime to avoid prosecution for a major crime.

The fact that the confession has such a reduced influence on the Swedish crime procedure has some advantages, but certainly also some disadvantages. Amongst the advantages there is the improved possibility of avoiding false or wrongful confessions (e.g. that the suspect confesses to avoid the risk of being sentenced for a more severe crime, which is an obvious risk to consider in a system of plea bargaining and long prison sentences), that all crimes are handled equally in court and that a confession is regarded and scrutinized as any other evidence.[22] Amongst the disadvantages we find higher costs, a lower clear-up rate—as confessions do not pay off the 'natural' defence is denial, which means that the police have to prove the crime without any help from the defence—and that the suspect usually lacks all motivation to make any contribution to the investigation.

But the most important disadvantage is maybe to be found on another level—the ethical one. *If the criminal procedure does not promote the confession of a crime committed it also is counter to the importance of admitting guilt*, to the moral obligation of taking responsibility for your own acts and the consequences of these actions. Not giving the confession a part in the solving of a criminal case certainly produces some anti-therapeutic effects. The most essential effect is of course that the victim will not have full clarity and rehabilitation, but it can be negative for the defendant as well, not to reveal his involvement and intention. Maybe he has to live with a burden of guilt for the rest of his life.[23] That is why a defence counsel has to ask himself if this long-term ethical perspective should not be a part of his judicial strategy for the defence, if it should not be a part of his mandate to examine the need of the client to lift the burden of guilt from his shoulders.

Of course this is a very difficult and sensitive commission. If even the defender, his own representative, starts to question a firm denial it could be interpreted as treason and lead to a gap in confidence so large that the mandate of the counsel cannot be executed. The defence counsel cannot function as an extra judge and even less as an extra prosecutor, but has to be loyal to the client in spite of the crime and attitude. Still there are limits to this loyalty.

Ten years ago some members of the Swedish Bar Association launched a campaign in favour of 'convicted but innocent' men in incest cases. They claimed that judges had too strong a confidence in children and their mothers in these cases, that the standards of proof had been lowered and that the consequences were that numerous innocent men had been wrongly convicted for sexual offences towards children. There was not any proof of these allegations,[24] but these lawyers entered a debate—which already was at stake within the behavioural sciences—with a categorical stand-point as a general support for all suspects and convicts of child sexual abuse. As the action was combined with active recruiting of clients in this field, it could be regarded simply as a unsound

---

22. It should be noted that the defendant is never heard under oath in the Swedish criminal trial (nor the victim, only other witnesses).
23. This burden—and whether it is a myth or not—is discussed below.
24. One factor to mention though is that, between 1993 and 2004, eight convicted men were awarded a new trial, and were acquitted since the victim had withdrawn or changed her testimony.

marketing campaign against more moderate lawyers. The more serious effect, however, was that many suspects (and those convicted against their denial) were persuaded that they were victims of a moral panic, and in this manufactured 'witch-hunt', confession could never be an option.

At this point, Madeleine Leijonhufvud, Professor of Penal Law (whose textbook on ethics is used in legal education at the universities),[25] entered the debate and claimed that those lawyers 'who have made their business to get suspects of incest acquitted may, in their ardour, commit ethical mistakes in disfavour of the client'.[26] As an example, Leijonhufvud used a case in which a man had admitted that a nine-year old girl had held his penis, but where the defence counsel secured his acquittal with the 'explanation' in court that it was the girl who had taken the initiative, that she had put her hand into his trousers and that his penis was never erect. According to Leijonhufvud 'half a confession' during the police investigation was transformed in court—by the strategy of the defence counsel putting the blame on the child—into a 'life lie'.

This argument was met with very divergent reactions amongst lawyers; some did agree, while others spoke about 'biased humbug from the academic world' and firmly pointed out that 'the only mission of the defence counsel is to stand up for the rights of the suspect'.[27]

During the past decade there have been some surges of that debate, but it is not adequate to say that in Sweden there is an ongoing movement towards a more ethical or holistic view of the role of the defence lawyer. The 'classical', more limited, view of the defender as a 'freedom fighter' is as dominant as it was ten years ago.[28] Whether it can be in the interest of the suspect to confess is merely a question of strategy: Is it possible to gain anything by confessing? Can it lead to a more lenient sanction? As the answer to that question in Sweden often is a clear 'no', the interest of raising the question is limited.

To make it interesting for the defence counsel to work with 'truth' as the goal of the process, there probably is a need for some evidence that truth is profitable, in other words, that it could be in the interest of the suspect to confess. Furthermore it must be possible to combine a long-term strategy in the best interests of the client with the role of the defence, both in procedure (within the adversary system) and in practice (meaning that there are knowledge and resources for curative efforts). Considering the first part, knowledge, there is no research in Scandinavia upon the relevance of a criminal confession from a psychological point of view, stating for example that a confession produces a higher quality of life. It is a general postulate, based on Christian values and cultural presumptions, that only a person who takes responsibility for his evil actions (and even better if he asks for forgiveness) is able to live a life of well being and happiness, but if this is a need amongst criminals, and what effects the confession produces, has not been studied.[29] This lack of research is probably connected to the methodological problem of finding an adequate control group—guilty persons who decided not to

---

25. M. Leijonhufvud, *Etiken i juridiken* (*Ethics in law practice*), 3rd edition, Stockholm 2005.
26. *The Journal of the Swedish Bar Association* (*TSA*) nr 5 1995 p. 12.
27. R. Fröman in TSA nr 6 1997 p. 18.
28. In theory the moral agent is performing another role than that of a freedom fighter, but in (Swedish) practice the professional standpoint of the moral agent it is more connected to a an attitude of judicial realism than to a moral or social guidance.
29. There is some research, however, on factors influencing the tendencies of confessing or denying, showing for example that a more humane, therapeutic attitude by police officers promotes confessions while an authoritarian style prevents them, see Ulf Holmberg, 'Police interviews with victims and suspects of violent and sexual crimes', (dissertation) Stockholm 2004.

confess—and therefore the general assumption that 'you feel better if you tell the truth' is used as a gauge for criminals as well. However, this 'catharsis' myth about purification through truth-telling could perhaps be reduced to an ideological justification of condemning, an expectation for surrender and a hope for the universal goodness of mankind. Perhaps most criminals do not feel like Raskolnikov but are comfortable with denying their guilt? The empathy they were lacking in committing the crime they are lacking still, and if they feel sorry for somebody, they feel sorry for themselves.

Anyway, the 'burden of guilt'—the assumption that you feel better if you confess—is not in general strong enough to make Swedish defence counsel consider it. But they should, and not only in cases where the evidence is too strong to evade conviction. *If there is a glimpse of empathy in the suspect's mind it is better to break the criminal career as soon as possible, so as not to make the burden too heavy in the future.*

When it comes to the practical possibilities for a Swedish lawyer to work in a wide spectrum of law and psychology there are limitations, too. As almost all defence lawyers are financed by the state and are paid per working hour from their appointment in a case until the end of the main hearing (according to a fixed tariff), there are no resources available for psychological or other curative consultations, nor for work after the trial. In other words, there is no space for other contributions than strictly judicial ones—unless you have very strong ambitions to widen the role of the defender to a more therapeutic approach. Most defenders will have a final conversation with the client to explain the consequences of the verdict, e.g. the risk of conviction if prosecuted for a new offence (if acquitted) or the possibilities to appeal (if convicted), but not many have the opportunity (on a pro bono-basis) to discuss his or her life situation. Such an ambition by lawyers met by supplementary funding by the state would probably be cost-efficient as well as pro-active at a macro level.

How to promote a confession and/or a long-run choice?

The defence counsel is often put in a position where he or she has to make strategic choices that will influence the future life of the client. Such a situation occurs when it could be possible for a defendant to receive treatment instead of a prison sentence—in Sweden drug addicts can have a sentence of probation connected to rehabilitation instead of a prison sentence,[30] and persons with a severe mental disturbance can never be sentenced to imprisonment, only to compulsory forensic psychiatric treatment (with no time limit and with the court as a release board).[31] In these circumstances some conflicts between the evaluations of the counsel and the wishes of the client can emerge. Most of the time, they agree that the better option is to have treatment instead of imprisonment, but it is not as self-evident that a mentally disturbed person wants to be classified as mentally ill. On the other hand there may be some clients who want that classification as the time in treatment will be more lenient and probably shorter than a prison sentence. When it comes to these choices the attitude of the client towards the crime can have a major impact. The drug addict who shows regret and a will to with-

---

30. A person can, after a socio-medical examination (decided by the court), be sentenced to compulsory treatment if the alternative is prison. If the treatment plan is not followed the sentence can be reversed to imprisonment. (A treatment sentence can also be combined with imprisonment up to 3 months or with civil services). The examination is performed before the trial, but serves only as an alternative sanction after a conviction.

31. A commission at the Justice Department proposed in 2004 that mentally disturbed offenders should be sentenced to prison as well and that their care should be provided in prison, but still no proposal for a change of law has been announced.

draw from his drug abuse certainly has a greater chance to be awarded rehabilitation than a defendant who is not able to express remorse and willingness to start anew. Therefore the defence counsel often has to coach his client into an attitude in court that expresses a personal conviction that the rehabilitation will be a success. The mentally disturbed client, on the other hand, may have to be persuaded to choose the alternative of rehabilitation (in cases where the lawyer has a definite opinion about the mental status of the client) and it can happen, in more extreme cases, that the counsel feels obliged to oppose the wishes of the client and plead for rehabilitation when his client would prefer a prison sentence.

In these situations a lawyer with therapeutic ambitions must be sensitive to the desires of the client, but must also be prepared to react against these wishes in a motivating dialogue encouraging the suspect to look upon the consequences in a long-term perspective. Even if it is up to the client to decide in the end (except in some cases of mental illness), the defence counsel has to try to convince the client about the advantages of the alternatives, making sure that the short-sighted alternative does not win automatically.

Another—more unusual—situation that causes a conflict between the more holistic view of the defence counsel and the wishes of the suspect is when the client confesses and accepts punishment for a certain offence, but the defender suspects that the confession is made only to protect the real perpetrator. In that case the defender should not accept the confession but—in spite of the wishes of the client—question it, not only to the client but in court as well. The same position should be taken when a lawyer is forced to defend someone who does not want a defence (or wants to defend himself). In Sweden, a professional legal representative is regarded as necessary in cases that would lead to a longer imprisonment (or to compulsory forensic care), which means that defence counsel will be appointed in those cases against the will of the suspect. *Legal defence in criminal cases is not only a civil right but also a civil obligation*—and of course a defence forced upon a person can create open conflicts in court.

The Swedish defence lawyer is not short of moral dilemmas. But the most frequent situation where there is a conflict between the social interest of solution of a crime (a correct verdict) and the role of the defender probably appears during the preliminary investigation, and more specifically during *the interrogation of the suspect*. If a defence counsel is present during that interrogation—which in Sweden ordinarily depends upon the risk that the suspect will be held in custody[32]—moments will appear where the suspect is 'at risk' of talking too much and will incriminate himself. A skilled interrogator perhaps can drive him into an emotional state where he is prepared to confess. If an opening appears, a defender can serve as a guard and eliminate 'negative' effects by saying, 'You don't have to answer that question', or asking for a pause in the interrogation. Through this 'obstruction', a pause and new instructions to the client, the defence counsel can make sure that the chance of the prosecutor knowing the truth of the matter never reappears.

This responsibility is heavy. Surely the defence counsel can justify his behaviour by referring to his function as a guardian of civil rights, but the effect of the intervention is not limited to concealing the truth about the event, but also to determine the destiny of several persons involved. A 'sabotage' of the investigation may be considered as a professional duty towards the suspect, but at the same time it can be regarded as a hostile and cynical act against the victim. Before interrupting an interrogation—consciously

---

32. See above.

or mechanically—the defence counsel should consider the consequences and ask himself if the intervention in question really is a reasonable element of his work for the defence. It is one thing to protest against undue methods of interrogation or to ask complementary questions; it is another to use the privileged position of the defence attorney to ruin the possibilities of clearing up a crime.

As I described earlier, it is difficult in Sweden to have a defence counsel appointed at the early stage of the investigation. The reason is not only the general restrictions (when the crime does not lead to detention) but also that the condition for an appointment is 'probable cause'. As a result many police interrogations are performed without any lawyer present.[33] However, *sex offences* represent an exception. As a suspicion of a sex offence is considered as highly socially stigmatising, it is not regarded as fair to the suspect to launch an allegation against him without the protection of a defence counsel by his side. This routine implies that many suspects will not be interrogated at all (as the suspicion has not reached the level of 'probable cause') and that the suspects interrogated will deny their involvement (if there is no overwhelming evidence such as DNA, witnesses or pictures).[34] A short conversation between counsel and suspect before the interrogation with the instructions, 'If you don't confess, the police will never have enough evidence to convict you' (child sexual abuse), or 'Admit intercourse if you had it, say she consented if you got that impression' (rape), will be enough to kill the investigation in most cases. The word of the abused child or the raped woman will not be enough to put the guilt of the suspect 'beyond reasonable doubt'.

The case will be closed and the defence counsel satisfied—he reached his goal to get his client off the hook. What will happen next, if the perpetrator returns to his family and abuses the child again or rapes his next date, is not the lawyer's problem. But should it not be?

Even if there are other players, especially within the social services, who have to guarantee the welfare and security of all citizens, especially the children's, the lawyer should be aware of his power: A criminal case is not a game to win or lose. The work of a defence counsel influences the lives of other people—a gain manifested in the acquittal of his client can be a fatal loss to others. The lawyer has to be careful in his fight for the interests of his client and realize that he is *a tool in other people's social conflicts*. Without knowledge and insights about socio-economic factors, environmental circumstances and psychological motives, the role of the defender is reduced to the role of a saboteur.

The interests of the victim are contrary to the interests of the defendant?

It is a common understanding, and also within jurisprudence, that if someone wins someone else will lose. The law procedure thus can been seen as a *zero sum game*[35] and in a criminal trial this means that if the guilty person goes free the victim has lost. And, consequently, the victim wins if the offender is convicted. Even though some lawyers tend to look upon trials this way, it is too much of a one-dimensional image.

---

33. Nor they are informed about the right to remain silent.
34. Of the *prosecuted* sex offence cases in Sweden during 2005–2006 only 16.4% contained a confession, in rape cases only 5.7%. In the *reported* cases in Stockholm 2004 concerning child sexual abuse, less than 5% of the offences were admitted. An analysis combining these parameters demonstrates that only approximately 10% of the reported sex crimes will be prosecuted (that is, the cases with a confession plus a minor part of the cases with a denial).
35. See, for instance, L. Sebba, *Third Parties. Victims and the Criminal Justice System*, Columbus 1996.

In many cases both parties lose no matter the outcome of the trial. In other cases, the victory is at most limited or temporary for one of the parties while the loss is permanent for the other. *In the best cases, both parties leave the process in a better position than they had before the conflict.* For a lawyer with a therapeutic mind, the latter should be the load-star of his work.

In some civil cases, for example concerning custody of a child, this aim in practice signifies to avoid trial—with all probability a trial would not only cement the conflict between the parents but also damage the child. In other civil cases a settlement—and the road towards it—can be a solution that gives both parties insights about themselves and lead to positive effects in the future, while in other cases, for example, concerning damages caused by a certain product, it can be important to the plaintiff to have a successful claim, allowing others in the same situation to receive compensation too and stopping a dangerous activity. The proactive and therapeutic effects are not seldom dependent on the ability of the lawyer to put the litigation in a broader social (and economic) perspective.

In criminal cases the perspective should be the same. But as a criminal procedure rarely produces any positive effects in itself—destructive (repressing and punishing) as it is in its character—the task of the lawyer is more difficult. It is easy to look upon victory or loss as a question reduced to acquittal or conviction, much harder to make the process a new, constructive platform, not only for the defendant but also for the victim. Even if the lawyer is aware of the social perspective on a macro level—and as a background explanation of the crime—it is often difficult to use it as a functional tool in the actual case. But as a lawyer you can always try to accomplish a 'sense of justice'; that all the participants leave the trial with the impression that it was a due process, everybody got to speak and all-important facts were presented.

In creating this feeling of fairness the defence counsel has to be aware of the fact that if he limits the defence to the welfare of the defendant he can cause harm to others. Attacking the testimony of the victim certainly is a crucial part of the defence counsel's duty, but that duty does not imply it is legitimate to discredit the victim as a person. The defence counsel must ask himself if the confrontation fulfils a legal aim or only serves to satisfy the need of the defendant to paint the victim black. Putting a moral guilt upon the victim by spreading prejudice in a rhetorical style does not serve justice. It is only a dramatization that causes trauma, maintains conflicts, encourages revenge, lowers the self-esteem and demonises the suspect in the eyes of the victim—and diminishes confidence in justice. Not violating the victim during the process by, for example, irrelevant discreditation during interrogation, should be an ethical standard of the therapeutic defender. Furthermore, there is no proof that a more humane appearance does not produce as good a result as the hostile one.[36] On the other hand, the purgatory of cross-examination expected by victims has an impact on the macro level, for example when it comes to reporting or not reporting a crime (especially sexual offences).

In Sweden there has recently been a debate about the ethics of the defence lawyer in encountering the victim in court, as a result of two cases drawn to public attention by the media. In the first case, a father was prosecuted for battering his 16-year-old daughter and the defence counsel argued that he should be excused with the statement 'that she was running around, dressed like a whore'. In the second case, the defence counsel held a brutal cross-examination with the victim about her sex life and drug habits,

---

36. Holmberg, "Police interviews" (2004).

when the charge against his client was kidnapping and procuring. The young woman had been drugged, abducted to a city 150 miles away, drugged again and sexually abused (as a prostitute) by several (other) men during one day. In this debate, it has been suggested that Swedish law should introduce some limitations in the cross-examination of rape victims,[37] but such a regulation is considered to violate the principles of free production and free evaluation of evidence.

This debate about defence ethics serves as a good illustration of the present situation in Sweden when talking about criminal procedure and the need for reforms. During the last fifteen years there has been a clear focus on victims' rights. Indeed one reason why most Swedish defence lawyers seem reluctant to take up a more therapeutic approach could be that they consider the broader perspective to be well guaranteed by the welfare system in itself, and also the balance in the process granted by the reform of 1988, which gives most victims a legal representative throughout the process. As soon as a crime against a person is committed, this victim can have a legal advisor, a lawyer funded by the state, appointed to them. This victim's counsel (målsägandebiträde) will appear on the same side as the prosecutor at trial and focus on the compensation claim, but within the bounds of their mandate is to see that the victim received the social and curative support needed.

In this situation, with two 'opponents', it maybe becomes even more natural for the defence counsel to concentrate upon the traditional defence work, disregard its negative consequences and reject a more holistic view upon the criminal procedure. At the same time, the improved position of the victim may produce more constructive long-term solutions in some cases, especially since many of the defence counsel (especially in smaller cities) also work as victim's counsel. A lawyer who one day represents a suspect and the next day a victim should be able to see the need of less short-sighted solutions than the ones that the trial can offer. Not least in cases where the criminal case is closed without prosecution, there is often a need for social or therapeutic measures in order to prevent future conflicts, future crimes. But not many lawyers in Sweden have the desire, time or competence to work that way. Nor is there a mediation process that could be used in these cases, which perhaps would be desirable. Not least in cases of violence against women, it is well-known that there exists a destructive relational pattern that has to be broken—if the woman withdraws the allegation it will probably result in a closed case, but also in a repeated offence.

Summary and conclusion

In Sweden there are many lawyers who shift between working as defence counsel and as victim's counsel. That is one of the reasons why there might be Swedish lawyers who have a more holistic view upon the outcomes of a criminal trial and work in a more therapeutic way, but you never hear about them. The debate about the role of the defender is dominated by the representatives of the more narrow-minded defence counsel ideals. In an aggressive tone, these members of the Bar repeat that it is always the wishes and the interests of the client that the counsel has to observe and follow. But even in that perspective, the lawyer must ask himself or herself: What is in the best interests of the defendant in the long run?

On the other hand: Everything is relative. Sweden probably provides a better platform for therapeutic jurisprudence than most other jurisdictions. The experience of the "treatment ideology" in the 70's and 80's at least created a consciousness of the links be-

---

37. Such rules have existed in the UK since 2000.

tween social situation and criminality. And as all Swedish lawyers are educated to be able to act as moral agents—and are well aware of the need for pro-active thinking to avoid relapses—it is natural for every defence counsel to plead for treatment instead of punishment. Any time there is an even remote possibility to prevent imprisonment—and thereby preventing further criminal acts—they will fight for that chance. The current "problem" is the tendency amongst defenders, starting some 10 years ago, to act as "hired guns", using the *unreflected* will of the defendant as the only gospel.

About the Editor

David B. Wexler is Professor of Law and Director of the International Network on Therapeutic Jurisprudence at the University of Puerto Rico in San Juan, Puerto Rico and Distinguished Research Professor of Law and Professor of Psychology at the University of Arizona in Tucson, Arizona.

In addition to *Rehabilitating Lawyers*, his books include: *Judging in a Therapeutic Key: Therapeutic Jurisprudence and the Courts* (with Bruce J. Winick, Carolina Academic Press, 2003), *Therapeutic Jurisprudence: Law as a Helping Profession* (with Dennis P. Stolle and Bruce J. Winick, Carolina Academic Press, 2000), *Law in a Therapeutic Key: Developments in Therapeutic Jurisprudence* (with Bruce J. Winick, Carolina Academic Press, 1996), *Essays in Therapeutic Jurisprudence* (with Bruce J. Winick, Carolina Academic Press, 1991), *Therapeutic Jurisprudence: The Law as a Therapeutic Agent* (Carolina Academic Press, 1990) and *Mental Health Law: Major Issues* (Plenum Press, 1981).

He received the American Psychiatric Association's Manfred S. Guttmacher Forensic Psychiatry Award; received the National Center for State Courts Distinguished Service Award; chaired the American Bar Association's Commission on Mental Disability and the Law; chaired the Association of American Law Schools Section on Law and Mental Disability; chaired the advisory board of the National Center for State Courts' Institute on Mental Disability and Law; was a member of the Panel on Legal Issues of the President's Commission on Mental Health; was a member of the National Commission on the Insanity Defense; served as Vice President of the International Academy of Law and Mental Health; received the New York University School of Law Distinguished Alumnus Legal Scholarship/Teaching Award; and served as a member of the MacArthur Foundation Research Network on Mental Health and the Law. He is an Honorary Distinguished Member of the American Psychology-Law Society, has been a consultant to the National Judicial Institute of Canada, and has served as a Fulbright Senior Specialist, lecturing on therapeutic jurisprudence in Australia and New Zealand. He has also addressed national audiences in the US, UK, Canada, Spain, Israel, Puerto Rico, and Chile; and his work has been translated to Spanish, Portuguese, Hebrew, and Urdu. Wexler wrote the first paper on therapeutic jurisprudence in 1987 and has worked exclusively in that area ever since.

Index

ABA Model Rule of Professional Conduct, 150
Aboriginal, 180, 352, 357, 361–363
Aboriginal communities, 357, 363
Aboriginal culture, 357
Aboriginal people, 357, 361–363
Acceptance of responsibility, 20, 29, 102
Acute cocaine addiction, 195, 197
Admission of guilt, 101–102, 113, 126, 203, 218, 230
Adolescent, 247, 329, 335–336, 341, 343–344, 347
Adolescent delinquent behavior, 341, 344
Adversarial advocacy, 56
Adversarial system, 53–54, 90, 261, 355, 357, 370
Adversarialism, 52, 60, 64, 85, 87–88, 147, 150
Adversary System, 4, 46, 48, 51–54, 57, 76, 108, 112, 379
Advocate, 14–15, 22, 40, 46, 48–49, 51, 54, 56, 82, 88, 104, 107, 109, 118, 127, 134, 151, 168, 179, 184, 207, 219, 263–265, 276, 283–284, 300–301, 328, 332–333, 335, 337, 339, 345–347, 349, 353–354, 358, 365
Affective advocacy, 328
Age-appropriate consultation, 341
Alcohol abuse, 181, 254
Alcoholism, 21, 105, 123, 166, 197, 204, 245, 247, 309–310
Allocution statement, 174–176, 178–180, 235
Alternative dispute resolution, 303–304, 306
American Bar Association's Model Rules of Professional Conduct, 126, 193
American lawyer, 371

Anti-therapeutic consequences, 7, 95, 99, 156, 161–162, 198, 291, 329, 356, 363
Anti-therapeutic effects, 365, 373, 378
Apology, 20, 23, 29–30, 102, 120–121, 133, 144, 155–156, 225–230, 310
Appeal, 13, 22, 30, 36, 38–40, 43, 104–107, 116, 167, 211, 217–218, 297, 299, 320–321, 368, 371, 380
Appellate court, 36, 38–40
Appellate lawyer, 39, 179
Assault, 30, 124, 167, 185–186, 226–227, 244, 252, 352, 363, 375
Attention Deficit Disorder, 187, 208, 210
Attorney-child interactions, 328
Attorney-child paradigm, 328, 334
Attorney-child relationship, 328, 336
Attorney-client dyad, 329, 331
Attorney-client interaction, 79
Attorney-client paradigm, 328, 331, 336–337
Attorney-client privilege, 265, 348, 371
Attorney-client relation, 23, 79, 88, 100, 104, 114, 121, 207, 296, 300, 327–329, 333–345
Australia, 16, 25, 144, 180, 230, 235, 243, 310, 351–358, 360–361, 363, 367
Australia's High Court, 360
Authoritarian lawyers, 331
Automatic sanctions, 62, 82
Autonomous decision-making, 255
Barrister, 351–359, 364, 366, 368–370
Barristerial activism, 360
Barrister's role, 355–356, 364, 370
Basic legal principles, 359
Behavior modification program, 59
Behavioral contract, 8, 18, 31, 33, 38, 103
Behavioral contracting, 18–20
Behavioral disorder, 309

Behavioral science theory, 304, 317
Bipolar, 187, 207–208
Brain damage, 188, 190
Brain Injury, 192, 208, 210, 226
Break and Enter, 185–186, 229
British model, 353
Bronx, 80, 106, 108, 116, 118, 125, 167, 261–262, 267, 269
Brooklyn, 51, 65, 118, 152, 296
Broward County Mental Health, 294
Burden of proof, 167, 206, 373
Bureau of Prisons, 41, 176, 239
Canada, 15–16, 171, 175, 180, 183, 185–186, 192, 225, 310, 351, 357
Canadian prison authorities, 187
Change agent, 23–24
Chicago, 199, 263–264
Child, 5, 14–15, 37, 44, 65, 68, 72, 97, 104, 106, 114, 134, 172, 183, 187, 210, 226, 234, 267, 308, 315, 326–349, 364–365, 376, 378–379, 382–383
Child advocates, 343, 346
Child Client, 327, 332
Child dependency, 308
Civil Jurisdiction, 356
Civil legal aid lawyer, 15
Civil legal service, 265, 346,
Civil right, 381
Client autonomy, 88, 114, 243–244, 333–334, 348
Client based practice, 259
Client decision-making, 90, 243–244
Client innocence, 243
Client Interview, 159, 335
Client-attorney privilege, 370
Client-centered, 18, 25, 52, 54, 56, 88, 107–108, 114, 118, 121–122, 131, 145, 149–150, 212, 244, 246–247, 251–253, 255, 257–258, 260, 267, 276, 288, 305, 309, 328, 331, 333–334, 336, 338–339, 343, 345
Client-centered approach, 88, 108, 114, 244, 246, 252–253, 255, 288, 309, 328
Client-centered counseling, 244, 246, 305, 309, 333, 343
Client-centered lawyering, 54, 88, 108, 122, 258, 343
Client-centered representation, 107–108, 122, 149, 212, 260

Client's guilty conscience, 228
Client's interest, 243, 359
Client's legal rights, 108, 219, 335
Client's progress, 181, 235
Client's rehabilitation, 310
Client-satisfaction, 328
Clinical depression, 194–195
Clinical education, 92, 108, 130, 164, 280, 282, 289, 292, 297, 302–303, 323
Clinical educator, 297
Clinical law, 21–22, 50, 100, 116, 144, 164, 303–304, 307, 311, 316–317, 323
Clinical law teaching, 304
Clinical legal education, 11, 20, 44, 92, 276–277, 280–281, 292, 304, 306, 315, 323
Coercion, 4, 20, 26, 35, 59–61, 104, 149, 331, 347
Cognitive capacity, 334, 338–340
Cognitive restructuring, 8, 34
Cognitively deprived, 166
Collaborative lawyer, 328, 333, 342
Collaborative model, 342–343
Communication Through Art, 265
Community Courts, 45, 51, 65–66, 146, 153, 171, 260
Community involvement, 262
Community service, 49–51, 59, 61, 64–66, 69, 73, 147–148, 184, 216, 219, 278, 315
Community support, 144, 151, 263, 278
Community-based system, 357
Compensation, 6–7, 48, 97, 336, 352, 356, 383–384
Compensation process, 356
Competence, 24, 50, 64, 87, 100, 115, 124, 126, 132, 139, 193, 214–215, 231, 244, 305, 325, 331, 340, 347, 384
Compliance, 7–8, 10, 12, 16, 19–20, 31, 33–36, 49, 61, 63, 71, 73, 95, 103, 121–122, 133–135, 138, 147, 149, 171, 181–182, 191, 199–200, 232, 239, 259, 312, 317, 320, 322, 338–339
Comprehensive law movement, 45, 97, 230, 282, 304
Conditional Bond, 194–195, 197, 203
Conditional discharge, 163–164, 168
Conditional release, 8, 17, 19–20, 40–42, 95, 104, 170, 315

INDEX 391

Confession, 211, 223–224, 347, 374, 377–382
Conflict-free representation, 338
Constitutional rights, 37, 48, 54, 77–78, 80, 98, 286, 328, 331, 334, 337–338, 343, 346–347
Constitutionality, 60, 148
Constrained discretion, 18, 170
Constructive solutions, 373
Contextual view, 55–56
Continental tradition, 371
Cooperative approach, 354
Cooperative effort, 29
COPAC, 195, 197, 201, 203, 205
Cost-effective, 275
Counseling techniques, 199, 306
Creative arraignment advocacy, 258
Creative conditions, 313
Creative drafting, 306
Creative lawyering, 308, 317
Creative alternatives to incarceration, 332, 345
Crime-solving process, 376
Criminal attorney, 163, 301
Criminal behavior, 14, 47–48, 66, 199, 245, 259, 310
Criminal Behaviour, 188–189, 377
Criminal defense advocate, 258
Criminal defense attorney, 43, 53, 55, 76, 110, 124, 126, 163, 165, 194, 197, 199, 244, 309–310, 317
Criminal defense paradigm, 46, 76, 145
Criminal Defense Practice, 50, 92, 108, 137–138, 143, 193–194, 198, 206, 244, 323
Criminal Harassment, 226
Criminal Justice System, 14, 20–22, 26, 28, 46–49, 51–59, 66, 70, 74–76, 78, 82, 85, 89–90, 93, 105, 111, 113, 115, 123, 128–129, 137, 145, 148, 154, 156–157, 160, 162, 189, 192, 205, 207, 210, 245, 250, 261–262, 265, 267, 269–271, 275–276, 278, 286–287, 289–291, 293–294, 316, 360, 362, 382
Criminal law clinic, 92, 130, 164, 303–304, 308, 316–318, 323
Criminal law clinical program, 311
Criminal law competencies, 303

Criminal law education, 11, 18, 20, 132, 324
Criminal Negligence, 228
Criminal Procedure, 29, 94, 113, 115, 175, 202, 324, 355, 373–375, 378, 383–384
Criminal sentencing, 17, 47, 121, 304
Criminal specialty court, 45, 48–49
Criminality, 9, 22, 31, 33, 42, 58, 86, 103–104, 122, 139, 172, 372, 375, 385
Critics, 54, 67, 74, 97, 281, 333, 335, 361, 365, 370
Critique, 5, 45–46, 52, 91, 94, 119, 129, 132, 138, 245, 286, 292, 295, 302, 327
Cross-cultural communications, 340
Cross-examination, 301, 326, 337, 371, 375, 383–384
Cultural Competence, 24, 100, 124, 132, 325, 340, 347
Cultural Diversity Project, 352
Cultural issues, 232
Cycle of failure, 262
Cycle of offending, 233
Decisional balance, 245, 248, 250, 253
Defence counsel, 187–191, 370–385
Defendant's family, 152–153, 194, 197, 199
Defense lawyering, 55, 90, 92–93, 110, 112, 114–115, 118–120, 122–124, 127, 129, 138, 144, 162, 259, 323
Deferral, 15–16, 25, 149, 212
Deferral of judgment, 25
Deferred revocation, 311–312, 319–322
Deferred sentence, 17, 30
Delinquent behavior, 246, 312, 330, 341, 344
Depression, 189–190, 194–197, 199, 210, 227–228, 307, 344, 365
Desk side manner, 306
Detached approach, 357
Dignitary interests, 331, 336
Disadvantaged people, 352
Dispute resolution, 24, 28, 303–304, 306, 316, 369
Diversion, 22, 25, 39, 43, 73, 101, 106–107, 110, 116, 132, 157–158, 205, 235, 246, 258–259, 269–270, 273, 276–277, 285, 309–310, 317–318
DNA, 159, 210, 217, 382

Domestic Violence, 14–15, 20, 22–23, 34, 43–45, 47, 60, 64–65, 69, 72–73, 99, 106, 146–147, 163, 208, 232–233, 241, 244, 246–247, 254, 267, 273, 288–289, 295, 297, 309, 313, 318, 325, 345
Domestic violence court, 34, 43, 65, 72–73, 106, 297, 309, 318
Drug addict, 200, 380
Drug counseling conditions, 181
Drug Court, 22–28, 35, 41, 47–49, 51–52, 54, 57–59, 61–64, 66, 68, 71–72, 74–76, 78, 80–84, 86, 88–90, 101, 104, 119–121, 132, 144–145, 150, 157–158, 160–161, 167, 180, 230, 232, 262, 266, 279, 283–289, 291, 293, 296, 300, 316, 352, 358, 370
Drug court plea, 101, 167
Drug Intervention Program, 71
Drug Treatment Courts, 25, 27, 35, 45, 74, 78, 81, 97, 100, 156–158, 160–162, 206, 282, 285, 288, 313, 318
Drug-rehabilitation, 163
DTC program, 25–27
Dual track system, 90
Due process, 4, 11, 22, 26, 41, 44–45, 48, 59, 65–66, 75, 77–78, 89, 95, 109, 112, 145, 147–149, 156–162, 164, 309, 311, 316, 319–322, 335, 337–339, 346, 349, 362, 373, 376, 383
Duty of Care, 188
Early intervention, 261, 269
Economic disadvantages, 372
Economic disincentives, 80, 87
Educational plan, 154
Effective interviewers, 307
Effective legal counsel, 243, 246
Effective representation, 79, 117, 125, 127, 137, 139, 213, 269, 309
Elder law, 308
Empathetic counselor, 341
Empathy, 20, 24, 29, 125, 227, 232–233, 238, 246, 249, 310, 328, 340, 344, 380
Empathy training, 29
Employment prospects, 152–154
Empowering, 44, 62, 265, 308, 334
Equal Treatment Benchbook, 362,
Ethic of care, 11, 130–132, 138–139, 231–232, 259, 303, 305

Ethical issues, 26, 50, 238, 277, 288, 291, 371
Ethical obligations, 45, 108, 150, 291–292, 353–354
Ethical principles, 162, 354
European Convention on Human Rights, 373
Expanded approach, 258
Experiential learning, 80, 293
External Brain Concept, 188
Externship Program, 43, 279, 284, 288, 294, 299, 309
Fairness, 49, 54, 56, 88, 95, 279, 281, 325, 328–330, 336–339, 369, 383
Family member, 19, 32, 200
Family violence, 106, 352
Family-focused responses, 347
Federal, 11–13, 28–30, 32, 39, 41, 46–48, 57–58, 69–71, 75, 85, 102, 113, 120, 123, 133, 144–146, 156, 171, 173–176, 180–183, 217, 225, 239–240, 242–243, 260, 263–264, 267, 284–285, 294, 308, 311, 313, 316, 323–325
Federal Court, 28, 32, 323, 325
Federal prison, 239, 242–243
Federal sentencing guidelines, 13, 28–30, 58, 102, 113, 174, 308
Fetal alcohol, 144, 186–188, 190–192
Fiduciary relationship, 357
Fifth Amendment rights, 332
Financial responsibility, 153, 242
Firearm violation, 11–12, 311
Florida, 11, 51, 66, 68, 118, 169, 294, 301, 324
Fulton County Conflict Defender, 267
Fundamental fairness, 337
Georgia Justice Project, 42–43, 106, 261, 267, 269
Gipuzkoa, 323
Goal Achievement, 310
Guardian advocate, 328, 332
Guilty plea, 29, 50, 59–60, 66, 73, 80–81, 101–102, 116, 119–120, 123, 148–149, 157–158, 160–161, 228, 230, 316
Hands on approach, 357
Harlem, 108, 110, 118, 260–261, 269, 278
Healing, 7, 22, 58, 138, 143, 157, 161, 164, 199–200, 211, 228, 230, 234, 238, 285, 293, 300, 304, 306, 316, 327

Healing to wellness courts, 316
High Court of Australia, 360
Holistic advocacy, 113, 133, 258, 261, 275, 318
Holistic law, 230, 304
Holistic legal skills, 316
Holistic sentencing, 262
Holistic team defense, 261
Holistic, 11, 21, 55, 108, 113, 130, 133–134, 145, 151–152, 168, 198–199, 230, 258, 261–263, 267–268, 275, 277–278, 304, 308, 316, 318, 331, 379, 381, 384
Homeless Court, 67
Hospitalization, 6, 95, 164, 168, 301, 332
Human needs, 31, 304
Humanistic orientation, 304
Humanizing Legal Education, 365
Hybrid system, 357
Immigration law, 308
Incarcerative sentence, 17, 32, 38, 40, 151
In-court representation, 315, 324
Indian Civil Rights Act, 313
Indian Country, 313
Individual autonomy, 94, 96–97, 330, 333, 342
Informational interviewing techniques, 195
Innovative plan, 36
Integrated approach, 250
Integrated service model, 258
Intention to change, 249–252, 254
Interdisciplinary outreach, 258, 261
Interdisciplinary partnerships, 328, 345
Interdisciplinary perspective, 303–306
Interdisciplinary work, 317–318
Interests of parents, 336
Interpersonal skills, 132, 171, 246, 303–304, 306–307, 310–311, 317, 327, 340
Interrogation, 347, 375, 381–383
Investigation phase, 373–376
Israel, 163–165
Israeli law, 164
Job counseling, 263–264
Joint submission, 226
Judge, 6–8, 10, 13, 16–18, 21, 26–27, 29–30, 32, 34–38, 43, 46–49, 52, 54, 56–59, 61–63, 65–66, 70–78, 80–83, 87–89, 100, 102–103, 111, 113, 115, 120, 127, 135–136, 138, 145–147, 149–155, 158–159, 163, 172–174, 176, 178–182, 194–198, 200–202, 205, 209, 211, 218, 221–222, 224–227, 233, 236–238, 241–242, 259, 263, 265, 270–271, 273, 279, 282, 287–288, 293, 296, 300–301, 308–310, 313–314, 317, 325, 330, 332, 335–336, 341, 343, 348, 354–355, 357–360, 366–367, 371, 373, 378
Judicial activism, 359–361, 365, 370
Judicial adventurism, 361
Judicial officer, 231–232, 235–238
Justice process, 233, 365
Justice system, 13–14, 20–22, 26, 28, 46–49, 51–59, 66, 69–70, 74–76, 78, 82, 85–86, 89–90, 92–93, 105, 111, 113, 115, 123, 128–129, 137–138, 145, 148, 154, 156–157, 160, 162, 168, 189, 192, 205, 207, 210, 230–231, 236, 245, 250, 261–262, 265, 267, 269–271, 273–276, 278, 285–287, 289–291, 293–294, 308, 316, 327–329, 332–339, 341, 344–346, 349–350, 352, 355–356, 358, 360, 362–363, 370, 382
Juvenile case, 329–330, 333, 336, 345–346
Juvenile Court system, 328
Juvenile drug courts, 344, 346
Juvenile Justice system, 21, 327–329, 332–339, 341, 344–346, 349–350
Juvenile law clinics, 313
Juvenile offenders, 69, 271, 311, 344
Juvenile parole revocation, 303–304, 311
Kidnapping, 384
Knox County Tennessee Public Defender Community Law Office, 264
Law office counseling skills, 304
Law school, 3, 14–15, 20, 22–24, 42–44, 84, 91–93, 106–108, 124–125, 130, 144, 153, 164, 247, 257, 259, 261, 279–281, 284, 288–294, 296, 302–303, 309–311, 313–314, 316, 318, 323–327, 343, 364, 369–370
Law student, 116, 298, 311, 315, 317, 324, 326, 355
Law student representation, 311
Lawyer reconnaissance mission, 151
Lawyer/client relationship, 305

Lawyering, 4, 11, 13–14, 19–20, 24, 26, 36–38, 45–46, 54–56, 85–88, 90–93, 95, 105–106, 108, 110–112, 114–115, 118–124, 127, 129–130, 133–134, 136–138, 143–144, 162, 232, 246–247, 257–261, 263, 275, 277, 279–281, 291, 294, 296, 300, 302–308, 310–311, 317, 323, 326, 328–329, 335, 338–340, 343–344
Legal Advisor Clinic, 323, 325–327
Legal anthropologists, 9
Legal check-ups, 306
Legal education, 11, 20, 24, 34, 44, 70, 92, 132, 143, 207, 247, 257, 276–277, 280–281, 284, 288–289, 292, 303–304, 306, 315, 323, 326, 343, 355, 364–365, 370, 379
Legal educators, 277, 279, 365, 370
Legal planning, 246, 306
Legal procedure, 5, 127
Legal process, 3, 10, 88, 95, 255, 258, 260, 283, 286, 289, 305, 307, 315, 330, 332–333
Litigation skills, 289, 296, 304, 308, 316
Long-run choice, 380
Magistrate, 27, 144, 194, 199, 230, 233, 236–238, 352
Magna Carta, 359
Manipulative, 136, 305, 364
Mason Court Revolution, 360, 365
Mass neurosis, 364–365
Mediation, 5, 59, 155, 233, 235, 301, 355, 369, 384
Mental Health, 6–7, 13–15, 18–19, 21, 26, 32, 41, 43, 45, 52, 59, 66–67, 73, 82–83, 89, 92–99, 106–107, 113–114, 117, 123, 132, 151, 154, 161, 167–168, 170–171, 189, 199–200, 204, 206–207, 210, 214–216, 218, 220, 232, 240, 242–243, 245–247, 249–251, 255, 258–259, 261, 263–264, 266, 269–270, 273, 276, 278, 280–281, 285, 289, 291, 293–294, 296, 298–302, 305–307, 309, 318, 334, 343–344, 357–358, 366–368
Mental Health Law, 6–7, 92, 94–97, 167, 280, 298, 301, 305–306, 366, 368
Mentally disturbed person, 380
Mentally ill client, 164, 207
Mentally impaired, 165, 168

Mentorship, 154
Miami, 4, 48, 51, 257, 279–280, 289, 294–295, 301, 303, 323, 326
Michigan Department of Corrections, 260, 270–271
Minority population, 86
Moral dilemma, 370
Motivation, 62, 86, 110, 134, 171–172, 181, 228, 231, 235, 245, 247, 252–253, 310, 330, 370, 378
Motivational counseling, 343
Motivational interviewing, 24, 136, 144, 171, 233, 244–245, 247, 249–252, 255, 264, 310, 343–344
Motivational methods, 344
Motivational support, 243
Motivational technique, 251
Multi-disciplinary, 64, 74, 196
Multi-systemic model, 345
Multi-systemic responses, 345
National Association of Drug Court Professionals, 49, 76, 86, 157–158
National Association of Sentencing Advocates, 263, 265, 278
National Legal Aid and Defender Association, 49, 109, 162, 257, 267–269, 278
Negotiation, 28, 43, 106, 116, 211, 215, 232, 277, 306–308, 317, 355, 369–370, 377
Neighborhood Defender Service of Harlem, 118, 260, 269, 278
Netwidening, 36
New York, 13, 48, 51, 65, 68, 71, 91, 110, 116–119, 144, 152–153, 167, 211–213, 239, 285, 315
New York City, 48, 65, 110, 116–119, 239
New York Public Defender Association, 211
New Zealand, 16–17, 180, 310
NLADA, 22, 49, 58, 60, 63, 74–76, 79, 81, 86, 88–90, 109, 115, 158, 257, 262, 267, 269, 272, 275, 278
Non-adversarial, 52, 57, 64, 84, 157, 167
Non-criminal violations of probation conditions, 181
Non-profit center, 266,
Offender's rehabilitation, 309
Oklahoma, 173, 209, 220–221, 364
Ombudsman, 312

Oñati International Institute for the Sociology of Law, 323
Ottawa, 132, 144, 180, 183, 185–186, 272
Over-represented, 49, 362
Paradigm, 46, 73–74, 76, 78, 87, 90, 127, 131, 145, 305, 328, 331, 334, 336–337, 339, 342
Paradigm shift, 73–74, 76, 87, 90
Parental control, 336, 348
Parental liability, 338
Parent-child privilege, 347
Parent-directed advocate, 333
Parent-directed alternatives, 338
Parole officer, 311–313, 319, 321–322
Parole revocation, 41–42, 303–304, 311–312, 318
Paternalism, 4, 97, 107, 114, 165, 168, 305, 310, 327, 330, 332–334, 337
Paternalism, 4, 97, 107, 114, 165, 168, 305, 310, 327, 330, 332–334, 337
Paternalistic advocate, 332–333
Paternalistic ideology, 334
Paternalistic judges, 327
PD office, 43
PDS, 72
Penitentiary population, 187
Performance Guidelines for Criminal Defense Representation, 93, 109, 158
Performance Standards for the North Carolina Indigent Defense Program, 211
Periodic review hearing, 16, 35, 312, 314–315
Personal choice and control, 253–254
Perspective taking approach, 122
Perth Drug Court, 180, 230, 358
Philosophy of Sentencing, 259
Physical disability, 186–187, 191
Plea agreement, 60, 116, 216, 310
Plea bargaining, 15, 21, 30, 73, 78, 83, 86, 91–92, 105, 127, 159, 244, 246, 263, 275, 305–306, 309, 316, 318, 354, 374, 378
Plea bargaining, 15, 21, 30, 73, 78, 83, 86, 91–92, 105, 127, 159, 244, 246, 263, 275, 305–306, 309, 316, 318, 354, 374, 378
Plea discount, 29
Plea negotiation, 28, 43, 106, 277
Plea of Guilty, 60, 73, 121, 126–127, 149, 216, 230, 232, 234, 238, 357, 369
Plea-bargained agreement, 149
Plea-based option, 101
Popcorn effect, 82
Positive development, 341
Positive therapeutic outcomes, 312, 329, 331, 333–334
Possession of heroin, 84, 166
Post-adjudication, 11, 22, 25–26, 35, 59–60, 78, 81, 85, 149, 156–158, 160, 162, 164, 167, 309
Post-guilty plea, 25
Post-offense rehabilitation, 30–31, 102, 123, 263, 308–309
Post-sentence stage, 313
Post-traumatic disorder, 363
Post-traumatic stress syndrome, 363–364
Poverty, 69, 109, 115, 121–124, 139, 141, 163, 165–166, 264, 324, 372
Pre-adjudication diversion, 158
Pre-adjudication model, 60, 71, 157–158, 164
Precontemplation stage, 252
Preliminary examination, 24, 131, 159, 270, 273
Prenatally exposed to alcohol, 191
Pre-Sentence Investigation Report, 174, 240
Pretrial stance, 60, 148
Prevention plan, 31–32, 245, 250–251, 255, 310, 314
Prevention principle, 31–32, 103,
Preventive law, 15, 24, 30, 95, 159, 198–199, 230, 246, 263, 275, 303–308, 310, 317, 326, 329, 373
Preventive law model, 15, 30, 159, 199, 246, 263, 275, 303–308
Preventive lawyer, 306–307
Preventive orientation, 306
Principles of constitutional law, 334
Principles of criminal defense, 162
Principles of law, 329, 336, 349
Prior criminal history, 85, 155
Prison inmate, 243
Prison life, 239, 242–243
Prison sentence, 239, 242–243, 268, 309, 371, 374, 380–381
Prisoner re-entry, 314

Prisoner reentry Court, 68
Proactive, 29, 146, 231, 246, 255, 282, 305, 371, 373, 377, 383
Probable cause, 75, 222, 224, 374, 382
Probation, 6–8, 10, 12, 16, 18, 20, 24–25, 31–39, 42, 57, 60, 65, 67–68, 71, 102–104, 112, 117, 120–123, 128, 130, 133–136, 144, 149–150, 158, 163, 168, 171, 173, 179–183, 187–188, 190–192, 198, 207–211, 215, 217, 219–220, 222, 224, 229, 235, 239, 241–242, 259–260, 263, 265, 267–268, 270–274, 285, 287, 301, 309–310, 316–318, 327, 329, 332, 335–336, 338, 349, 380
Probation Department, 239, 241
Probation progress reports, 130, 133–134, 181
Problem solving court, 16, 43, 60, 106, 232, 235–236, 238, 266, 282–284, 357
Problem-solvers, 150, 307
Procedural justice, 26, 39, 54, 56, 78, 84, 95, 131, 171, 231, 245, 330–331, 338
Procedural protection, 167
Procedural system, 371
Process of reform, 329
Professional ethic, 166
Progress report, 134, 144, 172, 181–182, 294
Prosecutors, 22, 48, 52–53, 59–60, 65, 67, 69, 73–74, 79–82, 85, 88–89, 120, 128, 144, 149, 151, 154, 161, 182, 191, 207–212, 266, 296, 308, 316–317, 326–327, 335–336, 346, 373–375
Prostitution Court, 73
Psychological defense mechanism, 307
Psychosocial problems, 281, 308
Psychic numbing, 364
Psychological development, 329
Psychological point of view, 379
Psychological resistance, 263, 307
Psychological sensitivity, 130, 132, 138–139, 306
Psychological wellbeing, 94, 304–306, 316
Psychologist, 12, 29, 33, 44, 144, 171, 190, 220–221, 237, 243, 310, 343
Psychology, 6–7, 22–23, 94–95, 141, 167, 169, 210, 220, 245–247, 251, 282, 298–299, 303–306, 313, 330, 340–341, 343, 349, 356, 380

Public defender, 15, 22, 43, 50, 52, 69–70, 72, 78, 80, 82, 91–92, 100, 106–108, 110, 113, 116–118, 125–126, 128, 130, 133, 143–144, 157–158, 162–163, 165, 167, 176, 181–183, 206–207, 211, 221, 223, 225, 239, 260, 262, 264–265, 267–273, 275–276, 278–279, 287, 293–295, 300–302, 318, 327, 346, 374
Public Defender Service, 69–70, 72, 108, 118, 327
Public safety, 21, 157, 208, 240, 334–335, 343
Public shaming technique, 61
Punishment, 21, 27, 29, 50, 58, 61, 65, 71, 112, 118, 147, 152, 156, 174–178, 204–205, 309, 332, 349, 357, 360, 375–377, 381, 385
Quality advocacy, 91
Quality legal representation, 92, 109
Quasi mental health issues, 97
Racial minority, 51
Rape victim, 384
Reasonableness, 13, 126, 193
Recovery Defense, 193, 198, 200–201
Red Hook Community Justice Center, 51, 65, 152
Re-entry, 16–17, 22, 40, 42, 170, 313–316
Re-entry court, 16–17, 22, 170, 313–315
Re-entry program, 313
Rehabilitation, 9–10, 16, 19, 21–22, 30–31, 34, 51, 58, 77, 93, 98, 102, 109–110, 112–114, 116–118, 120–124, 137, 140–141, 162–164, 168–170, 172–173, 178–180, 216–217, 219, 226, 230, 233–238, 243, 245–246, 248, 261, 263, 265, 287, 303, 308–310, 314, 316–318, 324, 328, 330, 332–333, 335, 337, 339, 341–342, 345, 353–354, 358, 376–378, 380–381
Rehabilitation plan, 234–238, 287
Rehabilitation-oriented packet, 28, 102
Rehabilitative alternatives, 309, 317
Rehabilitative potential, 22, 101
Rehabilitative process, 286, 332–333, 349
Rehabilitative program, 163–164, 168, 310
Rehabilitative role of the attorney, 22
Relapse prevention, 9–10, 19–21, 31–34, 42, 103, 105, 198–200, 205, 238,

245–246, 250–251, 255, 276, 309–310, 312, 314–315, 330, 342–343, 349
Remorse, 29, 121–122, 155, 189, 206, 226–228, 235, 381
Researchers, 15, 169, 270, 279, 326
Residential Drug Abuse Treatment Program, 240
Resistant client, 246–247, 250–251, 344
Responsivity to treatment, 170
Restorative justice, 29, 47, 51, 58, 61, 64, 68–69, 74–75, 84, 89, 132, 138, 145, 153, 172, 230, 235, 258–259, 265, 273, 304, 310, 316
Retribution, 65, 117, 206
Review hearing, 35
Revocation proceedings, 133, 181, 303
Revocation process, 311–312, 319
Reward, 14, 62, 365
Rewind exercise, 103, 307–308, 326
Rhode Island Public Defender Office, 268
Right of audience, 353–354
Right to counsel, 41, 49, 53, 109, 279, 332, 334, 337, 347
Rights to justice, 359
Robbery, 69, 173, 227–228, 376
Role of a barrister, 354–357, 366, 368–369
SCDIP, 71–72
Self-actualization, 122, 342, 345
Self-determination, 34, 82, 114, 231–234, 238, 305, 316, 325, 330, 333, 335, 348
Self-incrimination, 77, 80, 337, 348
Self-motivation, 341
Sentence leniency, 29, 102
Sentencing, 6, 8, 10, 12–13, 15–18, 21–23, 25, 28–32, 34, 36, 41–44, 47–48, 52, 56–58, 60, 68, 71, 73, 75, 78, 88, 92, 100, 102–103, 105–106, 110, 112–113, 116–118, 121, 123, 125, 127, 131–133, 135, 144–146, 148–156, 158–159, 164, 168, 171–176, 178–179, 184–186, 197, 206–208, 210–211, 213, 215–220, 225–230, 232–243, 245–246, 254, 257–260, 262–265, 270–271, 273–275, 277–279, 285, 301, 303–305, 308–309, 311, 313, 318, 324–325, 354
Sentencing Advocacy, 145, 148, 207–208, 265, 278
Sentencing consideration, 102

Sentencing guidelines, 12–13, 28–30, 32, 47, 57–58, 102, 113, 146, 174, 211, 239, 301, 308
Sentencing plan, 150, 152–155, 277
Sex offence, 382
Sexual Assault, 226–227, 252, 352
Sexually abused, 210, 384
Shift focus, 253
Short-sighted perspective, 373
Sixth Amendment, 41, 112, 126, 174, 330
Social Science, 15, 51, 62, 112, 120, 154, 170, 306
Social service, 14, 16, 32, 118, 128, 148, 264–265, 275, 277, 324
Social work, 7, 14–15, 18–19, 23–24, 34, 58, 110, 125, 134, 152, 169, 209–210, 258–259, 298–299, 303–304, 311, 315, 325, 335, 343, 346–347
Solicitor, 353–354, 356–357
Solicitor's function, 357
Spain, 16–17, 22, 41, 170, 323
Spanish law, 17
Special needs courts, 354
Specialized Justice, 46–47, 52, 57–58, 145
Specialty Court, 49–50, 55–56, 59–64, 69, 74–90, 145–152, 154–155
Specialty Court advocates, 56, 61–62, 76, 79–82, 84–86
Specialty court client, 90
Spectrum disorder, 187
Stakeholder, 81, 157
State Bar of Texas, 193–194
Statistics, 46, 49, 69–70, 86, 110, 154, 158, 163, 260, 268, 273, 285, 361–362, 367
Students, 14, 20, 23–25, 36, 38, 43, 84, 92–93, 100–101, 103, 107, 111, 117–118, 125–126, 128–129, 132, 143, 153, 246, 251, 255, 257, 259–260, 262, 276–277, 279–282, 284–302, 305, 307–308, 310–313, 315–318, 323–325, 327, 355, 365, 371
Substance abuse, 14, 41, 57, 59–60, 64, 67–68, 83, 123, 136, 148, 154, 157, 163, 171, 178, 182–183, 204, 208, 214, 232, 234–235, 238, 240–241, 248, 251, 263–264, 267, 281, 287, 301, 309–310, 317, 365
Successful discharge, 315

Sweden, 323, 370–371, 373–377, 379–384
Swedish criminal procedure, 374
Swedish lawyer, 371, 380
Tailored release conditions, 314
Teachable moment, 245, 250, 255, 341
Team approach, 62–64, 75, 145, 147, 180
Team-based advocacy, 258
Texas, 21, 116, 193–194, 198, 201–202, 204–206, 258
Texas Rules of Disciplinary Conduct, 194
Theft, 229, 375
Theory-inspired practice, 18
Therapeutic approach, 13, 64, 166–167, 184, 211, 232, 234, 237–238, 355–356, 380, 384
Therapeutic Court, 280, 287–288, 294–295, 297–299, 302, 316
Therapeutic sentence, 144, 181, 183–184
Therapeutic strategies, 232
TIPS, 18–19, 134, 143, 236, 317
TJ all the way, 105, 119, 126–127, 131, 139–140
TJ criminal lawyer, 3, 22–23, 28, 40, 100, 102, 104, 130, 132, 134–135, 144
TJ Criminal Lawyering, 14, 19, 105, 130, 137, 143
TJ defense lawyering model, 114–115
TJ defense theory, 115
TJ inspired practice, 164
TJ lawyer, 102–106, 119–122, 127, 132, 135–136, 163, 165–166, 168, 306
TJ principles, 45, 91–92, 96, 99, 111, 137, 314
TJ Theory, 94, 96–98, 100–101, 105
TJ-focused criminal defense, 93
TJ-friendly feature, 17
Tohono O'odham Tribal Court, 313
Traditional criminal lawyer, 140, 166
Traditional defense perspective, 226
Traditional lawyer, 130
Traditional system, 357
Transtheoretical Stages of Change Model, 233
Treatment Alternative, 59–60, 148
Treatment Court, 11, 21–22, 35, 40, 43, 50–52, 59–61, 63, 71–72, 76–81, 84, 89, 100–102, 104, 106–107, 125, 132, 143, 147–148, 156–162, 164, 167, 206, 208, 257, 262, 265, 285–288, 309, 317–318, 323, 346
Treatment, 6–9, 11–16, 18–19, 21–23, 25–28, 30–33, 35, 40–41, 43, 45–47, 49–52, 56–68, 70–90, 92, 95, 97–98, 100–102, 104–107, 109, 114, 117–120, 125, 128, 132, 135–136, 138, 141, 143–144, 146–152, 154–172, 174, 176, 178, 181–182, 184, 193–208, 210–213, 216–217, 219–220, 235, 239–240, 242, 245–247, 253–255, 257, 260, 262–266, 269–271, 274, 277–278, 281–289, 291, 294, 300–301, 305–306, 309, 313–314, 317–318, 323, 330–332, 335, 337–338, 341, 344–346, 349, 352, 362, 366–367, 372, 377, 380, 384–385
Trial Advocacy, 127, 131, 139, 264, 353
Tribal Codes, 313
Tribal courts, 17, 313, 316
Tribal jail, 313
Tribal judges, 314
Tribal reentry court, 303–304, 311
Tripartite analytical framework, 304
U.S. Department of Justice, 71, 157, 161, 266, 275, 294
UK, 33, 180, 351, 384
Unconstitutional, 37–38
Under-representation, 48
United Kingdom, 310
University of Miami, 257, 279–280, 289, 294–295, 303, 323, 326
Utah, 41, 124, 371
Utah Supreme Court, 41
Utilitarian value, 330
Vectors, 45, 230, 282, 304
Victim, 29–30, 35, 44, 65, 73, 86, 102, 120–121, 133, 138, 145–146, 150, 153, 155, 168, 173, 202, 225–230, 233, 235, 259, 263, 310, 314, 323–327, 343, 356–357, 362, 375, 378, 381–384
Victim impact evidence, 155
Victim impact statement, 30, 226–228, 324–325
Victim Legal Advisor Clinic, 323, 325–327
Victim of crime, 356
Victim participation, 323, 326
Victim Witness Assistance Program, 323, 325–326

Victorian Justice Department, 352
Violation Report, 181
Virginia Department of Criminal Justice Services Statistics, 285
Virginia, 47, 68, 71, 80, 153, 276, 278–279, 284–286, 289
Vocational counseling, 153
Waiver, 50, 79–80, 128, 157, 160, 211, 287, 332, 347
Washington State Institute for Public Policy, 169, 314
Washington, D.C., 61, 63, 65, 69, 80, 83, 144, 157, 257
Washtenaw, 269–275
Washtenaw Public Defender Office, 269, 272
Welfare, 14, 165, 182, 315, 363, 382–384
Western Australia, 16, 144, 180, 230, 235, 351, 356–358, 361, 367
White Australian Justice, 363
Whole client representation, 107, 259–260
William & Mary Law School, 279, 284, 289
Wisconsin, 37, 75, 109
Wisconsin Supreme Court, 37
Young offenders, 171, 187, 341
Youth ombudsman, 312
Zealous advocacy, 77, 87, 89–90, 131, 162, 206, 261, 277, 331
Zealous criminal defense, 46, 52, 140
Zealous defense, 54, 163, 168, 266, 274
Zealous representation, 61, 87, 90, 121, 127, 139, 156, 158, 160, 163–164, 169, 261
Zealous traditional advocacy, 260
Zealousness, 50, 53, 76, 87, 109